Understanding & Programming COM+

PRENTICE HALL PTR MICROSOFT® TECHNOLOGIES SERIES

NETWORKING

- Microsoft Technology: Networking, Concepts, Tools
  Woodard, Gattuccio, Brain

- NT Network Programming Toolkit
  Murphy

- Building COM Applications with Internet Explorer
  Loveman

- Understanding DCOM
  Rubin, Brain

- Web Database Development for Windows Platforms
  Gutierrez

PROGRAMMING

- Introduction to Windows 98 Programming
  Murray, Pappas

- Developing Professional Applications for Windows 98 and NT Using MFC, Third Edition
  Brain, Lovette

- Win 32 System Services: The Heart of Windows 98 and Windows NT, Third Edition
  Brain

- Multithreaded Programming with Win32
  Pham, Garg

- Visual Basic 6: Design, Specification, and Objects
  Hollis

- ADO Programming in Visual Basic 6
  Holzner

- Visual Basic 6: Error Coding and Layering
  Gill

- Visual C++ Templates
  Murray, Pappas

- Introduction to MFC Programming with Visual C++
  Jones

- MFC Programming in C++ with the Standard Template Libraries
  Murray, Pappas

- COM-CORBA Interoperability
  Geraghty, Joyce, Moriarty, Noone

- Distributed COM Application Development Using Visual Basic 6.0
  Maloney

- Distributed COM Application Development Using Visual C++ 6.0
  Maloney

- Understanding and Programming COM+: A Practical Guide to Windows 2000 DNA
  Oberg

- ASP/MTS/ADSI Web Security
  Harrison

- Microsoft Site Server 3.0 Commerce Edition
  Libertone, Scoppa

- Building Microsoft SQL Server 7 Web Sites
  Byrne

ADMINISTRATION

- Windows 2000 Registry
  Sanna

- Configuring Windows 2000 Server
  Simmons

- Tuning and Sizing NT Server
  Aubley

- Windows NT Cluster Server Guidebook
  Libertone

- Windows NT 4.0 Server Security Guide
  Goncalves

- Windows NT Security
  McInerney

- Supporting Windows NT and 2000 Workstation and Server
  Mohr

- Zero Administration Kit for Windows
  McInerney

- Designing Enterprise Solutions with Microsoft Technologies
  Kemp, Kemp, Goncalves

PRENTICE HALL PTR MICROSOFT® TECHNOLOGIES SERIES

Robert J. Oberg

Understanding & Programming COM+

A Practical Guide to Windows 2000 DNA

Prentice Hall PTR, Upper Saddle River, NJ 07458
www.phptr.com

Library of Congress Cataloging-in-Publication Data

Oberg, Robert J.
    Undersstanding and programming COM+: a practical guide to Windows 2000 DNA /
  Robert J. Oberg.
        p. cm. -- (Prentice Hall series on Microsoft technologies)
    Includes bibliographical references and index.
    ISBN 0-13-023114-2
      1. COM (Computer architecture) 2. Microsoft Windows (Computer file)
    3. Electronic data processing--Distributed processing. I. Title. II. Series.
    QA76.9.A73 O24 1999
    005.2'768--dc21   99-056388

Editorial/Production Supervision: *Joanne Anzalone*
Acquisitions Editor: *Mike Meehan*
Marketing Manager: *Bryan Gambrel*
Manufacturing Buyer: *Maura Goldstaub*
Cover Design: *Anthony Gemmellaro*
Cover Design Direction: *Jerry Votta*
Series Design: *Gail Cocker-Bogusz*

© 2000 Prentice Hall PTR
Prentice-Hall, Inc.
Upper Saddle River, NJ 07458

Prentice Hall books are widely used by corporations and government agencies for training, marketing, and resale.

The publisher offers discounts on this book when ordered in bulk quantities. For more information, contact Corporate Sales Department, Phone: 800-382-3419; fax: 201-236-7141; email: corpsales@prenhall.com or write Corporate Sales Department, Prentice Hall PTR, One Lake Street, Upper Saddle River, NJ 07458.

Product and company names mentioned herein are the trademarks or registered trademarks of their respective owners. The Electronic Commerce Game™ is a trademark of Object Innovations. Inc.

All rights reserved. No part of this book may be
reproduced, in any form or by any means, without
permission in writing from the publisher.

Printed in the United States of America

10 9 8 7 6 5 4 3 2 1

ISBN 0-13-023114-2

Prentice-Hall International (UK) Limited, *London*
Prentice-Hall of Australia Pty. Limited, *Sydney*
Prentice-Hall Canada Inc., *Toronto*
Prentice-Hall Hispanoamericana, S.A., *Mexico*
Prentice-Hall of India Private Limited, *New Delhi*
Prentice-Hall of Japan, Inc., *Tokyo*
Pearson Education Asia Pte. Ltd., *Singapore*
Editora Prentice-Hall do Brasil, Ltda., *Rio de Janeiro*

DEDICATION

In Memory of Fred R. Oberg
1910-1999

CONTENTS

Foreword xxiii
Preface xxv
About the Author xxxi

Part 1 Introduction to COM+ and Windows DNA *1*

ONE   What is COM+? *3*

The Object Foundations 4
Objects 4
Object-Oriented Languages 5
Components 7

Microsoft's Road to COM+ 8
Dynamic Link Libraries (DLLs) 8
Windows Open System Architecture (WOSA) 9
Object Linking and Embedding (OLE) 9
Component Object Model (COM) 11
Microsoft Transaction Server (MTS) 13
Microsoft Message Queue (MSMQ) 14

COM+ 15
COM+ Component Model 16
COM+ Services 16

The Power of COM: A Preview 18
Building a Web Browser 18
Software Components 22

What's Next 24

TWO   Three-Tier Applications and Windows DNA *25*

Evolution of Distributed Systems 26
One-Tier Systems 26

PC LANs 27
Two-Tier (Client/Server) Systems 28
Three-Tier Systems 33

Overall Structure of Windows DNA 35
General Services 35
"Glue" Technology 37

Windows DNA Layers 38
Presentation Layer 38
Business Logic Layer 40
Data Access Layer 45

Summary 46

THREE A Testbed for Windows DNA 49

Overall Configuration 50
Roadmap 51
Timeline 52

Windows 2000 53
Hardware Requirements 53
Windows 2000 Professional 53

Windows 2000 Server (Can Do Later) 55
Networking 56
Domain Name System (DNS) 57
Active Directory 58

Development Tools 61
Visual Basic 62
Visual C++ 62
Visual InterDev 63
Platform SDK 64

COM+ Preview 64

Summary 67

Part 2 COM Fundamentals 69

FOUR COM Clients: Concepts and Programming 71

A Bank Account Server 72

Exploring the Structure of a COM Server 73
Visual Basic Object Browser 73
OLE/COM Object Viewer (OLE View) 74
IDL for Bank Server 75

COM Terminology and Concepts 79
Interfaces 80
Classes 81
Objects 81
Instantiating an Object 82
Identifiers in COM 84
Object Lifetime 86
Interface Negotiation 87
Server 89
Type Library 89

COM Client Programming Model 90

Programming a COM Client 90
Visual Basic COM Client Program 90
Visual C++ COM Client Program (Console) 92
Visual C++ COM Client Program (Using MFC) 94

Additional Topics in COM Client Programming 95
Unicode 95
BSTR 97
COM Library Programming 97

Windows Registry and COM 98
Using OLE/COM Object Viewer 99
Registry Editor 101
Server Self-Registration 103

Summary 104

FIVE **C++ and the Component Object Model** *105*

Objects, Components and COM 106
Component Objects 106
Component Software 106
Component Object Model 107

C++ and COM 108
Classes and Interfaces 108
Class Identification 109
Encapsulation 109
Object Creation 109
Class Object 109
Object Lifetime 110
Versioning and Interface Negotiation 110
Reuse 111
Distributed Objects 111

Implementing a COM Class Using C++ 111
Account Object Example 112
COM Interfaces 112
Binary Representation of Interfaces 112
C++ Representation of Interfaces 113
Review Exercise for Virtual Functions 114
Review Questions 115
Answers to Review Questions 115
Globally Unique Identifiers 116
IUnknown and QueryInterface 117
Reference Counting 118
Class Factories 118
Implementing a COM Object 118
Interface Specification 119
Interface Implementation 120
Object Creation Function 123
COM Status and Error Reporting 124
Using a COM Object 125
Additional Interfaces 126

Summary 127

Contents **xi**

SIX   In-Process COM Servers   *129*

COM Server Concepts   129
Local/Remote Transparency   130
Class Factories   130
Bootstrapping an Object   130
Class Object   130
Class ID's and the System Registry   131
Structure of a Component   131
Registry   132
Registry Editor   132
Registry Entry Files   132
Important Registry Information   133

Implementing an In-Process COM Server Using C++   135
Class Factory Definition   136
Class Factory Implementation   136
Exported Functions of the DLL   138
Exposing the Class Factory to COM   139
Unloading Mechanism   139
Client Access to the Class Factory   140
CoCreateInstance   140
Execution Context   141
CoFreeUnusedLibraries   141
Linking to COM Libraries   141

Working with DLLs   141

Implementing an In-Process COM Server Using Visual Basic   142
Creating the Server   143
Client Test Program   146

Summary   147

SEVEN   Active Template Library   *149*

Active Template Library   150
MFC and ATL   150
Boilerplate COM Code   150
Implementing IUnknown   151
Class Declaration   151
Class Implementation   152

Instantiating an ATL-Based COM Object   152
CComObject   153
Example Program   153

Visual C++ and ATL   154
Visual C++ COM Support   155
ATL COM Server Demo   155
ATL Code Walkthrough   164

Multiple Interfaces and More about IDL   168
Adding a Second Interface in IDL   168
C++ Code for Second Interface   170

ATL COM Wrapper Classes   171
CComBSTR   172
Smart Pointers   172

Summary   173

EIGHT   Visual C++ COM Support   *175*

Visual C++ and COM Clients   175
Visual C++ COM Client Demo   176
Finishing the Client Program   178
Namespaces   179

Visual C++ COM Support Classes   180
_bstr_t   180
_com_error   180

Summary   181

NINE   EXE Servers   *183*

Application Integration and OLE   183
Windows Messages and DDE   184
OLE 1.0   185
OLE 2.0   186
OLE Demonstration   186
Application Integration and EXE Servers   187
EXE Servers and Surrogates   188
Interfaces for an OLE Server   188

Structure of an EXE Server   189
Marshaling   190

Contents **xiii**

"Demo" Object as a Local Server   191
Proxy   191
Registering a Class Factory   192
REGCLS Enumeration   193
Revoking Class Factory   193
A Better-Behaved EXE Server   194

EXE Servers Using ATL   196
EXE Server Demo   197
Self Registration for EXE Servers   198
Proxies and Stubs   199
EXE Server Files   201

Summary   202

TEN   Introduction to DCOM   *203*

Remoting an Existing COM Object   204
Existing COM Server   204
DCOM Demo   204
Security Issue   207
Registry Entries   209

Programming for DCOM   212
Client Specifies the Server   213
DCOM Implementation   216
DCOM and the Registry   220
Optimizing Network Traffic   220
Security   224

DCOM Architecture   224
Launching a Server over the Network   224
Server Operation over the Network   225
Multithreading Issues   226

Summary   227

ELEVEN   Automation and COM Programming Using Visual Basic   *229*

Automation   230
Properties and Methods   230
Late Binding   230

IDispatch 231
Type Information 231
Dual Interfaces 231
VARIANTs 232

Automation with ATL and VBScript 233
ATL Automation Server 233
"Thin" Client Using VBScript 234
VBScript Automation Processing 237
More About IDispatch 237

Visual C++ Automation Controllers (Optional) 237
Calling IDispatch Directly 238
Using CComDispatch Driver 239

Automation and Visual Basic 240
Properties 240
Events 242

Collections 246
Collections and Object Models 246
Enumerators 247
Implementing Collections 248

Summary 249

TWELVE Error Processing and Debugging *251*

Using the HRESULT 252
Facility Codes 252
Error Codes and Naming Conventions 253
Looking Up Error Codes 253
Displaying Error Descriptions 254

COM Error Interfaces 256
IErrorInfo 256
Returning Error Information 256
Retrieving Error Information 256
Implementing ISupportErrorInfo Using ATL 257
Returning Error Information Using ATL 257
COM Error Interfaces Example 258
Server Code Provides Error Information 260
Client Code Retrieves Error Information 261
Visual C++ Compiler Smart Pointer Error Support 262

Automation Exceptions 264

EXCEPINFO 264
MFC Support for Automation Exceptions 265

COM Error Handling in Visual Basic 268
Default Error Handling 268
Using On Error 269

Tracing and Debugging 272
ATL Tracing Support 272
Tracing in the SDK 273
Breaking into Program Execution 273
A Logger Component 276

Summary 278

THIRTEEN Multithreading in COM 279

Concurrent Programming 280
Race Condition Example 280
Serializing Access to Shared Data 280
Automatically Serializing Data Access 281
Windows Message Queue Demo 281

Apartments and Multithreading in COM 284
Apartments 284
Threading Models 286
Crossing Apartment Boundaries 289

Implementing Multithreading in COM 290
ATL Support for Multithreading 291
DLL Server Example, Step 1 292
DLL Server Example, Step 2 (Race Condition) 292
DLL Server Example, Step 3 (Marshal Interface Pointer) 295
DLL Server Example, Step 4 (Free Threads) 297

Summary 301

Part 3 Windows DNA and COM+ 303

FOURTEEN COM+ Architecture Fundamentals 305

Why COM+? 306
Scalability 306
Reliability 307
Complexity 308
Transactions: A Canonical Example 308

Declarative, Attribute-Based Programming 309
Apartments as a Model for Declarative Programming 309
Declaring Transaction Requirements 310

COM+ Catalog 310
Component Services Snap-In 311

COM+ Terminology 312
COM Terminology 313
COM+ Terminology 314
Types of COM+ Applications 316

COM+ Architecture 317
Context 317
Activation 319
Interception 321
Just-in-Time (JIT) Activation 323
Object Pooling and Construction 325

Summary 327

FIFTEEN A COM+ Tutorial 329

A Visual Basic COM+ Component 330
A Roadmap 330
An Unconfigured Component (#1) 331
A Configured Component (#2) 332
A Tour of Attributes (#3) 337
Activation and State (#4) 341

A Visual C++ COM+ Component 348
Creating the Example Program 348
Installing and Running the Example 349

IObjectControl and IObjectConstruct Interfaces   350
Object Construction   352
COM+ Administration Objects   354
Deploying a COM+ Application Remotely   356
Summary   357

SIXTEEN   Concurrency in COM+   *359*

Synchronization and Apartments   359
Multithreaded Bank Account Example   360
Synchronization through Apartments   360
Neutral Apartments   361

Synchronization and Activities   361
Activities   361

Programming Example   364
Each Thread in its own STA   365
All Threads Run in the MTA   366

Summary   367

SEVENTEN   Windows 2000 and COM+ Security   *369*

Fundamental Problem of Security   370
Authorization   371
Authentication   371

A Windows 2000 System Administration Tutorial   371
Administering User Accounts in Windows 2000   371
Workgroups, Domains, and the Active Directory   375

NT Security   377
NT Security Model   377
Security Demonstration   379

COM Security   383
Authorization   383
Authentication   388
Identity   388
Impersonation   392

COM+ Security   393

Electronic Commerce Game Case Study   393
Configuring COM+ Security   397
Role-Based Security   400
Programmatic Security   401
Identity in COM+   404
Impersonation   406

Summary   408

EIGHTEEN SQL Server and ADO Survival Guide   *411*

Getting Started with SQL Server 7.0   412
Query Analyzer   413
Enterprise Manager   414

Managing Databases Using SQL Server 7.0   415
Databases for Case Study   416
Creating a Database   417
Creating a Table   418
Inserting Data into a Table   419
Creating and Using SQL Scripts   420
Setting Up Databases for the Electronic Commerce Game   422

Uniform Data Access   424
ODBC   424
OLE DB   425
ActiveX Data Objects (ADO)   425

A Tutorial in Database Programming   427
Creating an ODBC Data Source   427
An Administration Program for the History Database   431

Programming with ActiveX Data Objects   432
ADO Object Model   433
Connection Object   434
Recordset Object   434
Errors Collection   439
Using Native SQL Server OLE DB Provider   441

A Three-Tier COM+ Application   442
Creating the Middle-Tier Server   443
Creating the Presentation-Tier Client   443
Using COM+ to Create a Remote Proxy   444
Running the Data Tier Remotely   444

Electronic Commerce Game Case Study   444

File DSN   445
Playing the Game   447
Summary   447

NINETEEN   Transactions in COM+   *449*

Principles of Transaction Processing   449
Transactions   450
Distributed Transaction Processing   451

Microsoft Transactions Technology   453
OLE Transactions   454
Microsoft Distributed Transaction Coordinator (MS DTC)   454

Automatic Transaction Processing Using COM+   456
Transactional Components   456
Life Cycle of an Automatic Transaction   459

Programming Transactions in COM+   461
Player Administration Program   461
Middle-Tier Components   462
Data Tier   466
Presentation Tier   466
"Auto Done" Flag for a Method   467

Summary   468

TWENTY   Web Applications Using COM+   *471*

Classical Web Technology   472
Hypertext and HTML   472
Internet Servers   477
HyperText Transfer Protocol (HTTP)   477
Common Gateway Interface (CGI)   479

An Internet Programming Testbed   481
Internet Explorer 5.0   482
Internet Information Services 5.0   482

Microsoft Web Technologies   489
Microsoft Client-Side Web Technologies   489
Microsoft Server-Side Web Technologies   499

Active Server Pages and COM+   505

Active Server Pages Object Model 505
Request and Response Using Active Server Pages 506
A Three-Tier Web Application Using COM+ 507
Summary 517

TWENTY ONE MSMQ and Queued Components 519

Message Queuing and MSMQ 520
Message Queuing 520
Microsoft Message Queue 521

Using and Programming MSMQ 524
Installing and Testing MSMQ 524
Administering MSMQ 525
Example Programs 525

Queued Components 534
Queued Components Architecture 534
Using Queued Components 535
Programming Example 538
Configuring a Queued Component 539

Summary 546

TWENTY TWO COM+ Events 547

Events and Connection Points in COM 548
Event Example 548
Connection Point Architecture 551

Loosely Coupled Events and the Publisher/Subscriber Model in COM+ 554
COM+ Event System Architecture 555
EventClass 556
Subscriptions 557
Subscribers 557
Publishers 558
Filtering 558

COM+ Event Example 559
EventClass 559
Subscriber 561
Publisher 565

Summary 567

TWENTY THREE COM+ and Scalability 569

Microsoft Clustering Technologies 569
Microsoft Cluster Server (MSCS or "Wolfpack") 570
Windows Load Balancing Service (WLBS or "Convoy") 572
Component Load Balancing (CLB) 573

COM+ Component Load Balancing 574
Load Balancing 574
Load Balancing Algorithm 575
Composing Clustering Technologies 575
Configuring Component Load Balancing 575
Fault Tolerance with Component Load Balancing 578
Design Issues for Load-Balanced Components 578
Performance 578

Object Pooling 579
Using Object Pooling 579
IObjectControl 580
Requirements for an Object That Is Pooled 581
Pooling and Load Balancing 582

The Significance of COM+ 582
The Effectiveness of COM 582
The Power of COM+ 583
Comparing Architectures 583
Raising the Level of Abstraction 584
The Importance of Quality 585

Summary 586

APPENDIX A Learning Resources 587

APPENDIX B Electronic Commerce Game Case Study 589

Setup 589
Databases 590
ODBC Data Sources 590

Player's Guide 591
Introduction 591
Playing the Game 592

Distributed Version of Game 597
Running the Data Tier Remotely 597

INDEX 599

FOREWORD

COM+ is perhaps the most exciting new technology to come from Microsoft, and I cannot think of anyone better qualified to write a great book on the subject than Bob Oberg. Bob combines the qualities of strong technologist, excellent writer and gifted teacher. Bob has taught and provided course materials for UCI Corporation for many years. He has always had great enthusiasm and also much patience for the needs of students struggling to learn new software technologies. These qualities have translated into book form very well.

What I like most about *Understanding and Programming COM+* is the breadth of its coverage, not only of COM+ but also the COM underpinnings and several related technologies of Windows DNA. The COM fundamentals portion of the book provides the best coverage of COM and DCOM I have seen anywhere. This did not surprise me because Bob has been involved in teaching COM, OLE and ActiveX for a long time. He delivered for UCI the first public offering of Microsoft's course "Implementing OLE in MFC Applications," and his own courses on COM and OLE, COM and DCOM, and Internet Programming Using ActiveX have been very well received by many students. Bob has always been very adept at quickly mastering new technologies, and he enthusiastically rose to the challenge of learning COM+ and presenting it with exceptional clarity.

COM+ is a big challenge to learn because the interesting applications involve issues like database transactions, security, Web programming, etc. Bob has included self-contained introductions to these important areas, making this book truly accessible. The CD-ROM has many excellent example programs, and these are thoroughly integrated into the book. There are many hands-on demos. Reading this book made me feel that I was taking one of Bob's classes. The first chapter likens the study of COM+ to taking a journey. I thoroughly enjoyed my journey in this book, and I think you will enjoy yours too.

Andrew Scoppa, President, UCI

PREFACE

This book is intended as a practical guide to learning COM+ for use in building three-tier applications that exploit Microsoft's Windows DNA architecture. It is based on many years of experience programming and teaching COM. This book is focused on the needs of developers, but it should also prove useful to others on a COM+ project, including architects and managers.

Learning this new technology can be very enjoyable and interesting, but also quite challenging because there are so very many concepts and tools involved. This book aims to be largely self-contained, providing basic tutorial information on everything needed to implement hands-on examples of the major services provided by COM+. (See the first chapter for a discussion of what COM+ is.) In particular this book incorporates a systematic treatment of the foundations of COM that are integral to COM+. Thus this book should be completely accessible to you, even if you have no prior COM experience. The core COM chapters are clearly identified, so if you are experienced with COM you can proceed directly to the new features of COM+.

The book is organized into three parts. The first part introduces COM+ and provides an overall introduction to Microsoft's Distributed interNet Applications architecture, or Windows DNA. This comprehensive architecture is Microsoft's blueprint for building robust three-tier distributed applications. COM+ provides the core infrastructure for the whole architecture. This introduction orients the reader to the whole subject—starting with the "forest." COM+ is introduced in its historical perspective as an evolution of object and component systems. There is also a chapter guiding you in setting up a testbed that can be used for hands-on work during the rest of this book. It is useful to start setting up the testbed early, because there are so many pieces that will ultimately be required. Any snags encountered can be fixed before they become a blocking problem.

The second part of the book provides thorough coverage of the fundamentals of COM which underpin COM+. The third part covers COM+ itself and shows how to build multiple-tier applications conforming to the Windows DNA model.

This book uses both C++ and Visual Basic as important development languages. One of the great strengths of COM is that it is language neutral, and different parts of an application can be developed in the most appropriate language. This approach works well in development, and it also is useful in learning the subject. We use both C++ and Visual Basic in Part 2. There is somewhat greater emphasis on C++ in Part 2, because C++ helps in understanding the concepts of COM better than Visual Basic, which hides so much. On the other hand, in Part 3 we focus more on Visual Basic, because we are interested in learning the important services provided by COM+ without getting bogged down by the more complex coding required by C++. For example, we use Visual Basic as a very simple interface for database access using ADO. A database access component implemented in Visual Basic can easily be called by a business object implemented in C++. Note that in "real life" you may in fact wish to reverse this usage. It will be more efficient to implement a database component in C++ using OLE DB, and the business logic might be implemented in Visual Basic. This book should make you comfortable with such mixed language development.

What about Java? It is indeed very feasible to implement COM components using Microsoft's version of Java, Visual J++. In fact the Java feature of a class implementing multiple interfaces makes Java a good fit for COM. But standard Java does not provide this COM support, and if you are using Java you may well be interested in its cross-platform capabilities. The future of Visual J++ is somewhat unclear, with some hints that Microsoft may in the future switch to its own language nicknamed "COOL." For these reasons, and to keep this book within scope, I decided to focus on C++ and Visual Basic.

Using both C++ and Visual Basic is well and good, but you are probably much more oriented toward one of these languages than the other. How does that affect the usability of this book for you? I've tried to structure this book so that it will be useful to both C++ and Visual Basic programmers. If you are a C++ programmer you should have no trouble creating simple Visual Basic client programs There is also complete coverage on implementing Visual Basic servers, which should prepare you for the use of Visual Basic in Part 3. If you are a Visual Basic programmer, read Part 1 completely, followed by Chapters 4, 6 and 9 through 13, focusing on the concepts. You should study Chapter 11 in detail. Then you should be well prepared for Part 3, which is primarily in Visual Basic.

Another important topic is database programming, and here too you may or may not have very much background. Or you may have used a desktop database such as Access but not SQL Server. Chapter 18 provides a complete tutorial to using SQL Server 7.0, which is actually a database that is very easy to use. There is also a discussion of OLE DB and ADO. Databases are used in the following two chapters on transactions and on Web application development.

Many companies are moving towards Web-based applications. Web applications have the tremendous advantage of ease of deployment. All that is needed on the part of a client is a Web browser, and clients can reach the application from anywhere in the world. The server capability can be arbitrarily powerful, using the full capabilities of COM+. Chapter 20, which covers both the fundamentals of Web programming and also the use of COM+ on the middle tier, is in fact the longest chapter in the book.

Two important technologies in Windows DNA on NT 4.0 are Microsoft Message Queue (MSMQ) and Microsoft Transaction Server (MTS). There is a hands-on introduction to MSMQ in Chapter 21. MSMQ is important in COM+ because it provides the infrastructure for Queued Components, and MSMQ may on occasion be used directly in COM+ applications where some of its extended features are required. MTS is a different story. It is completely subsumed in COM+ and disappears as a separate entity. Thus we do not have any specific discussion of MTS, except of a survey nature in Part 1. This book is focused on what is currently needed in COM+ application development moving forward. All of the fundamental concepts of COM discussed in Part 2 remain important, but MTS as such drops out.

An important consideration in learning a new technology is hands-on examples. There are many example programs throughout this book. Complete code is provided on the accompanying CD-ROM. There are a number of demonstrations in some chapters, which lead you through hands-on work. Most of the examples are deliberately kept quite simple and minimal, focusing on the concept at hand. On the other hand, small point examples do not really illustrate what is involved in creating a complete three-tier application. This book contains a complete case study of an Electronic Commerce Game™, which I hope you will find both instructive and enjoyable.

The COM+ examples provided in this book were developed using beta software (Windows 2000 Beta 3 and Release Candidate 1), and the usual caveats apply. Changes may be made to the final product. Indeed, Microsoft announced some changes late in the writing cycle. The In-Memory Database (IMDB) has been deleted from the final shipment of Windows 2000. Also, the Component Load Balancing (CLB) service is being moved to a separate product. Accordingly, I deleted the IMDB chapter from this book but retained the chapter containing information on CLB. The information provided is the best I have available at the time of writing. I am committed to maintaining up-to-date information about COM+ on my Web site, **www.ObjectInnovations.com**, which is mirrored at the publisher's Web site. The COM+ area contains corrections and updates to this book, corrections to the example programs, and new technical write-ups and example programs.

A NOTE ON THE CD-ROM

As is usual with programming books, there is a CD-ROM provided with this book. I don't know what your experience with book CDs has been, but mine has been quite mixed, to the point that now I rarely load the CD. It seems that in many cases making the examples work smoothly gets lost in the shuffle of writing the text for leading edge technology.

I have tried very hard to make this CD-ROM different, and if you don't load it, I believe you will be making a mistake. This book lives and breathes by sample programs, and running these programs, studying the code, and creating your own experiments will add immeasurably to your understanding of the material. And if you enjoy programming as well as its being your job, I think you will find it fun too. Even if you are a manager or architect I encourage you to do a little hands-on experimentation as you read this book. One of the nice things about Microsoft's development technology is that they have made it remarkably easy to do some interesting things. I'm sure that programmers in your group will be happy to help you get set up.

What gives me confidence that the example programs in the CD-ROM will work smoothly is that I have a lot of experience in producing code disks for industrial training courses. Some of the example programs come form these courses and thus have been classroom tested. Many others were created expressly for this book, but benefit from my experience in creating similar instructive examples.

If you happen to have taken an Object Innovations course you will notice some differences between the courses and this book. One is in the directory structure. For courses I have a master Examples directory, which is a repository for all the programs in the course, and an install script copies starter code where appropriate to lab working directories. In this book I have a simpler structure, with a separate directory for each chapter in this book.

A second difference is that there are no "labs" in this book. I decided to place my priorities on writing the text and creating the example programs rather than on labs. I hope you will find this a reasonable trade-off. If I had created lab instructions at the detailed level I provide for courses, they could have become out of date as new versions of the software comes out. A book by its very nature is more durable than an industrial course. But I hope the absence of structured labs will not prevent you from doing your own experiments as you read this book. It is when you start to write things yourself that your knowledge and skills grow to a higher level. And it is nice to do some of your experiments on "toy" code rather than on your next project.

The structure of the CD-ROM is very straightforward. Under the top-level **ComPlus** directory there is a chapter directory for each chapter in the book for which there are working code samples. The chapter directories in turn have subdirectories for each sample program in the chapter. Some of these have multiple steps. Some chapter directories also have a **Demos** directory, where you are encouraged to work along with a specific demo described in this book. The subdirectory **CaseStudy** contains the Electronic Commerce Game™.

The CD-ROM has a simple **install.exe** self-extracting file which will set up the example programs on your hard disk. You may choose the root directory. It defaults to **c:\ComPlus**. (If you choose a different root directory you will have to edit some pathnames in **.reg** files in Chapters 6 and 9. I am not aware of any other path dependencies, but I have not performed extensive testing.) I encourage you to run this **install.exe** file right away. You will then have at your immediate disposal a place to build and experiment with the sample programs and to do the demos. The CD-ROM also has the example programs expanded in the directory structure, so you can make changes on your hard disk freely and go back to the CD-ROM to get back any original files you need.

ACKNOWLEDGMENTS

A list of acknowledgments for a book like this either needs to be short or very long. The true list would be long indeed and would include many teachers, colleagues, authors, students, friends and family who have helped me in innumerable ways. I will instead give a short list of people who provided very direct help in the short, intense period of planning and writing this book.

I am grateful to Andrew Scoppa of UCI Corporation for suggesting the book and for Mike Meehan of Prentice Hall for helping me get the project off the ground. Michael Stiefel has worked with me in developing the COM curriculum that provided the foundation for much of this book. He was a blunt critic of early drafts of this book, which I did not enjoy, but his critiques proved immensely valuable. Ron Reeves took time from a busy schedule to jump in and start reading this book, providing useful suggestions. My father encouraged me to write this book, knowing from his own experience as an author what I would be letting myself in for but encouraging me nonetheless. My wife, Marianne, has provided enormous support and encouragement, not only in the writing of this book but also in starting my business. She has helped me to focus.

ABOUT THE AUTHOR

Robert J. Oberg was educated as a mathematician, receiving a Ph.D. from Harvard University in 1969 and an A.B. from University of California at Berkley in 1964. He received a National Merit Scholarship for undergraduate study, a National Science Foundation Fellowship for graduate study, and was elected to Phi Beta Kappa and Sigma Xi. He taught Mathematics at Knox College, Statistics and Operations Research at the University of Pennsylvania, and Computer Science at Framingham State College, serving as Chairman of the Computer Science Department.

Since 1982 he has worked in the computer industry. At Prime Computer he worked as a software engineer for the CPU Group, including projects such as the development of a pipeline simulator for a high-end CPU. At Wang Laboratories he did client/server work for the Imaging Group and was a member of a team developing an object management system. While at Wang, as a side project, he wrote a course in C++ programming. In 1993 he started his own company, Object Innovations (**www.ObjectInnovations.com**), a consulting and courseware firm specializing in object-oriented technologies such as C++, MFC, COM/COM+ and Java. He writes training courses in these areas and teaches for UCI Software Training. In the last several years he has focused mainly on courseware development, with an emphasis on Java, COM and COM+.

PART ONE

Introduction to COM+ and Windows DNA

In This Part

♦ **CHAPTER 1**
What is COM+?

♦ **CHAPTER 2**
Three-Tier Applications and Windows DNA

♦ **CHAPTER 3**
A Testbed for Windows DNA

The first part of this book introduces COM+ and provides an overall introduction to Microsoft's Distributed interNet Applications architecture, or Windows DNA. This comprehensive architecture is Microsoft's blueprint for building robust three-tier distributed applications. COM+ provides the core infrastructure for the whole architecture. This introduction orients you to the whole subject—starting with the "forest." COM+ is introduced in its historical perspective as an evolution of object and component systems. Windows DNA is surveyed as an organizing principle for understanding Microsoft's software that enables the construction of both traditional distributed systems and also Web-based application. There is also a chapter guiding you in setting up a testbed that can be used for hands-on work during the rest of the book. It will be useful to start setting up the testbed early, because there are so many pieces that will ultimately be required. Any snags encountered can be fixed before they become a blocking problem.

O N E

What is COM+?

We are starting out on a long journey together, studying Microsoft's comprehensive software component architecture called COM+, an evolutionary step from their Component Object Model or COM. The journey will not always be an easy one, because the subject is large and in places rather sophisticated. You will have to roll up your sleeves and do some work, not just read along. Euclid is reported as once telling a king who wanted an easy route to learning geometry, "There is no royal road to Geometry." There is no shortcut to really learning COM+. Microsoft provides many tools to greatly simplify the application development process. But in order to understand what you are doing, you really need to grasp the overall architecture of COM+ as well as specific programming techniques.

This first chapter is intended to help you get your bearings as we start out on our journey. The initial question of course is What is COM+? We will see that COM+ is actually part of a larger framework called Windows DNA. We'll discuss this larger framework in the next chapter, and then we'll start to delve into the details of COM+. But first let's try to understand at a high level what it is, anyway. I'll try to help you understand by treating the subject as a kind of story. A story is more interesting than a "how to" manual and easier to understand than a technical treatise. So the story will involve a little bit of history of some problems that software people have grappled with for a long time and of Microsoft's original contribution. This last point I find particularly interesting, because Microsoft in many ways has been a company that has gained success by imitating others but doing it with much persistence and great marketing. But with COM and then COM+ they have actually created something new under the sun.

This journey is yours as well as mine, and you should feel completely free to follow your own path. If I talk about history and you want to get on with it, do so! Skip ahead. If you're very comfortable with a topic, go on ahead. You can always come back when you need to. Likewise if a section seems pretty complicated and your eyes are glazing over, leave it for now and come back to it if you need to. (Don't worry—we start off pretty easy.) Let's begin!

The Object Foundations

COM+ is the current culmination of a long road that Microsoft has been following to create a very robust architecture for developing applications and systems. We will see that it involves some unique contributions that Microsoft has invented. But the foundations are some very classical ideas in software engineering, beginning with object-oriented programming.

Objects

A key notion that helps us to solve software problems (and indeed to make sense of the world around us) is *abstraction*. It's easier to understand something if I can strip away extraneous details and focus on what is of interest. If I am planning a trip from Boston to Philadelphia there are only a few simple things I need to think about at first. How will I travel? Plane? Train? Car? How long will it take by each form of transportation? How much time do I have available? It is a business trip, I do not have extra time, so I consider going by plane. There are many, many characteristics of each vehicle, but for my problem the paramount characteristic is speed. I don't care about the color of the vehicle. But maybe I care about which airline, because I have frequent flyer miles on some airlines, and I want to accumulate more.

So we see in our little example that we may have an abstraction of Vehicle. Every Vehicle has an attribute or characteristic called Speed. There are various specializations of Vehicle, such as Plane, Train, Car, and there is a hierarchical relationship. See Figure 1–1.

We commonly refer to such an abstraction as a *class*, which specifies the various characteristics and capabilities of something. One type of characteristic may refer to *data*, such as the Speed of any kind of Vehicle or the Number-OfEngines of a Plane. Another aspect of a class concerns its *behavior*. For example, actions which a Plane may do include Fly and Land. We sometimes refer to such actions as *methods*. A key feature of a class is that data and methods are grouped together in a single entity, which defines this particular

```
                    ┌─────────┐
                    │ Vehicle │
                    └────┬────┘
              ┌──────────┼──────────┐
         ┌────┴───┐  ┌───┴───┐  ┌───┴───┐
         │ Plane  │  │ Train │  │  Car  │
         └────────┘  └───────┘  └───────┘
```

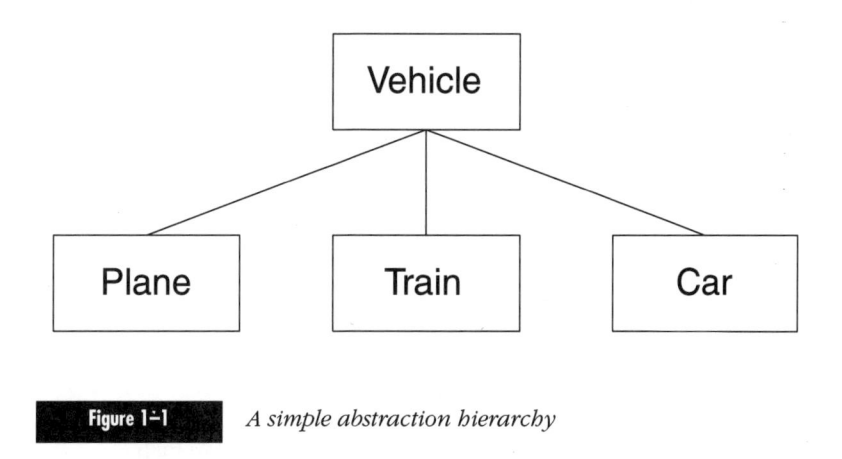

Figure 1-1   *A simple abstraction hierarchy*

abstraction. An object is a particular instance of a class. Each object has its own unique values for data.

The grouping together of data and methods facilitate *encapsulation*. Typically the data is hidden, walled off from the rest of the system. We say that the data is *private*. Methods to manipulate the data are *public* and may be called from elsewhere in the program. Encapsulation of data in this way offers two kinds of protection. The data itself is protected against corruption by other parts of the program, because they cannot touch the data directly. So preventing the data from becoming corrupt is reduced to making sure that the methods behave properly. A second form of protection is that the rest of the program is protected against changes in the representation of the data. As long as the public method interfaces remain the same, the program will still work correctly. The class honors a *contract*.

An unfortunate illustration of the consequences of not encapsulating is the year 2K bug. Many programs represented the year portion of dates by just two digits. This saved a little data storage space and worked fine as long as all dates were in the same century, but things break down when we cross over into a new century. When all this date data is touched by many parts of a program, a great deal of code must be changed in order to accommodate switching to representing a year by four digits.

Object-Oriented Languages

How do you write programs that make use of objects? So-called "data hiding" to achieve encapsulation can be implemented fairly easily in many programming languages. For example, in C you can declare data to be static and thus have file scope. Then you implement various functions in this source file that may access the data. The functions can be called from functions in other source files (they are "public"), but the data itself is "private" to the file where it is declared.

It is not quite so easy in C to implement class-type behavior, where you can create objects as instances of a class. It can be done through the concept of an opaque "handle" that is used to represent a data object. A special "CreateXXXX" function is implemented to create a particular type of object and return a handle. Internally, a handle table is maintained which associates a handle with a pointer to actual data. Outside there is no access to the pointer to the data, only to the handle. All functions that manipulate these "objects" take a handle as a parameter. This type of handle architecture is used extensively in the Windows C style API, including extension systems such as ODBC.

The first use of the class construct in a programming language occurred in 1967 in Norway in the language Simula, which was derived from Algol. Bjarne Stroustrup, the inventor of C++, used the language Simula in his Ph.D. thesis for coding simulation programs he wrote to model computer systems. He found that the Simula language was very expressive and permitted him to work at a high level of abstraction. But when it came time to run the programs to get the numerical results he needed for his thesis, he found that the performance was far too slow, and he would never be able to complete the work in time. So he recoded his programs in C. But he did something very intelligent. In place of handcoding, he wrote a translator program that would take a C-like program with extensions for classes (modeled after Simula) and translate it to pure C. The result was a language initially called "C with Classes," later to become C++. The translator program became the AT&T "cfront" compiler, that would translate C++ to C, thus facilitating the creation of C++ compilers for many different kinds of computers (because C itself is implemented on many machines). Later C++ compilers translated directly to machine language for the particular machine. Whether the translation is via a preliminary translation to C via cfront or directly, the end result is compiled machine language code for the target platform. Besides being compiled code, the design of C++ (remember Stroustrup and his need to complete his thesis) in several ways was steered toward *efficiency*.

Another important object-oriented language is Smalltalk. Unlike C++, which derived from C, Smalltalk (designed at the Xerox Parc research facility) was created from the ground up as a "pure" object-oriented language. In Smalltalk everything, even numbers, was implemented as objects. There was an extensive standard class library which was part of the language. There were also very rich program development tools such as class browsers and debuggers. The result was a very capable program development environment. Smalltalk code is not as efficient as C++, and the programming language is quite different from what most programmers are used to. Smalltalk remains as a niche language. There have been other object-oriented languages that have remained even more as niche players, such as Objective C and Eiffel.

The language currently gaining popularity most rapidly is Java. Java is object-oriented from the ground up, but unlike Smalltalk takes a more pragmatic approach to native data types, implementing them directly and not as objects. Java compiles into a portable intermediate language called "bytecode" that runs on a Java Virtual Machine, which interprets the bytecode on a particular platform. The result is that the same compiled Java program will run unchanged on many different computers—a feature very desirable in Internet applications. Java comes with a large and rapidly expanding standard class library. A downside of Java is lower performance.

Visual Basic is not commonly thought of as an "object-oriented" language, but in fact modern versions of the language are quite object oriented. As we shall see later, the Visual Basic object model is tied closely to COM, and works very well in a COM environment, both for using COM objects and for creating COM objects. (What is a "COM object"? Wait—we are getting ahead of our story.) Originally Visual Basic was interpreted, but later versions can produce compiled code. Visual Basic is exceptionally easy to program, in some ways almost like a 4GL.

Of all the object-oriented languages, C++ can produce the most efficient code.

Components

A few years ago the magazine *BYTE* ran a cover story entitled something like "Is Object-Oriented Programming Dead?" Inside they made the point that in many ways "objects" have not lived up to their hype. People had talked about how objects would facilitate code reuse. In fact objects have been compared to hardware "chips." Great economy is now achieved in hardware engineering by creating computers from chips rather than implementing custom circuitry. It was hoped that similar reuse could be achieved by software objects. But it never happened.

Meanwhile, Microsoft created a language called "Visual Basic" to simplify programming Windows applications. Central to the Visual Basic approach was drawing various Graphical User Interface (GUI) elements or "controls" (text boxes, list boxes, buttons, etc.) onto a form. These various controls could be attached to little pieces of code that would handle associated events. From the beginning, Microsoft recognized that the built-in controls were nowhere near comprehensive enough to satisfy the needs of Visual Basic programmers. So Microsoft defined a specification for a "VBX" (Visual Basic Extension) custom control. A VBX would plug into the VB development environment and behave just like an ordinary built-in control, but would do the special features designed for it. Like an ordinary control, a VBX had properties that could be set and events that could be handled by VB code.

Soon there were hundreds and then thousands of VBXs created and sold by Independent Software Vendors (ISVs). A VBX could be a simple graphical "widget" of some sort or could implement complex functionality such as Windows sockets. Any VBX could be easily plugged into a Visual Basic program.

The *BYTE* article highlighted VBXs as more successful in implementing the dream of reuse than objects. The article raised the hackles of many in the object-oriented community. VBXs were not "object oriented" (they lacked even the concept of a method, and they certainly did not support features such as inheritance and polymorphism). But they did facilitate reuse. They were commercially successful.

A VBX can be considered an example (albeit a somewhat crude one) of a software *component*. Loosely, a software component can be thought of as a piece of binary code that can be easily plugged into different applications.

Microsoft's Road to COM+

A VBX is a rather curious animal in the evolution towards COM+. It in fact represented a dead end. But it comes from something that is very seminal and basic to Windows, namely a DLL. And DLLs represent the first of a series of steps that lead directly to COM+.

Dynamic Link Libraries (DLLs)

A DLL is a special kind of software library that can be linked into an application at run time. It is more flexible and efficient than a traditional static library. Static libraries go way back to the early days, where programs were written on punched cards, and library code would be a deck of punched cards that could be loaded with one's program to provide some standard functionality. Programming languages typically come with a standard run-time library, such as the Standard C Library. A static library is linked into the executable of the application. Thus, if three applications each use the same code in a static library, each executable will contain its own copy of this code. In a DLL, a single copy of the code in the DLL is loaded into memory and multiple applications can share this copy. Another feature of a DLL is that linkage occurs at run time. This means that a new version of a DLL can be deployed without rebuilding applications that make use of the DLL. If strict compatibility is preserved, the existing application may now run faster, if for example, the new version of the DLL has better performance.

Unfortunately, if the new version of a DLL is not completely compatible, something difficult to ensure with complex software, installing a new application with new DLLs may break an older application with an older version of a DLL. Fixing the old application by restoring its DLL may break the new application.

Windows Open System Architecture (WOSA)

Dynamic link libraries represented Microsoft's first attempt at implementing components on the Windows platform. They offered advantages over traditional standard static libraries, and did offer a code reuse mechanism. However, they suffered various defects, such as the versioning problems described in the previous paragraph. Another limitation of DLLs is that they do not support "polymorphic" behavior. Polymorphism is another feature of object-oriented programming. With polymorphism, a client can make the same method call on different objects and get different behavior for each object type, appropriate for that kind of object. For example, consider a "Show" method. A text object may display text with a standard font. A vector graphics object may create a graphical rendering by performing graphics operations. A raster graphics object may display a picture by lighting up the appropriate pixels. And a video clip may start playing the video.

As an example of a case where polymorphic behavior is desired, consider accessing data in a shrink-wrapped application. A spreadsheet program like Excel would like to be able to read data from a database and populate the cells of a spreadsheet accordingly. The shrink-wrapped program has no prior knowledge of the database employed by the end user. One user may have an Access database and another user an Oracle database. Rather than create special versions of Excel for different databases, Microsoft adopted a common approach. It created a "middleware" database layer known as Open Database Connectivity or ODBC, which defines a common database API (Application Program Interface). ODBC provides a standard front-end interface for applications. The call-level interface uses SQL syntax based on X/Open and SQL Access Group (SAG) SQL CAE specification (1992), a subset of the SQL-92 standard. Back-end implementation is provided by installable drivers (dynamic link libraries). Figure 1–2 depicts the basic architecture of ODBC.

With ODBC an application can talk polymorphically to different databases. Through an administrative procedure (the ODBC Control Panel applet) a particular driver (for example, Access or Oracle) is associated with a data source, and at run time the Driver Manager will load the appropriate driver DLL. This approach is classic middleware. ODBC sits between the application and the database.

Object Linking and Embedding (OLE)

OLE 1.0 was introduced in June, 1991, as Microsoft's first attempt to provide an object-oriented mechanism for integrating applications. It introduced the concept of a compound document which can contain "objects" from other applica-

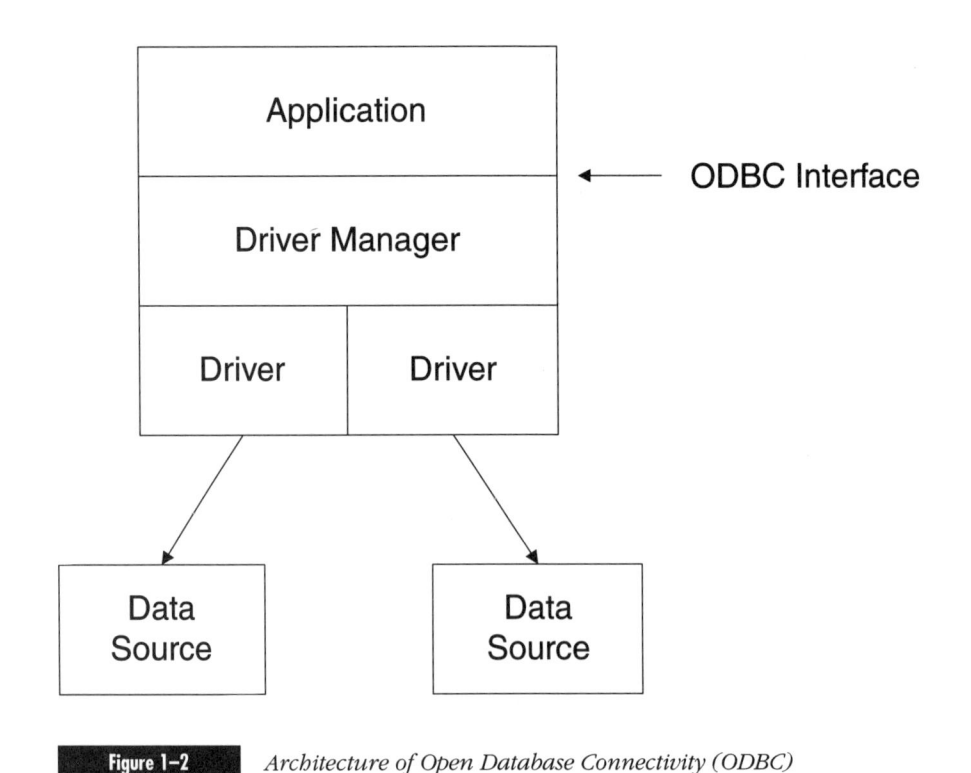

Figure 1-2 *Architecture of Open Database Connectivity (ODBC)*

tions. OLE derived from the work of PowerPoint developers who wanted to embed Microsoft Graph elements in their documents and overcome some limitations of previous integration techniques. Using the Clipboard, users could paste static "snapshots" of data from other applications into their documents.

Editing such data was very cumbersome—it would have to be edited in the original application and then pasted in again. There was no way to use the Clipboard to support "links," whereby changes in the original data would automatically be reflected in data in the container document. Another integration mechanism was Dynamic Data Exchange (DDE), which could be used to support links to original data, but the container needed its own code to render the data in proper format.

OLE 1.0 enabled a user to embed an *object* into a container. The object contained a static picture and also the original data needed to edit the object, along with a hook to bring up the original application when required. To edit the object the user typically double clicked with the mouse. The original application would then start up in a separate window. When done, the user could save, and data in the container document would be updated. An object could also be stored in a container as a *link*. The original data would be stored as a separate file, and only a link to this data placed in the container document. The container document can then be guaranteed to always have the latest copy of its linked object, automatically getting updates when the data is edited by its original application.

There were a number of limitations to OLE 1.0, which was implemented on top of Dynamic Data Exchange. DDE is inherently asynchronous—when you call a function, it returns immediately, and you must wait in a message loop, polling a status flag. DDE connections are rather fragile. OLE 1.0 relied exclusively on shared global memory for passing data between applications. Large blocks of data would have to be copied into memory prior to a transfer (where it might be immediately paged back onto disk). OLE 1.0 links were easily broken when files were moved. Editing of embedded and linked objects was intrusive to the user, because another application would start in a separate window to do the editing.

OLE 2.0

OLE 2.0 was introduced in May, 1993. Its primary original objective was to improve upon OLE 1.0. During its design, OLE 2.0 was extended far beyond its original domain of supporting compound documents, and OLE ceased to be an acronym for "Object Linking and Embedding." Significant improvements were made over OLE 1.0. DDE was replaced by the far more robust lightweight remote procedure call (LRPC) protocol. A new uniform data transfer (UDT) mechanism provided several alternatives to shared memory for efficient data transfer. A new moniker mechanism improved on link tracking. Visual editing or in-place activation was introduced to allow an embedded object to be edited in the context of the container application.

The most important thing about OLE 2.0 was not any feature or improvement over OLE 1.0 but the infrastructure that was created to support it. OLE 2.0 was based on a precisely defined model, COM or Component Object Model. This model was inherently extensible, and so it was realized that new component services could be introduced according to the architecture without making any fundamental changes. Hence the version number was dropped, and the technology came to be known as simply OLE.

Component Object Model (COM)

The Component Object Model, created as the foundation for OLE 2.0, can be viewed as Microsoft's third generation component architecture. The first generation "component" was a DLL, which provided a C function call interface. The second generation, WOSA, provided a number of important services such as ODBC and Windows Sockets. There was still a C function call interface. The third generation introduced "component objects." As we have seen, objects encapsulate data and behavior in a single entity. Without objects, you have to maintain multiple variables and pass them to isolated functions. By grouping related data and functions into an object, you create an abstraction that simplifies programming and allows you to extend your programming model to include your own new data types.

COM extends this object structuring capability. Objects can have multiple *interfaces*, each of which supports a particular feature through a related group of functions. An object can support multiple interfaces, and if a client has a pointer to one interface it can obtain a pointer to another interface through a function **QueryInterface**. This simple concept of multiple interfaces and a query mechanism is extremely useful, because it supports the evolution of software components through the introduction of additional interfaces without breaking existing clients. For example, an OLE compound document server may or may not support in-place activation. Originally no OLE servers did, because in-place activation was not a feature of OLE 1.0. For a server to support in-place activation it must provide additional interfaces, which a new version of the server application may do. This will not break an old client application, because the old client never queries for the new interfaces. A new client will work with a new server, because when it queries for the additional interfaces it will find them, and can then activate the server object in-place. A new client can also work with old servers, because when it queries for the new interfaces and does not find them, it can open up the server object in the old way, that is, in a separate window.

Another very important feature of COM is that it is a *binary* standard, allowing programs implemented in different programming languages to interoperate. Thus, different COM components could be created in C, C++, Visual Basic, and Java (Microsoft's version, Visual J++) by different software vendors. Any of these components can be used in any language that supports COM. This binary standard is a major improvement over object-oriented programming languages, which define objects at the source-code level, limiting the potential for wide scale interoperability.

With Windows NT 4.0, Microsoft introduced DCOM or Distributed COM, which extends COM over a network. From the beginning, COM used an RPC mechanism involving proxies and stubs to cross process boundaries. With DCOM, the RPC is extended to cross a network. The basic architecture remains the same, and the calling semantics of a client program invoking an object is the same whether the object is in the process, in a different process, or on a different machine. This feature of COM is known as *location transparency*.

A central feature that should be appreciated about COM is that it is *not middleware*. COM does not stand between the client and the server, as an ORB (Object Request Broker) in CORBA or as ODBC does in WOSA. The COM run time is involved in setting up the connection between the client and the server, and then it gets out of the way. In the case when the COM component is running in the same process as the client, there is literally no extra overhead—it is exactly the same as calling a virtual function in C++. In the case where the component is out of process or on another machine, the only overhead is the RPC involved in going across the process or network boundary.

ACTIVEX

The marketing mavens at Microsoft muddied the water by coining the phrase "ActiveX" to describe Microsoft's Internet technology initiatives to enable creation of "active" Internet applications. The classic Internet was basically a huge information store. Through a browser program you could navigate to Web sites all over the world and download HTML pages that would be displayed. These pages can contain links to other pages, and so you "surf" the net. Gradually more functionality was introduced. For example, forms could be created on HTML pages allowing you to enter data, for example information to order a product. You could then submit your information, and a server program would process your order. HTML forms were a pale reflection of the richness of a classical GUI program. One thing that Microsoft wanted to enable was a very rich user interface, comparable to Windows. So they invented technology to enable an OCX (OLE Custom Control, the successor to VBX) to be displayed on a Web page. They renamed these controls to "ActiveX controls." They were so pleased with this new name that they rechristened all of OLE to be called ActiveX, and there was Active This and Active That. Don't worry about this terminology. It is all marketing!

Microsoft Transaction Server (MTS)

Microsoft's technology originated on the desktop and has been expanding upward to workgroups and now to the enterprise. Creating enterprise applications on a server involves many complex programming challenges not faced on the desktop. Server applications have to be multithreaded, so that they can service many users concurrently. Scaling is a major consideration, so that the application won't fail as more people start to use the system. Scalability becomes a major factor for Web applications where users may be all over the world. Security is a significant issue. Most server applications work with databases, and in fact a single application may need to manage transactions that affect multiple databases. Microsoft's solution is a new software platform called Microsoft Transaction Server or MTS.

MTS greatly simplifies the creation of server applications built using COM. The programmer can create COM components as DLLs designed for a single user application, without worrying about issues such as multiple threads. No particular coding has to be done to provide for security. Using a tool called the MTS Explorer the COM component can be imported into an MTS "package." The client program then talks not directly to the COM component but to an MTS "surrogate" process which manages all of the complex multiple-user issues, such as creating new threads for new clients. Also using MTS Explorer, a package can be configured for security. Roles can be assigned (for instance, Manager, Auditor, Employee) and selective access to components within the package can be granted based upon the role of a particular user. MTS also manages interaction with databases and can "pool" scarce resources such as database connections. MTS provides a simple model for managing distributed transactions.

Microsoft Message Queue (MSMQ)

Message queuing is a conceptually simple model for building distributed systems. An application creates a message and sends it to a queue. Another application can read the message from the queue. The receiving application can then send another message to another queue. This other queue may be read by the original sender or by yet another application. Message queuing is asynchronous. As soon as the message has been posted in the queue, the sending application can go on to other work, without waiting for the message to be read. Message queuing permits offline work—a message can be queued while the application is not connected to the network, and then routed to its queue once a network connection is reestablished. Message queuing can be very robust. The queue can be saved in persistent storage, and queue operation can be retried when the system is back after a failure.

Message Queuing and RPC are both valid high-level models for communication among applications, and each has its uses. DCOM is an object-oriented communication model built on RPC. For synchronous operations where the caller depends on results from the server before proceeding, you typically should use RPC. If the sending and receiving applications may run at different times, use message queuing. If the sender does not care which receiver processes a message, use message queuing. In message queuing the sender posts a message to a queue, which may be read by many different servers. With RPC, the client typically talks to a specific server.

A major issue in many distributed systems is interoperability. Data can be accessed from multiple systems using a standard data access technique such as ODBC. But what if the business rules are running on a "foreign" system? Message queuing provides a simple model that is implemented on many systems. There is a whole category of "middleware" products called "message-oriented middleware" or MOM, designed for interoperability across diverse systems.

Microsoft Message Queue (MSMQ) is Microsoft's implementation of message queuing on Windows platforms. There are three major components to MSMQ:

- An API for applications to send and receive messages.
- Messages that get created by an application and are then sent to other applications.
- Queues to which messages are sent and from which they are retrieved.

Queues are managed by a queue manager. There are two forms of the MSMQ API, a classical C interface and a COM interface. With the latter, MSMQ services can be invoked by any client program that can use COM, including Visual Basic and Visual C++.

COM+

We finally come to COM+, which can be viewed as Microsoft's next-generation component architecture. Basically, what COM+ does is to integrate MTS into COM and to provide a messaging alternative for COM calls, based on MSMQ. The result is a quite seamless system in which it becomes as easy to implement server applications as it is to implement client applications. There are also many services provided which will enable highly scalable applications to be built.

The encompassing term for COM+ related technology in Windows 2000 is *Component Services*. I believe you can get a sharper understanding of just what COM+ is if you separate out "component" from "services." In fact I believe that a lot of confusion about Microsoft's overall system architecture can be avoided if we can sort out the core infrastructure from the multitude of services that are provided. A more full-blown roadmap is provided by Windows DNA, which we will begin to examine in the next chapter. Right now, I would just like to sort the technologies we have already discussed into components and services. This list is meant to be suggestive, not definitive. It is for the purpose of helping me to make a point.

Components	Services
DLLs	ODBC
COM	OLE
	MTS
	MSMQ

A place where I believe this distinction helps is in looking at COM and OLE. When OLE came out, a lot of books on the subject appeared, all with "OLE" in their title. It took a long time for a book about COM itself to come out. Thus people tended to think that OLE was the key technology. OLE was (and remains) incredibly difficult. Kraig Brockschmidt valiantly tried to debunk what he called the "OLE is difficult myth." The problem is that OLE really is very complex, inevitably so because of its problem domain, that of compound documents, the geometry of placing document components on a page, in-place activation, merging menus, etc. The gem in OLE was the component infrastructure used to support this set of services. That infrastructure is COM, and the imbalance of books has been more than rectified, with many books on COM, and it is a long time since I have seen a new book on OLE.

COM+ Component Model

What I have always found so elegant about COM is that it is *not* middleware. It provides a mechanism for a client and server to connect, and then it gets out of the way. The result is an extremely flexible component architecture that can be used for very fast in-process components as an improvement over DLLs and that can also be used for DCOM servers over a network. The same model applies in both cases.

But for complex enterprise applications, there are myriad cases where middleware is very valuable. ODBC is an excellent example, and it is only the tip of the iceberg—the complex processing that must be performed to implement distributed applications, including the handling of transactions, concurrency, security, message queuing, event notification, and many others. It would be a prohibitively expensive development effort for every application to implement these services itself. Hence there is a role for *system* services.

The genius of COM+ is that it provides an architecture, called *interception*, that enables it to intervene when it is needed and not otherwise. COM+ components run in what is known as a *context*. A context can be thought of as a set of run-time constraints. If a component and its client are running in the same context, a method call is made directly, with no intervention by COM+ and no overhead. If they are running in different contexts, the call on the way in goes through an "interceptor," which can do whatever preprocessing is necessary to satisfy the run-time constraints. And on the way back the return also goes through the interceptor for any needed postprocessing. The result is middleware when and only when it is needed—the best of both worlds.

The other key feature of the COM+ component model involves the way the run-time constraints get specified. That happens not through a programming interface but by *declaring* the values of some attributes. These attribute values are stored in a configuration database called the catalog. At run time, COM+ can figure out what interception is needed based on these configuration parameters.

COM+ Services

The model just outlined is very elegant, but it does not mean anything by itself without at least some understanding of the services that can be performed by these interceptors. So let's look very briefly at some of the main services.

TRANSACTIONS

"Transactions" gave the name to Microsoft Transaction Server, and they remain a key service in the successor of MTS, namely COM+. Transactions are units of work in applications. They are atomic and either completely succeed or completely fail. Many different kinds of data stores, not just traditional databases, are candidates for participating in transactions. And, in a distributed environment, data can reside in many different data stores, and transactions can span them. So how do you program transactions? These different data stores all have their own interfaces, which are different, so we have a potential for middleware to harmonize the differences, with a resulting uniform API for participating in transactions. But this approach remains at the programming level.

MTS and now COM+ provides a different approach. A component declares an attribute such as "requires a transaction." Then at run time, through an interceptor, COM+ calls the necessary services to enlist the component in a transaction. Application level programming is not required.

SECURITY

Another vital concern in enterprise applications is security, protecting the various resources of the application against unauthorized access. Again there are two approaches: programming security through an API or declaring security attributes. COM+, following MTS, provides a high-level role-based security model. For a given resource, you can specify various roles, such as Manager, Clerk, Auditor, etc., all of whom are allowed some access to the resource. The applications can treat these different roles appropriately. Membership in the different roles can be configured administratively. The result is a flexible and easy-to-use security system.

CONCURRENCY

Enterprise applications involve many users, who inevitably will be accessing some resources at the same time. The resulting need for writing "thread-safe" code can be daunting, if it must be done at the application level. COM+ provides a nonprogramming solution through more attributes such as "requires synchronization." An interceptor can intervene and acquire locks to enforce synchronization, resulting in great simplification for the application programmer.

MESSAGE QUEUING

We have seen that MSMQ provides message queuing services that allow great flexibility in how a client requests services of a server. For example, the client may be temporarily disconnected from the server, but can still place a request in a queue, which the system can guarantee will be satisfied sometime. The programmatic approach is for the application programmer to learn the MSMQ API and make calls as necessary. The COM+ approach is again to provide some attributes which can be declared. A "queued component" has the attribute that a method call will result in a request being placed on a queue. It is COM+, through an interceptor, not the application program, that calls MSMQ. The result again is considerable simplification in the programming model for the application programmer.

OTHER SERVICES

We could go on at considerable length, but you should get the general idea. Part 3 of this book discusses these services in some detail. Some of the other services include a "publish and subscribe" event service and a load-balancing service. The common denominator is that these are services that are important for developing robust, scalable enterprise applications, they are difficult to program at the application level, and COM+ makes it easy to access these services through its declarative, attribute-based programming model.

The Power of COM: A Preview

Hopefully at this point you have a good first cut understanding of what COM+ is. The road to a detailed understanding includes learning the fundamentals of COM itself, because every COM+ component *is* a COM component. COM+ adds configuration attributes and very powerful run-time services, but in order to participate in these services you must implement a COM component. Part 2 of this book covers the fundamental concepts and programming techniques of COM in detail. This study is rather long, in order to teach the subject matter at the required depth to write robust programs. It might be nice to have a little preview of what can be gained from all this work.

Building a Web Browser

The beauty of COM+ is that it builds on COM, which has already proved itself very capable for enabling complex applications to be built from reusable components. I believe that COM has been the crown jewel of Windows system architecture and has powered Microsoft's efforts to move very quickly into new areas, such as Internet technology. As a demo of the power of COM, I invite you right now to sit down at your computer and create your own simple Web browser!

We'll use Visual Basic 6.0. If you are a C++ bigot (like I used to be) and have never programmed in Visual Basic, please spend a little time familiarizing yourself with Visual Basic. There is a nice *Programmers Guide* provided with the online documentation that should be more than enough to get you started. The environment is so easy to use you may in fact be able to guide yourself through it with just the little hints I give in various demos. You may want to look ahead to my "hello" program in Chapter 3.

We will use both C++ and Visual Basic in this book to illustrate different features of COM and COM+. Since Visual Basic operates at a higher level of abstraction than C++, it is often useful to do something in Visual Basic to illuminate the central features without getting bogged down in extraneous code.

The magic that will enable us easily to build our own Web browser application comes from the way Microsoft architected Internet Explorer, beginning with version 3.0. A key component is an ActiveX control called the Web Browser Control, which you can use in your own programs.

INSTALLING THE CD-ROM

If you have not already done so, now would be a good time to install the CD-ROM that comes with this book. See instructions at the end of the preface. The structure of the CD-ROM is very straightforward. Under the top-level **ComPlus** directory there is a chapter directory for each chapter in the book for which there are working code samples. The chapter directories in turn have subdirectories for each sample program in the chapter. Some of these have multiple steps. Some chapter directories also have a **Demos** directory, where you are encouraged to work along with a specific demo described in this book. The subdirectory **CaseStudy** contains the Electronic Commerce Game™.

The CD-ROM has a simple **install.exe** self-extracting file which will set up the example programs on your hard disk. You may choose the root directory. It defaults to **c:\ComPlus**. (If you choose a different root directory you will have to edit some pathnames in **.reg** files in Chapters 6 and 9. I am not aware of any other path dependencies, but I have not performed extensive testing.) I encourage you to run this **install.exe** file right away. You will then have at your immediate disposal a place to build and experiment with the sample programs and to do the demos. The CD-ROM also has the example programs expanded in the directory structure, so you can make changes on your hard disk freely and go back to the CD-ROM to get back any original files you need.

WEB BROWSER DEMONSTRATION

Do your work in the **Chap1\Demos\MyBrowser** directory. Example code can be found in the directory **Chap1\MyBrowser**.

1. Start up Visual Basic 6. Create a new Standard EXE project. Change the name of the project to "MyBrowser." Change the Caption property of Form1 to "My Web Browser." Save your program in **Chap1\Demos\MyBrowser**. (Save again when you are all done.)
2. Bring up the Components dialog (menu Projects | Components). Put a check by Microsoft Internet Controls. See Figure 1–3. Click OK. The WebBrowser control is now added to the tools palette (it is a little globe).

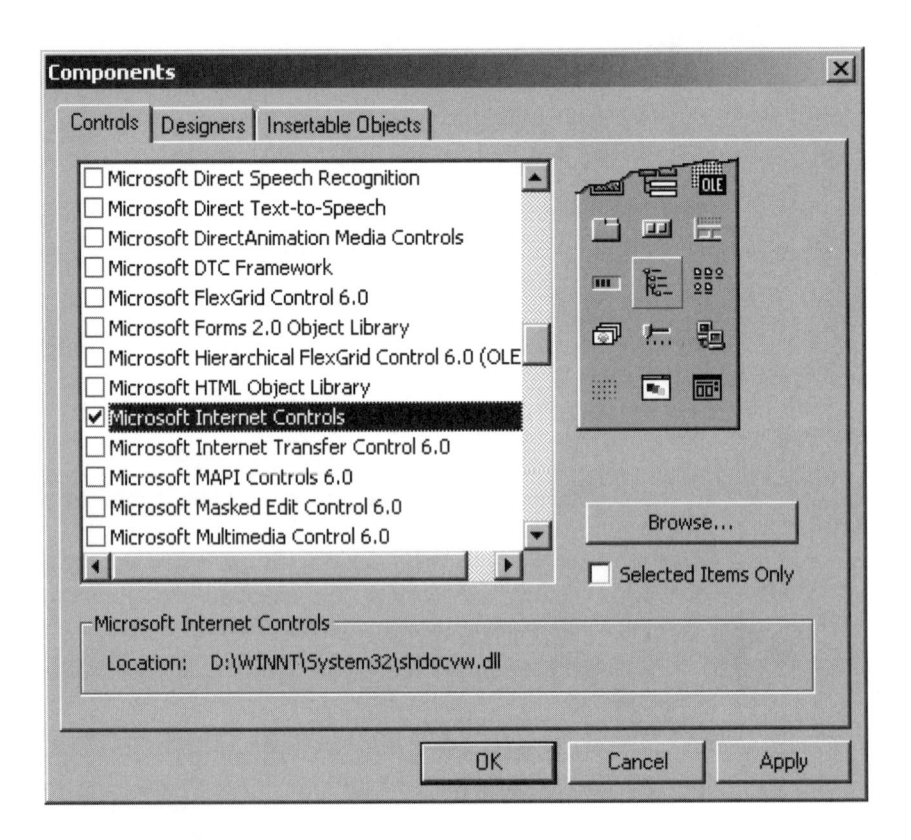

Figure 1-3   *Adding an ActiveX control to your project*

3. Now draw controls for a label "URL," a text box where the user can type in a URL, a button "GO," and a WebBrowser control. You may wish to expand the form a little. See Figure 1–4.
4. Give names "txtURL" and "cmdGo" to the textbox and button respectively. Accept the default name "WebBrowser1" for the WebBrowser control.
5. Bring up the Object Browser to get information about the methods of the new control (menu View | Object Browser). In the libraries dropdown at the top, select "SHDocVwCtl." For Classes choose "WebBrowser" and scroll through the methods. "Navigate" looks promising. See Figure 1–5.

The Power of COM: A Preview 21

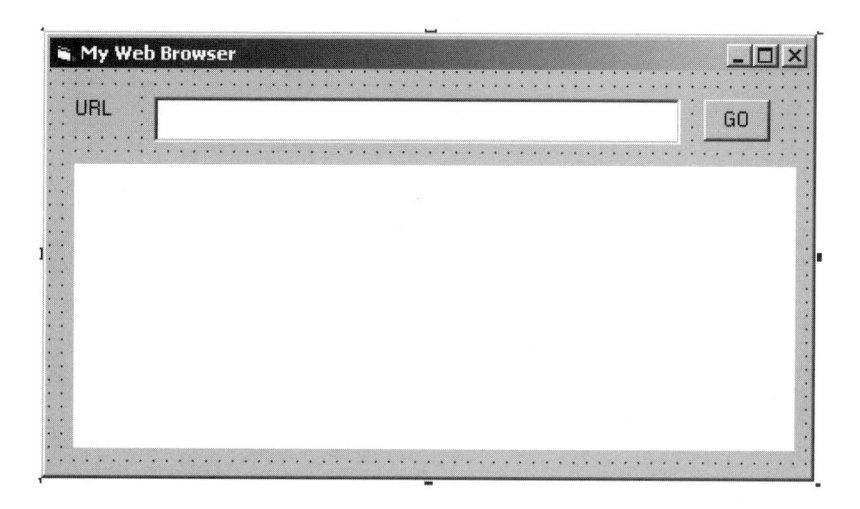

Figure 1-4   *Adding controls to the form*

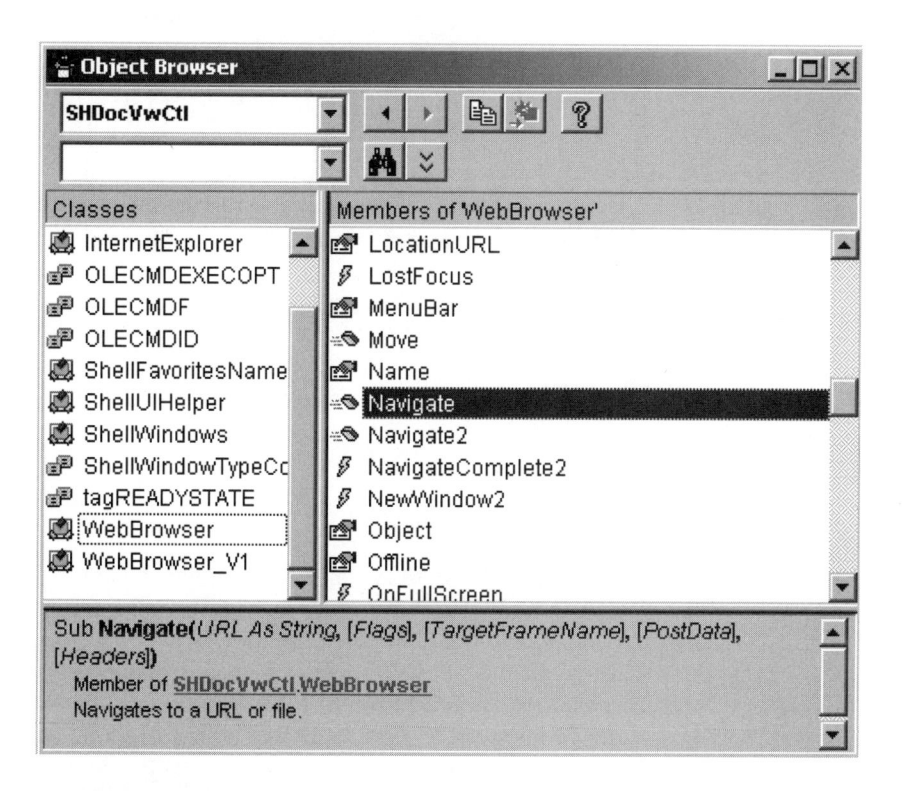

Figure 1-5   *Using the Object Browser*

6. Add a command handler for the "GO" button and the following intuitive code:

   ```
   Private Sub cmdGo_Click()
      WebBrowser1.Navigate (txtURL)
   End Sub
   ```

   Did you notice the "Auto completion" dialog that came up after you typed "WebBroswer1" and the period? A list is presented of the possible methods, and you can select from the list, without having to type in.

7. Connect to the Internet and run the program. Type in the URL of your favorite Web site and click "GO." See Figure 1–6.

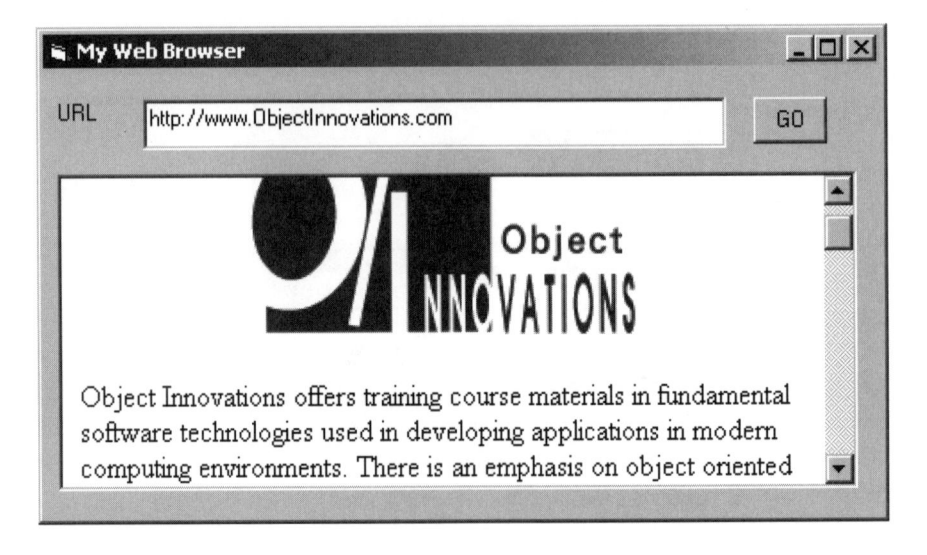

Figure 1–6 *Using your new app to browse the Web*

Software Components

I hope you enjoyed the little demo. It actually illustrates quite a bit about Microsoft's component architecture. The Visual Basic application development environment is thoroughly integrated with COM. The Components dialog displays a list of all the ActiveX controls that are registered in your system. An ActiveX control is a special kind of COM component that is quite rich in features. It can be plugged into a development environment and be used like the built-in controls. When you selected "Microsoft Internet Controls" from the Components dialog, all the ActiveX controls contained in the DLL shdocvw.dll (the DLL is shown in the Location box) are added to your project, including the WebBrowser control. These new controls show up on the Tools palette just like the built-in controls. The Object Viewer shows all the objects available to you. Built-in entities like textboxes and buttons are objects as well as COM objects that are added. A feature in COM known as a type library is used by viewer programs like Object Viewer to give information about the objects in the system.

There are several features of software *components* that make them more than simple objects from classical object-oriented languages. One is that they are language independent. They can be used from many different languages. They are distributed as binary executables. They are completely encapsulated black-box entities. (Class libraries such as Microsoft Foundation Classes or MFC are specific to a language such as C++ and usually distribute their source code. A template library like Active Template Library or ATL has to distribute the source code, because the C++ template mechanism requires source code for template instantiation.) The source code is the ultimate documentation for the user of the class library, and inheritance can introduce nuances in behavior. Providing the source code surrenders intellectual property of the vendor of the class library. In contrast, a completely black-box component both protects the vendor and also makes a more clear-cut contract of component functionality for the user. Components can provide extremely rich functionality, as we've seen with the Web Browser control. Another feature of components is that, as we have seen with ActiveX controls, they can actually "plug in" to the development environment.

This last point about the integration of a component architecture with tools is extremely important. Implementing and using components "by hand" may be intricate and difficult. An analogy is writing computer programs in machine language or assembly language. By using a compiler and various development tools like an IDE (integrated development environment), the writing and debugging of computer programs is greatly simplified. It does not matter that the underlying machine language may be quite complex.

I should have mentioned Ada in the survey of object-oriented languages. Although the original Ada had strong support for encapsulation, it was not "object oriented" because there was no class construct by which objects could be instantiated. However the revised 9x Ada does support objects, and Ada is actually a very powerful object-oriented language at this point. Ada is used in some large military and government systems but has not become a popular commercial language. I believe the use of Ada was hindered by the lack of strong tool support initially. In the development of Ada, great attention was paid to the language specification. There was also a tools specification called APSE (Ada Programming and Support Environment). Unfortunately this specification received much less attention, and so a uniform tool suite among vendors did not emerge.

In contrast, Microsoft has placed enormous emphasis on providing tools supporting COM and has also published the complete COM specification.

Microsoft has supported other tool vendors in supporting COM in their environment. Thus, whether it is Delphi (based on another object-oriented language, Object Pascal—my survey really is rather incomplete!) PowerBuilder, Progress, SAP R/3, you name it, there will probably be COM support (as long as the platform is Windows).

The last point is interesting. COM has basically been a Windows component architecture. COM has been ported to other environments. Microsoft itself ported COM to the Macintosh and has arranged with third parties like Software AG to port COM to Unix and MVS. So far Microsoft has not released COM+ to other vendors (as of this writing), so it is unclear how strong COM on other platforms will really be. Cross-platform support is not the strong suit of COM. For interoperability with other platforms, you should consider various strategies, such as doing COM within your Microsoft systems and bridging to CORBA for legacy systems. As pointed out earlier, MSMQ can be useful for integrating to foreign systems. This book is about COM+ on Windows platforms, and interoperability with other platforms will not receive further attention.

What's Next

At this point you should have a general appreciation for what COM/COM+ is and where it fits in the evolution of object-oriented and component systems. You've also seen a demonstration of how really powerful COM is, especially when combined with development tools. In the rest of this book we will discuss the details. The next chapter puts COM+ into the context of Windows DNA (Distributed interNet Applications) architecture, Microsoft's comprehensive framework for enterprise application development. We'll see how Windows DNA is geared towards the development of three-tier applications. After this general architectural overview, you'll set up a testbed for working with Windows DNA. The testbed will actually be quite extensive, involving Windows 2000, Visual Studio with both Visual C++ and Visual Basic, MSMQ, SQL Server 7.0, and some other components. Although some of what we do will only require a single tool (like the VB demo we did in this chapter), the full exploration of the subject will require an extensive testbed.

T W O

Three-Tier Applications and Windows DNA

We saw that COM is a powerful technology. With COM we can encapsulate very complex software such as a Web browser into an easy-to-use software component. Many of the current applications of COM technology have been in client programs using COM components such as ActiveX controls. COM+ extends this power to the server, simplifying the development of complex multiple-tier applications. This chapter surveys issues in distributed applications, tracing the evolution from one-tier to two-tier (client/server) to modern three-tier architectures. The three tiers are Presentation (for the user interface), Business (for the application logic), and Data Access (for the data).

One of the most important distinctions in three-tier applications is the technology used in the presentation tier. Traditional client/server applications have emphasized a rich client that exploits fully the capabilities of a modern graphical user interface, such as Microsoft Windows. There are a number of issues with these rich (or "fat") clients, and modern practice is evolving towards "thin" clients, especially clients relying on a Web browser for presenting a standard user interface. These so-called Web-based applications make use of HTTP as the protocol for communicating to the middle tier. The rest of the system is the same in both cases, with business and data objects in the middle talking to data in the third tier. This chapter explores these and other issues in three-tier applications and examines Windows DNA as Microsoft's architecture for building three-tier applications. We will look at all three tiers and explore the Microsoft technologies for implementing each tier.

Evolution of Distributed Systems

Early computers were not at all distributed. The user interacted directly with the computer. In the very earliest days, programs and data were entered directly in binary by toggling switches on the computer. Then various peripheral devices were created, allowing for easier interaction with the computer via punched cards and keyboards. Only a single user at a time would have access to the computer, and batch processing was the norm. It is interesting that the modern stand-alone PC is a throwback to this basic architecture, although the hardware and software makes for a much friendlier environment for interacting with the machine.

This section examines the evolution from single-user systems to multiple-user single-tier and then to two-tier (client/server) systems.

One-Tier Systems

The simplest kind of multiple-user system is a single-tier system in which all the processing and data reside at a central computer, typically a mainframe or minicomputer. Users interact with the central computer through terminals. Since all applications and data are kept at the central computer, this kind of system is very easy to manage. Figure 2–1 illustrates a one-tier system.

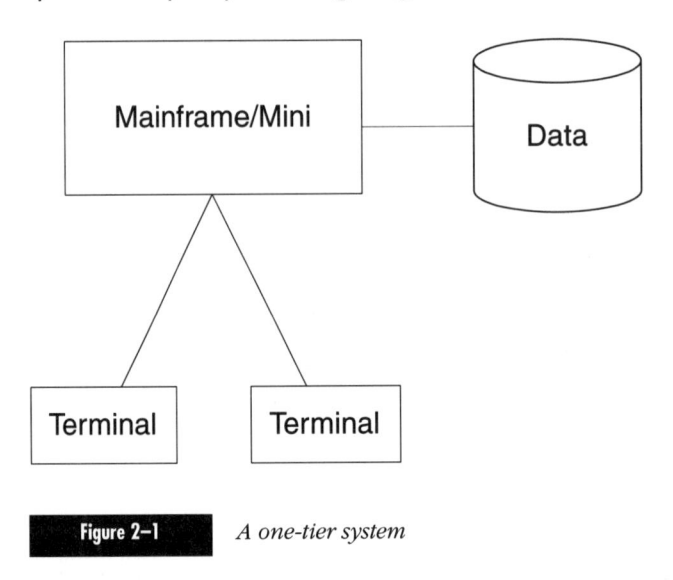

Figure 2–1 *A one-tier system*

There are a number of disadvantages to such a system. Since all processing is done on the central computer, the amount of processing power available to an individual user is limited. The central computer is also responsible for the presentation logic, which typically is character-based and therefore very simple.

There is a single point of failure: if the central computer goes down, all users are dead in the water. Because of the importance of the central computer staying up, it is typically a quite expensive system, such as a mainframe designed for maximum reliability. There is a basic lack of flexibility in such a system. The only applications available are ones that are centrally installed, and mainframe applications tend to be expensive, just as mainframe hardware is.

PC LANs

A response to the inflexibility of mainframe systems was the Personal Computer (PC). The big initial attraction of the PC was the variety of inexpensive applications that were available. Because of the low cost of the hardware, there quickly grew a large installed base of PCs, creating a large market for software. This large market resulted in low prices and great variety. Thus many useful applications could be purchased to run on an inexpensive PC, which proved very attractive to departments in large companies. An off-the-shelf application could be purchased that would do useful things without having to wait a long time for in-house development of an application, or securing the approval to buy an expensive mainframe application. Note that the initial growth of PCs came before the Graphical User Interface (GUI) was available. The appearance of easy-to-use GUI applications only fueled this enormous growth.

But the initial PC was a stand-alone machine, an intolerable limitation in a business environment. So the next step was to connect the PCs via a Local Area Network (LAN). The resulting configuration is shown in Figure 2–2. The server would be a file/print server, and a network operating system such as NetWare or LAN Manager would be used on the server with corresponding client software on each PC. Only files and printers would be shared. All the applications would still run on the individual PCs.

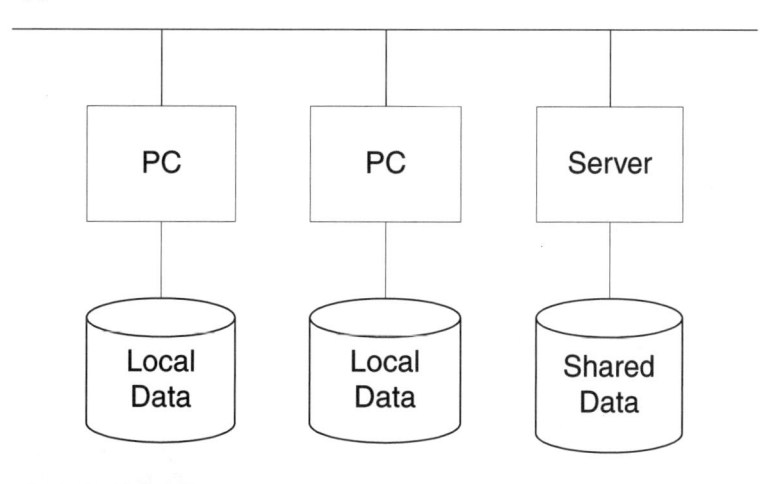

Figure 2–2   *A PC local area network*

Note that in such a configuration you could run a shared application on the server. But the only thing that resided on the server was the EXE of the application. You could cut down on the local storage requirements, but each PC ran its own image of the EXE in its own memory. A personal database application designed for one PC could run in a shared mode with suitable locking. But this kind of operation is extremely inefficient, because the data resides on the shared disk, and all processing is done on the PC; this means that data is continually being moved between the PC and the shared disk.

Two-Tier (Client/Server) Systems

At this point we are on the horns of a dilemma. On the one hand we have expensive, centralized mainframe systems. On the other we have inexpensive, flexible PC LAN systems. The inexpensive PCs are attractive, but we have to solve some fundamental problems, such as the inefficiency of continually moving large amounts of data over the LAN.

DATABASE SERVERS

The next step was to solve the problem of shared data being continually moved between the server and the PC. To make the issue concrete, consider a database table with 10,000 records. A query is made to find an individual record meeting some selection criteria. With the database executable image running in the memory of the PC, data must be moved from the shared disk to the PC in order to execute the query. It may not be as crude as moving all 10,000 records, but there is much more data movement than simply returning the single record meeting the selection criteria.

The solution was to break the application into two pieces. The database engine would run on the Server, and the user interface would run on the PC (now called the "client"), and these two pieces of the application would communicate with each other through some network protocol. In our database query example, both the data and the database engine reside at the server, and only the *results* of the query (a single record) are sent to the client, which displays the result to the user. Figure 2–3 illustrates a client/server system.

Although Figure 2–1 and Figure 2–3 look very similar, there is a vast difference between them. In fact, the step to client/server represents the largest conceptual leap in the whole evolution. All of the preceding systems had the characteristic of the entire application running on one computer, just like the case of the very first computer. With client/server, there are two independent, cooperating applications, one running on the server and one on the client, and these two applications must communicate with each other over a net-

Figure 2-3 *A two-tier (client/server) system*

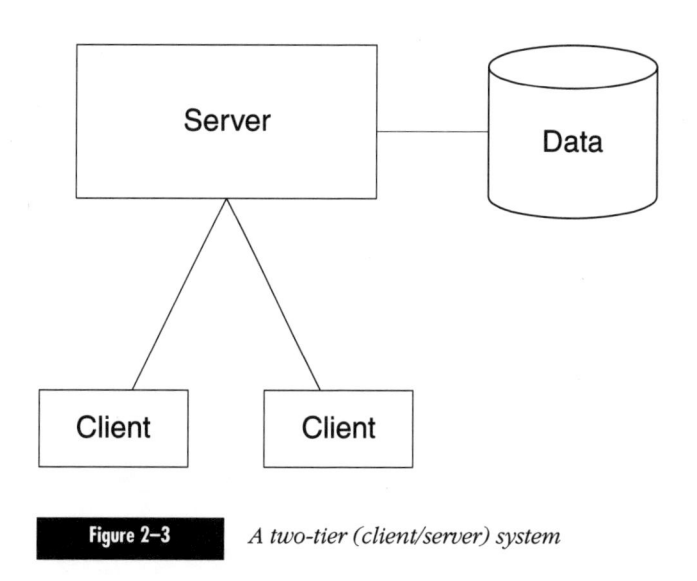

work. Although there are substantial advantages to such an architecture, as illustrated by the database query example, a client/server application is inherently very complex.

Fortunately the work of the application programmer is greatly simplified through the use of appropriate tools. For database applications, the DBMS (database management system) can provide the entire infrastructure. As a simple example, consider the SQL Server database **Game** installed on a remote computer. There is a table **Products** with columns **item** and **price**. We want to find the price of a cat carrier. For our demo we will make use of the Query Analyzer tool that is part of SQL Server 7. If you would like to do this demo now, please look ahead to Chapter 18 for instructions on setting up the **Game** database. Start Query Analyzer. You will be presented with a login screen, where you can select which SQL Server system you want to connect to. See Figure 2–4. In the "SQL Server" dropdown, specify the name of the computer where your database resides.

Next we choose the database **Game** from the "DB" dropdown and then enter a SQL query:

```
select * from Products where item = 'cat carrier'
```

We get back a result showing that the price is 30.00. See Figure 2–5.

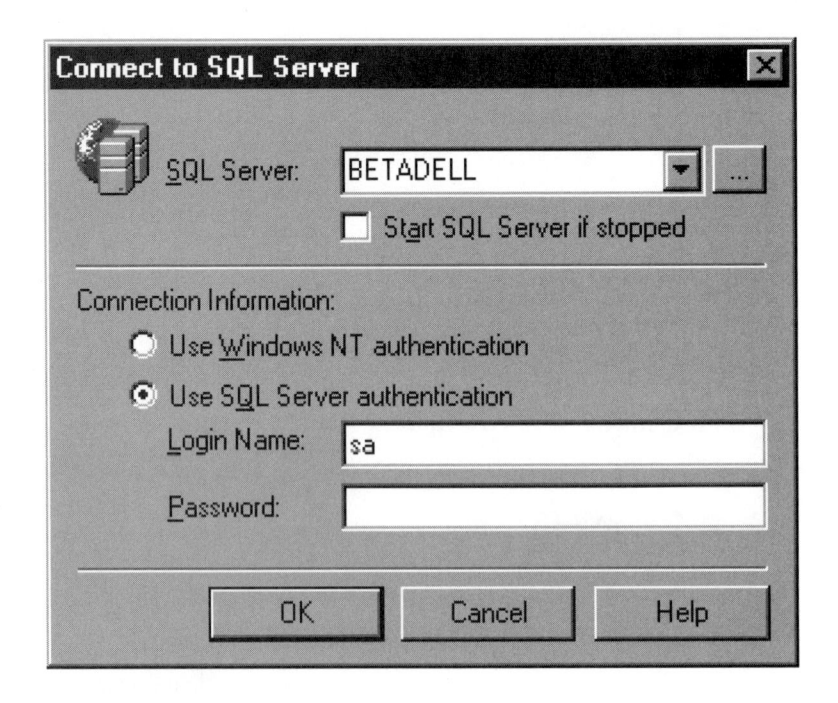

Figure 2–4 *Connecting to a remote DBMS*

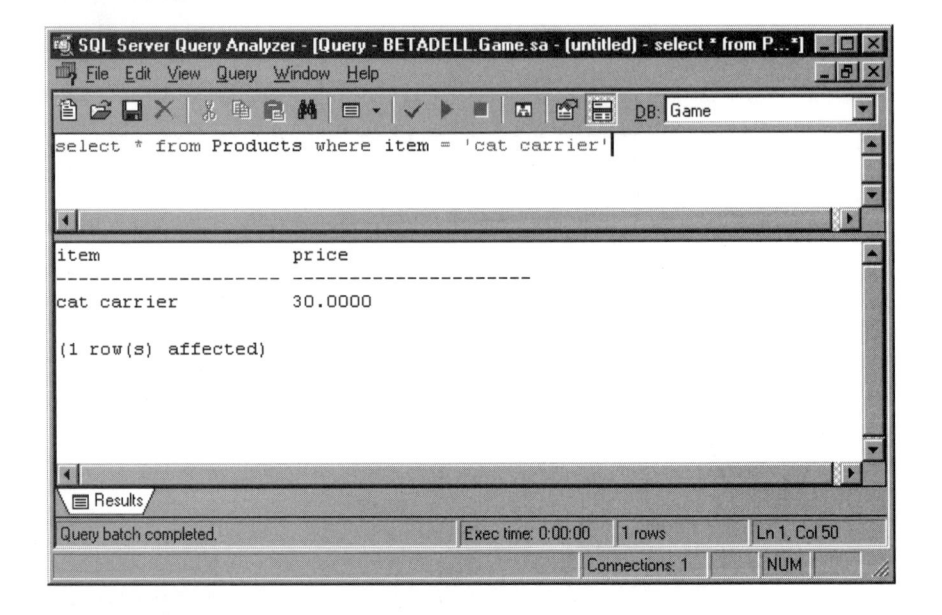

Figure 2–5 *A simple SQL query*

This simple example illustrates the essence of a client/server application. The server part of the application is the database engine running on the remote computer. The client part of the application is the query tool running on the local computer. The two pieces of the application communicate by a network protocol provided by the DBMS itself. The application program in this case is the simple SQL statement. The DBMS provides all the infrastructure.

Normally of course, the client application will not be a query tool but a custom application. Tools like Visual Basic and PowerBuilder make it easy to implement a GUI program that talks to a database. If we are always talking to the same DBMS (such as SQL Server or Oracle), we can rely on the network protocol provided by the DBMS itself. The DBMS will also supply a client API that can be used for invoking this protocol, resulting in a simple programming model. If our organization uses more than one DBMS, or if we want to structure our applications so that we are not tied to a particular DBMS but may be free in the future to move to a different one, we may choose to make use of middleware such as ODBC. Chapter 1 mentioned ODBC or "Open Database Connectivity" as part of Microsoft's WOSA (Windows Open System Architecture). Figure 1–2 illustrated the basic architecture. The line between the Driver and the Data Source could in fact cross a network boundary. Again it is the DBMS that is entirely responsible for the network communication.

It may appear that client/server provides quite a complete solution that is easy to program, thanks to the DBMS. But what if we want to solve a partial differential equation? No DBMS that I am aware of knows how to do that. This means that the code to solve the equation must be placed on the client, and we are back to the situation where there is much data movement from the server to the client. We would like for the client to be able to issue a command "solve equation." The data points needed reside on the server, and we would like the code to run on the server, with only the result sent back to the client.

There is another disadvantage to this simple kind of DBMS client/server architecture. With all the application-specific logic residing on the client, we get very "fat" clients. There are several drawbacks to such an approach. For one thing, too much might be demanded of the client, requiring more expensive computers at every desktop. Another issue concerns management. With multiple applications residing on desktop computers throughout an organization, maintenance and upgrades become a nightmare.

In fact, the disadvantages to client/server have been so great that the demise of the mainframe has not occurred. There are large hardware cost savings in a client/server system versus a mainframe system. But some of these savings evaporate when you have to invest in high-end clients, and much more of the savings disappear into the maintenance sinkhole. As a result the mainframe has had surprising longevity. Mainframes also make great servers, which is another reason they aren't dead.

APPLICATION SERVERS

Without retreating to the old one-tier solution, we would like to find a way to implement application functionality on the server, both to lower the demands on the client and also to simplify administration on the client. We are led to *application servers* that do more than share printers and files (PC LAN file/print server) or provide a DBMS (database server). We want to be able to code any desired functionality and run it on the server if desired. Specialized file servers such as NetWare have proved poor targets for applications, and the most popular application servers have been Unix and NT.

With application functionality running on the server, we are now faced with the network communication issue, which was solved for us by the DBMS for the case where all server functionality was performed in the database. One approach would be to augment the capability of a database, so that you have a general purpose programming language for the database engine, and you *could* code an algorithm for solving a partial differential equation inside a DBMS. Such an approach is technically feasible, and in fact some database zealots have ardently pushed for such an approach. The latest SQL standard is over 800 pages, compared to the original 100 pages or so that elegantly captured the core relational database requirements. Some simple business logic can be implemented in the database itself through stored procedures, but trying to make the database do everything is probably not a good idea. It goes against the whole modern programming approach of trying to make systems modular. And customers do not want to be locked into a single very complex DBMS.

So we are led back to servers providing application functionality outside the database, and the application must implement network communication. Network protocols themselves can be used, such as TCP/IP, SPX/IPX (NetWare) or NetBios/NetBEUI (LAN Manager). Or slightly higher level protocols like sockets or pipes can be used. All of this requires a high degree of specialized communications programming expertise, and the lower-level protocols are network specific. It becomes easier to program network communication using Remote Procedure Call (RPC), but even this level of programming is rather complex.

Still higher protocols can make the communications problem tractable. One example is Microsoft's DCOM, which we will preview in Chapter 3 and discuss in depth in Chapter 10. Other examples include the Object Management Group's CORBA (Common Object Request Broker Architecture) and Remote Method Invocation (RMI) in Java. Yet another approach is message-oriented middleware (MOM) such as IBM's MQSeries and Microsoft's MSMQ.

This alphabet soup of technologies illustrates the inherent complexity of client/server architecture. There is no panacea that will make it all simple. A development organization needs to choose a set of technologies that are appropriate to its requirements and then make the necessary investment to acquire suitable tools and to learn the technologies. In this book we are focusing on Microsoft technologies.

Actually, the term "application server" has come to mean more than a generic name for a server that performs functionality other than file/printer sharing or database. There is now a whole category of software products called "application servers" that provide many services and greatly simplify the development of distributed applications. Microsoft has provided Microsoft Transaction Server (MTS) and there are many different Java application servers on the market. We will discuss this more specialized use of the term when we examine three-tier applications.

Three-Tier Systems

Apart from the communications issue, which must be solved somehow in every distributed system, there are some intrinsic limitations in the two-tier approach. To focus our discussion, let's go back to the pure database type of application (no partial differential equations). We don't have to worry about communications, because the DBMS takes care of it. But there are a number of other significant issues. Database types of applications have a common structure. There of course is the data itself, residing in the database. There is the user interface residing on the client PC or workstation. And finally there is the business logic. In a one-tier system this business logic is implemented in the central computer, and in two-tier systems the logic is implemented primarily in the client (some processing may be done in stored procedures in the database).

We have already mentioned some of the "fat client" issues of a requirement for relatively high-end client PCs and the complexity of managing applications on many desktops. There is another significant issue in this type of design, and that is scalability. In a client/server system, every client is directly connected to the database. This is fine for a department type of application, but it may break down for an enterprise where there are a great many users, and it will certainly break down on the Internet where there can be an extremely large number of concurrent users at a peak time. The problem is that a database connection is a scarce resource. Also, with the client tied directly to the database, the client is limited to a particular kind of database. Some flexibility is provided by ODBC, but the client is still limited to the kind of data for which an ODBC driver is available.

A more flexible and scalable architecture is created by introducing a third tier, the "business" or "application" layer that sits between the presentation and data access layers as shown in Figure 2–6.

The Business layer separates the client from direct dependence on the database. Thus, the database can be changed without having any impact on Presentation layer code. Moreover, the Business layer can implement common "business rules" that may be utilized by many different client applications,

```
┌──────────────┐     ┌──────────┐     ┌──────────┐
│ Presentation │─────│ Business │─────│   Data   │
│              │     │          │     │  Access  │
└──────────────┘     └──────────┘     └──────────┘
```

Figure 2–6   *Three-tier architecture*

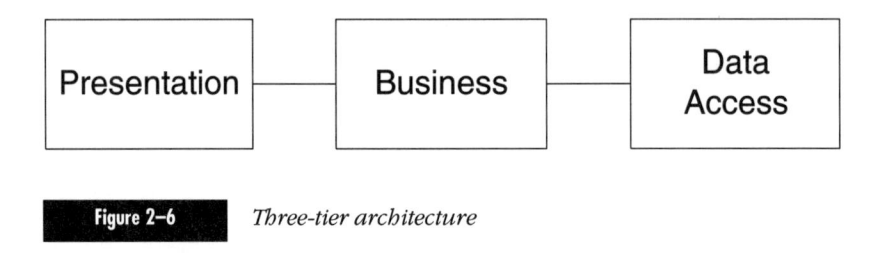

resulting in significant code reuse. If a business rule changes, only the Business layer has to be updated. The Business layer will be implemented on a server, so the desktop systems do not have to be touched for maintenance when business logic changes. Finally, the Business layer may perform optimization that can greatly increase the scalability of the system. For example, the Business layer may maintain a pool of database connections. A connection is used for a particular client when that client needs access to the database. When that particular data access is complete, it is not necessary to tear down the connection, only to return it to the pool. Thus, a limited number of connections can service a large number of clients, because not all the clients need access to the data at the same time.

APPLICATION SERVERS IN THE MIDDLE TIER

Although three-tier architecture is conceptually very simple, the implementation is complex. There are many issues. One is network communication, which we have already discussed. Another is the database connection pooling mentioned above. Multithreading is another issue, because there are multiple clients accessing the Business layer at the same time, and the DBMS does not help us out with concurrency issues once we introduced the extra layer. The Business layer may talk to multiple data sources, and so there may be a need for managing distributed transactions. And so on.

It would be difficult to implement three-tier applications if it was necessary at the application level to deal with issues like the ones discussed above. Fortunately, such system-level programming tasks can be managed by the system. A good analogy is with the DBMS, which handles issues of communication, concurrency, and transactions. Such issues do not have to be dealt with by the programmer in one-tier and two-tier systems. The new product category of *application servers* provides similar capabilities in the middle tier.

Microsoft's application server solution for NT 4.0 is Microsoft Transaction Server or MTS. The follow-on to MTS is COM+, the subject matter of this book. There are many pieces required for implementing three-tier applications, and Microsoft has organized its solutions under the rubric "Distributed interNet Applications (DNA) architecture." The rest of this chapter will survey the main parts of Windows DNA, including a very important variation on three-tier applications designed to exploit the Internet, so-called Web-based applications.

Overall Structure of Windows DNA

Windows DNA is a very grand vision involving a great many sophisticated technologies. It is more than simply Microsoft's implementation of the three-tier model. It will be reasonably straightforward for us to trace through the three tiers and outline the relevant technologies in each tier. But there are also important general services and "glue" technologies, which apply to more than one tier. So before going through the tiers, we will briefly sketch these general services and glue technologies. The overall structure of Windows DNA is illustrated in Figure 2–7.

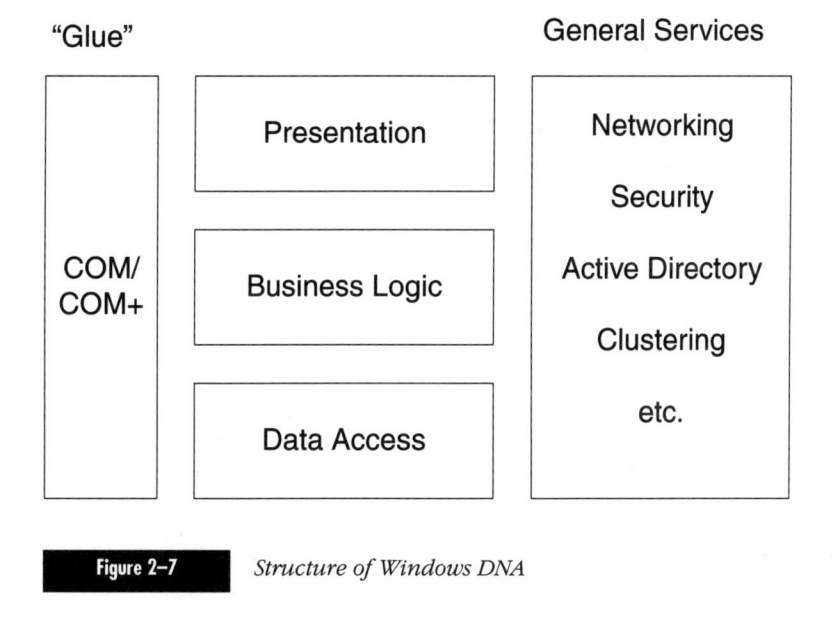

"Glue" — COM/COM+

Presentation
Business Logic
Data Access

General Services — Networking, Security, Active Directory, Clustering, etc.

Figure 2–7 *Structure of Windows DNA*

General Services

The general services include the base Win32 API and many other services that are layered on top of Win32. Some of the important services are specific to a particular tier. In this section we will look at some of the principal services that apply to more than one tier.

NETWORKING

The fundamental service important to distributed processing is of course networking. The networking services are built on top of the basic network protocols. Increasingly, TCP/IP is the most important protocol. Windows DNA is concerned with two higher-level protocols. The first is HTTP (HyperText

Transfer Protocol), the industry standard protocol connecting Web clients and servers over the Internet. The second is DCOM, a Microsoft-specific object-oriented protocol built on top of RPC. DCOM is a natural extension of COM and will be discussed in Chapter 10. We will see that there are two basic types of DNA applications: thin clients making use of HTTP and rich clients making use of DCOM.

SECURITY

A very important aspect of distributed systems is security. Issues in security include authenticating users (making sure they are who they say and are entitled to system access), gate-keeping access to data and services, and protecting data as it is transmitted (for instance, by encryption). Core security is provided by the operating system. Windows NT/2000 provides a layered security system, allowing for different security providers which support a special interface SSPI (security support provider interface). Windows NT has relied on NTLM (NT LAN Manager) and Windows 2000 introduces the more powerful Kerberos security provider. DCOM provides a higher-level security mechanism that applies to objects. Microsoft Transaction Server and COM+ provide an even higher-level and easier-to-use security model. Security is discussed in Chapter 17.

ACTIVE DIRECTORY

A very important new service in Windows 2000 is the Active Directory. Windows grew up as a desktop operating system, with only a single user. It was then extended to a local area network connecting multiple users into a *workgroup*. Such a network configuration is peer-to-peer, with no central repository of users. NT Server introduced the concept of a *domain* in which there is a repository of users, but the size of this repository is limited, and a large enterprise must have many domains, which become difficult to administer. The Active Directory is a central repository which can manage *all* users in an entire enterprise. Facilities are provided for replicating this repository to enhance performance and robustness. The Active Directory is object oriented and can hold many different kinds of entities, not just users. It becomes a very general storehouse for system information. The study of the Active Directory is beyond the scope of this book, but we will see in Chapter 3 that we must install the Active Directory on one of our computers in order to have a fully functional testbed in which we can manage multiple user accounts. Active Directory is also necessary for Microsoft Message Queue.

CLUSTERING

Another important issue in large systems is scalability. How do we handle a very large number of concurrent users? Windows DNA provides various technologies to enhance scalability, and we will explore some of them in Part 3. One important Microsoft technology is the Cluster Server, which is software to enable multiple computers on a LAN to cooperate in processing, so called "loosely coupled multiprocessing." Clustering does not require special hardware, unlike tightly coupled multiprocessing, in which there are multiple CPU chips in one computer. Clustering can also be configured to support a degree of fault tolerance. Microsoft clustering technologies are discussed in Chapter 23.

"Glue" Technology

Another dimension to Windows DNA is the "glue" technology that enables multiple pieces of software to collaborate to achieve an objective. In Microsoft software, the preeminent glue technology is the Component Object Model (COM) and its big brother, COM+.

COM

The core underlying technology used in all three tiers of DNA is COM. We will be discussing COM in considerable detail in Part 2. The simple way to think of COM right now is that it is *fast, object-oriented,* and *packaged*. It is fast, because it can be called in-process. It is an evolution of object-oriented technology, as we saw in Chapter 1. This means that COM objects typically are part of an "object model" and thus have an organized structure. Finally, COM components come in a nice physical package such as a DLL, which can be conveniently plugged into an application, bought from a third party, etc.

COM+

There are two ways to look at COM+. One way is as a collection of services that provide support for sophisticated distributed applications, greatly simplifying the life of an applications programmer by removing the need to code multithreading, connection pooling, etc. As such, COM+ primarily addresses issues in the middle tier and can be thought of as the merging of MTS into COM. The more fundamental way to look at COM+ is as an extension of the COM model to support declarative programming based on attributes. An object and its client each live in their own programming context, with their own assumptions about threading, transaction requirements, etc. COM+ makes it possible for the object and its client to each declare their own attributes. If there is a perfect match, a direct call takes place. If there is not a perfect match, some work must be done to adjust the contexts so that they can work together correctly. COM+ introduces the concept of an *interceptor* which is invoked automatically by the system when required to reconcile contexts. Interceptors are provided by the system, and no coding needs to be done by the application programmer to address context mismatch issues.

COM+ is discussed in detail in Part 3, and the fundamental architectural features of attributes, contexts, and interceptors are covered in Chapter 14.

Windows DNA Layers

In this section we describe the specific Microsoft technologies and tools that are relevant to developing and implementing three-tier applications. The range and scope of these technologies and tools is very broad, so we will not attempt an exhaustive summary. Rather we will focus on the major ones that make up the contents of this book.

Presentation Layer

There are two broad kinds of clients, what Microsoft calls "thin clients" and "rich clients." Apart from avoiding pejorative connotations of the word "fat," rich clients refer more to the technology used to create the user interface than to how much code is running on the client.

RICH CLIENTS

Rich clients are Win32 applications that have access to all the resources of the client computer. They are just like any other Win32 application, except they are also clients of a three-tier application. Their most immediately striking feature is their full-blown graphical user interface. Microsoft has been very aggressive in moving forward the look and feel of its Windows applications, adding many Visual features and nuances. The modern Windows user interface has gone far beyond the classical WIMP (Windows, icons, menus, and pointing device). Commonplace features today include toolbars, status bars, tooltips, context menus, and many special controls like treeviews. Compare any modern Windows app with a typical HTML form that you see on the Web, and you will immediately grasp what I am talking about. (But Web-based interfaces, too, thanks largely to stimulus by Microsoft, are moving rapidly forward.)

The traditional way of building a rich client is through a high-end development system such as Visual Basic or Visual C++, augmented by add-ins such as ActiveX controls. A new approach that Microsoft has begun to emphasize is using Office applications as a front-end. Office applications have long been customizable by power users through macros. Originally Microsoft had incompatible macro languages among its different Office products. Today all Office products use the common language VBA (Visual Basic for Applications), which Microsoft has also licensed to other Windows application vendors.

The advantage of rich clients is their functionality, in terms of both user interface and also the ability to perform whatever additional processing on the client is appropriate for the application. The disadvantage is the requirements that are placed on the client computer, an issue that is particularly significant with Internet applications. If you are an e-commerce store you want to sell to as many customers as you can, without requiring them to run a modern Windows operating system on a fully functional PC and to obtain from you or download a large Windows application, which they must install and maintain (something gets corrupted, so they have to reinstall it, etc.). You want life for your customers to be simple. Just a Web browser is all they should need.

THIN CLIENTS

There are different possible kinds of thin clients. An example, of course, is a terminal. Microsoft has in fact purchased some technology (Windows Terminal Server) which enables Windows applications to run on a central server and to put up a GUI on clients. Such a configuration provides the advantage of central administration, at the expense of processing demands on the server, bandwidth issues between client and server, etc. But more and more "thin client" is coming to mean an application that runs on a Web server and puts up its user interface through HTML pages in a Web browser. The e-commerce merchant has his dream of an application that can run "anywhere."

For a while, it was thought that such Web applications could be enhanced through various kinds of components that could be plugged into the browser, such as Netscape plug-ins, ActiveX controls, Java applets, etc. The problem is that none of this technology is standard, and so you cannot achieve universal reach by employing it. The same applies to client side scripting. These issues will be discussed in more detail in Chapter 20.

Another approach is through enriching HTML itself. HTML 4 defines "dynamic" HTML or DHTML. Through this technology, you can design Web pages with a much richer user interface that will run inside any compliant browser. There is not yet complete consistency in implementations of DHTML, and of course older browsers do not support it. Note that it is possible for a Web server to find out what kind of browser is being used by the current client, and so it is feasible to customize the Web page that is returned accordingly.

The Microsoft technology for thin clients is its Web browser, Internet Explorer (IE), now at version 5.0. What is unique about this portion of Windows DNA is that part of the idea of thin clients is for Web applications to be able to run on *any* Web browser. Hence one option for Web pages is plan vanilla HTML (version 3.2,). The idea is for a thin client to be able to run anywhere, and to run better on Microsoft platforms using IE.

SCRIPTING AND COMPONENTS

Both rich clients and thin clients can be enhanced through use of appropriate technology. In particular, they can make use of COM components, which we will study in Part 2. Rich clients can call COM components through standard techniques, while thin clients can invoke COM components through a scripting mechanism, using a language like VBScript or JavaScript.

An easy way to put some logic onto a Web page is through scripting, which can be done on both the client and the server. Client-side scripting is part of the presentation layer and is very easy to learn and to implement. It can also be very useful to enhance the overall performance of a Web-based application. As a simple example, consider validating input fields on an HTML form. The standard technique is for all validation to be done on the Web server. The user does not find out about any errors until after the form has been submitted. Through scripting, data can be validated on a field-by-field basis as the user fills out the form.

There is a discussion of scripting in Chapters 11 and 20. Please remember that if you are creating a thin client which you wish to run in *any* Web browser, you should avoid depending on client-side scripting.

Business Logic Layer

The middle tier or "business logic" layer is the most important piece in three-tier architecture, and is what differentiates three-tier from its predecessors. Most of the new services provided by Microsoft are for the middle tier, and that is where most of our focus will be in this book. The three principle general services that Microsoft provides for the middle tier are Component Services (COM+), Microsoft Message Queue (MSMQ) and Internet Information Server (IIS). We will begin with IIS, which is conceptually the easiest to understand.

INTERNET INFORMATION SERVER

Internet Information Server is Microsoft's full featured Web server, now at version 5.0. It is integrated into Windows 2000 Server. IIS is the application server supporting thin clients, which communicate with it via Hypertext Transfer Protocol (HTTP). Clients send requests to the server using this protocol. A request may simply ask for an HTML page to be served up, or it may contain data gathered from an HTML form. A request may also ask for a program to be executed, perhaps by going through the Common Gateway Interface (CGI). If a program is executed, an HTML page can be generated on the fly, containing data extracted from a database and the results of computations. HTTP is a stateless protocol, with the connection between the client and server terminated after each response from the server. Figure 2–8 illustrates the basic operation of Web clients and servers at a generic level, which is not specific to Microsoft.

```
            ┌─────────┐
            │  Web    │
            │ Client  │
            └────┬────┘
                 │
   HTTP          │
                 │
            ┌────┴────┐      ┌─────────┐
            │  Web    ├──────┤ Program │
            │ Server  │      │         │
            └────┬────┘      └────┬────┘
                 │                │
                 │   ┌──────┐     │
                 └───┤ Data ├─────┘
                     └──────┘
```

Figure 2-8   *Web clients and servers*

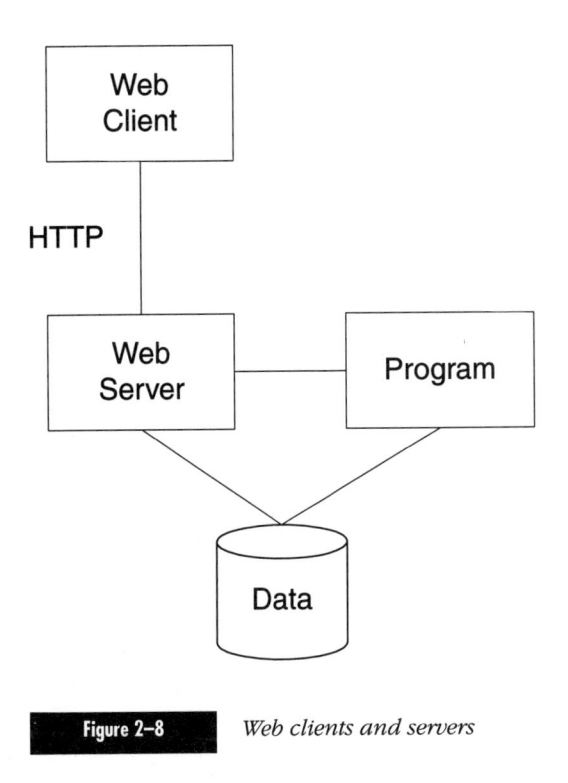

This basic HTTP protocol and the use of CGI to invoke a program on the Web server is plain generic Internet technology, which is supported by every Web server. Microsoft has added significant extensions to the server. While there are trade-offs to using Microsoft's client extensions (your application may not run on all Web browsers), in general you have control over what *server* your application runs on, and so if you choose Windows as your server platform, you can gain considerable functional benefit by employing Microsoft's server-side technologies.

The most fundamental of Microsoft's server extensions is ISAPI (Internet Services Application Programming Interface), which provides a higher-performance alternative to CGI. While CGI spawns a separate *process* to handle each request, ISAPI makes use of a DLL to run in-process. ISAPI remains Microsoft's highest performing Web application solution, and if you have a bottleneck in your Web application you should consider writing that portion directly at the ISAPI level. An ISAPI DLL makes direct calls to the Win32 API, and can of course utilize COM components just like any Windows program. But for most of your server work you will probably want to use *Active Server Pages* (ASP), which are implemented using ISAPI, to achieve much greater productivity in your Web server application programming.

Active Server Pages is a scripting environment for creating HTML pages to be returned to a Web client. An ASP page can be a mixture of HTML and scripting commands. The same scripting languages (VBScript and JavaScript) that can be used on the client can be used on the server. Thus, writing Active Server Pages is quite easy. The main drawback to use of a scripting language is performance. A script is *interpreted*, not compiled, and thus is much slower than compiled code. Hence only fairly simple operations should be performed directly by the script. Where speed is required, the script should call out to compiled code, and the way this is done is through COM components.

MICROSOFT TRANSACTION SERVER AND COM+

Microsoft Transaction Server (MTS) is Microsoft's NT 4.0 solution for simplifying the development of middle tier components. It is an add-on to NT 4.0, provided by the NT 4.0 Options Pack. In Windows 2000 MTS disappears as a separate entity. Its features have become integrated into COM itself, which is now called COM+. In Part 3, we discuss COM+ in detail. In this section we will give an overview of MTS, which will be our only coverage in this book.

The middle tier is the most challenging for the programmer. In the presentation tier the program only has to worry about a single user. There is considerable complexity in a graphical user interface, but by this time many tools (for example, Visual Basic and MFC) are available to greatly simplify the job. Likewise, the Data Access tier has considerable inherent complexity, but modern database systems are very powerful and provide many tools. The primary challenge with regard to the Data Access tier is providing uniform access to many different types of data, a topic we will discuss later in this chapter.

But the middle tier presents many new challenges, and MTS/COM+ provide solutions. The first challenge is dealing with *transactions*, which gave MTS its name. Transactions are the fundamental structuring concept that enables the development of complex multiple-user applications that access data. At its most basic, a transaction assures *atomicity*. A transaction is all or nothing. If you transfer money from one account to another, you do not wish for the debit to occur, a glitch to happen on the system, and you never get the compensating credit. Database management systems have supported transactions for many years, so you may think at first that transactions are a feature of the Data Access layer. But think again. Suppose you are ordering a product via the Web, and fulfilling your order involves many separate steps, each carried out on a different computer system. We are now in the realm of *distributed transactions*. It is for this kind of application that three-tier really shines. In a client/server system the client would be very complex, not only providing a user interface but also talking to multiple databases. Let us look at how such a system might be architected in three tiers. Figure 2–9 illustrates the basic architecture.

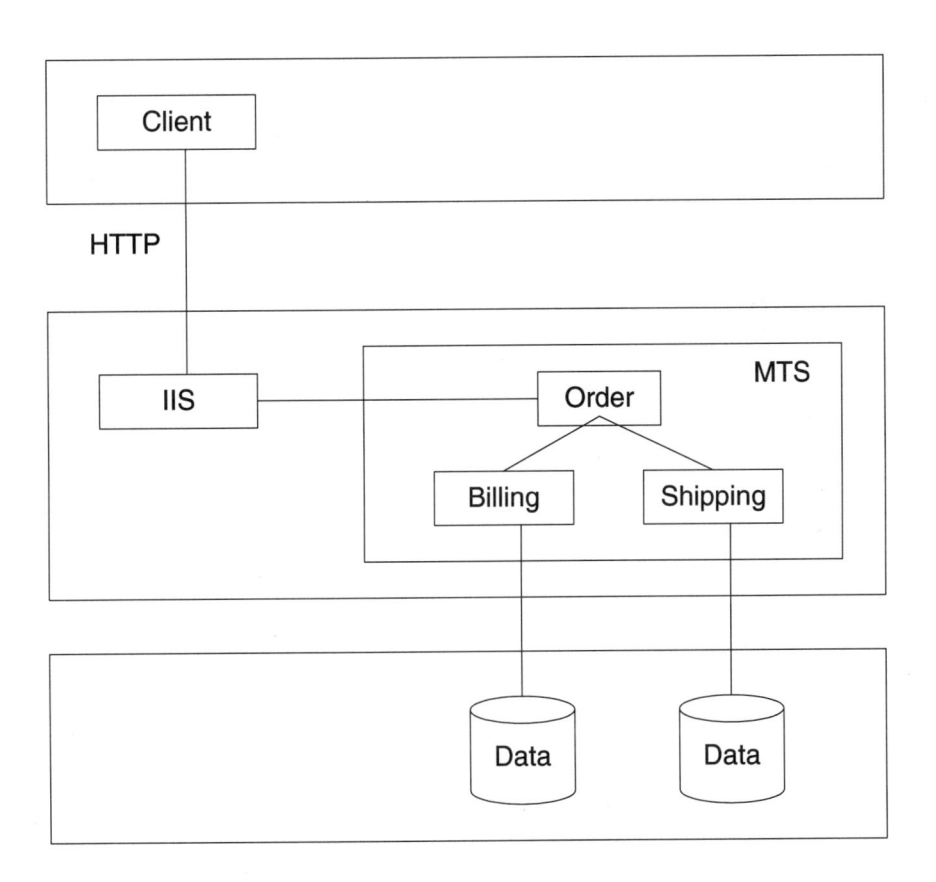

Figure 2-9 *A three-tier ordering application*

The server piece of the application is implemented on the middle tier through three business objects, Order, Billing and Shipping. These objects run inside a transaction. Thus if the order is posted to the Shipping application, but the Billing application discovers the customer credit card is not approved, the order will not ship, and any updates made to the Shipping database will be backed out. These objects run under MTS (or COM+). Let us look at some of the services MTS provides and why they are necessary (or what would have to be done by the application programmer if MTS were not in the picture).

First is the transaction itself. If there were only one database, the DBMS could handle the transaction aspect. But in our example there are two separate databases, and these may reside on different computers. Transactions to different databases are implemented through Microsoft Distributed Transaction Coordinator (MSDTC). The business objects could talk to MSDTC directly, but that would involve coding that is somewhat complex. MTS makes it very simple. You *declare* that the Order object "requires a transaction." You delegate work to the subsidiary objects Billing and Shipping. Each of these are declared as "supports transactions." This means that if they are called by a component running under a transaction, they will be enlisted under the same transaction, and the entire processing for Order will either all succeed or all fail. There is a little bit of coding required, but it is trivial. If an object succeeds in its work, it calls **SetComplete**. If it fails, it calls **SetAbort.** If all the objects call **SetComplete**, the transaction will succeed; otherwise, it will fail.

Another issue handled by MTS is concurrency control. There may be many clients placing orders concurrently, and the application as a whole has to deal with any conflicts that can arise. Notice that in a client/server system the application may not have to explicitly deal with concurrency, because it can be handled by the DBMS. But now client requests are not going directly to the database but to business objects. Thus these business objects have to deal with concurrency. MTS will handle the concurrency for any objects placed under its management.

Another issue is connection management. This is an area where a client/server system may not scale. Database connections are a scarce resource, and you may run into a problem if too many clients try to connect to the database at the same time. In the three-tier case, many clients may be connected to the Order component at the same time, but MTS will "activate" an object instance only when required. MTS also maintains a pool of database connections which it will hand out to the active objects. When the object is deactivated, the connection will be returned to the pool. The application must cooperate by calling **SetComplete** or **SetAbort** as soon as work has been completed, so that the object will be deactivated.

MICROSOFT MESSAGE QUEUE

The remaining key piece of Microsoft technology for the middle tier is Microsoft Message Queue (MSMQ). MSMQ, like MTS, is part of the NT 4.0 Option Pack. Unlike MTS, MSMQ remains a separate entity in Windows 2000, and is in fact a standard part of Windows 2000, like IIS.

What MSMQ brings to the party is asynchronous, one-way, message-oriented communication. MSMQ can be viewed as an alternative communications protocol to DCOM and HTTP, with quite different characteristics. DCOM is a connection-oriented protocol which preserves state. HTTP is stateless. Both DCOM and HTTP are synchronous and can return a result. This means the client is blocked until the server returns. It also means that both the client and server must be running in order for the call to succeed. MSMQ is asynchronous. A call is made by placing a message in a queue, and the call returns immediately with success or failure. Success simply means that MSMQ succeeded in placing the message on the queue. The client is not blocked. Note also that the server does not have to be running at the time the call is made. When the server comes up later, it will look for messages on the queue. Finally, the message is one-way—it does not return a result, because the server is not directly invoked by placing the message in the queue. If a result is desired, the server can send a message to the client.

There are many business situations where this asynchronous queuing model is appropriate. Consider again the order entry application illustrated in Figure 2–9. It may take some time to get a result back from Shipping. Rather than make the customer wait while the Shipping application processes, it may be better to submit the shipping request via a queue, and then the customer gets back an acknowledgment immediately. Later on if there is a problem, the Shipping application may send a message to the Order application.

Notice that I started referring to Order, Shipping, etc. as "applications." Another nice feature of MSMQ is that it facilitates integrating with legacy applications. MSMQ interoperates with other message queuing systems, such as IBM's MQSeries. In fact, MSMQ can be regarded as Microsoft's entry in "message-oriented middleware" (MOM), a popular mechanism for integrating applications.

COM+ has a technology called "queued components" which makes it much easier to use MSMQ. If a COM interface has all methods which don't return any results (no "out" parameters), then that interface can be given the attribute of "queued." Then client calls to that interface will automatically be routed through a queue, which COM+ creates. Besides obviating the need to make API calls to MSMQ, going through a queued component eliminates the need to marshal parameters into a message block.

Data Access Layer

Microsoft supplies a number of important technologies to support the Data Access layer in three-tier applications. Microsoft's strategic DBMS product is SQL Server, now at version 7.0. Unlike previous versions of SQL Server, which ran only on NT, SQL Server 7.0 also runs on Windows 95/98. On the other hand, SQL Server runs only on Windows platforms, unlike a DBMS such as Oracle, which runs on many different platforms. SQL Server is optimized to make full use of Win32. For example, SQL Server makes direct use of Win32 threads, and so does not have to go through a "thread package" which might be part of an implementation of a DBMS that has to run on many systems, including some that do not implement multithreading at the operating system level. We will use SQL Server 7.0 as the DBMS in the example programs in this book. Chapter 18 contains a simple tutorial on using SQL Server 7.0, which is quite easy to use.

More important than implementing its own DBMS, Microsoft has defined several important data access interfaces that are widely supported in the industry. The first such interface Microsoft defined was Open Database Connectivity (ODBC), which was briefly described in Chapter 1. ODBC is a C language interface which is somewhat complicated to code. For C++

programmers, Microsoft defined some MFC classes which can simplify the job in some situations. For Visual Basic programmers, Microsoft incorporated an ODBC backend to its Jet database engine used in Access and exposed to VB programmers through DAO (Data Access Objects). Besides being somewhat difficult to program without an added layer, ODBC suffers from the limitation of being tied to a relational database model. This is fine if the DBMS is in fact relational, but it makes writing an ODBC driver for a nonrelational data source very complicated.

Microsoft's fundamental, modern data access technology is OLE DB, a very flexible low-level COM interface. Although originally the only OLE DB data provider went through ODBC, now there are native OLE DB providers for many database management systems, including SQL Server and Oracle. OLE DB is the fastest object-oriented database interface where native providers exist. Layered on top of OLE DB is ActiveX Data Objects (ADO), which provides a very easy-to-use object model. ADO can be used from both Visual Basic and C++. The ADO object model is somewhat similar to DAO, but it has been improved. For one thing, the ADO object model is flatter, so you do not have to go through an object hierarchy so much in order to do what you want.

The most important feature of Microsoft's data access technology is that it facilitates accessing virtually any data source, whether a relational database or not, through the same interface. Microsoft calls this feature *Uniform Data Access* or UDA.

Summary

This chapter discussed the rationale for three-tier computer systems and outlined Microsoft's Windows DNA architecture, which provides a convenient way to organize the diverse technologies that can be used to implement three-tier designs. The three tiers are Presentation, Business Logic (the middle tier), and Data Access. Rich clients can make full use of Win32 and go through DCOM to communicate with the middle tier. Thin clients can run on any system for which there is a modern Web browser and use HTTP to communicate with a Web server. Internet Information Server (IIS) is Microsoft's full-featured Web server, which ships as a standard part of NT Server and of Windows 2000. Microsoft Transaction Server (MTS) is part of the NT 4.0 Option Pack and provides significant functions to simplify the development of the middle tier part of distributed applications, including simple support of transactions, transparent handling of concurrency, and pooling of database connections. In Windows 2000, MTS disappears as a separate entity and is merged into COM+. The third important middle-tier technology provided by Microsoft is Microsoft Message Queue (MSMQ), which facilities developing message-based applications implementing a one-way, asynchronous interface between client and server. For the Data Access layer, Microsoft supplies its own DBMS, SQL Server, and specifies important data access interfaces such as OLE DB and ADO, which are supported by many vendors. Besides technologies for the three tiers, Windows DNA consists of COM/COM+ "glue" and general services such as networking, security, and the Active Directory.

In the next chapter you will begin setting up a testbed that you can use while you read the rest of this book. We will then delve into the details of many of the technologies outlined in this chapter, with an emphasis, of course, on COM and COM+.

THREE

A Testbed for Windows DNA

*T*his chapter guides you through setting up a testbed for studying Windows DNA. Since our focus is on COM+, we will work primarily on Windows 2000, a new and sophisticated version of Windows. Our various example programs exercise many different features, and we use several important tools. While we need a network to illustrate the distributed features, this is not absolutely necessary to run all the examples. Although you do not need the complete setup right away, I suggest you start working on it now, so that if you encounter any snags you will have time to resolve them before they become a blocking issue. Guidance for setup of certain specific features, such as SQL Server, Internet Information Services, and MSMQ, is provided in later chapters as the need arises.

Besides specifying the various operating system features and tools that you will need, this chapter also provides a number of simple tests which you can try out to help verify that you have a good configuration. Although a 3-node network is recommended for the richest way to illustrate the various technologies, almost everything can be done on a 2-node network, and in fact most of the work can even be accomplished on a single computer. So do not despair if you don't have a full-blown lab at your disposal.

Overall Configuration

The core requirement is at least one computer running Windows 2000. Two machines running Windows 2000 is best, so that you can test distributed applications. Windows 2000 works best when it is installed on all the computers in an enterprise. You will not be able to test the distributed features of COM+ without two Windows 2000 machines.

On the other hand, one of the basic architectural features of COM/COM+ is "location transparency." That means a COM client calls a server in exactly the same way, whether the server is running in-process, in an EXE on the same machine, or on another machine on the network. As a result, you can create an application that has three logical tiers, even though all three tiers reside on the same machine. Thus the core concepts of the book can be exercised on one Windows 2000 machine with suitable operating system components and tools installed.

Although location transparency means that you do not have to rearchitect your COM component to run remotely, COM components not designed for distribution will not perform well. While DCOM enables you to have remote components, COM+ provides more general mechanisms for deploying COM+ applications remotely This process can be largely automated through the new Windows 2000 Installer. Even if you don't have a second computer, you can "read along" for those parts of the book discussing the true distributed parts of COM and COM+.

If you have access to a third computer on your LAN, you can physically deploy your database on one computer, your business logic on a second computer, and your client on the third computer to illustrate a completely distributed system. If NT 4.0 is installed on your third computer, you can explore interoperability between Windows 2000 and NT 4.0. You may feel more comfortable running your standard applications on a familiar operating system.

The rest of this chapter goes through the details of what software you should have installed. Note that I do not give precise instructions for installing Windows 2000 and its various components. Such information can quickly become out-of-date as new versions of Windows come out. You should rely on the documentation that comes with the product. My intent is to provide a guide through the logical structure of the product.

I begin with a roadmap that provides a brief summary of a recommended configuration that will serve as a robust testbed for the rest of this book. I also outline lesser configurations that will still enable you to exercise most of the concepts. Not everything has to be installed right away, and we give a timeline that outlines when you will need various components. I then provide a specific overview of Windows 2000 Professional, Windows 2000 Server, networking, and Active Directory. Next the development tools are outlined, and some test programs are provided. Finally I give a short preview of COM+.

Roadmap

The following roadmap summarizes a recommended configuration for three computers. As already mentioned, you can definitely cut back to two computers. With one computer, you could install everything on a single machine. You would then be unable to exercise the distributed features, including an independent MSMQ client, but you would still be able to create and test a logical three-tier application.

I find it convenient to have Visual Studio installed on each computer, so that you automatically have the required DLLs and can use just-in-time debugging. If you install SQL Server 7.0 on each computer, you can exercise distributed transactions. You may wish to start out with Computer #1 as your primary machine, which will take you through Part 2, and then switch to Computer #2 for doing Part 3.

COMPUTER #1: FIRST WINDOWS 2000 MACHINE

1. **Windows 2000 Professional**
2. **Visual Studio**
3. SQL Server 7.0
4. MSMQ Independent Client

COMPUTER #2: WINDOWS 2000 DOMAIN CONTROLLER

1. **Windows 2000 Server**
2. **Active Directory**
3. **Domain Controller**
4. **Visual Studio**
5. **Platform SDK**
6. SQL Server 7.0
7. Internet Information Services 5.0
8. MSMQ Server

COMPUTER #3

1. NT 4.0 Server or Workstation or Windows 2000 Professional
2. Your standard applications
3. Visual Studio
4. SQL Server 7.0

Not shown on the above lists are Internet Explorer and networking, both of which are integrated into Windows NT and Windows 2000. We use both.

Timeline

You won't need the complete setup until Part 3, and only then if you are interested in exploring every feature. In this chapter we'll go over a basic setup, shown in bold under Computer #1. We will also discuss basic setup of Computer #2 in this chapter, but you won't need to actually do the work until the time shown. Additional setup will be described when it is needed. In a few places there will be a preview"which provides an illustration out of sequence (for instance, we illustrated the "creating your own Web browser" application in Chapter 1). These previews are provided to pique your interest, not to impose a burden. Do these previews "hands-on" only if you have enough experience to work your way through them on the basis of the hints provided.

Here is an outline giving a timeline of when you will actually need various features as part of the systematic development.

CHAPTER 3. A TESTBED FOR WINDOWS DNA

In this chapter you should set up at least one Windows 2000 machine along with Visual Studio. This basic one-machine testbed will carry you through Chapter 13, with the exception of Chapter 10.

Although you won't need it until later, I suggest you also go ahead and set up a second Windows 2000 machine at this point, if your resources permit. This second machine should run Windows 2000 Server with Active Directory, and should be set up as a domain controller. It is a good idea to also install the Platform SDK, which has the most up-to-date documentation and sample programs, including the documentation on Component Services (COM+).

CHAPTER 10. INTRODUCTION TO DCOM

In this chapter you will need the second computer, networked to the first. As indicated above, the recommended operating system for your second computer is Windows 2000 Server.

CHAPTER 17. WINDOWS 2000 AND COM+ SECURITY

At this point you should have a computer running Windows 2000 Server (or Advanced Server). You will need Active Directory, and will "promote" this machine to be a domain controller. You will then be in a position to administer domain user accounts and work with security settings. If you are using only a single computer and have been running Windows 2000 Professional, you should upgrade it to Windows 2000 Server.

CHAPTER 18. SQL SERVER AND ADO SURVIVAL GUIDE

In this chapter, you will set up SQL Server on one or more machines. Databases will be emphasized in this and the following two chapters.

CHAPTER 20. WEB APPLICATIONS USING COM+

In this chapter, you will use Internet Information Services 5.0, and of course you will also be using Internet Explorer.

CHAPTER 21. MSMQ AND QUEUED COMPONENTS

In this chapter, you will set up MSMQ server on your machine running Windows 2000 Server. If you wish to explore how MSMQ can be used to deliver messages across the network, you should also set up an MSMQ independent client on your machine running Windows 2000 Professional.

Windows 2000

Your first task is to install Windows 2000, which comes in four versions, Professional, Server, Advanced Server, and Datacenter Server. I recommend Windows 2000 Professional and Server as the versions which will enable you to exercise all the features covered in this book without bringing extra baggage. I suggest you start with Windows 2000 Professional. After you have explored Windows 2000 Professional for a while, you may then go ahead and install Windows 2000 Server on a second machine, and set up networking between the two machines.

Hardware Requirements

The most important hardware consideration for good performance with Windows 2000 is plenty of memory. I recommend at least 128 Mb for the things we'll be doing in this book. A large amount of disk space will also be convenient. 2 Gb will suffice, but 4 Gb would be better, so that you can install MSDN onto your hard disk. Consider disk compression on one partition (needs NTFS). You should have at least a 200 MHz CPU, but faster is better.

Windows 2000 Professional

This is the most "lightweight" version of Windows 2000. It is intended as an upgrade path from Windows 95/98 and also from Windows NT Workstation. It is a fully adequate environment for programming and testing COM programs and for exercising many of the COM+ services.

After Windows 2000 Professional has been installed, you will see a welcome screen when you boot. See Figure 3–1. This screen will keep coming up, until you clear the checkbox "Show this screen at startup."

If you are relatively new to the Windows environment, you might want to take a tour by clicking the link "Discover Windows." If you are familiar with Windows but new to Windows 2000, you may also want to briefly check out the new features shown in the tour.

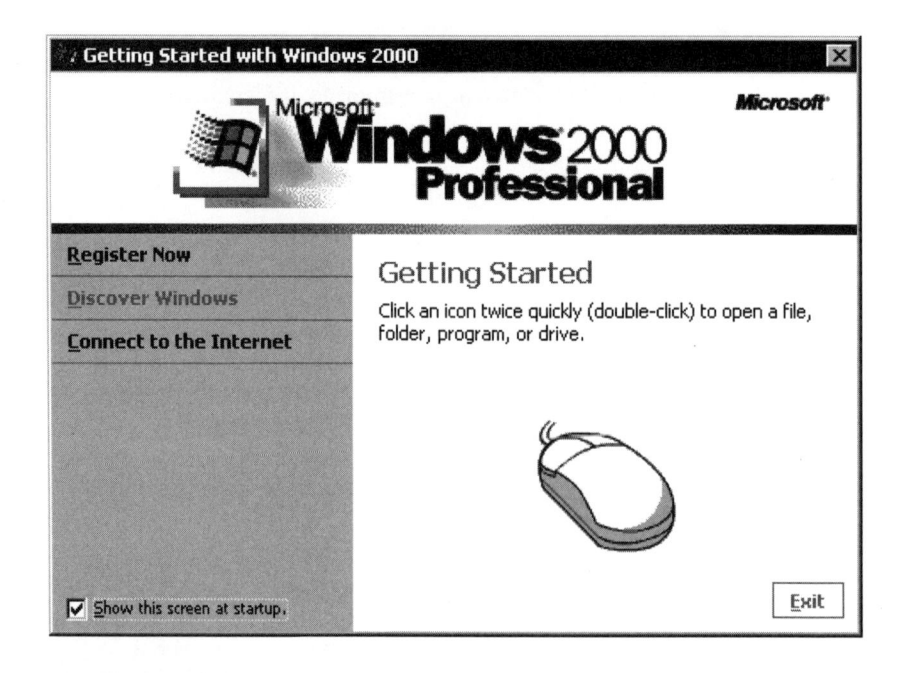

Figure 3–1 Welcome screen for Windows 2000 Professional

FINDING YOUR WAY AROUND WINDOWS 2000 PROFESSIONAL

If you are familiar with previous versions of Windows NT, you may find the new arrangement of various utilities somewhat confusing at first. For one thing, there are a number of tools in a folder called "Administrative Tools," which you won't find from the Start menu but from the Control Panel. See Figure 3–2.

Another feature of Windows 2000 is the ubiquitous use of Microsoft Management Console (MMC). Many administrative tools are now "snap-ins" to MMC, rather than stand-alone tools. All of the tools shown in the Administrative Tools folder are in fact MMC snap-ins. In Part 3, we will make extensive use of the Component Services administrative tool (or "COM+ Explorer," a shorter name we will frequently use). Many tasks can be done from the "Computer Management" snap-in. Figure 3–3 illustrates accessing the Disk Administrator from the Computer Management tool.

On the whole, you will likely find that a little experimenting is all you need to find your way around Windows 2000 Professional. There is a help system available, which you can access from Start | Help.

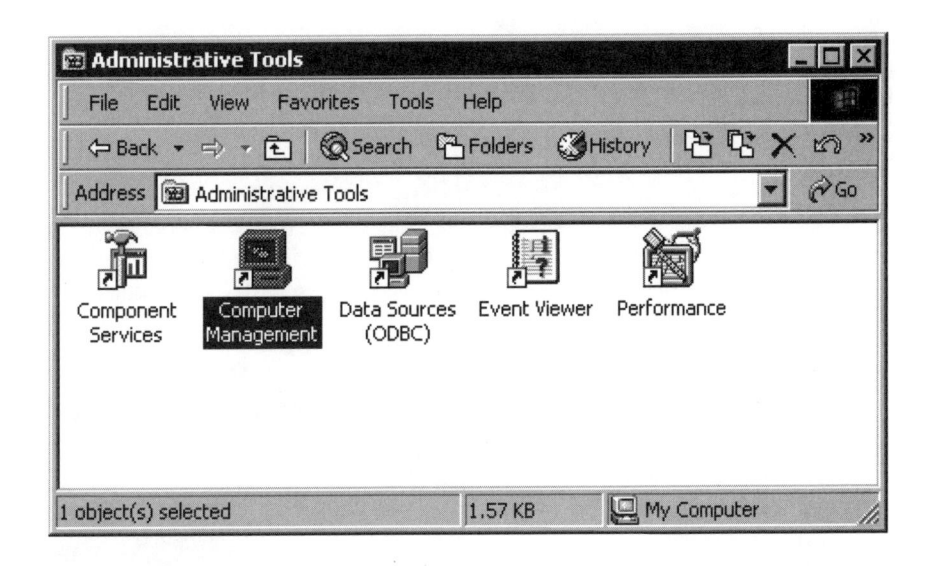

Figure 3-2 *You can find Administrative Tools from the Control Panel*

Windows 2000 Server (Can Do Later)

You will eventually need Windows 2000 Server. If you only have a single computer for your testbed, you can upgrade from Windows 2000 Professional. If you have a second computer, install Windows 2000 Server on your second computer, which will become your primary machine.

If you are installing Windows 2000 Server on your second computer, you should complete your work in this section by the time you start Chapter 10. If you are only using one computer, you can wait until Chapter 17, when you will need Active Directory.

Whenever you boot Windows 2000 Server, you will see a screen entitled "Windows 2000 Configure Your Server." This screen will always come up, unless you uncheck "Show this screen at startup." You can always get the screen back from Start | Administrative Tools | Configure Your Server. This screen provides a convenient "wizard" interface to a number of configuration functions, but all of the configurations can also be done directly.

I won't attempt to provide a tutorial on how to use Windows 2000 Server (a very big subject). It will help a lot if you have had some experience with earlier versions of NT Server. You will need to spend quite a bit of time with the on-line documentation, and you might want to reinstall Windows 2000 once or twice to get more practice or to tweak things. While working with the Beta version, I found the Microsoft Press book *Microsoft Windows*

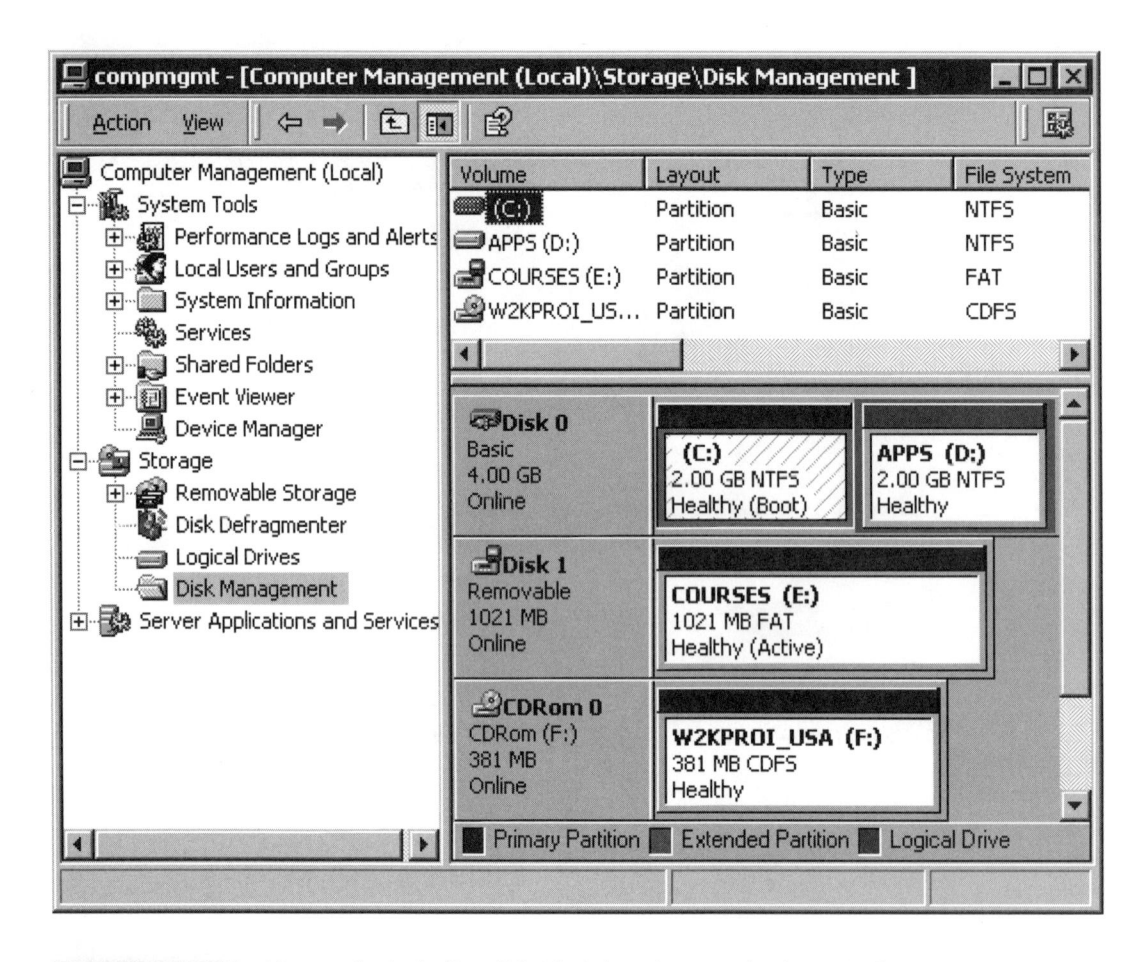

Figure 3–3 *Many tasks, including disk administration, can be done via Computer Management snap-in*

2000 Beta Training Kit helpful. I assume there will be a similar book for the released product.

Networking

To illustrate the distributed features of COM+, you of course need to have networking installed. You should have TCP/IP installed. If you are working on a computer connected to a department LAN, you can get help from your administrator. If you are administering your own small LAN yourself, try to keep things simple. For example you can assign specific IP addresses to your machines. (I use the addresses 131.107.2.200, 131.107.2.201, and 131.107.2.203 with subnet mask 255.255.0.0.). If you are not connected to the Internet, these numbers can be arbitrary.

Once the network is installed you should be able to "ping" the computers on your network. Bring up a command console (if you cannot find it from the Start menu you can type "cmd" from "Run"). You can then type "ping," followed by either the computer name or the numerical IP address. See Figure 3–4.

```
Command Prompt
Reply from 131.107.2.203: bytes=32 time<10ms TTL=128
Reply from 131.107.2.203: bytes=32 time<10ms TTL=128
Reply from 131.107.2.203: bytes=32 time<10ms TTL=128
Reply from 131.107.2.203: bytes=32 time<10ms TTL=128

C:\>ping betadell

Pinging betadell.oi.com [131.107.2.201] with 32 bytes of data:

Reply from 131.107.2.201: bytes=32 time<10ms TTL=128
Reply from 131.107.2.201: bytes=32 time<10ms TTL=128
Reply from 131.107.2.201: bytes=32 time<10ms TTL=128
Reply from 131.107.2.201: bytes=32 time<10ms TTL=128

C:\>ping 131.107.2.201

Pinging 131.107.2.201 with 32 bytes of data:

Reply from 131.107.2.201: bytes=32 time<10ms TTL=128
Reply from 131.107.2.201: bytes=32 time<10ms TTL=128
Reply from 131.107.2.201: bytes=32 time<10ms TTL=128
Reply from 131.107.2.201: bytes=32 time<10ms TTL=128

C:\>
```

Figure 3–4   *"Pinging" computers on your network*

Domain Name System (DNS)

Domain Name System (DNS) is a distributed database implemented on top of TCP/IP that is used to translate computer names to numerical IP addresses. Since DNS uses the same naming conventions as used on the Internet, once you have DNS installed, you will be able to connect to servers on your LAN using the same kind of naming as you use to connect to servers on the Internet.

Names in DNS are created in a hierarchy, with periods separating the levels of the hierarchy. At the top of the hierarchy is the *root domain*, represented by a period. Next come *top-level* domains such as "com" (for commercial organization), "org" (noncommercial organization), "gov" (government organization), "edu" (educational institution), etc. There are also country codes such as "uk" (United Kingdom), etc. A *second-level* domain specializes the top-level domain with a unique name identifying a particular organization. Examples of second-level domains are "microsoft.com," "harvard.edu," etc. Finally, at the lowest level is a *host name*, which refers to a particular computer on the Internet or on a private LAN.

You can install DNS by dropping down the options under "Networking" in the left panel of the "Configure Your Server" screen and clicking "DNS." During the installation process, you will need to make up a name for your domain, and assign an IP address for your DNS server, which should be your main computer running Windows 2000 Server.

If you go directly to the Active Directory Wizard, the wizard should set up DNS for you. You will need to activate DNS.

Active Directory

Windows 2000 Server provides *Active Directory* as its directory service. Active Directory identifies all resources on a network. Active Directory consists of a distributed database called the Directory, that stores information about network resources. Active Directory also has software services that make the information in the Directory accessible to users and applications. The resources stored in the directory are referred to as *objects*. Examples of objects are users, groups, printers, databases, etc.

Computers and other resources on a network are organized into *domains*. A domain represents a portion of the resources in the entire Directory, and is managed by one or more computers, running Windows 2000, known as *domain controllers*. All domain controllers for a particular domain are peers, and each has a replica of the domain's portion of the Directory. A domain represents a region of security. For example, user accounts are established on a per-domain basis. When a user has succeeded in logging on to a particular domain controller, that user then has access to all resources that have granted that user permission.

Active Directory provides a single point of administration for all resources on the network. All the domains are interconnected, and an administrator can administer all resources from a single logon. Before Active Directory, an administrator would need a separate administrator account for each domain, which became very cumbersome for a large enterprise with many domains.

Active Directory uses DNS as its domain naming service. Active Directory uses the standard Lightweight Directory Access Protocol (LDAP), which makes it possible for Active Directory to interoperate with other directory services, such as Novell's Network Directory Service (NDS). Active Directory also supports HTTP, which makes it possible for any object in the network to be viewed in an HTML page in a Web browser.

The logical structure of Active Directory is based on domains. The physical structure is based on *sites*, which can be thought of as one or more IP subnets. If you are administering a small test LAN, normally all the computers on your little LAN will be on the same subnet and will comprise a single Active Directory site.

INSTALLING ACTIVE DIRECTORY

The use of Active Directory in Windows 2000 makes the process of setting up a domain controller somewhat different from what it was in NT 4.0. As with NT 4.0, you need a Server version of the operating system. But, unlike NT 4.0, the choice of making a particular computer a domain controller is made *after* you install the operating system. A computer is made a domain controller by installing Active Directory. You will then have the choice of adding a domain controller to an existing domain, or creating the first domain controller of a new domain. By installing Active Directory, you are "promoting" your standalone server to be a domain controller.

You can launch the wizard to guide you through the process of setting up Active Directory from the "Active Directory" selection in "Configure Your Server."

JOINING A DOMAIN

Once you have installed Active Directory on your primary computer and promoted it to a domain controller, you can have the other computers on your LAN join this domain. This is a two-step process. First you have to create new computer objects in Active Directory for your other computers, an operation performed on the domain controller. Then you have to change the properties of the other computers to join the domain.

To create a new computer object from the domain controller, bring up Active Directory Users and Computers (from Start | Programs | Administrative Tools). Open up the tree view for your domain, select "Computers," and right click over "Computers." Choose New | Computer from the context menu. Type in the name of the computer you want to add to the domain. If you like, you can also change the group of users having the right to join the computer to the domain. The default is the group "Domain Admins."

Now go to the other machine. For an NT 4.0 machine right click over Network Neighborhood on the desktop, choose Properties, select the Identification tab, and click "Change." On a Windows 2000 machine right click over "My Computer," choose Properties, select the Network Identification tab, and click the "Advanced" button. You can then select the radio button, making the computer a member of a domain in place of a workgroup. Type in the name of the domain. You will then be asked to supply the user name and password of the user authorized to join this computer to the domain. If you left this as the default, you can enter the name of the domain administrator ("Administrator," if you did not change it) and the password. You will then be welcomed to the new domain. The new setting will take place when you reboot the computer. Then on your logon you can expand the dialog box, and you will have a choice of an account on the workgroup (local machine) or on the domain.

If you log in using a domain account, don't be surprised to see all your desktop settings, shortcuts, etc. be different, as they are managed on a per-user basis, and the domain account represents a different user.

MANAGING USERS

Once Active Directory has been installed, you use it to manage all network resources, including user accounts. You can access Active Directory management functions through the "Configure Your Server" screen, but most typically once you've done the major configuration of your machine you will probably close that screen by default. Then you can get to the various services of Active Directory from the Start menu. To manage user accounts go to Start | Administrative Tools | Active Directory Users and Computers. See Figure 3–5.

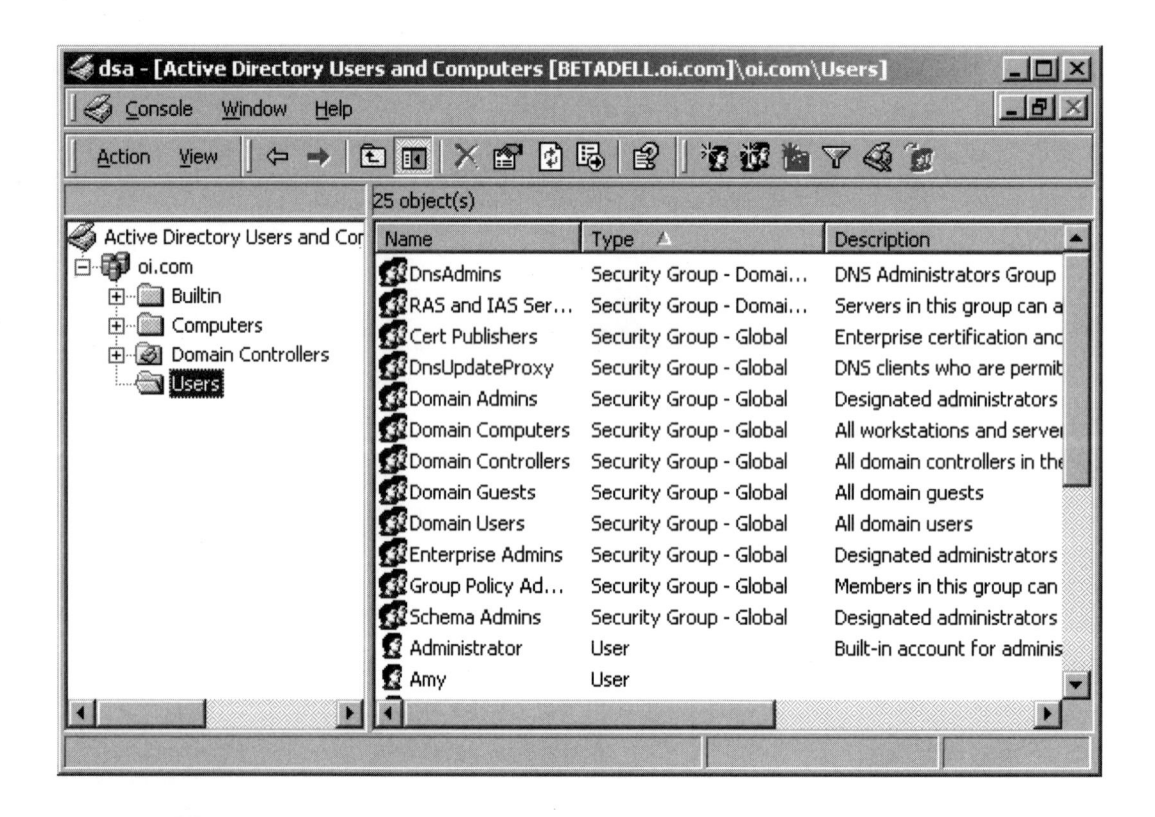

Figure 3–5   *Managing user accounts through Active Directory*

Notice the tree view in the left pane showing the domains which this administrator can manage. An "Enterprise Administrator" will be allowed to manage all the domains in the Directory. In the example shown on the screen capture there is a single domain, oi.com. To add a user you can select and then right click over "Users" in the left pane, and from the context menu that comes up, choose New | User. You can then fill in appropriate information in the "Create New Object (User)" window that comes up.

Development Tools

The core Microsoft development suite is Visual Studio, version 6.0 or later. The two parts of Visual Studio we will need are Visual C++ and Visual Basic. You may also install Visual InterDev as the editor for HTML and ASP (Active Server Pages) files, if you wish. I recommend the Enterprise editions of these tools, but you can accomplish most of the tasks in this book with the Standard editions. Microsoft changes from time to time the definition of "editions" of their development tools. For up-to-date information on Visual Studio, Visual C++, and Visual Basic visit Microsoft's Web sites **msdn.microsoft.com/vstudio**, **msdn.microsoft.com/visualc** and **msdn.microsoft.com/vbasic**. If you are doing COM+ development, you are probably developing for the enterprise, and will need many other Microsoft tools as well, such as SQL Server. The most economical way to obtain the full-blown Microsoft development environment is through the MSDN Universal subscription (**msdn.microsoft.com**).

Visual Studio is now integrated with the MSDN Library. The on-line documentation now *is* MSDN. After completing installation of Visual Studio, a screen will come up for installing MSDN. You should go ahead and install MSDN at this time. If you have enough hard disk space, it will be convenient to install onto your hard disk so that you don't have to swap CD-ROMs.

Although we use both Visual Basic and Visual C++ extensively in this book, if your primary focus and interest is in just one of these languages, you can follow the book by concentrating on the language of your choice. If you are a C++ programmer, I will try to entice you into considering some use of Visual Basic, because of its extraordinary ease of use. Save the heavy ammunition of C++ for where you need it.

Once you have Visual Studio installed, it is a good idea to build and run a few small programs. In the following sections I outline some simple examples. While presenting these sample programs, I also review briefly some concepts about Visual Studio, such as the different project types, etc.

Building Sample Programs

To Build or not to Build

When you buy a software package, you purchase binary code. When you are furnished with development samples you normally have the source code. If there is also a binary file (DLL or EXE), should you use it or build it? I generally recommend you build the project, because there might be some incompatibilities in the binary with your current development environment (different version of a library, etc.). Possible incompatibilities is an ever-present issue in a book such as this one, where the examples have been built using beta software. To help keep you out of trouble, I normally do not supply the binary. An exception is with Visual Basic ActiveX DLLs, where the binary is required to avoid generating different "GUIDs" (discussed later).

Visual Basic

The two most common types of projects you will be building with Visual Basic are an ActiveX DLL (server) and Standard EXE (client). As a simple example of an ActiveX DLL, open up the project **HelloVB.vbp** in directory **Chap3\HelloVB**. Build this project. (From menu choose File | Make HelloVb.dll. Say yes to replace existing DLL.) That will result in the server being "registered" and hence available to client programs. Since the DLL already exists, you could just register it by running the batch file **reg_hello.bat**.

As an example of a Standard EXE, open up **HelloClientVB.vbp** in directory **Chap3\LateClientVB**. You may run the project from within the IDE (integrated development environment), or you may create an EXE from File | Make HelloClientVB.exe. A simple form will come up, allowing you to exercise the Visual Basic server (VB) or the Visual C++ server (VC). Click the VB button. You should receive a little greeting from the Visual Basic COM server. See Figure 3–6.

Of course, clicking the "VC" button won't work yet, because we have not yet built the Visual C++ server. In this client program we are using "late binding," so we won't notice the missing server until we try to run it. After you have built the Visual C++ server, you could try the "early binding" form of the program, in **Chap3\EarlyClientVB**. We will discuss early binding and late binding in Chapter 11.

Visual C++

The two most common types of projects you will be building with Visual C++ are an ATL COM AppWizard (server, either a DLL or an EXE) and an MFC App-

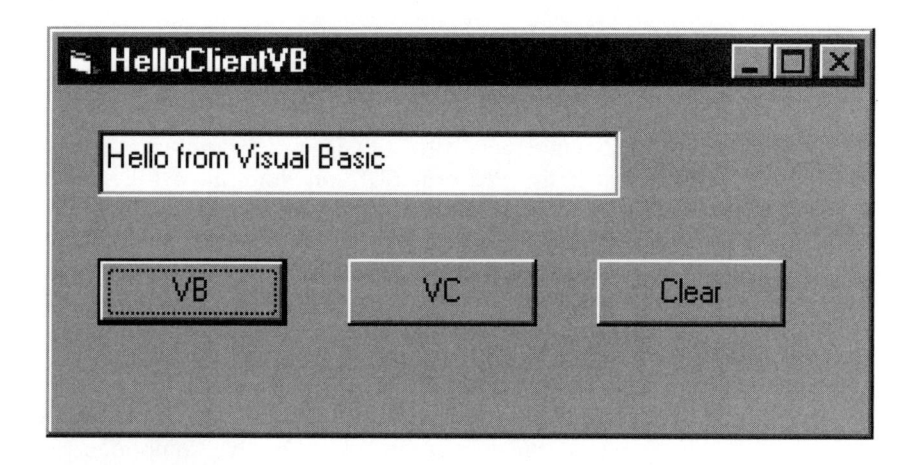

Figure 3–6   *Visual Basic client invokes VB COM server*

Wizard exe (client). We have parallel Visual C++ "hello" server and client. For the server, open up the project **Hello.dsw** in directory **Chap3\HelloVC**. Build the project (menu Build | Build Hello.dll), which will register the server.

As an example of an MFC AppWizard (exe) project, open up **HelloClientVC.dsw** in directory **Chap3\HelloClientVC**. With Microsoft Foundation Classes (MFC) you can create several kinds of programs, including Multiple Document Interface (MDI), Single Document Interface (SDI), and Dialog-Based. We will be using Dialog-Based applications in this book. Build the project (again Build | Build...). Then run the program. A form will come up that is similar to the VB client test program. You should be able to exercise both the VC server and the VB server. If you go back to the VB client program, you should be able to exercise both servers from there, too.

This little "hello" program illustrates how COM is language neutral. You can create COM servers and clients in different languages, and a client in one language can call a server in another language.

Visual InterDev

Visual InterDev is part of Visual Studio and has a number of features to simplify the development of Web applications. We will discuss Web applications in this book, but we don't need Visual InterDev. If you do have it installed, you can benefit from a couple of features. One is the color coding of HTML and Active Server Pages files. Since HTML syntax is rather picky, the color coding can be beneficial (also available in Visual C++). Another feature is useful when working with Active Server Pages. Microsoft's "IntelliSense" technology, which pops up a little yellow box showing available methods, parameters, etc., is available when you are writing scripts for Active Server Pages.

Platform SDK

The final development tool you should install is the Platform SDK. You won't need it in Part 2, but it will be vital for Part 3. The Platform SDK provides the complete documentation for COM+ and a number of sample programs. You should install the Platform SDK on your most fully configured computer, where you will exercise various advanced features such as MSMQ.

COM+ Preview

Let's take our first hands-on peek at COM+. We don't have to do any special installation or configuration. COM+ is part of the core Windows 2000 infrastructure, and it is automatically installed when you install Windows 2000. There is another MMC snap-in called simply "Component Services" (or sometimes the "COM+ Explorer") that is used for administering COM+ applications.

Make sure that your "Hello" examples are working. We are going to create a COM+ application out of the **HelloVB.dll** component. Bring up the Component Services snap-in from Start | Programs | Administrative Tools | Component Services (if you are using Windows 2000 Server) or from Start | Settings | Control Panel | Administrative Tools | Component Services (if you are using Windows 2000 Professional). Open up the tree view until you can see the COM+ Applications that are preinstalled. See Figure 3–7.

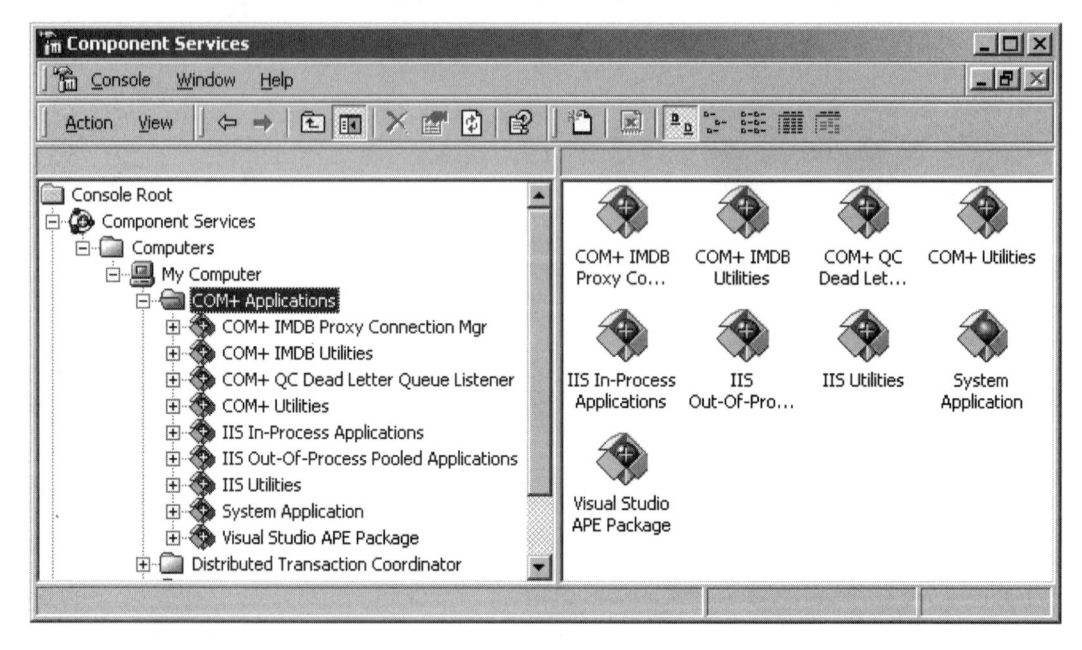

Figure 3–7 *Component Services snap-in manages COM+ applications*

The next job is to create a COM+ "application" (called a "package" in MTS) that contains the **HelloVB.dll** component. First create an empty COM+ application by selecting and then right-clicking over "COM+ Applications" and choosing New | Application. In the wizard that comes up, enter the name "HelloVB" for a new empty application, and accept all the defaults. You will see "HelloVB" added to the tree view. Select "HelloVB" in the tree view. Right-click over "Components" underneath "HelloVB" and choose New | Component (or you may use the "Action" menu). In the COM Component Install Wizard, click on "Install new components(s)." In the "Select files to install" dialog that comes up, navigate to **Chap3\HelloVB**, select **HelloVB.dll**, and click "Open." Click "Next" and "Finish." Repeat this process to also install **Hello.dll** from **Chap3\HelloVC\Debug**. When you are done you should see two little ball icons in the right pane. See Figure 3–8.

Now run the client program **HelloVBClient.exe**. You should see identical behavior to what happened when we called the COM object directly, without it being installed as a COM+ application.

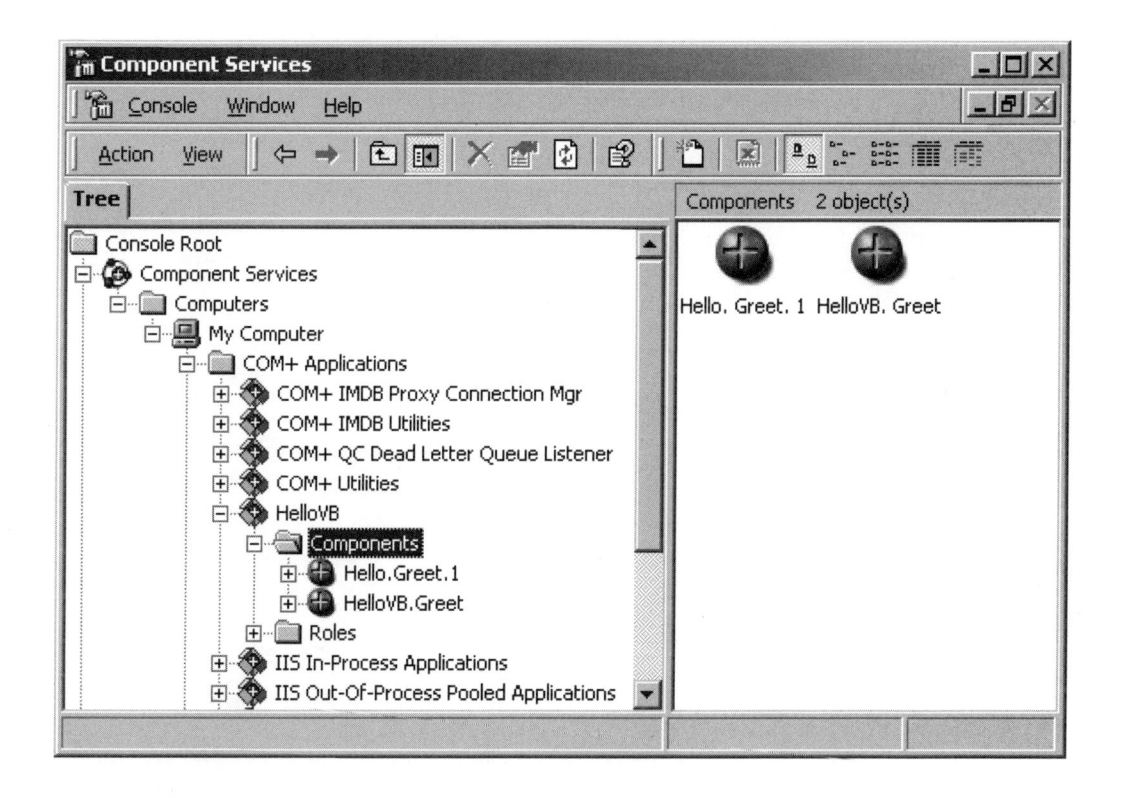

Figure 3–8   *Two components have been installed in the "HelloVB" application*

In some later examples you will see the ball "spin" when the client program is running. That does not happen in our example, because the client program that calls the server is "in and out"—an object is created, used, and immediately destroyed.

DEPLOYING ON A REMOTE COMPUTER

Installing the COM component in the COM+ application appears to be no big deal—we get the same behavior that we always have. But we will see in Part 3 that there are profound capabilities enabled when a COM component is "configured" in this way. For now, we will illustrate one benefit. It becomes very easy to deploy a COM+ application on a remote machine.

We will "export" our simple application. Select and right-click over "HelloVB" in the tree view. Choose "Export" from the context menu. In the wizard that comes up, browse to the **Deploy** directory in the book lab directory **ComPlus**. Assign the name "HelloVB" for the application file to be created. Note the **.msi** extension, which will be used by Windows 2000 Installer. Choose "Application proxy." We are going to enable a client program on Computer #2 to talk to the server on Computer #1. See Figure 3–9.

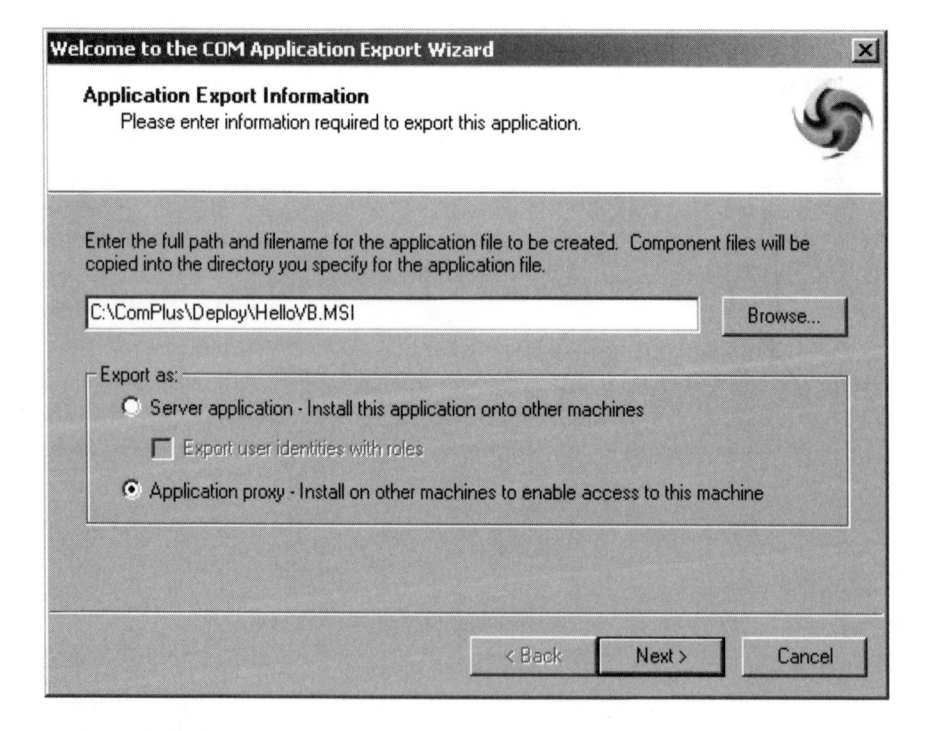

Figure 3–9   *Creating an application proxy to deploy a client remotely*

Click Next and then Finish. Now copy the files **HelloVB.msi** and **HelloVBClient.exe** (from folder LateVBClient) to a test directory on Computer #2. Try running the client program on Computer #2 (click the "VB" button). It will fail. Now double click on **HelloVB.msi**. The Windows 2000 Installer will be invoked and "proxy" code will be installed on Computer #2. This is COM "glue" code that will enable the client to remotely invoke the server. Try running the client again. Now it should succeed.

Like all good Windows software, the application proxy can be uninstalled. Open up "Add/Remove Programs" in the Control Panel. You can select the proxy and remove it. See Figure 3–10.

Summary

This chapter provided a brief guide for setting up your testbed for studying COM+ and Windows DNA throughout the rest of this book. A fully featured

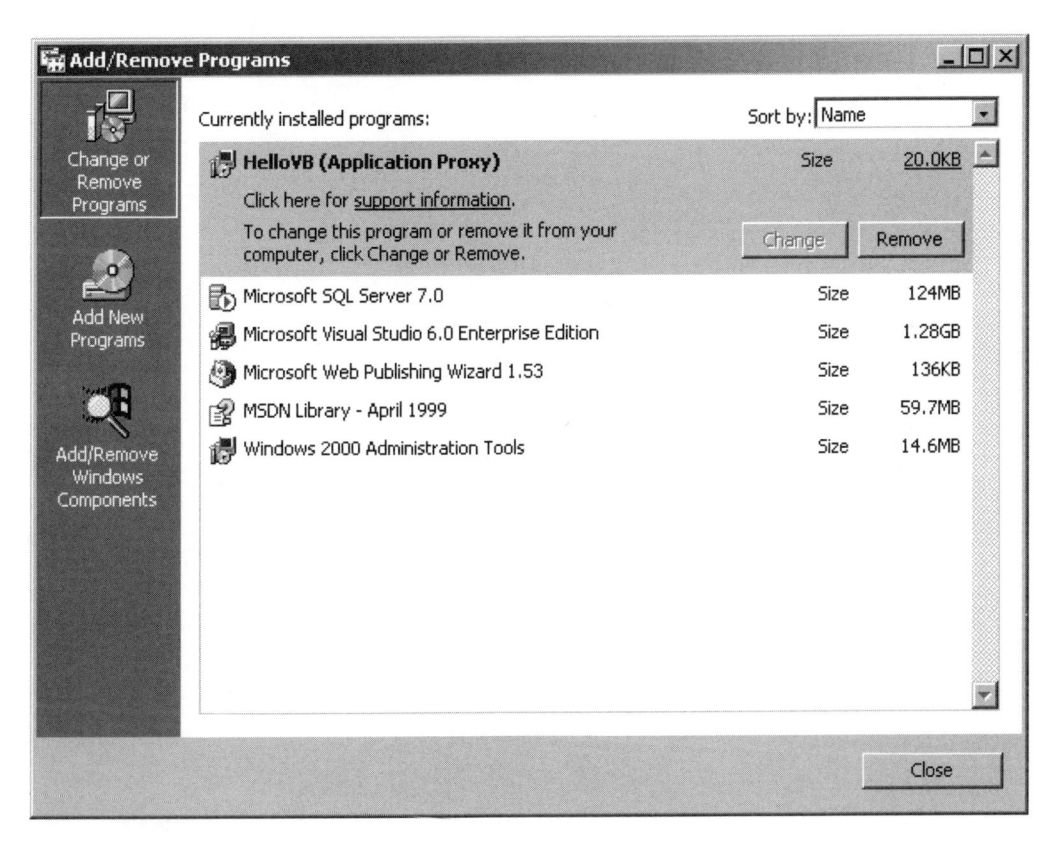

Figure 3–10 *You can remove the application proxy like any other program*

configuration was outlined, that included three computers. Because of the key COM feature of "location transparency," most aspects of Windows DNA programming can be exercised on a single machine, so you can definitely get by with much less than the recommended maximum. A timeline suggested when you will need various features as you read through this book. For Part 2, which covers the fundamentals of COM, you can do very nicely with a single computer running Windows 2000 Professional. The chapter on DCOM will need a second computer. The more full-blown configuration involving Windows 2000 Server, Active Directory, and the like will not be required until Part 3.

The chapter also outlined the development tools you will need, including Visual Basic and Visual C++, and some simple test programs were provided for each. Finally a short preview of COM+ was given, including deploying an application to run remotely across the network.

You are now ready to begin Part 2, with a study of the fundamentals of COM, which underpin COM+ and Windows DNA.

PART TWO

COM Fundamentals

In This Part

- **CHAPTER 4**
  COM Clients: Concepts and Programming

- **CHAPTER 5**
  C++ and the Component Object Model

- **CHAPTER 6**
  In-Process COM Servers

- **CHAPTER 7**
  Active Template Library

- **CHAPTER 8**
  Visual C++ COM Support

- **CHAPTER 9**
  EXE Servers

- **CHAPTER 10**
  Introduction to DCOM

- **CHAPTER 11**
  Automation and COM Programming Using Visual Basic

- **CHAPTER 12**
  Error Processing and Debugging

- **CHAPTER 13**
  Multithreading in COM

The second part of this book provides thorough coverage of the fundamental principles of COM which underpin COM+. You need this knowledge in order to work with COM+, because every component that is imported into the rich COM+ environment must be a standard COM component in the first place. All of the standard tools for building straight COM components, including the Active Template Library and Visual Basic, are used for creating COM+ components. More than that, you need to understand the basic concepts of COM in order to understand COM+. I have tried to make this book self-contained, so you are not forced to cobble together an understanding of COM and COM+ from multiple sources. Everything you need to know about COM to succeed in working with COM+ is contained in Part 2 of this book. If you already have experience in COM please feel free to go directly to Part 3, coming back to Part 2 when you feel a need.

I cover all the essential topics at both a conceptual level and at a hands-on programming level. The programming examples are all very simple and concrete. I dissect them to find out what makes them "tick." This experience should give you a good grounding for the more sophisticated examples in Part 3.

I use both Visual C++ and Visual Basic. Both languages are vitally important for developing in the Microsoft environment, and a typical scenario that is facilitated by COM is to use both languages in a large project. Certain key components which are critical to the performance of the system may be built using C++, and large parts of application code may be created using the high-productivity environment of Visual Basic. Thus it is important to learn how these languages work together through COM.

I include a thorough introduction to DCOM and provide an in-depth discussion of multithreading in COM. There is a practical treatment of the important topics of error handling and debugging.

FOUR

COM Clients: Concepts and Programming

The most fundamental aspect of programming with COM is writing client programs that call COM objects. In fact, in the Microsoft environment COM has become so ubiquitous that many programmers use COM already without realizing it. For example, Visual Basic is built on COM. When you use many Windows controls on a form, you are not using the Win32 control directly but are using an ActiveX wrapper of the control. So even if you don't implement COM objects, you most certainly will use them. The purpose of this chapter is to explain the COM programming model at a level of abstraction suitable for implementing COM client programs. You will learn how to write COM clients in both Visual Basic and Visual C++. You will also learn how to use some tools that can help you better understand the COM objects in your system.

It is fairly easy to spell out a step-by-step approach to creating COM clients, especially in Visual Basic, and it is pretty straightforward in C++ too. The trick is to gain a real *understanding* of what is going on. I will try to help you understand by first dissecting an example program and then summarizing the core terminology and concepts. These concepts will be very important for the rest of this book. Then comes the actual code for implementing COM clients in Visual Basic and in Visual C++. We cover some more details about COM client programming, such as Unicode and BSTR for strings and the essentials of memory management in COM. Finally, we look at the role of the Registry in storing vital information about COM servers.

A Bank Account Server

The example program for this chapter is a simple bank account server. The server implements two classes. The first provides a greeting, similar to the "hello" servers discussed in the previous chapter. This class provides a welcome to the bank. The second class manages the account itself, providing methods to make deposits and withdrawals and to obtain the balance. A second interface can be used to show the current balance in a message box.

The server is in the folder **Chap4\Bank**, and the clients are in the folders **Chap4\BankClientVb** and **Chap4\BankClientVc**. Build the server. (Double click on **bank.dsw** in **Chap4\Bank** to open up the "bank" project in the Visual C++ development environment. Then choose menu item Build | Build Bank.dll.) Run the Visual Basic client program (the two clients have similar functionality). See Figure 4–1.

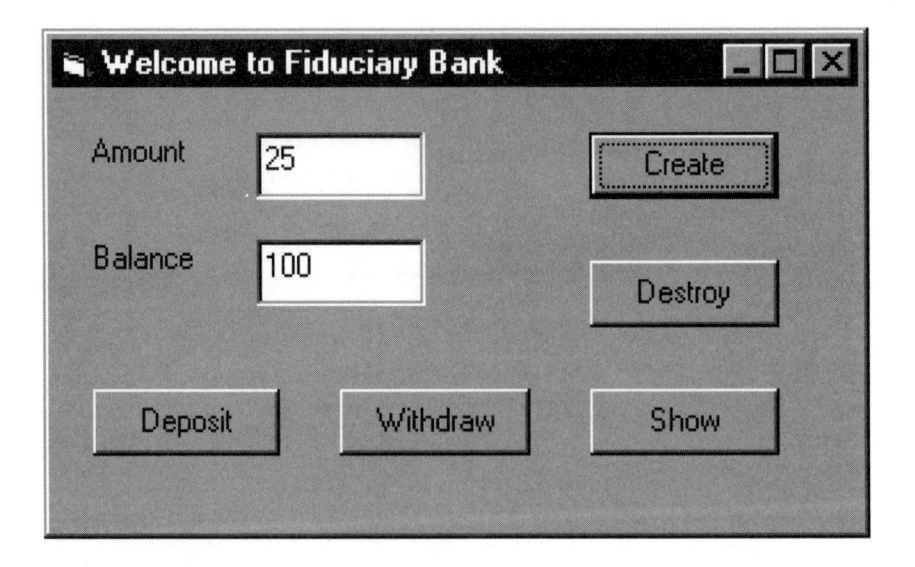

Figure 4–1   *Client program for a bank account server*

When you run the program, you should first see message boxes announcing the creation and destruction of a Greet object. This object is used to provide the welcome message, which is displayed as the title of the window. You create an Account object by clicking the Create button. The starting balance of 100 is then shown. You can make deposits and withdrawals, and you can show the balance in a message box. When you are done, you click the Destroy button. There are also message boxes announcing creation and destruction of the Account object. These message boxes are provided by the server to help you understand the life cycle of a COM object.

Exploring the Structure of a COM Server

In this section you will explore the structure of a COM server, which can be thought of as a means of providing "library" functions that can be used off-the-shelf. The goal of a COM server is to provide reusable code for your programs, similar to what can be accomplished by a static library (such as the C run time) or by a dynamic link library (such as the DLLs that are part of the Windows system and applications). The functionality of a COM server can be described by a *type library*, which gives a specification of classes, interfaces, and methods.

We will follow an inductive approach to learning about the structure of a COM server. We will use some tools to dissect our bank account server, discovering entities like "class" and "method." After a survey of our example server, making use of the tools, we will then cover more systematically some of the basic terminology and concepts of COM. After that, we can outline the simple programming model for a client program to invoke functionality from a COM server, and we will look at actual Visual Basic and Visual C++ implementations.

Visual Basic Object Browser

A useful tool for viewing the structure of COM servers is built right into Visual Basic. It is called the *Object Browser* and can be accessed from the View menu. Open up the project **BankClientVb** and bring up the Object Browser. From the dropdown choose "BANKLib," the type library for our bank account server example. Select the "Deposit" method of the "Account" class. Then in the bottom pane you will see displayed the parameters for this method. See Figure 4–2.

CLASSES, METHODS, AND PROPERTIES

The Object Browser shows us *classes*. So we see that a COM server, as described by its type library, implements classes. Selecting a class shows us its *methods* and *properties*. A method can be thought of as a function and a property as data. For example, the **Greet** class has the property **Greeting**, while the **Account** class has methods **Deposit**, **Withdraw** and **GetBalance**. A method that basically returns data could be implemented as a property.

When a particular method is selected, the Object Browser will show us the "signature" of the method, indicating the parameters and their data types. For example, the **Deposit** method takes a single parameter of type **Long**.

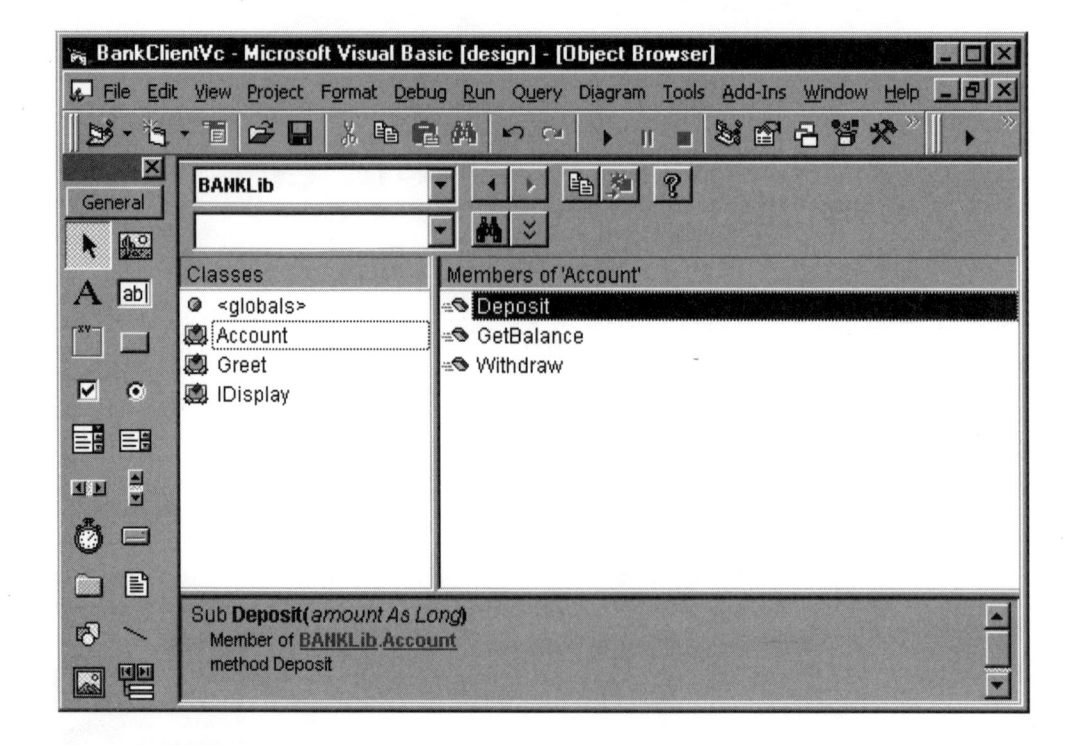

Figure 4–2 *The Visual Basic Object Browser*

Unfortunately, the Object Browser does not indicate whether a parameter is called **ByVal** or **ByRef**.

OLE/COM Object Viewer (OLE View)

More detailed information about a COM/Server can be obtained by using the OLE/COM Object Viewer. This program can be started from the Tools menu of Visual C++ and also from the Start menu (Start | Programs | Microsoft Visual Studio | Microsoft Visual Studio Tools | OLE View). There are many features available in this tool. Right now we just want to use the tool to view a type library. (Caution: Type Library Viewer has been known not to work on Windows 95, but you should be using NT or Windows 2000 anyway.) After starting OLE View you can bring up the Type Library Viewer from menu File | View TypeLib. Navigate to directory **Bank** and open up either **bank.tlb** or **Debug\bank.dll**. (For this server created using Visual C++, the type information is available both in the DLL file and also in a special type library TLB file. For Visual Basic servers there is only a DLL file. An EXE server will have its type information in the EXE.) You will then get a much more detailed display of information. See Figure 4–3.

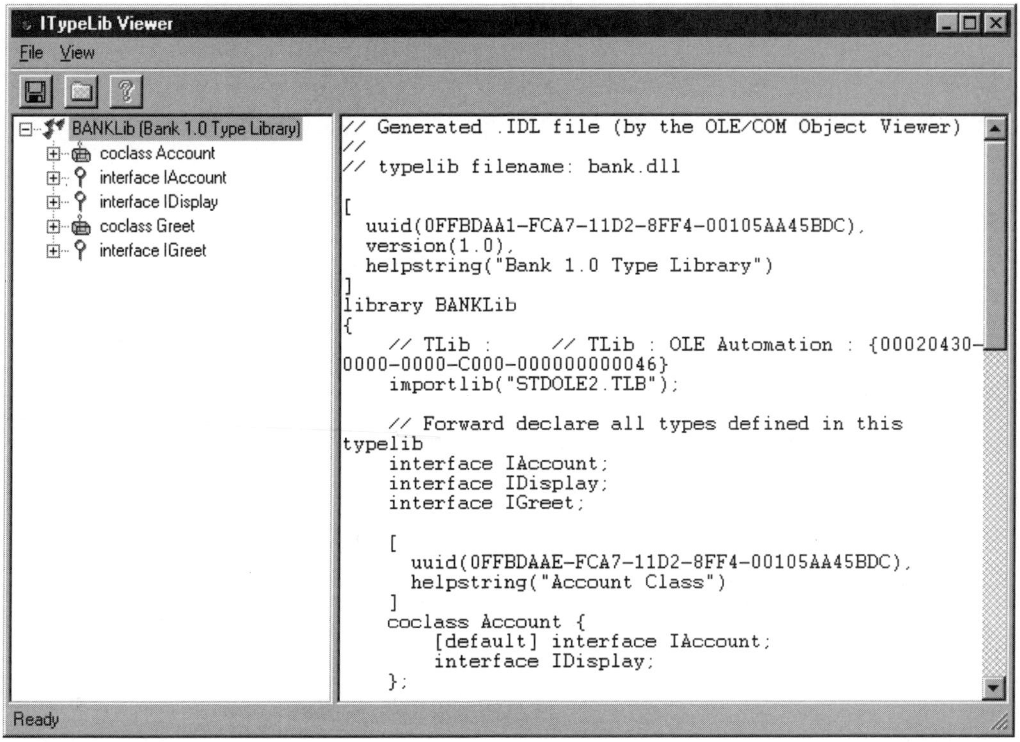

Exploring the Structure of a COM Server   75

```
// Generated .IDL file (by the OLE/COM Object Viewer)
//
// typelib filename: bank.dll

[
  uuid(0FFBDAA1-FCA7-11D2-8FF4-00105AA45BDC),
  version(1.0),
  helpstring("Bank 1.0 Type Library")
]
library BANKLib
{
    // TLib :     // TLib : OLE Automation : {00020430-
0000-0000-C000-000000000046}
    importlib("STDOLE2.TLB");

    // Forward declare all types defined in this
typelib
    interface IAccount;
    interface IDisplay;
    interface IGreet;

    [
      uuid(0FFBDAAE-FCA7-11D2-8FF4-00105AA45BDC),
      helpstring("Account Class")
    ]
    coclass Account {
        [default] interface IAccount;
        interface IDisplay;
    };
```

Figure 4–3   *OLE/COM Object Viewer*

The tree view in the left pane provides a convenient way for navigating the library. The corresponding IDL (Interface Definition Language) in the right pane gives a detailed specification. If you are curious about what a large type library would look like, you could try out one of the Office "object library" files such as **Msword8.olb** for Microsoft Word or the ADO library **msado15.dll.**

IDL for Bank Server

Interface Definition Language or IDL is the language used for precisely specifying a COM server. It does not contain any implementation—it is pure specification, something like a header file in a C or C++ program. Later on we will work with IDL when we create COM servers. Right now let's examine the IDL code for the example Bank server. With the root of the tree view selected, BANKLib (Bank 1.0 Type Library), the entire IDL will be shown in the right-hand pane. You may use the clipboard to copy the text to another file, if you like. Select the text and use the standard keyboard shortcut for Copy, Ctrl+C.

The IDL file is shown below. Don't worry about understanding the details right now, just try to follow the general discussion. Some of the interesting portions are shown in bold.

```
// Generated .IDL file (by the OLE/COM Object Viewer)
//
// typelib filename: bank.dll

[
  uuid(0FFBDAA1-FCA7-11D2-8FF4-00105AA45BDC),
  version(1.0),
  helpstring("Bank 1.0 Type Library")
]
library BANKLib
{
    // TLib :    // TLib : OLE Automation : {00020430-0000-0000-C000-000000000046}
    importlib("STDOLE2.TLB");

    // Forward declare all types defined in this typelib
    interface IAccount;
    interface IDisplay;
    interface IGreet;

    [
      uuid(0FFBDAAE-FCA7-11D2-8FF4-00105AA45BDC),
      helpstring("Account Class")
    ]
    coclass Account {
      [default] interface IAccount;
      interface IDisplay;
      };

    [
      odl,
      uuid(0FFBDAAD-FCA7-11D2-8FF4-00105AA45BDC),
      helpstring("IAccount Interface")
    ]
    interface IAccount : IUnknown {
        [helpstring("method Deposit")]
        HRESULT _stdcall Deposit([in] int amount);
        [helpstring("method GetBalance")]
        HRESULT _stdcall GetBalance([out] int* pBalance);
        [helpstring("method Withdraw")]
        HRESULT _stdcall Withdraw([in] int amount);
    };

    [
      odl,
      uuid(42135D00-2F41-11D1-A01B-00A024D06632),
```

```
        helpstring("IDisplay Interface")
    ]
    interface IDisplay : IUnknown {
        [helpstring("method Show")]
        HRESULT _stdcall Show();
    };


    [
      uuid(7A5E6E82-3DF8-11D3-903D-00105AA45BDC),
      helpstring("Greet Class")
    ]
    coclass Greet {
        [default] interface IGreet;
    };


    [
      odl,
      uuid(7A5E6E81-3DF8-11D3-903D-00105AA45BDC),
      helpstring("IGreet Interface")
    ]
    interface IGreet : IUnknown {
        [propget, helpstring("property Greeting")]
        HRESULT _stdcall Greeting([out, retval] BSTR*
pVal);
    };
};
```

IDENTIFYING THE TYPE LIBRARY

First comes the identification of the type library itself, which is done in three different ways. The fundamental way of identifying any entity in COM is through a *universally unique identifier* or UUID (sometimes also called a globally unique identifier or GUID). This 128-bit quantity is guaranteed to be unique anywhere, and gets around the problem of name clashes. But for the purposes of displaying information to humans, a more friendly name is appropriate. The helpstring ("Bank 1.0 Type Library") gives a name which can be used by viewer programs. You can see this long name used in Visual Basic in the References dialog, which can be brought up by the menu Project | References. See Figure 4–4.

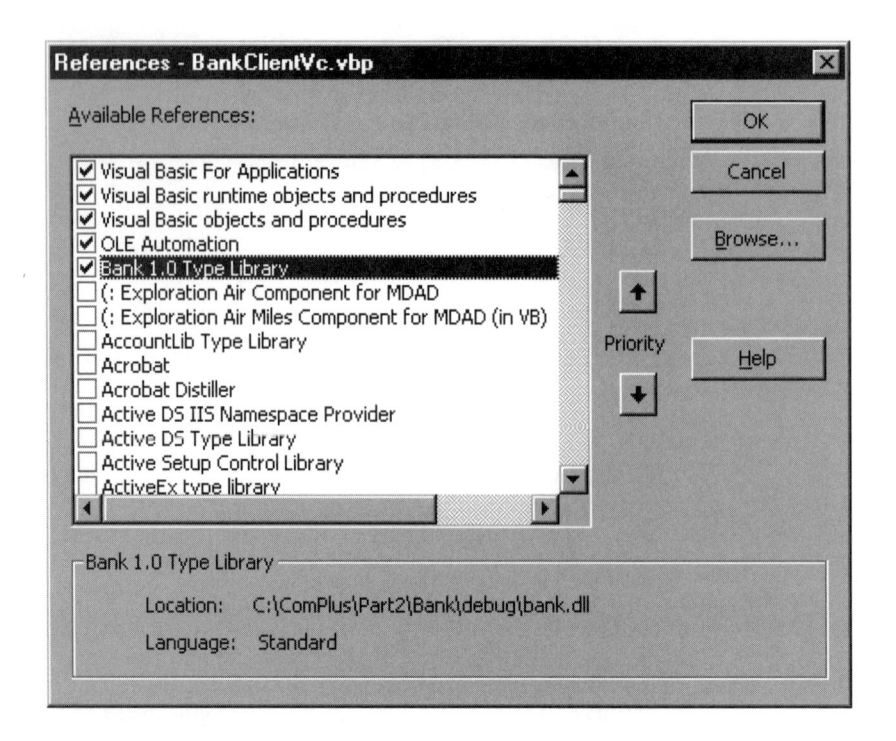

Chapter 4 • COM Clients: Concepts and Programming

Figure 4-4 *References dialog uses the long name for type library*

When you are creating a COM client program in Visual Basic, the first thing you have to do is to add references to any COM servers that you will use.

The third name is the means by which the library is referenced in programs. This name is displayed by the Object Browser (Figure 4–2). The library name is used in program code if it becomes necessary to disambiguate a class name. For example, suppose we are using two different libraries which both have a COM class named **Account**. Then to uniquely name the particular class in the **BANKLib** library, use the name "BANKLib.Account."

Having three names like this is common in COM. You can think of the UUID as a "machine" name, the long name given by the helpstring as a "user" name, and the third name as a "program" name. You can never mistake the UUID for one of the other two names, but the user name and program name can become confused. Be careful!

IDENTIFYING THE COCLASS (COM CLASS)

Next comes the COM class or "coclass." There may be several of these in one library. Each class is named in three ways. First comes the machine name or UUID. For a class, this identifier is often referred to as the class ID or CLSID.

Next comes the user name ("Account Class"). Then there is the name used in programs ("Account"). (To make matters really confusing, for classes there is in fact a *fourth* name called the program ID, which will be discussed a little later.)

INTERFACES

Besides identifying the class, the IDL also specifies which *interfaces* the class supports. An interface is something specific to COM. If you are familiar with object-oriented languages like C++, you know about classes, and how classes can have methods (or "member functions"). In a language like C++, there is no grouping of the methods of a class. But in COM you don't speak about methods of a class, but about methods of an interface. Related methods are grouped into an interface. This approach gives a greater logical organization to the functionality supported by a class. The **Account** class supports two interfaces, **IAccount** and **IDisplay**. Note the naming convention of beginning the name of an interface with the letter "I."

The first interface, **IAccount**, is designated as the "default" interface. In a Visual Basic program, you gain access to the methods of the default interface through a reference to the class itself. This point will become more clear when we look at Visual Basic client code.

METHODS

The next specifications are the precise "signatures" of the *methods*, identifying each parameter, its data type, and whether the parameter is input, output, or both input and output.

PROPERTIES

There is a special notation for the *properties*. The **IGreet** interface has a single read-only property called **Greeting**.

SUMMARY

Our example bank account server has a single type library (like all COM servers). There are two classes, **Account** and **Greet**. The **Account** class supports two interfaces, **IAccount** (with three methods) and **IDisplay** (one method). The **Greet** class supports one interface, **IGreet**, with a single property.

COM Terminology and Concepts

Hopefully, our exploration of the example bank account server, including dissecting the IDL description, will have given you a good start at understanding the structure of a COM server. Our goal in this section is to give a concise summary of the key terminology and concepts of the Component Object

Model (COM). Be warned that there is some confusion and inconsistency in how terms are used in the literature on COM. The term "object" is sometimes used when "class" is meant, and then there is the term "component," which does not appear to have acquired a universally accepted and consistent meaning. The terminology presented here provides a consistent standard for use in this book. I hope it will also serve to help you get your bearings when you read other writings about COM.

Interfaces

The most fundamental concept in COM is that of an *interface*. An interface can be thought of as a precise contract between a server and its clients. Once defined, an interface must remain immutable. If there are to be changes, a new interface must be defined. An interface consists of a group of *methods*. A method can be thought of as a function, with parameters of specified types. An interface is described in *Interface Definition Language* or IDL. Here is an example of the IDL for the **IAccount** interface.

```
interface IAccount : IUnknown
{
  HRESULT Deposit([in] int amount);
  HRESULT GetBalance([out] int* pBalance);
  HRESULT Withdraw([in] int amount);
};
```

HRESULT is the standard return type for interface methods and indicates an error code or success code. Visual Basic programs do not deal with HRESULTs directly. HRESULT will be discussed in the section on Visual C++ clients below. (In the IDL shown by the OLE/COM Object Viewer tool that was created from the type library there was added "_stdcall," which represents the standard "calling convention," specifying how arguments are placed on the stack, etc. This is a directive to the compiler, and, since _stdcall is the default, can be left out.)

IUNKNOWN INTERFACE

In COM, all interfaces derive from the special interface **IUnknown** and hence have, in addition to their own methods, the three methods of **IUnknown**. The following is the IDL representation of **IUnknown**.

```
interface IUnknown
{
  HRESULT QueryInterface(REFIID iid, void** ppvObject);
  ULONG AddRef();
  ULONG Release();
};
```

The first method supports "interface negotiation," which enables a client to find additional interfaces. The remaining methods support reference counting, which enable the client to control object lifetime. These topics will be discussed below.

Classes

An interface is an abstract specification. Interfaces are implemented by *classes*. A class in COM is similar to a class in object-oriented programming languages. A class encapsulates data and behavior in a single entity. Without classes, you have to maintain multiple variables and pass them to isolated functions. By grouping related data and functions into a class, you create an abstraction that simplifies programming and allows you to extend your programming model to include your own new data types.

COM extends this familiar programming model by providing that classes can implement multiple interfaces, each of which supports a particular feature through a related group of functions. For example, in our bank account server, the **Account** class implements the two interfaces **IAccount** and **IDisplay**, and also **IUnknown**. IUknown is supported by every COM object. See Figure 4–5.

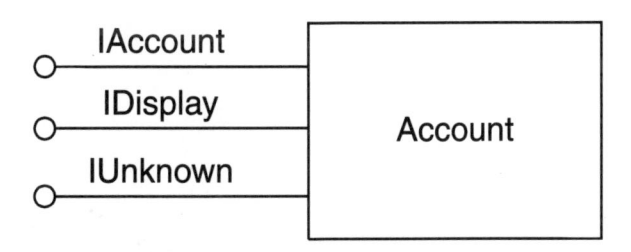

Figure 4–5 *Account class implements three interfaces*

Objects

An *object* is an "instance" of a class. A class can be thought of as code. It provides the capabilities described by the interfaces the class supports. But to do any work, you need to create at least one instance of the class. Such an object instance has particular associated data. Another object instance will have its own data. For example, consider running two instances of the client program concurrently. (To run two instances of a VB program, you could either start two sessions of Visual Basic, or else you could build the EXE file, and start the EXE file twice using Windows Explorer.) With each you can create an object. In our example, the new object always starts out with a balance of 100. With the first object make two deposits, and with the second make two withdrawals. Clearly we have two separate object instances, each with their own data. Since, Figure 4–6.

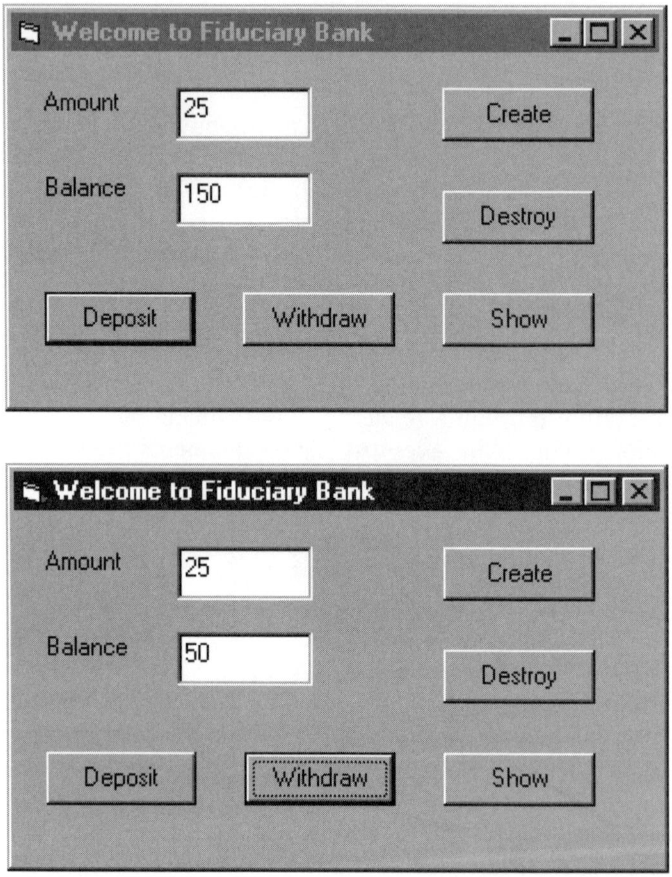

Figure 4–6 *Two object instances of the Account class*

Instantiating an Object

A client program needs to be able to instantiate an object instance of a class. The COM run time system provides an API function, **CoCreateInstanceEx** (or a simpler, older function, **CoCreateInstance**), which can be used directly in a C++ program. A Visual Basic program can use the **New** operator or the **CreateObject** function. We will look at all three of these, because they give insight into another important topic: How do you identify classes and interfaces?

A very important point is that what comes back from instantiating an object is not a reference to the object but rather to a particular *interface*. This distinction is quite important and can lead to confusion, particularly in Visual Basic where there is no direct language support for interfaces, as we shall see shortly.

COCREATEINSTANCE (C++)

First we will look at using C++ to instantiate an object. This will bring us much closer to how COM works, without the Visual Basic "sugar coating." For simplicity we will use the older function, **CoCreateInstance**. Later in this book where we discuss DCOM, I will explain the modern function **CoCreateInstanceEx**.

Here is the code for instantiating an object of the **Account** class. You will find the complete code in the **CBankClientDlg::OnCreateObject** function of **BankClientVc**. The interface pointer is declared in **BankClientDlg.h**.

```
IAccount* m_pAccount;
...

HRESULT hr;
hr = CoCreateInstance(CLSID_Account, NULL,
                      CLSCTX_SERVER, IID_IAccount,
                      void **) &m_pAccount);
```

Note that the class is identified by a class ID and the interface by an interface ID.

NEW (VISUAL BASIC)

The first way to instantiate an object in Visual Basic is to use the **New** operator. First you must have added a reference to the type library (menu Project | References). See Figure 4–4 earlier in the chapter. This brings in the **BANKLib** library, which includes the **Account** class (see Figure 4–2, which showed use of the Object Browser). The following code, taken from the **BankClientVb** project, then does the job. Note that the class is identified by its name.

```
Dim objAccount As Account
...
Set objAccount = New Account
```

Visual Basic speaks of obtaining an "object reference" to an object of class **Account**. This terminology is misleading, because, as we have seen, in COM you work with references to *interfaces*. Recall from our exploration of the IDL for the bank account server that **IAccount** is the "default" interface of the **Account** class. This means that the "object reference" to an **Account** object is really an interface reference to **IAccount**. When we look at the complete code for the Visual Basic client, we will see how to obtain and use a second interface in Visual Basic.

CREATEOBJECT (VISUAL BASIC)

A second way to instantiate an object in Visual Basic is through the **CreateObject** function. This was actually the original way to instantiate objects in Visual Basic, and is still the only way to instantiate objects using VBScript. Originally Visual Basic only used a special form of COM known as "Automation" and could only talk to COM servers whose classes provided "dispatch" interfaces. Automation is less efficient than straight COM but is more flexible, supporting something known as "late binding," in which the kind of class is only determined at run time (a requirement for a scripting language in an application such as Internet Explorer, which has no way of knowing what kinds of objects may be used on HTML pages). This topic is discussed in Chapter 11.

It turns out that the **CreateObject** function can also achieve "early binding," if a reference to the type library has been added to the project, like we did above. Then the following code will instantiate an object. This code is also in the **BankClientVb** project and is used for instantiating an object of the class **Greet**. Note that the class is identified by its program ID in the **CreateObject** function and by its name when the object reference is declared.

```
Dim objGreet As Greet
Set objGreet = CreateObject("Bank.Greet.1")
```

Identifiers in COM

These examples have illustrated several kinds of identifiers that are used in COM. We can now explain these various identifiers.

GLOBALLY UNIQUE IDENTIFIER (GUID)

Programming languages refer to variables, classes, and other language elements by human-readable names. Name clashes are an ever-present possibility but can be managed within the context of a single development project. COM classes implement binary components that need to be unique across a very wide domain. Interfaces and other entities in COM require an identification mechanism that will prevent accidental name collisions. The Distributed Computing Environment (DCE) of the Open Software Foundation provides a solution through the concept of the "universally unique identifier" (UUID), which is a 128-bit quantity that can be generated algorithmically in a manner to virtually assure uniqueness. Microsoft adopted this mechanism for COM, calling the identifier (somewhat less grandiosely) a "GUID" (globally unique identifier).

There are different kinds of GUIDs for various entities in COM. So far we have encountered GUIDs for type library, class (class ID or CLSID), and interface (interface ID or IID).

Programming in C++, you may refer directly to these GUIDs in your code. Typically you will use a manifest constant defined in a header file to refer to the GUID. In a high-level environment such as Visual Basic, you will program using human-readable names, but the Visual Basic environment will use the corresponding GUIDs when talking to COM on your behalf.

PROGRAM ID (PROGID)

Closely associated with the CLSID is a program ID or ProgID. The ProgID is a string that can be used as a proxy for the CLSID. The ProgID is often of the form "application.class" or "application.class.N," where "application" refers to a particular application or server and "class" refers to a particular class implemented by that server. There may also be a version number appended. An example of a ProgID is "Bank.Greet.1."

CLASS NAME

The IDL for a server contains a "coclass" statement, which is used to give a name to the coclass (COM class). The two coclasses in our bank server example are **Account** and **Greet**.

```
coclass Account {
        [default] interface IAccount;
        interface IDisplay;
    };
...
coclass Greet {
        [default] interface IGreet;
    };
```

Visual Basic uses the coclass name when you **Dim** an object reference and when you use the **New** operator.

"USER" NAMES

All of the identifiers discussed up until now are used for programming. An end user would never see either a GUID, a ProgID, or a coclass name. But there are some COM entities that may in fact be exposed to an end user An excellent example are compound document classes used in OLE. An end-user of an OLE client (or "container") application such as Microsoft Word can insert "objects" created by other applications. To do so, the user invokes the menu item Insert | Object, and a dialog comes up showing all of the OLE classes on the system. The names shown are the "user" names of the classes (sometimes called the object "type"). See Figure 4–7. Various user names are created via helpstrings in IDL.

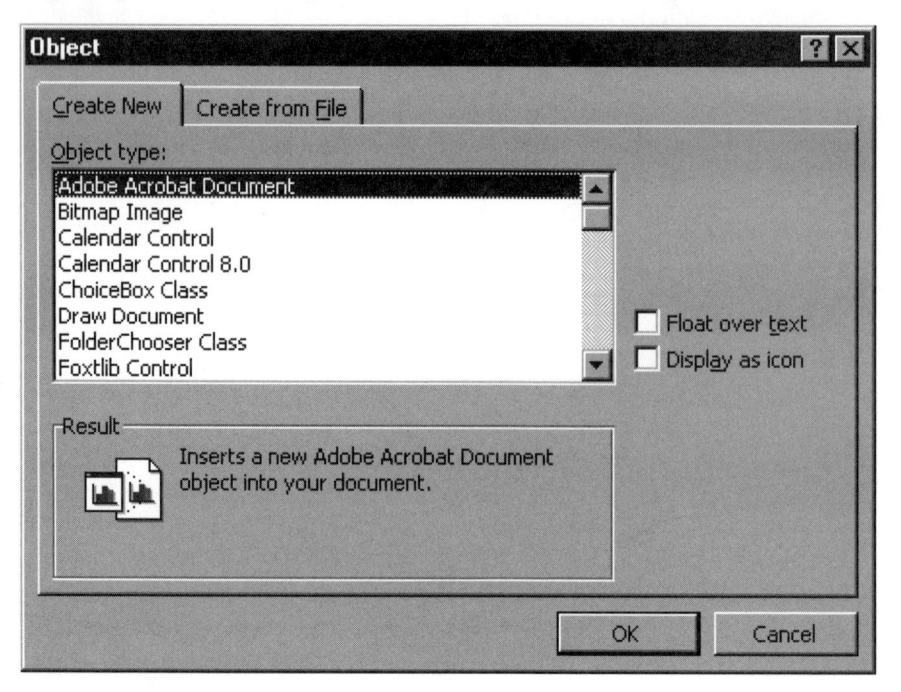

Figure 4–7 *"User" names of classes are employed in OLE*

Object Lifetime

A feature of COM is that both client and server participate in managing the lifetimes of COM objects. Neither can do so by itself. Clearly a server cannot delete an object unless the client is done with it. So a client tells the server when it is done with an object. But that does not mean that the server can delete the object, because *another* client may be using it. The solution is for the server to maintain a reference count for each object. The fundamental **IUnknown** interface provides two methods for manipulating the reference count. **AddRef** increments the reference count. **AddRef** is called when an object is instantiated, so it begins at 1. Whenever a client "copies" an interface reference, it should call **AddRef**, because now the object will be referenced again. When a client is done using an interface pointer, it calls **Release**. When all clients have released all their references to an object, the reference count will stand at 0, and the server can then safely delete the object.

COM Terminology and Concepts

OBJECT LIFETIME IN VISUAL BASIC

A nice feature of Visual Basic is that in many cases object lifetimes are managed for you automatically, without a requirement for any special coding on your part. If you **Dim** an object reference as a local variable within a procedure or function, the object reference will be released when you go out of scope of that procedure or function.

If you have an object reference at global scope, you may have to do some management yourself. You "release" a reference by setting it to **Nothing**. Thus, the Visual Basic client program **BankClientVb** implements the handler for the "Destroy" button as follows:

```
Dim objAccount As Account 'global scope

...

Private Sub cmdDestroy_Click()
    Set objAccount = Nothing
    txtBalance = ""
End Sub
```

Interface Negotiation

The fact that a COM class can support multiple interfaces means that there has to be a mechanism for a client that has a reference to one interface of the class to obtain a reference to another interface. Obtaining another interface pointer is accomplished through a process known as "interface negotiation" by using the third method of **IUnknown**, namely **QueryInterface**.

```
HRESULT QueryInterface(REFIID iid, void** ppvObject);
```

The first parameter is used to pass in an interface ID of the requested interface. The second parameter is used for passing out a pointer to the interface, if it is supported. If the requested interface is *not* supported, the HRESULT that comes back will indicate a failure.

QUERYINTERFACE USING VISUAL C++

A Visual C++ program calls **QueryInterface** directly. As an example, look at the implementation of **OnShow**.

```
void CBankClientDlg::OnShow()
{
   // Query for second interface
   HRESULT hr = m_pAccount->QueryInterface(
                      IID_IDisplay,
                      (void**) &m_pDisplay);
   if (FAILED(hr))
```

```
  {
    MessageBox("QueryInterface failed");
    return;
  }
  if (!m_pDisplay)
    return;
  hr = m_pDisplay->Show();
  if (FAILED(hr))
  {
    MessageBox("Show failed");
    return;
  }
  m_pDisplay->Release();
  m_pDisplay = NULL;
}
```

QUERYINTERFACE USING VISUAL BASIC

A Visual Basic program does not call **QueryInterface** directly. In fact, Visual Basic does not even directly expose the notion of "interface" at all. Interfaces are represented in Visual Basic by means of classes. When it reads a type library, Visual Basic will expose a "class" for each interface. The default interface will be assigned a class with name corresponding to the coclass. Thus the VB class corresponding to the **IAccount** interface is **Account**. For other interfaces, VB will assign a class name that is the same as the name of the interface. Hence the VB class corresponding to the **IDisplay** interface is simply **IDisplay**. The Visual Basic code to do a **QueryInterface** is then quite simple. You **Dim** a reference to the desired interface, and do a **Set** to the original reference. Here is the code for handling the "Show" button:

```
Private Sub cmdShow_Click()
    If Not objAccount Is Nothing Then
        Dim ifcDisplay As IDisplay
        Set ifcDisplay = objAccount
        ifcDisplay.Show
    End If
End Sub
```

Note that there is a little robustness in this code. Rather than blindly set the new reference to **objAccount**, we first check that it is valid (that is, is not **Nothing**).

Also note the naming convention. Bowing to tradition, in VB we call the reference to the default interface **objAccount** and refer to it as an "object reference." We have no such scruples with the **IDisplay** interface. We use a prefix **ifc** to suggest that it is referring to an interface.

Server

We can now describe what a *server* is in COM. It is simply a program module (in Windows it is a DLL or EXE) which provides the executable code for one or more classes. Note the hierarchy that is involved. A server can implement multiple classes. A class can support multiple interfaces. An interface can have multiple methods. Figure 4–8 shows the overall structure of our example bank account server. (For simplicity **IUnknown** is not shown.)

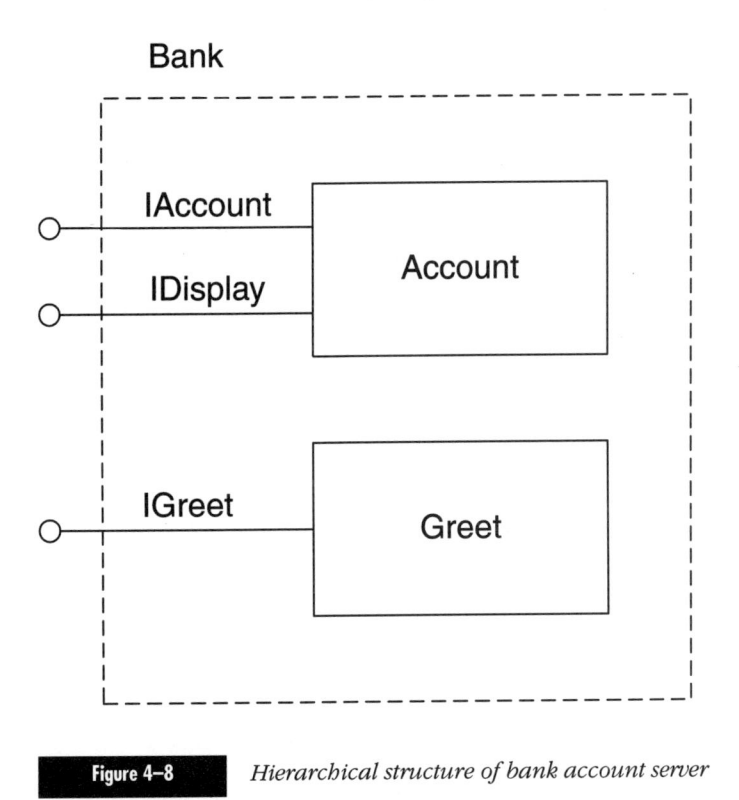

Bank

- IAccount ── Account
- IDisplay ── Account
- IGreet ── Greet

Figure 4–8 *Hierarchical structure of bank account server*

Type Library

The code for the server will be in a program module. Typically it will be in a dynamic link library (DLL). Besides the code itself, COM makes extensive use of a *description* of the code. This description is called *type information* and is saved persistently as a *type library*. The library itself has a GUID, a name ("BANKLib" for our example) and a user name ("Bank 1.0 Type Library"). The library stores a description of the classes implemented by the server, the interfaces supported by the classes, the methods of the interfaces, and the precise signatures (parameters and data types) of these methods. The default interface of each class is specified.

COM Client Programming Model

We are now in a position to describe very concisely the programming model for a COM client. There are six main things you may need to do. Depending on your programming environment or application framework, some of these steps may be done for you automatically. (One note on terminology is that, in C++, an interface is referenced through a *pointer*. So far we have been using the language neutral term "interface reference," and for the default interface in Visual Basic have used the term "object reference." Now that we are getting closer to the actual coding, we will tend to use the term interface pointer when we are referring to C++.)

1. Initialize the COM run-time system. The COM API call for this is **CoInitialize** (or **CoInitializeEx**). An MFC application can call **AfxOleInit**. Visual Basic does the initialization for you automatically.
2. Obtain an initial interface reference (or pointer). In C++, you do this by calling **CoCreateInstance** or **CoCreateInstanceEx**. In Visual Basic, you use the **New** operator or call **CreateObject**.
3. Through the interface pointer you can now invoke methods of the interface.
4. If you need to call methods of other interfaces, do a **QueryInterface**. In C++, you call **QueryInterface** through the interface pointer, and, in Visual Basic, you perform a **Set** operation.
5. When you are done using an interface pointer in C++ you call **Release**. In Visual Basic, you either just let it go naturally out of scope, or you explicitly **Set** it to **Nothing**.
6. When done using COM, you uninitialize COM by calling **CoUninitialize**. This step is done automatically by Visual Basic and by MFC.

Programming a COM Client

We can now give complete programming examples of calling a COM server. We provide three sample programs. The first is the Visual Basic client program, **BankClientVb**. The second is a Visual C++ console program implemented using MFC, **BankConsoleVc**. Finally we give a Visual C++ GUI program implemented by MFC, **BanckClientVc.**

Visual Basic COM Client Program

The example program is **BankClientVb**. It is created as a standard EXE project. You must add a reference to the bank server type library ("Bank 1.0 Type Library") using Project | References. See Figure 4–4. You put the controls on the form as shown in Figure 4–1. Then the complete code that you need is shown below.

```
Option Explicit
Dim objAccount As Account

Private Sub cmdCreate_Click()
    Set objAccount = New Account
    UpdateBalance
End Sub

Private Sub cmdDeposit_Click()
    'WARNING: We don't check for valid object reference!!
    'See code for Withdraw and Show for correct pattern
    objAccount.Deposit txtAmount
    UpdateBalance
End Sub

Private Sub cmdDestroy_Click()
    Set objAccount = Nothing
    txtBalance = ""
End Sub

Private Sub cmdShow_Click()
    If Not objAccount Is Nothing Then
        Dim ifcDisplay As IDisplay
        Set ifcDisplay = objAccount
        ifcDisplay.Show
    End If
End Sub

Private Sub cmdWithdraw_Click()
    If Not objAccount Is Nothing Then
        objAccount.Withdraw txtAmount
        UpdateBalance
    End If
End Sub

Private Sub Form_Load()
    'Note use of ProgId and CreateObject
    Dim objGreet As Greet
    Set objGreet = CreateObject("Bank.Greet.1")
    Form1.Caption = objGreet.Greeting
    txtAmount = 25
End Sub

Private Sub UpdateBalance()
    Dim balance As Long
    objAccount.GetBalance balance
    txtBalance = balance
End Sub
```

By this time the code should be quite self-explanatory. One point to note is that there is some defensive coding. The "Show" and "Withdraw" handlers check for a valid object reference. Thus if you run the application and do not create the object, "Show" and "Withdraw" will just do nothing. But you will get an error if you click "Deposit" without first "Create." The textbox for Balance is shown blank when there is no object, and the current balance is shown when there is an object.

There is no other error checking in the program. To make it more robust you should make use of the Visual Basic **On Error** capability. Error handling is very important in COM, and Chapter 12 will be devoted to it.

Visual C++ COM Client Program (Console)

The example program is **BankConsoleVc**. It is created as a Win32 Console Application project. In our C++ program, we will not be working with the type library but will get the required information from a header and code file from the server project. Our client program has the files **bank.h** and **bank_i.c** copied over from the server project (**Bank**). The file **bank.h** contains the declarations of the interfaces **IAccount**, **IDisplay** and **IGreet**. Don't worry about trying to understand this file—it is pretty arcane code generated by the MIDL RPC compiler (more about MIDL later). As a client programmer, all you need to do is to include this where you are declaring interface pointers. The second file, **bank_i.c**, contains the definitions of the GUIDs. It should be included in only one compilation unit and hence should not be included in a header file (if you do that, you may get a "symbol multiply defined" error message). Since this project has only one source code file, we include both **bank.h** and **bank_i.c** in **BankConsole.cpp**. The key header file to include for the COM library is **objbase.h**.

The complete code is shown below. It should be fairly easy to understand. One nuance is the proper handling of character strings. In COM all strings are Unicode strings, and some strings are a particular kind of Unicode string known as a BSTR. The **Greet** class passes back the welcome message as a BSTR, which must be converted. We discuss Unicode and BSTR a little later.

```
// BankConsole.cpp

#include <stdio.h>
#include <objbase.h>
#include "bank.h"
#include "bank_i.c"
#include <comdef.h>

int main(int argc, char* argv[])
{
   // Initialize COM
```

Programming a COM Client

```
HRESULT hr = CoInitialize(NULL);
if (FAILED(hr))
{
  printf("CoInitialize failed\n");
  return 0;
}
// Instantiate Greet object, obtaining interface pointer
IGreet* pGreet;
hr = CoCreateInstance(CLSID_Greet, NULL, CLSCTX_SERVER,
                      IID_IGreet, (void **) &pGreet);
if (FAILED(hr))
{
  printf("CoCreateInstance failed\n");
  return 0;
}
// Display welcome message, and then release
BSTR bstr;
hr = pGreet->get_Greeting(&bstr);
if (FAILED(hr))
{
  printf("get_Greeting failed\n");
  return 0;
}
else
{
  _bstr_t greeting(bstr);
  printf("%s\n", (const char*) greeting);
  pGreet->Release();
}

// Instantiate Account object, obtaining interface ptr
IAccount* pAccount;
hr = CoCreateInstance(CLSID_Account, NULL,
                      CLSCTX_SERVER,
                      IID_IAccount, (void **) &pAccount);
if (FAILED(hr))
{
  printf("CoCreateInstance failed\n");
  return 0;
}
// Use interface pointer to call methods
// First get and display initial balance
int balance;
hr = pAccount->GetBalance(&balance);
if (FAILED(hr))
{
  printf("GetBalance failed\n");
  pAccount->Release();
  return 0;
}
```

```
  printf("balance = %d\n", balance);
  // Deposit 25
  hr = pAccount->Deposit(25);
  if (FAILED(hr))
  {
    printf("Deposit failed\n");
    pAccount->Release();
    return 0;
  }
  // Obtain balance after deposit
  hr = pAccount->GetBalance(&balance);
  if (FAILED(hr))
    printf("GetBalance failed\n");
  else
    printf("balance = %d\n", balance);

  // Query for IDisplay, call Show, and then release
  // interface pointers
  IDisplay* pDisplay;
  hr = pAccount->QueryInterface(IID_IDisplay,
                                (void **) &pDisplay);
  if (FAILED(hr))
  {
    printf("QueryInterface failed\n");
    pAccount->Release();
    return 0;
  }
  hr = pDisplay->Show();
  if (FAILED(hr))
    printf("Show failed\n");
  else
    pDisplay->Release();
  pAccount->Release();
  return 0;
}
```

Visual C++ COM Client Program (Using MFC)

The example program is **BankClientVc**. It is created as a standard MFC AppWizard (exe) project. In Step 1, choose "Dialog based" as the application type. In Step 2, clear the checkbox for About Box (for simplicity). Accept the default of support for ActiveX controls. We are not using ActiveX controls, but selecting that option has the convenience of bringing in an MFC header file that we need. Accept all the other defaults.

As in the console case, we need the files **bank.h** and **bank_i.c**. The file **bank.h** is included where you are declaring interface pointers, in this case the dialog class definition file **BankClientDlg.h**. The second file, **bank_i.c**, contains the definitions of the GUIDs. It should be included in only one compilation unit and hence should not be included in a header file (if you do that, you may get a "symbol multiply defined" error message). We include it in **BankClientDlg.cpp**.

An MFC program can include the header file **afxdisp.h** for the COM libraries (see **stdafx.h**). An MFC program can initialize COM via the function **AfxOleInit**. MFC takes care of uninitializing COM. The rest of the program is functionally similar to the console program but is structured differently. Where the console program is straight down, the MFC program implements a GUI and so there is code in handler functions for the various buttons. Initialization of COM is done in **CBankClientApp::InitInstance** and the **Greet** object is used to initialize the window title in **CBankClientDlg::OnInitDialog**. The rest of the program should be easy to understand if you know MFC and understand the use of COM in the console program. You may examine the code files in the **BankClientVc** project.

Additional Topics in COM Client Programming

There are several other topics pertaining to COM client programming that should be discussed. We examine how strings are represented in COM as Unicode or BSTR strings. For converting the strings, we will need some API functions. We also need to look at memory management. Frequently in COM a server will allocate memory which a client must free. COM provides a special memory management interface, **IMalloc**, which can be used for such cooperative memory management. Memory management, string conversions, and other services are performed by library functions. We will see how the COM library is organized into API functions and COM interfaces. Some important functions are provided by the Win32 API or by wrapper functions such as provided by MFC.

This section will be of interest primarily to Visual C++ programmers. Everyone should look at the final section on the Registry.

Unicode

Unicode is a 16-bit character standard that is widely used. NT and Windows 2000 use Unicode natively for representing strings. COM has adopted this standard. This means that if you pass a string to a COM API or method, you should pass it as a Unicode string. If you get a string back from such a call, it will be in Unicode. By default, Visual C++ applications use "multibyte," which is standard 8-bit characters for ANSI and additional bytes where required. Unless you are building your application as a Unicode application, you will need to convert between Unicode and multibyte.

CONVERTING USING WIN32

The Win32 functions **MultiByteToWideChar** and **WideCharToMultiByte** convert between multibyte and Unicode. For sample code, see the **UseCmd** project in **Chap4** directory. This console program lets the user enter a ProgID, calls a COM API function to convert to a CLSID, converts the CLSID to a string representation of it, displays it, and then goes on to instantiate the object.

Here is an example of converting to Unicode:

```
char progid[80];
WCHAR wbuf[80];
...
// Convert progid to Unicode and obtain CLSID
CLSID clsid;
MultiByteToWideChar(CP_ACP, 0, progid, -1, wbuf, 80);
```

Here is an example of converting from Unicode:

```
LPOLESTR ostr;
char buf[80];
...
WideCharToMultiByte(CP_ACP, 0, ostr, -1, buf, 80,
    NULL, NULL);
```

CONVERTING USING MACROS

MFC (also ATL) provides a series of macros, to simplify character conversion. To use these macros you must include the header file **afxpriv.h**. Before invoking any of the macros, declare local storage for doing the conversion via the macro **USES_CONVERSION**. Then you can use macros such as **OLE2CT**, **T2OLE**, etc., to do conversion between "traditional" strings T and OLE strings.

An illustration of converting this way is provided in the file **BankClientDlg.cpp** in the **BankClientVc** project.

```
#include <afxpriv.h>
...
BSTR bstr;
hr = pGreet->get_Greeting(&bstr);
if (FAILED(hr))
  MessageBox("get_Greeting failed");
else
{
  // _bstr_t greeting(bstr);
  USES_CONVERSION;
  SetWindowText((const char*) OLE2CT(bstr));
  ::SysFreeString(bstr);
...
```

BSTR

A special kind of Unicode string is a BSTR (or Basic String). The characters are stored as 16-bit Unicode characters. Rather than using a null terminator, a BSTR has a 16-bit prefix giving a count of the number of *bytes* in the string. Thus a BSTR could be used for passing binary data that may have embedded nulls. Visual Basic uses BSTR for representing string data. Many COM API functions and methods use BSTR for passing string data. In Visual C++, a BSTR has a null appended to it, and the character pointer points to the first character (just after the byte count). Thus a BSTR can be treated in a Visual C++ program like an ordinary Unicode string.

When a BSTR is passed via COM, there are some special memory management considerations. Memory for the string is allocated in the server, and the memory should be freed by the client. A BSTR is allocated using the Win32 API function **SysAllocString** and is freed using **SysFreeString**.

BSTR

Visual C++ provides a number of useful utility classes to assist in COM programming. One of these is **_bstr_**, which wraps a BSTR. There are various constructors, conversions (for instance, overridden cast operator), and a destructor which automatically deallocates. To use these COM utility classes, you should include the header file **<comdef.h>**. An alternate way of coding the above example follows:

```
#include <comdef.h>
...
BSTR bstr;
hr = pGreet->get_Greeting(&bstr);
if (FAILED(hr))
  MessageBox("get_Greeting failed");
else
{
  _bstr_t greeting(bstr);
  //USES_CONVERSION;
  SetWindowText((const char*) greeting);
  ...
```

Note that when you use this Visual C++ support class, the BSTR memory deallocation is done automatically by the class destructor.

COM Library Programming

We have been examining programming considerations for COM clients which call COM servers. There are similar considerations for programs that call upon the COM library. The first thing to understand is the basic structure of the COM library. Like any other library in the Windows environment, the COM library has a number of ordinary API functions which you can just call. What is different about the COM library is that most of its functionality is provided by COM classes, which you invoke through interface pointers. The basic pattern to invoke a method of one of these built-in classes is to do the following:

1. Call an API function to get an interface pointer.
2. Through this interface pointer, call methods.
3. When you are done, release the interface pointer.

The **UseCmd** example program that we saw before illustrates this pattern.

```
LPOLESTR ostr;
hr = StringFromCLSID(clsid, &ostr);
...
// Free the OLE string by obtaining an IMalloc pointer
LPMALLOC pMalloc;
hr = CoGetMalloc(MEMCTX_TASK, &pMalloc);
pMalloc->Free(ostr);
pMalloc->Release();
```

A number of COM library API functions serve to wrap a series of calls. Thus the above sequence of three calls to get an interface pointer, call a method, and then release the interface pointer can be replaced by an API call:

```
CoTaskMemFree(ostr);
```

Windows Registry and COM

The Registry is a configuration database for Windows. It was introduced with Windows 3.1 and has come to largely supplant .INI files for storing configuration information. A drawback of .INI files is that they are text files that can easily become corrupted. The Registry is a binary database that can only be accessed programmatically and by a special tool called the Registry Editor (REGEDIT). You need Administrator privileges in order to use the Registry Editor.

The Registry stores important information about COM servers. Basically, it connects the various GUIDs, the other names, and the server itself. To provide an orientation to how this information is stored in the Registry we will trace through the various Registry, entries for our Bank server. The tools we will use are OLE/COM Object Viewer and REGEDIT. We will also see how COM servers register and unregister themselves.

In a sense, information about COM and the Registry is more important when programming COM servers than when programming clients. The server is responsible for providing a mechanism for proper information to be placed in the Registry. Once a server has been properly installed, a client program should be able to just use the server according to the programming model described in this chapter, without any regard to how information is stored in the Registry. But if something does not work, it will be very helpful to you if you know what information should be in the Registry, so you can do some troubleshooting.

Information in the Registry is organized according to "keys" and "values." We will see many examples of keys and values as we trace through the entries.

Using OLE/COM Object Viewer

Earlier in the chapter we used OLE/COM Object Viewer to examine information about the type library for the Bank server. Now we will use it to examine other information. We will also see that it can be used in a more active way—for example, to actually instantiate an object.

Bring up OLE/COM Object Viewer (from Tools menu in Visual C++ or from Start | Programs | Microsoft Visual Studio | Microsoft Visual Studio Tools | OLE View). From the View menu make sure that "Expert Mode" is checked. Adjust the tree view in the left pane so that you see the top nodes "Object Classes," "Application IDs," "Type Libraries," and "Interfaces," and, immediately under Object Classes, the nodes "Grouped by Component Category," "OLE 1.0 Objects," "COM Library Objects," and "All Objects." See Figure 4–9.

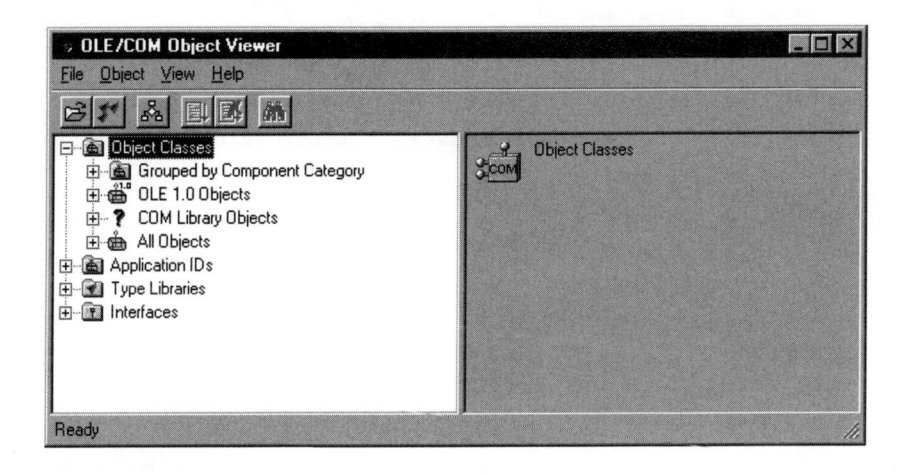

Figure 4–9 *Top-level nodes in OLE/COM Object Viewer*

Chapter 4 • COM Clients: Concepts and Programming

Now expand "All Objects" (you need to be in Expert Mode) and look for "Account Class." Here is a place where being familiar with the various names by which the class is known proves useful. OLE/COM Object Viewer shows the "user name" (longer, friendly name). If you look for the ProgID "Bank.Account.1" you will be out of luck. In the right pane, you will be shown in one place all the information about this class that is scattered in various places in the Registry. See Figure 4–10.

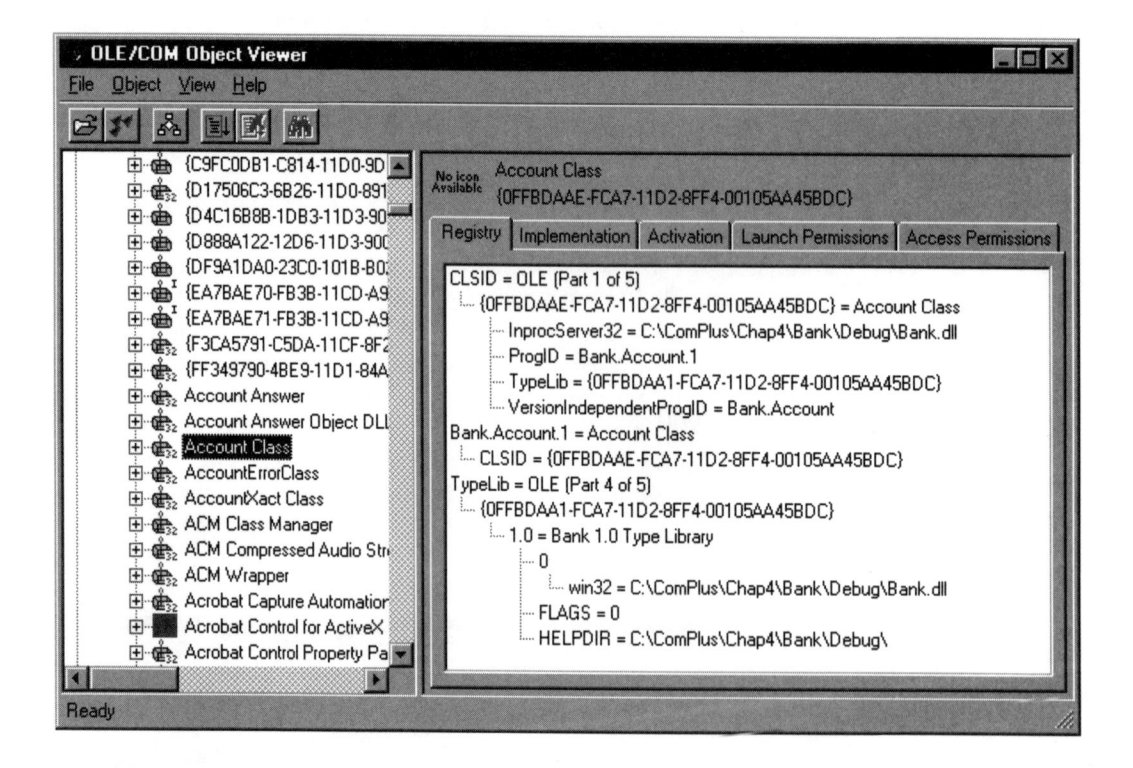

Figure 4–10 *Registry information for Account Class*

The information for "Account Class" is organized in the Registry under three nodes: "CLSID," "Bank.Account.1," and "TypeLib." We will use the Registry Editor shortly to view some of this same information (less conveniently), but right now let's trace through just what information is shown.

CLSID

Under "CLSID" is a key which is the numerical GUID representing the class, shown in hex. The corresponding value is "Account Class," the user name. There are several subkeys. The first is "InProcServer32" whose value is the path to the server. This is actually the most important entry in the Registry for the Account class. When a client calls **CoCreateInstance** and passes the CLSID, the COM run time can go to the Registry and find the path to the server, which it can proceed to load.

The next subkey is the ProgID, where we find "Bank.Account.1." There is also a "version independent" ProgID, which does not have the number suffix. Finally, there is TypeLib, which gives the GUID for the type library.

BANK.ACCOUNT.1

Under this key we simply find the CLSID. This is typical of redundancy you find in the Registry. The Registry is a hierarchical database designed for very fast lookup, not a normalized relational database.

TYPELIB

Here we find information about the type library, including the friendly user name "Bank 1.0 Type Library." Under the "Win32" key there is a path to the type library, which is available in the DLL itself.

INSTANTIATING AN OBJECT

You can use OLE/COM Object Viewer to instantiate an object. When the class is selected in the left pane you can double-click, click the "+" in the tree view node, or right-click and select "Create Instance." If you do that for the Bank server you will see a message box announcing creation of the object. To release the object, right-click and choose "Release Instance." For the Bank server you will see a message box announcing destruction of the object.

Registry Editor

Now let us see how information is stored in the Registry, as viewed by the lower-level tool, the Registry Editor. You can start the Registry Editor from OLE/COM Object Viewer from the File menu. You can also run it using Run from the Start menu. Type in **regedit** as the program to be run. When you start the Registry Editor, you will see a tree view in the left pane showing a number of "hives." HKEY_CLASSES_ROOT is the hive of importance to COM. See Figure 4–11.

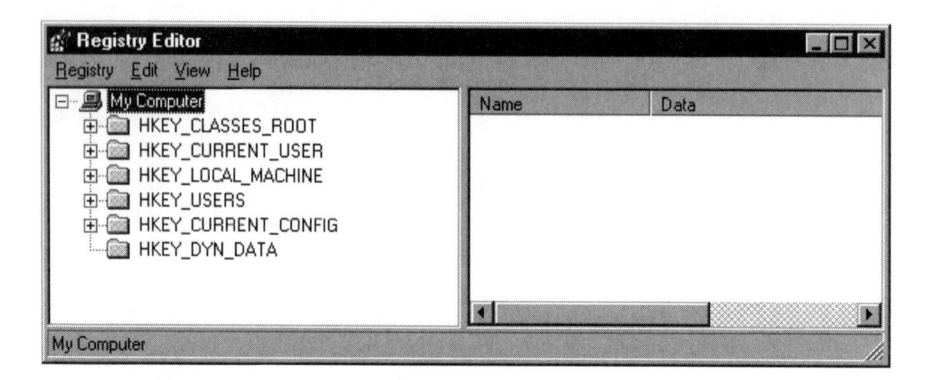

Chapter 4 • COM Clients: Concepts and Programming

Figure 4-11   *The "hives" are shown in the Registry Editor*

Opening up HKEY_CLASSES_ROOT, you will see a number of file extensions followed by ProgIDs. The ProgID is the easiest thing to key off when using the Registry Editor directly. Look for "Bank.Account.1." You can then find the numerical CLSID. See Figure 4–12.

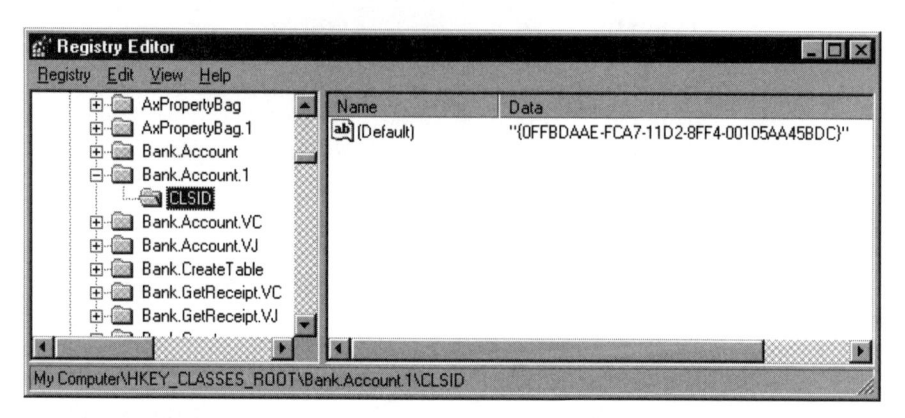

Figure 4-12   *You can find the numerical CLSID from the ProgID*

Now that you know the numerical CLSID, you can find the other core information, such as the path to the server. In the left pane open up the node "CLSID" and scroll down until you find the numerical CLSID that you are looking for. In the right pane you will see the desired information. See Figure 4–13.

Windows Registry and COM

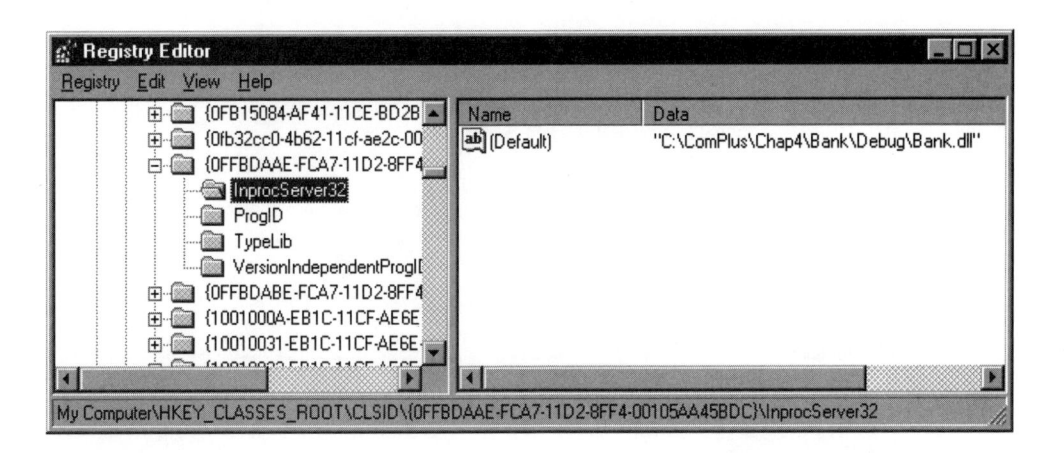

Figure 4-13 *Most important information in the Registry is stored under the CLSID*

Server Self-Registration

An important feature of COM servers is that they are "self-registering." This makes it easy for registry information to be put into and taken out of the Registry. A DLL COM server is supposed to support entry points **DllRegisterServer** and **DllUnregisterServer** to register and unregister the server, respectively. You can invoke these functions using the tool **regsvr32.exe**. To register **bank.dll**, type

```
regsvr32 path\bank.dll
```

To unregister use the **/u** command line option:

```
regsvr32 /u path\bank.dll
```

In the examples in this book I have provided batch files to register and unregister the server.

To try self-registration out, in the **Bank** directory double click on **unreg_bank.bat**. This will unregister the server, as should be confirmed by a message box. Now try running the Visual Basic client program **BankClientVb.exe**. You will get an error message. See Figure 4-14.

Look for Registry information for "Account Class" in OLE/COM Object Viewer (Refresh if necessary). You won't find it. Now register the server again by double-clicking on **reg_bank.bat**. Now you should be able to find the Registry information, and if you run the client program it should work again.

Figure 4–14 Cannot instantiate an object for an unregistered COM server

Summary

This long chapter covered a lot of ground. There were two basic agenda items. The first was to be able to write COM clients using both Visual Basic and Visual C++. The second was to *understand* what you are doing. The most important thing to remember from this chapter is the basic programming model for a client to call a COM server. You have to instantiate an object from a COM class. You do that in C++ by calling **CoCreateInstance(Ex)**, and in Visual Basic by using the **New** operator or **CreateObject**. What you get back is a reference to an *interface*. Through this interface reference (pointer in C++), you can call methods. When you are done using this interface, you release it. In C++, you call **Release**. In Visual Basic, you just let the reference go out of scope, or **Set** it to **Nothing** (if reference has global scope). A COM class can support multiple interfaces, and the **QueryInterface** mechanism allows you to access these other interfaces.

We also looked at some programming details, such as the use of Unicode and BSTR for strings in COM. We briefly examined the use of the Registry for storing information about COM classes, including the path to the COM server.

The next two chapters will cover implementing COM servers. Chapter 5 covers some of the details about the COM protocol and how it is implemented in C++. Visual Basic programmers can skip this chapter, or just skim it for the general ideas. Chapter 6 covers the actual implementation of a COM server in C++ (hard) and Visual Basic (easy).

If you are a C++ programmer, don't despair, because Chapter 7 introduces the Active Template Library, which will make it easy to implement COM servers in C++.

FIVE

C++ and the Component Object Model

This chapter is for C++ programmers. It addresses two questions. The first is: "Why should I care about COM—why don't I simply continue to build my systems in straight C++?" If you reach an affirmative answer to the first question, you come to the second: "How do I implement COM in C++?" Writing COM clients in C++ is quite straightforward, as we saw in Chapter 4. But implementing servers in C++ is quite a different story. There is a lot of infrastructure that must be provided. In C++ this infrastructure is not completely abstracted away as it is in Visual Basic. Higher level tools like Active Template Library (ATL) remove much of the drudgery, but in order to use ATL effectively you need to have a basic understanding of what ATL is doing for you.

We will describe COM as an object-oriented foundation of component software. We will see that a "component" has many of the characteristics of an "object" but is more. Components provide the foundation for reusable software in a way that was dreamed of in object-oriented languages like C++ and Smalltalk but never fully achieved. We will compare the object models of C++ and COM. For this discussion you should have a good understanding of C++ as an object-oriented language. You do not need a great deal of fluency in C++ in order to understand the concepts, but of course to implement the program examples you must have C++ programming knowledge. We'll review the basic principles of the C++ object model as we go along. In particular we will take a look at virtual functions and the C++ vtable, because the vtable data structure defines the binary layout of COM interfaces. It is this binary specification that gives COM its language independence.

There are several key concepts that lie at the foundation of COM. These include the notion of a COM *interface*, the role of *globally unique identifiers*, and the **IUnknown** interface and its role in interface negotiation and reference counting. These concepts are part of the COM "protocol" and apply to any communication about a COM client and object. In this chapter, the object will in fact be part of the same application as the client, and there is no "server" involved. The COM libraries are not used. Hopefully, by focusing on just the basic aspects of this important COM protocol you can come to a firm understanding of it. In the next chapter we will introduce additional aspects of the COM protocol, such as class factories, which are required when the COM object is implemented in a server.

After a discussion of the basic features of the Component Object Model, we will go on to give a detailed programming example. To implement two or more interfaces on an object, we will see that the C++ feature of multiple inheritance is very useful.

Objects, Components and COM

In this first section, we discuss briefly what an "object" is and the fact that a "component object" is more. We look at the goal of reusability.

Component Objects

Objects encapsulate data and behavior in a single entity. Without objects, you have to maintain multiple variables and pass them to isolated functions. By grouping related data and functions into an object, you create an abstraction that simplifies programming and allows you to extend your programming model to include your own new data types.

COM extends this object structuring capability. "Component objects" can have multiple interfaces, each of which supports a particular feature through a related group of functions. COM defines a binary standard, allowing a component object implemented in one programming language to be called by a client written in another language.

Component Software

A dream of the software industry has been the creation of reusable components that can be assembled to build applications. There is an analogy with hardware components implemented as integrated circuits (chips). Much talked about, this goal has been elusive for both technical and commercial reasons. Object-oriented programming languages define objects at the source-code level, limiting potential for wide-scale interoperability. Software by its very malleability is frequently changed, creating significant versioning problems for would-be components. Industry standards supported by many vendors are required for the commercial production of interoperable components.

COM provides the technical underpinnings for component software, and Microsoft's position in the software industry offers promise of significant vendor support for the COM standard. Indeed this support has materialized, as evidenced by the large number of third-party ActiveX controls, wide support of COM in application development tools, and plans for use of COM in many industries and applications.

There are other important component frameworks in use today. CORBA (Common Object Request Broker Architecture) is an object-oriented interoperability standard that crosses many platforms. It is useful for integrating legacy applications into a modern distributed environment.

Although more a language than a component framework, Java also delivers on many aspects of component software. Java Beans are components that work in Java GUI programs in a manner similar to ActiveX controls in Windows programs. Enterprise Java Beans are distributed components that are similar to DCOM components.

There is passionate debate in the industry of the merits of these different technologies. This book is focused on COM and COM+ and will not discuss CORBA and Java. A rather simple way to think about where these technologies fit is to view COM as the architecture of choice for working within the Microsoft world. COM is implemented on other platforms, but not nearly as maturely as on Windows. CORBA is useful for integrating across platforms. Both COM and CORBA work with multiple languages. Java, of course, is focused on the Java language.

Component Object Model

The Component Object Model (COM) is the foundation on which Microsoft's modern system architecture is built, providing:

- the concept of an interface, consisting of a group of related functions a client can use to obtain services from a server
- an architecture by which an object can support multiple interfaces, with a client able to obtain a pointer through a function, **QueryInterface**
- a reference counting mechanism which ensures a server is available until all clients are finished
- memory management facilities, enabling memory to be allocated by a server and freed by a client
- a model for reporting extended error and status information
- a mechanism by which objects can communicate transparently within a process, across processes, or across a network

- a mechanism that allows a specific application or DLL that implements a service to be dynamically identified and loaded into the running system
- a mechanism to dynamically create object instances (class factory)

C++ and COM

C++ and COM both support object-oriented programming, but their goals, philosophy and structure are quite different. C++ supports object-oriented programming within the context of a programming language. COM is a binary standard that is designed to support interoperability of components developed in different programming languages, by many different developers, and running through multiple versions. Both C++ and COM are designed to be efficient. C++ follows its C heritage for efficiency, has static binding as the default, supports inline functions, has no automatic garbage collection, etc. COM is not "middleware" but gets out of the way as soon as a connection is established between a client and a component. COM uses the binary layout of the C++ vtable, making it easy to implement COM objects in C++.

In this section we will compare the underlying object models of C++ and COM in several respects:

- classes and interfaces
- class identification
- encapsulation
- object creation
- class object
- object lifetime
- versioning and interface negotiation
- reuse mechanisms
- distributed objects

Classes and Interfaces

Both C++ and COM have the notion of a *class* from which objects can be instantiated. In C++, a class represents *both* an interface and an implementation. An abstract class can be used to specify an interface without an implementation. In COM, the fundamental notion is of an interface, which specifies a contract without an implementation. A class can implement several interfaces. Thus functionality can be factored into several independent interfaces.

There is an interesting relationship between multiple interfaces and multiple inheritance. In C++, a class has just one interface, the public member functions. There is no logical grouping of functionality into subunits. But if the class is derived from multiple base classes, the base classes can represent these subunits. Java does not support multiple inheritance, but it does have the concept of an interface that is independent of a class, and a class can support multiple interfaces. In this way the object models of Java and COM are quite similar. Conceptually, Java is an excellent language for implementing COM classes, and in fact Microsoft has defined extensions to Java in its Visual J++ to do exactly that.

Class Identification

In C++, classes are constructs of a programming language and are identified by human-readable names. Name clashes are an ever-present possibility but can be managed within the context of a single development project. The ANSI C++ namespace mechanism provides a means of managing names of classes imported from several independent sources.

COM classes implement binary components that need to be unique across a very wide domain. COM classes are identified by "globally unique" long binary numbers. Likewise, unique binary numbers identify COM interfaces and other entities such as component categories and type libraries.

Encapsulation

A prime goal of C++ (or any object-oriented language) is to support encapsulation. Normally, data in C++ programs is private and is only accessed and manipulated through public member functions. But such encapsulation is only a convention, and it is perfectly legal to have public data members.

Encapsulation in COM is stricter. An object's data is *always* private and can only be accessed through methods of interfaces.

Object Creation

In C++, objects are always part of the same program and are created by a *constructor*. A constructor is invoked implicitly for global and automatic variables. A constructor is explicitly invoked via the **new** operator to create an object on the heap.

COM objects may be created in another module (a DLL or another EXE) and require an elaborate bootstrapping mechanism. A separate "class factory" object is first created by the COM run-time system. Then a method of the class factory interface is used to instantiate a COM object belonging to the specified class.

Class Object

In C++, there can be *static* data members. A static data member exists on a per class as opposed to a per-instance basis.

In COM, there is a *class object*. There is only one class object no matter how many object instances are created. The class object is normally used for implementing the class factory.

Object Lifetime

In C++, objects exist until a destructor is invoked. A destructor may be invoked implicitly when an object goes out of scope or explicitly by the delete operator.

COM has a reference counting mechanism to control the lifetime of an object. Whenever there is a new use of an object, the reference count is incremented. Whenever the object is no longer used in a given context, the reference count is decremented, and when the reference count reaches zero, the object is destroyed. The client program is responsible for explicitly calling functions to increment and decrement the reference count.

Versioning and Interface Negotiation

C++ has no language support for versioning issues. Versioning is a difficult issue in traditional software development environments. Consider an existing library component that is used by many customers. Adding new features to the library can break existing applications, requiring minimally a relink of the code. Failing to add new features can make the library less competitive. DLLs can be updated without forcing relinks, but DLLs are tied to a filename, causing issues for maintaining a system with different versions of a DLL that are used by different clients. For example, suppose a customer buys a new application that uses a different version of a DLL that is currently used by an existing application. When the new application is installed, the old DLL may be overwritten by the new DLL. The old application may mysteriously stop working. There are many variations of this scenario in the Windows environment, all of them frustrating.

Through "interface negotiation," a COM component can be updated with additional interfaces. New applications can take advantage of the additional interfaces. Old applications, not knowing about these new interfaces, will never "query" for them and will not break. This capability enables client applications and server applications to evolve independently, with different versions of clients and servers working with each correctly.

As an example, consider the evolution of two Windows applications supporting OLE. A server application and a client application both support the OLE 1.0 style of compound documents in which editing of an embedded object is done in a separate window. Now suppose the server is upgraded to support "in-place activation," in which editing is done right within the client's window. The existing client cannot take advantage of this new functionality, but it will continue to work with the new server. Now suppose the client application is also upgraded to support in-place activation. There are now old and new servers and old and new clients. A new client will query for the additional interfaces to support in-place activation. If they are present (it is talking to a new server), the client will run correctly in-place active. But if the new client is talking to an old server, when the query for the new interfaces fails, the client can revert to the old style of activation in a separate window.

Reuse

C++ supports reuse through inheritance. Inheritance is very easy to use. It is a "white box" mechanism: The implementation data structures of the base class are exposed through the header file, and the programmer must be cognizant of the semantics of base class functions that are overridden.

COM supports reuse through containment/delegation and aggregation. Both mechanisms are strictly "black box." Containment/delegation is straightforward, but may involve much repetitive code when there are many methods. Aggregation permits direct use of methods of the reused object but is complex to implement manually. MFC and ATL provide support for aggregation.

Distributed Objects

The C++ object model is for single programs. There are many ways to implement distributed programs using C++, but all the means for distribution (sockets, RPC, CORBA, etc.) involve features external to the language.

COM inherently supports distributed objects, which may reside:

- in a DLL that runs in the same process as the client
- in an EXE that runs on the same machine as the client
- in an EXE that runs on a different machine (Distributed COM or DCOM)

A significant part of this book is devoted to various aspects of DCOM. Indeed, a major goal of COM+ is to provide facilities to simplify implementing distributed systems.

Implementing a COM Class Using C++

The rest of this chapter is concerned with the details of implementing a COM class using C++. Going through this code will help you to understand the COM protocol much more concretely. In practice you will not have to implement COM classes yourselves at this level, because higher-level tools such as Active Template Library (ATL) will do much of the grunt work for you. But studying this code will help you to really understand how COM works.

Even if you are not interested in studying the details of the code, you should read through this section, because many important concepts are covered, including COM interfaces, globally unique identifiers (GUIDs), and **IUnknown**. We will also review the fundamental C++ concept of virtual functions and the vtable.

Account Object Example

Our illustration will be a bank account object similar to the one we worked with in the previous chapter. The sample object holds a bank balance as its data with the following methods of an interface **IAccount**:

- GetBalance
- Deposit

Later we will extend the example to add another method, **Withdraw**, to the **IAccount** interface, and we will also add a second interface, **IDisplay**.

COM Interfaces

A COM object consists of one or more interfaces. An interface consists of one or more member functions or *methods*. The object's data is private and can only be accessed through methods of interfaces. The name of an interface conventionally begins with letter I. Figure 5–1 illustrates the two interfaces supported by the Account object.

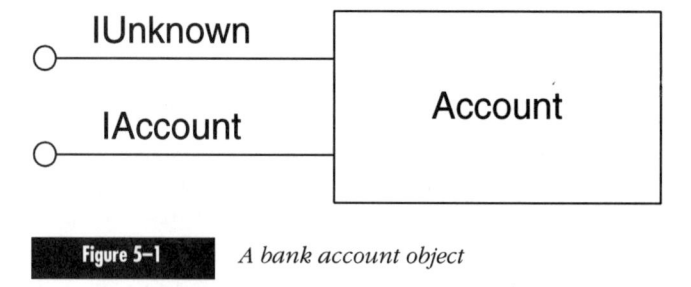

Figure 5–1   *A bank account object*

IUnknown is a standard interface (which must be supported by *every* COM object) and has the following methods:

- QueryInterface
- AddRef
- Release

IAccount is a custom interface and has the following methods:

- GetBalance
- Deposit

Binary Representation of Interfaces

The methods of an interface are always accessed through an interface pointer. The interface pointer points to an area of memory of the object instance which contains a pointer to the object's vtable. The vtable contains an array of function pointers that point to code implementing the methods of the interface. The vtable is associated with the "class" corresponding to the object—

there is a single vtable for all object instances. See Figure 5–2 for a depiction of the vtable.

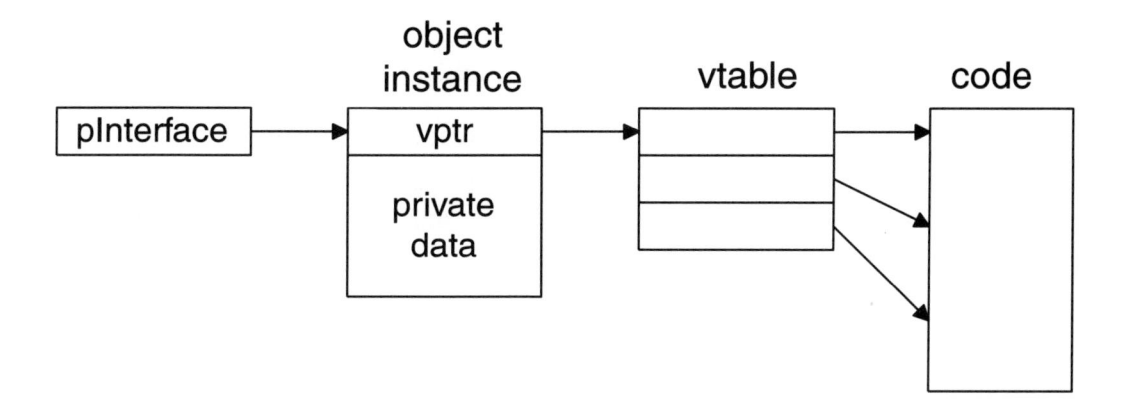

Figure 5–2 *vtable representation of interfaces*

C++ *Representation of Interfaces*

COM is designed so that its binary representation of interfaces is exactly the same as the standard vtable used by most C++ compilers. Declare an abstract class (with pure virtual functions) to specify the interface.

```
class IAccount : public IUnknown
{
public:
  virtual HRESULT GetBalance(int* nBal) = 0;
  virtual HRESULT Deposit(int amount) = 0;
};
```

Declare a concrete class derived from the interface class to implement the interface.

```
class CAccount : public IAccount
{
public:
  HRESULT GetBalance(int* nBal);
  HRESULT Deposit(int amount);
private:
  int m_nBalance;
};
```

Member functions of the interface then can be invoked directly through an interface pointer.

```
IAccount* pBalance;
int balance;
hr = pAccount->GetBalance(&balance);
```

Review Exercise for Virtual Functions

C++ virtual functions are demonstrated by the following simple program **virtdemo.cpp** in the **Chap5\Demos\VirtDemo** directory. (See **Chap5\VirtDemo** for a final version of the program.) Build and run it as a Console Application.

```
// virtdemo.cpp
#include <iostream.h>

class B
{
public:
  void f();
  void g();
private:
  long x;
};

class D : public B
{
public:
  void f();
  void g();
private:
  long y;
};

void B::f() {cout << "B::f" << endl;}
void B::g() {cout << "B::g" << endl;}
void D::f() {cout << "D::f" << endl;}
void D::g() {cout << "D::g" << endl;}

int main()
{
  B b, *pb;
  D d, *pd;
  pb = &b;
  pd = &d;
  b.f();
  d.f();
  pb->f();
```

```
    pd->f();
    pb = pd;// legal??
    pb->f();
    pd = pb;// legal??
    cout << "size B = " << sizeof(B) << endl;
    cout << "size D = " << sizeof(D) << endl;
    return 0;
}
```

Review Questions

1. Before building it, predict any compiler errors. Comment out any offending lines and build again.
2. Before running it, predict the output, paying particular attention to the second call **pb->f( )** after the pointer assignment.
3. How can you change the definition of the base class to get the "expected" output from

    pb->f()

    after the pointer has been reassigned to point to a D object?

Answers to Review Questions

1. The second pointer assignment is illegal. If it were permitted, you could call a member function of a derived class with a pointer that points to a base class object. The base class may not support the member function of the derived class, and you could get a run-time crash. The C++ compiler detects such an error at compile time. Comment out this second pointer assignment, and you should get a clean compile.
2. You might expect that when the pointer is reassigned to point to a "D" object, you will get the "D" version of the function invoked. But stubbornly the "B" version gets invoked in both cases, as shown by the output when you run the program:

    ```
    B::f
    D::f
    B::f
    D::f
    B::f
    size B = 4
    size D = 8
    ```

    There is static binding, and **pb->f( )** will always call the "B" version of the function, because the pointer is of type **B***.
3. To get the desired behavior, declare the functions *virtual* in the base class and run again. Now there is dynamic binding and **pb->f( )** will call

the "D" version of the function if the pointer has been assigned to point to a "D" object. Output:

```
B::f
D::f
B::f
D::f
D::f
size B = 8
size D = 12
```

The size of the objects is increased by 4 bytes, because each object instance now holds a "vptr" (pointer to a vtable). See Figure 5–3. Now go back to Figure 5–2 and review the structure of a vtable in C++.

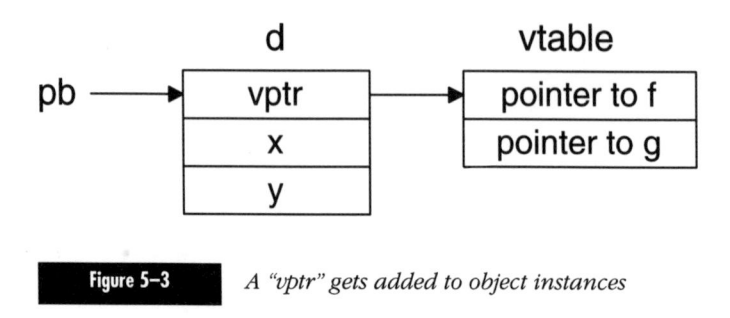

Figure 5–3 *A "vptr" gets added to object instances*

Globally Unique Identifiers

Interfaces and other entities in COM require an identification mechanism that will prevent accidental name collisions. The Distributed Computing Environment (DCE) of the Open Software Foundation provides a solution through the concept of "universally unique identifier" (UUID), which is a 128-bit quantity that can be generated algorithmically in a manner to virtually assure uniqueness. Microsoft adopted this mechanism for COM, calling the identifier a "GUID" (globally unique identifier).

Visual Studio provides a Windows utility GUIDGEN to generate a GUID (there is also a command line utility UUIDGEN). Microsoft has retained the capability to allocate a block of GUIDs.

GUIDGEN

You may wish to add GUIDGEN to the Tools menu in Visual Studio. Use menu Tools | Customize. **Microsoft Visual Studio\Common\Tools\Guidgen.exe** is the location in Visual Studio 6.0. Select the format you wish for the

GUID and click "Copy." The GUID will be placed on the Clipboard, from which you can paste it into your code. See Figure 5–4.

```
// Sample GUID from the GUIDGEN utility
// {E8132BB0-E39C-11ce-B776-FAB1C10CF9E4}
static const GUID <<name>> =
{ 0xe8132bb0, 0xe39c, 0x11ce, { 0xb7, 0x76, 0xfa, 0xb1,
0xc1, 0xc, 0xf9, 0xe4 } };
```

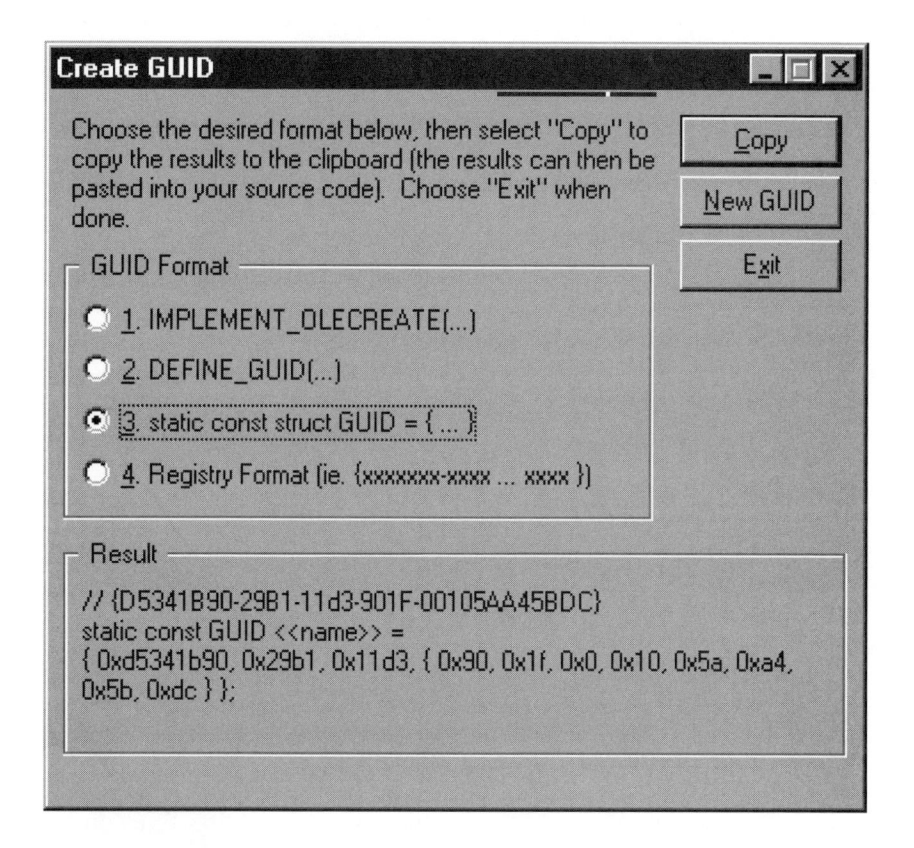

Figure 5–4 *GUIDGEN tool from Visual Studio*

IUnknown and QueryInterface

IUnknown is the fundamental COM interface, which must be supported by *every* component object. **IUnknown** provides a mechanism to obtain a pointer to any other interface that an object supports through the method **QueryInterface.** You pass **QueryInterface** the interface ID (a GUID representing an interface) of the interface you wish to obtain. If the object supports the interface, you get back a pointer to the interface. If the object does not support the interface, you get back an HRESULT indicating that the interface was not found and a NULL pointer.

Thus if you are able to obtain a pointer to a particular interface, you are guaranteed to be able to call any methods of the interface, which is not true in some object systems. For example, in the Win32 API there are numerous "handles." These handles represent opaque identifiers for various kinds of objects. But there is no assurance if you get a handle that it is valid. Hence the Win32 functions, if they are to be robust, may do some validation of the handle that they are passed. This validation code represents a cost in programmer time, in memory size, and in run-time performance.

Reference Counting

IUnknown also supports *reference counting* through its other two methods:

- **AddRef** increments the reference counter.
- **Release** decrements the reference counter, and deletes the object if the count has become zero.

Reference counting is important in COM, because an object may be in use in several places and should not be destroyed until all users are done with it.

Class Factories

Classes are identified to other programs by a unique class ID (or *CLSID*), a particular kind of GUID. To instantiate an object given its CLSID, you need a *class factory*. The class factory is provided as a separate object that implements the **IClassFactory** interface. We will study class factories in the next chapter.

A class factory is not needed for an object that is created locally without recourse to a CLSID. In COM, there are a number of API functions to instantiate special kinds of objects and some interfaces have methods to instantiate objects. You can implement a special creation function for your object that has no CLSID.

Implementing a COM Object

Implementing a COM object with no CLSID in C++ involves the following steps:

1. Declare an abstract class (with pure virtual functions) to specify the interfaces supported by the object, including **IUnknown**.
2. Declare a concrete class derived from the interface class to implement an object supporting the interface.

3. Implement the concrete class, which involves implementing both **IUnknown** and any other interfaces supported by the object.
4. Implement a special purpose object creation function that will instantiate one of your objects and return an interface pointer. (This will be replaced by the class factory mechanism when the object has a CLSID and is implemented in a server.)
5. Define an IID (interface ID) for any custom interface (you may use the GUIDGEN tool).

Interface Specification

There are several ways to specify COM interfaces. The first is to use standard macros that can specify an interface in either C or C++. The C++ expansion of the macros is quite simple because the vtable mechanism is built into C++. The C expansion is rather complicated because vtables have to be explicitly constructed in C code using a table of function pointers. A second approach is to use C++ specific syntax directly. The third is to use Microsoft's "Interface Definition Language" (IDL). For clarity we will use a combination of C++ syntax and standard macros.

Interface Definition Language facilitates defining an interface in a way that a tool (RPC compiler) can be used to create the language interface definitions and proxy and stub code for interprocess communication. Microsoft's RPC compiler MIDL.EXE ships with Visual C++. The MIDL compiler greatly simplifies creating custom interfaces that are implemented in separate executables. MIDL and IDL will be discussed later in this book. We saw one example of IDL already in Chapter 4.

INTERFACE SPECIFICATION OF IACCOUNT

The interface is specified by an abstract base class.

```
// bank.h
class IAccount : public IUnknown
{
public:
  // IAccount methods
  STDMETHOD(GetBalance)(int* pBalance) = 0;
  STDMETHOD(Deposit)(int amount) = 0;
};
```

The abstract base class **IUnknown** (defined in standard header files) specifies pure virtual functions for the **IUnknown** methods. If you want to see where various classes and macros are defined, you can use the Visual C++ Source Browser (right-click over the symbol you are interested in and choose "Go to Definition Of ...").

STANDARD MACROS

A number of standard macros are defined in **objbase.h**:

- **STDMETHOD(method)** is used to define a method that returns an HRESULT (used in header file).
- **STDMETHOD_(type, method)** is used to define a method that returns some other type (used in header file).
- **STDMETHODIMP** are corresponding macros for use in the implementation file.
- **REFIID** is a constant reference to an interface ID.
- **HRESULT** ("handle to a result") is a LONG, which is the standard return type for most COM functions.

```
// Win32 versions

#define STDMETHODCALLTYPE      __stdcall
#define STDAPICALLTYPE         __stdcall
#define STDMETHOD(method)
    virtual HRESULT STDMETHODCALLTYPE method
#define STDMETHOD_(type, method)
    virtual type STDMETHODCALLTYPE method
#define STDMETHODIMP           HRESULT STDMETHODCALLTYPE
#define STDMETHODIMP_(type)    type STDMETHODCALLTYPE
#define REFIID                 const IID &
```

INTERFACE NAMING CONVENTIONS

By convention, interface names in COM begin with the letter I followed by a capital letter, with remaining characters in mixed upper and lower case. Examples are **IUnknown**, the root interface, and **IClassFactory**.

Another convention is to create a typedef for interface pointers by dropping the leading "I," inserting "LP" (for long pointer, a carryover from 16-bit Windows), and making the rest of the name all upper case.

```
typedef IAccount FAR * LPACCOUNT;
```

We normally won't bother creating typedefs for our own interfaces, but you will often see it for standard interfaces (LPUNKNOWN, LPDISPATCH, etc.).

Interface Implementation

Now we will look at how to *implement* interfaces in COM. This will involve implementing not only the methods we define but also the standard methods of **IUnknown**. We will work through our little Account object example and create a running program. After examining the initial example, we will extend it by adding another method (easy) and another interface (more interesting). See **Chap5\BankCom** for our example. There are two steps.

CONCRETE CLASS

The interface is *specified* by an abstract class. For implementation we need a concrete class.

```
// Account.h : Declaration of the CAccount

class CAccount : public IAccount
{
public:
  CAccount()
  {
    m_nRef = 0;
    m_nBalance = 100;
  }

public:
  // IUnknown methods
  STDMETHOD(QueryInterface)(REFIID, void**);
  STDMETHOD_(ULONG, AddRef)();
  STDMETHOD_(ULONG, Release)();

  // IAccount methods
  STDMETHOD(GetBalance)(int* pBalance);
  STDMETHOD(Deposit)(int amount);
protected:
  ULONG m_nRef;      // reference count
  int m_nBalance;    // bank balance
};
```

Note that we have two data members. One is specific to our class and is used for holding the bank balance. The other is standard for *every* implementation of a COM class. It holds the reference count.

IMPLEMENTATION OF QUERYINTERFACE

We have to implement the methods of **IUnknown**. First comes **QueryInterface**. The input parameter is an interface ID, and the output parameter is an interface pointer. The only interfaces that we support are **IUnknown** and **IAccount**. When an interface pointer is returned, there is a new reference to the object and we must increment the reference count, which we do by calling **AddRef**.

```
// Account.cpp : Implementation of CAccount

#include "stdafx.h"
#include "guid.h"
#include "bank.h"
#include "account.h"
```

```
// CAccount

STDMETHODIMP
CAccount::QueryInterface(REFIID iid, void** ppv)
{
  if (iid == IID_IUnknown)
    *ppv = this;
  else if (iid == IID_IAccount)
    *ppv = this;
  else
  {
    *ppv = NULL;
    return E_NOINTERFACE;
  }
  AddRef();
  return NOERROR;
}
```

IMPLEMENTATION OF REFERENCE COUNTING

The remaining functionality of **IUnknown** is reference counting, which involves implementing **AddRef** and **Release**. **AddRef** is trivial—we just increment the reference count. **Release** is a little more interesting. We decrement the reference count. If it becomes 0, we then destroy the object, which we accomplish by deleting the **this** pointer. This code is somewhat strange in C++—for a method to delete the object through which it is invoked—but it is perfectly legal and is an appropriate idiom for what we need to accomplish here.

```
STDMETHODIMP_(ULONG) CAccount::AddRef()
{
  return ++m_nRef;
}

STDMETHODIMP_(ULONG) CAccount::Release()
{
  if(--m_nRef == 0)
  {
    delete this;
    Trace("Object destroyed", "CAccount");
    return 0;
  }
  return m_nRef;
}
```

For demonstration purposes, we have a **Trace** function. This function can be implemented as a message box, as is done here, or could be written to a log file or to whatever is appropriate.

```
// stdafx.cpp

#include "stdafx.h"

void Trace(const char* msg, const char* title)
{
   ::MessageBox(NULL, msg, title, MB_OK);
}
```

IMPLEMENTATION OF IACCOUNT METHODS

Next comes the implementation of the specific methods of our interface. This is the easy part.

```
STDMETHODIMP CAccount::GetBalance(int* pBalance)
{
   *pBalance = m_nBalance;
   return S_OK;
}

STDMETHODIMP CAccount::Deposit(int amount)
{
   m_nBalance += amount;
   return S_OK;
}
```

Object Creation Function

In order to instantiate a COM given its CLSID an object must be created through a generic mechanism, known as a "class factory," which we will discuss in Chapter 6. Our client program in Chapter 4 created an object using the class factory mechanism when it made use of the function **CoCreateInstance** to instantiate an object belonging to a particular COM class.

With a COM object having no CLSID, creation of an object can be handled by a special purpose function. The purpose of this function is to create the object and return an interface pointer to it. The new object is to start off with a reference count of 1, which we can accomplish by calling **QueryInterface**, which does an **AddRef** as we previously saw. Note that if **QueryInterface** fails, we should delete the newly created object. Our trace code announces the creation of the new object.

```
BOOL CreateAccount(IAccount** ppAccount)
{
  HRESULT hr;
  if (ppAccount == NULL)
     return FALSE;

  // Create object
  CAccount* pAccount = new CAccount;
  if (pAccount == NULL)
     return FALSE;

  // Get interface, which calls AddRef
  hr = pAccount->QueryInterface(
          IID_IAccount, (void**) ppAccount);
  if (SUCCEEDED(hr))
  {
     Trace("Object created", "CAccount");
     return TRUE;
  }

  else

  {
     delete pAccount;
     return FALSE;
  }
}
```

COM Status and Error Reporting

Our code has involved use of the COM status and error reporting mechanism. Most COM API functions and interface methods return a value of the type HRESULT, as illustrated in the methods of the **IAccount** interface. An HRESULT is simply a 32-bit integer that has the same structure as a Win32 error code. Bit 31 (most significant) is the "severity" bit, with 0 indicating success and 1 indicating failure. Bits 30–16 hold a "facility," indicating which group of status codes this result belongs to (Microsoft reserves to itself the definition of facility codes). Bits 15–0 hold the status code, which describes precisely what happened, error or otherwise. This code can be defined by anyone who specifies a COM interface. The code applies only to that particular interface. Since there are multiple success and error codes, there is a special naming convention. E_XXXX means function failed, and S_XXXX means function succeeded. For example S_OK is a code for a general success, and E_FAIL is a code for a general failure. You will find that there are many specific codes as you become familiar with COM API functions and methods.

For programming convenience, the COM SDK provides macros **SUCCEEDED** and **FAILED** that can be used to test for success or failure. The following is typical code:

```
HRESULT hr = somefunction();
if (FAILED(hr))
{
  MessageBox(NULL, "failed...",...);
  ....
}
else
  // call has succeeded
```

Using a COM Object

We have now described completely all the steps in specifying a COM interface, implementing that interface, and providing a mechanism for creating the COM object that supports that interface. To complete the picture, we need to examine how to *use* such a COM object. Use of such a COM object with no CLSID is actually very similar to what we did in Chapter 4, except in place of using **CoCreateInstance** to instantiate an object we make use of our special object creation function. Follow these steps:

1. Call the creation function of the COM object to obtain an interface pointer.
2. Call the objects methods through the interface pointer.
3. When you are done using the interface pointer, call the **Release** method.
4. If you need to use methods of another interface on the object, use **QueryInterface**.
5. Be sure to release any additional interfaces you obtained.

TEST PROGRAMS FOR COM OBJECTS

There are various strategies for writing test programs for COM objects:

- Write a console application (command-line interface).
- Write a GUI application using MFC.
- Write a GUI application using Visual Basic.

We used all three approaches in Chapter 4, and we will use these approaches as convenient throughout the rest of this book. Console applications are easy, and Visual Basic programs are easy. It is also quite easy to write simple dialog-based MFC applications, but you have to know the rudiments of MFC and the various Visual Studio tools for working with MFC, such as AppWizard, ClassWizard, and the resource editors. This book does not assume you have such a background, and indeed you do not need a lot of MFC experience to write and modify simple dialog-based test programs. Pre-written GUIs are provided for the example programs and exercises.

COM ACCOUNT OBJECT EXAMPLE PROGRAM

Build and run the program in **Chap5\BankCom\Step1**. This is an MFC dialog program that contains both the client and server code for the example COM object we have been discussing in this chapter. The user interface also has buttons "Withdraw" and "Show" for testing an additional method of **IAccount** and a second interface **IDisplay**. Run the program and examine the code. Figure 5–5 shows the simple user interface of this program.

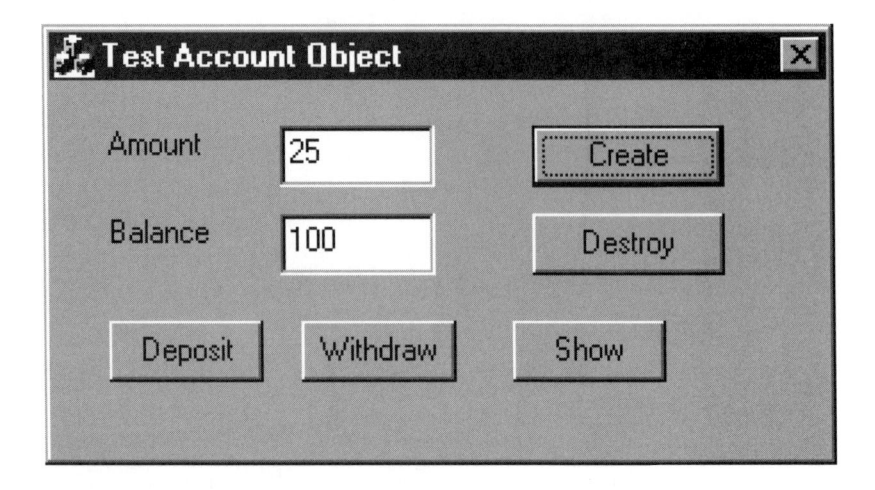

Figure 5–5   A COM Account Object

Additional Interfaces

Implementing a COM object with additional interfaces is actually quite straightforward. You will need to declare an abstract class (pure virtual functions) to specify each additional interface supported by the object. For example, the following code declares a new interface **IDisplay** with a method **Show**.

```
class IDisplay : public IUnknown
{
public:
   STDMETHOD(Show)() = 0;
};
```

You will also need to create an interface ID for the new interface. You can do that by means of the GUIDGEN tool.

Next you use multiple inheritance to make your concrete class derive from *all* the interfaces supported by the object. For example, the **CAccount** class derives from both interfaces **IAccount** and **IDisplay**.

```
class CAccount : public IAccount,
       public IDisplay
{
...
```

You will have to modify your implementation of **QueryInterface** to allow for all interfaces. Finally, you just have to implement the methods of the additional interfaces.

There is an issue involving multiple inheritance. You need to cast the interface pointer you return, because the vtables are different. The following code is a correct implementation of **QueryInterface** for the Account object with interface **IAccount** and **IDisplay**.

```
STDMETHODIMP
CAccount::QueryInterface(REFIID iid, void** ppv)
{
  if (iid == IID_IUnknown)
    *ppv = (IAccount*) this;
  else if (iid == IID_IAccount)
    *ppv = (IAccount*) this;
  else if (iid == IID_IDisplay)
    *ppv = (IDisplay*) this;
  else
  {
    *ppv = NULL;
    return E_NOINTERFACE;
  }
  AddRef();
  return NOERROR;
}
```

For an example of a COM class with multiple interfaces see **Chap5\BankCom\Step2**.

Summary

C++ and COM both support object-oriented programming, but their goals, philosophy, and structure are quite different. A COM interface is a group of related functions that specify a particular feature supported by an object. The binary representation of interfaces is identical to the vtable mechanism used by most C++ compilers, making it easy to implement interfaces in C++. A globally unique identifier (GUID) is a 128-bit ID that uniquely identifies a COM entity and guards against name collisions. **IUnknown** is the fundamental interface that must be supported by every component object. **QueryInterface** is used to obtain a pointer to other interfaces that an object supports. **AddRef** and **Release** are used to implement reference counting of COM objects.

In this chapter we implemented a COM *class* but not a COM *server*. In the next chapter we will implement an in-process COM server (DLL), using both Visual C++ and Visual Basic.

SIX

In-Process COM Servers

*T*he previous chapter illustrated a COM class with no CLSID. This class was called directly by the client, and there was no need for the COM run-time libraries. COM simply provided the protocol adhered to be the object and its client. When the object is a server, located in a DLL or separate EXE, COM is involved at run time to make the connection. In this chapter we will learn how to implement a COM class in a DLL.

A particularly important topic in this chapter is the **IClassFactory** interface, which provides the standard COM mechanism for creating COM objects. We will examine the steps that occur when an application creates an object that is implemented in a DLL. We will provide a complete implementation of a COM class in a DLL. We will make use of the OLE/COM Object Viewer to explore classes on our system, and we will use the system registry to store and access information about COM classes and interfaces.

Our coding is at a low level, illustrating how COM works. We will then see how to implement in-process COM servers using Visual Basic, and in the following chapter we will make use of the Active Template Library to simplify implementing COM servers in C++.

COM Server Concepts

In this first section, we go over some basic concepts of COM servers. Many of these concepts apply whether the server is implemented as a DLL or an EXE, with only the details of implementation differing. In the following section, we examine in detail the code required to implement a DLL server.

Local/Remote Transparency

COM classes (other than purely local ones known only within an application) are implemented in *servers*. An *in-process server* is located in a DLL, which is mapped into the address space of the client. A *local server* runs as a separate EXE in its own address space. A remote server runs as a separate EXE (provided by DCOM beginning with NT 4.0) on another machine. *Local/remote transparency* allows a client to access and use servers without regard to the boundaries between them. How a server runs (in-process, local, or remote) is called its *execution context*.

Class Factories

A COM class with no CLSID called directly by its client can be instantiated through a special creation function that is known within the application. Chapter 5 illustrated such an object.

Classes implemented in servers use a class factory for object instantiation. The class factory is itself an object which supports a special interface **IClassFactory** that is well-known to COM. The COM run-time system can query for this interface. **IClassFactory** has two methods:

- **CreateInstance** instantiates an object and returns an interface pointer.
- **LockServer** provides for a separate "lock count" that can be used to keep a server in memory even when there are temporarily no object instances, thus improving performance.

Bootstrapping an Object

Recall that a server consists of one or more classes. Each class supports one or more interfaces, which implement particular features of the class. A separate class is used for implementing the class factory interface. If we attempted to implement a class factory as an additional interface for our class, we would need to instantiate our object to get the factory to instantiate our object. Figure 6–1 depicts the class factory.

Class Object

The class factory is sometimes referred to simply as the *class object*. There is only one class object per class. The class object can be used to represent class data, like static members in C++. The class object is created directly by COM. The class object can support additional interfaces. There may be cases where a "singleton" object is all that is required, and then the class object need not implement **IClassFactory**.

COM Server Concepts 131

Figure 6-1 *A class factory*

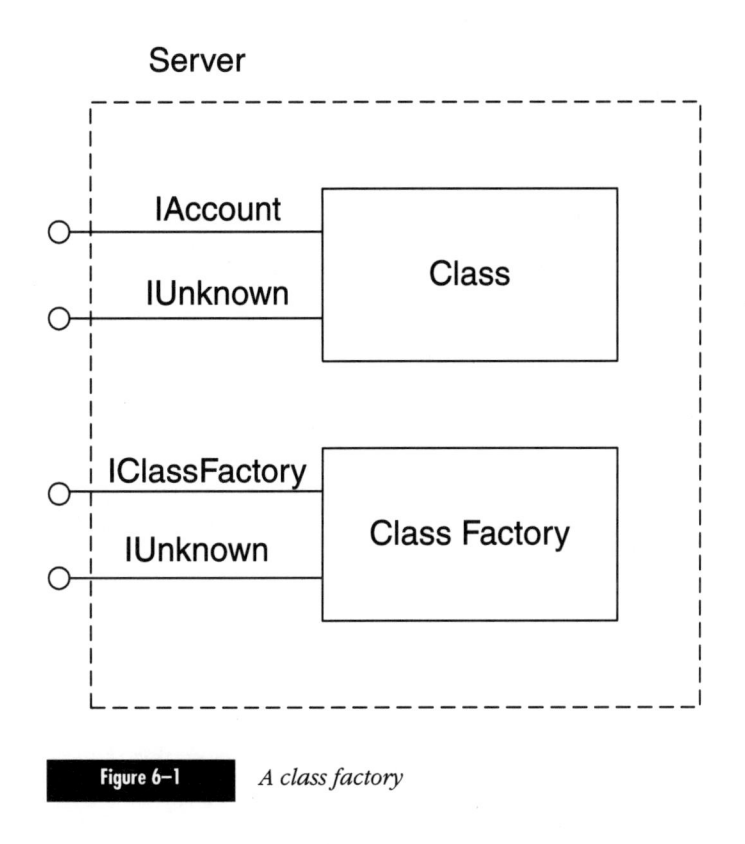

Class ID's and the System Registry

Components are identified by a unique *class ID* (or CLSID), a particular kind of GUID (128-bit identifier). Entries in the *system registry* set up an association between a class ID and the module (DLL or EXE) that implements the corresponding class. The system registry is a Windows database that stores system configuration information.

A client that knows the class ID of a component can ask COM to access the component. A part of Windows known as the "Service Control Manager" (SCM, pronounced "scum") does all the work to find and run the server, have it create the object, set up local/remote transparency, and return an interface pointer. Once the interface pointer is returned to the client, COM gets out of the way (except for local/remote transparency when the server is not in-process).

Structure of a Component

COM components have the same basic structure whether they are implemented as DLLs or EXEs, although some important details differ:

- a class ID for the component
- Registry entries to associate the class ID with the server module (DLL or EXE) that implements the component
- an implementation of a class factory object supporting the **IClassFactory** interface
- a mechanism that COM can use to access the server's class factory
- an unloading mechanism that facilitates removing from memory a server that is no longer serving any objects

Registry

The *Registry* or *registration database* is a central repository for Windows configuration information. The Win32 Registry also can store application profile information formerly stored in .INI files. Each piece of information is identified by a *key*, which may have a *value* associated with it. The arrangement is hierarchical, so that keys can contain other keys. The Windows Registry is organized as trees, called *hives*. The following are the most important root nodes:

- HKEY_USERS contains profiles for all users on the machine.
- HKEY_CURRENT_USER is an alias for the profile information (formerly stored in WIN.INI and private .INI files) of the current user.
- HKEY_LOCAL_MACHINE contains hardware and system software configuration information (formerly in SYSTEM.INI).
- HKEY_CLASSES_ROOT contains information needed for shell applications (such as File Manager) and OLE applications.

Registry Editor

The Registry can be viewed and edited through the Registry Editor REGEDIT.EXE. The registry editor should be used with caution. Changes are made immediately with no undo. Export and import commands from the Registry menu can be used to backup and restore the registry—a *good* practice (but beware that a restore will not delete new keys—consult system administration documentation). You can start the Registry Editor using Run from the Start menu (type REGEDIT.EXE). You can also start the Registry Editor from OLE/COM Object Viewer (File | Run The Registry Editor).

Registry Entry Files

Information can be entered into the Registry through *registry entry files*, which have a .REG extension. Double click on a .REG file in Windows Explorer to invoke the Registry Editor to merge a .REG file into the Registry. A registry entry file begins with the keyword REGEDIT followed by lines containing keys and values to be merged. Subkeys are separated from parent by a back slash (\). Values are separated from the key by an equal sign (=). The following is an example of a registry entry file:

COM Server Concepts

```
REGEDIT
HKEY_CLASSES_ROOT\Account.Answer.Object\CLSID = {67EF3200-
   2B8C-11d1-A01B-00A024D06632}
HKEY_CLASSES_ROOT\CLSID\{67EF3200-2B8C-11d1-A01B-
   00A024D06632} = Account Answer Object DLL
HKEY_CLASSES_ROOT\CLSID\{67EF3200-2B8C-11d1-A01B-
   00A024D06632}\InprocServer32 =
   c:\complus\chap6\bankdll\Debug\bank.dll
HKEY_CLASSES_ROOT\CLSID\{67EF3200-2B8C-11d1-A01B-
   00A024D06632}\ProgId = Account.Answer.Object
HKEY_CLASSES_ROOT\Interface\{40D92120-2863-11d1-A01B-
   00A024D06632} = IAccount
HKEY_CLASSES_ROOT\Interface\{40D92120-2863-11d1-A01B-
   00A024D06632}\NumMethods = 3
HKEY_CLASSES_ROOT\Interface\{5723B700-2878-11d1-A01B-
   00A024D06632} = IDisplay
HKEY_CLASSES_ROOT\Interface\{5723B700-2878-11d1-A01B-
   00A024D06632}\NumMethods = 1
```

Important Registry Information

You can view relevant information by bringing up the OLE/COM Object Viewer program. As a little demo, build the DLL server in **Chap6\BankDll**. Merge the registry entry file **bank.reg** (shown above) into the Registry by double-clicking on it. Then bring up OLE/COM Object Viewer and look under "All Objects" for "Account Answer Object DLL." Instantiate an object (double click or right click and choose "Create Instance"). You should then see the information shown in Figure 6–2.

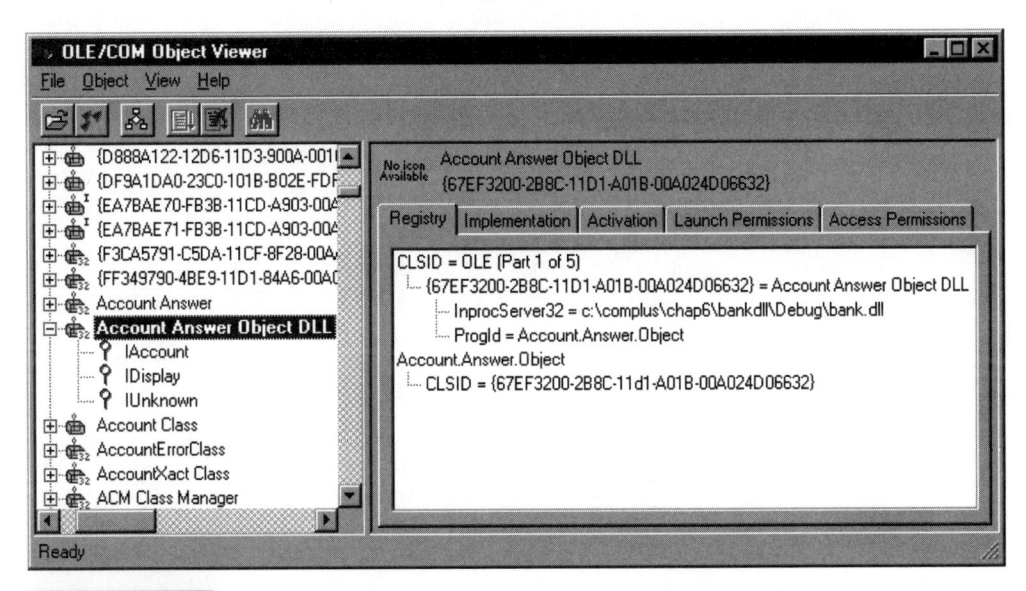

Figure 6–2 *Registry information shown in OLE/COM Object Viewer*

There are several ways by which you can refer to a COM class. Three of these are illustrated by this example. The fundamental identifier for a class is the CLSID, the 128-bit GUID that uniquely identifies the class anyplace in the world, on any system. The disadvantage of using the CLSID directly is that it is cumbersome. An alternative is the program ID or ProgID. This name is not intrinsic to the class but is tied to it through the registration process. For the bank account object, the ProgID is "Account.Answer.Object." A third name, that typically will be a little longer, we may call the "user name." This name is intended to be a little more user friendly than the ProgID and is shown in the Registry as a value associated with the CLSID as a key. Note that the OLE/COM Object Viewer employs the user name of an object in the left pane. In our example the user name is "Account Answer Object DLL." If you forget that the Viewer uses this name, and the user name is quite different from the ProgID, you may search and search for an object that you *know* is there.

There are other names that are important in COM, as we discussed in Chapter 4. There is the "coclass" name used in Visual Basic. There is a name assigned to the type library that is used in Visual Basic. There is also a "version-independent program ID." When we create code for a COM class using ATL in Chapter 7, we will see these other names again.

The Registry is a hierarchical database designed for very fast lookup. There is considerable redundancy and cross reference. The Registry is not a normalized relational database.

One of the most important pieces of information in the Registry for a COM class is the pathname to the server. For a DLL server, look under the key "InprocServer32" for the path to the server. When you are implementing a DLL server, one of your important tasks is to arrange for the registration of this path. One way of doing so is to create a registry entry file. A preferred alternative is to provide for programmatic registration, which can be facilitated by tools such as ATL. We discuss ATL in the next chapter.

INTERFACES IN THE REGISTRY

The most important GUIDs stored in the Registry are CLSIDs. They are key to enabling COM to find the proper server, given a CLSID. The Registry also provides key **Interfaces** where IIDs (interface IDs) can be stored. All the standard COM interfaces are there and a viewer program like OLE/COM Object Viewer can use this information to display the interfaces supported by a class.

Note that COM does not provide a direct mechanism to find out the interfaces supported by a class. If you know a specific interface, you can find out if a class supports it by calling **QueryInterface**. But you cannot go on a fishing expedition to just ask the object "give me a list of the interfaces you support." But COM does provide various ways to enable an object to supply this information indirectly, if it chooses to do so. The simplest is to just put entries in the Registry listing its interfaces, as illustrated by the sample registry entry file shown above. Another mechanism is to use *type libraries*, which we discussed in Chapter 4.

Implementing an In-Process COM Server Using C++

In this section, we go through the details of implementing an in-process COM server using C++. The COM server must support **IUnknown** and the particular methods of the interfaces provided by our class. This part of the job is identical to what we did in the previous chapter. The principal new feature is the implementation of a class factory. There are also some features required of a DLL server. One of these is a special function used for returning a pointer to the class object, an essential feature for supporting the class factory mechanism. Another function that must be provided by the DLL is one used for unloading the DLL. A module definition file is created to export these special functions.

The example used in this section is the bank account class we used in the previous chapter. We add the additional features required to make the class into a DLL server. Along the way, we review a little bit about the use of DLLs, including how to debug them.

The final version of our example is in **Chap6\BankDll**. You should have already built and registered the server as part of investigating registry entries. Now build the test program that is part of the same project, and run the test program. (See Figure 6–3.) The program behaves like the example from Chapter 5, but the implementation is different. In Chapter 5, the COM class was part of the test application. Now the COM class is in a separate DLL server. We've added some additional trace statements showing loading the DLL, creating the class factory object, and destroying the class factory object.

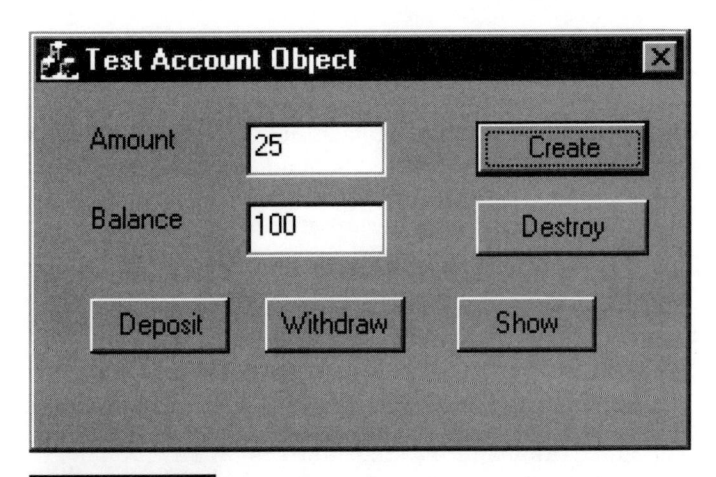

Figure 6–3 *Test program for in-process COM server*

Class Factory Definition

We need a header file to define the C++ class used for implementing the class factory object. This is a concrete class. It must implement the **IUnknown** methods as well as the **IClassFactory** methods. The implementation of **IUnknown** is identical to what we have already done and won't be repeated here.

```
// account.h

class CAccountClassFactory : public IClassFactory
{
public:
    CAccountClassFactory()
    {
      m_nRef = 0;
      Trace("Class factory object created");
    }

    // IUnknown methods
    STDMETHOD(QueryInterface)(REFIID, void**);
    STDMETHOD_(ULONG, AddRef)();
    STDMETHOD_(ULONG, Release)();

    //IClassFactory members
    STDMETHOD(CreateInstance)(LPUNKNOWN, REFIID,
            void**);
    STDMETHOD(LockServer)(BOOL);

protected:
    ULONG m_nRef;          // reference count
};
```

Class Factory Implementation

Next we look at the implementation of the class factory. **IUnknown** has one small change, which we will look at a little later.

```
// Account.cpp : Implementation of CAccount
...

// Count number of objects and number of locks.
ULONG g_cObj=0;
ULONG g_cLock=0;
...
STDMETHODIMP
CAccountClassFactory::CreateInstance(LPUNKNOWN
          pUnkOuter, REFIID riid, void** ppvObj)
{
```

```
    CAccount* pObj;
    HRESULT hr;
    *ppvObj = NULL;
    hr = E_OUTOFMEMORY;

    // we don't support aggregation
    if (NULL != pUnkOuter)
        return CLASS_E_NOAGGREGATION;
    pObj = new CAccount;
    if (NULL == pObj)
        return hr;

    hr = pObj->QueryInterface(riid, ppvObj);
    if (FAILED(hr))
        delete pObj;
    else
        g_cObj++;
    return hr;
}

STDMETHODIMP CAccountClassFactory::LockServer(
          BOOL fLock)
{
    if (fLock)
        g_cLock++;
    else
        g_cLock--;

    return NOERROR;
}
```

The **CreateInstance** method is very similar to the special-purpose creation function we implemented in Chapter 5. The output is an interface pointer to a newly created object. Notice that the caller can specify which interface is to be returned. The first parameter is a pointer to the "controlling unknown," which is used in conjunction with *aggregation*. We assume that we will always be passed NULL for this value and return an error otherwise. In COM, aggregation is a special technique for reusing classes. For the most part we ignore aggregation in this book. Aggregation is an important part of the infrastructure of COM, and certain system classes make essential use of aggregation.

There are two counters in our implementation. We count the number of objects and the number of locks. The purpose of these counters is to support the unloading process. We don't want the DLL to remain in memory when it is not needed. The object counter **g_cObj** counts the number of object instances, and is incremented whenever an object is created. The lock count is used in connection with the **LockServer** method. The parameter **fLock** specifies whether to increment or decrement the lock count. The client program may use the lock count mechanism as an optimization to lock the server into memory, ensuring it will not be unloaded if temporarily there are no objects, but the client has reason to believe there soon will be objects again.

Exported Functions of the DLL

Normally functions in a DLL are exposed to the outside world by *exporting* them. An application can use these functions by importing them. This procedure is used all the time in Windows, and in fact the entire Win32 API is provided by exported DLL functions. A requirement to use an exported function of a DLL is to know the DLL that is being used, so that the application can either link to an import library at build time or else explicitly load the DLL at run time.

COM works differently. The client does *not* need to know which DLL is actually being used to implement a server. Indeed, an essential aspect of the COM model is "polymorphism." A client program can be written to behave polymorphically with respect to its objects. For example, an OLE compound document container can contain different kinds of objects (a spreadsheet, a drawing, etc.). Each of these objects is implemented by its own server, and the client can work with *any* OLE compound document server—even new ones that were implemented after the container application was written. It is COM that connects the client to the server. The client does not connect directly.

In the case of a DLL, the COM run time will at the appropriate time return an interface pointer to a COM object, and this object is in the *same address space* as the client. This means that the vtable mechanism will dispatch a call from the client to the appropriate function. The function does *not* have to be exported by the DLL.

However, the DLL does need to export certain well-known functions for use by the COM run time system. We meet two in this chapter (for getting the class object and for checking whether the DLL can be unloaded). We will meet two more in the next chapter (for registering and unregistering the DLL).

MODULE DEFINITION FILE

The functions **DllGetClassObject** and **DllCanUnloadNow** should be exported. That can be done by means of a *module definition file*.

```
; bank.def

LIBRARY         BANK
DESCRIPTION     'BANK DLL Server'

EXPORTS
   DllCanUnloadNow     @1 PRIVATE
   DllGetClassObject   @2 PRIVATE
```

Exposing the Class Factory to COM

COM needs a standard mechanism to access the component's class factory. A DLL provides this mechanism through exporting a function **DllGetClassObject**:

```
HRESULT DllGetClassObject(rclsid, riid, ppv)
```

The first parameter, **rclsid**, identifies the CLSID of the object class to be loaded. The second parameter, **riid**, specifies the interface that the caller is to use to communicate with the class object. Most often, this is IID_IClassFactory. The third parameter, **ppv**, points either to the pointer of the requested interface, or to NULL if an error occurs.

The following code implements **DllGetClassObject** for our account class example.

```
STDAPI DllGetClassObject(REFCLSID rclsid,
                        REFIID riid, void** ppv)
{
    HRESULT hr;
    CAccountClassFactory *pObj;

    if (CLSID_Account != rclsid)
        return E_FAIL;

    pObj = new CAccountClassFactory;

    if (NULL == pObj)
        return E_OUTOFMEMORY;

    hr = pObj->QueryInterface(riid, ppv);

    if (FAILED(hr))
        delete pObj;

    return hr;
}
```

Unloading Mechanism

A server is no longer needed when the lock count maintained by **LockServer** is zero, and the object count for the objects is zero. COM determines whether to unload the server by calling the **DllCanUnloadNow** function exported by the DLL.

```
STDAPI DllCanUnloadNow()
{
    // Can unload if there are no objects and no
```

```
    // locks
    SCODE    sc;
    if (g_cObj == 0 && g_cLock == 0)
        sc = S_OK;
    else
        sc = S_FALSE;

    return sc;
}
```

Client Access to the Class Factory

The client gains access to the class factory through the COM API function **CoGetClassObject**.

```
LPCLASSFACTORY lpClassFactory;
DWORD dwContext = CLSCTX_INPROC_SERVER |
              CLSCTX_LOCAL_SERVER;
HRESULT hr = CoGetClassObject(
    CLSID_Account,
    dwContext,
    NULL,              // used in DCOM
    IID_IClassFactory,
    (void**) &lpClassFactory);
```

Once a class factory pointer has been obtained, an object can be instantiated via the method **CreateInstance**, and finally the class factory pointer must be released. It is useful to call **CoGetClassObject** when you wish to instantiate several object instances.

CoCreateInstance

Very commonly you don't want to go through the somewhat cumbersome three-step process of obtaining a class factory pointer, calling the method **CreateInstance**, and then releasing the class factory pointer. The COM API provides a convenient wrapper function that does everything needed to instantiate a single object and return an interface pointer. This wrapper function is **CoCreateInstance**, which we first saw in Chapter 4 when we discussed writing COM client programs.

```
HRESULT hr = CoCreateInstance(
    CLSID_Account,
    NULL,// pUnkOuter (no aggregation, so NULL)
    CLSCTX_INPROC_SERVER | CLSCTX_LOCAL_SERVER,
    IID_IAccount,
    (void**) &m_pAccount);
```

Execution Context

Both **CoGetClassObject** and **CoCreateInstance** take a parameter which allows the client to specify the *execution context*. By using the flag CLSCTX_INPROC_SERVER, the client would specify *only* an in-process server (DLL). This means that if the server is implemented as an EXE server, the call would fail. By this means, the client can exert some control over the execution-time characteristics of the server. The principal of local/remote transparency means that the syntax for calling a COM object is identical no matter where the object resides. But the *performance* is not identical. An in-process server is very fast, a local EXE server is slower, and a remote server is slowest.

CoFreeUnusedLibraries

The COM run-time system is responsible for unloading in-process servers when it is safe to do so. COM calls **DllCanUnloadNow**. If it is OK to unload, COM then goes ahead and unloads the library. A client program can force COM to check for unloading at any time by calling the API function **CoFreeUnusedLibraries**.

Linking to COM Libraries

When using class factories and other COM run-time facilities, you must link to COM libraries. For class factories (**CoCreateInstance**, **CoGetClassObject**, etc.) you need to link to the import library **ole32.lib**. The following pragma statements can be placed in **stdafx.h** to perform the linking without having to adjust project settings.

```
#pragma comment(lib, "oledlg.lib")
#pragma comment(lib, "ole32.lib")
#pragma comment(lib, "oleaut32.lib")
#pragma comment(lib, "uuid.lib")
#pragma comment(lib, "urlmon.lib")
```

This step is unnecessary when using MFC or ATL. For example, **afxdisp.h** contains the above pragma statements.

Working with DLLs

This section presents a brief demo which reviews a few considerations for working with DLLs. When you call a DLL directly, you have to worry about the DLL being in a directory where it can be found. (With COM servers you have to worry instead about maintaining proper information in the Registry.) The Visual Studio development environment makes it easy to set breakpoints for debugging DLLs. In the demo we examine that feature too.

Open the project in **Chap6\Demos\BankDll**. It is a DLL version of the Account COM object from Chapter 5. It is *not* a server yet—the COM class factory mechanism is not yet in place. There is a "bank" project and a "test" project in the workspace.

1. Build the "bank" project, creating **bank.dll** in Debug directory.
2. Build the "test" project and try to run it. (You can run it by double-clicking the .EXE file in Windows Explorer.) It fails. You get an error message complaining that the DLL cannot be found. There is a search path for DLLs. They must be located in the Windows directory, the Windows\System directory, etc. The directory where the calling EXE resides is always OK.
3. Copy **bank.dll** to the Test\Debug directory and try again. Now it should work.
4. Next we'll try to debug the DLL. In the "bank" project set a breakpoint at the beginning of the **Deposit** method.
5. Try to run the "bank" project under the debugger. You will be prompted for an executable. Navigate to test.exe and click OK. (You can also set the executable for debugging a DLL from menu Project | Settings, Debug tab.)
6. The test program should come up. Click the "Deposit" button. You don't hit the breakpoint. Why not?
7. The object has not been created. Click "Create" and then try "Deposit" again. Now you should hit your breakpoint.

Implementing an In-Process COM Server Using Visual Basic

It is very easy to implement COM servers using Visual Basic. You do not have the fine-grained control that you do when using C++, but in many cases a server implemented using Visual Basic will be perfectly adequate.

The key concept from Visual Basic that you will need is *class module,* which is the Visual Basic form of the familiar "class" from object-oriented programming and COM. There are two kinds of Visual Basic projects for COM servers, "ActiveX DLL" (in-process DLL server) and "ActiveX EXE" (out-of-process EXE server). Each comes with an initial class module. You add methods to the class module. To implement an additional interface, you first define the new interface by means of another class module. You then specify that your original class "implements" the additional interface and write appropriate code.

In the following demonstration, you will create a Visual Basic version of our bank account server. Do your work in **Chap6\Demos\BankVb**. A starter version of a client test program is provided in **Chap6\Demos\BankCli-**

Implementing an In-Process COM Server Using Visual Basic

entVb. Completed solutions can be found in **Chap6\BankVb** and **Chap6\BankClientVb**.

Creating the Server

First you create the server DLL. For simplicity, this section goes straight through creating the full DLL. You may wish to break off and test incrementally after you have implemented some of the features, but then you will need to deal with "version compatibility" issues. Each time you build your new DLL you will get new GUIDs, adding information to the Registry. It would be best to unregister your DLL after each test, before you add a new feature. When you are all done you can set the version compatibility to "binary," as described below. Testing the DLL is described in the next section.

CREATE A NEW ACTIVEX DLL PROJECT

From File | New Project choose "ActiveX DLL." See Figure 6–4.

Rename your project to **BankVb** and rename your class to **Account**. Save your project in **Chap6\Demos\BankVb**. Accept the filenames **Account.cls** and **BankVb.vbp**.

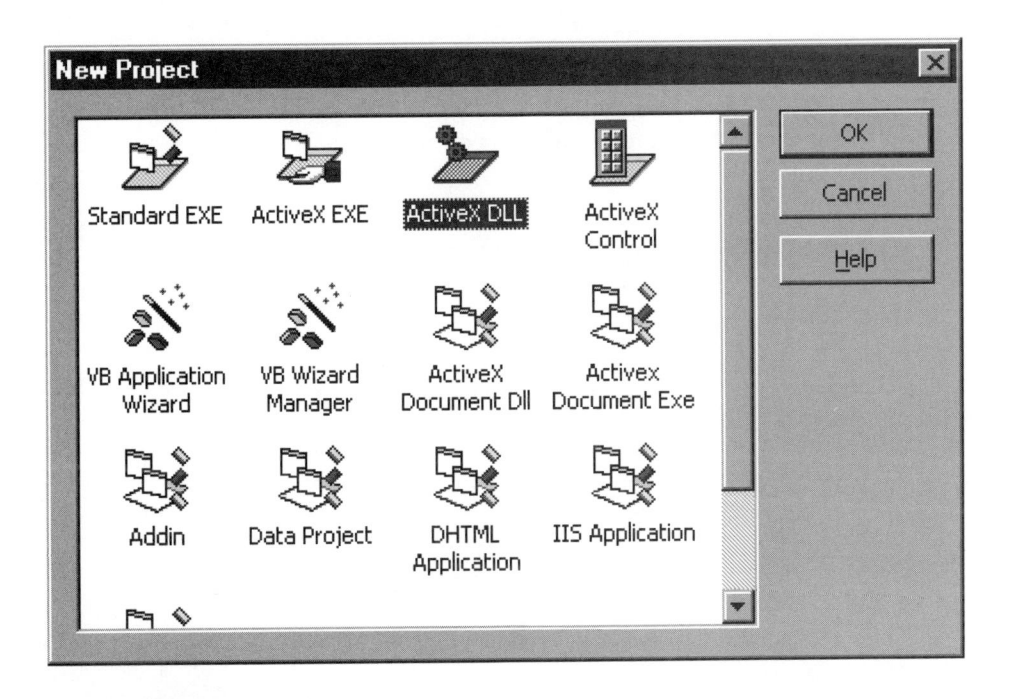

Figure 6–4 *A new ActiveX DLL project*

PROVIDE CODE FOR ACCOUNT CLASS

Add the following code to the **Account.cls** class module. A private variable is declared to hold the balance, which is initialized to 200 when the class is created. Message boxes announce creation and destruction of an Account object. The **Deposit**, **Withdraw**, and **GetBalance** methods are implemented.

```
Private gBalance As Long

Public Sub Deposit(ByVal amount As Long)
    gBalance = gBalance + amount
End Sub

Public Sub Withdraw(ByVal amount As Long)
    gBalance = gBalance - amount
End Sub

Public Sub GetBalance(ByRef balance As Long)
    balance = gBalance
End Sub

Private Sub Class_Initialize()
    gBalance = 200
    MsgBox "Account object created"
End Sub

Private Sub Class_Terminate()
    MsgBox "Account object destroyed"
End Sub
```

CLASS MODULE FOR IDISPLAY INTERFACE

Next add a new class module to your project (Project | Add Class Module). Change the name of this class to "IDisplay." Add code for a **Show** method. For the body, just have a comment (prevents the editor from deleting the otherwise empty method). Save the file under the name **IDisplay.cls**.

```
Public Sub Show()
    'You don't need to implement here
End Sub
```

IMPLEMENT IDISPLAY IN ACCOUNT CLASS

Finally, we provide an implementation of the **Show** method in the Account class module. Near the top add the line of code "Implements IDisplay." Then, in the left-hand dropdown in the code window, select "IDisplay." Since there is only one method, you will automatically see "Show" in the right-hand dropdown. This will add the "Show" method to the **Account** class. See Figure 6–5.

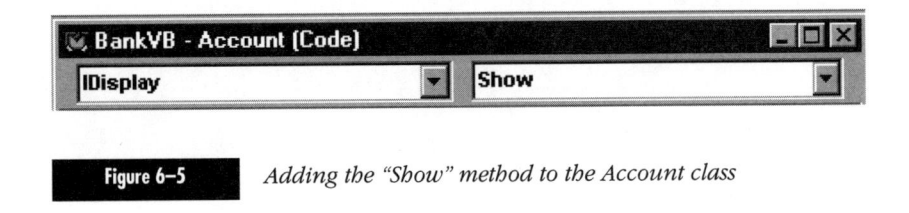

Figure 6–5 *Adding the "Show" method to the Account class*

You can now implement the Show method in Account by putting up a message box.

```
Implements IDisplay
...
Private Sub IDisplay_Show()
    MsgBox "Balance is " & gBalance, , "IDisplay::Show"
End Sub
```

BUILDING THE DLL

You can now build the DLL. From the File menu choose "Make BankVb.dll."

SETTING BINARY VERSION COMPATIBILITY

Now that your server is complete, it is very important that you specify "binary compatibility." Otherwise you will get new GUIDs generated when you rebuild your DLL, causing great confusion. Select menu item Project | BankVb Properties. In the dialog that comes up choose the "Component" tab. Select "Binary Compatibility" for version compatibility. See Figure 6–6.

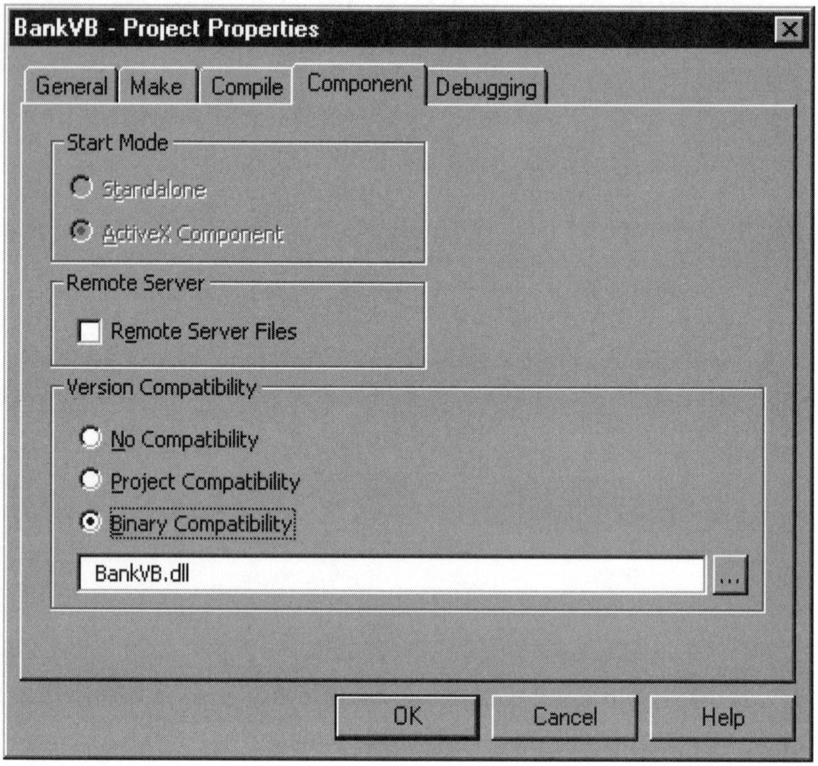

Figure 6–6 *Setting "binary compatibility" in your component*

Client Test Program

As a first test you can look up your server in OLE/COM Object View. Look for "BankVb.Account." Note that Visual Basic creates a "user name" that is the same as the ProgID. This can cause confusion if this leads you to believe that the two are always the same.

For the main test, open up the program in **Chap6\Demos\BankClientVb**. This is the same test program that was used in Chapter 4 for testing the C++ version of the Bank server. We have commented out the code that displays a welcome message in the title bar, because we did not implement the **Greet** class in our Visual Basic server (you can easily add such code if you want to). If you run the program as is, you will access the original C++ bank server (assuming it is still registered). You need to change the project references. From the menu Project | References bring up the "References" dialog. Uncheck "Bank 1.0 Type Library" (the C++ server) and put a check by "BankVb." See Figure 6–7.

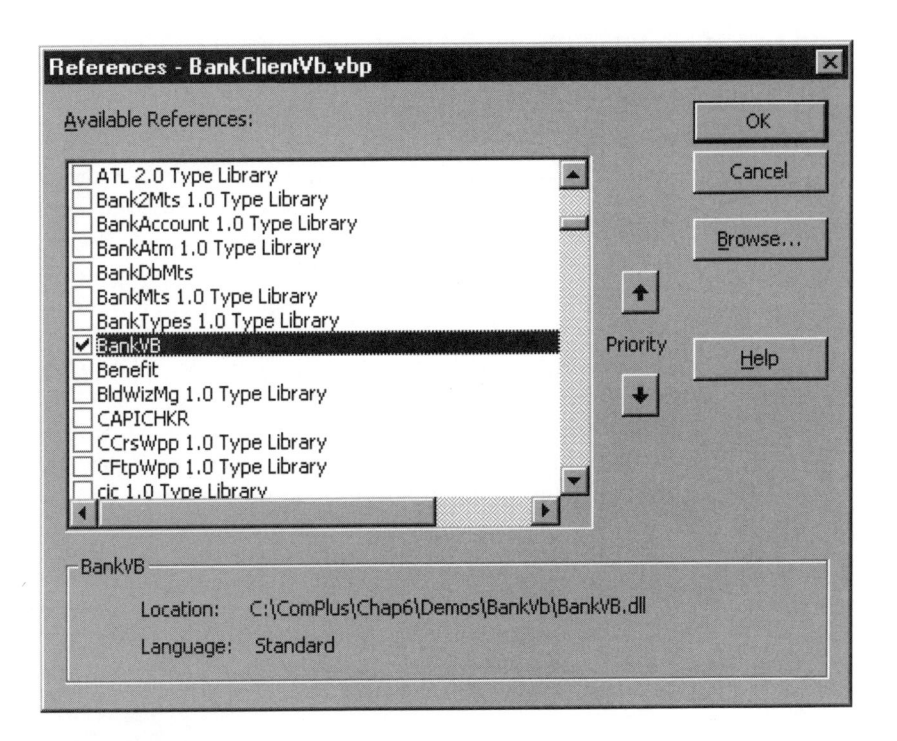

Figure 6–7 *Setting a reference to type library of BankVb*

You should now be able to run the client test program and exercise the Visual Basic version of the Bank server that you just created. (Note that the Visual C++ server has a starting balance of 100, while the Visual Basic server has a starting balance of 200, helping you to distinguish between them.)

Summary

In this chapter we completed the basic picture of how COM works. All of the most essential ingredients are now in place. In Chapter 4 we saw how to *use* COM classes in a server. In Chapter 5 we began discussing how to *implement* COM classes by going through in detail the **IUnknown** mechanisms of interface negotiation and reference counting. To enable the client to create one of our objects, we supplied a special-purpose creation function. In this chapter, we examined in detail class factories which are a general-purpose mechanism for creating objects in a server. The Registry contains information that associates a class ID with a server. When the client wishes to create an object given a class ID, it calls the COM API function

CoGetClassObject and COM loads the server (which it finds from the Registry) and returns a class factory pointer.

Visual Basic makes it easy to implement in-process COM servers. You create an "ActiveX DLL" project. You add methods to the class module. To implement an additional interface you first define the new interface by means of another class module. You then specify that your original class "implements" the additional interface and write appropriate code.

An important feature of COM is location transparency. The COM class may be located in a DLL, in an EXE on the local machine, or it may reside on a remote machine. In the coming chapters we will examine these other cases. First, however, we will introduce the Active Template Library, which greatly simplifies the task of implementing COM servers in C++, supplying for us much boilerplate code, such as that required for **IUnknown** and class factories. One of the things ATL does for us is to make it easy to use Interface Definition Language (IDL) to specify custom interfaces and to invoke the MIDL RPC compiler to create proxies and stubs. These proxies and stubs can be used to get us across process boundaries, enabling us to explore local and remote EXE servers.

SEVEN

Active Template Library

In the previous two chapters we discussed how to implement COM objects at the raw COM level. It is important to do this at least once in order to fully understand the mechanisms of COM. However, for practical application development this level of coding is much too low level, and there is too much "boilerplate" code required for common features such as **IUnknown** and class factories. To increase programmer productivity, higher-level tools are essential. For C++ programmers, the tool of choice is the Active Template Library or ATL. In this chapter, we discuss the basic structure of ATL and its use in implementing. COM servers. We begin with a simple use of ATL without any of the Visual C++ wizards. The wizards are very useful, but by beginning with some ATL programming "by hand" you can gain a better understanding of how ATL works. We then go on to make use of the wizards. ATL also makes it much easier to implement "self-registration" by your components, greatly simplifying registering and unregistering. ATL works very well with Interface Definition Language (IDL) and the Visual C++ ATL project will automatically invoke the MIDL compiler on your IDL file. The result is that it becomes very easy to build proxies and stubs, a feature we will exploit in Chapter 9 when we discuss EXE servers. ATL also provides some useful wrapper classes for interface pointers and for some COM data types such as BSTR.

Active Template Library

The Active Template Library (ATL) is a C++ template library for building COM objects. ATL is included as part of Visual C++ 5.0 and higher. ATL can help you build small, self-contained COM objects. With ATL, all code is normally compiled into a single binary without requiring any run time. ATL is both flexible and powerful. Support is provided for advanced COM features such as alternative threading models and aggregation.

MFC and ATL

Microsoft Foundation Class (MFC) Library is an application framework for building Windows applications. MFC encapsulates most of the Windows API and provides additional high-level classes to support features such as the document/view architecture. MFC provides extensive high-level support for OLE and ActiveX, greatly simplifying the creation of complex applications that use features such as object linking and embedding. MFC does provide low-level COM support, but it is not integrated into Visual C++ (no wizards). MFC has a large memory footprint (MFC42.DLL is almost a megabyte in size).

The Active Template Library is designed specifically for creating COM objects. It is powerful, lightweight, and there is wizard support. There is only limited encapsulation of the Windows API, including a simple message map facility.

MFC AND ATL IN THIS BOOK

We use both MFC and ATL in this book. For implementing COM objects in C++, we typically use ATL. We use MFC to easily create test programs, providing a dialog-based user interface. But the MFC code is supplied, so little knowledge of MFC is required. Initially, we create ATL-based COM objects without use of any of the ATL Visual C++ wizards. Without the wizards, we can examine minimal ATL-based COM objects and so better understand ATL from the ground up.

Boilerplate COM Code

Implementing a COM object involves much repetitive coding. Basic **IUnknown** functionality must always be supplied. Class factories require additional boilerplate code. Advanced features such as aggregation require additional standard code, some of which can be quite extensive. ATL provides a reusable implementation of all this standard functionality.

Implementing IUnknown

To use the ATL implementation of **IUnknown**, we will make our implementation class derived from the ATL class **CComObjectRootEx** as well as from the interfaces our object supports.

```
class ATL_NO_VTABLE CAccount :
  public CComObjectRootEx<CComSingleThreadModel>,
  public IAccount,
  public IDisplay
{
...
```

A template parameter specifies the threading model (we use the simplest case here). Multithreading is discussed in Chapter 13.

To enable ATL to implement **QueryInterface** via a table lookup, we must install entries in an "interface map" for each interface to be supported by our object.

```
BEGIN_COM_MAP(CAccount)
  COM_INTERFACE_ENTRY(IAccount)
  COM_INTERFACE_ENTRY(IDisplay)
END_COM_MAP()
```

Class Declaration

The rest of the class declaration is identical to the non-ATL case, except we don't need our own reference count.

```
// account.h

class ATL_NO_VTABLE CAccount :
  public CComObjectRootEx<CComSingleThreadModel>,
  public IAccount,
  public IDisplay
{
public:
  CAccount() : m_nBalance(0)
    {
    }

BEGIN_COM_MAP(CAccount)
  COM_INTERFACE_ENTRY(IAccount)
  COM_INTERFACE_ENTRY(IDisplay)
END_COM_MAP()

public:
// IAccount
  STDMETHOD(Withdraw)(int amount);
```

```
  STDMETHOD(GetBalance)(int* pBalance);
  STDMETHOD(Deposit)(int amount);
// IDisplay
  STDMETHOD(Show)();
protected:
  int m_nBalance;
};
```

Class Implementation

The class implementation is much simpler, because we only have to provide implementation of our own methods (which is identical to the non-ATL case).

```
// account.cpp

STDMETHODIMP CAccount::Deposit(int amount)
{
  m_nBalance += amount;
  return S_OK;
}

STDMETHODIMP CAccount::GetBalance(int * pBalance)
{
  *pBalance = m_nBalance;
  return S_OK;
}

STDMETHODIMP CAccount::Withdraw(int amount)
{
  m_nBalance -= amount;
  return S_OK;
}

STDMETHODIMP CAccount::Show()
{
  char buf[80];
  wsprintf(buf, "Balance = %d\n", m_nBalance);
  Trace(buf, "IDisplay::Show");
  return S_OK;
}
```

Instantiating an ATL-Based COM Object

A special creation function is implemented in a manner similar to that done for raw COM. (We are avoiding class factories for didactic purposes. We examine ATL support for class factories in the next section.)

```
__declspec(dllexport) BOOL CreateAccount(
                    IAccount** ppAccount)
{
  HRESULT hr;
  if (ppAccount == NULL)
    return FALSE;

  // Create object
  CComObject<CAccount>* pAccount =
           new CComObject<CAccount>;
  if (pAccount == NULL)
    return FALSE;

  // Get interface, which calls AddRef
  hr = pAccount->QueryInterface(IID_IAccount,
           (void**) ppAccount);
  if (SUCCEEDED(hr))
    return TRUE;
  else
    return FALSE;
}
```

CComObject

The "implementation class" **CAccount** is actually an abstract class. The ATL base class **CComObjectRootEx** does not actually implement **IUnknown** but rather provides generic helper functions that can support an actual implementation. Hence **CAccount** has no implementation of the pure virtual functions of **IUnknown** and so is an abstract class. Thus the **new** operator in the above code is not applied to the class **CAccount** but rather to the ATL template class **CComObject**, which takes **CAccount** as a template argument.

There are several possible variations of how **IUnknown** will be implemented. The normal case is that of a heap-based object. But there are alternatives, such as a stack-based object that cannot be **AddRef**ed, an object that can only be created as part of an aggregate, etc. ATL provides template classes **CComObjectXXX<T>** to support these different variations. **CComObject** implements the normal case. Pass your implementation class as the template argument.

Example Program

See **Chap7\BankAtl\Step2** for an example of a simple COM class implemented using some of the features of ATL. This program is somewhat similar to the example in Chapter 5. There is no class factory implemented. The COM class is implemented in a DLL, but this DLL is called directly by the client program; it is not loaded by the COM run time. There is no information placed in the Registry.

Build the server and the test program and try to run the test program. You will find that it won't run because the DLL cannot he found. Copy the DLL to the **Test\Debug** directory and run the test program again. This time it should work (see Figure 7–1). Note that this program is a little simpler than the one we used in the previous chapter. There are no buttons for "Create" or "Destroy." The object is instantiated as part of program initialization, and the object is released as part of termination.

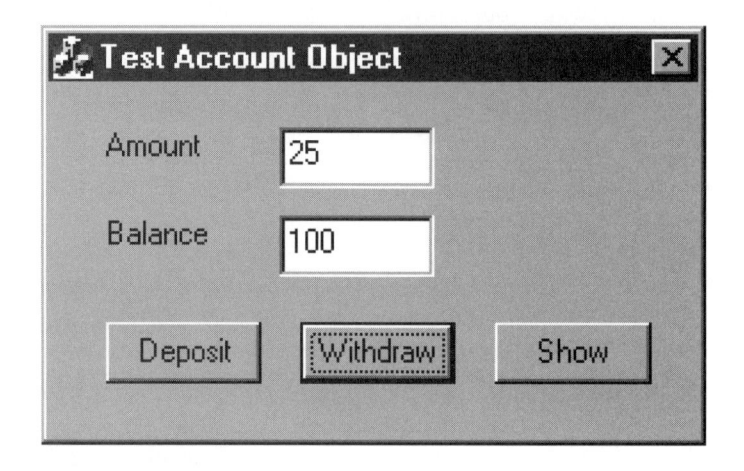

Figure 7–1 *A simple object implemented using ATL*

Visual C++ and ATL

In this section, you will learn about the support provided by Visual C++ to simplify COM programming using ATL. With ATL and the wizard support provided by Visual C++, it becomes very easy to implement a COM server from scratch. Such a COM server automatically supports self-registration, which is a great improvement over the use of registry entry files. The compiler support in Visual C++ also simplifies the creation of COM client programs, a topic we will cover in the next chapter. Support is provided by ATL for implementing class factories. You will also start learning about Interface Definition Language (IDL). In order to add more interfaces to a COM object you will need to manually edit the IDL file created by a wizard. The IDL file is also used to create proxies and stubs, which will be explored in Chapter 9.

The work in this section is "hands on," creating a server similar to the Bank server that we used as an example back in Chapter 4.

Visual C++ COM Support

Beginning with Version 5.0, Visual C++ provides significant support to simplify COM programming.

- An "ATL COM AppWizard" creates a skeleton project for implementing a COM server.
- An "ATL Object wizard" automates adding code for a COM object with a class factory.
- IDL is automatically generated, simplifying the specification of COM objects and the generation of code necessary for remoting COM objects across process boundaries.
- A type library is automatically created that is useful for browsers and for creating client programs.
- An import directive reads a type library and automatically generates "smart pointer" code that simplifies management of interface pointers by client programs. (This last topic will be discussed in Chapter 8.)

ATL COM Server Demo

To demonstrate creating and using a COM object via ATL:

1. Create a COM DLL server using the ATL COM AppWizard.
2. Add code for a COM object using the ATL Object wizard.
3. Create a dialog-based client application using AppWizard that will import a type library to simplify use of the COM object (Chapter 8).

Do your work in the **Chap7\Demos** directory. Completed server projects are in **Chap7\BankWiz** and client projects in **Chap7\BankWizClient** and **Chap8\SmartClient**.

Registry Hygiene

Unregister Previous Bank Server

Before you begin this demo it would be a good idea to make sure that the previous Bank server is not registered. You can unregister it by running the batch file **unreg_bank.bat** in the directory **Chap4\Bank**.

If you don't unregister the old server, you will have two servers registered with different GUIDs but the same names of various sorts (ProgID, coclass, etc.), leading to great confusion!

Our demo COM account object will have the following characteristics (same object we've worked with before, but now it will be easier):

- The object keeps track of an account balance.
- An interface **IAccount** has methods to deposit, get the balance, and withdraw.
- An interface **IDisplay** has a single method to show the balance in a message box.

The demo will just implement the **IAccount** interface with **Deposit** and **GetBalance** methods. You are invited to work along as you read.

ATL COM APPWIZARD

Create a new project, "Bank," in the **Demos** directory using ATL COM AppWizard, creating subdirectory **BankWiz**. See Figure 7–2.

Accept the defaults in Step 1. Click Finish and then OK. See Figure 7–3.

This creates a skeleton DLL with required entry points for COM support, but not yet any COM object. See Figure 7–4.

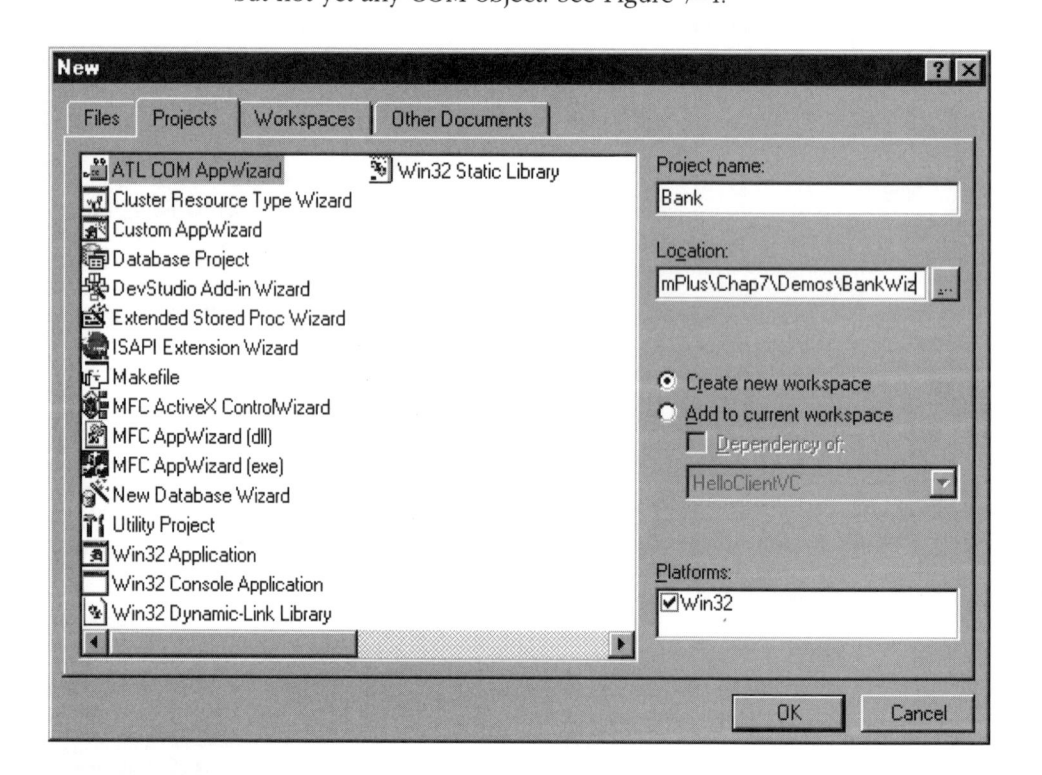

Figure 7–2   *A new ATL COM AppWizard project*

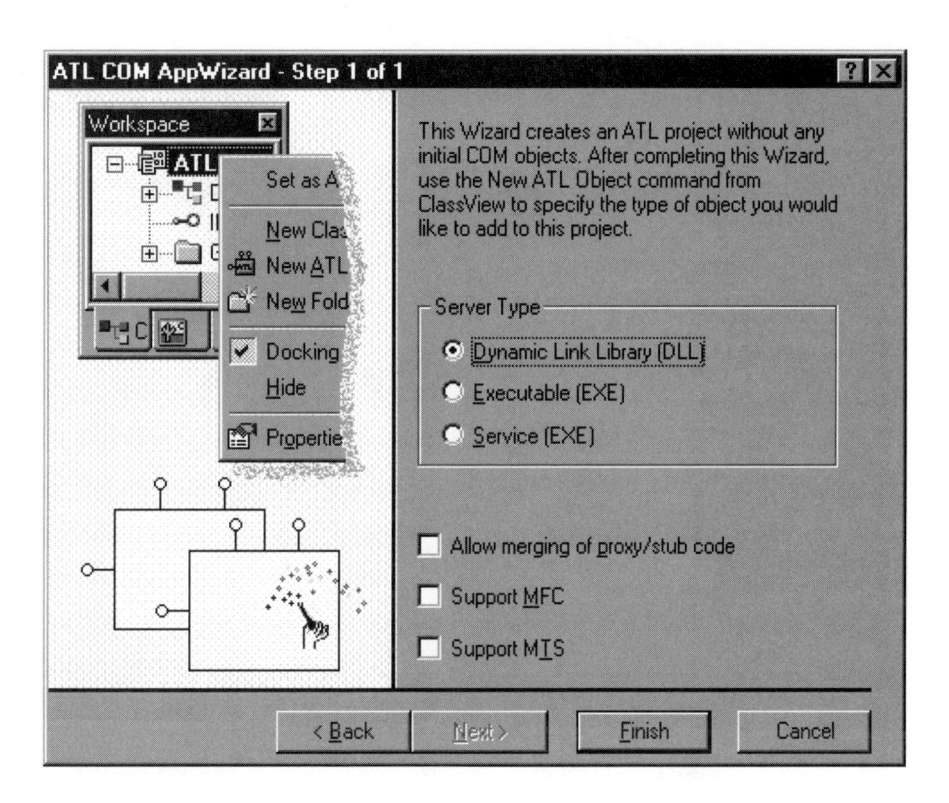

Visual C++ and ATL   **157**

Figure 7–3   *ATL COM AppWizard Step 1*

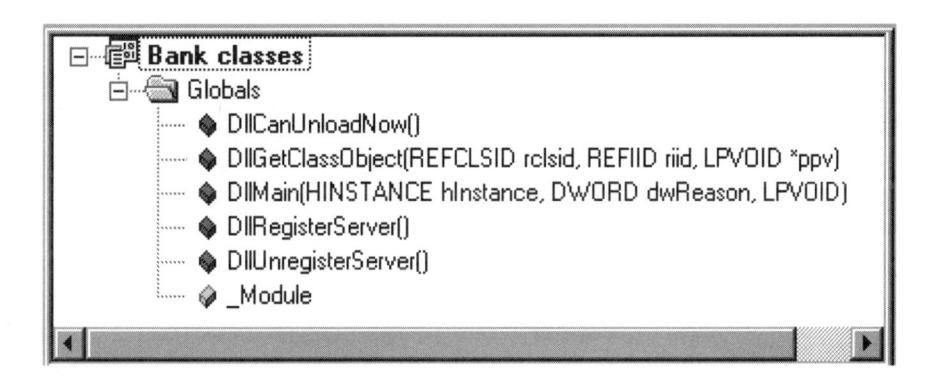

Figure 7–4   *A skeleton DLL*

ATL OBJECT WIZARD

Add support for a COM object via Insert | New ATL Object ..., which will bring up the ATL Object Wizard. See Figure 7–5.

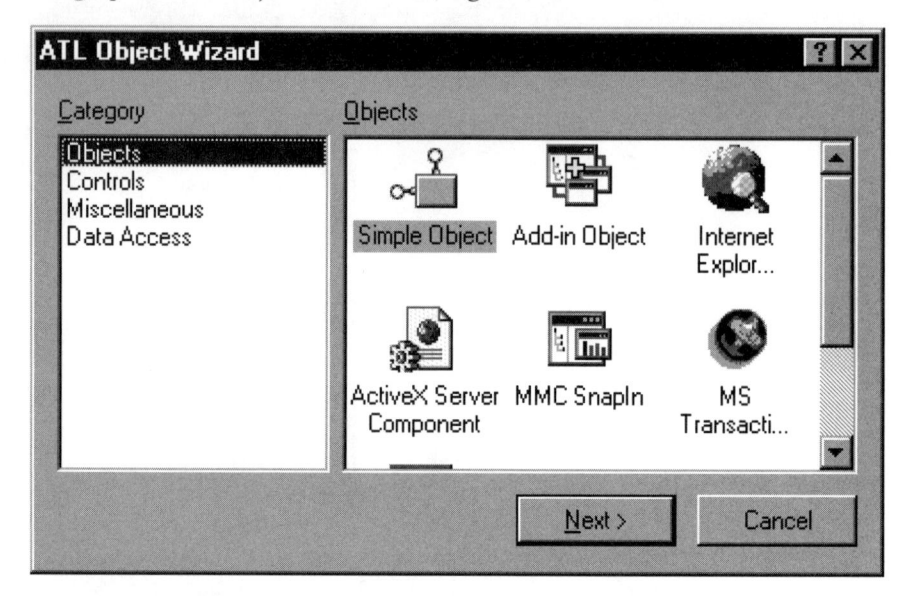

Figure 7–5 Inserting an object with ATL Object Wizard

Select "Simple Object" and click Next. Assign "Account" as the short name, **IAccount** for the interface, and accept the defaults for the other names that will be generated. See Figure 7–6.

CLASS NAMES

Note the various names that are chosen once you enter "Account":

- "Account Class" is the name that will be shown to a user (for instance, in the OLE/COM Object Viewer).
- "Account" is the "coclass" name. This is the name of the class that you will use in a Visual Basic client program.
- "Bank.Account" is the version independent program ID.
- "Bank.Account.1" is the program ID.

ATTRIBUTES

Click on the Attributes tab. Choose the simplest options (not the default):

- Single Threading Model
- Custom Interface
- No for Aggregation

See Figure 7–7.

Visual C++ and ATL **159**

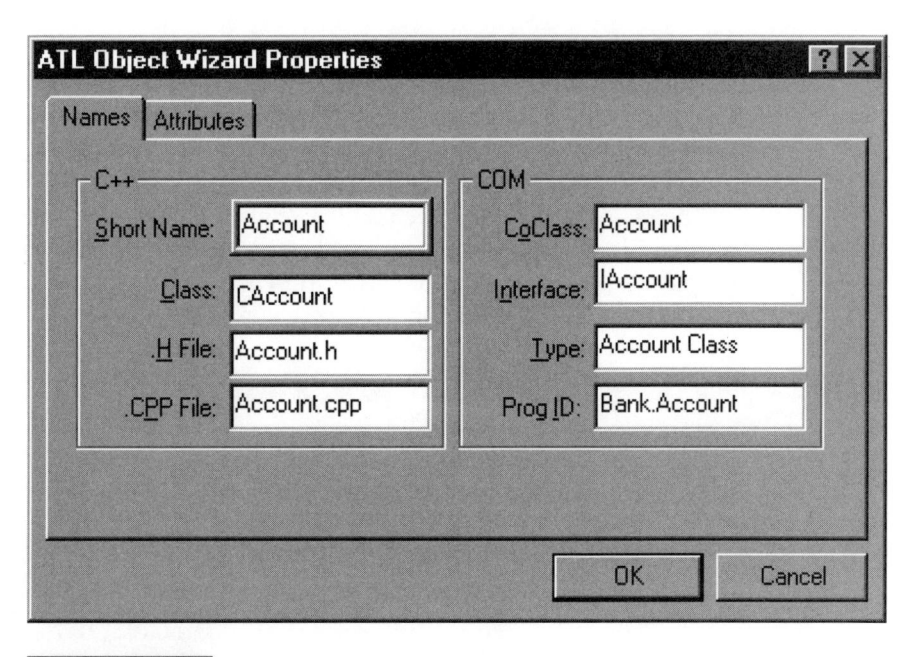

Figure 7–6 *An Account object*

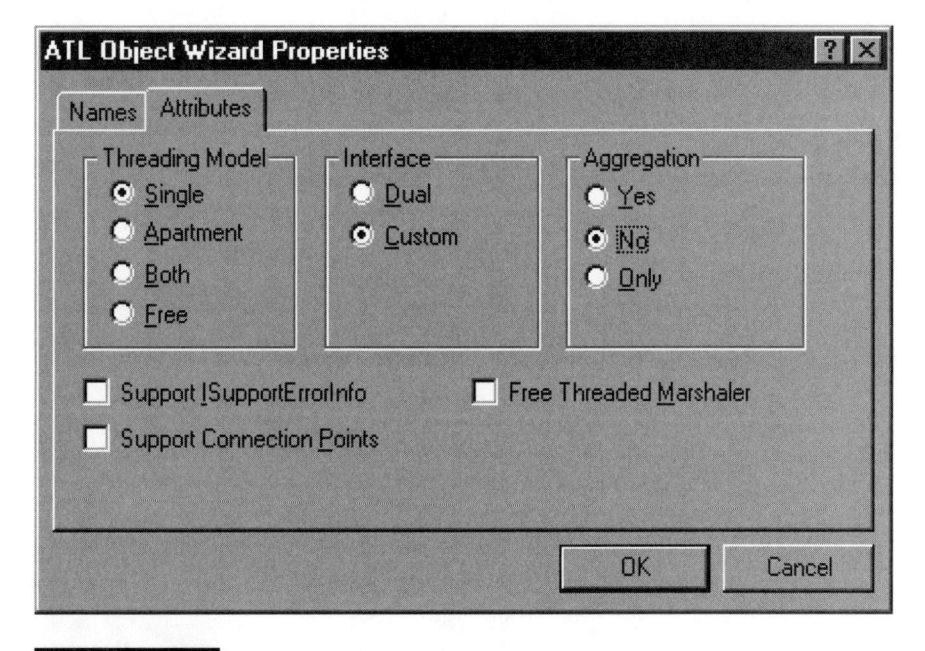

Figure 7–7 *Attributes for a new ATL object*

BUILDING THE SERVER

Click OK and then build the DLL. You have created a COM object without writing any code! Use the OLE/COM Object Viewer to examine your new object. Make sure that you are in "Expert Mode" (View menu). Find the class name "Account Class" (under "All Objects"). Single-click to see the registry entries. Double-click (or click the + in the tree view) to instantiate a COM object belonging to this class and query for all the interfaces in the registry that this object supports (**IUnknown**). Note that the custom interface **IAccount** is not in the registry. See Figure 7–8.

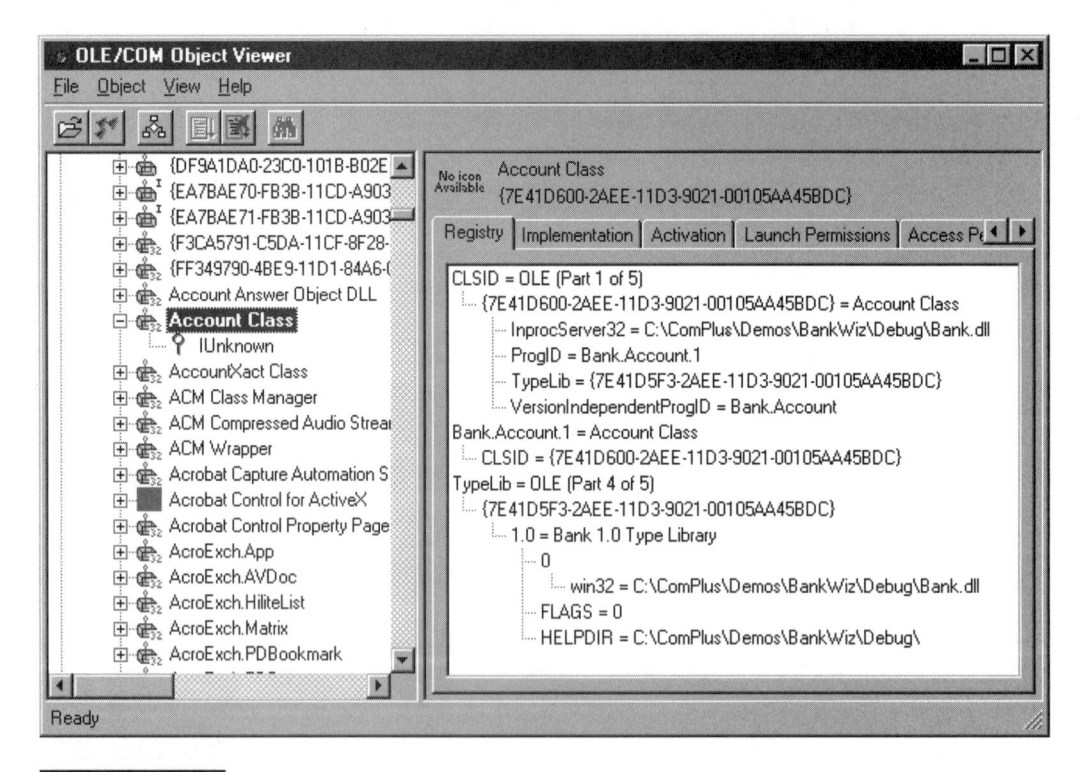

Figure 7–8 *An ATL object in OLE/COM Object Viewer*

DEFINING THE METHODS

The next step will be to add methods to the **IAccount** interface. Right click over **IAccount** in the Workspace pane, and choose "Add Method..." from the context menu. Add the **Deposit** method, which takes one **int** input parameter (IDL syntax). See Figure 7–9.

Similarly, add the **GetBalance** method which takes one output parameter that is a pointer to an **int**. See Figure 7–10.

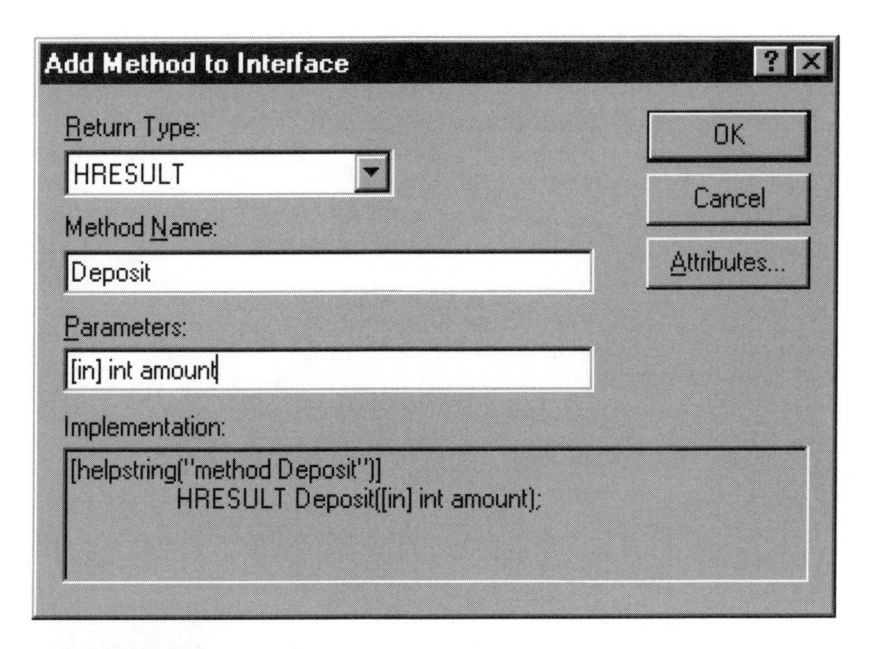

Figure 7-9 *Adding **Deposit** method to **IAccount** interface*

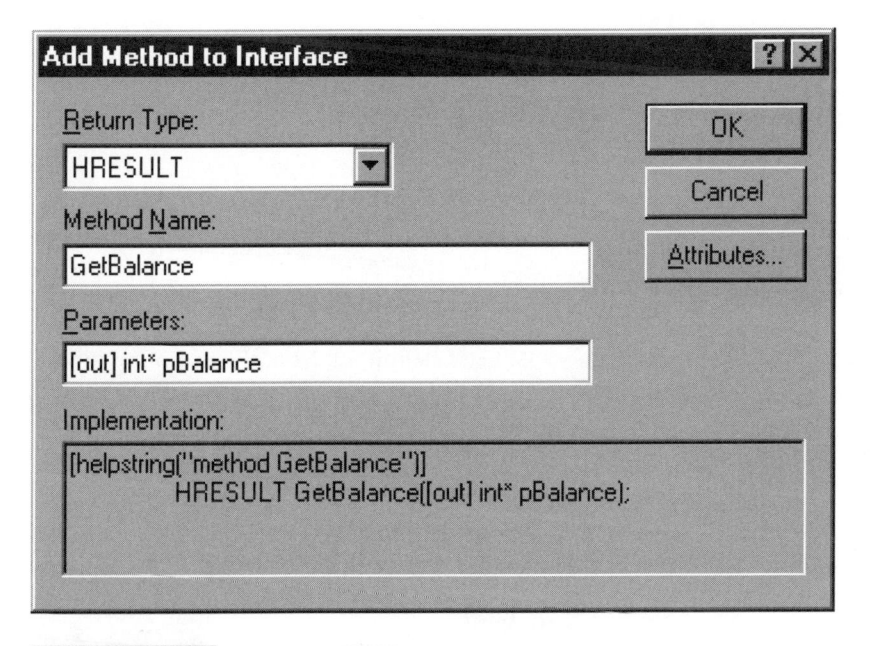

Figure 7-10 *Adding **GetBalance** method to **IAccount** interface*

IDL FILE

Examine the IDL file **bank.idl** that is generated. (For simplicity some "helpstring" entries are not shown.)

```
// bank.idl : IDL source for bank.dll
//
...
  [
  uuid(A1F11F1C-2E6A-11D1-A01B-00A024D06632),
  helpstring("IAccount Interface"),
    pointer_default(unique)
  ]
  interface IAccount : IUnknown
  {
    HRESULT Deposit([in] int amount);
    HRESULT GetBalance([out] int* pBalance);
  };
[
  uuid(A1F11F0F-2E6A-11D1-A01B-00A024D06632),
  version(1.0),
  helpstring("bank 1.0 Type Library")
]
library BANKLib
{
...
  [
  uuid(A1F11F1D-2E6A-11D1-A01B-00A024D06632),
    helpstring("Account Class")
  ]
  coclass Account
  {
    [default] interface IAccount;
  };
};
```

DEFINING THE IMPLEMENTATION CLASS

Examine the COM class definition. Note the use of multiple inheritance. Add a data member to hold the balance and initialize it to 100 in the constructor.

```
// Account.h : Declaration of the CAccount
...

class ATL_NO_VTABLE CAccount :
  public CComObjectRootEx<CComSingleThreadModel>,
  public CComCoClass<CAccount, &CLSID_Account>,
  public IAccount
{
public:
```

```
      CAccount() : m_nBalance(100)
      {
      }

DECLARE_REGISTRY_RESOURCEID(IDR_ACCOUNT)
DECLARE_NOT_AGGREGATABLE(CAccount)

BEGIN_COM_MAP(CAccount)
   COM_INTERFACE_ENTRY(IAccount)
END_COM_MAP()

// IAccount
public:
   STDMETHOD(GetBalance)(/*[out]*/ int* pBalance);
   STDMETHOD(Deposit)(/*[in]*/ int amount);
protected:
   int m_nBalance;
};
```

IMPLEMENTING THE METHODS

The last step is to implement the two methods. Skeletons have already been created for you.

```
STDMETHODIMP CAccount::Deposit(int amount)
{
   m_nBalance += amount;
   return S_OK;
}

STDMETHODIMP CAccount::GetBalance(int * pBalance)
{
   *pBalance = m_nBalance;
   return S_OK;
}
```

Build the DLL. You have now created a fully functional in-process COM server equivalent to the server whose code is provided in the directory **Chap7\BankWiz\Step1**.

CLIENT TEST PROGRAM

If you would like to test your server now, you can use it in a client program by calling **CoCreateInstance** to instantiate an object and obtain an interface pointer, use the methods through the interface pointer, call **Release** when you are done using the interface pointer, etc. A suitable client test program is provided in **Chap7\BankWizClient\Step1**. You will have to copy the files **bank.h** and **bank_i.c** from the server directory to the client directory.

ATL Code Walkthrough

We will go through the main features of the ATL code generated by the wizards. The basic structure is the same as the ATL project we built by hand in the first section of this chapter, with some significant enhancements.

bank.cpp	Exported functions **DllGetObject**, **DllCanUnloadNow** etc., object map, **CComModule**
bank.def	Module definition file
bank.idl	IDL file
account.h	COM object class definition and interface map
account.cpp	COM object class implementation
account.rgs	Registry script file

MIDL GENERATED CODE

Several additional files are generated when the IDL file is processed by the MIDL compiler

bank.h	Interface definitions
bank.tlb	Binary type library describing the objects and their interfaces (if there is a library statement in the IDL)
bank_i.c	Definitions of all GUIDs (use in only one compilation unit)
bank_p.c	Implementation for proxy/stub code
dlldata.c	Marshaling code for parameters of interfaces

The last two files are significant for the case of an EXE server where we need marshaling across process boundaries, a topic that we will discuss in Chapter 9.

CCOMMODULE AND OBJECT MAP

```
// bank.cpp : Implementation of DLL Exports.

...

CComModule _Module;

BEGIN_OBJECT_MAP(ObjectMap)
  OBJECT_ENTRY(CLSID_Account, CAccount)
END_OBJECT_MAP()
...
```

CComModule maintains an object map containing information about COM objects and their class IDs, lock counts, etc. There should be exactly one instance of **CComModule**, at global scope. **CComModule** plays a role a little analogous to **CWinApp** in MFC.

DLLMAIN

The **CComModule** instance is initialized and uninitialized. Appropriate thread protection is turned on or off.

```
// bank.cpp : Implementation of DLL Exports.

...

// DLL Entry Point

extern "C"
BOOL WINAPI DllMain(HINSTANCE hInstance,
         DWORD dwReason, LPVOID /*lpReserved*/)
{
  if (dwReason == DLL_PROCESS_ATTACH)
  {
    _Module.Init(ObjectMap, hInstance);
    DisableThreadLibraryCalls(hInstance);
  }
  else if (dwReason == DLL_PROCESS_DETACH)
    _Module.Term();
  return TRUE;    // ok
}
...
```

DLLCANUNLOADNOW AND DLLGETCLASSOBJECT

ATL provides implementations of the functions **DllCanUnloadNow** and **DllGetClassObject**, which must be supported by every in-process COM server.

```
// bank.cpp : Implementation of DLL Exports.

...

// Used to determine whether the DLL can be
// unloaded by OLE

STDAPI DllCanUnloadNow(void)
{
return (_Module.GetLockCount()==0) ?
            S_OK : S_FALSE;
}

// Returns a class factory to create an object of
// the requested type

STDAPI DllGetClassObject(REFCLSID rclsid,
         REFIID riid, LPVOID* ppv)
{
  return _Module.GetClassObject(rclsid,riid,ppv);
}
```

SELF-REGISTRATION

A very important feature of COM objects is that they be "self-registering." In fact, it is a *requirement* for ActiveX controls. Self-registering means that the component itself contains code to both register and to unregister the component. For a DLL, self-registering is supported by implementing two additional entry points:

- **DllRegisterServer** to register
- **DllUnregisterServer** to unregister

The following code is generated by the wizard, which works in conjunction with **CComModule** and the registry script file.

```
// bank.cpp : Implementation of DLL Exports.

...

// DllRegisterServer - Adds entries to the system
// registry

STDAPI DllRegisterServer(void)
{
// registers object, typelib and all interfaces in
// typelib
   return _Module.RegisterServer(TRUE);
}

// DllUnregisterServer - Removes entries from the
// system registry

STDAPI DllUnregisterServer(void)
{
  _Module.UnregisterServer();
  return S_OK;
}
```

The **CComModule** implementation of registration is based on a registry script file.

```
// account.rgs
HKCR
{
  Bank.Account.1 = s 'Account Class'
  {
    CLSID = s '{A1F11F1D-2E6A-11D1-A01B-00A024D06632}'
  }
  Bank.Account = s 'Account Class'
  {
    CurVer = s ' Bank.Account.1'
```

```
  }
  NoRemove CLSID
  {
    ForceRemove {A1F11F1D-2E6A-11D1-A01B-00A024D06632} =
s 'Account Class'
    {
      ProgID = s ' Bank.Account.1'
      VersionIndependentProgID = s
                      ' Bank.Account'
      InprocServer32 = s '%MODULE%'
      {
      }
    }
  }
}
```

REGSVR32

The tool REGSVR32.EXE can be used to call **DllRegisterServer**. A command-line argument takes the path to the The tool is already on the Tools menu under "Register Control." Use the command-line switch /u to call **DllUnregisterServer.**

For convenience, I have created tiny one-line batch files **reg_xxxx.bat** and **unreg_xxxx.bat** for our DLL servers. You can then register and unregister them by merely double-clicking on the appropriate batch file in Windows Explorer.

IMPLEMENTING ICLASSFACTORY

To use the ATL implementation of **IClassFactory**, we make our implementation class also derive from the ATL class **CComCoClass**. Template parameters specify the implementation class and the CLSID.

```
// account.h
...

class ATL_NO_VTABLE CAccount :
  public CComObjectRootEx<CComSingleThreadModel>,
  public CComCoClass<CAccount, &CLSID_Account>,
  public IAccount
{
...
```

To enable **CComModule** to maintain a set of class object definitions, we must install entries in an "object map" for each COM object with a CLSID.

```
BEGIN_OBJECT_MAP(ObjectMap)
  OBJECT_ENTRY(CLSID_Account, CAccount)
END_OBJECT_MAP()
```

Multiple Interfaces and More about IDL

In this section, we will see how to add support for more interfaces using ATL. We will need to edit the IDL file, which will give us an opportunity to examine IDL some more. We will see how a type library is specified, how the type library is identified for use in Visual Basic, and the role of the coclass. To finish implementing a second interface, we also have to add some more C++ code, including making the implementation class also derive from the new interface and adding another entry to the COM map.

Adding a Second Interface in IDL

We will begin by editing the **bank.idl** file. If you like you could carry out these steps as you read by working in **Chap7\Demos\BankWiz** (or **Chap7\BankWiz\Step1**).

1. Make a copy of the portion of the file that defines the **IAccount** interface and change the name to **IDisplay**.
2. Change the uuid (use the GUIDGEN tool).
3. Delete the methods (temporarily you have an empty new interface).
4. Add the new interface to the "coclass Account" (the second interface will not have the **default** attribute).
5. Build the server. You can now use OLE/COM Object Viewer to examine the new type library (File | View TypeLib) to verify that the new interface has been properly defined.

```
// Bank.idl : IDL source for Bank.dll
//

// This file will be processed by the MIDL tool to
// produce the type library (Bank.tlb) and marshalling code.

    [
      uuid(42135D00-2F41-11d1-A01B-00A024D06632),
      helpstring("IDisplay Interface"),
      pointer_default(unique)
    ]
    interface IDisplay : IUnknown
    {
    };

[
  uuid(0FFBDAA1-FCA7-11D2-8FF4-00105AA45BDC),
  version(1.0),
  helpstring("Bank 1.0 Type Library")
]
library BANKLib
```

```
{
  importlib("stdole32.tlb");
  importlib("stdole2.tlb");

  [
    uuid(0FFBDAAE-FCA7-11D2-8FF4-00105AA45BDC),
    helpstring("Account Class")
  ]
  coclass Account
  {
    [default] interface IAccount;
    interface IDisplay;
  };
};
```

TYPE LIBRARY

The **library** statement in the IDL file specifies a *type library*. A type library contains in binary form a description of COM classes, their interfaces and the methods of the interfaces. A type library can be read by tools such as Visual Basic. When you open up the "References" dialog in Visual Basic (from the Project menu), the list box of available references shows the various type libraries that are registered in the system (under the uuid shown before the **library** statement, underneath the **TypeLib** key in the Registry). The help string in the IDL file is used for the display in the list box. Thus the Account class will be found under the name "Bank 1.0 Type Library" (as we saw in Chapter 4).

COCLASS AND VISUAL BASIC

The **coclass** is used by Visual Basic to identify the Visual Basic class used in a client program. Visual Basic does not work directly with interfaces. You only have classes. The methods you can use are those of the **default** interface, as specified in the IDL. If you want to use methods of another interface in Visual Basic, you must **Dim** an object reference to the second interface and **Set** it to the original object reference (doing a **QueryInterface** under the hood). We saw similar code in **Chap4\BankClientVb**.

```
Option Explicit

Dim objAccount As New Account

Private Sub cmdDeposit_Click()
    objAccount.Deposit txtAmount
    Dim balance As Long
    objAccount.GetBalance balance
    txtBalance = balance
End Sub
```

```
Private Sub cmdShow_Click()
    Dim ifcDisplay As IDisplay
    Set ifcDisplay = objAccount
    ifcDisplay.Show
End Sub

Private Sub cmdWithdraw_Click()
    objAccount.Withdraw txtAmount
    Dim balance As Long
    objAccount.GetBalance balance
    txtBalance = balance
End Sub

Private Sub Form_Load()
    Dim balance As Long
    objAccount.GetBalance balance
    txtBalance = balance
End Sub
```

C++ Code for Second Interface

Continuing with the demo, we edit the C++ code in **account.h**.

6. Make the class **CAccount** also derive from **IDisplay**.
7. Add a COM_INTERFACE_ENTRY for **IDisplay** to the COM_MAP. Save.
8. You can now add the **Show** method by right-clicking over **IDisplay** in the tree view in the Workspace pane (use the **IDisplay** inside of **CAccount**). The **Show** method takes no parameters.
9. Implement the **Show** method by displaying the balance in a message box. In the title of the message box identify the interface and method: "**IDisplay::Show**."

The project at this point is close to **Chap7\BankWiz\Step2**. It is just lacking a **Withdraw** method, which you may add, if you wish.

```
// Account.h : Declaration of the CAccount
...

class ATL_NO_VTABLE CAccount :
  public CComObjectRootEx<CComSingleThreadModel>,
  public CComCoClass<CAccount, &CLSID_Account>,
  public IAccount,
  public IDisplay
{
public:
    CAccount() : m_nBalance(100)
        {
        }
```

```
DECLARE_REGISTRY_RESOURCEID(IDR_ACCOUNT)
DECLARE_NOT_AGGREGATABLE(CAccount)

DECLARE_PROTECT_FINAL_CONSTRUCT()

BEGIN_COM_MAP(CAccount)
    COM_INTERFACE_ENTRY(IAccount)
    COM_INTERFACE_ENTRY(IDisplay)
END_COM_MAP()

public:
// IDisplay
    STDMETHOD(Show)();
// IAccount
    STDMETHOD(Withdraw)(/*[in]*/ int amount);
    STDMETHOD(GetBalance)(/*[out]*/ int* pBalance);
    STDMETHOD(Deposit)(/*[in]*/ int amount);
protected:
    int m_nBalance;
};

...

// Account.cpp : Implementation of CAccount
...

STDMETHODIMP CAccount::Show()
{
    char buf[80];
    wsprintf(buf, "Balance = %d\n", m_nBalance);
    ::MessageBox(NULL, buf, "IDisplay::Show", MB_OK);
    return S_OK;
}
```

The server project at this stage can be found in **Chap7\Bank-Wiz\Step2**. It is almost but not quite up to the functionality provided in **Chap4\Bank**. It still needs an **IGreet** interface, which is provided in Step 3 of the sample code on the CD-ROM.

ATL COM Wrapper Classes

ATL provides wrapper classes that can further simplify several aspects of COM programming. There are wrapper classes for certain COM data types and for interface pointers. As we see in the next chapter, Visual C++ provides a number of classes of its own with similar features. These ATL wrapper classes are defined in **atlbase.h**.

CComBSTR

We saw in Chapter 4 that COM makes use of Unicode for passing character strings, and many functions and methods use a special form of Unicode called BSTR. Recall that a BSTR (or Basic String) has a 16-bit byte count prefix. At the Win32 level, memory is allocated for a BSTR by the function **SysAllocString**, and memory is freed by calling **SysFreeString**.

ATL provides a wrapper class, **CComBSTR**, that will internally store a BSTR, which gets allocated in the constructor and deallocated in the destructor. There are various functions for copying, appending, etc. There is an implicit cast operator that converts a **CComBSTR** into a BSTR. Check out the online documentation.

For an example of the use of **CComBSTR** see Step 3 of our Bank server example, which is equivalent to the **Chap4\Bank** that we saw before. A second class, **Greet,** is implemented, with a property **Greeting**, which is a BSTR. The following is the code that implements **get_Greeting**.

```
STDMETHODIMP CGreet::get_Greeting(BSTR *pVal)
{
  CComBSTR bstr("Welcome to Fiduciary Bank");
  *pVal = bstr.Detach();
  return S_OK;
}
```

The first line creates a **CComBSTR** from an ordinary string. Memory is now allocated for the internal BSTR. The second line assigns this BSTR to the output parameter. Without the **Detach**, the BSTR would be deallocated upon exiting the function, which is not the correct behavior. The protocol in COM calls for the server to allocate the BSTR and for the client to free it. The **Detach** call fixes the problem, because afterward the BSTR is no longer part of the **CComBSTR** object, and so will not be deallocated by the destructor.

Visual C++ provides a similar wrapper class, **_bstr_**. The ATL class is somewhat lighter weight.

Smart Pointers

Working with raw interface pointers is error prone, because you have to be very careful in calling **AddRef** and **Release** appropriately. ATL provides a "smart pointer" class, **CComPtr**, which "wraps" the interface pointer by an object with the intelligence to call **AddRef** when it is assigned and to call **Release** when it goes out of scope. The class **CComQIPtr** has the additional feature of overloading the assignment operator, so if a smart pointer of one type is assigned to a smart pointer of another type, **QueryInterface** will be called.

Visual C++ provides its own wrapper class, **_com_ptr_t** for smart pointers, which again is somewhat more heavyweight. What is nice about the

Visual C++ compiler support for smart pointers is that code for using them can be placed into your project automatically when you "import" a type library. We examine this feature in the next chapter.

Summary

In this chapter we learned about the Active Template Library (ATL), which is a powerful and flexible C++ template class library that can help you build small, self-contained COM objects. With ATL and the wizard support provided by Visual C++, you can easily implement a COM server from scratch. ATL automates implementation of class factories and self-registration. A key feature in working with ATL is the Interface Definition Language, which specifies interfaces, type libraries, and coclasses. The type library and coclass are especially important when using Visual Basic.

ATL also provides useful wrapper classes for interface pointers and for certain COM data types such as BSTR. In the next chapter we look at similar wrapper classes supplied by Visual C++ itself and some wizard support provided for importing a type library.

E I G H T

Visual C++ COM Support

*In Chapter 7, you learned about the use of ActiveX Template Library to greatly simplify the implementation of COM servers. This chapter covers various features in Visual C++ that make it easier to implement clients. One very important feature is "smart pointers," which take much of the drudgery out of client-side programming. For example, a smart pointer will automatically call **Release** when it goes out of scope, simplifying the life of the programmer. Smart pointers can also transparently do a **QueryInterface** when you do a pointer assignment. Visual C++ has an "import" feature which will read a type library and automatically set up smart pointer support. Visual C++ also provides some support classes to simplify working with COM data types such as BSTR. The end result is a C++ COM programming environment that has some of the ease-of-use features that Visual Basic programmers enjoy.*

This is a short chapter, but keeping it separate from Chapter 7 will help you remember that the Visual C++ compiler COM support is independent of ATL.

Visual C++ and COM Clients

Visual C++ offers significant compiler support to simplify the process of creating COM clients:

- An import directive can import a *type library* and automatically create appropriate C++ wrapper classes.
- "Smart pointers" can be used to encapsulate interface pointers, relieving the programmer of the burden of doing **AddRef** and **Release**.
- The C++ exception mechanism is used to simplify the handling of errors.

Visual C++ COM Client Demo

We give a complete demonstration using Visual C++ compiler "smart pointer" support for creating a COM client program.

- Do your client work in **Chap8\Demos\SmartClient** directory (backed up in **Chap8\SmartClient\Prelim**).
- The server directory is **Chap7\Demos\BankWiz** or **Chap7\BankWiz\Step1**.
- The finished demo is in **Chap8\SmartClient\Step0** directory.

STARTER PROJECT

1. Examine the starter project, which provides the GUI for exercising the Account object.

USING THE TYPE LIBRARY

2. Copy the file **banks.tlb** from server directory to client directory.
3. Add the following include and import directives to **stdafx.h**. The directive is for the special Visual C++ compiler support of COM clients.

   ```
   #include <afxwin.h>
   #include <afxext.h>
   #include <afxdisp.h>
   #import "bank.tlb" no_namespace
   ```

4. Build your project to make sure that you get a clean compile at this point.

USING THE SMART POINTER

5. Do a simple test of using the COM server by performing the following operations in **OnInitDialog**:
    - Create pointer to COM object.
    - Call **GetBalance** method.
    - Display balance in a message box.

   ```
   // TODO: Add extra initialization here
   SetDlgItemInt(IDC_AMOUNT, 25);
   IAccountPtr pAccount("Bank.Account.1");
   ```

```
int balance;
pAccount->GetBalance(&balance);
CString strBal;
strBal.Format("%d", balance);
MessageBox(strBal, "Balance");
...
```

The "smart pointer" class **IAccountPtr** was created when the type library was imported. The program ID "Bank.Account.1" is passed as an argument to the constructor.

TESTING AND ERROR HANDLING

6. Build and run. The program shuts down immediately (crashes), without producing any output.
7. Put our COM code inside a try block and provide a **catch** handler. If ATL code fails, it will throw an exception of type reference to **_com_error**. This ATL class has a member function **ErrorMessage** which will return a character string error message.

```
try
{
  IAccountPtr pAccount("Bank.Account.1");
  int balance;
  pAccount->GetBalance(&balance);
  CString strBal;
  strBal.Format("%d", balance);
  MessageBox(strBal, "Balance");
}
catch (_com_error &ex)
{
  MessageBox(ex.ErrorMessage());
}
```

8. Build and run. Now we get a nice error message. See Figure 8–1.

We did not initialize OLE.

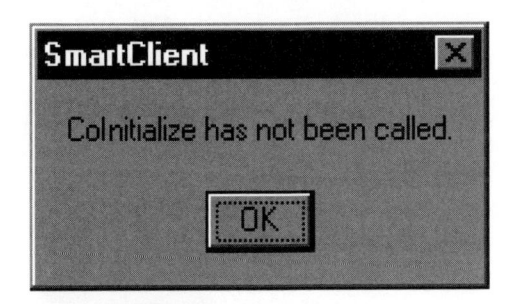

Figure 8–1 *Error message*

9. Since our client is an MFC application, we can initialize OLE by calling **AfxOleInit** in **InitInstance**.

   ```
   BOOL CBankClientApp::InitInstance()
   {
     if (!AfxOleInit())
     {
       AfxMessageBox("AfxOleInit failed");
       return FALSE;
     }
   ...
   ```

10. Build and run. Now the application should work. See Figure 8–2.

Figure 8–2   *Message box displaying starting balance*

Finishing the Client Program

The demo program did a minimal test of being able to connect to the server. It is straightforward to implement a GUI test program that fully exercises the server. See the program in **Chap8\SmartClient\Step2** (which runs against the server in **Chap7\BankWiz\Step2**). The most interesting feature is how the smart pointers get initialized. There is no **CoCreateInstance** or **QueryInterface**. Everything takes place in the constructor of the dialog class.

```
CSmartClientDlg::CSmartClientDlg(CWnd* pParent /*=NULL*/)
  : CDialog(CSmartClientDlg::IDD, pParent),
  m_pAccount("Bank.Account.1")

{
  m_pDisplay = m_pAccount;
...
  m_hIcon = AfxGetApp()->LoadIcon(IDR_MAINFRAME);
}
```

Namespaces

In our example program we used a **no_namespace** directive when we imported the type library. That slightly simplified our code. However, if we are using two or more COM servers in the same program, there is a potential for name clashes. The "Hello" example from Chapter 3 provides an illustration. The client program **HelloClientVC** calls a VB server and a VC server. If we ignore the namespace issue, our program will not compile (multiply defined symbols). An easy fix is to make use of namespaces. Do not suppress the namespace in the **#import** directive. In the C++ code you can then employ **using namespace**.

```
void CHelloClientVCDlg::OnVb()
{
  using namespace HelloVB;
  try
  {
    _GreetPtr spGreet("HelloVB.Greet");
    _bstr_t greeting = spGreet->GetGreeting();
    SetDlgItemText(IDC_GREETING,
        (const char*) greeting);
  }
  catch (_com_error &er)
  {
    MessageBox(er.ErrorMessage());
  }
}
```

DISAMBIGUATING IN VISUAL BASIC

A similar issue arises in a Visual Basic COM client program. Visual Basic does not support namespaces, so the solution is to fully qualify names, using the library name as a prefix. The following code is from **EarlyClientVB** in Chapter 3.

```
Private Sub cmdVB_Click()
    On Error GoTo ErrorHandler
    Dim objGreet As New HelloVB.Greet
    txtGreeting = objGreet.Greeting
    Exit Sub
ErrorHandler:
    MsgBox Err.Description
End Sub

Private Sub cmdVC_Click()
    On Error GoTo ErrorHandler
    Dim objGreet As New HELLOLib.Greet
    txtGreeting = objGreet.Greeting
    Exit Sub
```

```
ErrorHandler:
    MsgBox Err.Description
End Sub
```

Visual C++ COM Support Classes

Visual C++ provides a number of COM support classes. We have looked at the smart pointer class **_com_ptr_t**. In Chapter 11, we mention **_variant_t**. In this section we discuss **_bstr_t** and **_com_error**. Use the header file **comdef.h**.

_bstr_t

The class **_bstr_t** wraps the BSTR data type. It is similar to the ATL class **CComBSTR** but somewhat more heavyweight. One natural application of this class is to simplify coding the common situation where a BSTR is returned by a COM method or API call. The constructor will initialize a **_bstr_t** from a BSTR. Then you can convert to a multibyte string via the cast operator **(const char *)**. Finally, the BSTR gets deallocated by simply letting the **_bstr_t** go out of scope.

The "hello" client program **HelloClientVC** from Chapter 3 that we looked at above also provides an illustration of using **_bstr_t**.

```
void CHelloClientVCDlg::OnVb()
{
  using namespace HelloVB;
  try
  {
    _GreetPtr spGreet("HelloVB.Greet");
    _bstr_t greeting = spGreet->GetGreeting();
    SetDlgItemText(IDC_GREETING,
               (const char*) greeting);
  }
  catch (_com_error &er)
  {
    MessageBox(er.ErrorMessage());
  }
}
```

_com_error

COM does not throw exceptions. It communicates the occurrence of errors through the HRESULT. In addition, there are some special COM interfaces that a class can optionally support which can provide extended error information. We study this COM error mechanism in Chapter 12.

The Visual C++ COM support classes will throw an exception of type **_com_error** when they encounter an error. Additionally, if the server class supports extended COM error interfaces, they will obtain this additional error information and store it in the exception object. The method **ErrorMessage** will return a string giving a descriptive error message.

The same example code from **HelloClientVC** that we have been looking at for namespaces and **_bstr_t** also illustrates use of **_com_error**.

```
void CHelloClientVCDlg::OnVb()
{
  using namespace HelloVB;
  try
  {
    _GreetPtr spGreet("HelloVB.Greet");
    _bstr_t greeting = spGreet->GetGreeting();
    SetDlgItemText(IDC_GREETING,
        (const char*) greeting);
  }
  catch (_com_error &er)
  {
    MessageBox(er.ErrorMessage());
  }
}
```

Summary

This chapter showed you how to use COM support provided by the Visual C++ compiler to simplify implementing COM client programs. A number of features work together to make your life easier. By importing the type library of the server you automatically gain access to smart pointers. You do not have to work with the smart pointer class **_com_ptr_t** directly but can make use of some classes with mnemonic names derived from names in the type library. Name clashes can be resolved with C++ namespaces. The smart pointers remove the need to explicitly call **CoCreateInstance** or **QueryInterface**. Visual C++ also provides some convenient support classes for data types, such as the **_bstr_t** class that wraps BSTR. All of the Visual C++ COM support classes throw an exception when they encounter a COM error through an HRESULT error return. Thus you can use C++ exception handling in your client program.

The support classes provided by Visual C++ are similar to those provided by ATL, but in general the Visual C++ classes are geared more to ease of use, while the ATL classes are oriented towards high performance and small code size. For example, the ATL classes do not throw exceptions.

Fortified with the capability to use ATL, we now move onward to some additional topics in COM programming, including creating EXE servers and DCOM.

NINE

EXE Servers

In the preceding chapters we examined the basic COM protocol, implemented in-process COM servers at the raw COM level, and learned about ATL. We now have all the tools needed to take the next step, which is to implement an out-of-process COM server in a separate EXE. COM servers implemented as EXEs are historically important because of the original coupling of COM with OLE, which was concerned with EXE servers. We begin with a discussion of various approaches to integrating applications, including DDE and OLE. We then examine the issues involved in creating EXE COM servers and the differences from DLL servers. Next we show how to implement EXE servers for objects supporting standard interfaces, both at the raw COM level and using ATL. Then we see how IDL can be compiled by the RPC compiler MIDL to create proxies and stubs, enabling us to implement EXE servers with custom interfaces.

Application Integration and OLE

Windows began as a desktop computing environment, putting a graphical user interface on top of DOS. The original Windows applications were stand-alone, and different Windows applications were not able to talk to each other (except to pass data back and forth using the Clipboard). It soon became apparent that it would be useful to allow applications to communicate with each other programmatically. Dynamic Data Exchange, or DDE, was Microsoft's first attempt at a standard protocol allowing Windows applications to communicate with each other. DDE was based on sending Windows messages. OLE 1.0 was a more sophisticated protocol for application integration, supporting compound documents, but it was based on DDE for interprocess communication. OLE 2.0 substantially improved upon OLE 1.0 and introduced COM. In all of these cases it was *applications*, that is EXE modules, that were communicating with each other. In this section we will briefly examine the issues and techniques for integrating EXE applications.

Windows Messages and DDE

Consider two separate Windows applications that would like to communicate with each other. How might such communication be implemented? There are a number of techniques, including operating system primitives like memory-mapped files, pipes, mailslots, etc. In the Win32 environment, a very basic form of interprocess communication is Windows messages, because every Windows application has a message queue, and one application can send messages to a window of another application.

For a concrete illustration of how two Windows applications can communicate in this way, look at the Windows bank server in **Chap9\Wsrv**. This workspace has two projects, the server "hello" and the client "wcli." Both are EXEs. Build both applications and start the server and then the client. Arrange the windows side by side, and in the client click the "Get Balance" button. The starting balance of 100 is obtained, and the server window shows the most recent message "GetBalance." See Figure 9–1.

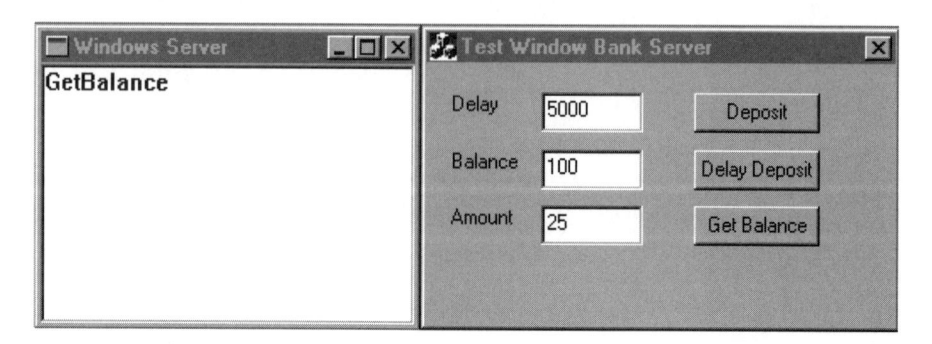

Figure 9–1   *Communicating via Windows messages*

These two applications communicate via a private protocol that only they understand, making use of three registered Windows messages. Applications are free to make up whatever private protocols they wish to use, but such protocols are not general purpose. Microsoft defined a *standard* protocol for Windows applications to communicate with each other, called Dynamic Data Exchange, or DDE. Many Windows applications implemented this protocol. It was somewhat difficult to program and not very robust. For example, depending on the volume of message traffic, you could get timeout problems and the like. Another limitation is that both applications have to know the data formats used, making for a tight coupling between them.

OLE 1.0

OLE 1.0 was introduced in June, 1991 as Microsoft's first attempt to provide an object-oriented mechanism for integrating applications. OLE 1.0 introduced the concept of compound documents, which can contain "objects" from other applications. It derived from the work of PowerPoint developers who wanted to embed Microsoft Graph elements in their documents. OLE 1.0 attempted to overcome limitations of previous integration techniques

Using the Clipboard, users could paste static "snapshots" of data from other applications into their documents. Editing such data was very cumbersome—it would have to be edited in the original application and then pasted in again. There was no way to use the Clipboard to support "links," whereby changes in the original data would be automatically reflected in data in the container document. DDE could be used to support links to the original data, but the container needed its own code to render the data in proper format.

OBJECT LINKING AND EMBEDDING

OLE 1.0 enabled a user to *embed* an *object* in a container. The object contained a static picture and also the original data needed to edit the object, along with a hook to bring up the original application when required. To edit the object, the user typically double-clicked with the mouse. The original application would then start up in a separate window. When done, the user could save, and the data in the container document would be updated.

Despite its advances over previous techniques, there were a number of limitations:

- OLE 1.0 was implemented on top of DDE, which is inherently asynchronous. When you call a function, it returns immediately, and you must wait in a message loop, polling a status flag.
- OLE 1.0 relied exclusively on shared global memory for passing data between applications. Large blocks of data would have to be copied into memory prior to a transfer (where it might be immediately paged back onto disk).
- OLE 1.0 links were easily broken when files were moved.
- Editing of embedded objects in a separate window was intrusive to the user.

OLE 2.0

OLE 2.0 was introduced in May, 1993. Its primary original goal was to improve upon OLE 1.0. During its design, OLE 2.0 was extended far beyond its original domain of supporting compound documents (OLE is no longer an acronym for "Object Linking and Embedding"). Significant improvements were made over OLE 1.0:

- DDE was replaced by the far more robust lightweight remote procedure call protocol.
- A new uniform data transfer (UDT) mechanism provided several alternatives to shared memory for efficient data transfer.
- A new moniker mechanism improved upon link tracking.
- Visual editing or in-place activation was introduced to allow an embedded or linked object to be edited in the context of the container application.
- Above all, OLE 2.0 was based on a precisely defined model (COM or Component Object Model),

Being based on COM, OLE 2.0 was *extensible*. As a result, new features could be incrementally introduced, simply by defining additional interfaces. As a result, the version number was dropped, and the technology is now just called OLE.

OLE Demonstration

The detailed study of OLE is beyond the scope of this book. We are concerned with another facet of COM technology, leading to the development of multiple-tier applications using COM+. To gain a flavor of what OLE is like, you may wish to spend a few minutes on a simple demonstration. The example programs we use are two standard MFC examples that ship with Visual C++. The programs are HIERSVR and OCLIENT. Both are in the OLE section of the MFC sample programs. A third program is STR, in the **Chap9** directory.

1. Build HIERSVR and run it stand-alone. Running it will automatically register it. Try adding a few nodes, and save as a file **hier1.hie**.
2. Build STR and run it stand-alone. Type in a few characters, and change the color if you wish. Save as a file **str1.str**
3. Build OCLIENT and run it. Use Edit | Insert New Object to bring up the "Insert New Object" dialog. Choose "Insert from file" and navigate to **hier1.hie.** Insert one copy as an embedded object and one as a link (see the check box). Insert **str1.str** as an embedded object.
4. Double-click on an embedded object. Both servers support in-place activation, so you will see the menu and toolbar change to support editing the embedded object within the container's window, using the server. See Figure 9–2.

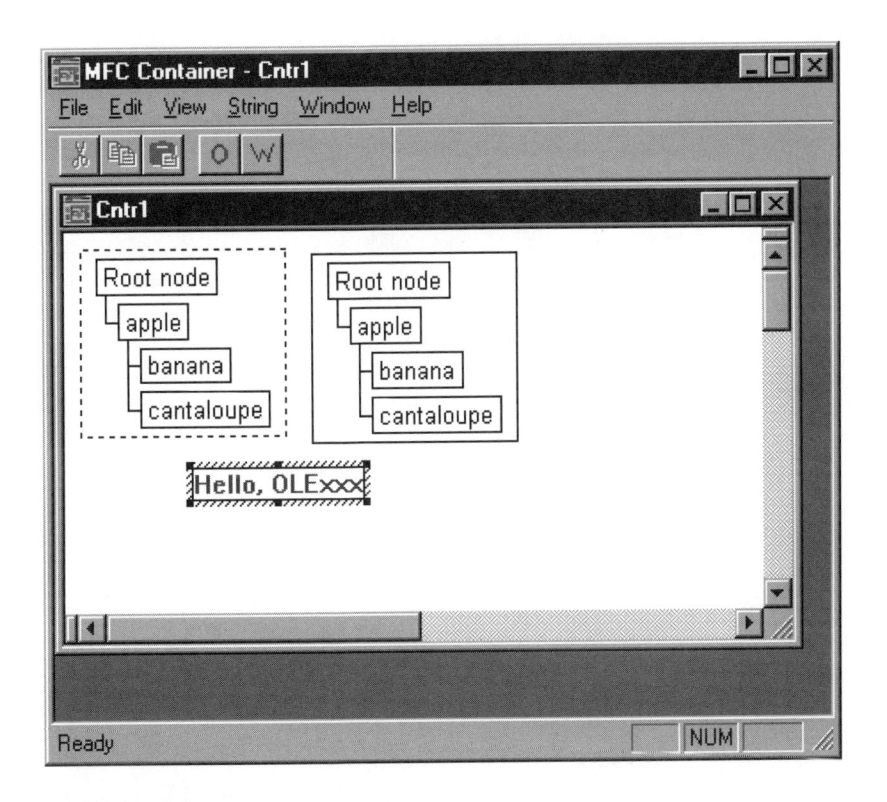

Figure 9–2 *Embedded and linked objects, one of them is in-place active*

5. Make some changes to the object you are editing, and save the container document. Close the container document file and then reopen it. You should see that your changes have indeed been saved. Now open up the original file (**str1.str**). The original data is still there. In the container you have been working with an *embedded* object, complete with its own data, which is completely independent of the data in the file. The file was just used as an original source of data, which was copied into the container.

6. Now double-click on the linked object (shown by the dotted surrounding lines). The server application opens up in a separate window. Make some changes and save. You are editing the original file—you are working with a *link*.

Application Integration and EXE Servers

Both STR and HIERSVR are EXE servers. They are complete applications, which either can run stand-alone as ordinary applications or can run when they are invoked by a client application such as OCLIENT. When they are running as servers, there is interprocess communication taking place, which is the subject of this chapter. OLE 1.0 used Windows messages (DDE) for interprocess communication. This communication was inherently limited to a single machine. You cannot send a Windows message to an application on another machine. (Something called "network DDE" was invented, but that did not use Windows messages to get across the network.) OLE 2.0 used COM as the protocol, and COM uses Remote Procedure Call (RPC) to communicate from one process to another. RPC is not limited to one machine, but can cross a network.

The OLE-style integration can empower the end user to do more, by being able to interact with multiple applications in a relatively transparent way. In-place editing is much more seamless than opening a special window. There is a shift from "application-centric" to "document-centric." The user is concerned with editing a document; while doing so, many different applications may come and go (acting as servers).

However, providing EXE servers is somewhat after the fact. We have these huge desktop applications with many features. The features are exposed via COM interfaces. This works but is not optimal. It is not really component-based software. The real explosion of components has been in controls (ActiveX controls, sometimes called OLE controls or OCXs). These are DLL servers, not applications.

EXE Servers and Surrogates

There is another role for EXE servers. That is to enable clients to call across a network. You cannot make a direct call to an in-process server from another address space, much less across a network. You need to use RPC. You might be led to believe that if you want your sever to be callable across the network you must implement it as an EXE, but you would be wrong. There is a COM entity known as a *surrogate* which is an EXE that can serve as a shell outside of a DLL. Then a client can call the surrogate remotely, which in turn calls the DLL inside the surrogate's process. In Part 3 we will see that COM+ provides a surrogate for DLL servers.

Another advantage of EXE servers can also be handled by surrogates. A problem with DLLs is that the server and client are in the same address space. Thus there is no isolation. The server could overwrite the client's address space, and conversely. The latter is more serious—one rogue client could bring down a server that is being used by many clients. A surrogate can provide isolation.

Interfaces for an OLE Server

An OLE compound document server must implement many interfaces in order to support the very rich integration that OLE provides. We can use OLE/COM Object Viewer to see these interfaces. See Figure 9–3, which shows the interfaces for the simple STR server. You could look under "All Objects," but it will be easier to find under "Embeddable Objects." Look for "Str Answer Document." In the next section we will discuss the significance of some of the Registry entries.

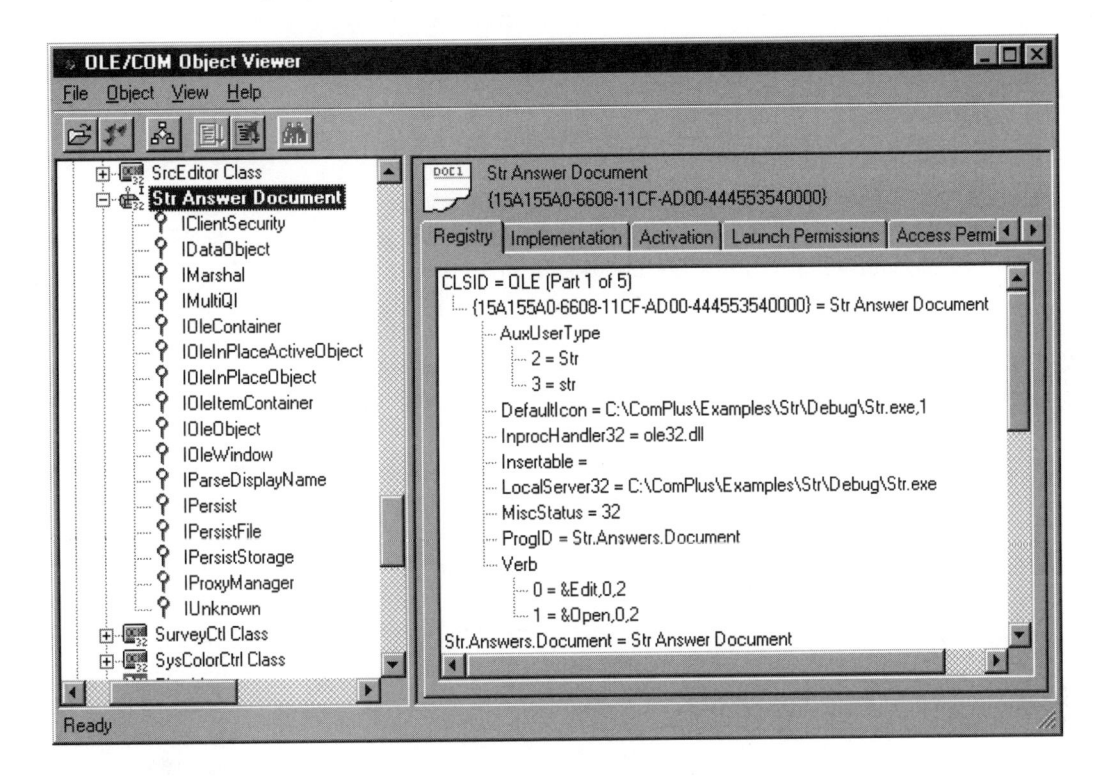

Figure 9-3 *An OLE compound document server*

Structure of an EXE Server

In this section we look at the structure of an EXE server. Although there is much in common with DLL servers, many of the details are different. An EXE server is an application in its own right, and we have to worry about issues such as not showing the application's window when it is launched as a server. Above all, an EXE server and the COM run time must provide for the *marshaling* of data between the server and the client. This marshaling is provided by COM itself for all *standard* interfaces. We will illustrate the mechanism used by an EXE server by implementing a simple "demo" object that supports only a couple of standard interfaces. In the following section, we discuss using the RPC compiler MIDL to create proxies and stubs for marshaling *custom* interfaces.

There are several differences when a COM object is implemented as a local server (EXE) instead of as an in-process server (DLL):

- A registry entry under the key **LocalServer32** points to an EXE file where the object is implemented.
- An EXE must instantiate all its class factories on startup and register them with COM.
- During shutdown, an EXE must revoke its class factories.
- An EXE has a main window and a message processing loop. The main window must not be shown when the EXE is launched by COM.
- An EXE must take steps to unload itself when its object count and lock count are both 0.

Marshaling

Marshaling is the mechanism that enables a client in one process to transparently invoke methods on objects implemented in another process. A client always makes in-process calls to some kind of object. The object may be a complete implementation (in-process server); an *object handler*, which provides a partial implementation; or a *proxy*.

An example of an object handler is provided by OLE compound documents. If an object is *active*, the server is running, and the user can edit the object. But if the object is not active it can still be seen in the container's window. Indeed, the server might not even be installed on the user's system—the user may have received the document via e-mail from another user. But the user can still see a *picture* of the embedded object. If you look in the Registry for "Str Answer Document" (see Figure 9–3) you will notice the key **LocalServer32** which points to **Str.exe** as you would expect. This is the application that will run when the server is active. There is another key **InprocHandler32** which points to **ole32.dll.** This is the object handler, which is provided by the standard **ole32.dll** and hence is available on every system. This object handler provides a partial implementation of the object's functionality. It cannot do very much, but it can display a metafile, which is stored in the container document as part of the embedded object.

If the object is in another process, the *proxy* implements interprocess communication to a *stub* in the object's process, which makes in-process calls to the object itself. For the standard interfaces, the proxies and stubs are provided by COM itself. For custom interfaces we have to provide them. We will see later in the chapter that the proxies and stubs can be generated by the MIDL compiler. Thus all we need to do is provide the proper IDL and arrange for registration of the proxy and stub.

"Demo" Object as a Local Server

We illustrate a local server with an object that supports only the **IUnknown** interface. The sole purpose of this server is to illustrate object creation by a local server. You may extend your object to support one other standard interface, **IPersist**. For demonstration purposes, you can build the project in **Chap9\DemoSdk\Step1** and run the registration file **demosdk.reg**. If you open up the object "Demo Object SDK EXE" in OLE/COM Object Viewer, you will see that the main window is shown, and the server application does not unload when you release the interface pointer. See Figure 9–4.

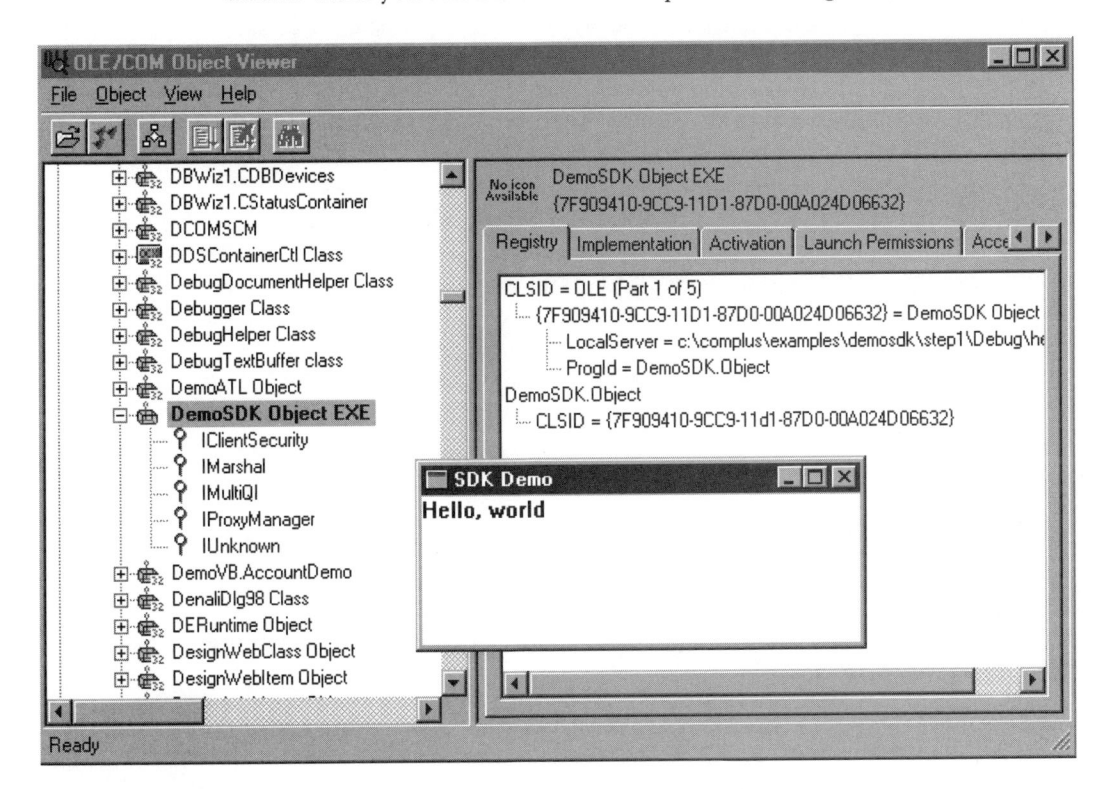

Figure 9–4 *An ill-behaved EXE Server*

Proxy

For a COM object with *standard* interfaces, the COM run time itself provides a proxy for the server. The proxy runs in-process and supports several additional interfaces beyond the interfaces supported by the object. Open up the object "Demo Object SDK EXE" in OLE/COM Object Viewer (refer again to

Figure 9–4). Besides the interface **IUnknown** supported by the object itself, the COM marshaling run time provides the interfaces **IMarshal**, **IClientSecurity**, **IMultiQI**, and **IProxyManager** in the proxy. We discuss marshaling in the next chapter.

Registering a Class Factory

As with a DLL server, the EXE server must implement a class factory. But the mechanism for getting the class factory pointer to the client is somewhat different. An EXE cannot "export" functions like a DLL can. Instead, as part of program initialization the application instantiates a class factory object and then *registers* it with COM. The COM run time system maintains a data structure known as the Active Object Table that stores the CLSID and the associated class factory pointer. Then when a client calls **CoGetClassObject**, the COM run time will first see if this CLSID is in this table. If it is, the class factory pointer is returned.

If the CLSID is not in the Active Object Table, the COM run time will look in the System Registry for the CLSID and the key **LocalServer32**. It finds the path to the server EXE, which then starts up. As part of its initialization, the server registers its class factory. The COM run time tries again, and this time succeeds in finding the class factory pointer.

The following is the initialization code for **demosdk**. Note that the very first initialization that must be done is to initialize COM with **CoInitialize**.

```
BOOL Init()
{
  HRESULT hr;
  hr = CoInitialize(NULL);
  if (FAILED(hr))
  {
    MessageBox(NULL, "CoInitialize failed", "DemoSDK",
             MB_OK);
    return FALSE;
  }

    g_pClassFactory = new CDemoClassFactory;

    if (g_pClassFactory == NULL)
        return FALSE;

    // Since we hold on to this pointer, we should AddRef it.
    g_pClassFactory->AddRef();

    hr = CoRegisterClassObject(CLSID_DemoSDK,
        g_pClassFactory,
        CLSCTX_LOCAL_SERVER,
        REGCLS_MULTIPLEUSE,
```

```
            &g_dwRegister);

    if (FAILED(hr))
        return FALSE;

    return TRUE;
}
```

A "cookie" **g_dwRegister** is returned if registration is successful. This cookie is a DWORD that can be used at program termination to revoke the registration.

REGCLS Enumeration

The fourth parameter in the call to **CoRegisterClassObject** is one of the variables of an enumeration data type that specifies how the class is to be registered. The two most common values for this parameter are REGCLS_SINGLEUSE and REGCLS_MULTIPLEUSE. In the "single use" case, multiple instances of the server EXE will be started in order to service multiple clients, that is, one instance of the server can only service a single client. "In the multiple use" case, the same instance of the EXE can service multiple clients.

Revoking Class Factory

On program termination, the class factor(ies) must be *revoked*. This will remove the CLSID from the Active Object Table. If an application neglected to revoke its registration, the COM run time would erroneously return a class factory pointer to a class factory object that no longer exists. Note that a single application EXE server might support several different COM classes, and so it might register several class factories.

```
void UnInit()
{
  // Opposite of CoRegisterClassObject; class factory
  // reference count is now 1
    if (g_dwRegister != 0)
        CoRevokeClassObject(g_dwRegister);

    // The last Release, which frees the class factory.
    if (g_pClassFactory != NULL)
        g_pClassFactory->Release();
  CoUninitialize();
}
```

A Better-Behaved EXE Server

Step 1 of **Chap9\DemoSdk** illustrates the basic elements of an EXE server. Code is provided to implement a class factory, to register it on program startup, and to revoke it on program termination. But an intrusive window is displayed when the server starts up.

HIDING THE MAIN WINDOW

When an application is launched by OLE, you may wish to hide the main window. The command-line flag **/Embedding** or **-Embedding** is used when launched by OLE. In an SDK Windows applications you should check for these flags prior to calling **ShowWindow**.

```
int APIENTRY WinMain (HINSTANCE hInstance,
                      HINSTANCE hPrevInstance,
                      LPSTR lpszCmdLine, int nCmdShow)
{
...

   hwnd = CreateWindow ("DemoClass", "SDK Demo",
                        WS_OVERLAPPEDWINDOW,
                        CW_USEDEFAULT, 0,
                        CW_USEDEFAULT, 0,
                        NULL, NULL, hInstance, NULL) ;
   g_hWnd = hwnd;

   // MessageBox(NULL, lpszCmdLine, "Command line", MB_OK);

   // Check command line for /Embedding or -Embedding

   if (!strstr(lpszCmdLine, "/Embedding")
     && !strstr(lpszCmdLine, "-Embedding"))
   {
     ShowWindow (hwnd, nCmdShow) ;
     UpdateWindow (hwnd) ;
   }

   while (GetMessage (&msg, NULL, 0, 0))
   {
     TranslateMessage (&msg) ;
     DispatchMessage (&msg) ;
   }
   return msg.wParam ;
}
```

Build the Step 2 version of the server and register by merging **demosdk.reg** into the Registry. Now use OLE/COM Object Viewer to create an object. You will see a message box announcing object creation, but no intrusive window is shown. Good. Release the object. You get a message box saying the object has been destroyed. Is everything well? Not quite. Bring up the Task Manager (or the Process Viewer). The server process **hello.exe** is still running. See Figure 9–5. Kill it.

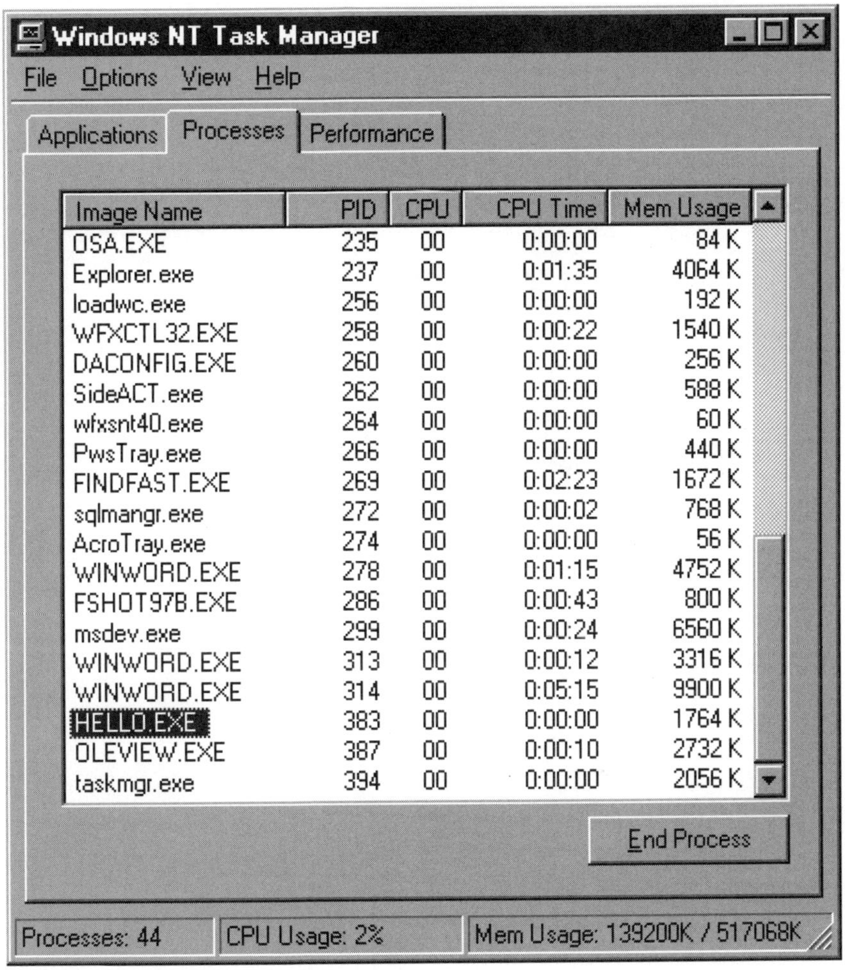

Figure 9–5 *An EXE server that has not unloaded*

UNLOADING THE APPLICATION

To handle unloading, implement a helper function that will close the application when the object count and lock count both reach 0. Unloading is implemented in Step 3, which also implements the **IPersist** interface discussed in the next section.

```
// Unloading mechanism. Call this function whenever
// object count or lock count reaches 0

void ObjectDestroyed()
{
  if (g_cObj == 0 && g_cLock == 0 && IsWindow(g_hWnd))
      PostMessage(g_hWnd, WM_CLOSE, 0, 0);
}
```

Call this function from **IUnknown::Release( )** ...

```
STDMETHODIMP_(ULONG) CDemo::Release()
{
  if(--m_nRef == 0)
  {
    delete this;
    --g_cObj;
    ::MessageBox(NULL,
      "Demo object destroyed","Info",MB_OK);
    ObjectDestroyed();
    return 0;
  }
  return m_nRef;
}
```

... and also from **IClassFactory::LockServer( )**

```
STDMETHODIMP CDemoClassFactory::LockServer(BOOL fLock)
{
    if (fLock)
        g_cLock++;
    else
        g_cLock--;

  if (g_cLock == 0)
    ObjectDestroyed();

    return NOERROR;
}
```

EXE Servers Using ATL

It is very easy to implement an EXE server using ATL. Choose Executable (EXE) in ATL COM AppWizard. Add objects and methods just like you would for a DLL. For custom interfaces, build and register a proxy/stub DLL.

EXE Server Demo

We will first do a brief demo of using ATL to create an EXE server with standard interfaces. It is similar to the "Demo" object we created above at the raw level. It will support **IUnknown**. To make it slightly more interesting, we also implement the standard interface **IPersist**, which is the simplest of all the standard interfaces. It has only one method, **GetClassID**, which simply returns the CLSID of the object. (**IPersist** is not a useful interface in itself. It serves as a base interface for a number of interfaces in COM's persistence architecture, including **IPersistStorage**, **IPersistStream**, and **IPersistFile**.)

Do your work in the **Demos** directory. A solution can be found in the directory **Chap9\DemoATL**.

1. Use the ATL COM AppWizard to create a new project "DemoATL." In Step 1, choose "Executable (EXE)" for the Server Type. See Figure 9–6.

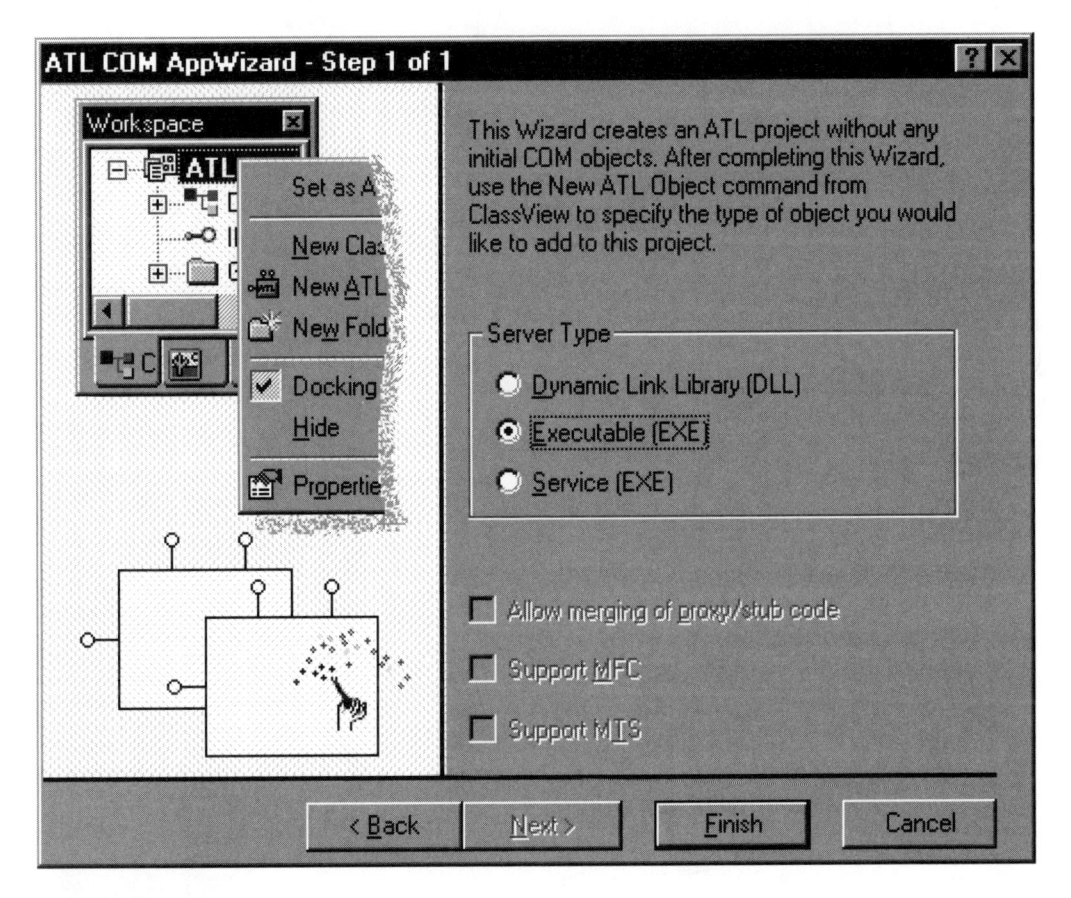

Figure 9–6   *ATL COM AppWizard for an EXE project*

2. Insert a new ATL object "Demo." Change the type to "DemoATL Class" (no period) and (version independent) ProgID to "DemoATL.Object" (with a period). Change the interface to "**IPersist**." The ProgID will be "DemoATL.Object.1." See Figure 9–7. The attributes will be Single Threading Model, Custom Interface, and No Aggregation.

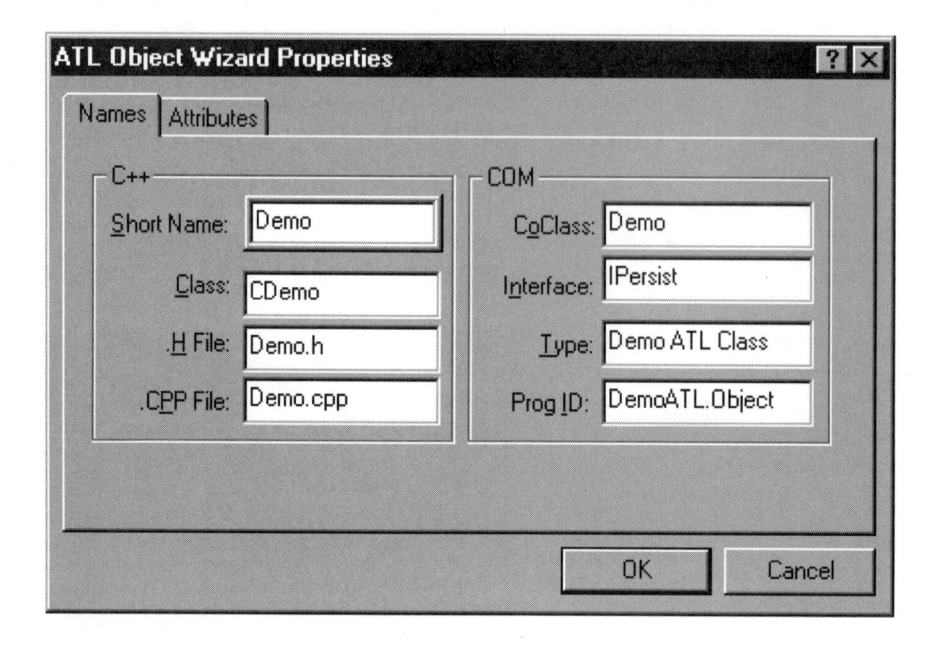

Figure 9–7 *Properties for the new object*

3. Add a method **GetClassID** with an out parameter CLSID ***pClassID**.
4. Implement **GetClassID** to return CLSID_Demo as the CLSID.
5. Delete **IPersist** interface (including the preceding attributes) from the IDL file. Build, and test using OLE/COM Object Viewer. Remember to look for the user name "DemoATL Class." You can also test by our own program **Chap4\UseCmd**. Use the ProgID "DemoATL.Object.1."

Self Registration for EXE Servers

As with a DLL server, an EXE server should support self-registration. The mechanism is somewhat different. Rather than export DLL functions to register and unregister, the EXE should take command-line arguments:

/RegServer   to register the server
/UnregServer to unregister the server

An ATL COM AppWizard project automatically implements self-registration for EXE servers, as it does for DLL servers. You may verify the above commands for the EXE server that you just created. First unregister the server and look for it in OLE/COM Object Viewer. Then register it and look again. The **Chap9\DemoATL** directory contains one-line batch files for registering and unregistering.

Proxies and Stubs

The last part of our story of EXE servers is the topic of proxies and stubs. They are not needed for DLL servers, because the client and server are in the same address space. They are needed for EXE servers because we have to marshal our calls across the address space barrier. For *standard* interfaces, the COM run time does this for us automatically. For custom interfaces we must create a proxy/stub DLL to do the marshaling. Visual C++ and ATL make this easy. The MIDL RPC compiler generates the needed code for us. The Visual C++ ATL COM AppWizard even creates a make file for us. All we have to do is run the make file and register the resulting proxy/stub DLL. If we put two custom build steps into our project, the whole process is automated. We illustrate this with a simple EXE server that returns the name of the computer the server is running on. We also use this example in the next chapter when we discuss DCOM.

CUSTOM INTERFACE EXAMPLE

We will create a server **Name.exe** that hosts a COM class with the custom interface **IMachine**. This interface has a single method, **GetName**, that returns a string containing the name of the machine on which the server is running. The following steps describe how to implement this server. You can follow along and create your own server in the **Chap9\Demos** directory. The final project is available in **Chap9\Name**.

1. Use the ATL COM AppWizard to create a new project "**Name**." In Step 1, choose "Executable (EXE)" for the Server Type.
2. Insert a new ATL object "**Machine**." Accept all the default names. The attributes will be Single Threading Model, Custom Interface, and No Aggregation.
3. Add a method **GetName** with an out parameter **BSTR* pName**.
4. Implement **GetName** with the following code. We use the Win32 function **GetComputerName** and the ATL wrapper class **CComBSTR**.

```
STDMETHODIMP CMachine::GetName(BSTR *pName)
{
  char buf[MAX_COMPUTERNAME_LENGTH + 1];
  DWORD size = MAX_COMPUTERNAME_LENGTH + 1;
  ::GetComputerName(buf, &size);
```

Chapter 9 • EXE Servers

```
       CComBSTR bstr(buf);
       *pName = bstr;
       return S_OK;
}
```

   5. Add the two following custom build steps to run the make file building the proxy/stub DLL and register it. See Figure 9–8. You can bring up the dialog box shown from the menu Project | Settings.

```
nmake Nameps.mk
regsvr32 Nameps.dll
```

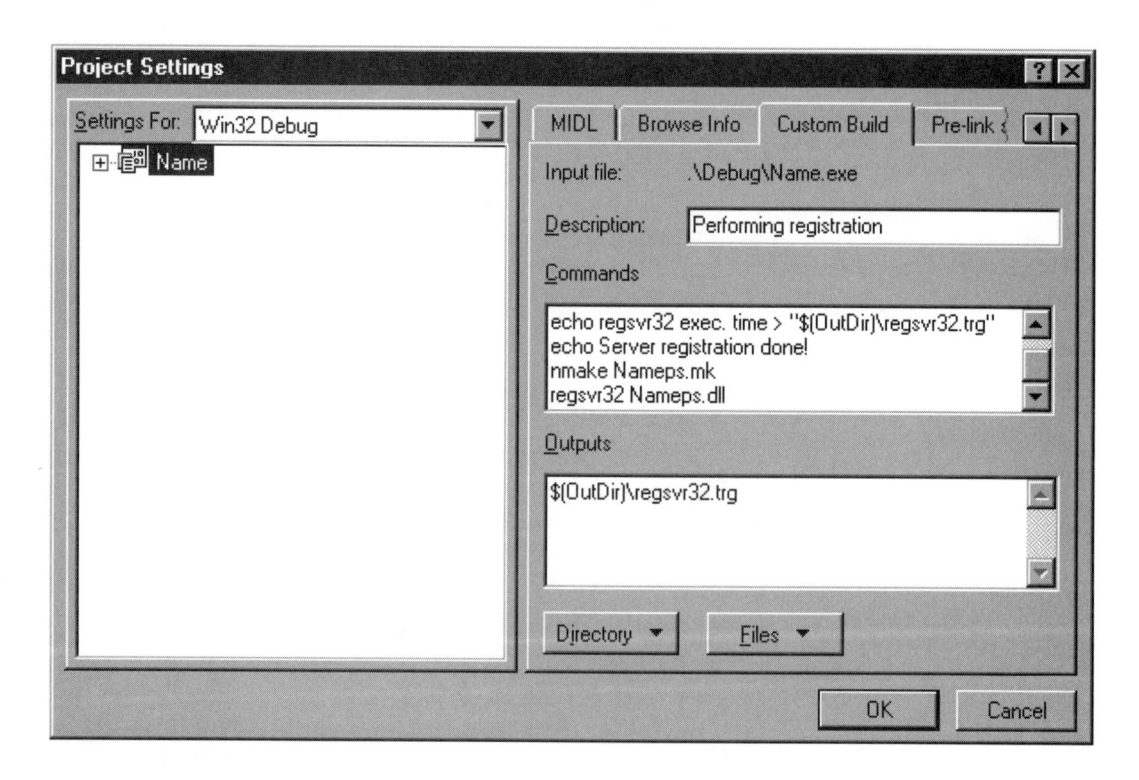

Figure 9–8 *Adding custom build steps for the proxy/stub DLL*

   6. Build the project. You can then examine the Registry entries using OLE/COM Object Viewer. A test program is provided (**Chap9\NameTest**). To apply the test program to your own server, copy the files **name.h** and **name_i.c** to the test directory. The test program is set up to work with the server in **Chap9\Name**. Figure 9–9 shows the output from running the test program.

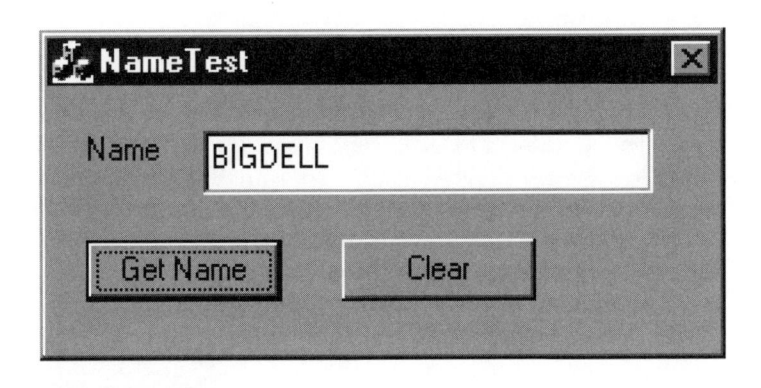

EXE Servers Using ATL

[Figure 9-9: NameTest dialog with Name field "BIGDELL", Get Name and Clear buttons]

Figure 9-9 *Test program to obtain name of server computer*

EXE Server Files

There are a number of important files associated with an ATL EXE server project besides the source code. The important files for the **Name** project include the following. The first files are created by the wizards:

Name.rgs	Registry script file
Name.idl	Interface definitions
Nameps.mk	Make file for proxy/stub DLL

The following files are created by the MIDL compiler:

Name.h	Interface definitions
Name_i.c	Definitions of all GUIDs (use in only one compilation unit)
Name_p.c	Implementation for proxy/stub code
dlldata.c	Marshaling code for parameters of interfaces

The following files are created by building the project:

Name.tlb	Binary type library describing the objects and their interfaces (if there is a library statement in the IDL)
Name.exe	Server executable file
Nameps.dll	Proxy/stub DLL

Summary

EXE servers are historically important because they were the first ones to be implemented using modern OLE, based on COM. There were predecessor technologies such as DDE, but OLE was the first to deliver robust application integration. But such EXE servers are not quite what is meant today by "component software." They provide in effect an "API" into an existing application, rather than create reusable primitive components. But it is important to understand the architecture of EXE servers because all distributed applications employ them, whether implemented by the programmer or provided by the system through a surrogate, as in COM+.

We examined in some detail the structure of EXE servers and implemented at the raw COM level a simple EXE server supporting only standard interfaces. The biggest structural difference from DLL servers is that an EXE server creates all class factories on program startup and registers them with COM. Other differences include hiding the main window and implementing correct unloading procedures. Then we looked at the use of ATL for implementing EXE servers. Custom interfaces can be supported by using MIDL to create a proxy/stub DLL.

In the next chapter we carry local/remote transparency a step further and introduce distributed COM or DCOM. All the hard work is done by the system, and knowledge of how to create EXE servers running locally will immediately translate into creating DCOM servers.

T E N

Introduction to DCOM

W_e come at last to distributed computing. One of the nice things about COM is that the features that support distributed computing were not an afterthought but are an integral part of the object model. As a result, everything you have learned up until now remains valid in the distributed case. In fact, the way a client calls an object is exactly the same whether the object is across a network, in a local EXE server, or even in a DLL in the same address space. We have called this feature of COM "local/remote transparency."

In this chapter we take our first look at DCOM. We cover it in much greater depth in Part 3, including the vital topic of security, and with an emphasis on the many powerful features provided by COM+ to support distributed applications. But DCOM is such an integral part of COM that it is appropriate to begin our discussion now while we are examining fundamentals. We first show how to distribute an *existing* application without making any code changes. The fact that this can be done, and in fact is very easy, is quite remarkable. The key to making this happen is the Registry. We will then look at the programming features of DCOM. There are some additional data structures, interfaces, and API functions that can provide greater flexibility and superior performance. We also discuss some of the things that the DCOM infrastructure itself does to promote efficiency. Finally, we discuss the overall DCOM architectural model, including topics such as the role of the Service Control Manager (SCM), how data is moved across the network, the role of surrogates for giving access to a DLL server, the DCOM network architecture, and some of the issues of multithreading.

Remoting an Existing COM Object

To demonstrate how COM and DCOM are related, let us remote an existing EXE server. The server simply returns the name of the machine it is running on. For the server program we will make some Registry entries on the local and remote machines, but we will leave the server itself unchanged. We will not have to make any changes to the client.

Existing COM Server

Our COM server is the **Name** program we developed in Chapter 9 (**Chap9\Name**). The class has a single interface, **IMachine**, with one method, **GetName**, which returns a string giving the name of the computer on which the server is running. The client program is **Chap9\NameTest**, which has a simple form with a button you can click to fetch the machine name.

DCOM Demo

1. On a remote machine create a directory **Test** with subdirectory **Debug**. Copy **Name.exe** to the **Debug** directory, and copy **Nameps.dll** and **NameTest.exe** to the **Test** directory. Also copy the four registration batch files to **Test**.
2. Register the server by running **reg_name.bat** and register the proxy/stub by running **reg_nameps.bat**. At the remote machine run **NameTest.exe**. You should be able to get the name of the remote machine. This is not DCOM—you are just running the client and server together on another machine.
3. Now return to your local machine, and make sure that the server and proxy/stub are registered. Run **NameTest.exe** and verify that you can display the name of the local computer.
4. We will now configure the client computer to run the *remote* server in place of the local one. This is easy to do by running **dcomcnfg.exe**, which you can start using "Run." In the dialog that comes up, find "Name" in the list of applications. See Figure 10–1.
5. With "Name" selected, click the Properties button. Clear the check for "Run application on this computer" and check "Run application on the following computer." Click the Browse button and find the remote computer where you registered the server. See Figure 10–2. Click OK and OK.

Remoting an Existing COM Object **205**

Figure 10–1 *DCOMCNFG program*

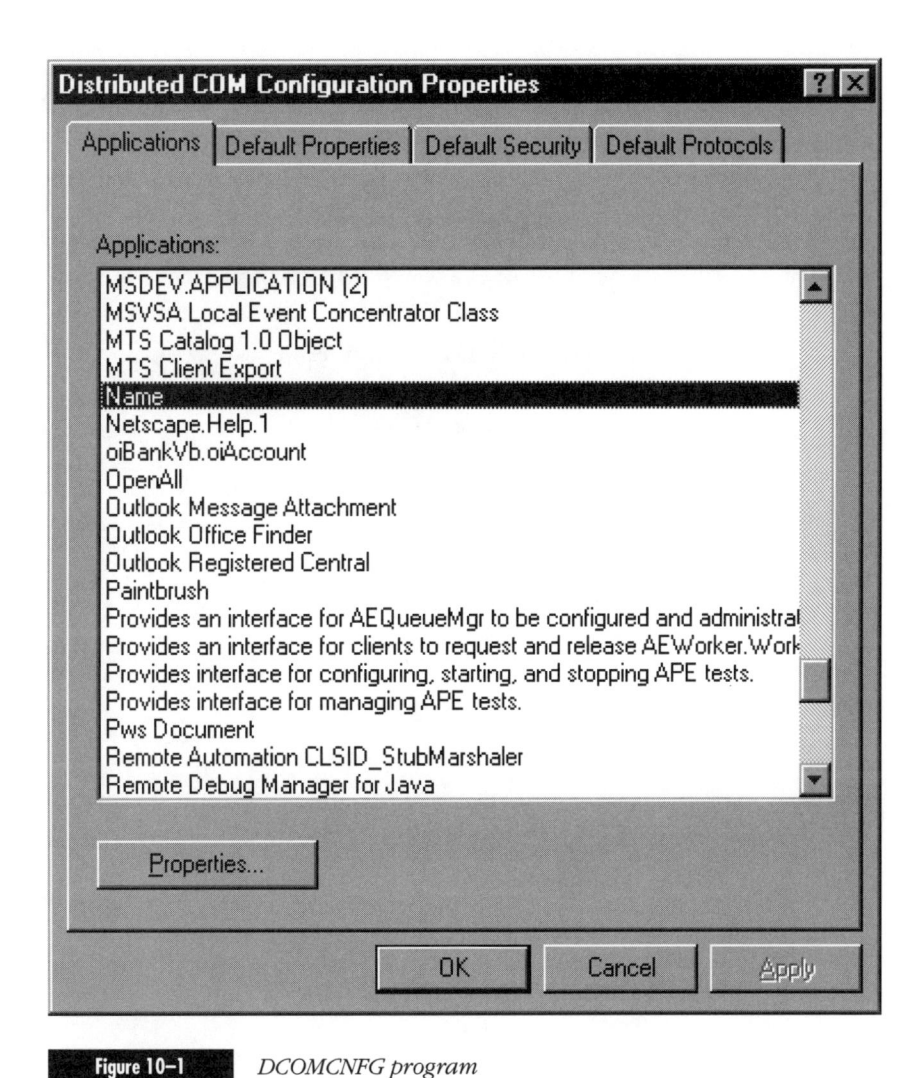

6. Now run the client **NameTest.exe** program on the local computer and click "Get Name." After a pause, you should see the name of the remote computer come up. Through DCOM you are calling the server on the remote machine. See Figure 10–3.

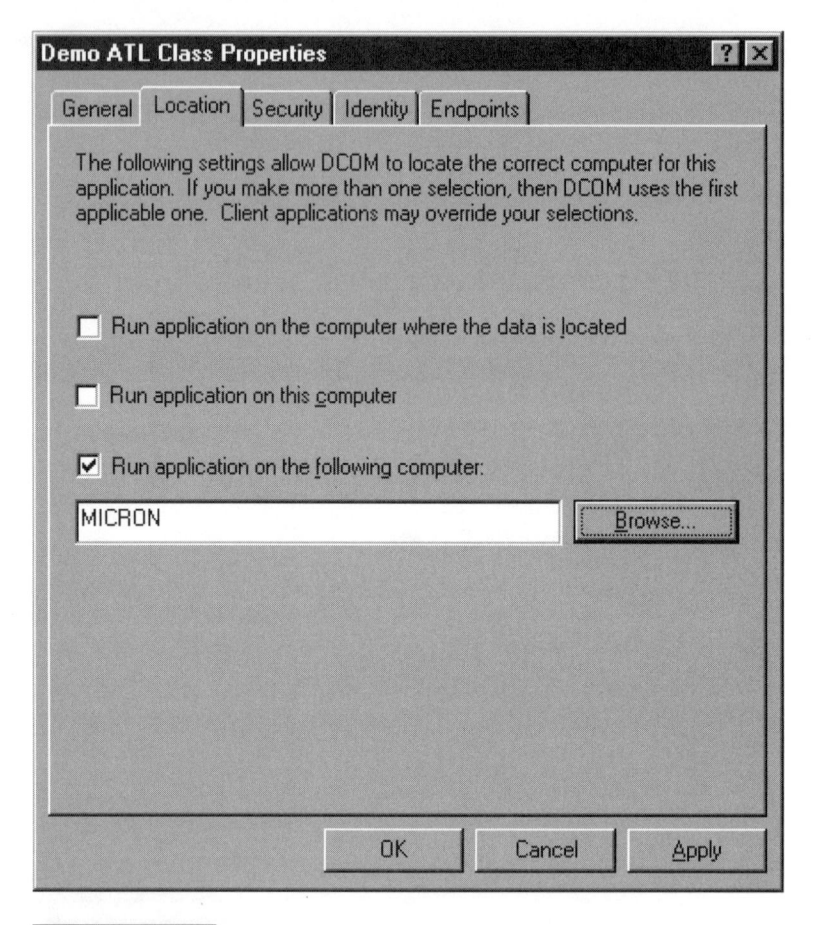

Figure 10-2 *Configuring server to run remotely*

Figure 10-3 *Displaying the name of the remote computer*

Security Issue

If you are using Windows 2000 as the server machine for **Name.exe**, there may be an issue with the default security settings, and the above demo may not run. If you have difficulty with the demo, bring up **dcomcnfg.exe** and choose the third tab, "Default Security." See Figure 10–4.

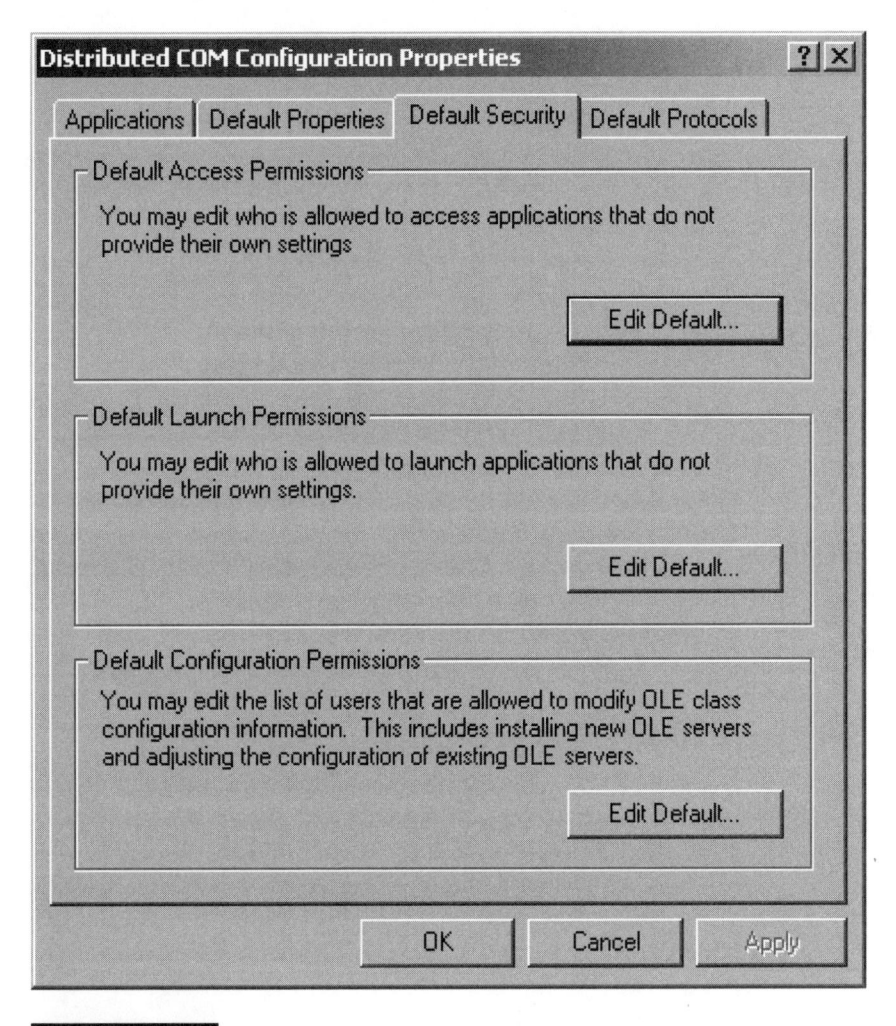

Figure 10–4   *Setting default security using DCOMCNFG.EXE*

Click on "Edit Default" in the "Default Access Permissions" area. The "Registry Value Permissions" window will come up showing you a list of groups and users who by default have access permission to DCOM servers.

See Figure 10–5. (If you don't see any entries in this window, you may be on Windows 2000 Professional and not have access to the user administration tools. Try working on your Windows 2000 Server machine.)

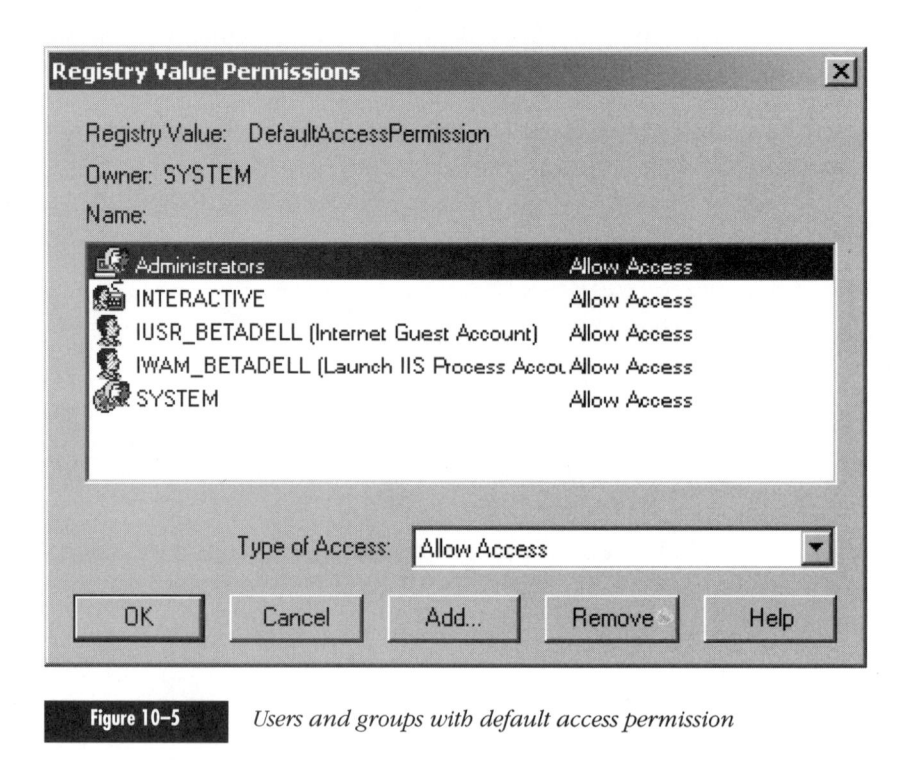

Figure 10–5 *Users and groups with default access permission*

The user account under which the client program runs should be on this list (either as a user or through a group the user is a member of). On Windows 2000, you may find that "Administrators" (or "Domain Administrators") may not be given default access permission out of the box. If that is the case on your machine, click the "Add" button and add an appropriate group or user. You must reboot the machine for the change in setting to take effect immediately. Similarly you should check "Default Launch Permissions" and add a user or group if necessary.

Besides default permissions, the DCOM security system allows you to make security settings individually for particular server applications. When you bring up Properties for an application, besides setting the "Location" you can set the "Security." You can either use default access and launch permissions or else set up custom permissions.

Security is discussed in detail in Chapter 17.

Registry Entries

It is appropriate entries in the Registry that makes all of this work. The batch files made entries in the Registry by invoking self-registration of the EXE server and the proxy/stub DLL. Some changes were made to the Registry by running the DCOMCNFG program. We begin by looking at the Registry entries on the remote machine, where the server is configured in the ordinary way. As usual, OLE/COM Object Viewer is a useful tool. We then examine the entries on the local machine that cause calls to the object to be directed to the remote server.

PROXY/STUB REGISTRY ENTRIES

The first thing to decipher is how the proxy/stub gets invoked. The proxy/stub is keyed from the *interface ID*. After all, it is method calls on interfaces that get marshaled. Start OLE/COM Object Viewer, open up "Interfaces" (at the very end of the list in the left panel), and you will see a list of interfaces arranged alphabetically by name. Look for "IMachine." See Figure 10–6.

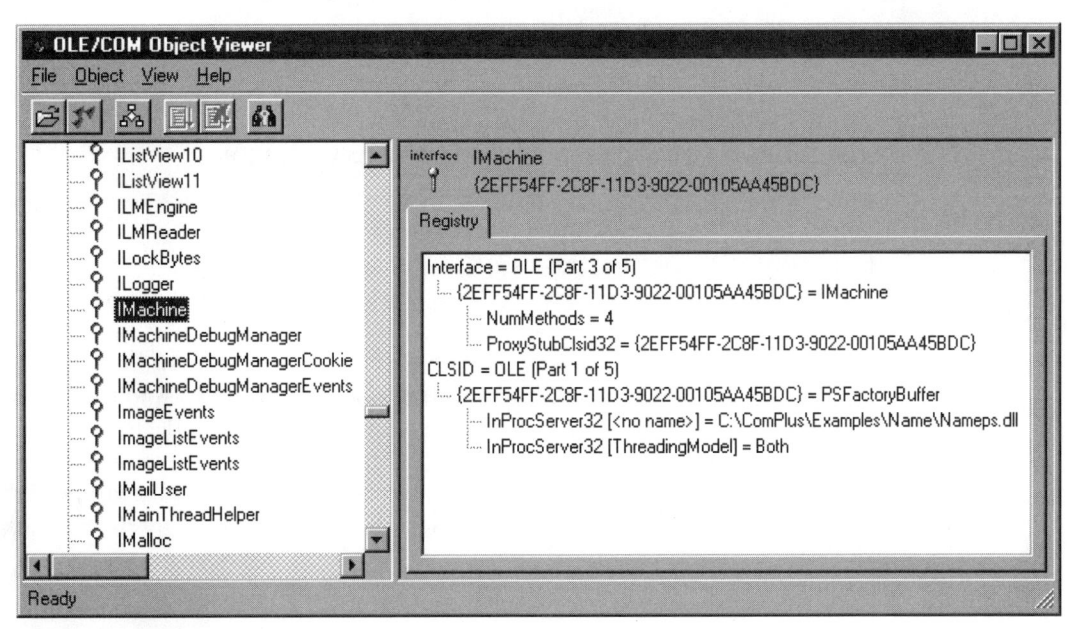

Figure 10–6 *An interface ID in the Registry*

Look for the key **ProxyStubClsid32** and find the numerical CLSID value. This is the CLSID of a DLL server—the proxy/stub DLL. To prove this, start the Registry editor and look for this CLSID. See Figure 10–7. Under the CLSID you will find an **InProcServer32** key, which sure enough points to the proxy/stub DLL, **nameps.dll**. If you look back at Figure 10–6 you will see that OLE/COM Object Viewer looks up this CLSID for us.

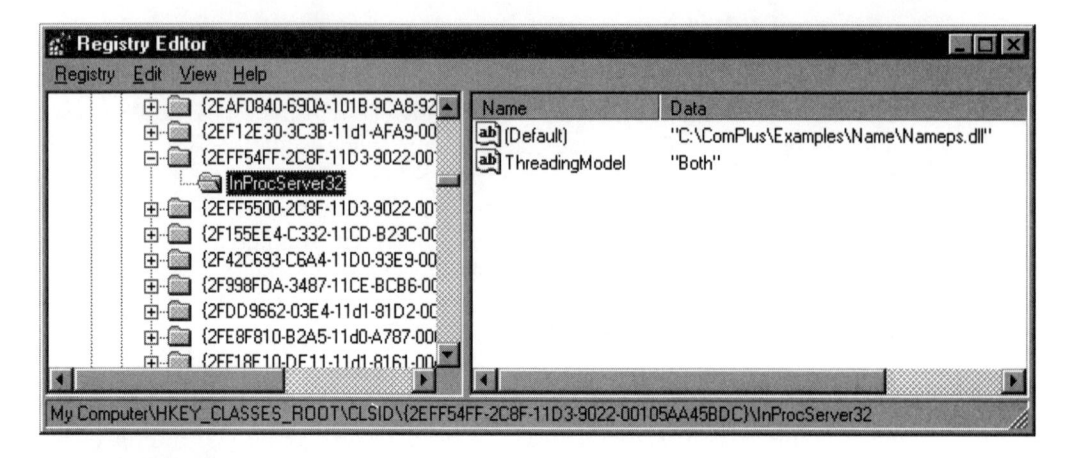

Figure 10–7   *Proxy/stub class ID directs us to the proxy/stub DLL*

APPID REGISTRY ENTRIES FOR A LOCAL EXE SERVER

Now let us examine the CLSID of the EXE Server (on the remote machine, which has not been configured for DCOM). In OLE/COM Object Viewer look for "Machine Class." We will see the familiar CLSID, ProgID, TypeLib, etc. But there is a new kid on the block—an "Application ID" or **AppID**. See Figure 10–8.

If we root around we won't find much interesting. There is just a string "Name" associated with the numerical AppID. You can find this string in a list of AppIDs in OLE/COM Object Viewer. In fact, Application IDs are one of the major groupings of entities in OLE/COM Object Viewer. See Figure 10–9. But you won't find anything interesting underneath the AppID. At this point the AppID is merely a placeholder. It becomes interesting for DCOM.

Remoting an Existing COM Object 211

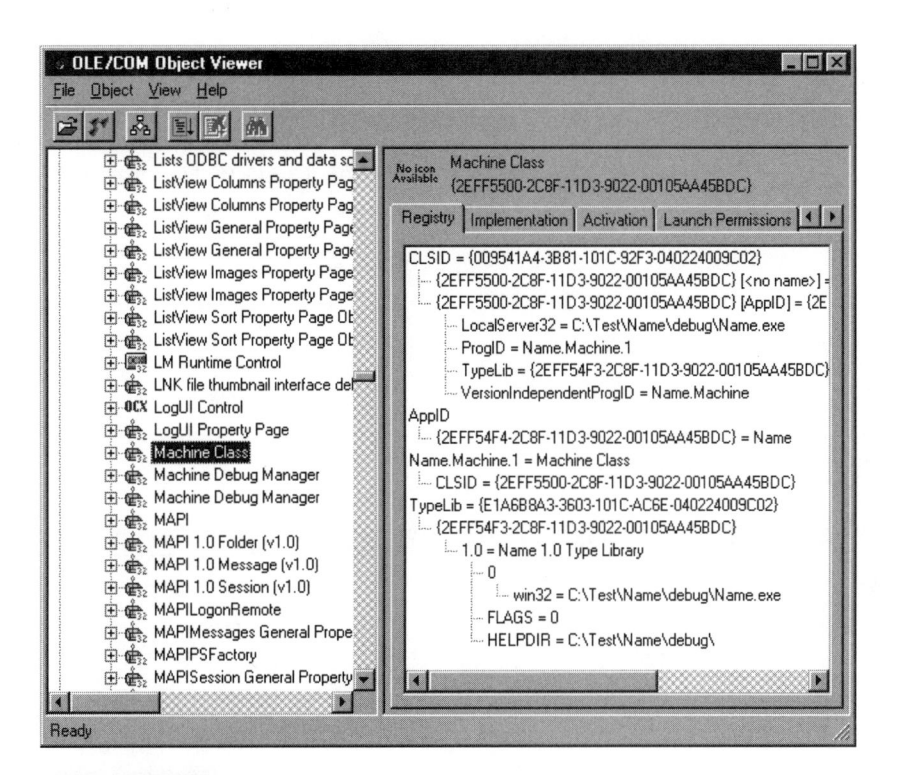

Figure 10-8 *An EXE server has an AppID*

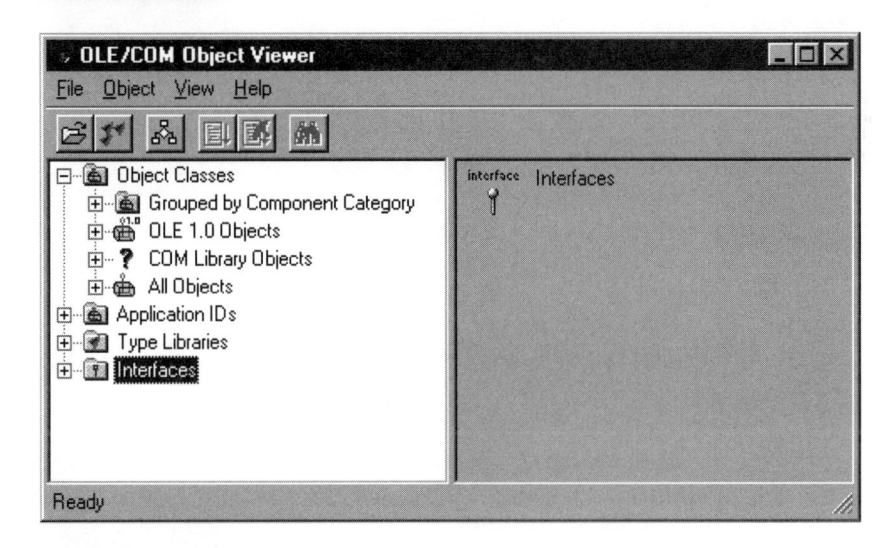

Figure 10-9 *The four major kinds of GUIDs shown in OLE/COM Object Viewer*

APPID AND REGISTRY ENTRIES FOR DCOM

We can now see the role of **AppID** in configuring an EXE server to run remotely. You have already configured your client machine to run **Name.exe** remotely. You did that using the DCOMCNFG program. Run DCOMCNFG again. The first window shows a list of Applications, shown by their string representation. This is merely a listing of all the entries under the **AppID** key in the Registry, as you can verify by comparing the list shown by DCOMCNFG with the entries under "Application IDs" in OLE/COM Object Viewer.

Now look for the entries for our **Name** application. You will see a named value "Remote Server Name" which is assigned to the name of the remote computer ("MICRON" on my network). That is exactly the name that is shown when we run the client program to find the name of the server. See Figure 10–10.

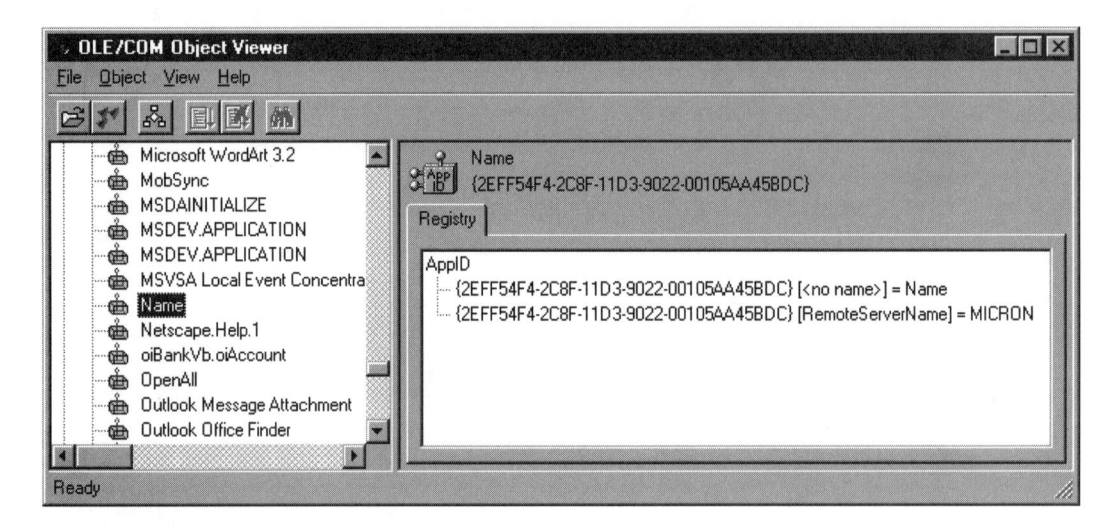

Figure 10–10 *The AppID is used to identify the computer on which the remote server runs*

Programming for DCOM

We have just seen how easy it is to make an existing COM object run remotely, without any DCOM specific code. However, when you know you are working in a DCOM environment, there may be optimizations that you would like to make so that your distributed application will run better. After all, the "transparency" between local and remote is only in the fact that they both run, not *how* they run. In this section, we will examine various programming considerations for DCOM.

Among the programming considerations are:

- The client may want to specify the server.
- Optimizations exist to minimize network traffic.
- Security access can be implemented on the client or server side.
- Programmers do not have to write network RPC code.
- Multithreading on the server is a significant issue.

Client Specifies the Server

The client can decide whether it wants to use the Registry settings for the server location, or specify the server location itself. To illustrate, let us first go back to DCOMCNFG and restore the settings for our **Name** server to always run locally (on this computer). See Figure 10–11.

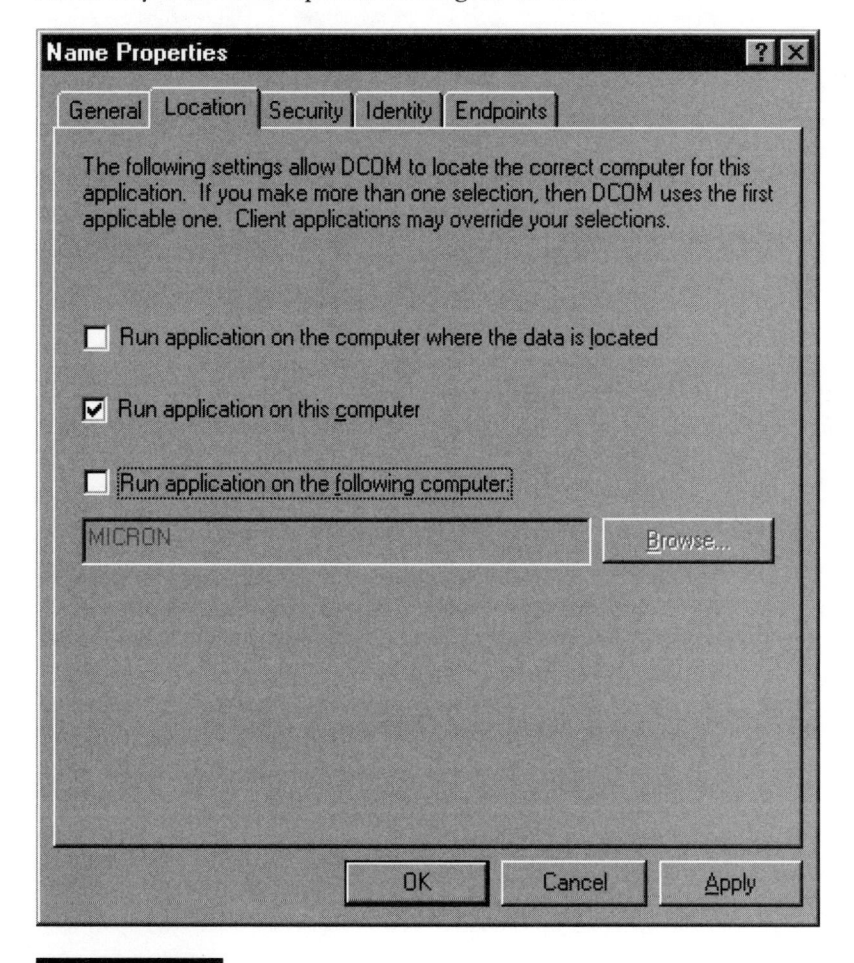

Figure 10-11 *Restoring Registry settings to run locally*

Chapter 10 • Introduction to DCOM

Now build the version of the **NameTest** client application in this chapter (**Chap10\NameTest**) and run it. With the Local/Remote option you can choose whether to rely on the Registry settings or to specify the server. See Figure 10–12.

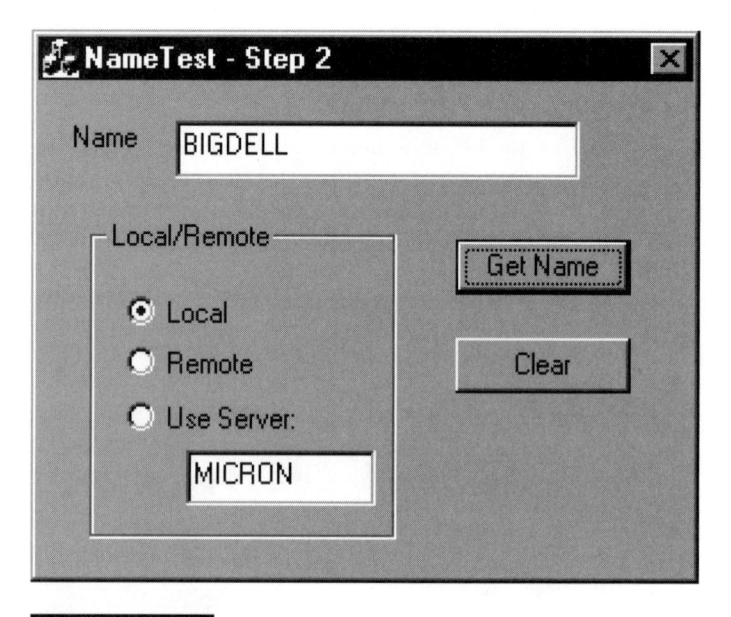

Figure 10–12 *Using Registry settings or specifying server*

Let us exercise this program a little with these Registry settings. Type in the name of your remote server and choose the "Local" option. You retrieve the name of the local computer, because that is the machine on which the server is running. Now choose "Use Server" option. The program will now run code that uses the server name to decide where the server should be run (we will shortly examine the code). Try it. The name retrieved should indeed be the same name you typed in for the server. Now try typing in some other name, either for a computer where the server is not installed, or just some random name. The function **CoCreateInstanceEx** fails. Finally try the "Remote" option. Again **CoCreateInstanceEx** fails, because the Registry was not configured for running remotely.

For the final set of experiments, change the Registry settings again. Go back to DCOMCNFG. This time check *both* "Run application on this computer" and "Run application on the following computer," where you specify the name of your remote computer. See Figure 10–13.

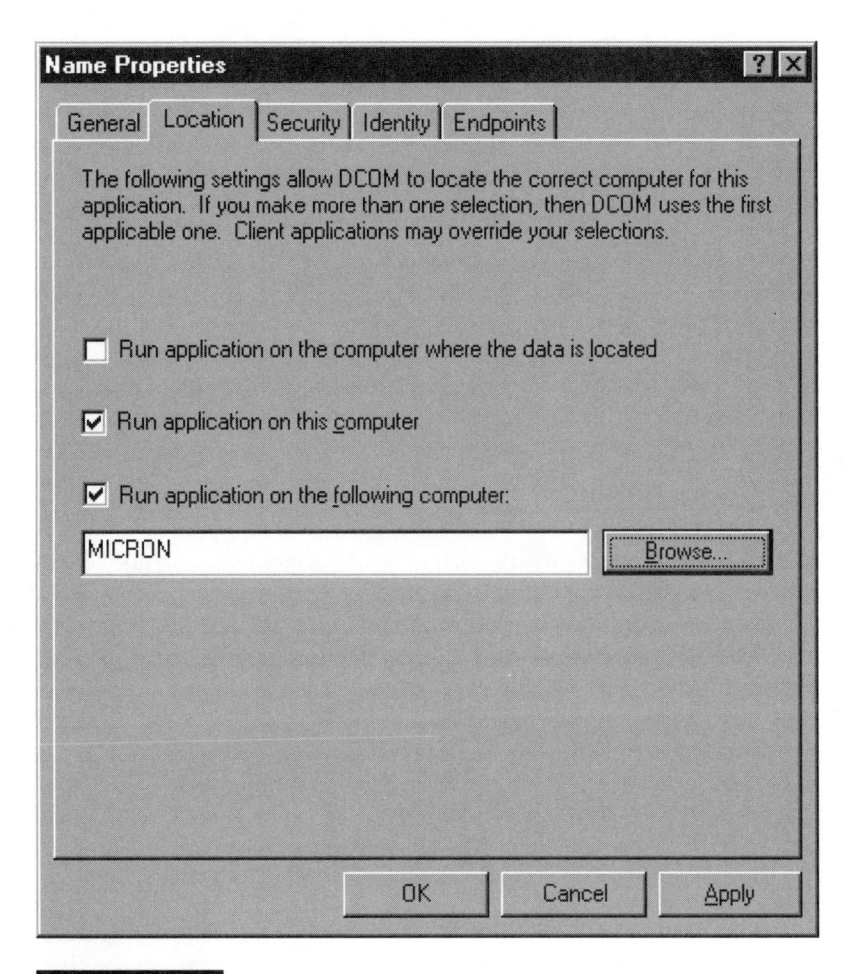

Figure 10-13 *Registry settings for both local and remote operation*

Now you should be able to exercise all three of the options "Local," "Remote," and "Use Server." The first option will return the name of the local computer. The second option will return the name of the computer that is specified in the Registry for running the application. The third option will return the name of whatever computer you specify as your server. If you have another computer available on your network for testing purposes, you could install the server on this computer too and verify that you can indeed reach any computer that you specify.

The very important capability of DCOM demonstrated in this example is that it is perfectly feasible to specify at *run time* the computer on which a server application may run. A natural question arises at this point: what about load balancing? Rather than either hardwiring a specific computer into the Registry or having the client application determine where the server should be run, it would be preferable in many cases to have the *system* determine where the server should run. We would like the system to choose a lightly loaded server in order to achieve better performance. This kind of load balancing is one of the features that is provided by COM+ and is discussed in Chapter 23.

DCOM Implementation

It is instructive to examine the code of the client program just demonstrated. There are a number of features that are used in the code. The first is a new execution context. If the client wishes to allow the object to run remotely, CLSCTX_REMOTE_SERVER can be specified as one of the flags in the context parameter. The second feature is a data structure, COSERVERINFO, that can be used for specifying the name of the remote machine. The third feature is an extended version of the API for instantiating objects, **CoCreateInstanceEx**. Instead of returning a single interface pointer, this function returns an array of interface pointers, specified in another new data structure, MULTI_QI.

EXECUTION CONTEXT

There are four possible execution contexts for an object:

CLSCTX_INPROC_SERVER	Code for this object runs as a DLL in the same address space as the client.
CLSCTX_INPROC_HANDLER	Code is an "object handler," which is a DLL that provides a partial implementation of the object's functions.
CLSCTX_LOCAL_SERVER	Code for this object runs as an EXE on the same machine as the client.
CLSCTX_REMOTE_SERVER	Code for this object runs as an EXE on a different machine.

The most common ones, and the only ones we will use in this book, are the three server choices. The flag CLSCTX_ SERVER is a combination of the three server options. The execution context is used as a parameter by the client when calling **CoGetClassObject**, **CoCreateInstance** and **CoCreateInstanceEx**. It is also used as a parameter by an EXE server when calling **CoRegisterClassObject**.

COSERVERINFO

This data structure is used to identify a remote machine. It can also be used to override the default activation security settings. The following is the structure definition:

```
typedef struct _COSERVERINFO
{
  DWORD dwReserved1;
  LPWSTR pwszName;
  COAUTHINFO  *pAuthInfo;
  DWORD dwReserved2;
} COSERVERINFO;
```

The field of interest to us is **pwszName**, which is used to specify the name of the remote machine.

COCREATEINSTANCEEX

The key function for client-side control of DCOM is an extension of the basic API function **CoCreateInstance**.

```
HRESULT CoCreateInstanceEx(
    REFCLSID rclsid,           // CLSID of object to be created
    IUnknown* pUnkOuter,       // controlling unknown
    DWORD dwContext,           // execution context
    COSERVERINFO* pServerInfo// name of remote machine
    ULONG cmq,                 // count of number of interfaces
    MULTI_QI* qi               // array of MULTI_QI structures
);
```

We will pass NULL for the second parameter since we are not doing aggregation. The fifth and sixth parameters allow us to get an array of interface pointers, which is an optimization to minimize network traffic.

_WIN32_DCOM Flag

A Preprocessor Constant
To use certain extended DCOM functions such as **CoCreateInstanceEx**, you must define the preprocessor constant _WIN32_DCOM.
You can do this in Project | Settings, C/C++, Preprocessor category.

MULTI_QI

This data structure is what allows getting back an array of interface pointers with one trip across the network. The first parameter is an input parameter for passing the interface ID of requested interface. The second parameter is an output parameter to get back the corresponding interface pointer. The third parameter gives the HRESULT from querying for the particular interface pointer.

```
typedef struct _MULTI_QI
{
    const IID* pIID;
    IUnknown * pItf;
    HRESULT hr;
} MULTI_QI;
```

CLIENT CODE EXAMPLE

The code for the client program should now be easy to understand. It is an MFC dialog-based application. See file **NameTest.Dlg.cpp** in **Chap10\NameTest**. There is an **enum** data type for the radio button choices, and then all the interesting code is in the handler for the "Get Name" button.

```
// NameTestDlg.cpp : implementation file
...

enum ServerTypes {Local, Remote, CoServerInfo};

void CNameTestDlg::OnGetname()
{
  IMachine* pMachine;
  HRESULT hr;

  COSERVERINFO serverinfo;
  COSERVERINFO* pServerInfo;
  DWORD dwContext;
  MULTI_QI qi = {&IID_IMachine, NULL, 0};

  UpdateData();

  if (m_LocalRemote == Local)
  {
    pServerInfo = NULL;
    dwContext = CLSCTX_LOCAL_SERVER;
  }
  else if (m_LocalRemote == Remote)
  {
```

```cpp
    pServerInfo = NULL;
    dwContext = CLSCTX_REMOTE_SERVER;
  }
  else if (m_LocalRemote == CoServerInfo)
  {
    serverinfo.dwReserved1 = 0;
    serverinfo.dwReserved2 = 0;
    serverinfo.pwszName =
      m_ServerName.AllocSysString();
    serverinfo.pAuthInfo = NULL;
    pServerInfo = &serverinfo;
    dwContext = CLSCTX_REMOTE_SERVER;
  }
  else
    return;

  hr = CoCreateInstanceEx(CLSID_Machine, NULL, dwContext,
        pServerInfo, 1, &qi);
  if (SUCCEEDED(hr) && SUCCEEDED(qi.hr))
  {
    pMachine = (IMachine* )qi.pItf;
    BSTR bstr;
    hr = pMachine->GetName(&bstr);
    if (SUCCEEDED(hr))
    {
      _bstr_t name(bstr);
      SetDlgItemText(IDC_NAME,
          (const char*) name);
    }
    else
    {
      MessageBox("GetName failed");
      SetDlgItemText(IDC_NAME, "??");
    }
    pMachine->Release();
  }
  else
  {
    MessageBox("CoCreateInstanceEx failed");
    SetDlgItemText(IDC_NAME, "??");
  }
}
```

DCOM and the Registry

As with COM, the location of the server in the file system is specified in the Registry. Which machine to launch the server on is specified either in the Registry or by the client in a call to **CoGetClassObject** or **CoCreateInstanceEx**.

Various security options for an object can be specified in the Registry (launch permissions, access permissions, impersonation). Security is a large and important topic which we discuss in Chapter 17.

The Registry contains a "master switch" which you can use for disabling DCOM on your machine, if you wish. Set **EnableDCOM** under HKEY_LOCAL_MACHINE\SOFTWARE\MICROSOFT\OLE to "**N**." Setting the key back to "**Y**" reenables DCOM. You can set this flag in DCOMCNFG through the "Default Properties" tab of the first screen that comes up when you start DCOMCNFG.

Optimizing Network Traffic

A very important consideration in DCOM is the optimization of network traffic. There are two aspects to this optimization. The first is coding by the application programmer. DCOM provides several extensions that enable a programmer to minimize trips across the network. The second aspect is optimization performed by the DCOM infrastructure itself.

PROGRAMMER OPTIMIZATIONS

A common aspect of COM programming is obtaining interface pointers. An initial interface pointer is obtained by **CoCreateInstance**. As we have seen, DCOM provides the extended function **CoCreateInstanceEx** that allows several interface pointers to be obtained in one trip across the network.

For an example, look at the DCOM version of the bank account example. Our object supports two custom interfaces, **IAccount** and **IDisplay**. The semantics of the **Show** method of **IDisplay** has been changed to return the balance rather than put up a message box, which would be inappropriate behavior for a remote server. The test client allows you to choose the program ID at run time, so you could test with several different servers on different nodes on your network. You may choose a local or remote server. When you connect to the servers the starting balance will be shown. When you make a deposit or withdrawal, the balance is not automatically shown. You must use the "Show" button. See Figure 10–14.

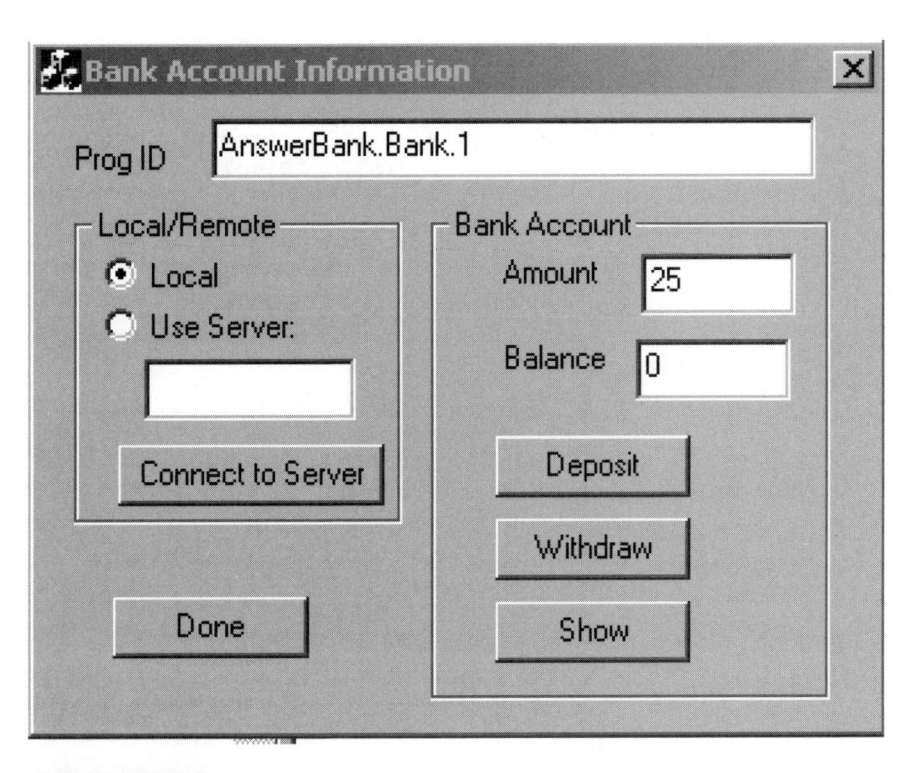

Programming for DCOM

Figure 10-14 *Client program for DCOM version of bank account server*

The DCOM version of the server is in the folder **Chap10\Accdcom\Server** and the client program is in the folder **Chap10\Accdcom\Client**. Here is the code from the client (file **dcomcDlg.cpp**).

```
void CDcomcDlg::OnConnect()
{
  CLSID clsid;
  HRESULT hr;

  UpdateData();

  hr = AfxGetClassIDFromString(m_progid, &clsid);
  if (FAILED(hr))
  {
    MessageBox("Could not get class id");
    return;
  }

  COSERVERINFO serverinfo;
```

```
            COSERVERINFO* pServerInfo;
            DWORD dwContext;

            MULTI_QI qi[2] =   {{&IID_IAccount, NULL, 0},
                                {&IID_IDisplay, NULL, 0}};

            if (m_nLocalRemote == 0)
            {
              pServerInfo = NULL;
              dwContext = CLSCTX_LOCAL_SERVER;
            }
            else
            {
             serverinfo.dwReserved1 = 0;
             serverinfo.dwReserved2 = 0;
             serverinfo.pwszName =
                m_strServer.AllocSysString();
             serverinfo.pAuthInfo = NULL;
             pServerInfo = &serverinfo;
             dwContext = CLSCTX_REMOTE_SERVER;
            }

            hr = CoCreateInstanceEx(clsid, NULL, dwContext,
                                    pServerInfo, 2, qi);

            if (SUCCEEDED(hr))
            {
              m_pAccount = (IAccount* )qi[0].pItf;
              m_pDisplay = (IDisplay* )qi[1].pItf;

              int nBalance = -1;

              m_pAccount->GetBalance(&nBalance);
              SetDlgItemInt(IDC_BALANCE, nBalance);
            }
            else
              MessageBox("Could not connect to server.",
                  "OnConnect");
        }
```

IMULTIQI

You can get multiple interfaces at one time when you create an object by using **CoCreateInstanceEx**. After an object is created, you can get a new interface by calling **QueryInterface**, which gives one interface at a time. You can also query for multiple interfaces by using the interface **IMultiQI** which has the single method **QueryMultipleInterfaces**. This call can return multiple interfaces in an array of MULTI_QI.

A nice thing about **IMultiQI** is that it is available for free. It does not have to be implemented by an object you implement (unlike **IUnknown**, which you must implement yourself). Every COM object proxy provides this interface. You can see this interface in OLE/COM Object Viewer if you open up an EXE server. See Figure 10–15, which is for the EXE version of the bank account server.

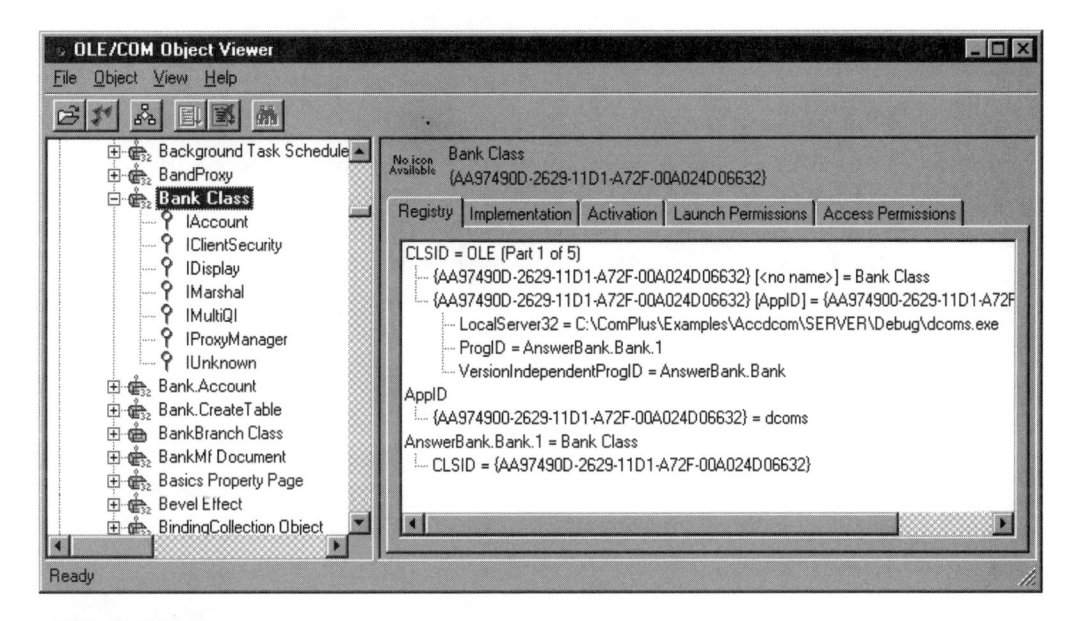

Figure 10–15 *IMultiQI is available for free*

OPTIMIZATIONS BY THE DCOM INFRASTRUCTURE

Besides providing data structures and functions that you can use to optimize network traffic in DCOM, the system infrastructure itself performs some optimizations for you automatically. Consider the issue of reference counting. DCOM caches all calls of **Release** by a client, and does not actually send any **Release** calls over the network until the client has driven its usage to zero. As a result, the actual reference count on the server is not guaranteed to be current, but that does not matter, because the only use for the reference count is to delete the object when it is no longer in use.

Another issue concerning deleting objects arises in DCOM. What happens if a client goes away without releasing its objects? This could happen, for example, if there is a network failure or if a client crashes. The server object then never receives **Release** from this client, and so the object will never be destroyed. Over a period of time, this could become a problem, resulting in much wasted memory on the server.

The DCOM solution is for the client to periodically "ping" the server announcing that it is alive. If the client misses sending three consecutive ping messages, the system presumes that the client is no longer alive, and it releases the references held by the client. This "ping" traffic could be considerable, and DCOM optimizes it by piggybacking all pings from all clients on one machine in a single tightly packed ping packet.

Security

Security is a very important issue in DCOM. There are two basic issues. Are users who they say they are? Can they do what they want to do? Since security is built into Windows NT, client security can be checked when launching DCOM servers. After launching, a server can always make NT security calls over the network. DCOM understands NT security to ensure that clients and servers are authenticated and authorized. In addition, access rights can be set on Registry keys. You can also check security on a per-call basis. Security can be specified on the client or the server side.

Since Windows 95/98 has no intrinsic security, you cannot automatically launch DCOM servers. On the other hand, Windows 2000 has substantially enhanced security, including the Kerberos security system. Security will be examined in detail in Chapter 17.

DCOM Architecture

We have seen how easy it is to remote an existing COM object by making some settings in the Registry, which is easy to do through the DCOMCNFG utility. We have also looked at how to explicitly program for DCOM using some of the data structures, functions, and interfaces. In this final section, we examine some of the architectural elements of DCOM, so that we can better understand what is happening when a client talks to a remote server via DCOM.

Launching a Server over the Network

Recall that the Service Control Manager (SCM) is the system service that is responsible for launching a COM server on a machine. SCM plays a vital role in DCOM. The Service Control Manager on the local machine tells the Service Control Manager on the remote machine to launch the server. If the server on the remote machine is an in-process server, the SCM launches a *surrogate* process between the client on the local machine and the in-process server on the remote machine. DCOM comes with a default surrogate **dllhost.exe**. This default surrogate is used by COM+, as we will see in Part 3. You can write your own custom surrogate for individual objects.

Under NT, the Service Control Manager is launched at startup. Under Windows 95/98, the SCM is launched after a call to **CoRegisterClassObject.** You can launch the SCM (**rpcss.exe**) manually, or add it to HKEY_LOCAL_ MACHINE\Software\Microsoft\Windows\CurrentVersion\RunServices to have it start at Windows startup.

Server Operation over the Network

DCOM determines if a client or server has died and provides the necessary notification. DCOM detects if a client has died through the ping mechanism described above. DCOM chooses the appropriate RPC protocol. Client and server have no knowledge of how the network communication is accomplished.

HOW IS DATA MOVED BETWEEN MACHINES?

Data must be marshaled between the client process on the client machine and the server process on the remote machine. Two issues are involved here. The first issue is that code has to be written to marshal the data and move it via the RPC mechanism. DLLs are used to marshal the data and move it. The DLL on the client side is called a proxy, on the server side, a stub. The RPC mechanism is hidden behind the proxies and stubs. There are some tracks of this process through the **IMarshal** interface that you can see when you open up an EXE server in the OLE/COM Object Viewer (see Figure 10–15). Just as with **IMultiQI**, you do not need to implement **IMarshal** yourself. The system-supplied marshaler works transparently with RPC. If you want to do something special, you can implement custom marshaling.

The second issue is that a description of the data is needed so that complex data structures can be moved. Data is described with the *Interface Description Language* in a platform- and language-independent manner. Microsoft's IDL compiler (MIDL) will generate the proxy and the stub with the appropriate descriptions so that the data can be marshaled. MIDL can also generate type libraries.

DCOM NETWORK ARCHITECTURE

Conceptually, the DCOM network architecture is very simple. The client makes an interface call to the proxy, which talks to RPC. RPC uses the underlying network protocol (for instance, TCP/IP) to cross machines. On the server machine, RPC talks to the stub, and the stub makes an interface call to the server.

From the client's perspective, the proxy is the object. The proxy object has to be registered on the client's machine. From the server's perspective, the stub is the client. The server object has to be registered on the server's machine. Figure 10–16 depicts this basic architecture.

Figure 10-16 *DCOM network architecture*

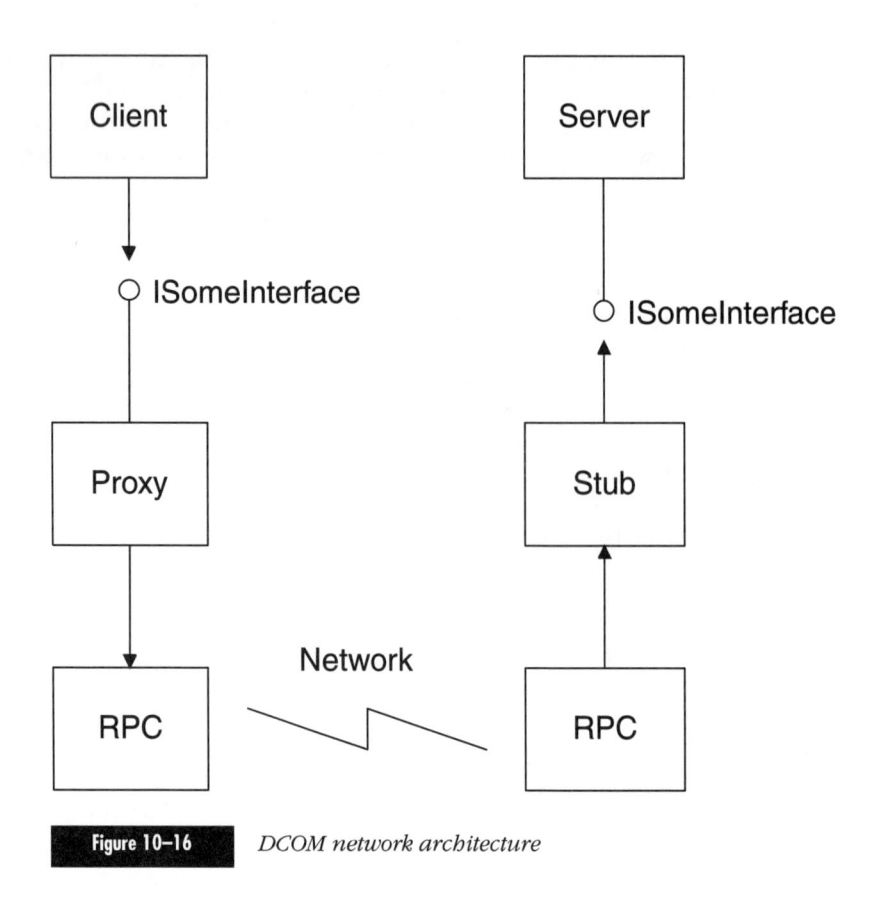

Multithreading Issues

What is wrong with the following standard COM code fragment?

```
ULONG ImyInterface::Release()
{
  m_lRef--;
  if (m_lRef == 0);
  {
    delete this;
    return 0;
  }
  else
    return m_lRef;
}
```

m_lRef decrement is NOT guaranteed to be an atomic operation. How much of a problem this is depends on how the COM object is invoked by different threads (Single, Apartment, or Free Threading Models). To avoid such problems, use **InterlockedIncrement** and **InterLockedDecrement** API functions instead of the increment and decrement operators.

This is a simple example of the type of problems that multithreading can pose.

WHY IS MULTITHREADING IMPORTANT IN DCOM?

DCOM components should be scalable. As time goes on, servers will want to handle several clients without blocking them. DCOM component methods might be invoked from different threads from the one they were created on. DCOM can compensate for the lack of multithreading support in components with marshaling and serialization of method calls, but this entails a performance penalty. Multithreading in COM is discussed in detail in Chapter 13.

Summary

DCOM is an integral feature of COM. COM objects can *automatically* be configured to be called by clients over a network without any change whatsoever in the code of either the client or server. The key to this remarkable fact is the system Registry and the COM run-time system. Through the Registry, you can configure the machine on which a server will run. There are a number of additional data structures, interfaces, and API functions that pertain to DCOM. By making use of these you can achieve greater flexibility and superior performance. The DCOM architectural model is quite simple, leveraging RPC to provide for the transparent calling of an object through a proxy.

DCOM is one of the fundamental protocols used by COM+ (the others are HTTP and MSMQ). In Part 3, we do a substantial amount of distributed programming, which rests on DCOM. This chapter should provide you with a good fundamental understanding for this later work.

ELEVEN

Automation and COM Programming Using Visual Basic

*A number of important concepts of COM programming address concerns of Visual Basic programmers. A common scenario is to create a component in one environment, such as Visual C++ and ATL, and see it deployed for use by client programs written in a number of different languages, including Visual Basic and scripting languages. Scripting languages, such as VBScript and JavaScript, present a particular challenge, because they must be able to utilize COM components without benefit of a compilation step. This means that the client program must be able to do "late binding" to the server. COM provides an interface **IDispatch** to support late binding. However, early binding is much more efficient, and so most COM components implement both a dispatch interface and a regular vtable interface—a so called "dual interface." The dispatch mechanism in COM is provided by a technology known as Automation, providing a way for users of applications to "automate" frequently performed tasks. More broadly, Automation is concerned with meeting the needs of Visual Basic programmers, including the basic model of methods, properties, and events. Automation is also concerned with a number of special data types, including VARIANT, Currency, and the BSTR that we have already seen. Automation provides a simple list mechanism known as a collection.*

There are five main sections to this chapter. The first section discusses the fundamental principles of Automation, including late binding (dispatch interface) and the VARIANT data type. The second section illustrates using a

COM Automation server implemented with ATL from an HTML page programmed with VBScript. This is the classic case where Automation is *required*, as VBScript is an interpreted language. In the third section, we gain a little more insight into the low-level infrastructure of Automation by examining a Visual C++ client program that calls **IDispatch** directly. We also provide an example program that illustrates creating a C++ automation controller using the ATL wrapper class **CComDispatchDriver**. In the fourth section, we review the basic property, method, and event model of Visual Basic and see how to implement COM classes that provide properties, methods, and events. Finally we discuss collections, including how to implement a collection in a server and how to access a collection in a client. Many standard COM servers have an "object model" that features both simple classes and collections.

Automation

Applications frequently provide mechanisms for advanced users to "automate" frequently used tasks. A macro language is used to program functionality in an application. But how can you automate a task that involves several applications? *Automation* provides a standard means for applications to expose their functionality. Data can be exposed through *properties*. Functions can be exposed through *methods*. The server is called a "programmable component" or "Automation object." The client is called an "Automation controller." The controller can be programmed in a high-level language, such as a dialect of Visual Basic, invoking functions in several different servers.

Properties and Methods

Individual Automation objects provide properties, which expose state through set and get functions, and methods, which perform actions. Properties and methods have names which are known outside the object. Properties have a type and methods have a signature that specifies the return type, number of parameters, and types of parameters. Properties can also have parameters.

Late Binding

To achieve programmability via a macro-like mechanism, Automation objects need to support "late binding" to their clients. A general-purpose application like a word processor cannot be compiled with knowledge of specific objects, as would be required for calling custom COM interfaces ("early binding"). Likewise, an interpreted language like VBScript cannot be compiled with knowledge of specific objects. Through late binding, an automation controller uses a single COM interface that allows invoking the properties and methods exposed by the object.

IDispatch

The fundamental COM interface that supports late binding is **IDispatch**. This interface does not have individual methods for the properties and methods of an Automation object. Rather **IDispatch** provides access to properties and methods through a single very general **Invoke** method. **Invoke** references properties, methods, and parameters by numeric IDs, called the dispatch IDs or dispids. The method **GetIDsOfNames** converts a property or method name and the associated parameter names to numerical values. Two other methods give access to *type information*. **GetTypeInfoCount** determines whether type information is available (1) or not available (0). **GetTypeInfo** retrieves the type information, if it is available.

Type Information

Type information is the Automation standard for describing exposed objects and their properties and methods. Besides exposing type information through methods of the **IDispatch** interface, COM supports special interfaces for providing type information. **ITypeInfo** provides information about the members of an object described in a type library. **ITypeLib** provides information about the objects in a type library. **ICreateTypeInfo** creates type information within a type library. **ICreateTypeLib** creates a type library.

Although type information originated with Automation, it is now considered fairly standard for other COM objects to provide type information, usually through a type library. We have already seen how ATL helps create a type library by compiling IDL code. We have also seen how Visual Basic programs use a type library (**New** operator), and Visual C++ clients that use smart pointers, import a type library.

Dual Interfaces

There are trade-offs in using a dispatch interface versus an ordinary COM vtable interface. A dispatch interface can be used by a wider variety of clients, including interpreted environments like VBScript. A vtable interface is more efficient, because it enables a direct call into the object without having to go through the elaborate dispatch mechanism. A *dual interface* is derived from **IDispatch** and can provide the best of both worlds. Properties and methods are implemented as additional COM methods after the four **IDispatch** methods. A dispatch interface is also provided, with properties and methods implemented by forwarding to the corresponding COM methods. Thus a class supporting a dual interface can be called with either early or late binding.

Besides the slight increase in code size caused by supporting both kinds of interfaces, there is a restriction on parameters. Parameters cannot be arbitrary C/C++ data types but must be restricted to the ones allowed by Automation.

VARIANTs

The key to understanding Automation is that Automation was created to support Visual Basic. Originally, Visual Basic was strictly an interpreted language, and hence late binding was a necessity. Also, Visual Basic is inherently an untyped language. It is perfectly legal to use variables in Visual Basic without declaring them to be of a particular type. (Modern VB programming practice recommends that you use the **Option Explicit** feature that forces you to declare variables.) A variable not declared to be of a specific type is treated as a VARIANT.

IDispatch::Invoke must pass a variety of data types as arguments and return values for Automation methods and properties. **IDispatch::Invoke** uses a VARIANT structure that is a tagged union. A VARIANT is defined as:

```
typedef struct tagVARIANT VARIANT;
typedef struct tagVARIANT VARIANTARG;
```

The VARTYPE field of the VARIANT determines the data type stored in the structure. COM provides several functions to ensure proper handling of Variants, including **VariantClear**, **VariantCopy**, **VariantInit** and **VariantChangeType**. ATL provides a variant wrapper class **CComVariant**. Visual C++ provides its own wrapper class **_variant_t**.

TAGVARIANT STRUCTURE

You can get an idea of the various types of data supported by a VARIANT by examining the **tagVARIANT** structure.

```
struct tagVARIANT {
  VARTYPE           vt;
  unsigned short    wReserved1;
  unsigned short    wReserved2;
  unsigned short    wReserved3;
  union {
    unsigned char   bVal;         //VT_UI1
    short           iVal;         //VT_I2
    long            lVal;         //VT_I4
    float           fltVal;       //VT_R4
    double          dblVal;       //VT_R8
    VARIANT_BOOL    boolVal;      //VT_BOOL
    SCODE           scode;        //VT_ERROR
    CY              cyVal;        //VT_CY
    DATE            date;         //VT_DATE
    BSTR            bstrVal;      //VT_BSTR
    IUnknown*       punkVal;      //VT_UNKNOWN
    IDispatch*      pdispVal;     //VT_DISPATCH
    SAFEARRAY*      parray;       //VT_ARRAY|*
    unsigned        char* pbVal;  //VT_BYREF|VT_UI1
```

```
    short*            piVal;       //VT_BYREF|VT_I2
    long*             plVal;       //VT_BYREF|VT_I4
    float*            pfltVal;     //VT_BYREF|VT_R4
    double*           pdblVal;     //VT_BYREF|VT_R8
    VARIANT_BOOL*     pboolVal;    //VT_BYREF|VT_BOOL
    SCODE*            pscode;      //VT_BYREF|VT_ERROR
    CY*               pcyVal;      //VT_BYREF|VT_CY
    DATE*             pdate;       //VT_BYREF|VT_DATE
    BSTR*             pbstrVal;    //VT_BYREF|VT_BSTR
    IUnknown**        ppunkVal;    //VT_BYREF|VT_UNKNOWN
    IDispatch**       ppdispVal;   //VT_BYREF|VT_DISPATCH
    SAFEARRAY**       pparray;     //VT_ARRAY|*
    VARIANT*          pvarVal;     //VT_BYREF|VT_VARIANT
  void*               byref;       //Generic ByRef
  };
};
```

Many of the data types in the structure are self-explanatory. The rather terse name **CY** represents the Visual Basic **Currency** data type.

Automation with ATL and VBScript

We can illustrate many of the ideas of Automation and multiple language development with a lightweight COM server that is implemented using Visual C++ and ATL and deployed on an HTML page, programmed via VBScript. The COM class supports a *dual* interface, and the dispatch interface is required for the VBScript code, which only does late binding.

ATL Automation Server

Our example server is in the directory **Chap11\BankDual**. It was created as an EXE server using the ATL COM AppWizard and the ATL Object Wizard. The ProgID is "Account.Answer.1" and the Type (friendly name for the user) is "Account Answer." In the Attributes page the Interface type was specified as "Dual" (the default). Build the project, which will register the server. You can view the class in OLE/COM Object Viewer. Create an instance so that you can see the interfaces (see Figure 11–1). Notice that **IDispatch** is supported.

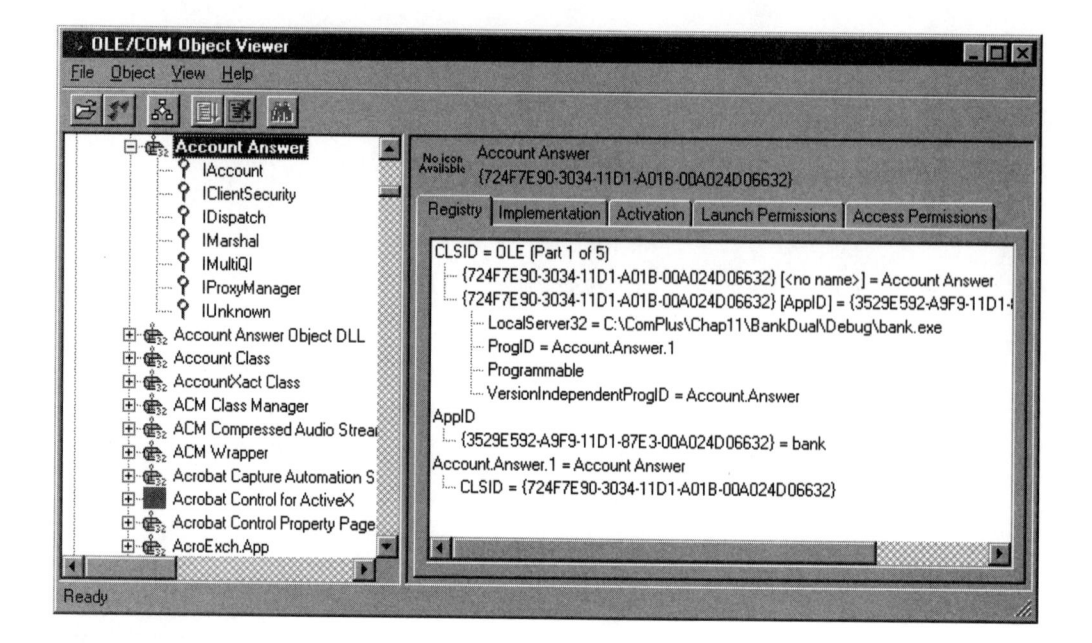

234 Chapter 11 • Automation and COM Programming Using Visual Basic

Figure 11–1 *Automation server supports IDispatch interface*

"Thin" Client Using VBScript

Our example client is in the directory **Chap11\BankHtml**. It is the HTML page **bank.htm**. Assuming you have Internet Explorer as your default browser, you can double-click on **bank.htm** in Windows Explorer and open this page in Internet Explorer. Notice that you do not have to compile anything for the client. An HTML form for exercising the bank server is brought up. See Figure 11–2.

Try clicking the "Create" button. If you have the default settings on Internet Explorer you will see a warning message about a possibly "unsafe" ActiveX control. See Figure 11–3. Go ahead and click "Yes" to allow it to run.

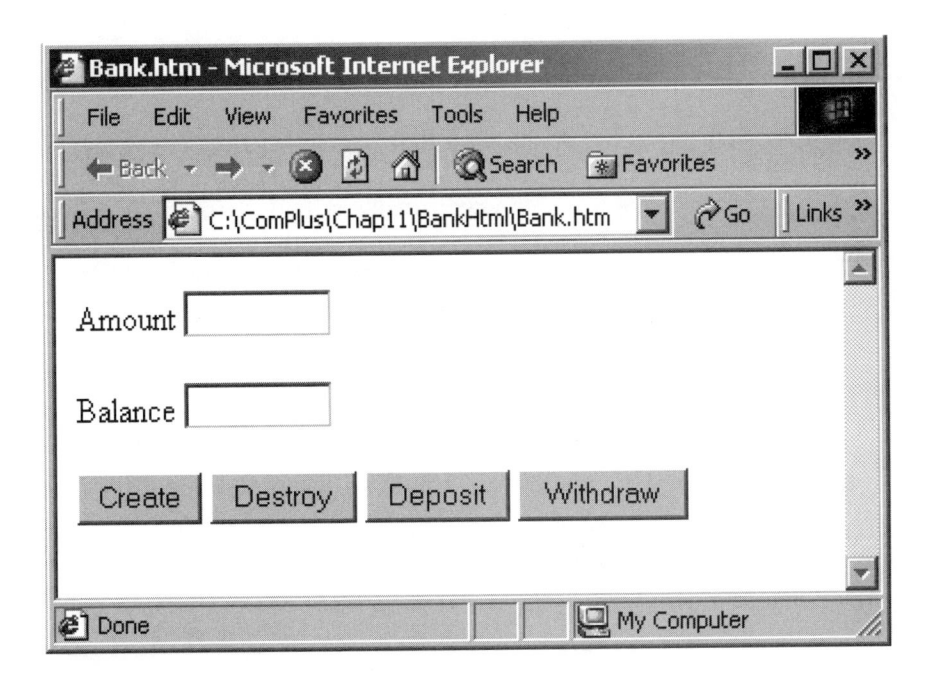

Figure 11–2 *Thin client for exercising bank Automation server*

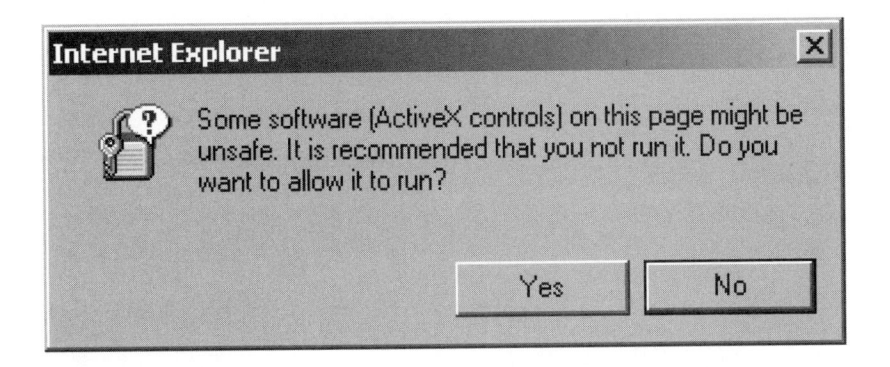

Figure 11–3 *Internet Explorer can warn user of possible safety issues*

An "Account" object should then be created, and you should be able to exercise the Deposit and Withdraw methods. The Balance property is used to display the current balance. When you are done, click the "Destroy" button.

Now examine the HTML source. The VBScript code is placed inside an HTML comment, so that it will be ignored by a browser that does not recognize VBScript. The **account** object is declared by a **Dim** statement. Notice that there is no type, as VBScript is an untyped language. Every variable in VBScript is of VARIANT data type, including object references. The object is instantiated by the **CreateObject** function, passing in the ProgID.

```
<!-- bank.htm -->
<HTML>
<HEAD>
<TITLE>Bank test page for Account object</TITLE>
<SCRIPT LANGUAGE="VBScript">
<!--

dim account

Sub btnCreate_OnClick
  set account = createobject("Account.Answer.1")
  Document.Form1.txtAmount.Value = 25
  Document.Form1.txtBalance.Value = account.Balance
End Sub

Sub btnDestroy_OnClick
  set account = Nothing
  Document.Form1.txtAmount.Value = ""
  Document.Form1.txtBalance.Value = ""
End Sub

Sub btnDeposit_OnClick
  account.Deposit(Document.Form1.txtAmount.Value)
  Document.Form1.txtBalance.Value = account.Balance
End Sub

Sub btnWithdraw_OnClick
  account.Withdraw(Document.Form1.txtAmount.Value)
  Document.Form1.txtBalance.Value = account.Balance
End Sub

-->
</SCRIPT>

<FORM NAME = "Form1" >
Amount <INPUT NAME="txtAmount" VALUE="" SIZE=8>
<P>
Balance <INPUT NAME="txtBalance" VALUE="" SIZE=8>
<P>
```

```
<INPUT NAME="btnCreate" TYPE=BUTTON VALUE="Create">
 <INPUT NAME="btnDestroy" TYPE=BUTTON VALUE="Destroy">
 <INPUT NAME="btnDeposit" TYPE=BUTTON VALUE="Deposit">
 <INPUT NAME="btnWithdraw" TYPE=BUTTON VALUE="Withdraw">
</FORM>
</BODY>
</HTML>
```

VBScript Automation Processing

It is instructive to examine briefly the underlying COM processing in this example of VBScript code. We will just look at what happens in the "Create" and "Destroy" handlers. We instantiate an object, obtain the value of the **Balance** property (using the name "Balance" rather than going directly through the binary vtable interface), and finally destroy the object by **Set**ting it to **Nothing**.

1. The ProgID "Account.Answer.1" is looked up in the Registry to find a CLSID, and then an interface pointer to the object is obtained through the class factory (**CoCreateInstance**).
2. **GetIDsOfNames** is called to find the dispid for **Balance**.
3. **Invoke** is called with the dispid for **Balance**.
4. If successful, the value is displayed. Otherwise VBScript throws an error based on the exception returned by **Invoke**.
5. When done, call **Release** is called through the interface pointer.

More About IDispatch

IDispatch::Invoke is the function that calls the Automation object. Properties, as well as methods, are implemented as function calls. Normally there are two functions per property (to set and get the value). Important parameters of **Invoke** include:

- The dispid of the property or method being called
- A pointer to an array of arguments to the property or method
- A pointer to a location to store results
- A pointer to a structure to hold exception information (this is Automation exception information, which is independent of C++ or NT exception handling)

Visual C++ Automation Controllers (Optional)

We can gain some additional insight into the low-level functioning of Automation by examining some Visual C++ code for Automation controllers. The first example illustrates calling a dispatch interface directly, at the raw COM level.

The second example illustrates using the ATL wrapper class **CComDispatch-Driver**.

Quite likely you will never need to call a dispatch interface from C++. Most modern objects do support a dual interface. You would of course need this information if you are implementing a scripting environment. Another reason for including this section because it offers insight into how the dispatch mechanism works.

Calling IDispatch Directly

Using the **IDispatch** interface at the raw COM level is straightforward but rather tedious. You have to fill in a number of data structures and then call the **Invoke** method. The example code should help you get up and running if you ever need to do this. The main reason for including the code sample is to illustrate the substantial overhead in going through **IDispatch** compared with the single vtable indirection of a standard COM interface. See **Chap11\UseDispCom** for the complete code. The essentials are shown below.

```
void main()
{
  ...
  HRESULT hr;
  VARIANT var;
  EXCEPINFO ei;
  UINT err;
  DISPPARAMS di = {NULL, NULL, 0, 0};
  var.vt = VT_EMPTY;
  ...

  // Use invoke to get Balance property
  // Rely on dispid is 1

  hr = pDisp->Invoke(
    1,                          // dispid
    IID_NULL,                   // reserved
    LOCALE_SYSTEM_DEFAULT,      // locale
    DISPATCH_PROPERTYGET,       // property get
    &di,                        // parameters
    &var,                       // returned value
    &ei,                        // exception info
    &err);                      // error index
  if (FAILED(hr))
  {
    cout << "IDispatch:Invoke failed" << endl;
    pUnk->Release();
    pDisp->Release();
    goto bottom;
  }
```

Visual C++ Automation Controllers (Optional)

```
long balance;
balance = var.lVal;        // VT_I4
...
```

Using CComDispatch Driver

ATL provides a wrapper class, **CComDispatchDriver**, that you can use for calling a dispatch interface. The example program is in **Chap11\UseDispAtl**, and the essentials are shown below. This example also illustrates use of the wrapper class **CComVariant**.

```
// use.cpp

#include "stdafx.h"

...

void exercise0(CLSID clsid);
char progid[80];

void main()
{
...
  cout << "ProgID: ";
  cin >> progid;
  cout << "You entered " << progid << endl;
  // Convert progid to Unicode and obtain CLSID
  CLSID clsid;
  MultiByteToWideChar(CP_ACP, 0, progid, -1, wbuf, 80);
  hr = CLSIDFromProgID(wbuf, &clsid);
  if (FAILED(hr))
  {
    cout << "ProgID not found: " << progid << endl;
    goto bottom;
  }
  ...
  // Exercise the object with this clsid
  exercise0(clsid);
  ...
}

void exercise0(CLSID clsid)
{
  // Use class factory to instantiate object
  // Use ATL smart pointer
  CComPtr<IDispatch> pAccount;
  HRESULT hr = CoCreateInstance(clsid, NULL,
              CLSCTX_SERVER,
              IID_IDispatch,
              (void **) &pAccount);
```

```
    if (FAILED(hr))
    {
      cout << "CoCreateInstance failed" << endl;
      return;
    }

    // Use ATL CComDispatchDriver class to get at
    // dispatch interface
    CComDispatchDriver pDisp(pAccount);
    CComVariant varResult;
    pDisp.GetProperty(1, &varResult);
    long balance = varResult.lVal;
    cout << "Balance = " << balance << endl;
}
```

Automation and Visual Basic

In this section, we review the fundamental programming model of Visual Basic and see how it maps to the elements of Automation. Every Visual Basic program makes use of properties, methods, and events. You set properties of forms and controls inside forms. You call methods. You write event handlers to handle events such as clicking a button.

Properties

We are familiar with methods as the functions associated with COM interfaces. Properties can be viewed as a particular kind of method which can be used to get and put values. Properties can take parameters, and they have a very simple syntax in Visual Basic.

To illustrate the different syntax, consider the simple example of "balance" in our bank account server. In the first case we have methods **GetBalance** and **PutBalance**. Assume there is a textbox **txtBalance** which is used to show the balance we obtain from the server or as a source for data we put to the server.

```
'Obtaining balance from server
Dim balance as Currency
objAccount.GetBalance balance
txtBalance = balance

'Putting balance to server
objAccount.PutBalance txtBalance
```

The alternative is to have **Balance** as a property. The above code then looks like the following.

```
'Obtaining balance from server
txtBalance = objAccount.Balance

'Putting balance to server
objAccount.Balance = txtBalance
```

Notice that in Visual Basic you can use properties on both the left- and right-hand side of assignment statements.

DEFAULT PROPERTIES

This example illustrates a feature of properties in Visual Basic and Automation. A property whose dispatch id is 0 is said to be a *default* property. You can refer to a default property simply by using the object reference itself. In the example above, the built-in textbox control has **Text** as its default property. Thus the following two lines of code are equivalent.

```
txtBalance.Text = balance'fully qualified
txtBalance = balance      'relies on Text as default
```

Default properties should be used with discretion. Although they can make code more concise, they also make code less obvious. We will not make any properties be default in any of our servers.

IMPLEMENTING PROPERTIES USING VISUAL BASIC

Visual Basic provides a special kind of **Property** procedure that you can use in a class module to implement a property.

```
Dim gBalance as Currency
...
Public Property Get Balance() As Currency
  Balance = gBalance
End Property

Public Property Let Balance(ByVal vNewValue As Currency)
  GBalance = vNewValue
End Property
```

READ-ONLY AND WRITE-ONLY PROPERTIES

You can make a property read only by deleting the **Property Let**. You could make a property write only (not often done) by deleting the **Property Get**.

IDL FOR A DISPATCH INTERFACE

You can use the Type Library Viewer from OLE/COM Object Viewer to view the Interface Definition Language (IDL) of an Automation server. You will see that an Automation server has a dispatch interface ("dispinterface"). Figure

11–4 shows the IDL for the example server discussed in the next section. Notice that **Balance** is a read-only property. It has a **propget** but no **propput** attribute.

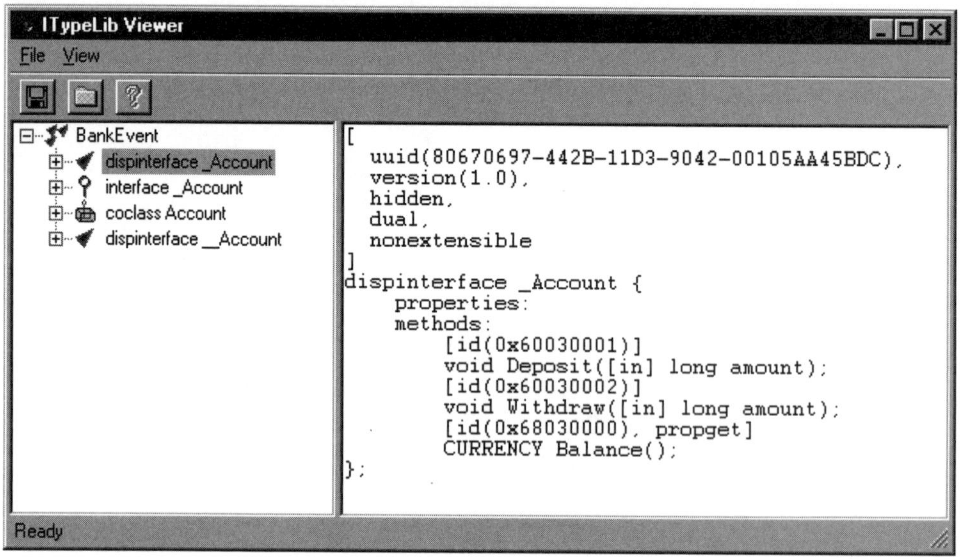
ITypeLib Viewer
File View
BankEvent
dispinterface _Account
interface _Account
coclass Account
dispinterface __Account
[
uuid(80670697-442B-11D3-9042-00105AA45BDC),
version(1.0),
hidden,
dual,
nonextensible
]
dispinterface _Account {
properties:
methods:
[id(0x60030001)]
void Deposit([in] long amount);
[id(0x60030002)]
void Withdraw([in] long amount);
[id(0x68030000), propget]
CURRENCY Balance();
};
Ready

Figure 11–4 *Interface Definition Language for a dispatch interface*

Events

A very important feature of Visual Basic is its ability to work with *events*. A fundamental feature of a graphical user interface is that it is the user and not the program that is "in charge." In a traditional user interface, the program is always in control. It presents the user with a fixed set of options at any given point. The user types in a command or chooses from a menu. The program does some processing, and then gives the user another chance to do input. This style of program is inherently sequential in structure.

A GUI type program is very different. The user can enter input in many different ways, via a menu, via a mouse click, via the keyboard, etc. The program at all times must stand ready to respond appropriately to any of these user actions. The Windows operating system provides a message system to deal with a GUI. Different user actions generate Windows messages, which are placed in a message queue. A Windows program must have a "windows procedure" which gets messages from this queue and does appropriate processing. C programmers write Windows procedures directly. C++ programmers use a class library to implement message handler functions that are provided by a class library such as Microsoft Foundation Classes (MFC) as a layer on Windows messages.

Visual Basic provides an "event" abstraction. User actions such as clicking a button, selecting an item from a list, etc. trigger an "event." A Visual Basic program can provide "event handler" procedures to deal with these events. A bare bones illustration would be a form with a single pushbutton "Button." The following Visual Basic code will put up a message box whenever the button is clicked. (See **Chap11\Button** if you would like to see an implementation of this tiny project.)

```
Private Sub cmdButton_Click()
    MsgBox "Button was clicked!"
End Sub
```

EVENTS IN COM SERVERS

Normally a COM client calls into a COM server, making use of a so-called "incoming" interface. But sometimes there may be an occurrence on the server which should be passed to the client. We say that the server "fires" or "raises" an event. The server specifies a special kind of "outgoing" or "source" interface which the client must implement.

Visual Basic makes it easy to provide events in a server. You declare one or more "event" procedures, and in the code you "raise" the event when required. For a sample program see **Chap11\BankEvent**. When a withdrawal results in a negative balance the **Overdrawn** event is raised. Notice that an event can take parameters.

```
Option Explicit
Private gBalance As Currency

Public Event Overdrawn(ByVal Balance As Currency)

Public Sub Deposit(ByVal amount As Long)
    gBalance = gBalance + amount
End Sub

Public Sub Withdraw(ByVal amount As Long)
    gBalance = gBalance - amount
    If gBalance < 0 Then
        RaiseEvent Overdrawn(gBalance)
    End If
End Sub

Private Sub Class_Initialize()
    gBalance = 100
    MsgBox "Account object created"
End Sub
```

```
Private Sub Class_Terminate()
    MsgBox "Account object destroyed"
End Sub

Public Property Get Balance() As Currency
    Balance = gBalance
End Property
```

CLIENT PROGRAM THAT HANDLES EVENTS

To implement a client program in Visual Basic that handles events, you must **Dim** your object reference **WithEvents**. You cannot include **New** as part of the **Dim** statement in this case, but must do an explicit **Set**. Once you have the **Dim WithEvents** statement in your client program, the code window will show all events for a particular object reference, allowing you to add event handlers See Figure 11–5.

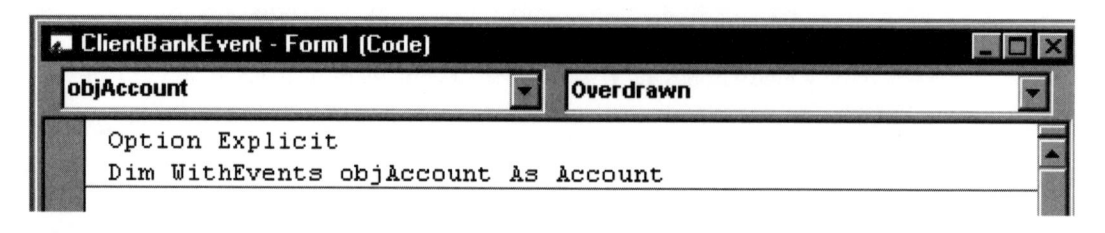

Figure 11–5 *Code window shows events*

You can examine the code for the Visual Basic client program in the directory **Chap11\ClientBankEvent**. This program allows you to make deposits and withdrawals, and if you overdraw the account, a message box is displayed.

```
Option Explicit
Dim WithEvents objAccount As Account

Private Sub cmdDeposit_Click()
    objAccount.Deposit txtAmount
    txtBalance = objAccount.Balance
End Sub

Private Sub cmdWithdraw_Click()
    objAccount.Withdraw txtAmount
    txtBalance = objAccount.Balance
End Sub

Private Sub Form_Load()
    Set objAccount = New Account
```

```
    txtAmount = 25
    txtBalance = objAccount.Balance
End Sub

Private Sub objAccount_Overdrawn(ByVal Balance As Currency)
    MsgBox "Account is overdrawn!" & vbNewLine _
        & "Balance = " & Balance
End Sub
```

IDL FOR AN EVENT INTERFACE

We can use the Type Library Viewer of OLE/COM Object Viewer to examine the IDL for the **BankEvent** COM server. Here is the complete text of the IDL:

```
// Generated .IDL file (by the OLE/COM Object Viewer)
//
// typelib filename: BankEvent.dll

[
  uuid(EA8166A5-4369-11D3-9041-00105AA45BDC),
  version(2.0)
]
library BankEvent
{
    // TLib :    // TLib : OLE Automation :
                 {00020430-0000-0000-C000-000000000046}
    importlib("STDOLE2.TLB");

    // Forward declare all types defined in this typelib
    interface _Account;
    dispinterface __Account;

    [
      odl,
      uuid(80670697-442B-11D3-9042-00105AA45BDC),
      version(1.0),
      hidden,
      dual,
      nonextensible,
      oleautomation
    ]
    interface _Account : IDispatch {
      [id(0x60030001)]
      HRESULT Deposit([in] long amount);
      [id(0x60030002)]
      HRESULT Withdraw([in] long amount);
      [id(0x68030000), propget]
      HRESULT Balance([out, retval] CURRENCY* );
    };
```

```
[
  uuid(EA8166A7-4369-11D3-9041-00105AA45BDC),
  version(1.0)
]
coclass Account {
  [default] interface _Account;
  [default, source] dispinterface __Account;
};

[
  uuid(80670698-442B-11D3-9042-00105AA45BDC),
  version(1.0),
  hidden,
  nonextensible
]
dispinterface __Account {
    properties:
    methods:
        [id(0x00000001)]
        void Overdrawn([in] CURRENCY Balance);
};
};
```

If you look at the IDL for the **coclass** you will see that now there are two interfaces. The first interface, **_Account**, is a dual interface, and so can be called efficiently by an early binding COM client and by a late binding client such as VBScript. The second interface, **__Account** has the **source** attribute, and is specifically a dispinterface.

Collections

An important feature of COM is *collections*, which enable you to work with lists of objects. Like other features of Automation, collections map directly to a corresponding feature in Visual Basic. This section introduces the concept of collections, discusses the COM topic of enumerators which underpin the implementation of collections, presents an example implementation of a collection using ATL, and gives an example of a Visual Basic client program that uses a collection.

Collections and Object Models

By exposing a *collection* object, you can provide access to more than one instance of an object. A collection object manages other objects. Collection objects support iteration over the objects they manage. The **IEnumVARIANT** interface provides a way to iterate through the objects contained by a collection object. Like other enumerators, **IEnumVARIANT** supports the methods

Next, **Skip**, **Reset**, and **Clone**. ATL makes it easy to implement enumerators, as we will see through an example later in this section.

Complex Automation servers expose their functionality through an *object model*. The model specifies a hierarchy of objects, some of which may be collections. We see examples of such object models everywhere in modern Microsoft software, from office applications (Word and Excel), Internet Applications (Internet Explorer, Active Server Pages), database access layers (Data Access Objects and ActiveX Data Objects), and many more.

Enumerators

Many COM applications have collections of pointers and other data. Examples include the object models mentioned above, streams in storage, and many others. Enumerators provide a *standard* pattern for applications to expose these collections. Since the exact format of an enumerator is dependent on exactly what is being enumerated, COM provides a pattern for enumerators to follow.

IENUMXXX

This pattern is defined by the **IEnumXXX**. Having a separate enumerator object separates the caller's ability to loop over a set of objects from the server's knowledge of how information is stored. All enumerators have the following methods:

- **Next** fetches the next specified number of items.
- **Reset** resets the enumeration sequence to the start. A reset enumerator might not retain the elements in the same order as before the reset method call.
- **Skip** skips over a specified number of items.
- **Clone** returns a copy of the current enumerator.

Each enumerator defines a sequence of the elements that the enumerator methods return. The enumerated collection of data may be static or dynamic. This data could include interface pointers. The enumerator itself is generally obtained from a method call on another object.

ATL ENUMERATOR CLASSES

ATL has several classes to help you build enumerators. **CComEnum** defines the enumerator. **CComIEnum** defines the abstract class that defines the enumeration interface. **CComEnumImpl** implements the enumeration interface. It is used by the **CComEnum** class. These classes are illustrated in the **Zoo-Coll** collection example presented below.

Implementing Collections

Collections make it possible for enumerators to be used by Automation controllers. A collection object exposes its underlying enumerator object through an **IDispatch** interface. If it makes sense, a collection object can have additions and deletions from any position. Just like the **IEnumXXX** interface, there is no one collection interface, it is a pattern to be followed by a specific collection object. Each item in the collection is stored as a VARIANT data type. Hence collections can be used with a wide variety of data types. Collections use an **IEnumVARIANT** enumerator to loop through the contained items. Collections also provide a means to access a specific item in the collection.

COLLECTION REQUIREMENTS

There are a number of requirements for collections in order for them to fit the standard pattern.

- The property or method that returns a collection is named with the plural name for the collected items (an Animal object is in the Animals collection).
- A collection must have a hidden **_NewEnum** property to get the enumerator **IEnumVARIANT**.
- A collection must support indexing with an **Item** method.
- A collection must have a **Count** property.
- If adding objects to a collection makes sense, implement an **Add** method.
- If removing objects from a collection makes sense, implement a **Remove** method.

COLLECTION EXAMPLE

A complete example of a collection is presented in **Chap11\ZooColl**. The server is implemented using ATL and is contained in the **Server** directory. A Visual Basic client is in the subdirectory **VbClient** and a Visual C++ client is in the subdirectory **VcClient**. Build the server and run the VB client. The initial collection has four animals. You can add and remove animals, and modify an animal. Note that the index for a Collection is based at 1. See Figure 11–6 for an illustrating of the collection after adding "Elephant" and modifying the third element from "Bears" to "Grizzly Bears."

You can study the Visual Basic code to see how to program with collections. The **For Each** loop is a particularly elegant language construct for iterating through a collection.

```
For Each Animal In Animals
    AnimalsList.AddItem Animal
Next Animal
```

Figure 11-6 *Visual Basic test program for a collection*

The **For ... Next** loop illustrates using the **Count** property and an index.

```
Dim i As Long
For i = 1 To Animals.Count
    AnimalsList.AddItem Animals(i)
Next i
```

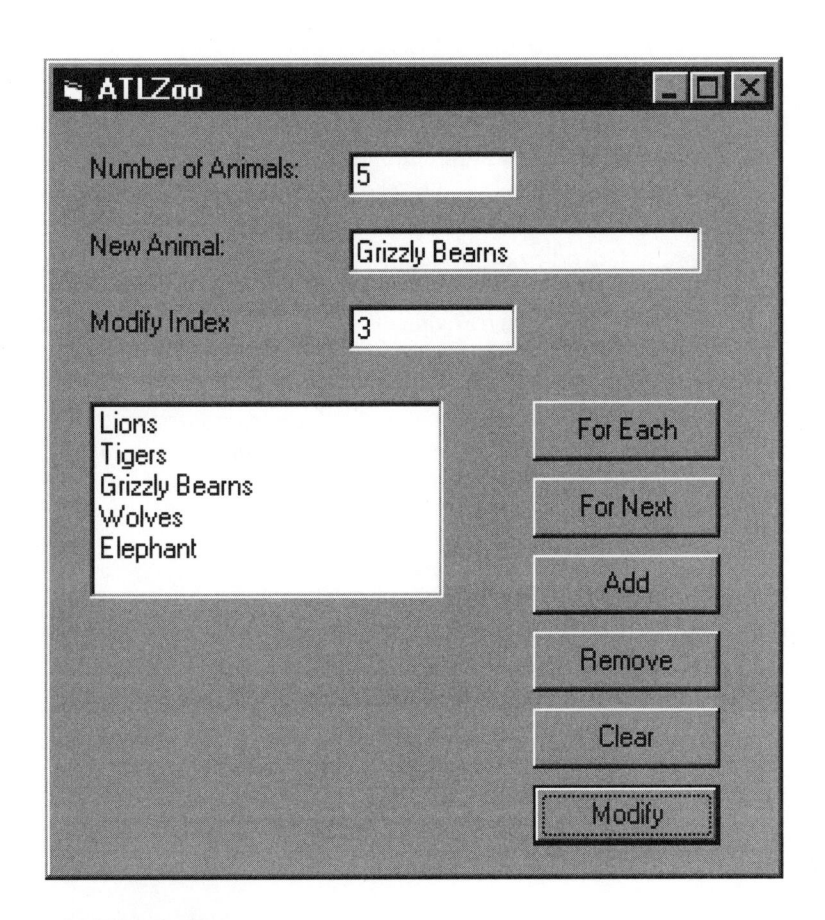

Summary

Automation is an important technology, providing the capability for a client (such as a "thin" client using VBScript on an HTML page) to connect to a COM server using late binding. Automation also supports untyped languages, through the "catch-all" VARIANT data type. Late binding relies on the very general **Invoke** method of the **IDispatch** interface. A dispatch interface makes a server available to scripting languages, but it is less efficient than a COM vtable interface. By providing a dual interface your server can in a sense provide the best of both worlds, at the cost of some increase in code size and limiting the data types of your parameters to those supported by Automation. It is easy to implement dual interfaces using ATL. The architecture of Automation is derived from the requirement to provide a close fit to the Visual Basic programming model, including the support of properties, methods and events. Collections provide a standard way in COM to deal with lists of objects.

One feature of Automation we have not yet discussed is its exception mechanism. This will be one of the topics treated in the next chapter, "Error Processing and Debugging." The topic of error processing is extremely important for multiple tier applications because there are so many possible sources of errors.

TWELVE

Error Processing and Debugging

U_p until now we have not paid very much attention to error processing. We have checked HRESULTs but not much more than that. We've essentially ignored error processing not because it is unimportant, but merely to simplify presenting the core concepts of COM. As we get closer to the COM+ portion of this book, it becomes more important to be serious about error processing. We will also discuss debugging techniques. Debugging can be viewed as finding and removing errors in program logic before your program ships. Error processing is providing code to deal with run-time error conditions that may arise when your application is deployed. It is important that your program deal with errors gracefully rather than crash. This is particularly vital in middle-tier components of enterprise applications. A crash that brings down a server can be massively disruptive. There will be more discussion of error processing in Part 3. We will see, for example, that the core concept of transactions has at its heart a mechanism to provide robust system performance in the face of failure of components.

We begin with a closer look at HRESULTs, including standard facility and error codes and techniques for displaying this information. We then examine standard COM error interfaces that can be used to provide richer error information than merely what can be returned by a single 32-bit number. We then examine ATL support for this COM error mechanism. We will then look at Automation exceptions and how handling of these exceptions can map to the appropriate mechanism in the implementation language. We will examine in particular exception handling in C++ and Visual Basic. The rest of the topic will be concerned with various debugging topics, including tracing and breaking into program execution.

Using the HRESULT

Most COM API functions and methods return an HRESULT. An HRESULT is a 32-bit quantity having the following format (bit 31 is most significant):

Bits	Meaning
31	Severity bit (0 = success, 1 = failure)
30 – 27	Reserved
26 – 16	Facility (area of responsibility for the error)
15 – 0	Code (specifics of the failure or success)

Success or failure is determined by testing the severity bit. You can use the macros SUCCEEDED or FAILED.

```
HRESULT hr = pInterface->SomeMethod();
if (FAILED(hr))
{
  // error handling
...
```

Facility Codes

Microsoft allocates facility codes because they need to be unique. The following facility codes are currently defined:

Value	Facility	Description
0	FACILITY_NULL	Common status codes like S_OK
1	FACILITY_RPC	RPC errors
2	FACILITY_DISPATCH	**IDispatch** interface errors
3	FACILITY_STORAGE	**IStorage** and **IStream** errors
4	FACILITY_ITF	Most status codes returned from interface methods (different interfaces have different HRESULT "address spaces")
	FACILITY_WINDOWS	Additional error codes for Microsoft defined interfaces
	FACILITY_WIN32	To handle error codes from Win32 functions as an HRESULT

Error Codes and Naming Conventions

To make up error codes for your own interface, use FACILITY_ITF. These error codes (bits 15–0) are unique to the particular interface, so you do not need to worry about clashes with other error codes. HRESULTS have the following naming convention:

```
<Facility>_<Severity>_<Reason>
```

- **<Facility>** is the facility name or another distinguishing identifier (omitted for FACILITY_NULL)
- **< Severity >** is a single letter S or E indicating success or error
- **< Reason >** is the identifier giving explanation of code

Here are some examples:

```
S_OK                 (FACILITY_NULL)
STG_E_FILENOTFOUND   (FACILITY_STORAGE)
DISP_E_EXCEPTION     (FACILITY_DISPATCH)
```

Looking Up Error Codes

If you get an error in program execution, naturally you will want to look up the description of the error. In many cases you can use the Error Lookup utility (from the Tools menu of Visual C++). See Figure 12–1.

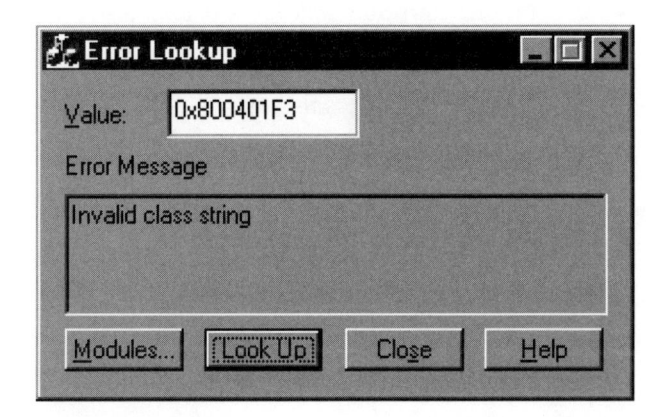

Figure 12–1 *Using Error Lookup for an HRESULT*

In some cases, the error may not be found via Error Lookup. You may then try the Find In Files command (from the Edit menu) to search for the numerical value (in hex) within the various include files. See Figure 12–2.

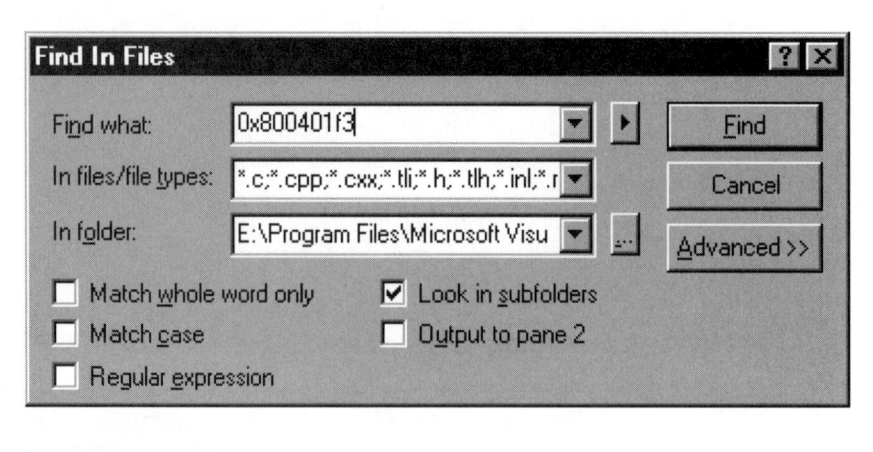

Figure 12–2 *Using Find In Files to look for an HRESULT*

Displaying Error Descriptions

Another strategy that is more convenient is to call the Win32 function **FormatMessage**. This will provide a descriptive string automatically. Like many Win32 functions **FormatMessage** takes many parameters and is rather complicated to call. Hence we provide a helper function **ShowError** that is more convenient to call. The command-line sample program in **Chap12\UseCmd** prompts for a ProgID and attempts to find and display the corresponding CLSID. If there is an error in the first HRESULT (which will occur if an invalid ProgID is entered), the **ShowError** function is called. See Figure 12–3. The helper function will display both a descriptive error message and the HRESULT in hex. (Note that a console program may display a message box.)

Figure 12–3 *Helper function displays descriptive error message and HRESULT*

```
// use.cpp

#include "stdafx.h"

void ShowError(HRESULT hr)
{
  if (hr == S_OK)
    return;
  if (HRESULT_FACILITY(hr) == FACILITY_WINDOWS)
    hr = HRESULT_CODE(hr);

  LPVOID lpMsgBuf;
  FormatMessage(FORMAT_MESSAGE_ALLOCATE_BUFFER |
    FORMAT_MESSAGE_FROM_SYSTEM |
    FORMAT_MESSAGE_IGNORE_INSERTS,
    NULL,
    hr,
    MAKELANGID(LANG_NEUTRAL, SUBLANG_DEFAULT),
    (LPTSTR) &lpMsgBuf,
    0,
    NULL );
  char buf[1024];
  wsprintf(buf, "%s\nhr = 0x%lx", (LPCTSTR)lpMsgBuf, hr);
  MessageBox( NULL, buf, "Error", MB_OK);
  LocalFree( lpMsgBuf );
}

void main()
{
  char progid[80];
  WCHAR wbuf[80];
  char buf[80];
  HRESULT hr;

  cout << "ProgID: ";
  cin >> progid;
  cout << "You entered " << progid << endl;

  // Convert progid to Unicode and obtain CLSID
  CLSID clsid;
  MultiByteToWideChar(CP_ACP, 0, progid, -1, wbuf, 80);
  hr = CLSIDFromProgID(wbuf, &clsid);
  if (FAILED(hr))
  {
    cout << "ProgID not found: " << progid << endl;
    **ShowError(hr);**
    return;;
  }
  ...
```

COM Error Interfaces

There are several COM interfaces that can be used to provide extended error information. **ISupportErrorInfo** is used to tell whether error information is available for a particular interface of an object. **ICreateErrorInfo** is used to create an "error object" that contains the extended error information. **IErrorInfo** is the interface whose methods expose the extended error information.

The error object is associated with a particular thread of execution. Thus in a multithreaded application there could be several error objects.

IErrorInfo

An error object supports the **IErrorInfo** interface, which has the following methods:

- **GetDescription** returns a text description of the error as a BSTR.
- **GetGUID** returns the GUID of the interface that defined the error.
- **GetHelpFile** returns path to a help file containing information about the error.
- **GetHelpContext** returns the help context ID identifying a particular entry in the help file.
- **GetSource** returns the ProgID of the object that caused the error.

Returning Error Information

To implement returning extended error information, perform the following steps:

1. Implement **ISupportErrorInfo** interface.
2. Call the API function **CreateErrorInfo** to create an error object, obtaining an **ICreateErrorInfo** interface pointer.
3. Use methods of **ICreateErrorInfo** to set the contents of the error object.
4. Call the API function **SetErrorInfo** to associate the error object with the current thread.

Retrieving Error Information

Retrieving error information involves the following steps:

1. Check HRESULT return code for an error.
2. Call **QueryInterface** looking for **ISupportErrorInfo** pointer.
3. Call **ISupportErrorInfo::InterfaceSupportsErrorInfo** to find out if error information is supported for the particular interface.
4. Call **GetErrorInfo** to obtain the error object for this thread most recently set by **SetErrorInfo**. You get back an **IErrorInfo** pointer.
5. Use **IErrorInfo** methods to obtain the detailed error information.

Implementing ISupportErrorInfo Using ATL

You implement the **ISupportErrorInfo** interface in ATL like you would implement any other interface. First, you add this interface to the multiple inheritance list for your implementation class.

```
class ATL_NO_VTABLE CAccount :
  public CComObjectRootEx<CComSingleThreadModel>,
  public CComCoClass<CAccount,
      &CLSID_AccountError>,
  public ISupportErrorInfo,
  public IDispatchImpl<IAccount, &IID_IAccount,
    &LIBID_BANKERRORLib>
{
...
```

Second, you provide the code to implement the methods of the interface. There is only one method, **InterfaceSupportsErrorInfo**. You check if the interface ID passed in matches any of the interface IDs (stored in an array) for which you will support error information. In the code below, you do support error info for **IID_IAccount**. The code shown is extensible. If you support error information for other interfaces, just add their interface IDs to the initializer list for the array.

```
STDMETHODIMP
CAccount::InterfaceSupportsErrorInfo(REFIID riid)
{
  static const IID* arr[] =
  {
    &IID_IAccount,
  };
  for (int i=0;i<sizeof(arr)/sizeof(arr[0]);i++)
  {
    if (InlineIsEqualGUID(*arr[i],riid))
      return S_OK;
  }
  return S_FALSE;
}
```

Returning Error Information Using ATL

ATL makes it very easy for your servers to use the COM error interfaces to return extended error information. For an example, see **Chap12\BankError**.

USING ATL OBJECT WIZARD

The error support code shown can be placed into your source file automatically by ATL Object Wizard. All you have to do is check "Support ISupportErrorInfo" in the Attributes tab of the ATL Object Wizard Properties dialog. See Figure 12–4.

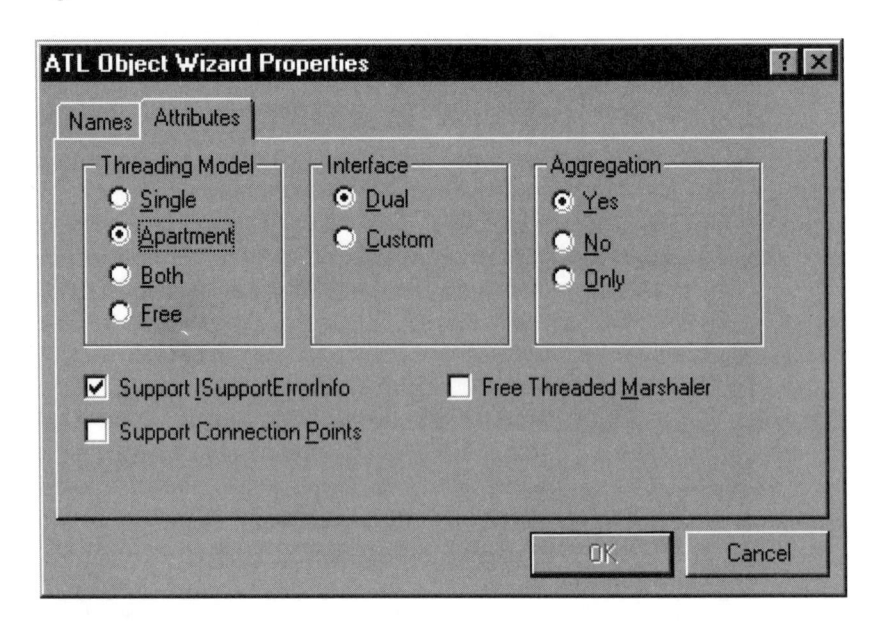

Figure 12–4 *ATL Object Wizard can automatically add error support code*

SETTING THE ERROR OBJECT

After you have added the **ISupportErrorInfo** support to your class, you can make use of the **Error** method in **CComCoClass** to accomplish all the steps described above under "Returning Error Information." In your method implementations when you return an HRESULT, you return a call to **Error(buf)**, where **buf** is a string buffer holding a description of the error.

COM Error Interfaces Example

The example program **Chap12\BankError** illustrates the details of using the COM error interfaces. We will also use this same program in the next section to illustrate Automation exceptions. The server implements the familiar bank account object with the **IAccount** interface, implemented as a *dual* interface. The following error checking is done:

- In **Deposit**, the amount must be positive.
- In **Withdraw** the amount must be positive and must also not exceed the current balance (that is, you are not allowed to overdraw the account).

RUNNING THE EXAMPLE

Build the server project "BankError" and also the client project "test" (both in the same workspace). Run the test program. The test program is implemented so that it can go through either the custom (vtable) interface or the dispatch interface. For now stick with the custom interface. See Figure 12–5.

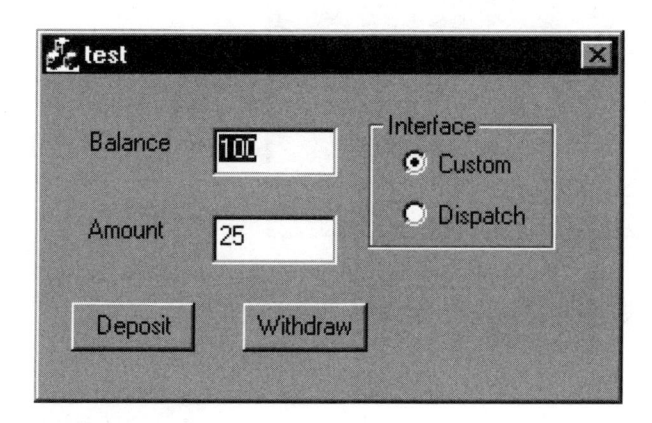

Figure 12–5 *Test program can use either custom or dispatch interface*

Verify that both Deposit and Withdraw work correctly with legal amounts. Now do several withdrawals until the balance would become negative. Our test program puts up two message boxes. The first one uses our **ShowError** helper function to display the HRESULT and the system message description. See Figure 12–6.

Figure 12–6 *System supplied message description is not specific*

Note that the system supplied description is not specific—it just says that an exception occurred. But a COM "exception" means that there may be additional error information. And indeed the second message box shows a more specific error message. See Figure 12–7.

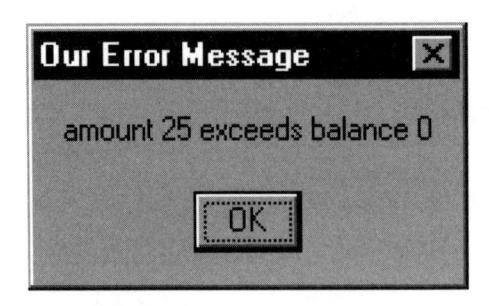

Figure 12–7 *Extended error information is provided for Withdraw error*

Next make the amount negative, and try Withdraw. Again you should see a suitable error message. Now try Deposit with a negative amount. This time the operation will silently fail (our client code does not do error checking for Deposit).

Server Code Provides Error Information

We already saw the code that the ATL Object Wizard provides when you check the box "Supports ISupportErrorInfo" when inserting a new ATL object into your project. An implementation is provided of the method **InterfaceSupportsErrorInfo**, which will return a "yes" answer that your interface does support error info.

You have to provide the code yourself to set the extended error information. Look in the file **account.cpp** in the **BankError** project for the implementation of the **Deposit** and **Withdraw** methods where errors are detected.

```
STDMETHODIMP CAccount::Deposit(long amount)
{
  if (amount > 0)
  {
    m_nBalance += amount;
    return S_OK;
  }
  else
  {
    TCHAR buf[80];
    wsprintf(buf, "amount %ld is not positive", amount);
```

COM Error Interfaces

```
      return Error(buf);
   }
}

STDMETHODIMP CAccount::Withdraw(long amount)
{
   if (amount > 0 && amount <= m_nBalance)
   {
      m_nBalance -= amount;
      return S_OK;
   }
   else if (amount > m_nBalance)
   {
      TCHAR buf[80];
      wsprintf(buf, "amount %ld exceeds balance %ld",
          amount, m_nBalance);
      return Error(buf);
   }
   else
   {
      TCHAR buf[80];
      wsprintf(buf, "amount %ld is not positive", amount);
      return Error(buf);
   }
}
```

The call to the **Error** method of **CComCoClass** accomplishes the low-level COM calls that create a COM error object and sets the descriptive error message. The return value of the call to **Error** is the HRESULT value 0x80020009 ("Exception occurred") that we saw in the first message box.

Client Code Retrieves Error Information

You can obtain extended error information (if available) by going through the appropriate COM interfaces. Use **ISupportErrorInfo** to find out if error information is available. Call **GetErrorInfo** to obtain an **IErrorInfo** pointer. Use **IErrorInfo** methods to obtain the detailed error information. Note that the semantics of the API function **GetErrorInfo** and the method **InterfaceSupportsErrorInfo** require a return of S_OK for success.

You can see an illustration of the appropriate code in the **OnWithdraw** handler in the test program **testDlg.cpp**.

USING ISUPPORTERRORINFO

```
// Query for ISupportErrorInfo
hr = m_pAccount->QueryInterface(IID_ISupportErrorInfo,
                                (void**) &pSupport);
if (FAILED(hr))
```

Chapter 12 • Error Processing and Debugging

```
{
  MessageBox("ISupportErrorInfo interface not available");
  return;
}
TRACE("ISupportErrorInfo interface is available\n");

// Now find out if error info available for
// IAccount interface
hr = pSupport->InterfaceSupportsErrorInfo(IID_IAccount);
if (hr != S_OK)
{
  MessageBox("Error info not available for IAccount");
  pSupport->Release();
  return;
}
```

USING IERRORINFO

```
// Now get the error object and its description
IErrorInfo* pError;
hr = GetErrorInfo(0, &pError);
if (hr != S_OK)
{
  MessageBox("GetErrorInfo failed");
  pSupport->Release();
  return;
}
TRACE("GetErrorInfo succeeded\n");
BSTR bstr;
hr = pError->GetDescription(&bstr);
if (FAILED(hr))
{
  MessageBox("GetDescription failed");
  pSupport->Release();
  pError->Release();
  return;
}
TRACE("GetDescription succeeded\n");

// Display the description
USES_CONVERSION;
MessageBox(OLE2CT(bstr), "Our Error Message");
SysFreeString(bstr);
pSupport->Release();
pError->Release();
```

Visual C++ Compiler Smart Pointer Error Support

The Visual C++ COM support class **_com_error** wraps the COM error interfaces, greatly simplifying writing client programs that retrieve extended error information. If you go through a Visual C++ smart pointer, any HRESULT error return will throw an exception of type **_com_error**. In Chapter 8 we saw an example of using this class to display descriptive error information using the **ErrorMessage** method. The following sample code from **Chap8\SmartClient** illustrates this:

```
void CSmartClientDlg::OnWithdraw()
{
  int balance;
  int amount = GetDlgItemInt(IDC_AMOUNT);
  try
  {
    m_pAccount->Withdraw(amount);
    m_pAccount->GetBalance(&balance);
    SetDlgItemInt(IDC_BALANCE, balance);
  }
  catch(_com_error &ex)
  {
    MessageBox(ex.ErrorMessage());
  }
}
```

Although useful, the **ErrorMessage** method simply calls the Win32 **FormatMessage** function. Thus all we get is the system message description. In the case of a COM exception, this will just be "Exception occurred," which does not convey any extended error information provided by the server. Fortunately, the **_com_error** error class does more. For one thing, the **ErrorInfo** member function returns the raw **IErrorInfo** pointer, and we can go from there. Even more convenient is the **Description** member function, which calls the method **IErrorInfo::GetDescription** for us. The description is returned as a **_bstr_** (the Visual C++ wrapper class for BSTR). If there is no error object containing extended error information, this string is empty, and we can revert back to **ErrorMessage** for the system error message.

For an illustration of using this Visual C++ smart pointer error support, see the third project "SmartClient" in the workspace for **Chap12\BankError**. This test program exercises only the custom interface, and it uses a Visual C++ smart pointer. Here is the code for exercising the **Withdraw** method.

```
void CSmartClientDlg::OnWithdraw()
{
  long balance;
  int amount = GetDlgItemInt(IDC_AMOUNT);
  try
  {
    m_spAccount->Withdraw(amount);
    m_spAccount->get_Balance(&balance);
    SetDlgItemInt(IDC_BALANCE, balance);
  }
```

```
catch(_com_error &ex)
{
  _bstr_t bstr = ex.Description();
  if (bstr.length() == 0)
    // no extended error info available
    MessageBox(ex.ErrorMessage());
  else
    MessageBox((const char*) bstr);
}
}
```

Note that again there is no error handling code for **Deposit** with an illegal negative amount. This time, instead of a silent failure, we will get a system supplied fatal error message. The smart pointer class throws an exception. Since we do not have an exception handler, we get the default error message.

Automation Exceptions

A feature of Automation is an exception mechanism. The seventh parameter in **Invoke** is a pointer to an EXCEPINFO structure. A dispatch method can communicate an error either by an error return code in HRESULT or by "raising an exception." To raise an exception, the method sets the return code to DISP_E_EXCEPTION and fills the EXCEPINFO structure with detailed information about the cause of the error. The client program will then deal with the exception in a manner appropriate to the implementation language. A C++ program can throw a C++ exception. MFC provides an exception handler that puts up a message box, so an uncaught Automation-generated exception will not end the client program. We will discuss how Visual Basic handles Automation exceptions in the next section.

EXCEPINFO

The EXCEPINFO structure gives detailed information about an exception. Some fields will remind you of member functions of **IErrorInfo**.

```
typedef struct FARSTRUCT tagEXCEPINFO {
  unsigned short wCode;           // error code
  unsigned short wReserved;
  BSTR bstrSource;                // source
  BSTR bstrDescription;           // description
  BSTR bstrHelpFile;              // help file path.
  unsigned long dwHelpContext;    // context ID.
  void FAR* pvReserved;           // Pointer to function that
                                  // fills in Help and
                                  // description info.
  HRESULT (STDAPICALLTYPE FAR* pfnDeferredFillIn)
      (struct tagEXCEPINFO FAR*);
```

```
       SCODE scode;              // A return value
                                 // describing the error
} EXCEPINFO, FAR* LPEXCEPINFO;
```

MFC Support for Automation Exceptions

MFC provides easy-to-use support for handling Automation exceptions. By using the debugger to step into the MFC code, we can see an example of code that works with the EXCEPINFO structure and calls **Invoke** directly.

To gain an appreciation of what MFC provides for you automatically, run the **BankError** client program again ("test"). This time try the Dispatch interface, set a negative value for amount, and click the "Deposit" button. While this operation failed silently for the custom interface, when we go through the dispatch interface, a message box comes up. See Figure 12–8.

Figure 12–8 *Message box supplied by MFC for uncaught Automation exception*

This message box was put up by MFC, not our program (we put a title "Our Error Message" in the message boxes we displayed, as you can see by trying "Withdraw" with the same illegal negative amount).

To investigate this phenomenon, run "test" in the debugger and set a breakpoint on the call to **Deposit**. Step in and you will come to a call to **InvokeHelper**.

```
void DAccount::Deposit(long amount)
{
  static BYTE parms[] =
    VTS_I4;
  InvokeHelper(0x2, DISPATCH_METHOD, VT_EMPTY, NULL,
    parms, amount);
}
```

Step into **InvokeHelper** and then into **COleDispatchDriver::Invoke-HelperV** and keep stepping until you come to **Invoke** itself. You should then see the initialization of the EXCEPINFO structure and the call to **Invoke**.

```
...
// initialize EXCEPINFO struct
EXCEPINFO excepInfo;
memset(&excepInfo, 0, sizeof excepInfo);

UINT nArgErr = (UINT)-1; // initialize to invalid arg

// make the call
SCODE sc = m_lpDispatch->Invoke(dwDispID, IID_NULL, 0,
     wFlags, &dispparams, pvarResult,
     &excepInfo, &nArgErr);
...
```

A little further down you will come to the code that actually throws the exception

```
if (FAILED(sc))
{
  VariantClear(&vaResult);
  if (sc != DISP_E_EXCEPTION)
  {
    // non-exception error code
    AfxThrowOleException(sc);
  }

  // make sure excepInfo is filled in
  if (excepInfo.pfnDeferredFillIn != NULL)
    excepInfo.pfnDeferredFillIn(&excepInfo);

  // allocate new exception, and fill it
  COleDispatchException* pException =
    new COleDispatchException(NULL, 0,
        excepInfo.wCode);
  ASSERT(pException->m_wCode == excepInfo.wCode);
  if (excepInfo.bstrSource != NULL)
  {
    pException->m_strSource = excepInfo.bstrSource;
    SysFreeString(excepInfo.bstrSource);
  }
  // remaining fields get filled in
  ...
  // then throw the exception
  THROW(pException);
```

COLEDISPATCHEXCEPTION

COleDispatchException is an MFC exception class (derived from **CException**) that is used to pass detailed information about Automation. The function **AfxThrowOleDispatchException** is used to throw a **COleDispatchException**. Data members exactly wrap the information provided by **IErrorInfo**.

m_wCode	error code specific to IDispatch
m_strDescription	text description of error
m_strHelpFile	help file containing extended help info
m_dwHelpContext	help context ID within help file
m_strSource	application that generated exception

USING COLEDISPATCHEXCEPTION

The client program that calls an Automation client through MFC helper functions can then deal with Automation exceptions very easily by using the standard C++ **try** and **catch** syntax. The following code is used for "Withdraw" in the "test" client, for the case of a dispatch interface.

```
try
{
  m_dispDAccount.Withdraw(amount);
  balance = m_dispDAccount.GetBalance();
  SetDlgItemInt(IDC_BALANCE, balance);
}
catch (COleDispatchException* e)
{
  MessageBox(e->m_strDescription, "Our Error Message");
  e->Delete();
}
```

Note that since an exception pointer is passed, you should call the **Delete** method of **CException**. Comparing the "Deposit" and "Withdraw" handlers, you can see the difference. For "Withdraw," we explicitly catch the exception and deal with it appropriately (in this case, just a message box). For "Deposit," we neglected to have exception handling code. This should be considered a defect in our program (done in the example for illustrative purposes). MFC provides some safety in such a situation through a default exception handler that puts up an error message derived from the information placed in the EXCEPINFO structure.

More broadly, we cn also compare the implementations of "Withdraw" in the "test" and "SmartClient" /client programs. The code in "test" used the underlying COM error interfaces directly, and thus was rather complex. This kind of error handling should be done for *every* error. It would not be practical at the application program level to perform such elaborate programming on every error. We did it once to illustrate how the underlying COM error

268 Chapter 12 • Error Processing and Debugging

interfaces work. The "SmartClient" provides a much more practical solution. Conceptually, it is similar to the approach taken by MFC. In both cases, C++ wrapper classes shield us from the low-level COM exception mechanism and we just have to write ordinary C++ exception handling code.

In the next section we will look at how another high-level application development framework, namely Visual Basic, deals with error handling in COM.

COM Error Handling in Visual Basic

Visual Basic has built-in support for the COM error interfaces, making it very easy to handle COM errors. Visual Basic does not give you an HRESULT when a COM error occurs, but rather a Visual Basic error is raised, which you can catch using the Visual Basic **On Error** statement. Any errors you do not handle yourself will be caught by the Visual Basic run time, which will display an error message (using extended error information, if available) and terminate the application.

Default Error Handling

First, let's look in detail at what happens if you do not provide any error handling in your code. Here is a minimal Visual Basic client program to exercise the **BankError** server. See **Chap12\BankClientVb\Step1**.

```
Option Explicit
Dim objAccount As AccountError

Private Sub cmdDeposit_Click()
    objAccount.Deposit txtAmount
    txtBalance = objAccount.Balance
End Sub

Private Sub cmdWithdraw_Click()
    objAccount.Withdraw txtAmount
    txtBalance = objAccount.Balance
End Sub

Private Sub Form_Load()
    Set objAccount = New AccountError
    txtBalance = objAccount.Balance
    txtAmount = 25
End Sub
```

Build the executable **BankClientVb.exe** (File | Make) and run this file through Windows Explorer. Try exercising a few good deposits and withdrawals. Then make several withdrawals, trying to force a negative balance. You will get a fatal error message from the Visual Basic run time. See Figure 12–9.

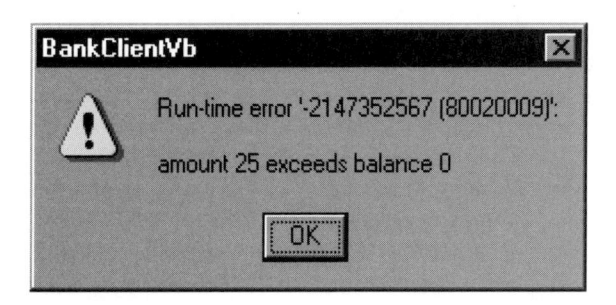

COM Error Handling in Visual Basic   **269**

Figure 12-9   *Visual Basic run time displays fatal message for unhandled error*

Notice that, without any work on your part, Visual Basic goes through the COM error interfaces to extract extended error information provided by the server. If you run the program from inside the Visual Basic development environment, you will see a different message displayed, allowing you the option of debugging the program, if you wish. See Figure 12–10.

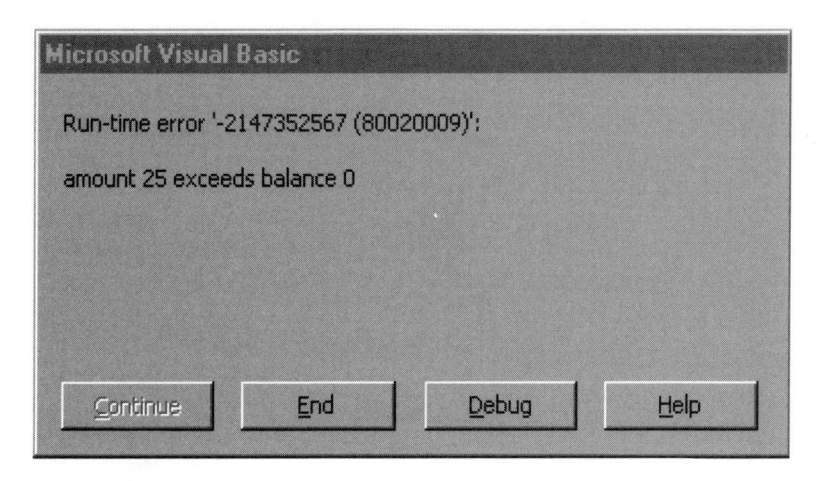

Figure 12-10   *Error message displayed when running within Visual Basic IDE*

Using On Error

Visual Basic provides an **On Error** statement that you can place before code that may raise an error condition. You also provide a **GoTo** and a label. If an error is encountered, the normal flow of execution stops and an immediate branch occurs to the code after the label. If no error occurs, execution continues sequentially. You should normally have an **Exit** statement just before the label, so in case of no error you do not have the error handling code execute.

Visual Basic also provides a built-in **Err** object, which is a wrapper for the underlying COM error object. Visual Basic provides a **Description** property which you can use to obtain the text description associated with the error, which can be supplied by the server as part of extended error information. The following code illustrates using **On Error** in Visual Basic. As with the Visual C++ example, we fail silently on "Deposit" (the MsgBox statement after the label is commented out) and put up an error message on "Withdraw."

```
Option Explicit
Dim objAccount As AccountError

Private Sub cmdDeposit_Click()
    On Error GoTo ErrorHandler
    objAccount.Deposit txtAmount
    txtBalance = objAccount.Balance
    Exit Sub
ErrorHandler:
    'MsgBox Err.Description
End Sub

Private Sub cmdWithdraw_Click()
    On Error GoTo ErrorHandler
    objAccount.Withdraw txtAmount
    txtBalance = objAccount.Balance
    Exit Sub
ErrorHandler:
    MsgBox Err.Description , , "Our Error Message"
End Sub

Private Sub Form_Load()
    Set objAccount = New AccountError
    txtBalance = objAccount.Balance
    txtAmount = 25
End Sub
```

If you run the Step 2 version of **BankClientVb.exe** (you have to build it), you should find the expected behavior. If you try to make an illegal withdrawal, you will get a nonfatal error message, the one we put up as our error handling code. See Figure 12–11.

If you run the Step 2 version from within the Visual Basic development environment, you may be surprised to see the default (fatal) Visual Basic message box displayed instead of the nonfatal one we created. Visual Basic has a setting on what to do with errors. The default behavior is to break on all errors, so you can conveniently go to the line of code where the error occurred (by clicking "Debug"). If you like you may change this default behavior, for instance, to break only on unhandled errors. You can bring up the appropriate dialog from Tools | Options, "General" tab. See Figure 12–12.

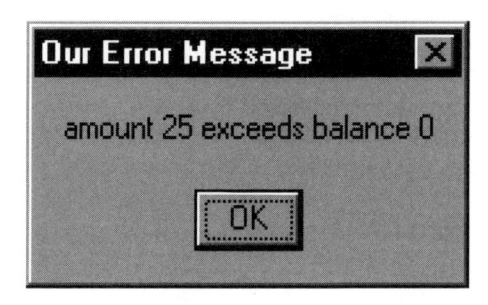

COM Error Handling in Visual Basic   271

Figure 12-11   *Message box displayed by our own error handling code*

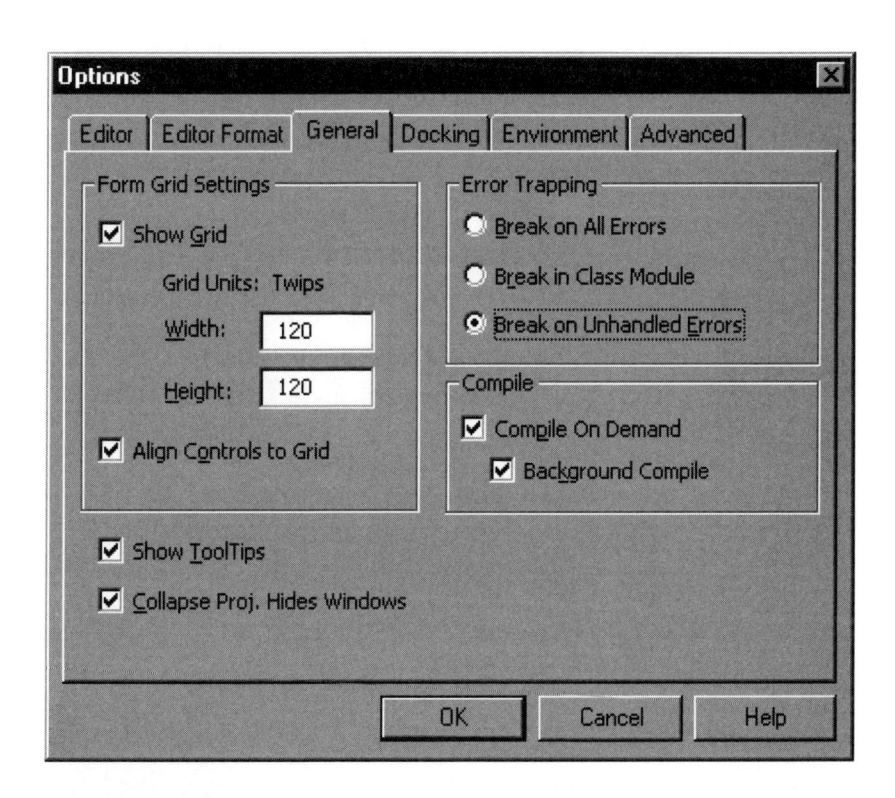

Figure 12-12   *Setting the option for when Visual Basic breaks after an error*

Tracing and Debugging

In this final section, we outline a few features in the Visual Studio and SDK development environment to help you debug your COM applications. ATL provides some useful tracing features, and there are various ways of breaking into the execution of a server so that you can use the debugger.

ATL Tracing Support

The ATLTRACE macro will write a formatted string to the output window while debugging. This macro works very much like the TRACE macro in MFC. You can use format control as in **printf**.

```
ATLTRACE("value = %d\n," value);
```

TRACING QUERYINTERFACE CALLS

ATL provides a special facility for tracing **QueryInterface** calls. For this to work, you must have all the common IIDs in the Interfaces section of the Registry. Normally this will be the case, but ATL provides a utility just in case. It is the command-line program **FINDGUID**, which you should run with the switch **-insert**. This only has to be done once, if at all.

Then in **stdafx.h** do a **#define** of the symbol **_ATL_DEBUG_QI** before you include **atlcom.h**.

```
// stdafx.
...

#define STRICT

#define _WIN32_WINNT 0x0400
#define _ATL_APARTMENT_THREADED

#include <atlbase.h>
extern CComModule _Module;
#define _ATL_DEBUG_QI
#include <atlcom.h>
...
```

TRACING OUTPUT

By using ATLTRACE (in the server), TRACE (in the MFC client), and the tracing of **QueryInterface**, you can obtain a good picture of fundamental COM activity in your program. The following trace shows the creation and use of a bank account object. An error was encountered. Bold output was produced by automatic ATL trace of **QueryInterface** calls. The nonbold output was the result of our own ATLTRACE and TRACE statements.

```
CComClassFactory - IUnknown
CComClassFactory - IClassFactory
CAccount object created
CAccount - IAccount
CAccount - IDispatch
CAccount - ISupportErrorInfo
ISupportErrorInfo interface is available
Error info is availble for IAccount
GetErrorInfo succeeded
GetDescription succeeded
CAccount object destroyed
```

Tracing in the SDK

Both ATL tracing and MFC tracing rely on the Win32 **OutputDebugString** function, which will send its output to the current debugger. In Visual C++, this means the Output Window when the Debug version of the program is running within the IDE.

The Platform SDK provides a utility called **DbMon**, which provides a debug window independent of Visual Studio. If you have the SDK installed on your system, you can bring up **DbMon** from the menu Start | Programs | Platform SDK | Tools | DbMon. Then any trace statements that wind up calling **OutputDebugString** will be displayed in the **DbMon** window if you are *not* running the program under Visual Studio. For example, if you bring up **DbMon** and launch **test.exe** (for **BankError** server), you will get the output shown in Figure 12–13.

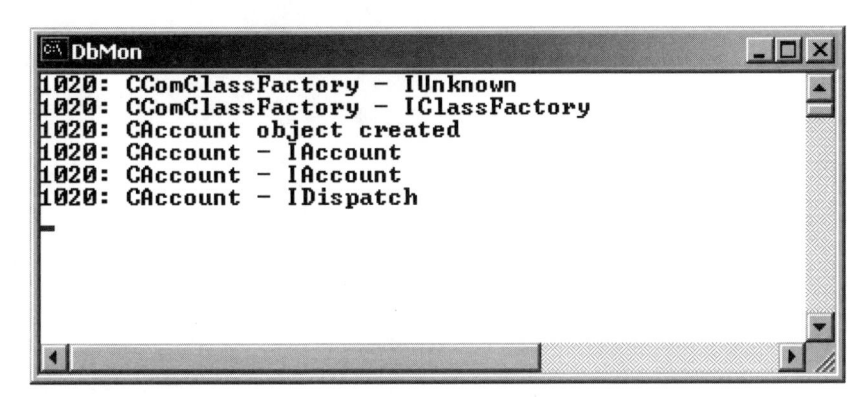

Figure 12–13   *Debug output shown by **DbMon** utility*

Breaking into Program Execution

When debugging servers, it can sometimes be tricky to break into execution of the server and use the debugger. A fundamental technique without relying on modern debuggers is judicious use of "print" statements. The previous section outlined tracing you can do, causing output to be directed to the Debugger, which can be displayed using **DbMon**. Another technique is to write to your own log file, using ordinary file I/O. If you close the file after every write, and reopen and append your new debug string, you can have a robust record of activity that will not be distorted by an output buffer not being flushed. So if you cannot break into the debugger, don't abandon hope. The following section will illustrate this logging technique and will provide a **Logger** component.

But it is nice to be able to use the debugger. Here are some tips.

SETTING A BREAKPOINT IN AN IN-PROCESS SERVER

You are in the best shape when your server is a DLL that runs in the same process as your own client (no surrogate). You can open your DLL project, set a breakpoint, and then specify your own client as the "Executable for debug setting" (Project | Settings, "Debug" tab). See Figure 12–14.

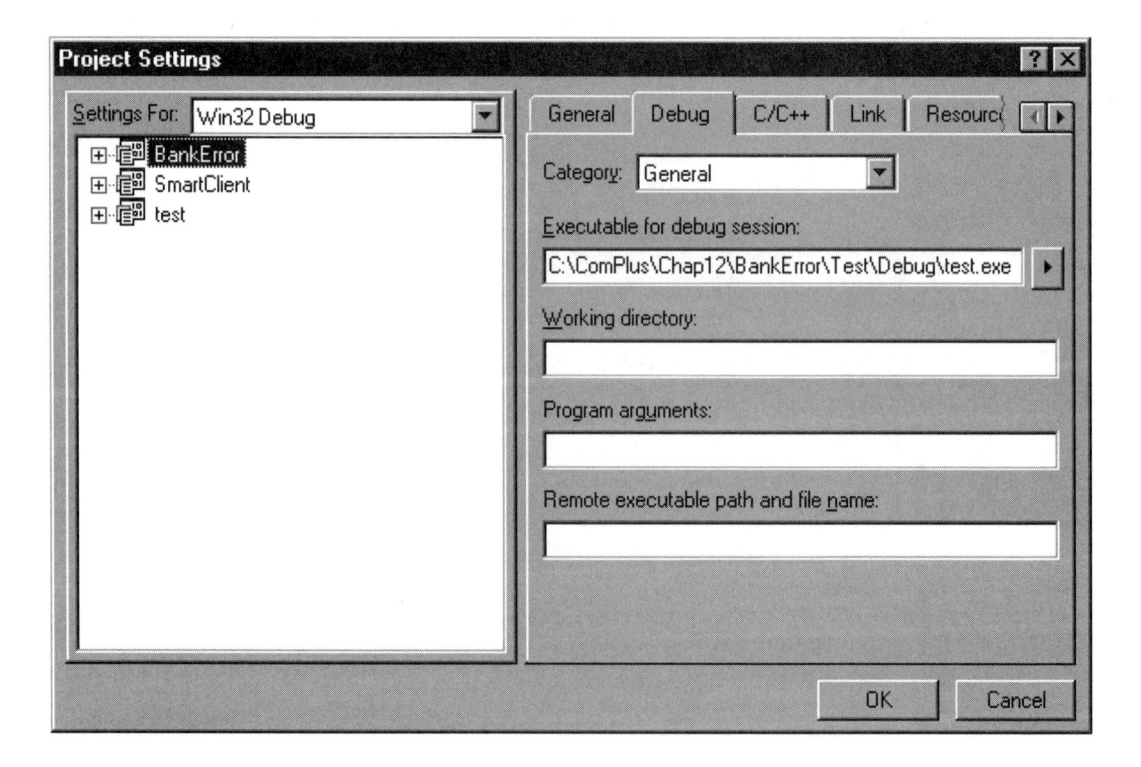

Figure 12–14   *Specifying the executable for debugging a DLL*

SETTING A BREAKPOINT IN AN EXE SERVER

A technique that can sometimes be applied for an EXE server is to set a breakpoint in the EXE server in one session of Visual C++. Then launch the server from Visual C++. Now start a *second* session of Visual C++ for the client. You may then be able to set breakpoints in both the client and the server. For this to work, when the client launches the server, the *same* instance of the server EXE must run. This will not always be the case, if for example the REGCLS parameter in **CoRegisterClassObject** was set to REGCLS_SINGLEUSE. In that case, the instance running under Visual C++ will sit there dumb and happy, and the breakpoint will never be hit. For the case of an OLE compound document server implemented as an MDI application, this technique usually works well.

USING THE DEBUGBREAK FUNCTION

Another technique for breaking into program execution is to call the Win32 function **DebugBreak** within the module you wish to debug. Rebuild your project and run your client program. When the **DebugBreak** call is hit, an application error message box will be displayed. See Figure 12–15.

Figure 12-15   *Application error dialog can get you into the debugger*

Click "Cancel," and you will indeed get into the debugger. You will come up in the midst of some assembly language. Don't despair. Single-step twice, and you will be into the routine where your **DebugBreak** was called. The display will be mixed assembly and source. For example, if you call **DebugBreak** at the beginning of the **get_Balance** function in the **BankError** server, here is what you will see:

```
36:         STDMETHODIMP CAccount::get_Balance(long * pVal)
37:         {
10001840    push        ebp
10001841    mov         ebp,esp
10001843    sub         esp,40h
10001846    push        ebx
10001847    push        esi
10001848    push        edi
38:             DebugBreak();
10001849    call        dword ptr [__imp__DebugBreak@0
                        (100373e8)]
39:             *pVal = m_nBalance;
1000184F    mov         eax,dword ptr [ebp+0Ch]
10001852    mov         ecx,dword ptr [ebp+8]
10001855    mov         edx,dword ptr [ecx+8]
10001858    mov         dword ptr [eax],edx
40:             return S_OK;
1000185A    xor         eax,eax
41:         }
```

You can now set other breakpoints in ordinary source windows and do regular source level debugging.

A Logger Component

In this final section we provide a simple Logger component. It writes to a file with the hardcoded path **c:\logfile.txt**. Each write involves opening the file, appending to it, and closing the file. Thus, there will be no anomalies from a buffer not being flushed. On the first write the file is created if it does not already exist. The method **Write** can be used to write out any string. The method **Writehr** can be used to write an HRESULT in both hex and also the system-supplied text associated with the error number.

As a COM component, it can be called from both Visual Basic and Visual C++. The Logger component itself is in the folder **Chap12\Logger**. A Visual C++ test program is in the **test** subdirectory as a separate project in the same workspace. A Visual Basic test program is in the folder **Chap12\TestLoggerVb**. Build the server project, which will register the Logger component.

LOGGING FROM VISUAL C++

Although the component is written in Visual C++, it is actually a little harder to call from Visual C++ than from Visual Basic, because strings are passed as the BSTR data type. We also supply a simple C++ wrapper class, **CLogging**. Normally, the logging would be done from a middle tier component written using ATL. If your C++ code is not using ATL, you should include the header file **atlbase.h** to get the ATL wrapper class **CComBSTR**, which is used to facilitate working with BSTRs.

Using the Logger component with the aid of a **CLogging** object **m_log** is very easy:

```
void CTestDlg::OnWrite()
{
  CString text;
  GetDlgItemText(IDC_TEXT, text);
  m_log.Write(text);
}

void CTestDlg::OnWritehr()
{
  m_log.Writehr("success", 0);
  m_log.Writehr("failure 1", 0x800401F3);
  m_log.Writehr("failure 2", 0x80080005);
}
```

The test program puts up a simple dialog to allow you to log strings and a few hardcoded HRESULTs. See Figure 12–16.

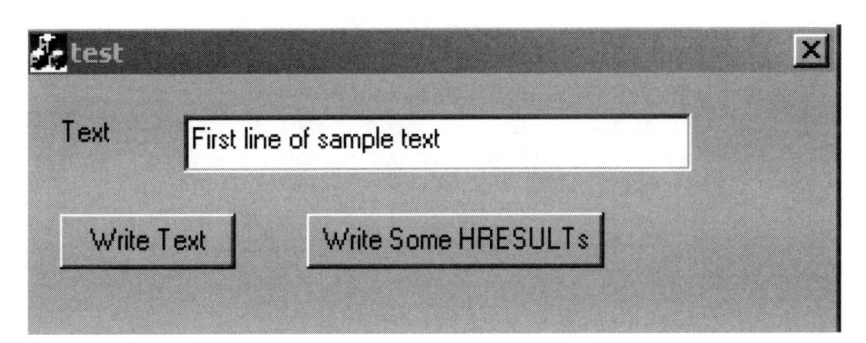

Figure 12–16 *Visual C++ test program for Logger component*

Enter a couple of strings, and then click "Write Some HRESULTs." You may then inspect **c:\logfile.txt**. Note that, by design, nothing is written to the log file in case of a successful HRESULT.

```
First line of sample text
Second line of sample text
----------
failure 1,   hr = 0x800401f3
Invalid class string
--------------------
failure 2,   hr = 0x5
Access is denied.
----------
```

LOGGING FROM VISUAL BASIC

Since BSTR is a native Visual Basic type, it is very easy to just directly use the Logger component. Here is the complete code of the Visual Basic test program:

```
Dim objLog As New Log

Private Sub cmdWrite_Click()
    objLog.Write Text1
End Sub

Private Sub cmdWritehr_Click()
    objLog.Writehr "success", 0
    objLog.Writehr "failure 1", &H800401F3
    objLog.Writehr "failure 2", &H80080005
End Sub
```

Summary

The fundamental means that COM uses for communicating error information is the HRESULT. The HRESULT is a 32-bit number consisting of a severity bit, a facility code, and an error code. You can make up your own error codes, but Microsoft defines the facility codes. There are a number of COM interfaces that can be used for transmitting extended error information. ATL provides some support for these error interfaces, making them easier to use. The Visual C++ **_com_error** class provides a simplification for the client code. Automation provides an exception mechanism. MFC will automatically throw a C++ exception in response to an Automation exception. Visual Basic automatically wraps the COM error interfaces for you, and you can do error handling using the Visual Basic **On Error** statement. You can do tracing of various sorts to help debug your COM servers, and there are various techniques that can help you break into the execution of a server. Another useful technique is to write information to a log file.

THIRTEEN

Multithreading in COM

Concurrency is an important issue in computer programming. In Windows you can write concurrent programs using multiple threads. Significant performance gains can be made by using multiple threads in your programs, but there is also greater complexity because of concern over thread safety. COM brings a new wrinkle to issues of multithreading, because clients and servers can be written independently, and each can have different approaches to threading. It is a challenge to enable these diverse servers and clients to coexist. COM provides an architectural element called an apartment *that serves as an abstraction for threading requirements and usage. A server may "declare" the apartment threading models for the classes it implements and the COM run-time system will harmonize the uses of these classes by different clients. This "declarative" style of programming is used extensively in COM+, and thus coverage of threading in COM will provide a nice transition to Part 3, where we discuss COM+.*

The chapter begins with a discussion of fundamental concepts of concurrency, including the problem of race conditions. A programming example illustrates a race condition. Windows messaging provides a natural synchronization mechanism, which can be used to prevent race conditions. After this background, we outline the concept of an apartment in COM and describe the different types of apartments and the different threading models of DLL servers. We then cover the programming of single threaded apartments, followed by a discussion of marshaling interface pointers between apartments. We conclude with a treatment of programming a multiple thread apartment.

Concurrent Programming

A classical issue in computer programming is concurrency. If a computer has more than one processor, performance can be improved by partitioning the computation into pieces that can be executed concurrently on different processors. Even if there is only one CPU, there are opportunities for concurrency using other hardware processors, such as I/O. For example, if a computation is blocked waiting for I/O, another computation can go forward.

A major issue in concurrency is shared data. If two computations access the same data, different results can be obtained depending on the timing of the different accesses, a situation known as a race condition. Race conditions present a programming challenge because they can occur unpredictably. Careful programming is required to ensure they do not occur.

Race Condition Example

Race conditions can easily arise in multithreaded applications, because threads belonging to the same process share the same address space and thus can share data. Consider two threads making deposits to a bank account where the deposit operation is not atomic:

- Get balance
- Add amount to balance
- Store balance

The following sequence of actions will then produce a race condition, with invalid results:

1. Balance starts at 100.
2. Thread 1 makes deposit of 25, interrupted after getting balance and adding amount to balance, but before storing balance.
3. Thread 2 makes deposit of 5000 and goes to completion, storing 5100.
4. Thread 1 now finishes, storing 125, overwriting the result of Thread 2. The $5000 deposit has been lost.

Serializing Access to Shared Data

Such race conditions can be avoided by serializing access to the shared data. Suppose only one thread at a time is allowed to access the bank account. Then the first thread that starts to access the balance will complete the operation before another thread begins to access the balance (the second thread will be blocked).

There are two ways such serializing of data access can be ensured:

- Automatically by the system
- Explicitly by application program code that uses mutual exclusion primitives such as critical sections

Concurrent Programming

There are trade-offs in the two approaches. The automatic serialization by the system is easy to implement for the application programmer. But it may lose concurrency due to *all* access to the shared data being prohibited when one method is accessing only part of the data.

Automatically Serializing Data Access

Windows itself serializes the handling of Windows messages through the **GetMessage/DispatchMessage** loop. You do not have to write "thread safe" Windows procedures. COM takes advantage of the serialization inherent in Windows message processing when it marshals method calls across process boundaries. Marshaling is implemented via message processing in a hidden window. Hence, one method call on a COM object will complete before another method begins execution. Under this approach, COM methods will not have to be "thread safe."

Windows Message Queue Demo

An example program illustrates how COM's use of Windows messages guards against the race condition in the "bank" example. See **Chap13\BankMt\Step0**, which contains two projects, "BankMt" and "test." "BankMt" is an EXE server for a bank object, and "test" is a dialog-based test program. See Figure 13–1.

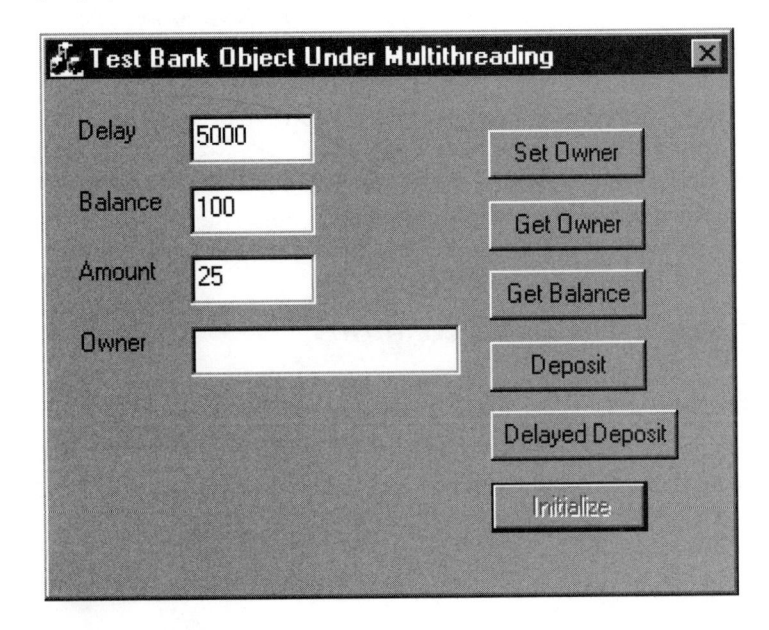

Figure 13–1   *Test program illustrates automatic serialization*

DELAYDEPOSIT

The method **DelayDeposit** makes it easy to simulate a race condition. After calculating the new balance in a local variable, the method goes to sleep before storing the new balance. While sleeping, the object is potentially vulnerable to the **Deposit** method going in and out. When the **DelayDeposit** method wakes up and stores its result, the work of the **Deposit** method could be lost.

```
STDMETHODIMP
CBankApt::DelayDeposit(long amount, long delay)
{
  long balance = g_balance;
  balance += amount;
  Sleep(delay);
  g_balance = balance;
  return S_OK;
}
```

EXERCISING THE TEST PROGRAM

1. Build the "BankMt" project. Notice that, as part of the build process, both the server is registered and a proxy/stub DLL is registered. The latter is necessary because the server is an EXE and the proxy/stub provides the marshaling code.
2. Build the "test" project.
3. Launch two instances of TEST.EXE. In both, click the Initialize button.
4. Try out clicking Deposit in both instances. Click GetBalance to show the current balance. Notice that both instances of the test program are accessing the same global data. Since the Deposit method is in and out so fast, you won't see any race condition.

TRYING FOR A RACE CONDITION

Now let's attempt to duplicate the race condition scenario described above. In Instance 1 leave the Amount at 25, and in Instance 2 enter 5000 for the amount. Now in Instance 1 click **DelayDeposit** and in Instance 2 immediately click **Deposit**. What happens?

The call to Deposit is blocked by COM until DelayDeposit returns. COM has enforced serial access to the methods, and the race condition has been avoided. No special coding was required in the method implementations to enforce a critical section.

Now try one more experiment. In Instance 1, again click **DelayDeposit** and in Instance 2 quickly click Get Owner. Even though the owner data is independent of the balance, COM will block the **get_Owner** call until **DelayDeposit** completes. We are losing concurrency that would be safe.

THE HIDDEN WINDOW

Using Spy++, you can see the hidden window that COM uses for marshaling. You can bring up Spy++ from the Tools menu in Visual C++. Use menu Spy | Processes and look for BANKMT. Expand the node in the tree view until you see the window shown. See Figure 13–2.

By right-clicking the mouse, we can bring up a message window and observe Window messages associated with method invocations. See Figure 13–3.

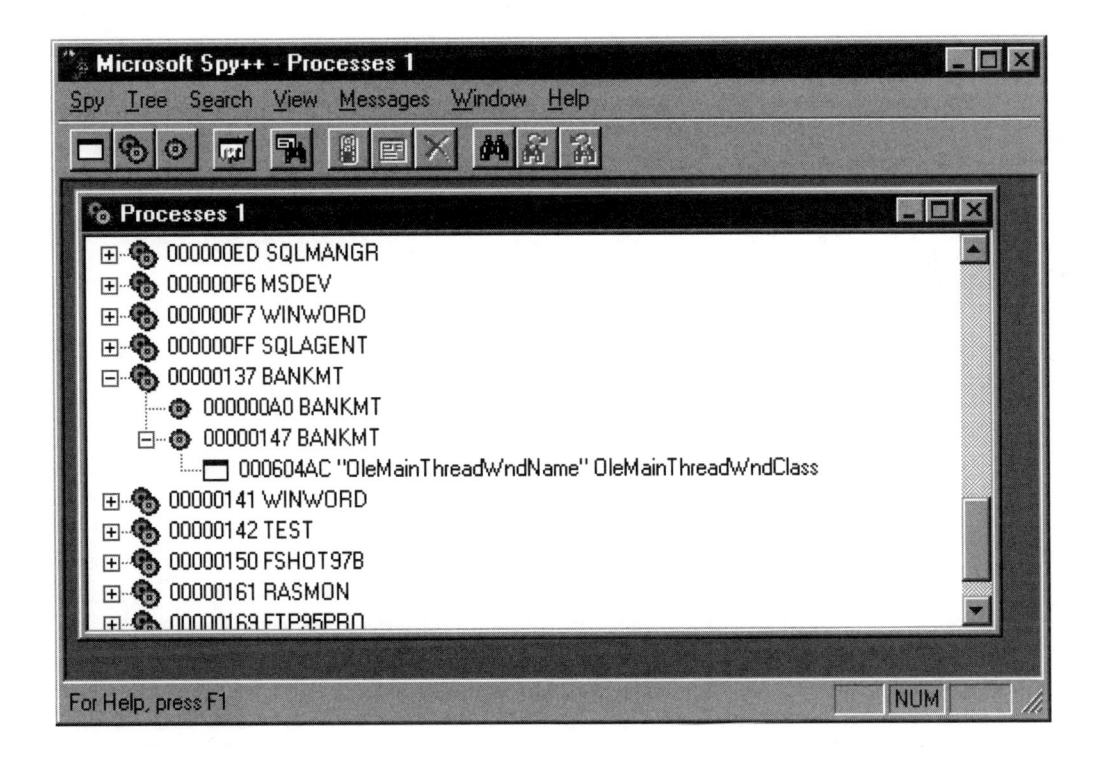

Figure 13–2 *The hidden window used for RPC across processes on one machine*

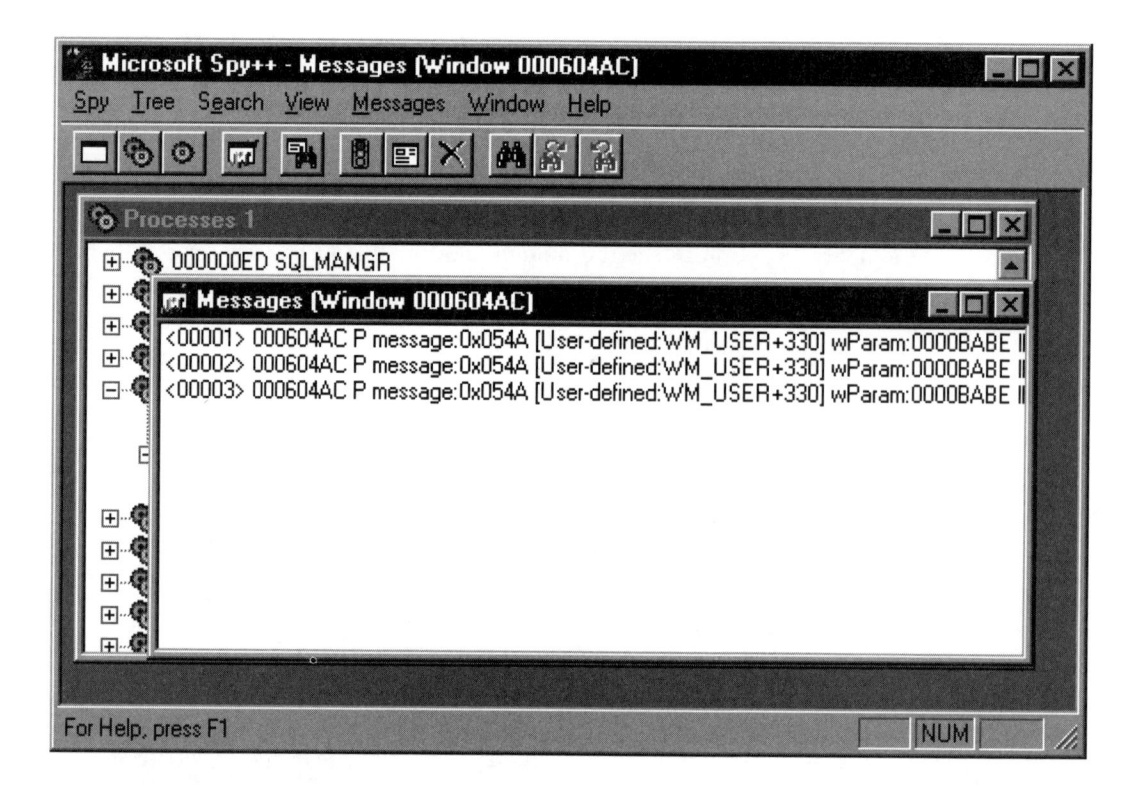

Figure 13-3 *Method calls translate into Windows messages*

Apartments and Multithreading in COM

We have seen that the Windows remoting architecture that makes use of Windows messages automatically serializes access to an object residing in another process. We are not guaranteed this serialization when the object resides in the same process and two threads in that process are concurrently accessing the object. We would like to be able to achieve two different outcomes with multiple threads, depending on our requirements. One outcome is easy programming with guaranteed serialization, as is the case when we cross a process boundary. The other is high-performance processing, when we are willing to take the trouble to put in thread synchronization code ourselves.

Apartments

COM achieves both objectives through the abstraction of *apartment* and the concept of a "threading model" for a class. An apartment groups objects that share the same concurrency requirements. The apartment an object resides in is part of the object's identity. In NT 4.0, there are two kinds of apartments, STA (single-threaded) and MTA (multithreaded). In a given process, there can be several STAs and only one MTA. Only one thread can execute in an STA, while many threads are allowed to concurrently execute in the MTA. A thread "enters" an apartment when it calls **CoInitializeEx**, with the second parameter indicating which kind of apartment. An STA is "created" when a thread enters it. The MTA is created the first time **CoInitializeEx** is called with second parameter asking for an MTA. The first STA created is called the "main STA." Figure 13–4 shows a process with four threads and three apartments. Thread 1 creates the main STA, thread 2 creates a second STA. Thread 3 creates the MTA, and thread 4 enters the already existing MTA.

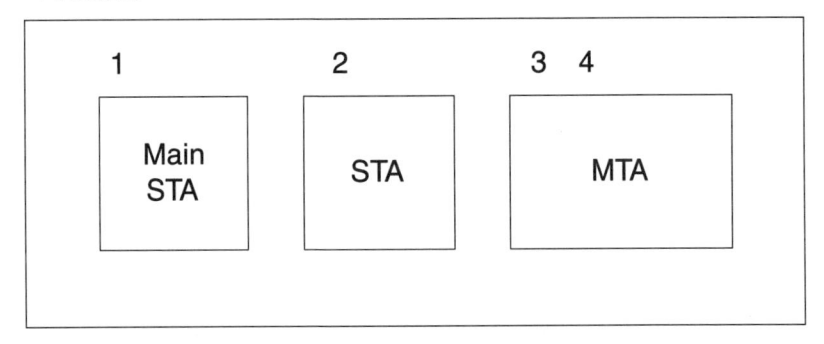

Figure 13–4 *A process with four threads and three apartments*

SINGLE-THREADED APARTMENTS

An STA enforces serialization of access to any object residing in it. COM enforces serialization through a Windows message queue that is associated with a hidden window that is created by every STA. The example program in the previous section illustrated such a hidden window, which we spied on. This means that there can be no concurrent access to methods of an object residing in an STA, and so you do not have to protect instance data against concurrent access. The result is a substantial simplification in programming effort:

MULTITHREADED APARTMENT

The MTA does not provide any enforcement of serialization. Multiple threads in the MTA can access the same object concurrently. Threads executing in the MTA are sometimes referred to as "free threads." Hence, the code implementing class methods which can be called directly by free threads must be thread safe; explicit coding for synchronization must be done, such as protecting shared data with critical sections, etc. The benefit of this increased effort of programming is potentially higher performance.

EXE AND DLL SERVERS

Apartments are not so important for EXE servers, because every method call to an EXE server is out-of-process and hence goes through the RPC/message queue mechanism, and COM is able to enforce serialization. Briefly, an EXE server indicates its apartment type by the parameter it passes to **CoInitializeEx**, and thus there are two threading models (single-threaded and multi-threaded).

The rest of this chapter focuses on DLL servers and in fact Part 3 also focuses on DLL servers, because they are the ones for which COM+ is geared to provide services.

Threading Models

Because of the different concurrency requirements of different apartment types and the resulting differences in how the COM run time should treat them, it is incumbent upon the server to specify the *threading model* of each of its classes. The threading model specifies the type of apartment in which its objects can execute. Note that a server can implement multiple classes, and each class can have its own threading model. Figure 13–5 shows the three classes implemented by the **BankMt** example server discussed in this chapter. The **BankApt** class supports the "Apartment" threading model and the **BankFree** and **BankNoCS** classes support the "Free" threading model.

A DLL server does not call **CoInitializeEx** itself (its client does). A DLL server indicates the threading model for its classes by placing appropriate entries in the Registry. Use the **ThreadingModel** named-value in the **InprocServer32** key. If the named-value is not present, the threading model is "Single;" otherwise, the model is indicated by the value, which may be "Apartment," "Free," or "Both." Figure 13–6 shows the Registry entries for the **BankApt** class, which has the "Apartment" threading model.

SINGLE THREADING MODEL

The classes in legacy COM servers will not have a **ThreadingModel** value in the Registry, and so their threading model will be "Single." This means that *all* instantiated objects belonging to this class will be placed in the main STA. Hence, there are no concurrency issues for the class whatsoever. Even static or global data in the class (such as object counts and lock count for the class factory) does not have to be protected against concurrent access. But this

BankMt DLL Server

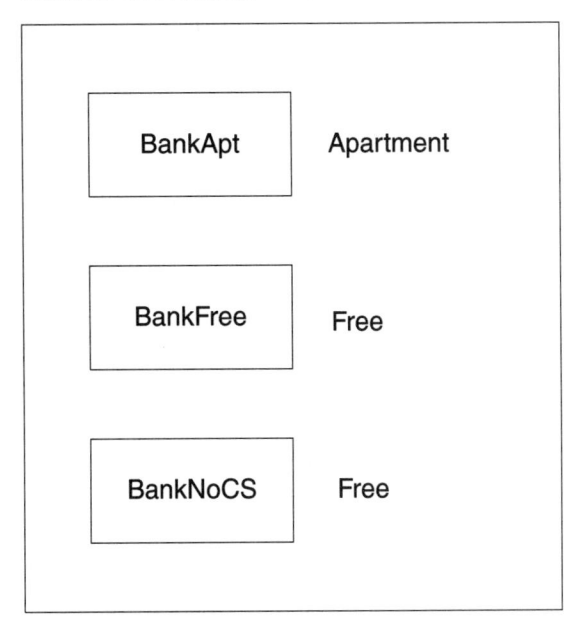

```
┌─────────────────────────────────────┐
│                                     │
│   ┌─────────────┐                   │
│   │   BankApt   │    Apartment      │
│   └─────────────┘                   │
│                                     │
│   ┌─────────────┐                   │
│   │  BankFree   │    Free           │
│   └─────────────┘                   │
│                                     │
│   ┌─────────────┐                   │
│   │  BankNoCS   │    Free           │
│   └─────────────┘                   │
│                                     │
└─────────────────────────────────────┘
```

Figure 13–5 *The classes in a DLL server can each have their own threading model*

means only a single thread can access such a COM object. As of NT 3.5, COM objects simply could not live on more than one thread.

APARTMENT THREADING MODEL

NT 3.51 introduced the apartment concept and the corresponding threading model, providing a great advance that allowed COM objects to live on multiple threads, each in its own STA. It is perfectly legal for a client on one thread to access an object on another thread (living in another apartment), but it must go through a proxy. The proxy makes use of message queue synchronization, and so access to the COM object is serialized. The genius of this approach is that it enables multithreaded COM applications without requiring the COM classes to worry about thread safety in the methods.

A DLL server that supports classes with the Apartment threading model does need to address some multithreading concerns, however. Multiple clients can instantiate an object concurrently, so you need to protect static and global data such as object and lock counts against concurrent access. **DllGetClassObject** and **DllCanUnloadNow** and the class factory methods must be thread safe. As we will see shortly, ATL provides thread-safe implementations for us.

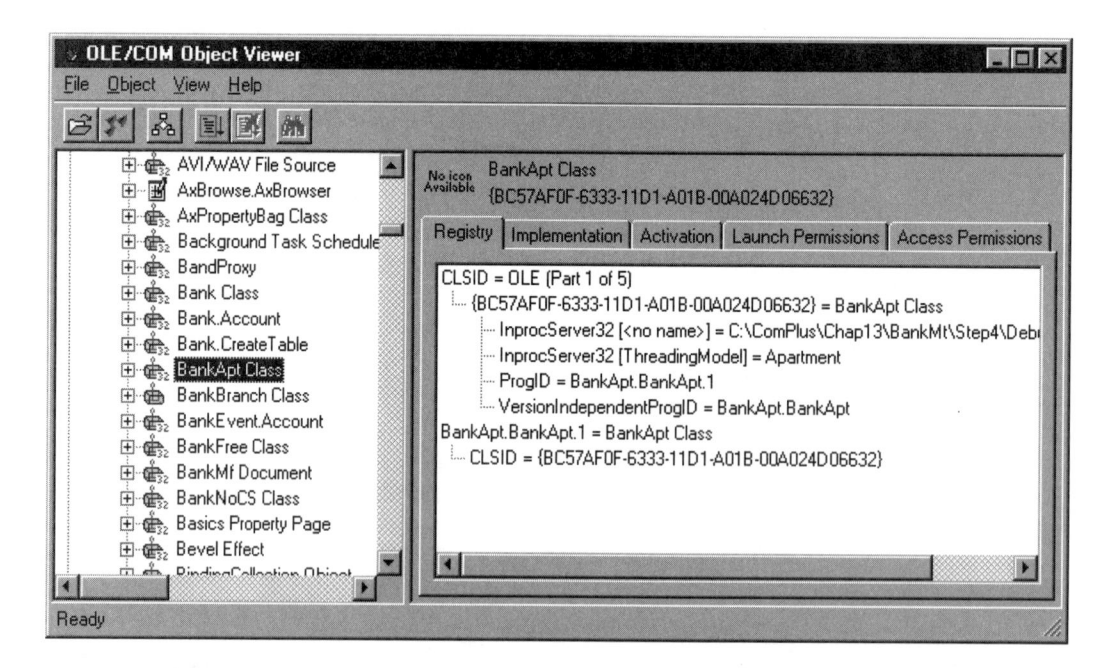

Figure 13–6 *Registry entries for a class with Apartment threading model*

FREE THREADING MODEL

Although the Apartment model made possible multithreaded COM applications, there are some performance limitations to this approach. The proxy is a rather blunt instrument to enforce serialization because it blocks *all* concurrent access to an object. An object may have many different pieces of encapsulated data. While one thread is accessing one piece of data, another thread could safely access another piece of independent data, but the object-wide blocking of the Apartment threading model prevents such concurrent access. To address such concerns NT 4.0, introduced the free threading model and the Multithreaded Apartment.

As we have seen, a process can have one Multithreaded Apartment (MTA) with several threads which can concurrently access the same object. In the Free threading model, all instantiated objects live in this MTA. This model provides excellent performance for the client that created the MTA (by calling **CoInitializeEx** with COINIT_MULTITHREADED) and for its worker threads. If there is a lot of processing done by these worker threads, this model can give good performance, because the worker threads have direct access to the object (no proxy), and there is fine-grained access (no object-wide lock).

What happens if a thread that lives in some STA calls the object? Such a call crosses an apartment boundary, and hence will have to go through a proxy.

"BOTH" THREADING MODEL

The last threading model under NT 4.0 is "Both." In this case, an instantiated COM object may live in any apartment, the MTA or any of the STAs. If any thread in the MTA instantiates the object, the object will live in the MTA. If a thread in some STA instantiates the object, it will live in that particular STA. Thus, a client living in an STA can call the object directly, not going through a proxy, unlike the case of the Free threading model, where the object always lives in the MTA.

CHOOSING A THREADING MODEL

The choice of appropriate threading model for a class depends on the application. No modern application should choose "Single"—that is strictly a legacy feature (it is simpler to implement, since the DLL itself does not have to be thread safe, but if you are using ATL, you do not have to worry about that anyway).

The Apartment model is appropriate in many cases. You do not have to worry about making your methods thread safe because COM serializes all calls to your object through the proxy mechanism. Yet your clients can implement multiple threads which call your object. The Apartment model is a good trade-off between ease of implementation and reasonable performance. If you are implementing your class using Visual Basic, the choice is made for you. Visual Basic only supports the Apartment threading model. Likewise, if you are implementing your class using MFC user interface classes, the threading model must be Apartment.

If you are using ATL to implement your class you have the full range of options and can consider "Free" or "Both." In both of these cases, you must write thread-safe code for your class methods. If you anticipate much access to your objects from both STA threads and MTA threads, "Both" is probably preferable. If you anticipate the bulk of the access to the objects will be from worker threads in the client that created the MTA, "Free" is likely a good choice.

NEUTRAL THREADING MODEL

Windows 2000 introduced another kind of apartment and a corresponding threading model called "Neutral." We will discuss the Neutral threading model, which is preferred under COM+, in Chapter 16.

Crossing Apartment Boundaries

A key feature of the Apartment architecture is that any calls to an object residing in another apartment must go through a proxy, as illustrated in Figure 13–7.

The case of an out-of-process server is a special case, because an object in another process is automatically in another apartment. The new feature is crossing apartment boundaries within a process. To permit cross-apartment

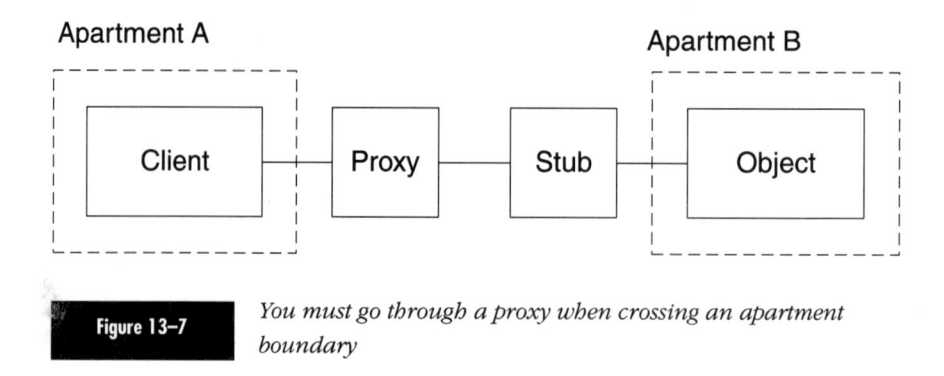

```
          Apartment A                                       Apartment B
          ┌ ─ ─ ─ ─ ─ ─ ─ ─ ─ ─ ─ ─ ┐                      ┌ ─ ─ ─ ─ ─ ─ ─ ─ ─ ─ ┐
          │  ┌─────────┐   ┌───────┐│  ┌───────┐   ┌──────┐│
          │  │ Client  │───│ Proxy │├──│ Stub  │───│Object││
          │  └─────────┘   └───────┘│  └───────┘   └──────┘│
          └ ─ ─ ─ ─ ─ ─ ─ ─ ─ ─ ─ ─ ┘                      └ ─ ─ ─ ─ ─ ─ ─ ─ ─ ─ ┘
```

Figure 13-7 *You must go through a proxy when crossing an apartment boundary*

calls within a process you need a proxy/stub DLL, just as with the case of an EXE server.

MARSHALING AN INTERFACE POINTER

In most cases, the COM infrastructure will handle marshaling issues through the proxy and stub automatically without any special programming required of you, other than generating and registering the proxy/stub DLL. There is one situation that can arise in crossing an apartment boundary within a process that does require special attention.

An interface pointer to an object in one apartment in a process is accessible to a thread in another apartment within the process because the apartments share a common address space. But your program must take care not to call the object through the interface pointer directly. Instead you must explicitly marshal the interface pointer. COM provides API functions (with very long names) for inter-thread marshaling within a process.

- **CoMarshalInterThreadInterfaceInStream** marshals an interface pointer into a stream object, from which it can be unmarshaled.
- **CoGetInterfaceAndReleaseStream** unmarshals an interface pointer from a stream object and releases the stream.

We will see the details of how to use these functions in the next section when we go through implementation details.

Implementing Multithreading in COM

In this final section, we go through some of the details of implementing multithreading in COM. The good news is that ATL does most of the heavy lifting for you. In the case of an Apartment threading model, it ensures that your DLL server is thread safe. COM itself takes the place of serializing access to your method calls, so you do not have to worry about thread safety there either. If you call an object in another apartment through an interface pointer stored in process-wide memory, you will have to take care of marshaling this interface pointer. If you have a class with threading model "Free" or "Both" you will need to ensure that your methods are thread safe. For example you may need to protect instance data by using a critical section.

We begin with an overview of the multithreading support provided by ATL. The rest of the section goes through an example program that illustrates the programming techniques required and demonstrates some of the concurrency issues that we have discussed.

ATL Support for Multithreading

ATL support for multithreading begins with the ATL Object Wizard. One of the attributes that you can set is the threading model. The four choices are the ones that we have previously discussed. See Figure 13–8.

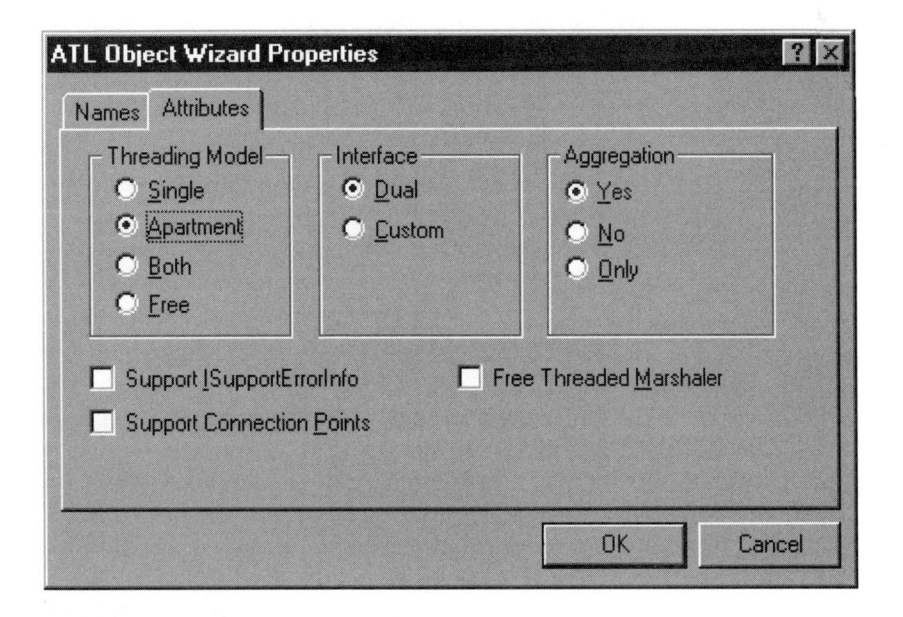

Figure 13–8 *ATL Object Wizard allows you to choose the threading model*

The choice you make for threading model is reflected in a class template parameter that is passed to **CComObjectRootEx**. For example, when you choose Single or Apartment model, the appropriate class to use for this parameter is **CComSingleThreadModel**. In the case of "Free" or "Both," the parameter will be **CComMultiThreadModel**. You can see this code in the class definition file.

```
class ATL_NO_VTABLE CBankApt :
  public CComObjectRootEx<CComSingleThreadModel>,
  public CComCoClass<CBankApt, &CLSID_BankApt>,
  public ISupportErrorInfo,
  public IBank
{
...
```

Now behind the scenes ATL will do the required work for you. First of all it will provide a thread-safe implementation of the functions exported by your DLL, such as **DllGetClassObject** and **DllCanUnloadNow**. Next, it will provide a thread-safe implementation of the class factories, including protecting variables storing the object counts and lock count. In the "Free" or "Both" cases, when object methods must be thread-safe, it will provide for thread safety in its implementation of **IUnknown**.

ATL also provides some useful utility classes, such as **CComAutoCriticalSection**, which makes it easy to implement critical sections.

DLL Server Example, Step 1

The rest of this section goes through the **BankMt** example server, illustrating many of the features in COM multithreading that we have been discussing. We will review some of the concepts as we go along. Step 0 of the example illustrated an EXE server, demonstrating the automatic serialization to an object provided by a proxy, the core concept that enables COM to transparently provide for thread safety in many situations. The rest of the example, Steps 1–4, is concerned with a DLL server.

First build the projects in **Chap13\BankMt\Step1**. Notice that, as part of building the server "BankMt," a proxy/stub DLL is registered. This is accomplished by a custom build step in the project. Next run two instances of the test program. Make some deposits from the first instance. Now get the balance in the second instance. You will see the original balance of 100. See Figure 13–9. What is happening?

In Win32, a DLL is mapped into the address space of the EXE that loads it. The two instances of the test program are separate processes, each with their own address space. Two separate objects are created, each with their own data.

DLL Server Example, Step 2 (Race Condition)

Next consider the case of one instance of the test program that spawns multiple threads, each accessing the same object. Build the two projects in **Chap13\BankMt\Step2**, and then do the following:

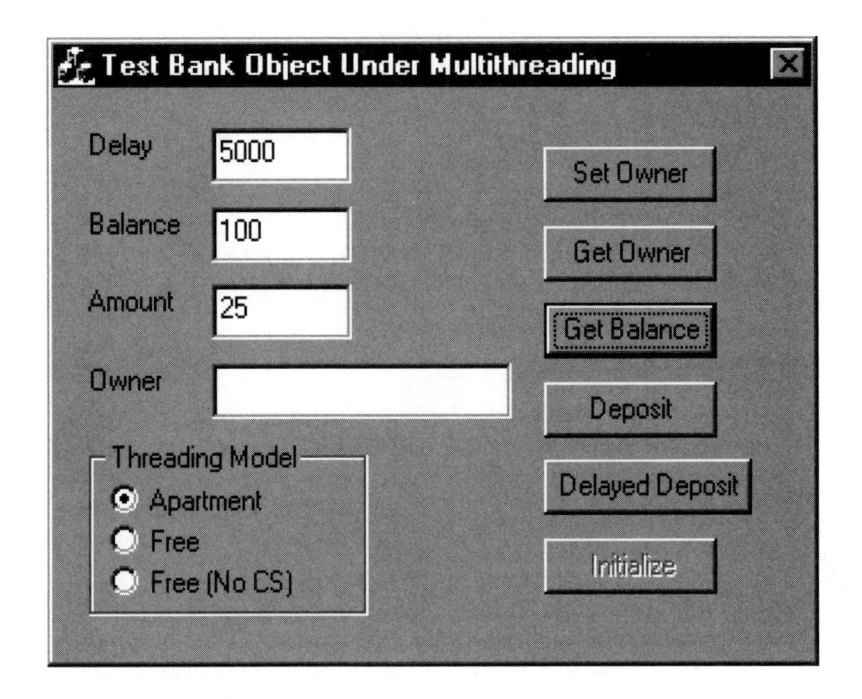

Implementing Multithreading in COM

Figure 13-9 *Why has the balance not been updated by the deposits?*

1. Run the test program and click Initialize. A "New Thread" button is enabled. You can start as many new threads as you like from the first thread.

2. Click New Thread. A new user interface thread starts (you will see it on the Task Bar).

3. Click the icon on the Task Bar to show the second dialog window. Arrange the windows so that you can see them both. Notice that you can distinguish the window associated with the initial thread by the presence of two additional buttons. See Figure 13–10.

4. Set Amount in the second window to 5000.

5. Click Delayed Deposit in the first window.

6. Immediately click Deposit in the second window. The call is not blocked, but returns immediately, showing an updated balance of 5100.

7. Wait until the Delayed Deposit completes in the first window. You will see balance in the first window of 125.

8. Click Get Balance in the second window. You will see indeed that the balance is 125. Your $5000 deposit has been lost.

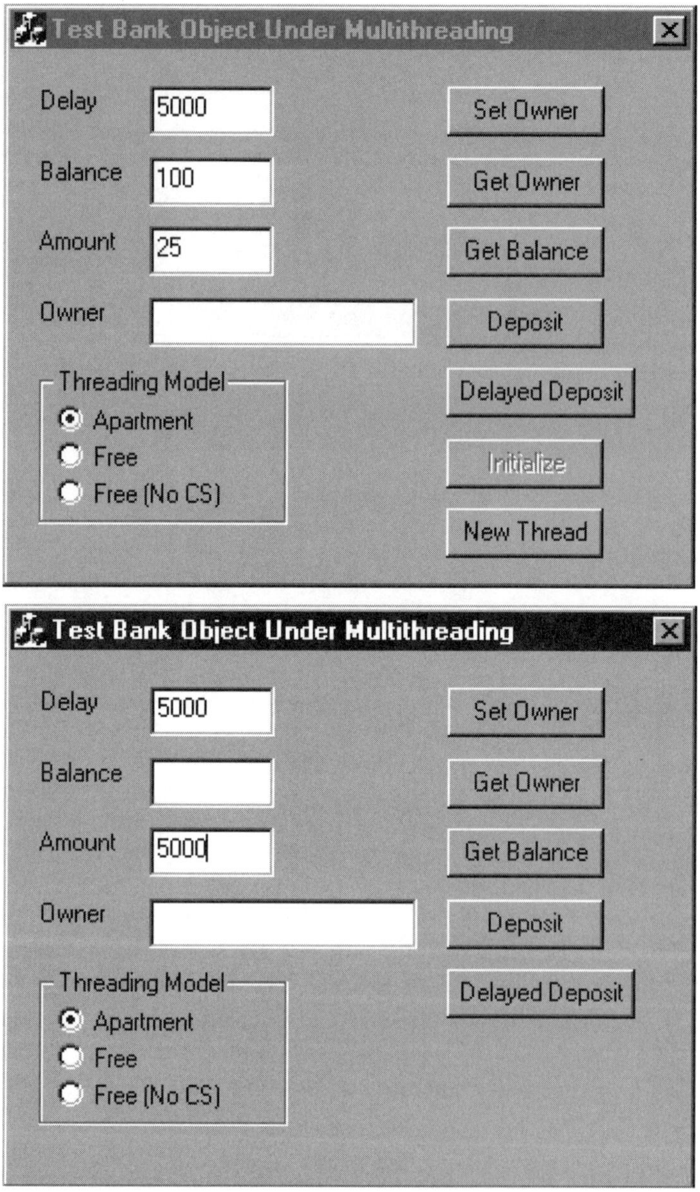

Chapter 13 • Multithreading in COM

Figure 13-10 Two threads accessing the same object

UNMARSHALED INTERFACE POINTER

A single instance of the bank object is created when the Initialize button is clicked. The interface pointer is stored as a static data member of the dialog class.

```
class CTestDlg : public CDialog
{
...
// Implementation
protected:
  void UpdateBalance();
  HICON m_hIcon;
  static IBank* m_pBank;
  BOOL m_bFirst;
...
```

When the second thread invokes the Deposit method, it uses the interface pointer *directly*.

```
void CTestDlg::OnDeposit()
{
  UpdateData();
  m_pBank->Deposit(m_amount);
  UpdateBalance();
}
```

DLL Server Example, Step 3 (Marshal Interface Pointer)

To take advantage of COM synchronizing access to methods through the Windows message queue, we must marshal the interface pointer. Marshaling takes place automatically when the server is out of process. COM provides API functions (with very long names!) for inter-thread marshaling within a process.

- **CoMarshalInterThreadInterfaceInStream** marshals an interface pointer into a stream object, from which it can be unmarshaled.
- **CoGetInterfaceAndReleaseStream** unmarshals an interface pointer from a stream object and releases the stream.

Step 3 of the project illustrates the use of these API functions. Before examining the code, build and run the project in **Chap13\BankMt\Step3**. This time when you run the test program, check "Marshal Interface Pointer" before you click "Initialize." Then start a new thread and try to duplicate the race condition. Click "Delayed Deposit" in the first window and then immediately click "Deposit" in the second window. The call by the second thread to the **Deposit** method blocks until the previous call to **DelayDeposit** finishes. The race condition is avoided.

Now again do a "Delayed Deposit" from the first thread. In the second thread immediately click "Get Owner." Even though it is harmless to access the independent owner name data that is not being updated by the first thread, the method call is blocked anyway. COM's synchronization is on an object-wide basis.

You can now examine the code in **testDlg.cpp**. The interface pointer is marshaled into a stream in **OnNewthread**.

```
void CTestDlg::OnNewthread()
{
  // marshal interface pointer for each new thread
  if (m_bMarshal)
  {
    HRESULT hr;
    hr = CoMarshalInterThreadInterfaceInStream(
            IID_IBank,
            (IUnknown*) m_pBank,
            &m_pStream);
    if (FAILED(hr))
    {
      MessageBox("Marshal failed");
      return;
    }
  }
  CClient* pThread = new CClient;
  pThread->CreateThread();
}
```

The interface pointer for the new thread is unmarshaled from the stream when the dialog for the new thread is brought up, in **OnInitDialog**.

```
BOOL CTestDlg::OnInitDialog()
{
...
// Unmarshal interface pointer if asked
    if (m_bMarshal)
    {
      HRESULT hr = CoGetInterfaceAndReleaseStream(
                    m_pStream,
                    IID_IBank,
                    (void**) &m_pBank);
      if (FAILED(hr))
      {
        MessageBox(Unmarshal failed",
        return TRUE;
      }
    }
    else
    {
      // Just copy interface pointer and AddRef it
      m_pBank = g_pBank;
      m_pBank->AddRef();
    }
```

```
    }
    return TRUE;
}
```

DLL Server Example, Step 4 (Free Threads)

The synchronization provided by COM using the Apartment model is nice because it is so easy to use. It is automatic when you are crossing a process boundary. You can implement it with two API calls when you are crossing thread boundaries within a process. The big drawback to Apartment model threading is loss of concurrency when separate method calls access independent data.

Free threads can often provide a higher-performance solution, with more work on your part. COM does not enforce any blocking behavior. You are responsible for making your methods thread safe, for instance, by providing critical sections for modifying shared data.

Build and run Step 4 of the demo program. This time choose "Free (No CS)" for Threading Model. Again start a second thread and do a Delayed Deposit on the first thread. Immediately click "Get Owner" on the second thread. You will get an immediate response with no blocking. See Figure 13–11.

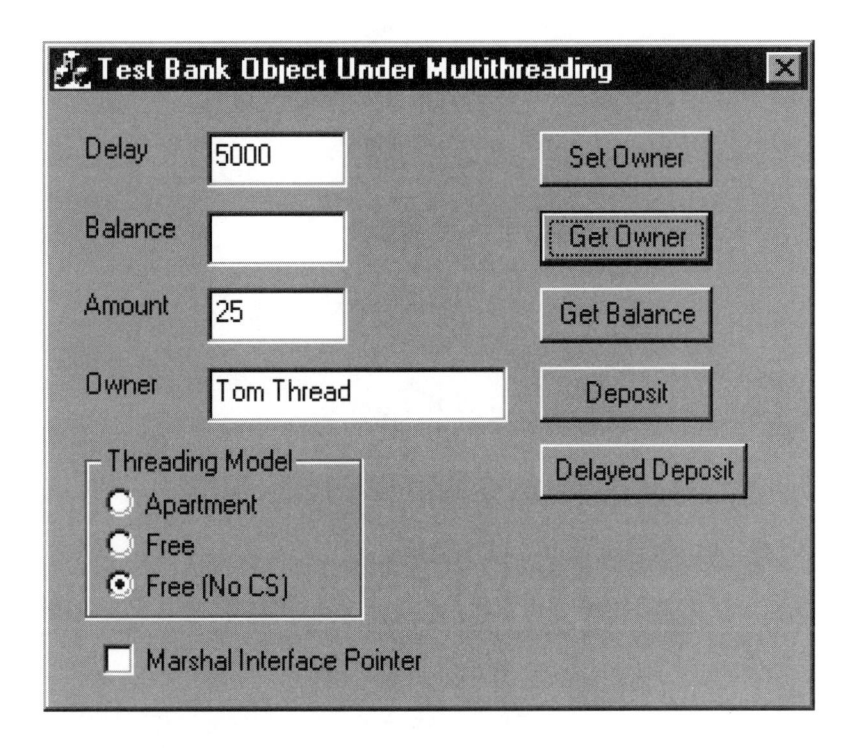

Figure 13-11 *No blocking when you access independent data*

But you will again have the race condition if you do a Delayed Deposit on one thread and Deposit on the other thread.

Run Step 4 of the demo program again. This time choose "Free" for Threading Model. Again start a second thread and do a Delayed Deposit on the first thread. Immediately click Deposit on the second thread. The call will be (correctly) blocked until the first deposit completes. Do another Delayed Deposit and immediately click Get Owner on the second thread. You will get an immediate response with no blocking (also correct, since owner data is independent of balance).

We will now walk through the most important features of the code for this example.

CLIENT: INITIALIZING COM

The client thread selects its threading model when it initializes COM.

```
void CTestDlg::OnInitialize()
{
  UpdateData();
  switch (m_model)
  {
  case ID_MODEL_APARTMENT:
    g_dwCoInit = COINIT_APARTMENTTHREADED;
    break;
  case ID_MODEL_FREE:
  case ID_MODEL_FREENOCS:
    g_dwCoInit = COINIT_MULTITHREADED;
    break;
  default:
    break;
  }
  HRESULT hr = CoInitializeEx(NULL, g_dwCoInit);
  ...
```

CLIENT: CREATING THE OBJECT

The server implements three different COM classes illustrating different ways of handling threading (Apartment, Free, and Free with no critical section). The client creates an object belonging to the appropriate class, depending on user choice.

```
  CLSID clsid;
  switch (m_model)
  {
  case ID_MODEL_APARTMENT:
    clsid = CLSID_BankApt;
```

```
    break;
case ID_MODEL_FREE:
    clsid = CLSID_BankFree;
    break;
case ID_MODEL_FREENOCS:
    clsid = CLSID_BankNoCS;
    break;
default:
    break;
}
hr = CoCreateInstance(clsid,
                      NULL,
                      CLSCTX_SERVER,
                      IID_IBank,
                      (void**) &m_pBank);
```

SERVER: C++ CLASSES

The server has separate C++ implementation classes for each of the COM classes. The only difference in class declarations is in the template arguments of **CComObjectRootEx** and **CComCoClass**.

```
class ATL_NO_VTABLE CBankApt :
    public CComObjectRootEx<CComSingleThreadModel>,
    public CComCoClass<CBankApt, &CLSID_BankApt>,
    public ISupportErrorInfo,
    public IBank
...

class ATL_NO_VTABLE CBankFree :
    public CComObjectRootEx<CComMultiThreadModel>,
    public CComCoClass<CBankFree, &CLSID_BankFree>,
    public ISupportErrorInfo,
    public IBank
...

class ATL_NO_VTABLE CBankNoCS :
    public CComObjectRootEx<CComMultiThreadModel>,
    public CComCoClass<CBankNoCS, &CLSID_BankNoCS>,
    public ISupportErrorInfo,
    public IBank
...
```

SERVER: ENFORCING MUTUAL EXCLUSION

In the Free threading cases, we must be careful to ensure mutual exclusion in access to shared data. There is shared data (the reference count) in ATL code implementing **IUnknown** (**CcomObjectRootEx**). There is shared data (balance and owner) in our own code.

ATL enforces mutual exclusion in its own code. The template parameter **CComMultiThreadModel** passed to **CComObjectRootEx** causes ATL to implement **IUnknown** in a thread-safe manner.

We are responsible for enforcing mutual exclusion in our code. Our class **CBankFree** is thread safe, and our class **CBankNoCS** is not.

CRITICAL SECTIONS

To make our code thread safe, we can create a critical section for each access to shared data. Lock the critical section before accessing the data. Unlock the critical section when finished with the data.

```
STDMETHODIMP CBankFree::Deposit(long amount)
{
  m_cs.Lock();
  g_balance += amount;
  m_cs.Unlock();
  return S_OK;
}
```

ATL provides a class **CComAutoCriticalSection** that makes it easy to implement critical sections.

```
class ATL_NO_VTABLE CBankFree :
  public CComObjectRootEx<CComMultiThreadModel>,
  public CComCoClass<CBankFree, &CLSID_BankFree>,
  public ISupportErrorInfo,
  public IBank
{
protected:
  static CComAutoCriticalSection m_cs;
  ...
```

Summary

Multithreaded COM objects need to deal with thread safety, and it is desirable to maximize concurrency. Standard marshaling in COM serializes access to objects, preventing race conditions without requiring COM methods to be thread safe. With Apartment threading, the system serializes COM methods. You can use COM API functions to marshal interfaces between threads in the same process. The Free threading model overcomes limitations of Apartment threading in achieving concurrency at the cost of requiring the programmer to make COM methods thread safe. ATL facilitates implementing a Free threading COM object by providing a thread-safe implementation of **IUnknown**. The class **CComAutoCriticalSection** simplifies using critical sections.

This concludes our coverage of the fundamentals of COM which underpin COM+. In the next chapter we begin our study of COM+. We will see that the "declarative" style of programming that COM uses to good advantage in handling multithreading is used extensively in COM+. And in Chapter 16 we will see how COM+ further simplifies handling concurrency.

In This Part

◆ **CHAPTER 14**
COM+ Architecture Fundamentals

◆ **CHAPTER 15**
A COM+ Tutorial

◆ **CHAPTER 16**
Concurrency in COM+

◆ **CHAPTER 17**
Windows 2000 and COM+ Security

◆ **CHAPTER 18**
SQL Server and ADO Survival Guide

◆ **CHAPTER 19**
Transactions in COM+

◆ **CHAPTER 20**
Web Applications Using COM+

◆ **CHAPTER 21**
MSMQ and Queued Components

◆ **CHAPTER 22**
COM+ Events

◆ **CHAPTER 23**
COM+ and Scalability

PART THREE

Windows DNA and COM+

The third part of this book provides a thorough introduction to the architecture and services of COM+ and its use in creating multiple-tier distributed applications that follow the Windows DNA model. The fundamentals of COM+ architecture are outlined, followed by a hands-on tutorial on programming using COM+, including the configuration and deployment of a distributed COM+ application. Concurrency in COM+ is discussed. COM+ Security is covered, including essential information about NT Security and Administration. A "survival guide" covers essential database programming techniques, including use of SQL Server, OLE DB and ActiveX Data Objects. The basic concepts of transactions are discussed along with the COM+ implementation. Web-based application development using COM+ is introduced. Microsoft Message Queue is introduced, and there is a discussion of Queued Components which integrate MSMQ into the COM+ programming model. The "publish and subscribe" event model used in COM+ is covered. Techniques for enhancing application scalability are studied, including component load balancing and object pooling. This book concludes with some thoughts about the overall significance of COM+.

FOURTEEN

COM+ Architecture Fundamentals

We now come to our detailed study of the architecture and services provided by COM+. This chapter provides a thorough conceptual overview of COM+ architecture. A good understanding of this material is essential to understanding and working with COM+ services. The next chapter presents a COM+ tutorial that reinforces these concepts through hands-on programming examples. After working with the examples in the following chapter, you may wish to come back and review the concepts presented in this chapter. This will ensure that you understand the fundamental architecture before you move forward to a detailed study of the many important COM+ services.

The chapter opens with the question "Why COM+?" In the process of answering this question, we review some of the issues in building distributed applications. We next discuss the fundamental principle of declarative, attribute-based programming. This is the programming model for working with COM+. By specifying attributes, you are able to hook into the services provided by the COM+ infrastructure without having to write a lot of tricky code that could easily have a lot of bugs.

The systematic overview of COM+ architecture begins with COM+ *applications*. COM+ applications are the top level of a hierarchy that includes components or classes, interfaces, and methods. Applications are the unit of administration and deployment in COM+. Underlying the attribute model is the concept of a *context*. A context is a description of the environment in which a COM+ object must operate. When you specify an attribute, you are specifying one aspect of an object's context. Since attributes in COM+ are much richer than in COM, the Registry is augmented by a system *Catalog* that provides a comprehensive repository for attribute information. When a client requires a different context from an object it is using, the system must intervene to bridge the gap, a process known as *interception*. To facilitate building scalable middle-tier components, you want to decouple the client's view of the object lifetime from that of the server. A client may wish to keep long-lived object references to avoid repeatedly paying the penalty of going through DCOM to create the object. The server, however, may not be able to afford the resources to keep a large number of objects live at the same time. By using the *activation* architecture and the "just-in-time activation" attribute, an object can be deactivated while the client's reference remains valid. *Object pooling* allows the server to save the expense of repeatedly creating objects by taking them instead from a pool of already created objects.

Why COM+?

Part 2 provided a quite detailed survey of the fundamental technology of creating and using COM components. This is vital knowledge for building distributed applications using COM+. In Part 1 we gave an overview of the challenges of building distributed applications and presented a summary of Microsoft's Windows DNA architecture, which is their blueprint for creating N-tier applications. We will not attempt to repeat or summarize that discussion here. After hacking your way among the COM "trees" and the rather dense underbrush some places, you may wish to review Chapters 1 and 2 to become reacquainted with the distributed application "forest."

In this opening section I'd like to discuss a few specific technical challenges in creating middle-tier server applications. These challenges provide the motivation for the architecture and features of COM+. The challenges can be grouped under the categories of scalability, reliability, and complexity.

Scalability

Hands-down, the driving force behind COM+ is *scalability*. And the driving force behind scalability is the Internet. I will venture to guess that if Microsoft had not been driving so hard to achieve success on the Internet, COM+ would not exist in the form that it does today.

To see why the Internet has been so important a technology driver, consider the challenges facing an enterprise application with a large but defined user base as compared to a Web application with an unknown user base. The former is challenging but can be planned for, and incremental software enhancements and hardware additions can be made as required. The Web is a totally different territory. A company puts up a Web site. It makes prudent capacity plans and the site proves wildly popular. That would be good news, but the site crashes under the heavy load. What might have been a triumph is instead an embarrassment or worse. This scenario has already been repeated many, many times.

Although a crash and a resulting outage for hours or days is the most spectacular manifestation of the problem, another important aspect is performance. The system may stay up but become very slow and unresponsive, and that too is a serious problem.

What is the solution? Buy extra mainframes as a hedge? How many will you need—one? two? ten? Cost is a very real business issue, and the problem cannot be solved by throwing hardware at it alone. A solution must also involve effective software. And appropriate software running on the cheapest of hardware platforms, the PC, represents the great opportunity for Microsoft to make significant inroads into the enterprise market, an opportunity that Microsoft is not ignoring.

We will see in this chapter and the ones that follow how COM+ helps achieve scalability, through techniques such as just-in-time activation, object pooling, and load balancing.

Reliability

An application that services many users, whether on the Web or within a large enterprise, is probably mission critical and, in any event, must be reliable, or considerable damage will result. In any large distributed system, many kinds of failures, such as hardware problems, communications outages, configuration errors, etc., are inevitable. The trick is to see to it that various component failures do not bring about a system failure or the loss of vital information.

Another aspect of reliability is minimizing the effect of avoidable failures, namely software bugs. The cost of bugs in a distributed enterprise system is much greater than in a desktop application. And unfortunately the opportunity for bugs is also much greater because these systems are so complex.

COM+ supports the development of reliable systems in a number of ways. It provides a large amount of tested, proven system code that applications do not have to implement themselves. COM+ supports transactions, which are the foundation for reliable and durable execution of work units in a distributed environment. COM+ supports component load balancing among application clusters, providing for the capability of an application to recover from a failure of one node in the cluster by redirecting the work to another node.

Complexity

A great challenge in modern distributed systems is their great complexity. Besides providing a very fertile ground for bugs, complexity makes the development of software systems very costly and time consuming. New software technologies that bring solutions to other problems also bring more APIs for the developer to learn. The result is a process that does not seem to converge, and despite many improvements in software methodology and tools, the perennial "software crisis" does not seem to abate.

COM+ actually does much to *simplify* the programming model. This aspect of COM+ may in fact turn out to be its greatest contribution. For example, COM+ supports *automatic transactions*, which enable the implementation of distributed transactions without specific application code. COM+ provides a simple security model. It supports synchronization of concurrent activities in a way that is very easy to apply.

Transactions: A Canonical Example

We have mentioned transactions a couple of times already. Transactions can be viewed as the key unifying principle in building robust distributed applications. They provide both a means of modularizing complex processing into simple logical units of work and a mechanism for ensuring correct operation of the overall system in the face of inevitable failures of individual components. They will be discussed in detail in Chapter 19. In this chapter, we will use transactions as an example of the kind of support that COM+ provides for implementing distributed applications.

A transaction can be thought of as a unit of work. Transactions must satisfy four fundamental requirements, which have come to be known as the ACID properties.

- **Atomic**. A transaction is all or nothing.
- **Consistent**. A transaction must not violate any integrity constraints of the state that is being managed.
- **Isolated**. Concurrent transactions must not expose any of their internal state to each other.
- **Durable**. Once a transaction has completed, any state modifications it made become permanent.

A simple example of a transaction is a transfer from one account to another, say from savings to checking. We want the whole operation to be atomic. If our savings account were debited and then some system glitch caused the credit to the checking account to fail, we would be unhappy to see a deduction from the one account without a corresponding credit to the other. If the whole operation is conducted as a transaction, the system would ensure that either both operations succeed or none are carried out.

Modern database systems normally provide a transaction mechanism within the database. You can group a series of operations together into a transaction. If all operations succeed, the transaction is *committed* and the changes become permanent. If any operation fails, the transaction is *aborted*, and the database reverts to its original state. A more challenging problem in transaction processing is to deal with *distributed* transactions, in which operations within the transaction are applied to different data stores, which may be of different types and may reside on different computers.

In this chapter we will illustrate some of the concepts of COM+ by showing how they apply to transactions.

Declarative, Attribute-Based Programming

The heart of the COM+ approach to programming is a model based on *declaring* requirements based on values of *attributes*. The COM+ run-time system implements these requirements for you. There are many advantages to such an approach. A prime advantage is that it is simpler for the programmer to declare values for attributes than it is to write complex, error-prone procedural code. This approach greatly reduces the complexity of the software. Equally significant is the fact that the code provided by the operating system will be more robust than what you can implement yourself in a reasonable time frame. The infrastructure type code that COM+ provides for you is inherently difficult to implement correctly, and it is very advantageous that the operating system has done it for you. You can also easily modify the attributes of the object without recoding. We will see later in this chapter that some of the attributes that you can specify can aid in making your application more scalable.

Apartments as a Model for Declarative Programming

A good example of using attributes to specify functionality is provided by the COM apartment architecture that facilitates writing safe, concurrent code without having to explicitly implement the synchronization part yourself. It is difficult to get this type of thread synchronization code right, so it is very advantageous that COM implements it for you.

SINGLE-THREADED APARTMENTS

Let's briefly review how you can achieve automatic synchronization of access to your class by seeing to it that it is created inside a single-threaded apartment (STA). You declare your class to have the "apartment" threading model by assigning the value "Apartment" to the ThreadingModel named-value key under the CLSID. This means that whenever an object is instantiated for your class, it will be inside its own STA. Only one thread is permitted to execute in this STA. If a client is running under this thread, it will execute methods of an interface directly. If another thread tries for concurrent access while the apartment's own thread is accessing the object, this other thread will go through a proxy, according to the rules of COM. This proxy makes use of the Windows message queue, which provides automatic synchronization. The second thread will have to wait until the first thread is finished. Essentially, the proxy enables COM to "intercept" the method call to synchronize it.

This architecture achieves thread synchronization without your application's having to implement it.

Declaring Transaction Requirements

COM+ carries this idea of attribute-based programming much further. There are many examples later in this book, and later in this chapter we examine in detail the architecture that enables attribute-based programming. Right now let's just see how you can declare transactional attributes for your component.

Suppose you have a component that implements operations on bank accounts. Suppose further the bank account information is stored in a database such as SQL Server, which is a Resource Manager that can provide transaction protection for operations on data that it manages. Then you can mark the "Transaction Support" attribute for the component as "Required." When your component runs, the COM+ runtime system will notice that your component requires a transaction, and a piece of system code known as an "interceptor" will enlist in a transaction for you. Then when the debit and credit operations are performed, they are running within this transaction. The result is that you are guaranteed that either both operations are performed or neither are, and you did not have to write any code to achieve this result.

COM+ Catalog

Standard COM stores all configuration information in the Registry. COM+ requires a great deal more configuration information for holding all the attribute settings of COM+ applications and components. This information is stored in a separate system database called *RegDb*. This database is not directly accessible. All access to configuration information in COM+ is made through a family of system objects known collectively as the *Catalog Manager* or simply the *Catalog*. The Catalog provides access to both RegDb and the Registry, as illustrated in Figure 14–1.

The Catalog administration objects can be accessed by programs and scripts. Thus all COM+ administrative procedures can be completely automated. The Catalog administrator objects form a hierarchy. The top-level

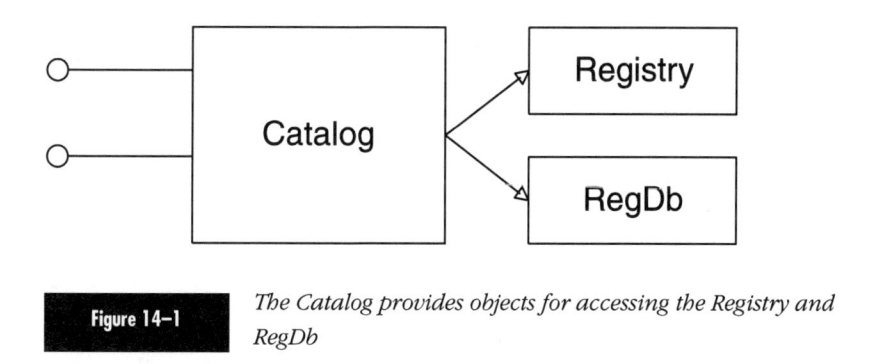

Figure 14–1 *The Catalog provides objects for accessing the Registry and RegDb*

object is a component called COMAdminCatalog. Collections are provided for applications, components, interfaces, and methods.

Component Services Snap-In

Windows 2000 provides a Microsoft Management Console snap-in that furnishes a user interface on top of the Catalog. This tool is sometimes called the "COM+ Explorer." It may also be referred to as the Component Services snap-in or the Component Services admin tool. The latter names are probably more descriptive, because the tool is used extensively to set configuration information, not just view it.

You can get a feel for the kind of information stored in the Catalog by viewing information for one of the built-in COM+ applications that ships with Windows 2000. Open up the tool from Start | Programs | Administrative Tools | Component Services. In the tree-view, otpen up Component Services, Computers, My Computer and COM+ Applications. You will see the currently installed COM+ applications (Windows 2000 ships with several COM+ applications that are preinstalled). See Figure 14–2.

You can drill down into the hierarchy by opening up a particular application, and then the components for it. Try the "System Application." You will see icons for these components in the right-hand pane. You can go into the left-hand tree view to open up an interface of a component and the methods within the interface. See Figure 14–3.

With COM+ Explorer, you can set attributes for the application and you can drill down and set attributes for the components in the application and for their interfaces and methods. You can view and set the attributes by opening up the appropriate Properties window. In the next chapter, we do some hands-on work in setting some attributes. Right now, let's just examine attributes for one of the components of the built-in System Application. In the tree view of COM+ Explorer, select the first component of the System Application, "Catsrv.CatalogServer.1." Right-click. From the context menu choose Properties. You will see a tabbed dialog box that groups the various attributes

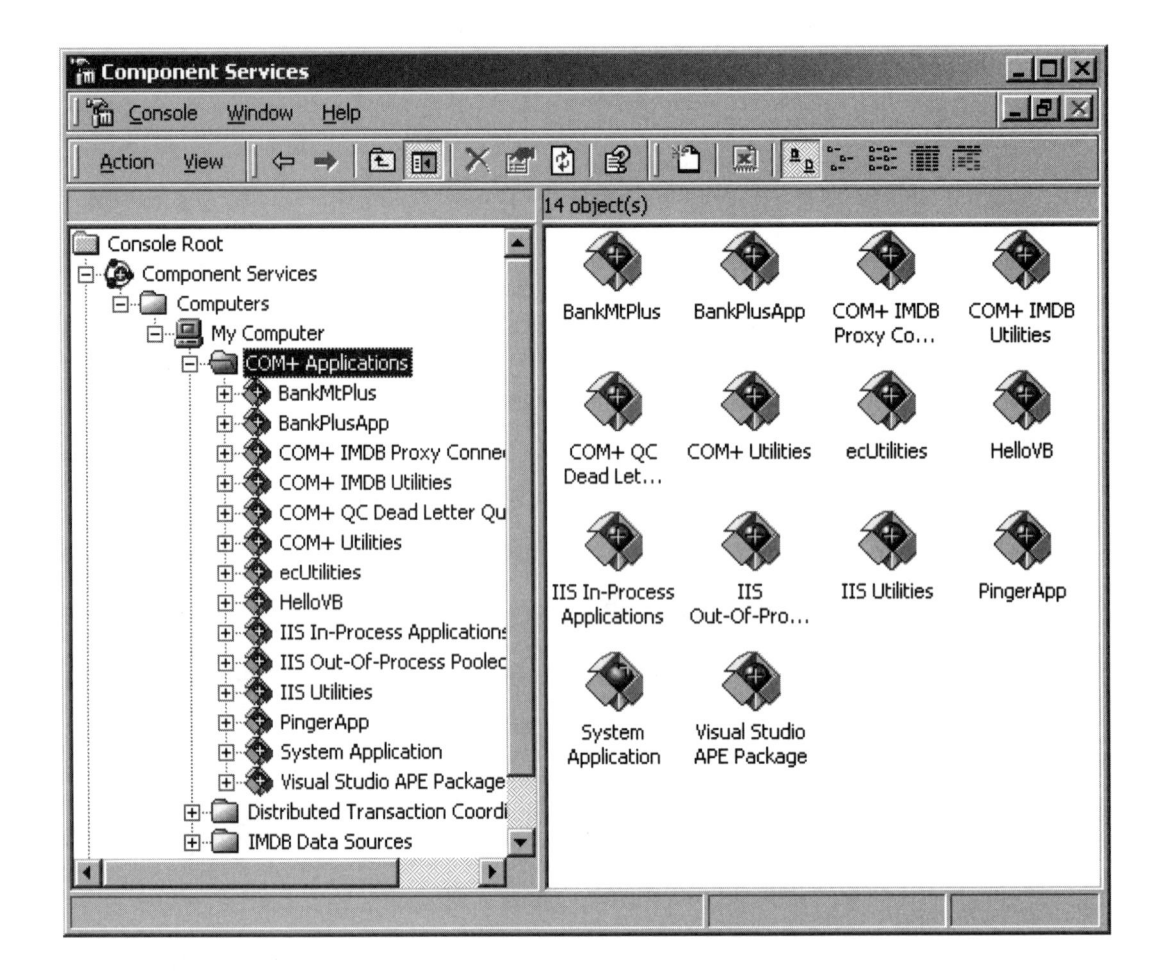

Figure 14–2 *COM+ Explorer shows the COM+ applications installed on your computer*

for the component that can be configured. Note that almost all the settings are grayed out, because you are not allowed to change attributes for the built-in System Application. Select the Transactions tab. Notice that the "Transaction support" attribute is set to "Required." See Figure 14–4.

COM+ Terminology

We will now begin our survey of the details of COM+ architecture, and will see how COM+ makes significant contributions to the challenges we discussed at the beginning of the chapter. Our starting point is rather mundane—the termi-

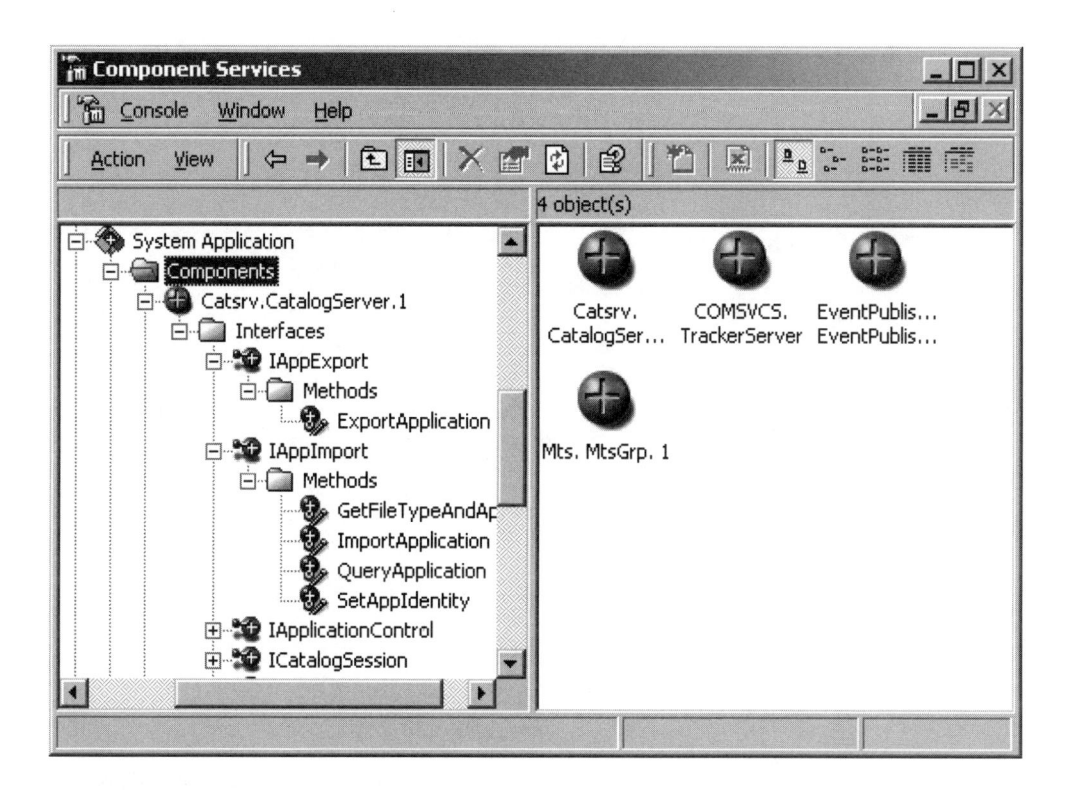

Figure 14-3 *Viewing application hierarchy in COM+ Explorer*

nology of COM+—but it is important to agree upon the meaning of some key terms before proceeding with a detailed discussion of the architecture.

COM Terminology

COM provides the hierarchy of server/class/interface/method. A *class* in COM is a concrete implementation of one or more abstract data types represented by *interfaces*. An interface has one or more *methods*, which represent the functions which the interface provides. Collectively, the methods, with their "signatures" describing parameters and return value, specify the "contract" that the interface represents. An *object* is an instance of a class and may have its own unique instance data. Such data is private to the object, and can only be accessed indirectly through the methods. An *apartment* groups objects that share the same concurrency requirements. The apartment an object resides in is part of the object's identity.

While class, interface, and method represent a logical structuring, the top element in the COM hierarchy, a *server*, is a purely physical container, a

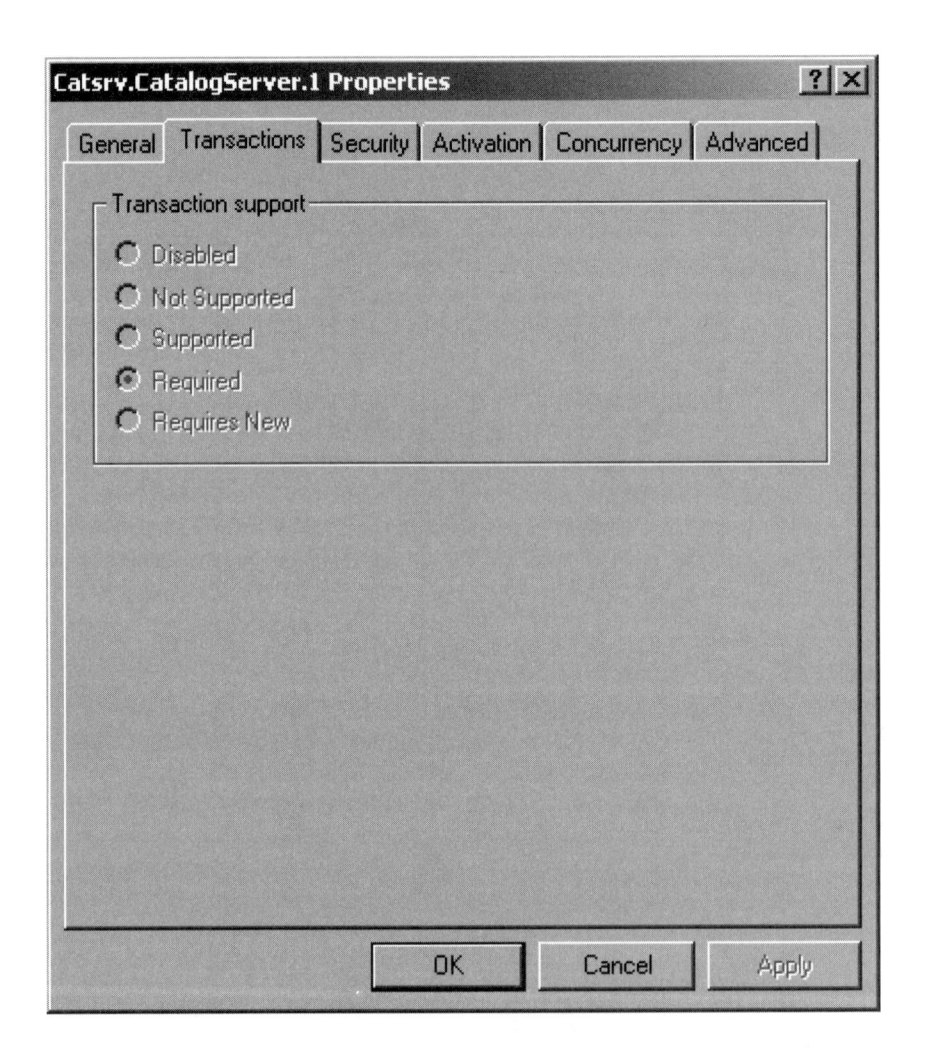

Figure 14-4 *Viewing attributes for a COM+ component*

binary code module that hosts one or more classes. A server may be either an EXE or a DLL.

COM+ Terminology

COM+ maintains the concepts of class, object, interface, method, and apartment. The concept of "server" is somewhat less important in COM+ than in COM. It should be regarded as an implementation detail about how some classes were packaged. In COM+ all of your classes must be implemented within DLL servers. If you require an EXE server, COM+ will run your components inside the standard "surrogate" DLLHOST.EXE.

APPLICATION

COM+ introduces the concept of *application*. Although this term is admittedly very overloaded, "application" has a specific meaning in COM+. An application is a group of classes that share a set of security, identity, and activation attributes. Thus, the basic COM+ hierarchy is application/class/interface/method.

COMPONENT

Most terms in COM/COM+ have a fairly straightforward and consistent usage. "Component" is rather a sore spot, because it is used in so very many different ways with varying nuances. The term is widely used throughout the industry. In general, a component is seen as a more practical and reusable entity than "object." Whereas "object-oriented" programming seems to many not to have lived up to its hype for bringing the dream of reusable software to fruition, industry experience with components seems more promising. A special kind of COM component, known as an "ActiveX control," has achieved massive adoption, with thousands of ActiveX controls developed by many third parties. Another kind of component from a different technology, "JavaBeans," also seems destined for widespread adoption. In this sense, a "component" is generally considered a reusable piece of binary software. By this definition, a simple DLL could also be considered a component, so a component is often considered as "something more." But precisely what this "something more" is remains open for discussion.

In Microsoft's Platform SDK, a component is described as a binary unit of code that creates binary objects, including code for self-registration. This maps essentially to a class. Technically, a COM class can be fairly bare bones, as we saw in Chapter 5 with our first C++ example that implemented the COM protocol (**IUnknown**) but had no class factory. A component should have the infrastructure to create objects (**DllGetClassObject** and class factory) and also be self-registering (**DllRegisterServer** and **DllUnregisterServer**). Note that some of this infrastructure is provided by the DLL as a whole and not by an individual class. A DLL may implement several classes.

The key point is that components are one-to-one with full-blown classes, and to every component in a COM+ application there is a unique class with a CLSID, ProgID, etc., and a corresponding Registry entry. The complete set of requirements for a component in COM+ is:

1. A component is a COM class implementing **IUnknown**.
2. A component is implemented in a DLL and has the infrastructure for creating objects, including a CLSID, class factory, and the DLL exported functions **DllGetClassObject** and **DllCanUnloadNow**.
3. A component is self-registering, with support for **DllRegisterServer** and **DllUnregisterServer**.

4. A component must provide a type library that is bound to the DLL.

5. A component must be able to marshal its interfaces. Dual interfaces are marshaled by Automation. You must supply and register a proxy/stub for custom interfaces.

Every class in an ActiveX DLL built using Visual Basic automatically fulfills these requirements. Likewise for classes in DLLs built using ATL. If your class has custom interfaces, you must build and register the proxy/stub.

CONFIGURED AND UNCONFIGURED COMPONENTS

A component that meets the requirements listed above is eligible to participate in COM+ services, but it won't actually do so until it has been installed into a COM+ application. A component can be added to an application either by using an administrative tool or programmatically by using the administrative API. Once a component has been installed in an application, it is referred to as a *configured component*. A component not installed in a COM+ application is called an *unconfigured component*.

Types of COM+ Applications

The principal type of COM+ application is a *server application*. A server application lives inside its own process, the standard surrogate DLL-HOST.EXE. A server application provides fault isolation, so if the server crashes, the client process will not be brought down. The client and server run in separate address spaces. A server application can be accessed via DCOM by clients on other machines. A server application provides the full range of interceptor services.

A *library* application runs inside the client's process. Thus there is no fault isolation, and only a limited set of interceptor services are available. A library application can only be accessed by clients on the same machine. The principal use of library applications is to provide reusable code for other COM+ applications rather than to provide services directly to clients.

An *application proxy* contains the information required for a remote client to access a server application. An application proxy provides a file which can be run on the client machine to install necessary information in the Registry, including CLSID, remote server name, and marshaling information.

Finally, there are a number of *preinstalled* COM+ applications. These include system applications for COM+ and IIS and a number of utilities. These applications cannot be modified or deleted.

COM+ Architecture

COM+ rests on three core concepts: *context, activation,* and *interception.* COM+ makes use of the interception mechanism to automatically invoke certain services on behalf of applications. In this chapter, we discuss the core concepts and two of the services, just-in-time activation and object pooling. In later chapters, we explore additional services, including synchronization, security, automatic transactions, queuing, loosely coupled events, and load balancing.

We'll first preview the overall architecture and then drill down and look at the core concepts and services in more detail.

We have seen that the fundamental principle of COM+ is declarative, attribute-based programming. The programmer declares the environment in which a component must run by specifying the configuration attributes for the component. This information is stored in the Catalog. When an object is created, COM+ checks the Catalog to see if the component being created is a configured component. If the component is found in the Catalog, the component is created and placed within a *context* that matches the configuration settings for the component. Associating an object with its context is called *activation.*

If the client of a COM+ component is in a different context from the component, COM+ uses *interception* to enable the incompatible components to work together. If the component and the client have identical run-time requirements, the component is created in the same context as the client and no interception is necessary.

If the component is not found in the Catalog, it is placed in a context for unconfigured components.

Context

A *context* is a collection of objects within an apartment that have similar run-time requirements. Every COM object that has been activated is associated with exactly one context, and a context resides in exactly one apartment. An apartment can contain several contexts, and a context can have several objects. Objects within different apartments necessarily have different contexts. Figure 14–5 illustrates the relationship of object, context, and apartment.

Every apartment has a *default context.* When an unconfigured component is activated, it will be associated with the default context, and this context is largely ignored. For a configured component, the properties of the context will be determined by attribute values for the component stored in the Catalog (and also possibly by attributes of a "parent" component, as is discussed below). Context for configured components provide the key for accessing COM+ services.

```
┌─────────────────────────────┐    ┌─────────────────────────────┐
│ Apartment                   │    │ Apartment                   │
│  ┌───────────────────────┐  │    │  ┌───────────────────────┐  │
│  │ Context               │  │    │  │ Context               │  │
│  │   ┌──────────────┐    │  │    │  │   ┌──────────────┐    │  │
│  │   │   Object     │    │  │    │  │   │   Object     │    │  │
│  │   └──────────────┘    │  │    │  │   └──────────────┘    │  │
│  │   ┌──────────────┐    │  │    │  └───────────────────────┘  │
│  │   │   Object     │    │  │    │                             │
│  │   └──────────────┘    │  │    └─────────────────────────────┘
│  └───────────────────────┘  │
│                             │
│  ┌───────────────────────┐  │
│  │ Context               │  │
│  │   ┌──────────────┐    │  │
│  │   │   Object     │    │  │
│  │   └──────────────┘    │  │
│  └───────────────────────┘  │
└─────────────────────────────┘
```

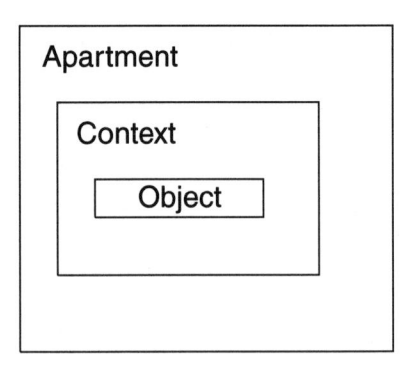

Figure 14–5 *Relationship of objects, contexts, and apartments*

CONTEXT OBJECT

A context is an abstraction that specifies a group of COM objects. Associated with a context is an actual COM object, called the "context object" (or "object context"), which holds all the attribute information associated with the context. (The context object represents what in MTS was called the "context wrapper.")

Code in a method can gain access to this context object through the API function **CoGetObjectContext** (or **GetObjectContext** in Visual Basic), which returns a pointer to the interface **IObjectContext**. You can than call the methods of **IObjectContext** to access and manipulate the properties of the context object. The interface **IObjectContext** carries over from MTS. In COM+, there are other more specialized interfaces, including **IObjectContextInfo**, **IContextState**, and **IObjectContextActivity**.

CALL CONTEXT

A portion of the context is valid on a per-call basis and is concerned with security, a topic we will discuss in Chapter 17. The API function **CoGetCallContext** returns a pointer to the interface **ISecurityCallContext**, which provides access to security methods and information about the security call context of the current call.

Activation

The important point to grasp in connection with context is that the context describes the "environment" of an object, not the object's own internal instance data (although it does affect the object's behavior). An object by itself does not have context. The process of associating an object with its context is called *activation*. The critical question for a newly activated object is "how am I being used today?" The object's environment is its context, and this context is crucial for determining the run-time behavior of the object.

Bringing an object to a "ready" state where it can carry out its methods is a two-step process in COM+. The first step is creation. An object is instantiated using a class factory, just as in straight COM. Next comes activation, when the object is associated with its context. Now the object is ready to do work, and the COM+ run time is ready to do additional work on the object's behalf through interception, when required. There is also a two-step termination process. The object is deactivated, which removes its context, and then the object is destroyed. Figure 14-6 shows the life cycle of an object in COM+.

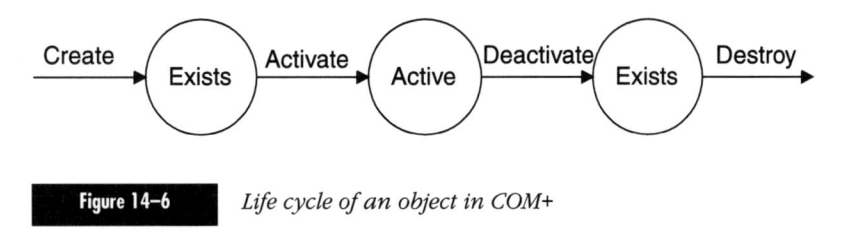

Figure 14-6 *Life cycle of an object in COM+*

Normally, activation occurs just after creation and deactivation just prior to destruction. But COM+ supports the capability of "object pooling," in which a pool of created objects can be maintained. When a client needs an active object, the server activates an object from its pool. When the client is finished with the object, the server does not destroy the object but merely deactivates it and returns it to the pool. Object pooling is discussed later in the chapter.

FLOWING CONTEXT PROPERTIES

The context for a newly activated object is determined by the component's attributes in the Catalog *and* possibly by the attributes of the "parent" object, if any. If an object is created directly by an end-client, the context will be determined strictly by the component's attributes. But if one object creates another, the situation is more complicated. The creating object itself has a context. Under some circumstances, the child will be created in its parent's context. This always happens for unconfigured classes because they have no independent means for specifying the context they want.

For configured classes, a run time check has to be made to see if the context of the parent is consistent with the requirements of the child. If consistent, the child will be activated inside its parent's context. If not consistent, a new context will be created for the child.

Sometimes when a new context is created, certain property values will flow to the child. We will see a number of examples. For now let's just preview something that can happen with transactions. A parent object can have an attribute "requires a transaction." This means that the COM+ run time will always activate this object in a context where the object will be enlisted in a transaction, and one of the properties of the context will be a transaction ID. Now suppose this parent object creates a child object that has the attribute "supports transactions." This new object will be activated inside a new context, but it will be enlisted within the transaction of the parent, and so it will "inherit" the transaction ID.

BANK ACCOUNT EXAMPLE

Let us look at our previous transaction example of making a transfer from savings account to checking account. For our illustration, we will assume there are three components, **Move**, **Debit**, and **Credit**, with respective methods **Transfer**, **Withdraw**, and **Deposit**. Here is hypothetical VB code for making a transfer of 25:

```
Dim objMove as New Move
objMove.Transfer 25
```

And here is the code for the **Transfer** method. Note that the transfer is implemented by creating two child objects and calling their methods.

```
Public Sub Transfer(ByVal Amount as Currency)
   Dim objDebit as New Debit
   Dim objCredit as New Credit
   objDebit.Withdraw Amount
   objCredit.Deposit Amount
End Sub
```

Now let us see how various transaction configuration settings affect how the components behave. There are three possible settings that will cause a component to run under a transaction in some circumstances.

- **Supports a transaction**. The component will run in its client's transaction. If the client is not running in a transaction, the component will not run in one either.
- **Requires a transaction**. The component will always run in a transaction. If the client is running in a transaction, the component will run in the same transaction. If the client is not running in a transaction, a new transaction will be created for the component.
- **Requires a new transaction**. The component will always run in a transaction of its own, especially created for it.

First let us assume that transaction attributes are configured as suggested earlier. The parent object **Move** "requires a transaction" and the child objects **Debit** and **Credit** "supports a transaction." Then **Move** will be activated within a context where a transaction is required, and the COM+ run time will do the work of enlisting in a transaction, obtaining a transaction ID of say **tid1**. When child objects **Debit** and **Credit** are activated, they will also run in a context with a transaction, and moreover it will be the *same* transaction, so the transaction ID property **tid1** will "flow" to their context. Then if they complete their work successfully, they will "vote" for the transaction to commit, and the whole transaction will commit, and the atomic operation will be carried out. If either child votes to "abort," the whole transaction will be aborted.

Now suppose that **Move** still "requires a transaction" but **Debit** and **Credit** "requires a new transaction." Now all three objects will run under transactions, but the child objects will now be running under *different* transactions, say with IDs of **tid2** and **tid3**. Now the outcome of **Debit** and **Credit** will not affect the outcome of **Move**, so we cannot guarantee the atomic behavior for **Transfer** that we would like. The transaction ID property has not "flowed" in this case from parent to children.

FORCING ACTIVATION IN CALLER'S CONTEXT

A configured class may set an attribute asking for it to always be created in its parent's context. This may be necessary if, for example, not all of the interfaces of the class can be marshaled. In this case creation will either succeed, in which case, the parent talks directly to the child, or creation may simply fail, with an appropriate return value indicating the cause.

Interception

When an object has been activated within a context, method calls to it from within the context are handled differently from calls made from outside the context. A call made from one object to another within the same context does not require any intervention by COM+ and the call is direct from the client to the object. Objects in different contexts have some incompatibility in their run-time environment. Hence, a call made across a context boundary requires *interception* by COM+ to mitigate the incompatibility.

Figure 14–7 illustrates an apartment with two contexts, A and B. Context A has two objects, 1 and 2. Context B has a single object, 3. The call from 1 to 2 is within the same context and hence is direct, requiring no intervention by COM+. The call from 3 to 2 crosses a context boundary and hence requires intervention by COM+ through an *interceptor*.

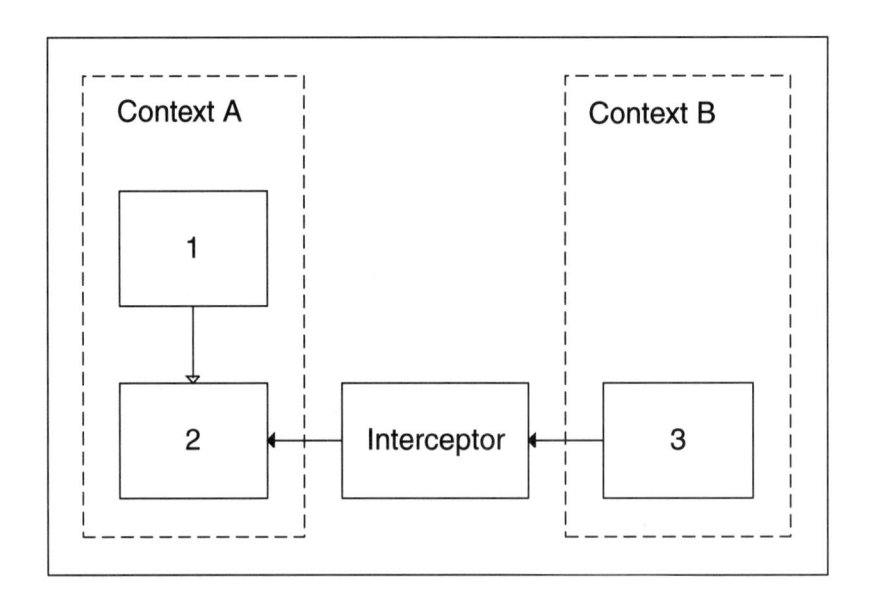

Figure 14-7 *A cross-context call requires an interceptor*

INTERCEPTORS

An *interceptor* is a lightweight proxy that is provided by the COM+ run-time system to resolve incompatibilities in a call across a context boundary. An interceptor exposes the same interfaces as does the target object. From the standpoint of the client it is completely transparent that an interceptor is being called rather than the object directly. The interceptor does preprocessing on the way into the object. The interceptor can also do postprocessing on the way back from the object to the client.

An interceptor is said to be "lightweight" because it does not necessarily involve a thread switch. The interceptor does exactly what is required to resolve an incompatibility and nothing more. An ordinary proxy involves at least a thread switch and possibly a process switch.

The interception mechanism is very generic in COM+ and can be used to resolve many different kinds of incompatibilities across contexts now and more in the future. In COM+ 1.0, interceptors can only be provided by COM+ itself and not by application programs. This may change in the future.

INTERFACE POINTER MARSHALING

If you pass an interface pointer as a parameter in a method call that crosses context, COM+ will automatically convert the interface pointer to a proxy, so when you call back into the context from outside you go through the interceptor.

If you share an interface pointer across a context boundary by some other means such as a global variable, you are responsible for marshaling the interface pointer yourself. This is exactly the same issue we discussed in Chapter 13 concerning sharing an interface pointer across an apartment boundary. The same marshaling and unmarshaling code we used there is applicable to the cross-context case.

Just-in-Time (JIT) Activation

A component may have an attribute enabling "just-in-time" activation or JIT. When JIT is enabled, the COM+ run time may present a client with the illusion that an object always exists, so that the client can maintain a long term object reference, while in fact the server has deactivated or even deleted the object, in order to conserve resources. Then when the client issues a method call on this object reference, the server "just-in-time" activates (or creates and activates) the object. This feature of COM+ may contribute to the ability of the application to scale.

Consider a very common situation: The client is talking to a database through a DCOM connection to a middle-tier object which talks to the database. A database connection is a scarce and expensive resource. Hence, the client may want to be careful to tear down its object connection to the middle-tier server when it is not needed, and then set it up again when required. But tearing down and setting up this object is expensive too, because the client is going over a network via DCOM to talk to the server. JIT provides a nice solution. The client may keep the object reference to the middle-tier server alive for a long time. The middle-tier server, through COM+, will deactivate the object that connects to the database when the method is done, and then reactivate the object when the next method request comes in.

Besides enabling greater scalability, JIT also simplifies the programming model for the distributed application. The client does not have to worry about maintaining a long term object reference. The client program can be implemented in a simple way, and the server and COM+ will provide good resource management.

Under COM+, your component is implemented in a DLL, which is hosted by the standard surrogate DLLHOST.EXE. This surrogate exposes the same interfaces as your component, and the client talks to the surrogate. The surrogate maintains a connection to all the clients, and only creates/activates a real object when needed (under JIT) as illustrated in Figure 14–8.

LIMITS TO SCALABILITY

Although JIT can enhance scalability, you should not regard it as a panacea. When an object is deactivated, the direct resources associated with the object can be released. But DLLHOST.EXE is maintaining an illusion to the client that the object is still alive. This means that the COM stub manager and interface

DLLHOST.EXE

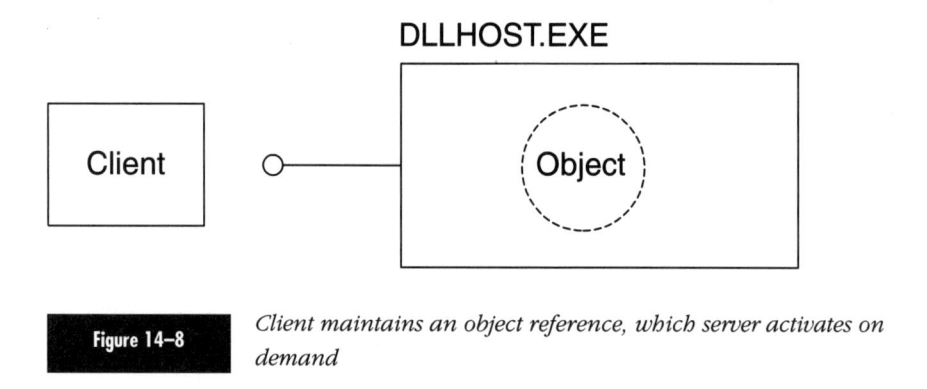

Figure 14–8 Client maintains an object reference, which server activates on demand

stubs must remain in memory until the client releases the proxy. This can consume several hundred bytes of memory per client.

"DONE" BIT

COM+ maintains a "done" bit in the object context. Under JIT, when this bit is set, the COM+ run time will go ahead and deactivate the object. The done bit may be set using any of several techniques:

1. Get an interface pointer to **IContextState** and call **SetDeactivateOnReturn**. This is the new mechanism provided in COM+, and affects only the done bit.

2. Get an interface pointer to the interface **IObjectContext** and call **SetComplete** or **SetAbort**. This technique was used in MTS and also sets the transaction "consistent" bit to vote to commit or to abort the transaction.

3. Administratively set the "auto done" property for the method in question. Then, when the method completes, the done bit will be set to true. The consistent bit will be set according to whether the HRESULT indicates success or failure. (You enable the auto done property from the properties for the method by checking "Automatically deactivate the object when this method returns.")

HOOKING OBJECT ACTIVATION AND DEACTIVATION

You may "hook" object activation and deactivation by implementing the **IObjectControl** interface in your class. The methods **Activate** and **Deactivate** will then be called on object activation and deactivation respectively. The **IObjectControl** interface also has the method **CanBePooled**, from which you return TRUE or FALSE, depending on whether or not your object supports object pooling.

STATE IN COM+ COMPONENTS

Traditionally, objects manage both state and behavior. State is held as instance data, and behavior is implemented through methods. Straight COM is entirely consistent with this model, and many COM classes maintain private instance data.

The requirements for highly scalable middle-tier components change this picture. State maintained in instance variables will not survive deactivation. The whole point of deactivation is to allow the system to reclaim resources, so that more clients can be supported concurrently. Thus whenever **SetComplete** or **SetAbort** is called, any instance data disappears. In particular, instance data will not survive across transaction boundaries. This requirement is important in preserving the "I" (isolation) in the ACID properties of transactions.

When needed, state can be maintained by a variety of means. The client may maintain state and pass it to the server as parameters in method calls. The server may maintain state in shared memory; COM+ provides a service called the Shared Property Manager (SPM) which supports such a capability. And finally, most typically, state is maintained persistently in a database.

Object Pooling and Construction

Just-in-time activation enhances scalability by allowing a server to manage a great many client connections without keeping an object instance "alive" for every client. The downside is that objects are continually being created and destroyed. If there is small overhead for the DLLHOST.EXE to create these in-process objects, there may be no problem. But if the overhead is large, it may be desirable to find an improved solution. It is also important that reinitialization be easy.

OBJECT POOLING

COM+ provides an automatic service that can maintain a pool of object instances for a component. If desired, some objects can be created when the component is initialized. When more objects are needed for clients, additional objects can be created and added to the pool, up to the maximum size of the pool. When an object is deactivated, it will not be destroyed but will be returned to the pool. When an object is activated, it will be taken from the pool and be given a chance to reinitialize. In this way, the overhead of creating and destroying objects is reduced. Object instances are "recycled." We will have a little more to say about object pooling in Chapter 23.

OBJECT CONSTRUCTION

One deficiency in straight COM is the inability to pass any information to a new object as part of its creation. In contrast, a constructor in C++ can take parameters, which can be used for doing custom initialization. COM+ adds some such capability through an interface **IObjectConstruct**. If you implement this interface in your class, when your object is constructed the **Construct** method of this interface will be called, being passed an interface pointer to **IObjectConstructString**. You call the method **get_ConstructString** to obtain a string, which may have encoded within it whatever information would be useful. The string can be configured for the component using the Activation tab of the Properties window for the component. See Figure 14–9.

A good example of using a constructor string would be to specify a connection string for a database.

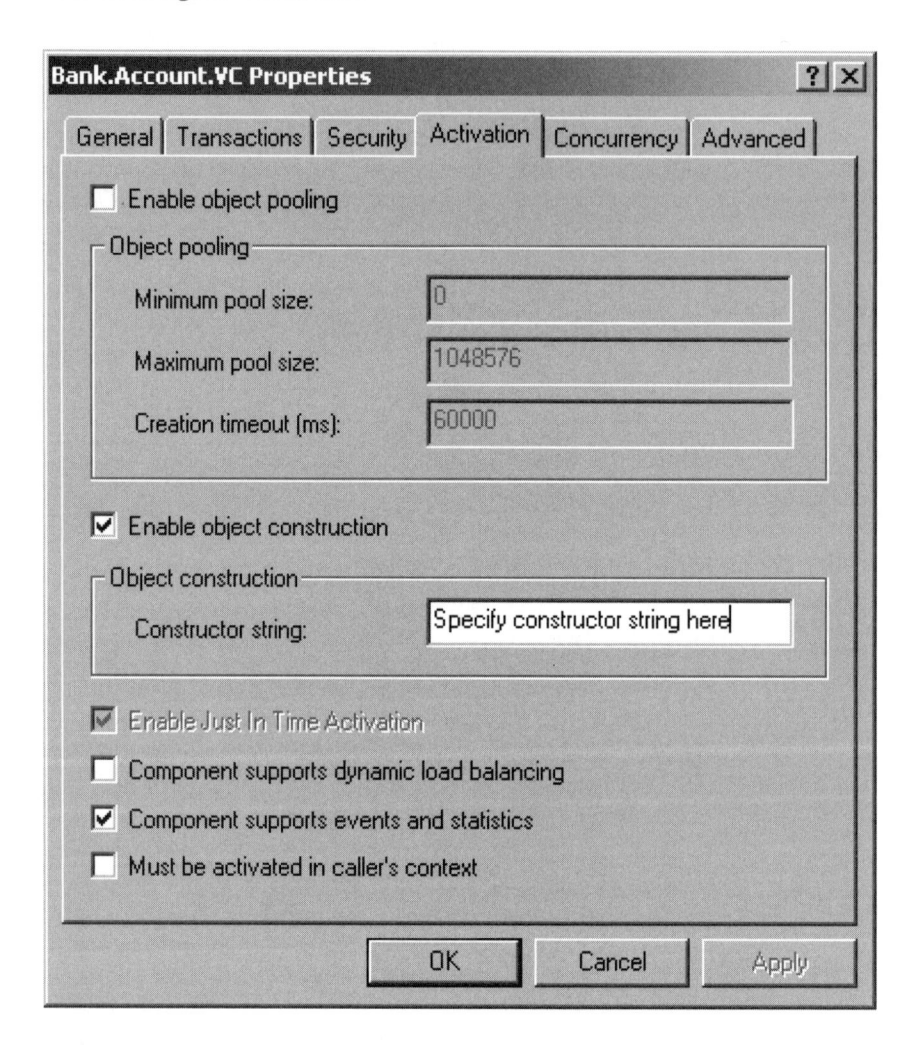

Figure 14–9 *Specifying a constructor string in the Component Services snap-in*

Summary

COM+ was created to address several significant issues in enterprise programming. The most important single driver for COM+ architecture is the issue of *scalability*. To build applications that can accommodate a very large number of simultaneous users, such as is the case with an application deployed on the Internet, requires a change in the programming model. The middle-tier needs to be able to manage object lifetime and temporarily discard object resources when they are not in use, and claim them again when the client needs them. COM+ achieves this objective through just-in-time activation, which can be provided automatically by the COM+ run-time infrastructure. Additional gains in scalability can be achieved for certain components through object pooling.

Other important goals for enterprise computing are *reliability* and dealing with the issue of *complexity*. COM+ addresses both of these issues through its programming model of declarative, attribute-based programming. In straight COM, configuration information is stored in the Registry. COM+ provides for much more configuration capability. These configuration settings or attributes are stored in the Catalog. A COM component is configured for COM+ by importing it into a COM+ application. Attributes can then be set through the Component Services administration tool (the "COM+ Explorer") or through an administrative API that is provided by a set of system administration objects. At run time, objects are instantiated in *contexts*, which reflect their run-time constraints based on their attribute values in the Catalog. Any call into a configured COM+ object must take into account the context, and to achieve compatibility with the requirements of the object being called, the call may go through an *interceptor* The interceptor is a lightweight proxy that does all the work necessary to comply with the requirements of the object. Through this interception process the COM+ system services are automatically invoked. This model deals with complexity, because it is much easier for a programmer to declare attributes than to write code. The model also enhances reliability, because the system code provided by the COM+ services is in many cases very intricate and difficult code, which can be error-prone when implemented by applications themselves.

This chapter stayed at the architectural level and tried to present in one place a compact survey of the core features of the COM+ programming model. The next chapter provides a hands-on tutorial to these concepts with a number of programming examples. The following chapters then go through the major services provided by COM+.

FIFTEEN

A COM+ Tutorial

In the previous chapter, we discussed in some detail the fundamental architectural model of COM+, but we did not do any hands-on work. In this chapter, we will begin working in the COM+ environment, starting to gain familiarity with both the tools and the programming techniques. The example programs should also serve to help solidify your understanding of the architecture. After completing this chapter, you may wish to reread Chapter 14 before going on to the more detailed coverage of specific COM+ services.

There are four main parts to this tutorial. In the first, we illustrate how to install a Visual Basic COM component into a COM+ application. We then add some COM+-specific code to illustrate some of the features of the COM+ architecture, such as just-in-time activation. We also do some experiments with COM+ Explorer, trying out various settings of attributes. Next we work with a C++ COM component of similar functionality. Being "closer to the metal," we'll be able to do additional experiments, including retrieving an initialization string in object construction. In both the Visual Basic and C++ cases, we will be writing messages to a log file. In the third section, we look at the system administration objects and examine a simple program example of retrieving information from the Catalog. Finally, we see how to deploy a COM+ application remotely.

A Visual Basic COM+ Component

Our first example is the VB bank account component from Chapter 6. We have modified it slightly so that no message boxes are displayed. Instead we use a "logger" component to write trace type output to a log file. (In general you should *not* display windows such as message boxes in server components. The server component may run on a different machine, and there may not be anyone there to close it. Worse, if the server does not run as the interactive user, the message box will not be displayed at all. The result is that the method that put up the message box will be waiting for someone to hit the OK button, but since it is not displayed the method will block forever, and the server will hang.)

A Roadmap

This first example is rather long, so I would like to provide you with a roadmap. Think of it as a tour with numbered stops along the way. You will find that there are three "steps" to the server code, but there are seven stops along our tour. In COM+ a lot is done by configuration, and so the same code will behave differently under different configurations.

1. We begin with trying out an unconfigured COM component. It is similar to our bank account example from Part 2, but our **IDisplay::Show** method writes to a log file rather than puts up a message box, for reasons discussed above.

2. In the second stop, we install the component in a COM+ application. There will be no new behavior. This is just an exercise in using the tools.

3. Next, we provide a tour of the various attributes that can be set. Don't take a lot of time over this. The purpose is just to give you a feel for the wide range of attribute information that is stored in the Catalog, not to try to understand what it is all for. The rest of this book will cover many of the areas of configuration encountered.

4. Next comes a hands-on exploration of the issues of activation and state. Here we see the ramifications of just-in-time activation. We demonstrate some Visual Basic code for using the context object.

5. Here we change the configuration to turn JIT off and see the results.

6. Here we write some Visual Basic code to implement the **IObjectControl** interface in order to hook into object activation and deactivation.

7. Finally, we do one more piece of configuration, setting the "auto done" property for a method.

Enjoy the trip!

An Unconfigured Component (#1)

Before trying our component under COM+, we will try it out as an unconfigured component. This is just straight COM.

USING THE LOGGER

We could use the **Logger** component from Chapter 12. For the sake of simplicity, and to make our example self-contained, we use a simple VB class **LogVb** with a single method **Writeln**, which simply takes a string argument. Information is written to the hardcoded file **c:\logfile.txt**. Every time you call **Writeln** the string gets appended as a new line onto the end of the file. If you want to start with a fresh file, simply delete the file. The first time **Writeln** is called, the file will be recreated. You can double-click on the file to bring up Notepad to examine the file.

If you would like to try out the simple logger stand-alone, you can use the test program in **Chap15\LogVb**.

TESTING THE BANK ACCOUNT COMPONENT

The server is in **Chap15\BankVbPlus\Step1** and the client is in **Chap15\BankClientVb**. Register the server by running **reg_BankVbPlus.bat**. For convenience, build the client (File | Make), and then run the client **BankVbClient.exe**. You should see a test window that looks like Figure 15–1. Click the "Create" button to create an object, make two deposits, show the balance, and make a withdrawal. Show the balance again, and close the

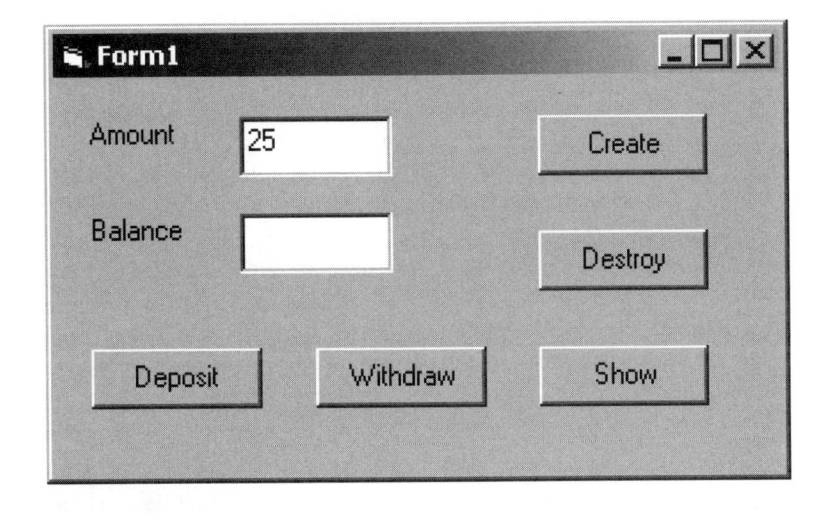

Figure 15–1   Test program for bank account object

application. Now examine the log file **c:\logfile.txt**. You should see the following record of what you did:

```
Account object created
Balance is 250 (IDisplay::Show)
Balance is 225 (IDisplay::Show)
Account object destroyed
```

A Configured Component (#2)

Now we will install our bank account component in the Catalog, which will make it a "configured component," having many attribute settings. Before exercising the test program again, we will examine a number of the attributes.

CREATING AN EMPTY COM+ APPLICATION

Bring up the COM+ Explorer from Start | Programs | Administrative Tools | Component Services. Open up the tree view Computers | My Computer | COM+ Applications. Select and then right-click over COM+ Applications. From the context menu choose New | Application. The COM Application Install Wizard will come up. Click Next. Click "Create an empty application." Assign the name **BankVbPlusApp**. Accept the default of Server Application. See Figure 15–2.

Click Next. In the next window accept the default of Interactive user for the application identity. Later, as part of our discussion of security, we will see that you probably will want to set up a specific user account for running the application. Click Next and then Finish. You now have a new, empty COM+ Application, as you can verify in COM+ Explorer.

INSTALLING A NEW COMPONENT

You will see "BankVbPlusApp" added to the tree view. Expand it by clicking the "+." Bring up the COM Component Install Wizard by selecting and right clicking over Components and choosing New | Component. Click Next. A dialog will come up giving you a choice of installing a new component, importing an existing component, or installing an event class. See Figure 15–3.

The choices presented may mislead you. In working with the unconfigured component, you registered it. Hence you may be tempted to choose the second button "Import component(s) that are already registered." This would not be a good idea, because doing so would not fully configure the component. In particular, information about interfaces and methods would not be installed. We discuss the third button in Chapter 22 when we discuss events.

Click the first button "Install new component(s)." Then in the "Select files to install" dialog that comes up, navigate to the folder **Chap15\BankVb-Plus\Step1**) and select the file **BankVbPlus.dll**. Click Open. You will now see

A Visual Basic COM+ Component   333

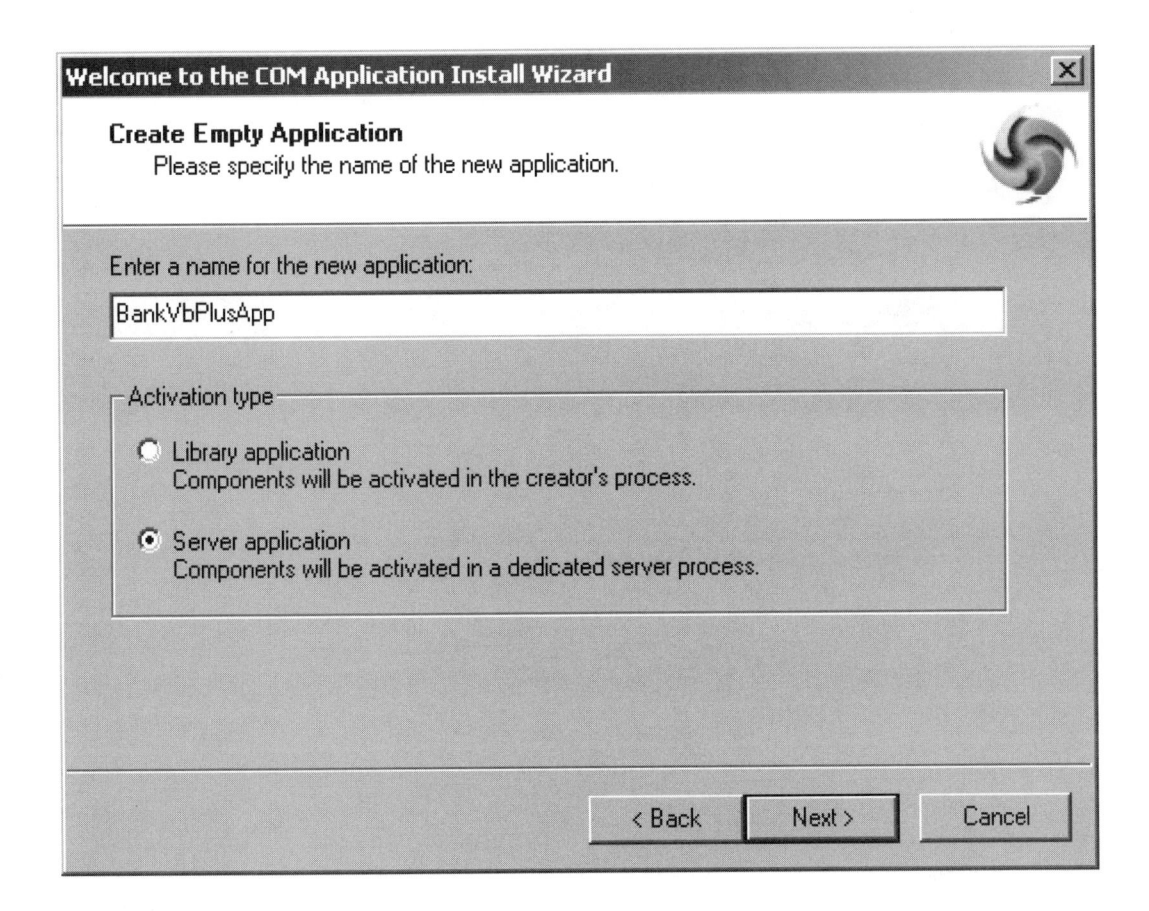

Figure 15-2 *Creating a new COM+ server application*

a list of files and components. In our case, there will be one file and two components (**Account** and **IDisplay**). See Figure 15-4. Click Next and then Finish.

(The second "component" is really an artifact of how Visual Basic implements COM classes. VB does not directly support interfaces, so the second interface, **IDisplay**, was implemented by defining another VB class. The **IDisplay** class does nothing, and the corresponding component can be deleted from the COM+ application.)

USING DRAG-AND-DROP

Alternatively, you can use drag-and-drop to install a component. Open up the Components folder in COM+ Explorer and a separate window in Windows Explorer where you can see the DLL file. With Components selected

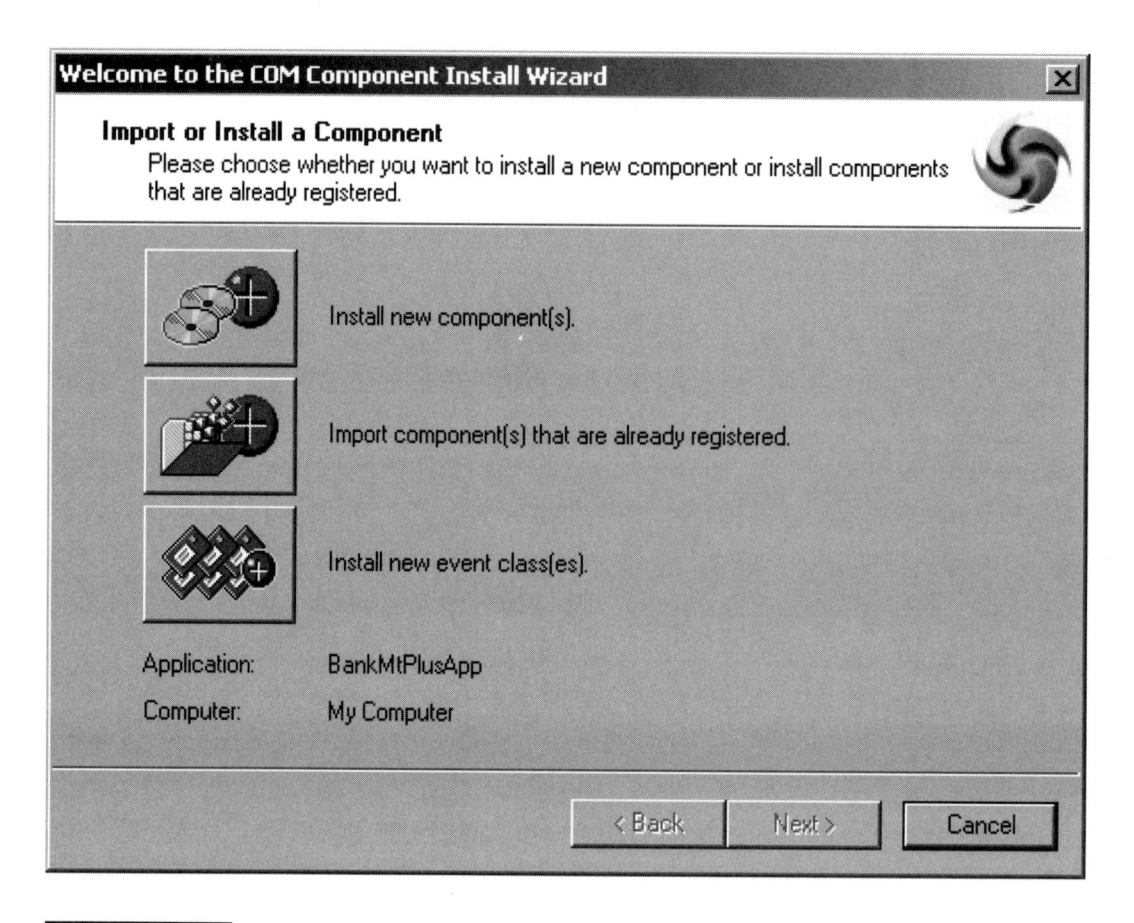

Figure 15–3 *Dialog for installing a new component*

in the tree view in the left pane, drag the DLL file into the blank area in the right pane.

INSTALLATION AND REGISTRATION

If you *install* the component, either using the Component Install Wizard or drag-and-drop, then the complete configuration information is under control of COM+. If you delete the component from the COM+ application, both the COM+ attribute information and the standard registry information will be removed—that is, the component will be unregistered. If you *imported* a component that had been previously registered and then delete the component from the COM+ application, the component will remain registered. As stated above, I recommend that you always *install* your components in a COM+ application so that they are fully configured.

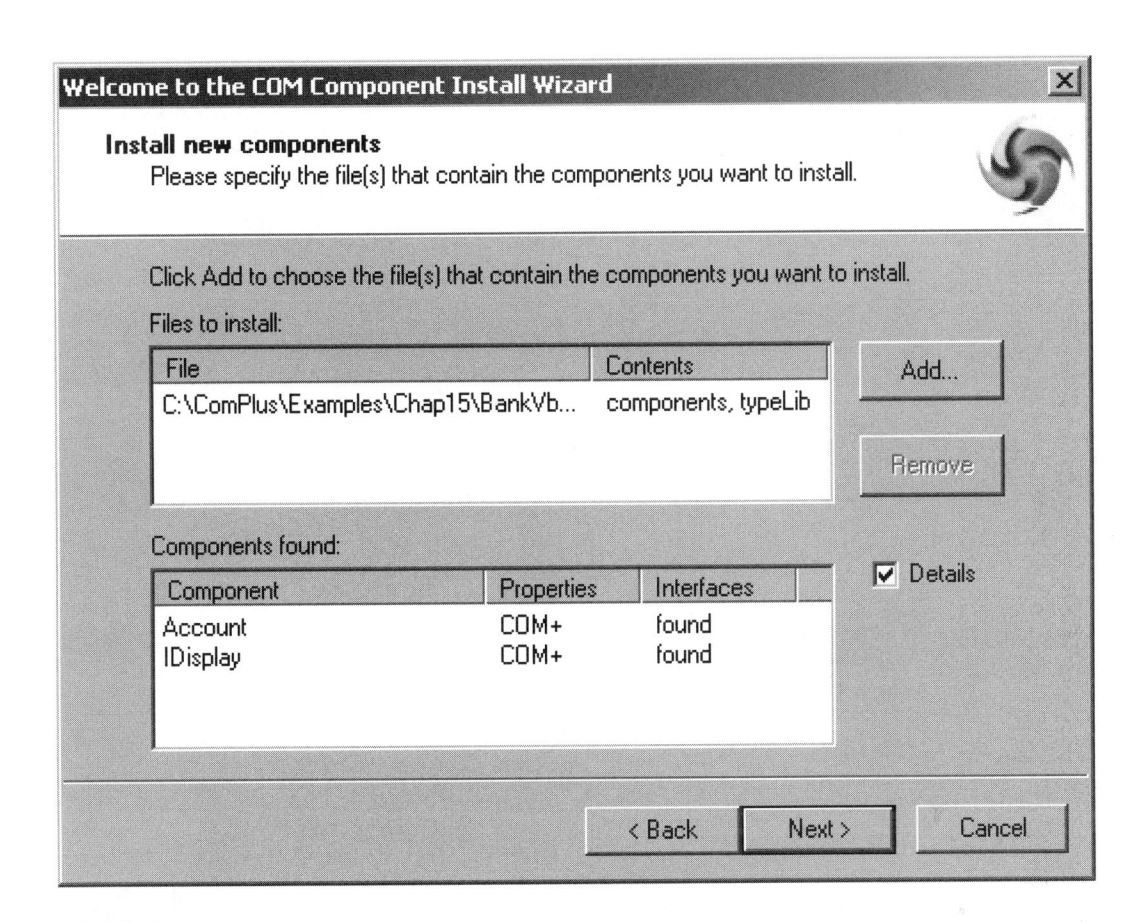

Figure 15-4 *Dialog for choosing files containing components to be installed*

A COM component can only be installed in *one* COM+ application. If you try to install the same component in another application, you will get an error message saying that the component is already registered. You cannot fix this by unregistering the component. If you try that, with the component still installed in another COM+ application, you will then get an error message "cannot load type library" when you try to install it in the second application. The only fix is to remove the COM component from the first application.

VIEWING THE COMPONENT(S) IN COM+ EXPLORER

You can view the component(s) you just installed in COM+ Explorer. After you click Finish from the Component Install Wizard, you should see the new components represented by balls in the right pane. (The View menu can be used to adjust how the components are shown. The balls correspond to the "large icon" view.) Delete the "artificial" component corresponding to the **IDisplay** interface. There will then be one component corresponding to the **Account** class. See Figure 15–5.

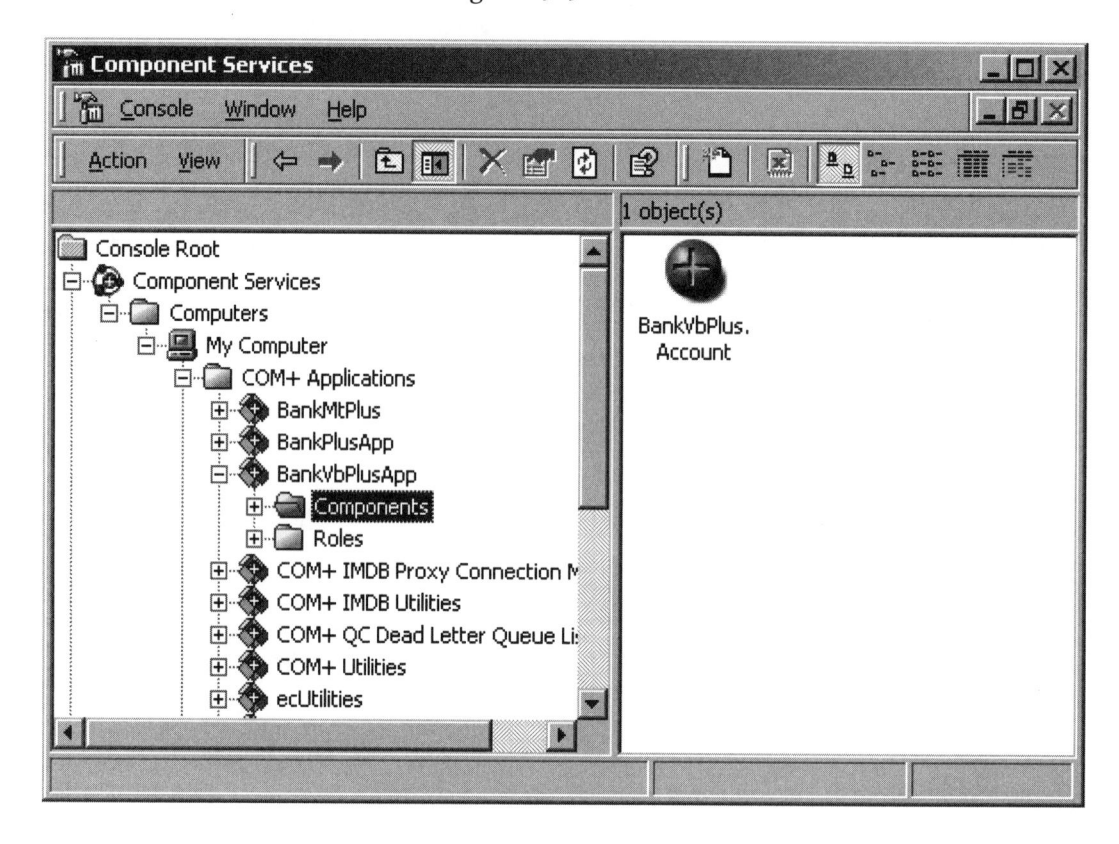

Figure 15–5 *A new component is now installed in your application*

RUNNING THE COM+ APPLICATION

Now you should be able to use the component just as before, only now is it a *configured* component installed within a COM+ application. Bring up the client program **BankClientVb.exe** and arrange your windows so that you can see both the client window and also the ball icon of your component inside COM+ Explorer. Click the Create button to instantiate a new bank account object. The ball should begin to spin. You should be able to exercise your object using Deposit, Withdraw, and Show. You can check the log file **c:\logfile.txt** to see that appropriate messages are being written there. When you are done, click Destroy. The ball will stop spinning. Close down the client application.

Now open up the server project **Chap15\BankVbPlus\Step1\BankVb-Plus.vbp**. Try to rebuild the DLL (File | Make BankVbPlus.dll). You get an error message saying permission is denied for the DLL. What is going on? You may want to try to figure out this conundrum before reading on.

A Tour of Attributes (#3)

We now have a configured component within a COM+ application. Recall the hierarchy of application/component/interface/method. There are many attributes that can be set at each level of this hierarchy. Without attempting to be exhaustive in your exploration, you should find it rather instructive to examine some of the attribute information that is available. You can do this within COM+ Explorer by opening up Properties for the particular level you are exploring.

APPLICATION ATTRIBUTES

In COM+ Explorer, right-click over BankVbPlusApp and choose Properties. A window will come up for BankVbPlus Properties. You will see six tabs for different kinds of properties. Making a pass through these tabs you will see a variety of configuration settings pertaining to the application as a whole. Some of the properties are:

- Application ID, a GUID that is used in DCOM
- A number of different security settings
- Identity (user account) under which application can run (this could be chosen as part of creating the application in the first place)
- Activation type of library or server (also could be chosen when creating the application)
- Queuing—the application can be configured to use MSMQ as the transport mechanism.
- Server process shutdown information (under Advanced tab)

The server process shutdown information pertains to the problem we experienced in being unable to rebuild the component DLL immediately after closing down the client. Recall that the component object runs inside an EXE surrogate host called DLLHOST.EXE.

In general, a COM+ server application will serve many clients. If temporarily there are no clients, it will probably be desirable to wait a while before bringing down the server, on the expectation that some new clients may soon arrive (minimize the performance penalty for starting up the object's host). The default is for the server to run for three minutes after the last client is done before shutting down. This setting can be configured. Go to the Advanced tab in the Properties window for the application. See Figure 15–6.

338   Chapter 15 • A COM+ Tutorial

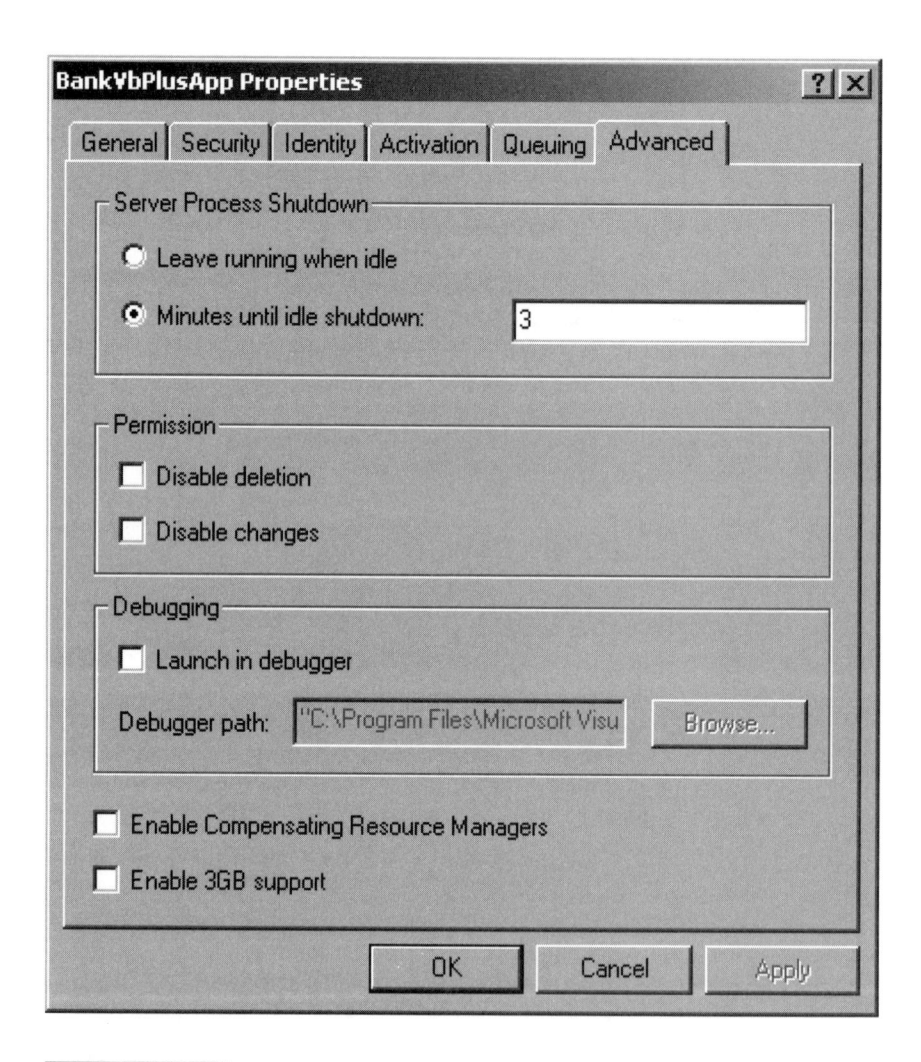

Figure 15-6   *You can set how long the server process will run while idle*

If you are interested you can do some experiments with this setting. You found out before that the process was still running by an indirect means—building the DLL failed due to no access permission (because the DLL was still in use). A more direct way to find out whether the process is still running is to use the Task Manager, which you can bring up by right clicking over an empty area of the task bar. Look for the process **dllhost.exe**. Note that you can sort the processes by clicking the "Image Name" header. Click twice, and the process names will be sorted in ascending alphabetical order.) One of these is always running, and you cannot terminate it. (It is the host for the components of a built-in application.) If your COM+ application is running you will see a second **dllhost.exe**. See Figure 15-7.

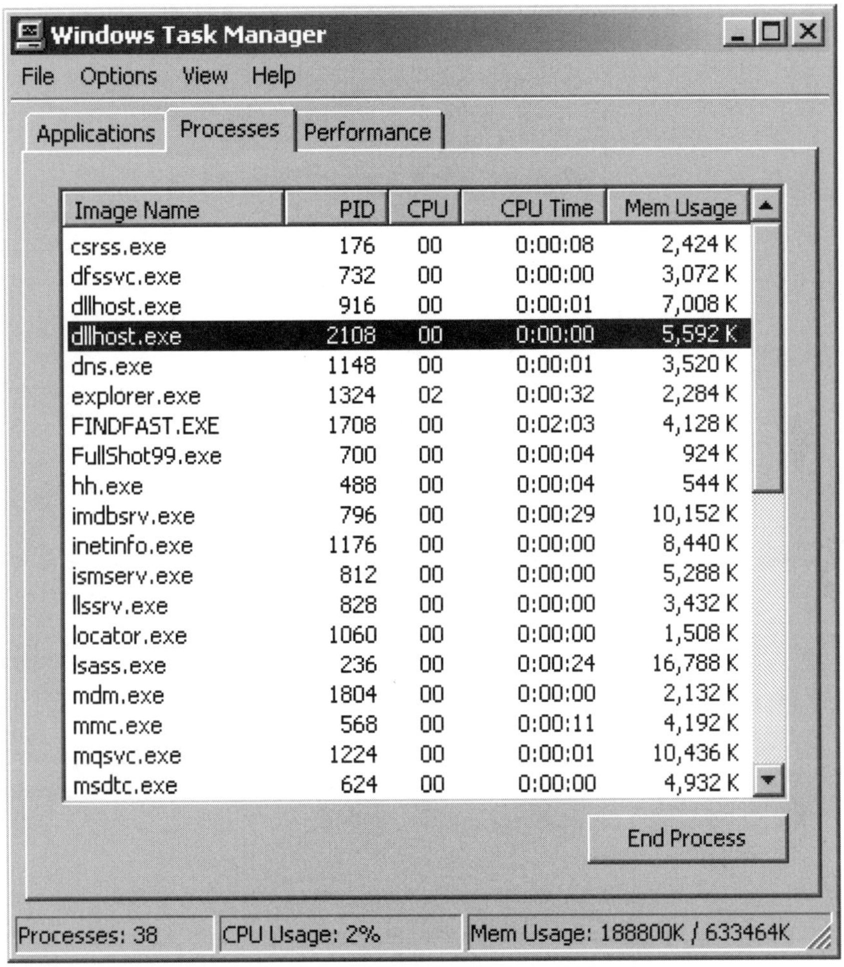
Windows Task Manager
File Options View Help
Applications Processes Performance
Image Name PID CPU CPU Time Mem Usage
csrss.exe 176 00 0:00:08 2,424 K
dfssvc.exe 732 00 0:00:00 3,072 K
dllhost.exe 916 00 0:00:01 7,008 K
dllhost.exe 2108 00 0:00:00 5,592 K
dns.exe 1148 00 0:00:01 3,520 K
explorer.exe 1324 02 0:00:32 2,284 K
FINDFAST.EXE 1708 00 0:02:03 4,128 K
FullShot99.exe 700 00 0:00:04 924 K
hh.exe 488 00 0:00:04 544 K
imdbsrv.exe 796 00 0:00:29 10,152 K
inetinfo.exe 1176 00 0:00:00 8,440 K
ismserv.exe 812 00 0:00:00 5,288 K
llssrv.exe 828 00 0:00:00 3,432 K
locator.exe 1060 00 0:00:00 1,508 K
lsass.exe 236 00 0:00:24 16,788 K
mdm.exe 1804 00 0:00:00 2,132 K
mmc.exe 568 00 0:00:11 4,192 K
mqsvc.exe 1224 00 0:00:01 10,436 K
msdtc.exe 624 00 0:00:00 4,932 K
End Process
Processes: 38
CPU Usage: 2%
Mem Usage: 188800K / 633464K

Figure 15–7 *You can see the **dllhost.exe** server process using Task Manager*

An alternative to the Task Manager is the Process Viewer tool, which you can bring up from Start | Programs | Microsoft Visual Studio | Microsoft Visual Studio Tools | Process Viewer.

COMPONENT ATTRIBUTES

You can open up the Properties window for your component either by selecting and right-clicking "BankVbPlus.Account" in the left pane (tree view), or you can right-click over the ball icon in the right pane. There are six tabs which show a variety of configuration information. Some of these are read only, and others are configuration information that you can set. Some of the properties are:

- General information such as path to the DLL, the CLSID and the AppID
- Transaction settings
- Security settings for the client
- Activation settings (including just-in-time activation)
- Object pooling
- Object construction (passing an initialization string to a new instance of the component)
- Concurrency settings

We will do some experiments with some of these settings later, but for right now let's continue our survey of the range of configuration settings for a COM+ application, working our way down the hierarchy.

INTERFACE ATTRIBUTES

In COM+ Explorer, open up the Interfaces node under "BankVbPlus.Account" in the tree view. You should then see the two interfaces, **_IAccount** and **_IDisplay**. (If you don't see these interfaces, you may have chosen "Import component(s) that are already registered" in the Component Install wizard. If that is the case, delete your component(s) and go back and choose "Install new component(s).")

Again you can open up a Properties window, this time by selecting and right-clicking the interface **_IAccount**. You will see three tabs' worth of configuration settings, which include:

- General information, such as the interface ID
- Queuing properties, which will be grayed out unless queuing was enabled for the application
- Security properties

METHOD ATTRIBUTES

Finally, you can examine attributes for individual methods. Open up the Methods folder under **_IAccount** and you will see the familiar methods of the account interface. At this point, the entire application/component/interface/method hierarchy will be open in COM+ Explorer. See Figure 15–8.

Right-click over the **Deposit** method and choose Properties from the context menu. This Properties window will have two tabs. Information that you can set includes:

- Automatically deactivation of the object when the method returns (this is how to set the "auto done" property, which we mentioned in the previous chapter when we discussed just-in-time activation)
- Security settings for the individual method

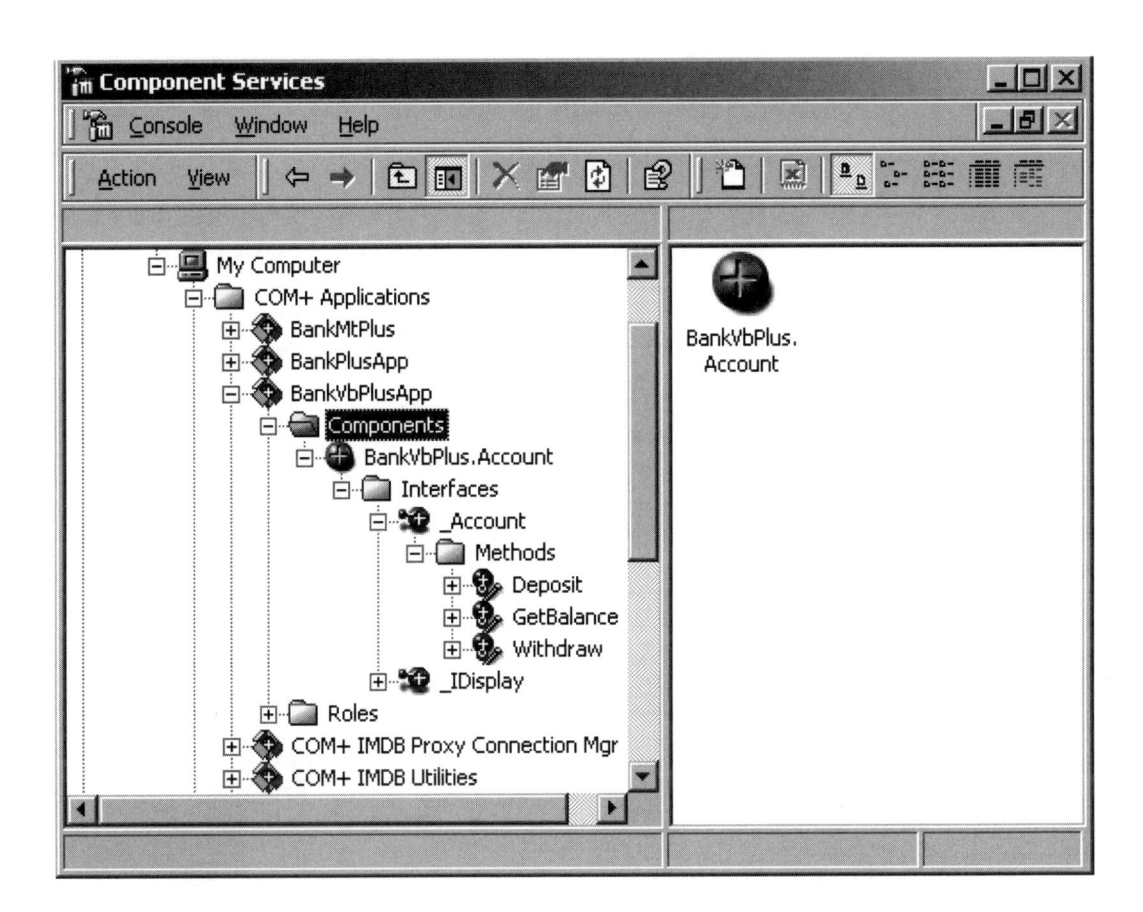

A Visual Basic COM+ Component 341

Figure 15-8 *Complete application/component/interface/method hierarchy*

This concludes our cook's tour of the various attributes that are available under COM+. As you can see, there is a great deal of configuration information that is stored in the Catalog and this information can be used by the COM+ run time to provide extensive services to your COM+ application.

Activation and State (#4)

The Step 1 version of the bank account server is a straight COM component, and we did nothing to make explicit use of any COM+ services. Step 2 obtains a reference to the context object and puts in a call to **SetComplete** after the new balance has been obtained. There are also trace statements to write the current balance to the log file after each transaction. Going through this example will help you to gain a better understanding of activation in COM+. It should also help elucidate the meaning and significance of "state" and "stateless." In order to make use of just-in-time activation, you will have to store state outside of the component.

PROGRAMMING WITH CONTEXT IN VISUAL BASIC

It is very easy to program with the object context in Visual Basic. The first thing you have to do is add a reference to the COM+ Services Type Library (Project | References). See Figure 15–9. (Recall from Part 2 that you need to bring in the type library to allow the Visual Basic run time to interact with the component using the names of the classes and methods.)

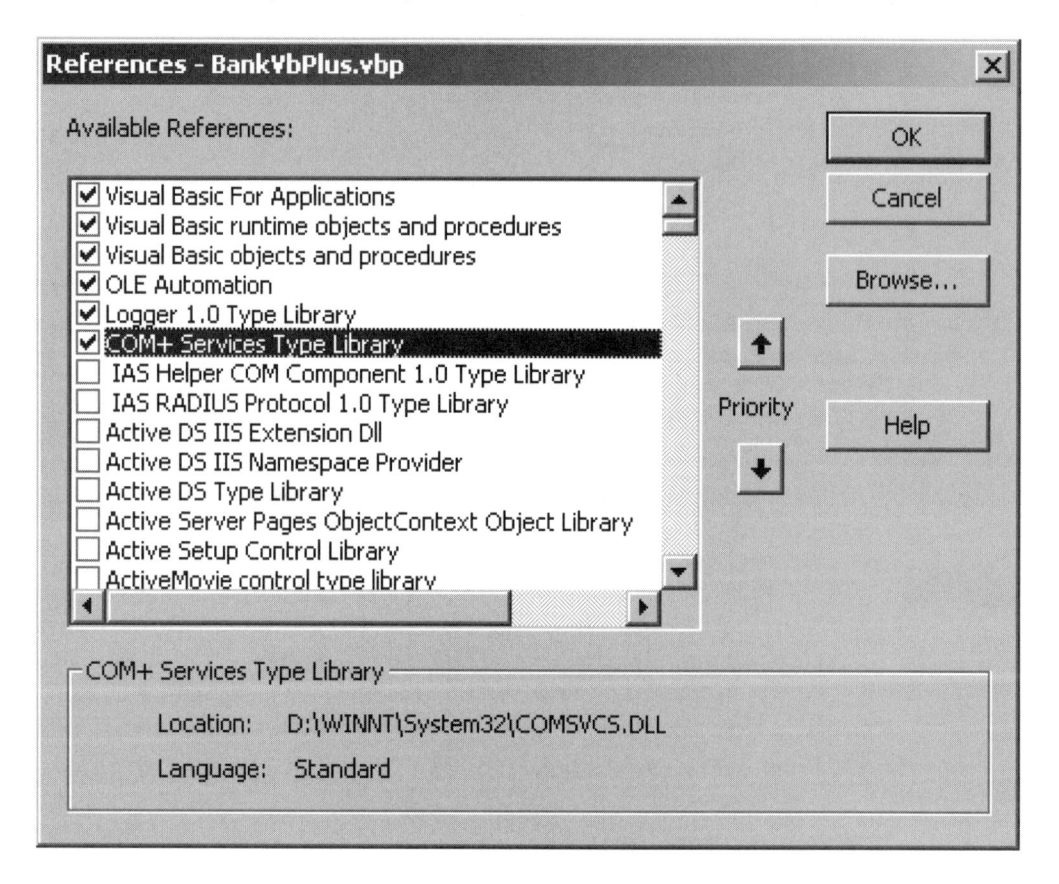

Figure 15–9 *Adding a reference to the COM+ Services Type Library*

In your Visual Basic code, you can then obtain an object reference to the context object by calling the function **GetObjectContext**. Through this reference, you can call methods such as **SetComplete**. The following is the code in **Chap15\BankVbPlus\Step2** for the **Deposit** and **Withdraw** methods. Notice that we call **SetComplete** after a deposit but not after a withdrawal. We are deliberately programming the two methods differently in order to show the impact of deactivation.

```
Public Sub Deposit(ByVal amount As Long)
    gBalance = gBalance + amount
    objLog.Write "Balance is " & gBalance & _
            "After Deposit"
    Dim objCtx As ObjectContext
    Set objCtx = GetObjectContext
    objCtx.SetComplete
End Sub

Public Sub Withdraw(ByVal amount As Long)
    gBalance = gBalance - amount
    objLog.Write "Balance is " & gBalance & _
            "After Withdraw"
End Sub
```

ACTIVATION AND DEACTIVATION AT RUN TIME

Now try to imagine what will happen when you install this Step 2 component into the **BankVbPlusApp** COM+ application in place of the Step 1 component. What will happen when you make several deposits and withdrawals?

To try it out, first delete the Step 1 component from the application. Then install the Step 2 component. Now run the client. What happens? Withdrawal works fine, but deposits seem to "stick" at 200, the starting balance. What is happening?

To be very concrete, let's obtain a specific log file. Delete the current **c:\logfile.txt** and then do the following: Withdraw, Withdraw, Withdraw followed by Deposit, Deposit, Deposit. The following is the complete log file.

```
Account object created
Balance is 175 After Withdraw
Balance is 150 After Withdraw
Balance is 125 After Withdraw
Balance is 150 After Deposit
Account object destroyed
Account object created
Balance is 225 After Deposit
Account object destroyed
Account object created
Balance is 225 After Deposit
Account object destroyed
Account object created
Account object destroyed
```

Everything behaves normally for **Withdraw**. But after each **Deposit**, the object is destroyed. It is created when it is needed, namely when the **Balance** property is invoked, in order to show the new balance in the dialog. Each time the object is created it starts out "fresh" with its starting balance of 200—thus the "sticky" 200 when we are doing deposits.

When **SetComplete** is called, the object is deactivated. If the object was pooled, it would not be destroyed at this point, only returned to the pool. But we are not pooling, so the object is in fact destroyed. (You would not have state preserved in the pooled case, either. You have no idea what object you will get next time, so keeping the balance with the object still will not work. The log file would look different, because you would not see the object being destroyed when it is deactivated.)

Note, however, that the client program is maintaining a long-term object reference, which it obtained when the user clicked the "Create" button. So the client "thinks" there is an object, while in reality there is none at this point. But as soon as the client calls a method, in this case the **Balance** property, the server has to create a real object so that the method call can succeed. The object is activated "just-in-time." (But the results are misleading. This is why COM+ works best with stateless objects; the state has to be fetched from the database or someplace else).

DISABLING JUST-IN-TIME ACTIVATION (#5)

The object creation/destruction behavior we have observed does not always occur. It depends on an attribute that can be configured. As a demo, let's turn this "just-in-time activation" attribute off. Bring up the Properties window for the "BankVbPlus.Account" component and go to the Activation tab. Uncheck "Enable Just In Time Activation." See Figure 15–10.

After disabling just-in-time activation, run the client program again, and repeat doing three withdrawals followed by three deposits. Now you get ordinary behavior again, with the object created at the beginning and staying around to the end. The state is preserved between all method calls. Here is the trace in the log file.

```
Account object created
Balance is 175 After Withdraw
Balance is 150 After Withdraw
Balance is 125 After Withdraw
Balance is 150 After Deposit
Balance is 175 After Deposit
Balance is 200 After Deposit
Account object destroyed
```

A Visual Basic COM+ Component **345**

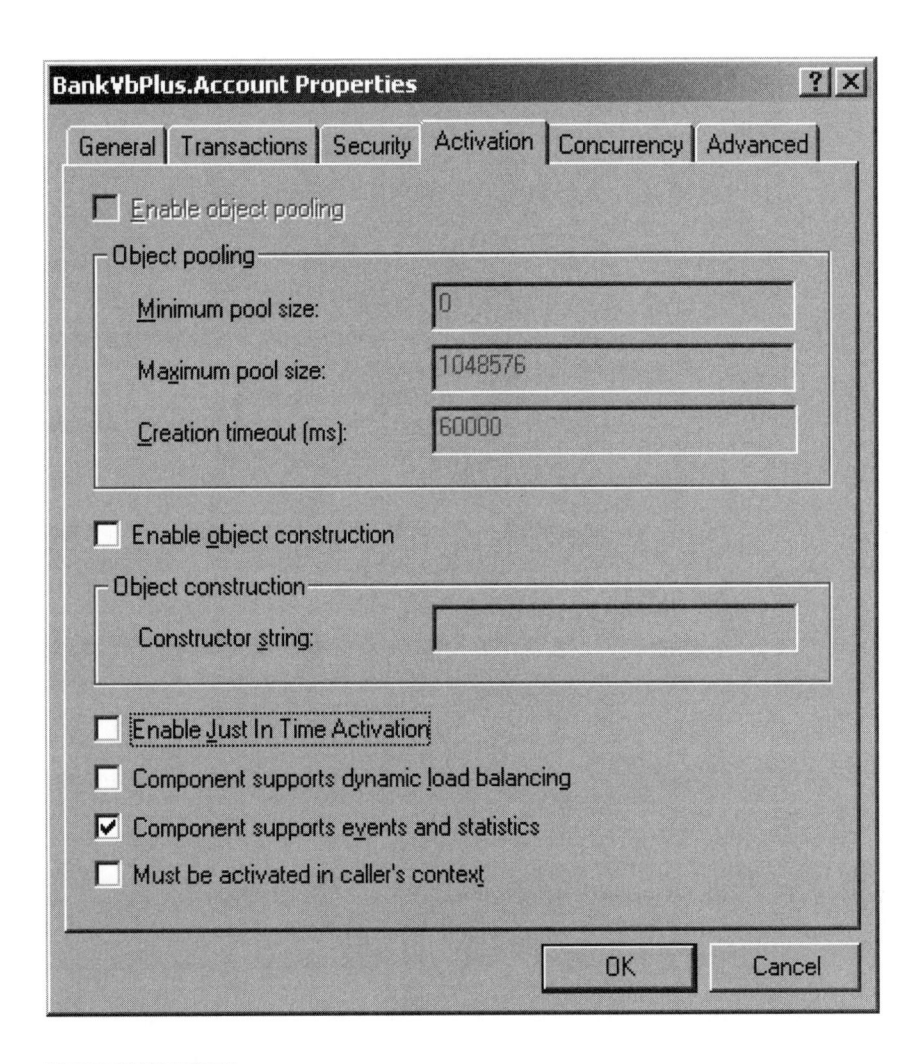

Figure 15-10: Just-in-time activation can be disabled

HOOKING INTO ACTIVATION AND DEACTIVATION IN VISUAL BASIC (#6)

COM+ provides the interface **IObjectControl** that a class can implement in order to hook into activation and deactivation. Visual Basic provides the class **ObjectControl**, which can be implemented by your VB class. Step 3 illustrates implementing **ObjectControl**, which involves implementing the methods **Activate**, **Deactivate**, and **CanBePooled**. Our implementation of the first two methods is by writing to the log file. For the third method, we return **False**. Here is the applicable code for the Step 3 project:

```
Option Explicit
Implements IDisplay
Implements ObjectControl
Dim objLog As New Log
Private gBalance As Long

. . .

Private Sub ObjectControl_Activate()
  objLog.Writeln "Account object activated"
End Sub

Private Function ObjectControl_CanBePooled() As Boolean
  ObjectControl_CanBePooled = False
End Function

Private Sub ObjectControl_Deactivate()
  objLog.Writeln "Account object deactivated"
End Sub
```

If we delete the Step 2 component from the COM+ application and install the Step 3 component, we will find that just-in-time activation is again enabled (the default). We can then run the client program and obtain a trace to the log file. So the output will be not quite so voluminous, we will trace one deposit followed by two withdrawals, with the following result:

```
Account object created
Account object activated
Balance is 225 After Deposit
Account object deactivated
Account object destroyed
Account object created
Account object activated
Balance is 175 After Withdraw
Balance is 150 After Withdraw
Account object deactivated
Account object destroyed
```

Since we are not pooling (indeed, a Visual Basic component cannot be pooled, as we will see in Chapter 23), an object is activated just after being created, and destroyed immediately after being deactivated.

AUTOMATIC DEACTIVATION (#7)

Up until now we have been deactivating our object by explicit code, calling **SetComplete**. COM+ provides an attribute in the Catalog that causes an object to be deactivated automatically when a method returns. This is a method attribute. Open up the Properties window for the method **Withdraw**

and check "Automatically deactivate this object when this method returns."
See Figure 15–11.

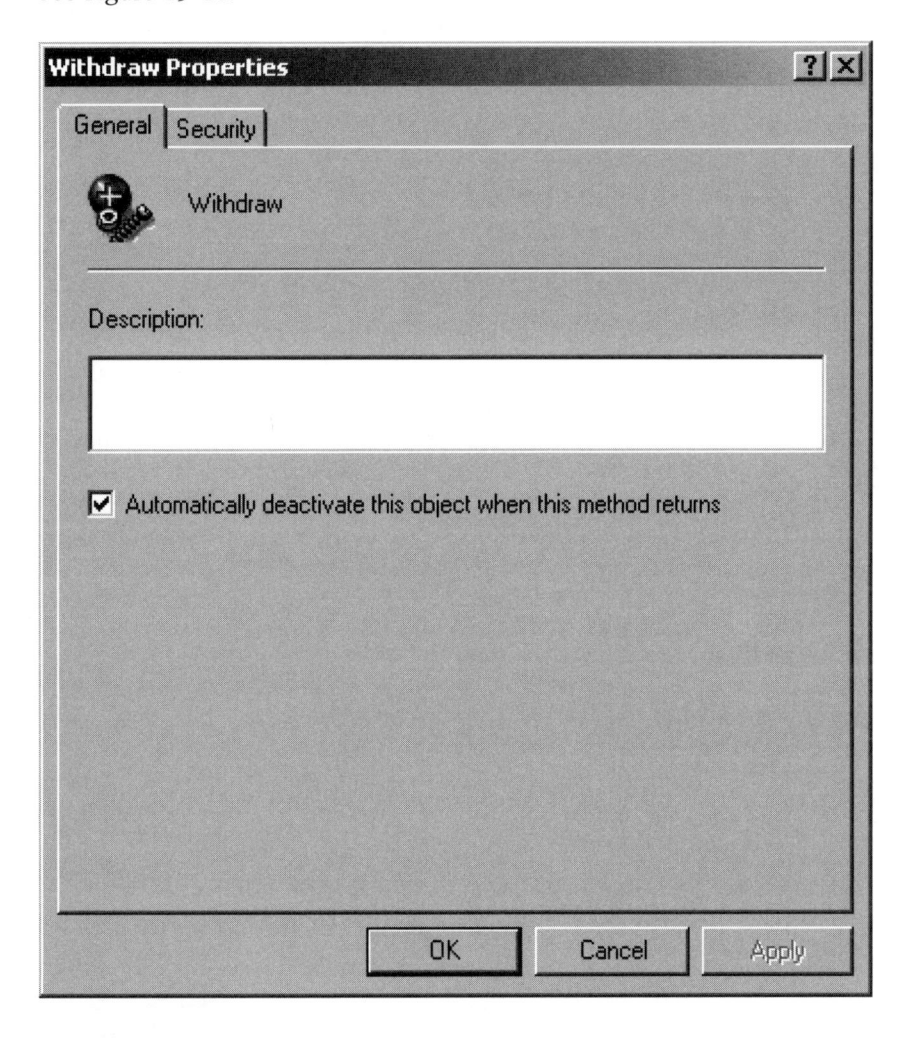

Figure 15–11   *You can enable automatic deactivation for a method*

Try this out, and run the client program again. Now the balance sticks at 200 for both **Deposit** (explicit call to **SetComplete**) and **Withdraw** (automatic).

Actually, when automatic deactivation is enabled, either **SetComplete** or **SetAbort** is called, depending on whether the method returns with a success or a failure. In either case, the object is deactivated ("done" bit is set to true). The difference between **SetComplete** and **SetAbort** has to do with transactions. **SetComplete** is called if this method votes to commit the transaction ("consistent" bit is set to true), and **SetAbort** is called if the method votes to abort the transaction ("consistent" bit is set to false). **SetComplete** and **SetAbort** will be discussed in greater detail when we cover transactions in Chapter 19.

The automatic deactivation attribute is sometimes called the "auto done" attribute.

A Visual C++ COM+ Component

This section provides a Visual C++ example that is essentially equivalent to the Visual Basic example just examined. One additional feature is illustrated, providing a string for object construction. The C++ example does not support the **IDisplay** interface, and the test program is a little simpler. Again, trace type output is written to a log file using the **Logger** component. The Logger component is a little more awkward to use from Visual C++ than Visual Basic, because the **Write** method expects a BSTR as its input parameter. We provide a simple C++ wrapper class **CLogging**, that simplifies using the Logger component.

The project is in **Chap15\BankPlus**. There are not multiple steps. There are three projects in the workspace, "BankPlus," "TestBank," and "Logger." Since the Logger component provided in Chapter 12 is implemented in Visual C++, we provide the code within this example, so the example is completely self-contained. The BankPlus project is dependent upon the Logger project, as you can see from Project | Dependencies.

Note that you will need to have the Platform SDK installed in order to build Visual C++ projects using Component Services libraries.

Creating the Example Program

Although we will not go through details of creating the example program, there is a practical tip to point out. The version of Visual C++ I used for writing this book, version 6.0, does not provide special support for creating components aware of COM+. But you can take advantage of support provided for MTS and make some conversions for COM+. This is easier than putting in all the code you need by hand.

When you create your ATL COM project, check the option to provide MTS support. When you insert a new ATL object, choose "MTS Transaction Server Component" for the type of object. See Figure 15–12.

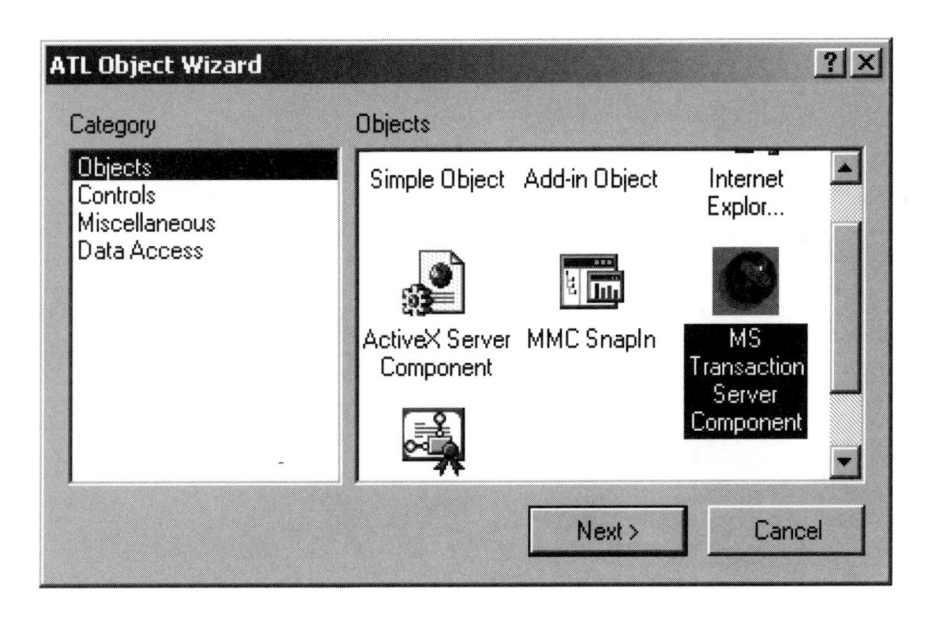

Figure 15–12 Taking advantage of MTS support for building COM+ component

Replace the MTS header file (**mtx.h**) by the one needed for COM+, namely **<comsvcs.h>**.

```
// AccountPlus.h : Declaration of the CAccountPlus
...
#include "resource.h"      // main symbols
#include <comsvcs.h>
#include "logging.h"
```

Installing and Running the Example

You should now be familiar with the procedures for creating COM+ applications and installing components, so we will not give detailed instructions again. Create a new empty COM+ server application, **BankPlusApp**. Build the DLL server and the test program. Install the DLL **BankPlus.dll** in the new COM+ application. You can now run the simple test program (see Figure 15–13). The ball in COM+ Explorer should immediately start to spin. You can do withdrawals, but the balance is stuck at 200 when you make deposits (because the component is configured for JIT and **SetComplete** is called at the end of the **Deposit** method). You can check the log file **c:\logfile.txt** when you are done.

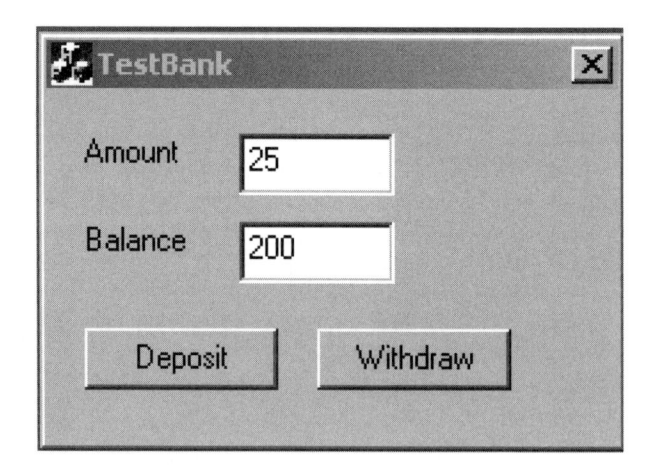

Figure 15-13 *Simple test program for C++ bank server*

IObjectControl and IObjectConstruct Interfaces

Your class should implement the interface **IObjectControl**. The trick of asking for an MTS Server Component in the ATL Object Wizard will bring in this support for you automatically. We also implement **IObjectConstruct**, for which we need to add support by hand. As usual in ATL, you should add the new interfaces to the derivation list for your C++ implementation class:

```
class ATL_NO_VTABLE CAccountPlus :
  public CComObjectRootEx<CComSingleThreadModel>,
  public CComCoClass<CAccountPlus, &CLSID_AccountPlus>,
  public IObjectControl,
  public IObjectConstruct,
  public IDispatchImpl<IAccount, &IID_IAccount,
                       &LIBID_BANKPLUSLib>
{
```

You should also add the interfaces to the COM map, and you should add prototypes for the methods of the interfaces to the class definition.

```
BEGIN_COM_MAP(CAccountPlus)
  COM_INTERFACE_ENTRY(IAccount)
  COM_INTERFACE_ENTRY(IObjectControl)
  COM_INTERFACE_ENTRY(IObjectConstruct)
  COM_INTERFACE_ENTRY(IDispatch)
END_COM_MAP()

// IObjectControl
```

```
public:
  STDMETHOD(Activate)();
  STDMETHOD_(BOOL, CanBePooled)();
  STDMETHOD_(void, Deactivate)();

// IObjectConstruct
public:
  STDMETHOD(Construct)(IDispatch * pUnk);
...
```

ACCESSING THE OBJECT CONTEXT

The standard way to access the object context in C++ is to keep a pointer member variable **m_pObjectContext** of type **IObjectContext***, which is initialized when the object is activated and released when the object is deactivated. Then, whenever you need to use a method of **IObjectContext**, you can just use this pointer.

```
HRESULT CAccountPlus::Activate()
{
  m_log.Write("Account object activated");
  HRESULT hr = GetObjectContext(&m_pObjectContext);
  if (FAILED(hr))
    m_log.Writehr("GetObjectContext failed", hr);

  return hr;
}

BOOL CAccountPlus::CanBePooled()
{
  return FALSE;
}

void CAccountPlus::Deactivate()
{
  m_log.Write("Account object deactivated");
  m_pObjectContext->Release();
}
...

STDMETHODIMP CAccountPlus::Deposit(int amount)
{
  HRESULT hr = S_OK;
  m_nBalance += amount;
  if (m_pObjectContext)
  {
    hr = m_pObjectContext->SetComplete();
    m_log.Writehr("Deposit...SetComplete", hr);
  }
  ...
```

Note that the semantics of this component are the same as for the Visual Basic version. We call **SetComplete** after a deposit but not after a withdrawal. Thus, when you run the client program (with default just-in-time activation for the server), the balance will "stick" at 200 when you make deposits, but not when you make withdrawals.

Object Construction

The C++ example illustrates a feature not present in the Visual Basic example, namely an implementation of the **IObjectConstruct** interface, through which you can receive a configuration string that is stored in the Catalog. We already looked at the standard ATL code for adding another interface to a class. Now let's look at the implementation of the single method, **Construct**, which is called just after the object is created and before it is activated.

The **Construct** method has an interface pointer parameter, which you can query for the interface **IObjectConstructString**. That interface has the method **get_ConstructString**, which you can call to obtain the string itself.

Our example code simply writes this string to our log file.

```
STDMETHODIMP CAccountPlus::Construct(IDispatch * pUnk)
{

  if (!pUnk)
    return E_UNEXPECTED;
  HRESULT hr;
  IObjectConstructString * pString = NULL;
  hr = pUnk -> QueryInterface(
                  IID_IObjectConstructString,
                  (void **)&pString);
  if (FAILED(hr))
  {
    m_log.Writehr("Construct...QueryInterface", hr);
    return hr;
  }
  if (pString)
  {
    BSTR bstr;
    hr = pString->get_ConstructString(&bstr);
    if (FAILED(hr))
    {
      m_log.Writehr("get_ConstructString", hr);
      pString->Release();
      return hr;
    }
    char buf[1024];
    USES_CONVERSION;
    wsprintf(buf, "construct string = %s",
    OLE2CT(bstr));
    m_log.Write(buf);
  }
```

```
else
  m_log.Write("null construct string");
pString->Release();
return S_OK;
}
```

CONFIGURING THE CONSTRUCTOR STRING

You can enable object construction and initialize the constructor string from the Properties window for the component. Go to the Activation tab. Check "Enable object construction" and enter your desired text for the constructor string. See Figure 15–14.

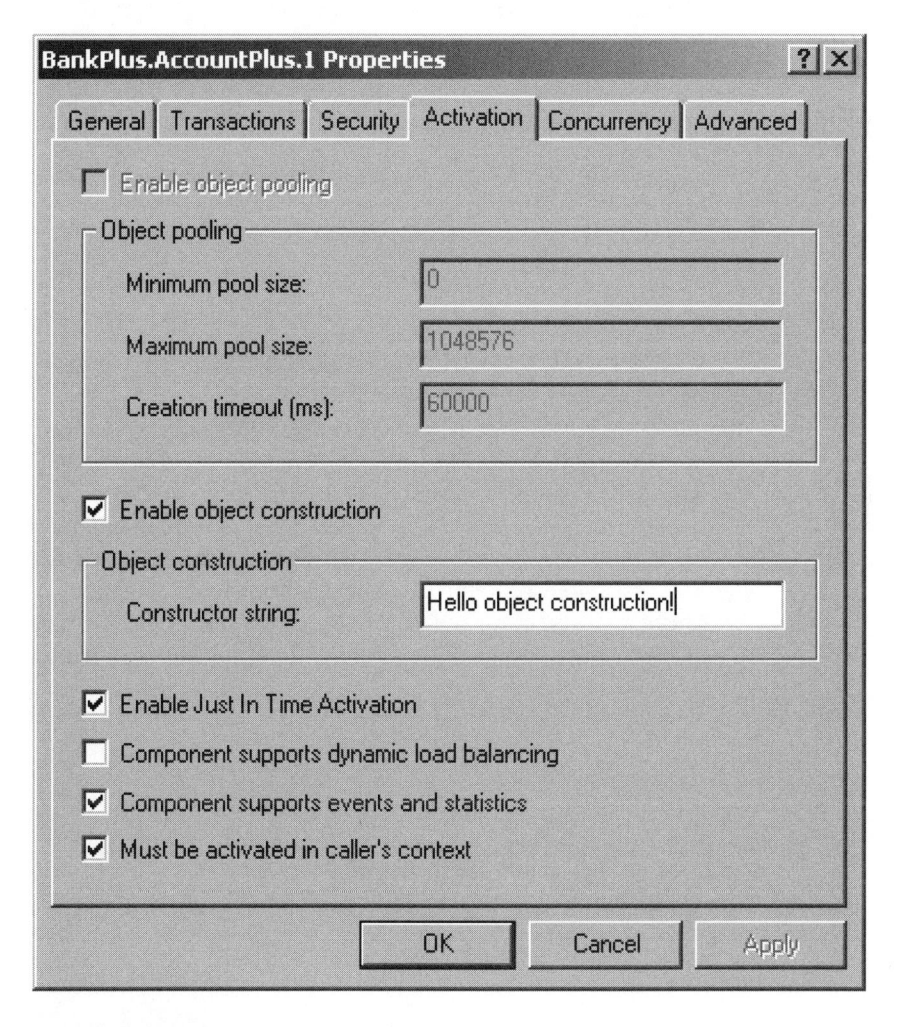

Figure 15–14 *Enabling object construction and specifying a constructor string*

RUNNING THE PROGRAM

After making this configuration change, prepare to run the client test program again. First delete the log file. Then run the test program. Make a single deposit and then exit. You should obtain the following log file. Note that, because of just-in-time activation, the object is destroyed after the deposit (because of the **SetComplete**), and the object is created in order to call the **GetBalance** method. The constructor string is received each time the object is created.

```
Account object created
construct string = Hello object construction!
Account object activated
After Deposit, balance = 225
Account object deactivated
Account object destroyed
Account object created
construct string = Hello object construction!
Account object activated
Account object deactivated
Account object destroyed
```

COM+ Administration Objects

COM+ provides an easy-to-use hierarchy of administration objects for working with configured COM classes. The COM+ Explorer simply provides a user interface on top of these objects. Everything you can do with COM+ Explorer you can do programmatically through the administration objects. For documentation see "Automating COM+ Administration" in the Platform SDK.

A sample program in **Chap15\MyAdmin** illustrates using these objects to obtain a list of all the COM+ applications installed in the system. Running this program shows a list of the COM+ applications. See Figure 15–15.

To use these objects, you need to add a reference to the COM+ 1.0 Admin Type Library. See Figure 15–16.

COM+ Administration Objects   **355**

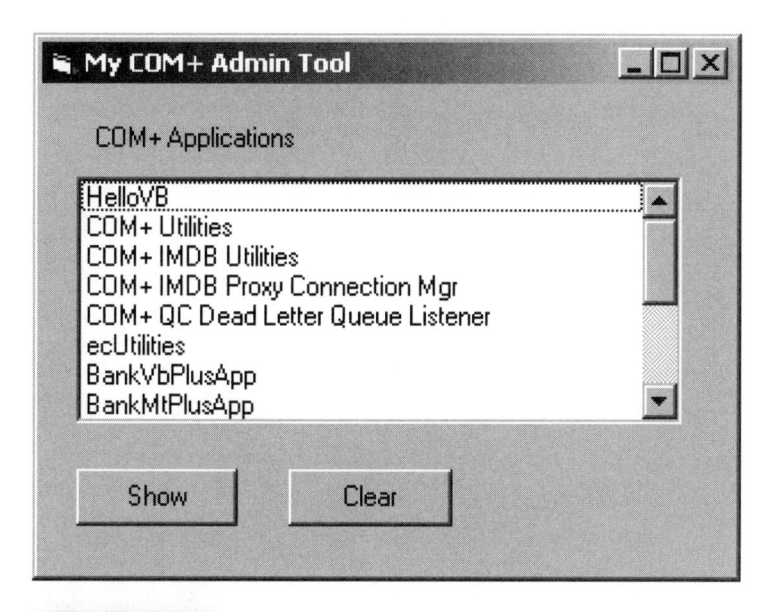

Figure 15-15   *Displaying a list of COM+ applications using administration objects*

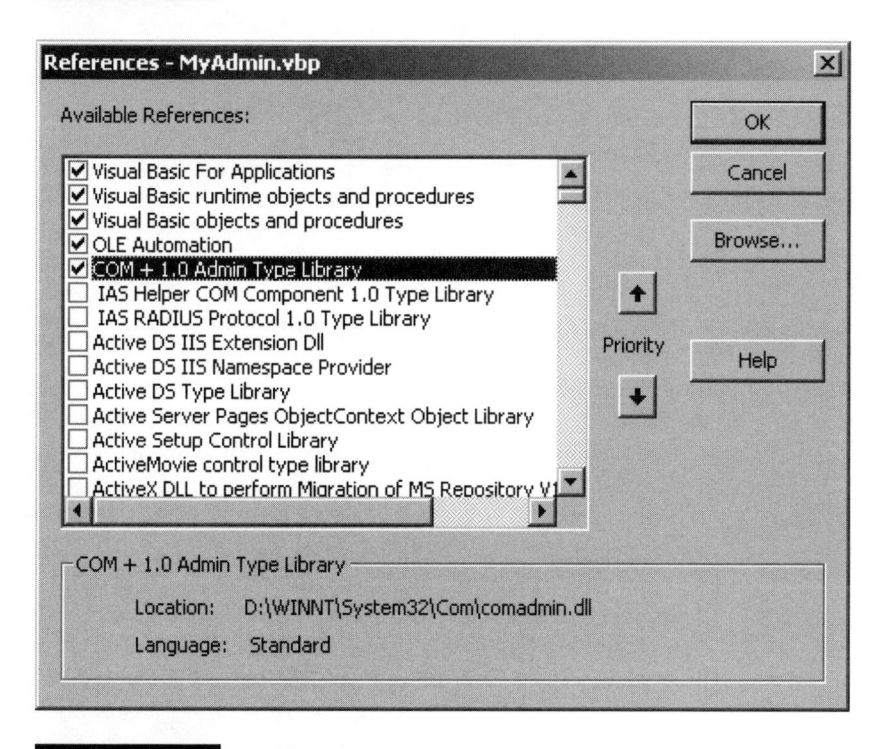

Figure 15-16   *Adding a reference to the COM+ 1.0 Admin Type Library*

The code itself is very easy. You create a root **COMAdminCatalog** object and then obtain an "Applications" collection object through the **GetCollection** method. You populate the collection and then you can simply iterate through the collection using a **For Each** loop.

```
Dim Catalog As New COMAdminCatalog
Dim Applications As COMAdminCatalogCollection

Private Sub cmdShow_Click()
   Set Applications =
      Catalog.GetCollection("Applications")
   Applications.Populate
   Dim app As COMAdminCatalogObject
   For Each app In Applications
   List1.AddItem app.Name
 Next app
End Sub
```

All of the configuring that we have been doing using the Component Services snap-in can be performed by using these objects, including installing applications and setting attributed properties.

Deploying a COM+ Application Remotely

The last topic we illustrate in this tutorial is deploying a COM+ application to run remotely. The process is considerably simpler than in straight DCOM. We will *export* our simple "BankPlusApp" application. Select and right-click over "BankPlusApp" in the tree view of COM+ Explorer. Choose "Export" from the context menu. In the wizard that comes up, browse to the **Deploy** directory in the book lab directory **ComPlus**. Assign the name "BankPlus" for the application file to be created. Note the **.msi** extension, which will be used by the Windows 2000 Installer. Choose "Application proxy." We are going to enable a client program on Computer #2 to talk to the server on Computer #1. See Figure 15–17.

Click Next and then Finish. Now copy the files **BankPlus.msi** and **TestBank.exe** to a test directory on Computer #2. Try running the client program on Computer #2). It will fail. Now double-click on **BankPlus.msi**. The Windows 2000 Installer will be invoked, and "proxy" code will be installed on Computer #2. This is COM "glue" code that will enable the client to remotely invoke the server. Try running the client again. Now it should succeed.

Like all good Windows software, the application proxy can be uninstalled. Open up "Add/Remove Programs" in the Control Panel. You can select the proxy and remove it. See Figure 15–18.

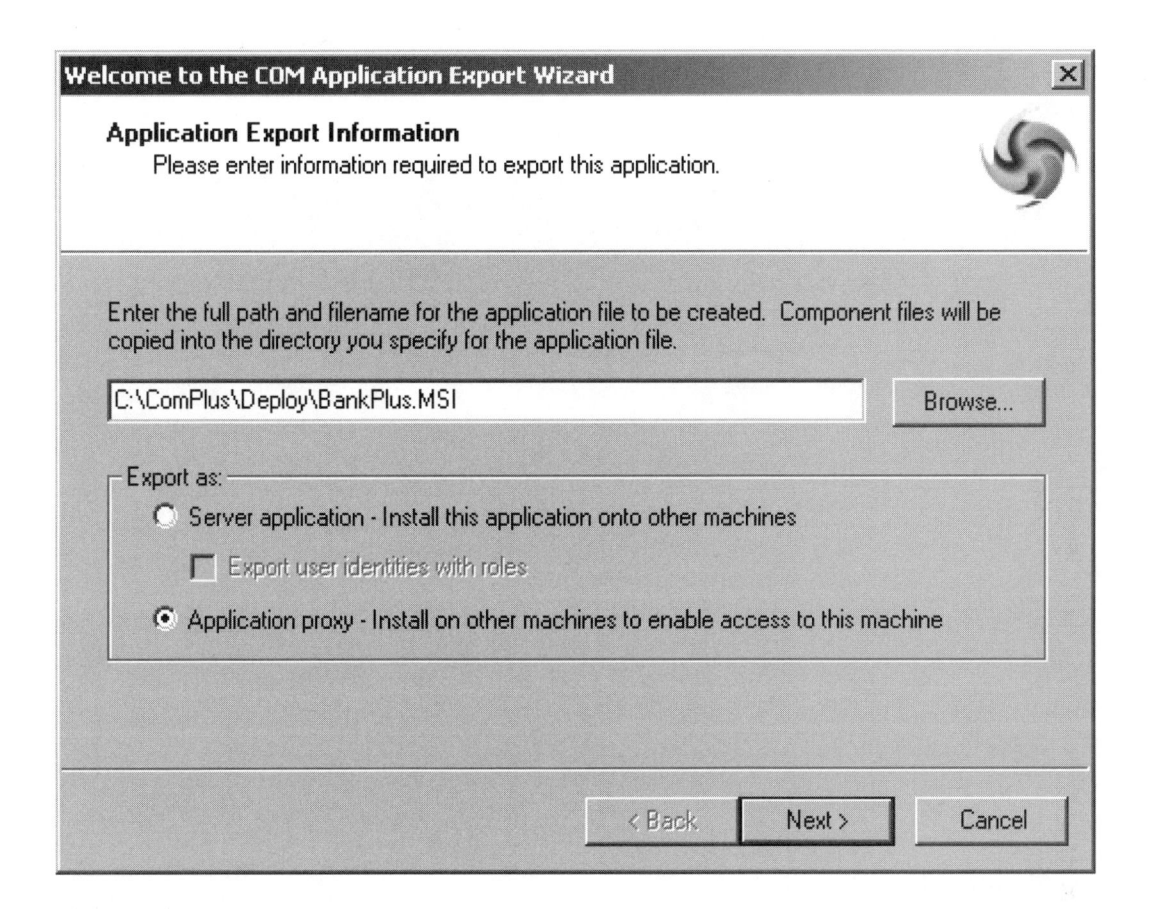

Figure 15-17 *Creating an application proxy to deploy a client remotely*

Summary

This chapter provided a hands-on introduction to working with COM+. The fundamental tool is the Component Services administration tool, or simply the "COM+ Explorer," which can be used for creating new COM+ applications, installing components, setting attributes, and exporting components so that they can be run remotely. Attributes can be set at all levels of the hierarchy: application, component, interface, and method.

We went through four examples. The first was our Visual Basic bank component. We demonstrated how COM+ activation works, including the issue of "state." We also showed how you can hook into the activation and deactivation process by implementing the **IObjectControl** interface (just

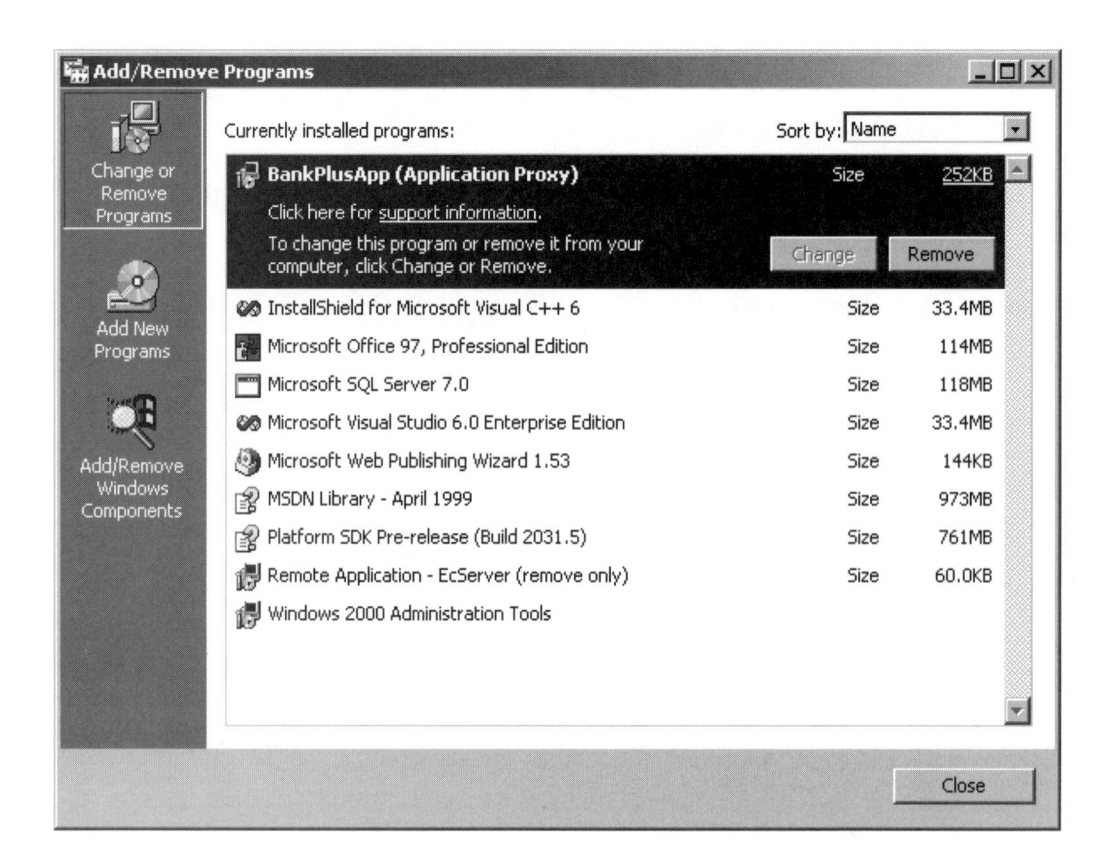

Figure 15-18 *Application proxy can be automatically removed from client machine*

ObjectControl in Visual Basic). The Visual C++ version of the bank component illustrated in addition passing a construction string to a new object through the **IObjectConstruct** interface. The third example provided an illustration of using the system administration objects. Finally we showed how to deploy an application so that it can run remotely.

In the next chapter we will discuss concurrency in COM+ and see how synchronization can be achieved by declaring an attribute.

SIXTEEN

Concurrency in COM+

We saw in Chapter 14 how the COM threading architecture of declaring concurrency requirements in the Registry (via the ThreadingModel key) provided a model for the more general and powerful declarative, attribute-based programming that is enabled by COM+. Just as crossing an apartment boundary in COM forces synchronization, so crossing a context boundary in COM+ triggers calling an interceptor.

In this chapter, we see how concurrency is handled in COM+. It turns out that apartments are less important in COM+ than in COM, and apartments are not the primary technique for enforcing synchronization. COM+ provides a *synchronization* attribute to further simplify multithreading and a new "neutral" apartment type that is more flexible, and should be the primary threading model for COM+ classes. COM+ also defines a new abstraction called an *activity*, which is used to group contexts having the concurrency requirement. We will discuss these concepts and provide a programming example.

Synchronization and Apartments

Classical COM relies on an abstraction called an *apartment* to deal with multithreading issues. We discussed apartments and COM multithreading in Chapter 13. If you feel somewhat hazy on the subject, it would be a good idea to go back and review that chapter before proceeding further. In this section, we review the basic concepts of COM apartments and the multithreading issues that motivate them. We will then introduce a new apartment type called the "Neutral apartment" that COM+ provides and is the preferred threading model for new components under COM+. Neutral apartments do not provide any support for synchronization. They merely get out of the way and permit the new COM+ synchronization mechanism based on activities to do its job, without contributing overhead.

Multithreaded Bank Account Example

To help make our discussion concrete, it will be based on a code example that will be examined in more detail later in the chapter. Our example is the multithreaded bank server from Chapter 13. A class **BankMtPlus** supports the interface **IBank,** having important methods **Deposit**, **DelayDeposit**, and **GetBalance**. We have two threads. In thread 1 we call **DelayDeposit**, which does the following:

1. Obtains the balance from shared memory
2. Increments the balance in local memory
3. Goes to sleep
4. Store the new balance in shared memory.

While thread 1 is sleeping, thread 2 goes in and out with a quick deposit (calling the method **Deposit**, which just increments the balance in shared memory, without sleeping). When thread 1 wakes up, it stores its new balance back in shared memory, overwriting the deposit made by thread 2. The deposit by thread 2 was effectively lost. For example, consider the following scenario for a race condition:

1. Balance starts at 100.
2. Thread 1 makes a deposit of 25 and is interrupted after getting balance and adding amount to balance, but before storing balance.
3. Thread 2 makes a deposit of 5000 and goes to completion, storing 5100.
4. Thread 1 now finishes, storing 125, overwriting the result of Thread 2. The $5000 deposit has been lost.

Synchronization through Apartments

In straight COM there are two solutions, both illustrated in Chapter 13. The first solution is to use the "Apartment" threading model. Each thread runs in its own single-thread apartment (STA). Each thread accesses the bank account class through an interface pointer. Since thread 2 runs in a different apartment, the interface pointer used by thread 1 must be marshaled to thread 2. Then when thread 2 calls into the bank account class, it goes through a proxy, which does a thread switch and waits on the message queue of thread 1 for the first call to finish. The race condition is avoided.

In the second solution, both threads run in the multithread apartment (MTA). Since the threads both reside in the same apartment, they use the raw interface pointer, with no proxy. Hence COM does not provide any automatic synchronization. Specific coding must be placed into the bank account class to prevent the race condition, for example by protecting the shared memory used for the balance by a critical section.

Neutral Apartments

There are possible performance issues in calling objects in both the MTA and an STA. Using an MTA and doing the work of implementing synchronization yourself is not guaranteed to buy you good performance, because calls coming to your object from outside the MTA will cause a thread switch. And of course *any* other thread calling into an STA will cause a thread switch.

COM+ provides a third apartment type, the Neutral apartment (NA), which never requires a thread switch. An object in the NA will always run on the thread of its caller. A process can have a single Neutral apartment. A class specifies the Neutral threading model by setting ThreadingModel = Neutral in the Registry. Then any object instances of the class are created in the NA.

Unlike the MTA and STAs, no thread calls the NA home. The only COINIT flags remain COINIT_SINGLETHREADED and COINIT_MULTITHREADED. So a thread will "live" in the MTA or some STA, depending on the COINIT flag it sets when it calls **CoInitializeEx**. A thread will "visit" the NA when it instantiates an object of a class specifying the Neutral threading model. But no thread switch will be involved.

Synchronization and Activities

Multithreading has always been a problematic area for COM. Even with the introduction of the MTA in Windows NT 4.0 it has been difficult to balance good performance with ease of programming. COM+ introduces attribute-based synchronization which does not rely on apartments. Apartments still exist in COM+, and contexts physically reside in apartments, but apartments no longer have to be considered as part of the logical programming model. You declare your component to have the Neutral model and specify a synchronization attribute as needed. This section describes the COM+ synchronization architecture based on activities.

Activities

COM+ provides an abstraction called an *activity* which is used to enforce serialization of method calls to an object. An activity is a group of contexts in which no concurrent execution is permitted. If a method is executing on an object in an activity, any other thread trying to make a method call into that object will be blocked until the first method finishes execution.

An activity can span several contexts, but a particular context can only be in at most one activity. It is possible for a context not to be in any activity at all. In that case, any thread in the apartment of the context can make a method call into an object of that context at any time. COM+ does not enforce synchronization in such a case. (The underlying COM will enforce synchronization in the case of a single-threaded apartment.) Figure 16–1 illustrates the relationship between activities, contexts, and objects. Note that while Objects 1–4 enjoy concurrency protection, there is no concurrency protection for Object 5, except what would be provided at the apartment level, if the context happened to reside in an STA.

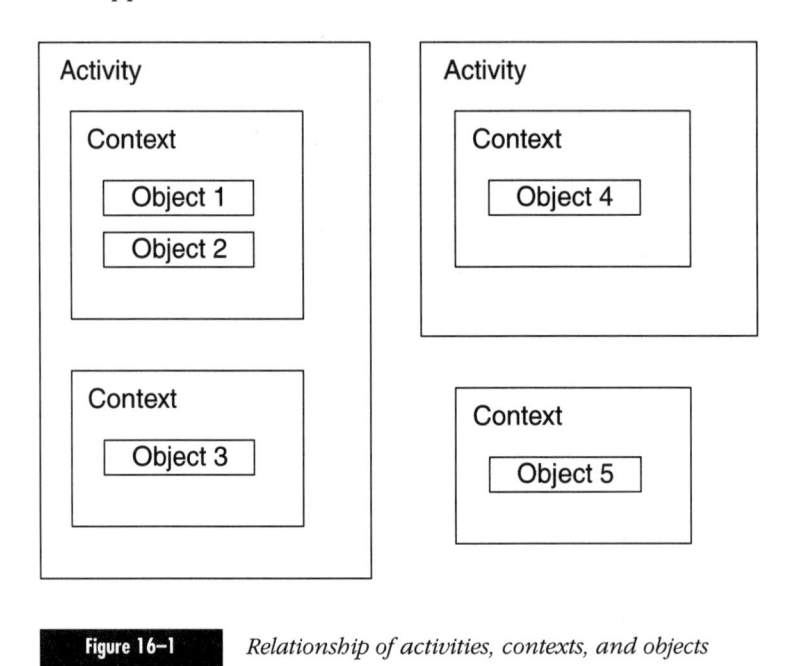

Figure 16–1 *Relationship of activities, contexts, and objects*

SYNCHRONIZATION ATTRIBUTE

If your component needs concurrency protection, you can have COM+ provide it for you by declaring a synchronization attribute. You specify a synchronization attribute through the Concurrency tab of the property window for the component, as illustrated in Figure 16–2.

Notice that the threading model is shown but cannot be configured in this window. The threading model is specified in the Registry.

The following choices are available for synchronization support:

Synchronization and Activities **363**

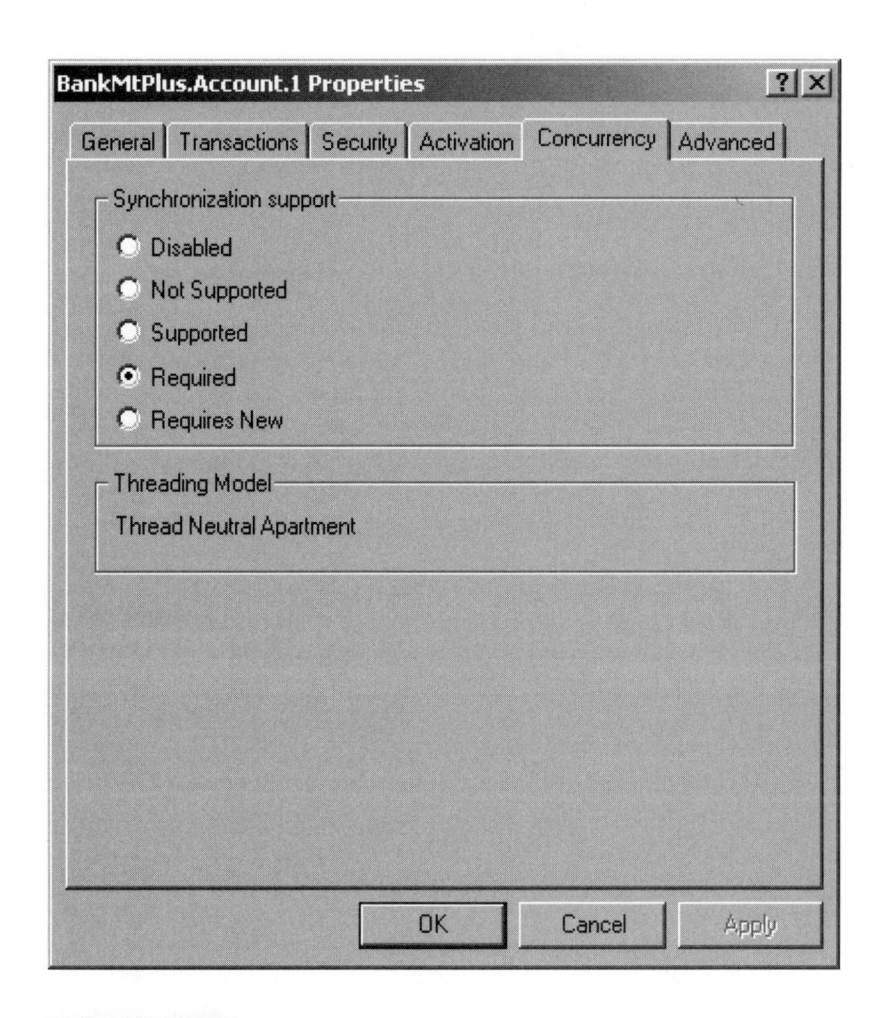

Figure 16-2 *Configuring the synchronization attribute*

- **Disabled**. As usual, this setting means that the attribute will not be considered by COM+ when associating the object with a context.

- **Not Supported**. The object's context will not be in an activity, and thus there will be no concurrency protection.

- **Supported**. The object will be in an activity if its parent is in an activity, and then the object's context will be in the same activity as the parent. If the parent is not in an activity, this object will not be in an activity.

- **Required**. The object will always be in an activity. If the parent is already in an activity, the object will share the activity of its parent. Otherwise, it will be in a new activity.

- **Requires New**. The object will always be in a new activity of its own. If the parent is in an activity, the object will be in a different activity. Thus no two threads can access the object at the same time, but it would be possible for one thread to access the parent and another thread to access this object concurrently.

RELATIONSHIP WITH OTHER ATTRIBUTES

The choices available for the synchronization attribute may be affected by the value of other attributes. If an object requires a transaction, it will likewise require an activity, because a transaction needs concurrency protection. Also JIT will force the requirement of an activity. If there were no activity protection, one method call might complete and cause the object to be deactivated out from under another executing method. In both of these cases, all options will be grayed out except for "Required" and "Requires new."

"RENTAL" THREADING MODEL

In early descriptions of the new threading model Microsoft used the term "rental" to describe an object which any thread type can visit (a thread whose permanent home is the MTA or an STA), but only one thread can call into the object at a time. This "rental threading model" is achieved through the two settings:

```
ThreadingModel = Neutral
Synchronization = Required
```

Programming Example

This section provides a programming example of how you can handle concurrency in COM+. The example program is in **Chap15\BankMtPlus**. There are two projects, "BankMt" and "test." This is the example that was mentioned at the beginning of the chapter. The server is built with the Neutral threading model. Set up the example by creating a new application, "BankMtPlusApp," in which you will install **BankMt.dll**. Accept the default attributes for the component, which will include "Required" synchronization support (Concurrency tab).

Run the test program. You will have an opportunity to select a value for the COINIT argument to CoInitializeEx for the client, and you can then click "Initialize." See Figure 16–3.

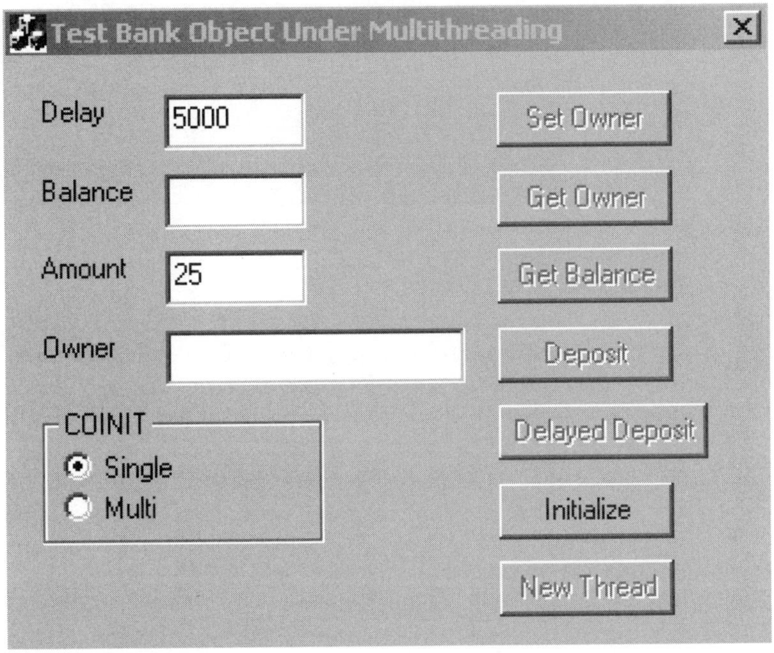

Figure 16–3 *You may choose a value for the COINIT flag*

Each Thread in its own STA

Select "Single" for the COINIT flag and click "Initialize." This will create a new object in the NA (Neutral apartment) and the main thread will be in an STA (single-thread apartment). You can exercise the various methods of the **IBank** interface. Now click "New thread." This will create a new thread, which will run in its own STA. Now try to exercise one of the methods, such as "Get Balance." You will get an error message, complaining about calling an interface that was marshaled for a different thread. See Figure 16–4.

Figure 16–4 *Trying to call an interface marshaled for a different thread*

This helpful error message points out exactly the problem. The method call is through the original interface pointer, which is stored in a global variable. If we were allowed to make this direct call without going through a proxy, we would be open to a race condition, as was illustrated in Chapter 13. One solution to this problem would be to marshal the interface pointer, as we did in Chapter 13. Then our method call would go through the proxy, which would provide synchronization. COM+ provides a simpler alternative.

All Threads Run in the MTA

Close both windows and start the test program again. This time select "Multi" for the COINT flag. Now all threads will be in the same apartment, the MTA. Click "Get Balance" in the second window, and the call succeeds, because the interface pointer is marshaled for the same apartment, the MTA. Click "Delayed Deposit" in the first window and then immediately "Deposit" in the second window. You will find that "Deposit" is blocked until "Delayed Deposit" completes. COM+ provides this blocking behavior for us through an interceptor. The interceptor sets up a lock because we selected the "Required" value for "Synchronization support" for our component.

Note that this blocking behavior is objectwide. If you go back to the first window and click "Delayed Deposit" again, and in the second window try "Get Owner," you will find that this call, too, is blocked. The COM+ synchronization support is not a cure-all. If you want to achieve finer granularity of blocking, you have to write the code yourself, like we did in Chapter 13. (But you can still use the NA to get a lighter weight proxy.)

Summary

The traditional mechanism in COM for dealing with concurrency issues has been apartments. This architecture works, and indeed the concept of achieving concurrency through declaring a threading model provided an inspiration for attribute-based programming in COM+. But there are a number of problems with this approach. Using the MTA and writing your own synchronization code is tricky. Relying on the STA relieves you from writing synchronization code, but you incur the overhead of a thread switch, and you may be forced to marshal your interface pointers. Even using the MTA does not guarantee great performance because if you call into your object from another apartment, you will incur a thread switch.

COM+ provides a solution that is both simpler and may offer better performance. An abstraction, an *activity*, defines a grouping of contexts within which concurrency is not allowed. By declaring that your component requires synchronization support, you will ensure that your object runs within an activity and gets concurrency protection. This protection is provided by a lightweight interceptor in place of a thread switch.

SEVENTEEN

Windows 2000 and COM+ Security

In this chapter, we discuss the vital topic of security. If you have been programming desktop applications, you may not have been concerned with security. If you have been programming enterprise applications, you are well-acquainted with the importance of security, but you may need to come up to speed on how to deal with security in Windows 2000. Our end goal is to achieve a good grasp of how security is programmed using COM+. We will see that in general it is remarkably simple, with the COM+ infrastructure transparently providing implementation of security, using the interception mechanism we have discussed. The problem is that COM+ makes security appear too simple, and if you need to delve just a little deeper you can quickly come to a sea of details. So in this chapter we take a fundamental approach to security, beginning with the underlying security architecture of NT, which has been enhanced in Windows 2000. We also look at COM security, which is at a higher level than NT but at a lower level than COM+. This background should give you a good grounding to face whatever security challenges you encounter in the Windows 2000/COM+ environment.

Another practical issue in working with security is understanding fundamental administrative procedures. Again, if you have been working as the sole user of a desktop Windows system, you likely won't have had to delve into working with user accounts and privileges and the like. And if you do have some experience in this area, you'll find that Active Directory brings some changes, and the layout of the administrative tools is decidedly different under Windows 2000. We provide a simple tutorial to help you in the basic administration you will need to secure the resources of your application.

Next we discuss COM security, which is at a higher level of abstraction and shares a number of features with those of COM+. Finally we come to the COM+ programming model itself, and see that it provides a good abstraction over the lower-level security infrastructure. Basic security tasks can be done by configuration and many tasks can be done by simple programming. If you need more elaborate security coding, the COM+ interfaces will allow you to get at the underlying mechanisms.

Fundamental Problem of Security

In the simplest terms, the basic problem of security can be expressed by the question: "Who is allowed to do what to whom?" An example is accessing files in an operating system. "Who" is a user. "What" is a file operation, such as Write. "Whom" is a particular file. There is a guard standing watch over the operation, called the *Security Reference Monitor*. The rules followed by the guard are spelled out in a *Policy*. In our file example, many operating systems have the concept of "access control list" (ACL) that can spell out in detail what users have what rights to a file resource. Figure 17–1 illustrates this basic issue of security, with the file example given as an illustration.

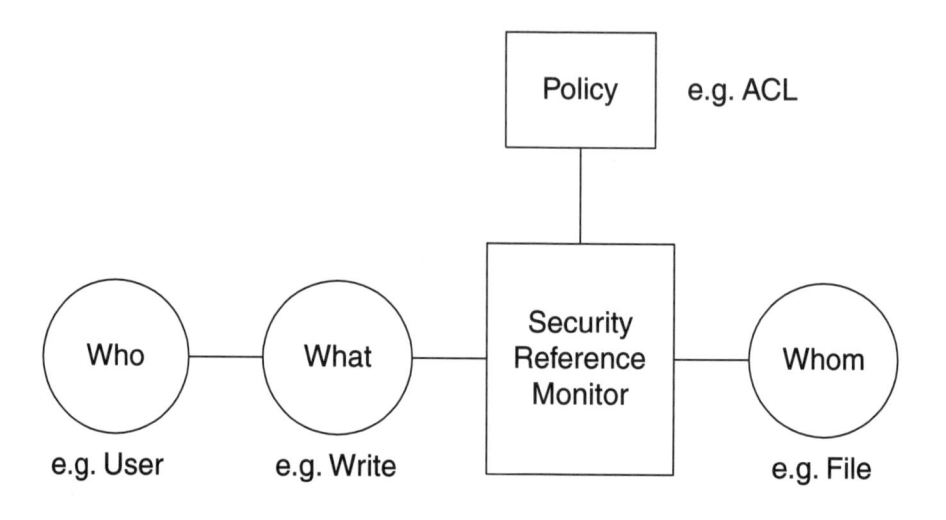

Figure 17–1 *Fundamental problem of security*

Authorization

The job of the Security Reference Monitor is to apply the policy to find out if the request is legitimate and should be allowed. This is the issue of *authorization*. A noncomputer example, of the same issue is the role of a security guard in a building granting access to people coming in. Only authorized persons, according to some policy, should be admitted.

Authentication

In order for the Security Reference Monitor to do its job, a more fundamental question must be answered first: are the parties who they say they are? This is the issue of *authentication*. In the building example the security guard may require a photo ID, which can be used to establish that the person asking admission really is who he says he is and not some imposter.

Issues of security are even more compelling in a distributed computing environment. Consider an online transaction over the Internet. Clearly the server wants to know who the client is before providing a service, such as permitting a piece of software that has been purchased to be downloaded. No pirates, please! And authentication can work both ways. The client may want to know the identity of the server. You don't want to type in your credit card number if you don't trust that the party at the other end is the party you think it is.

In this chapter, we will study how COM+ deals with both issues. But first let's examine the Windows NT/2000 fundamentals.

A Windows 2000 System Administration Tutorial

Any practical work you do with security in Windows 2000 requires that you know the basics of how to administer users and groups. You should also understand the role of workgroups and domains. In the demos we assume that you are working on a domain controller, and all the accounts you are creating are domain accounts.

Administering User Accounts in Windows 2000

Users in Windows 2000 are authenticated by proving who they are when they log on to the system. User *accounts* are provided, and every user is identified by the combination of a user name and a password. User accounts have certain privileges (or rights) to access various resources and to perform various operations.

A user account does not necessarily correspond to an actual person. Some user accounts exist for running server processes, for example. In Windows 2000, user accounts are created and managed through the MMC snap-in

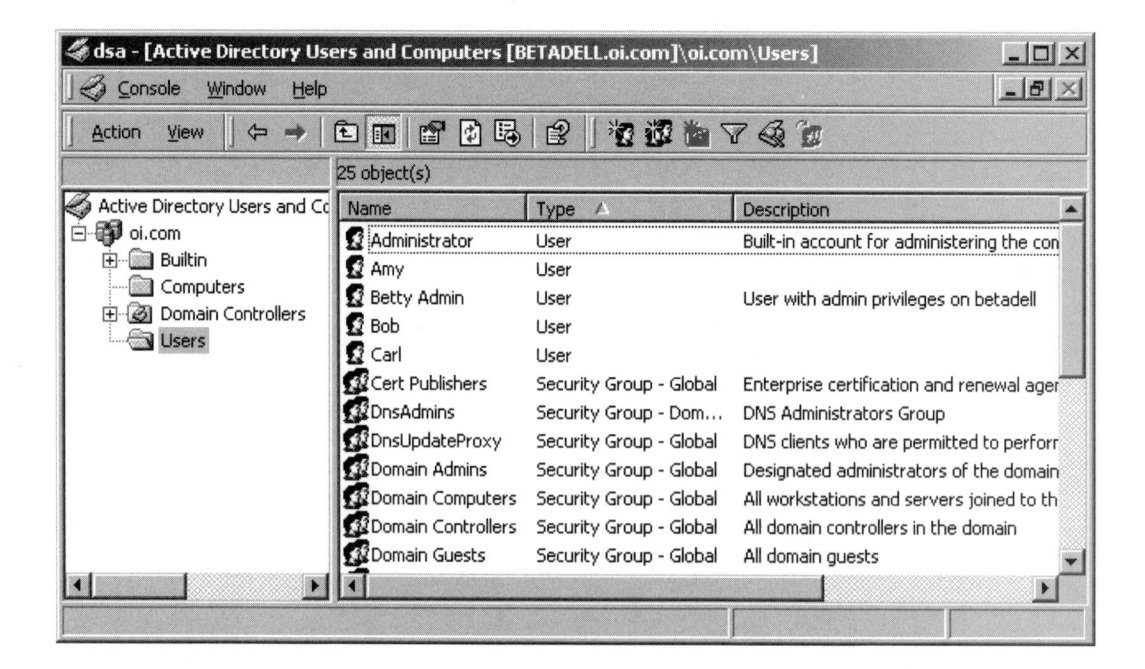

Figure 17-2 *Users are managed through Active Directory Users and Computers*

"Active Directory Users and Computers," which you can bring up from Start | Programs | Administrative Tools. See Figure 17–2.

ADDING USERS

We will illustrate Active Directory Users and Computers by using it to create six new user accounts. These accounts will be used later in our illustrations of COM+ security. In the tree view, select Users and right-click. From the context menu choose New | User. The "Create New Object (User)" screen comes up. Assign the following names: **amy, bob, carl, vicky, wanda**, and **admin**. The name and log-on name will be the same. See Figure 17–3. Accept all the other defaults, including blank password.

Once the account has been created, you can specify many more properties by right-clicking over the user and choosing Properties. As an example, add the description "Alternate administrator account" to **admin**. See Figure 17–4.

BUILT-IN ACCOUNTS

There are two built-in accounts that are intrinsic to the operating system. **Administrator** is the highest level account, with full access to the system. This account cannot be deleted, so you cannot lock yourself out of the sys-

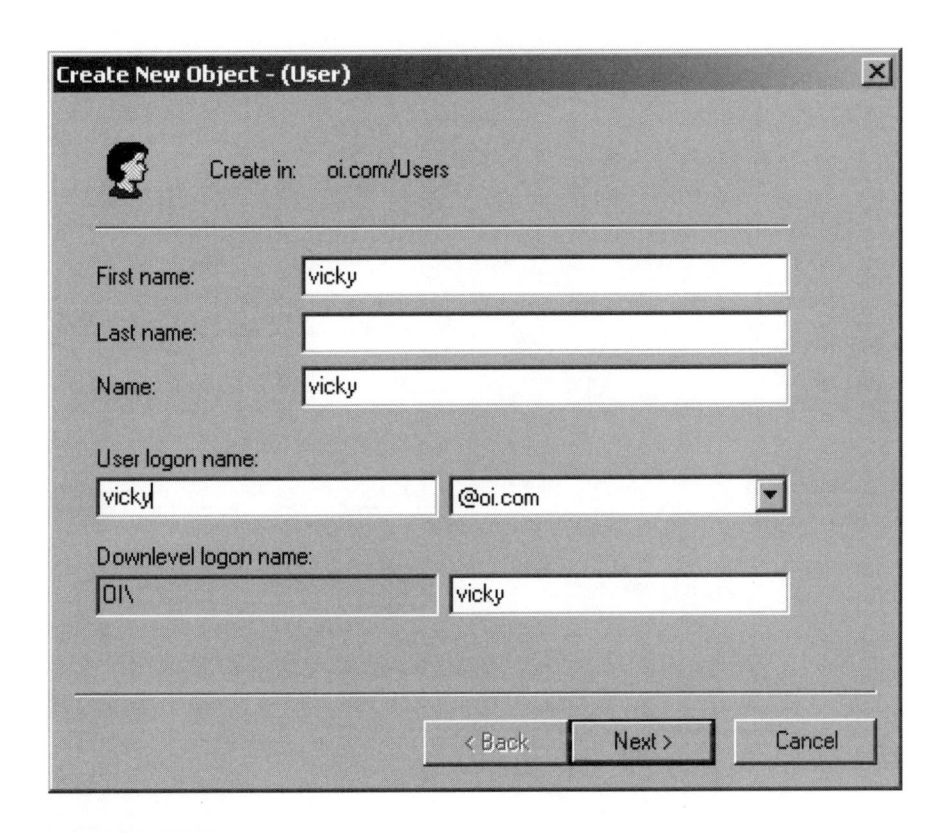

Figure 17-3 *Adding new users*

tem. **Guest** is a default account that gives some limited access to the system. By default it is disabled, but you can enable it if you want to. In addition, various special user accounts are created corresponding to various services. For example, there is an account under which Internet Information Services runs.

There is in fact a third built-in account which is always present, but hidden. **System** is an account that is used only by the system. You cannot log on using this account. It cannot be edited or deleted. The System account has unlimited access to the local machine but has no access to network resources.

GROUPS

Groups can be used to simplify the administration of user accounts. An account will typically be assigned membership in one or more groups. A group has associated rights, shared by the members of the group. There are a number of built-in groups, such as **Domain Admins**, **Domain Users**, etc. A newly created user account by default belongs to the group **Domain Users**.

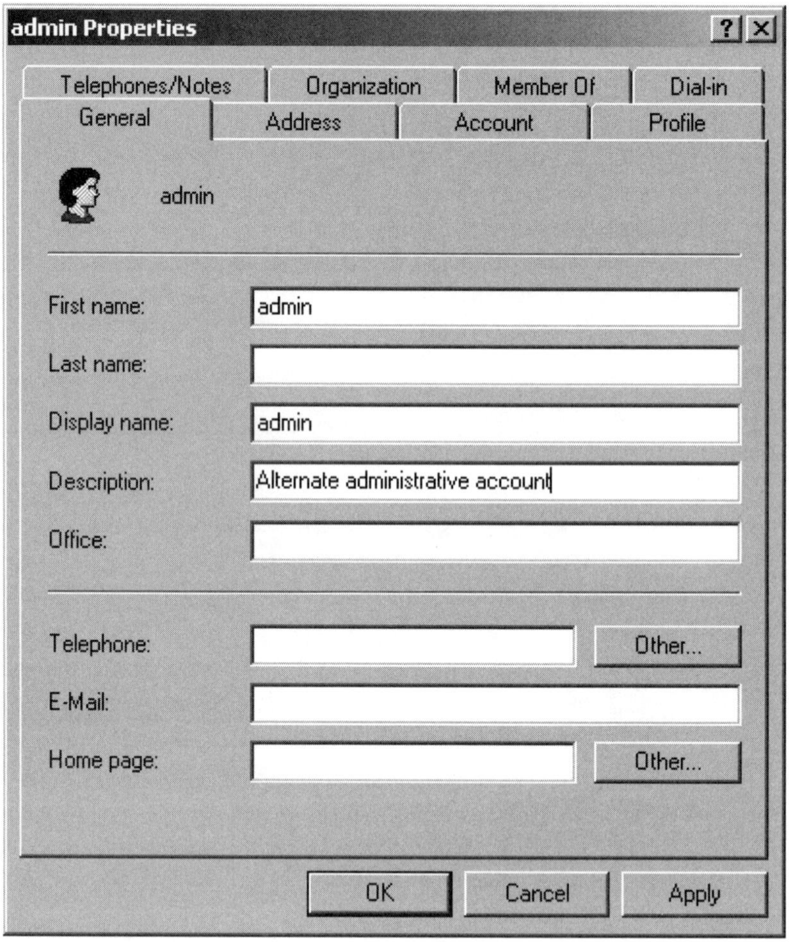

Figure 17–4 Specifying properties for a user account

We will leave **amy**, **bob**, **carl**, **vicky** and **wanda** as belonging to **Domain Users**, and we will change **admin** to also belong to **Domain Admins**.

To change the group membership of a user, bring up the Properties for that user and choose the Member Of tab. Click the Add button. In the "Select Groups" dialog, select the group you want, for example, **Domain Admins**, and click Add. You can add a number of groups in this way. When you are done, click OK. See Figure 17–5.

You can add a new group in a manner similar to adding a new user. In the tree view, right-click over "User" and from the context menu choose New | Group. The "Create Object (Group)" dialog comes up. Create a new

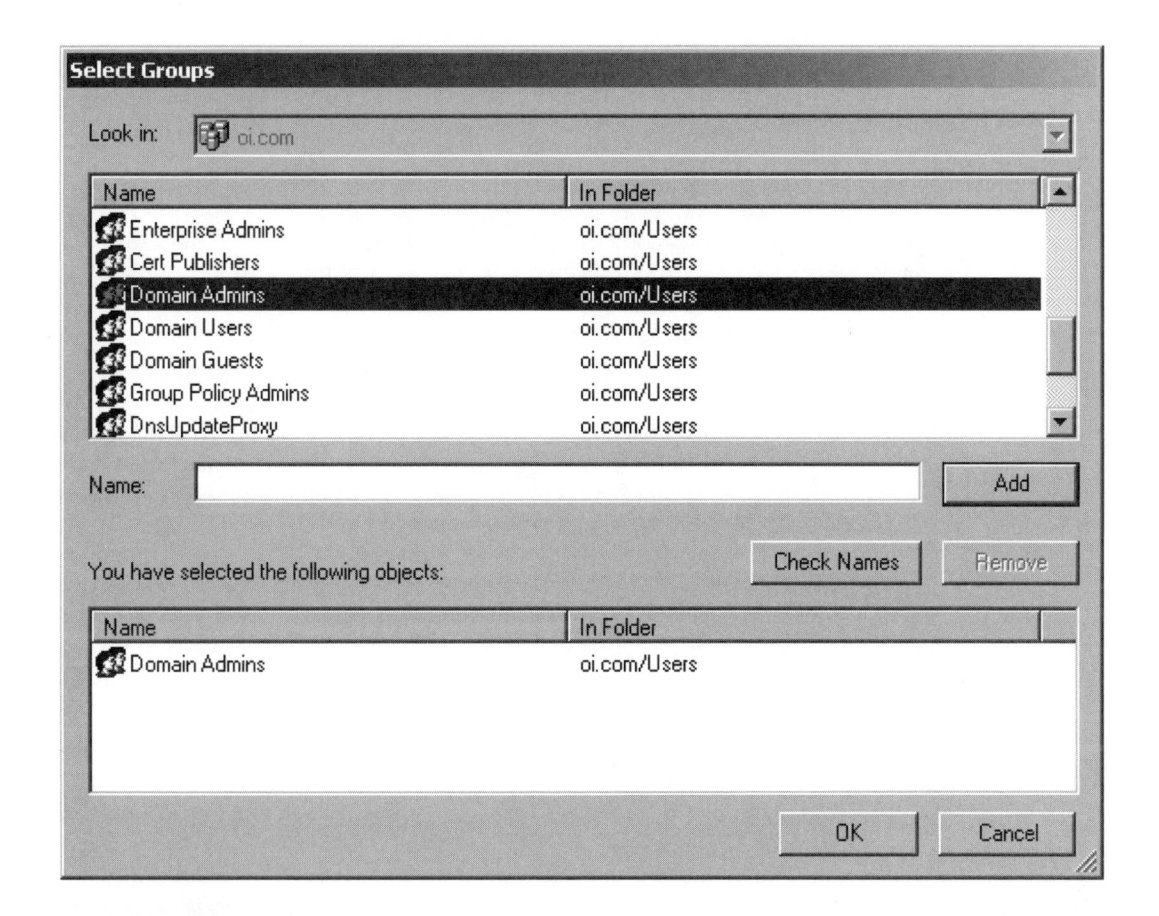

Figure 17-5 *Adding an existing user to a group*

group called **Cowboys**. Accept the default scope of Global and group type of Security.

As with a new user, once a new group has been created, you can modify its properties by right-clicking to bring up the Properties dialog. For this new **Cowboys** group add the description "Many rights—but BE CAREFUL with them!" Then click the Members tab and add **carl** to the new group.

Workgroups, Domains, and the Active Directory

When working with security, you are concerned with user accounts. It is important to understand the context in which a user account is valid. An account is valid either on a local computer or on a domain. A workgroup is a way of federating local computers. A domain brings them into a unified entity. The Active

Directory can unify a whole enterprise. This section provides basic background information on workgroups, domains, and the Active Directory.

WORKGROUPS

The simplest kind of NT network is a workgroup. A workgroup is *peer-to-peer*. A user on one machine gets access to the resources on another machine by logging on to the other machine with an account that is valid on that other machine. If you have logged on to one machine with a user/password that is not valid on another machine, when you attempt to access that other machine you will be given a logon prompt. To permit users in a workgroup to access multiple machines, they need to have accounts on each. If you log on to one machine in a workgroup with a user/password that is valid on other machines in a workgroup, you will be able to gain access to these other machines without a further log on. There is no such thing as a "workgroup account." Every account is specific to a particular machine.

DOMAINS IN NT 4.0

For some perspective, let's look briefly at how domains are organized in NT 4.0. An NT 4.0 domain is managed by a machine running NT Server that acts as *the primary domain controller* (PDC). A PDC holds "domain" accounts. A domain account is valid on all machines that are part of the domain. The PDC maintains a database of domain accounts and authenticates users when they log on.

There may also be one or more NT 4.0 Server machines functioning as *backup domain controllers* (BDC). A BDC holds copies of the domain accounts and can also authenticate users. A BDC reduces network traffic and load on the PDC. A BDC does not maintain accounts but is updated periodically by the PDC.

WINDOWS 2000 AND ACTIVE DIRECTORY

The main problem with NT 4.0 arises when scaling upwards to large enterprises with multiple domains. Since a domain account is only valid within one domain, an administrator needs multiple domain accounts, all of which have to be administered. Windows 2000 brings the *Active Directory*, which identifies all resources on a network. The Active Directory consists of a distributed database called the Directory that stores information about network resources. The Active Directory also has software services that make the information in the Directory accessible to users and applications. The resources stored in the Directory are referred to as *objects*. Examples of objects are users, groups, printers, and databases.

Computers and other resources on a network are organized into *domains*. A domain represents a portion of the resources in the entire Directory, and is managed by one or more computers running Windows 2000, known as *domain controllers*. All domain controllers for a particular domain are peers, and each has a replica of the domain's portion of the Directory. A domain represents a region of security. For example, user accounts are established on a per-domain basis. When a user has succeeded in logging on to a particular domain controller, that user then has access to all resources that have granted that user permission.

The Active Directory provides a single point of administration for all resources on the network. All of the domains are interconnected, and an administrator can administer all resources from a single log on. Without the Active Directory, an administrator would need a separate administrator account for each domain, which becomes very cumbersome for a large enterprise with many domains.

The logical structure of the Active Directory is based on domains. The physical structure is based on *sites,* which can be thought of as one or more IP subnets. If you are administering a small test LAN, normally all the computers on your little LAN will be on the same subnet and will comprise a single Active Directory site.

NT Security

We can now examine the NT security model, which is the foundation of security on all versions of NT, including Windows 2000. When it comes to distributed security, Windows 2000 adds the powerful Kerberos security provider as an alternative to LAN Manager security. But the core concepts at the operating system level remain the same. After discussing the basic concepts, we provide a demonstration which ties these concepts to the administrative procedures we discussed in the previous section.

NT Security Model

The core NT security model consists of a number of core elements:

- Security IDs (SIDs) to identify users and groups
- Access tokens assigned to users when they log on, specifying who they are and their rights
- NT objects (such as files, processes, threads, semaphores, etc.)
- Security descriptors, which define ownership of an object and who can access it
- Access control entries that consist of security descriptors and access masks specifying the actions allowed by a user or group
- Discretionary access control lists that identify which users or groups can be granted or denied access permissions
- System access control lists that identify who is audited for performing operations on an object

SECURITY ID (SID)

A security ID (SID) is a unique ID used to identify a user or a group. When a user or group is created on a machine or domain, a unique SID is created to identify that user or group. SIDs are used in Win32 API security functions. The Active Directory (the User Manager in NT 4.0) creates SIDs for you, and normally you never "see" one.

ACCESS TOKENS

When a user logs on to an NT system, it gets an access token, which specifies

- User ID
- Groups to which the user belongs
- Rights which the user has (which derive from rights assigned directly to the user and rights of groups to which the user belongs)

When a user launches a process, the process gets this access token and runs under the security context specified by that access token. A server process has its own access token with its security context. A server process can impersonate a client and perform actions under the security context of the client.

NT OBJECTS

In NT common operating system entities like files, processes, threads, etc., are considered *objects*. An NT object is an instance of an *object type*. An object type defines *object attributes* and *object services* for this type. Stock attributes common to all objects are stored in the *object header*, and attributes specific to a certain kind of object are stored in the *object body*.

The NT *object manager* provides services common to all objects, such as creating, destroying, protecting and tracking objects. When an object is created, the object manager returns a *handle* to the object. All access to an object is through its handle.

SECURITY DESCRIPTORS

One of the stock attributes of every NT object is a security descriptor. A security descriptor may be explicitly specified when the object is created, or it may inherit the security descriptor from the process that created it. A security descriptor specifies:

- A Discretionary Access Control List (DACL) that identifies users or groups granted or denied specific access permissions.
- A System Access Control List (SACL) that specifies auditing which will be performed.
- The Owner SID that identifies the user or group that owns the object. The owner can change the ACLs.

ACCESS CONTROL ENTRY (ACE)

An access control list (ACL) is a list of access control entries (ACEs). An access control entry consists of:

- An SID that specifies the user or group to which the ACE applies
- An access mask that specifies the access rights for the object (for example, read, write)
- The ACE header that specifies the type of ACE (allow, deny, or system audit) and the inheritance behavior

There are generic rights that apply to all objects, but the meaning is dependent on the particular type of object. Generic rights are Execute, Read, and Write. There are also standard and specific rights. Standard rights apply to all objects and have a standard meaning (for instance, Delete). Specific rights depend on the type of object.

DISCRETIONARY ACCESS CONTROL LIST

A Discretionary Access Control List (DACL) specifies who can and who cannot access an object to perform particular actions. Checking access by a process to a particular NT object involves walking the DACL for the object and comparing the access control entry against the access token of the process. The "deny" access control entries are examined first, and if one is found that applies to that access token, the walking stops and access is denied. If a suitable "allow" entry is found, access will be permitted. If an object has an empty DACL, access is denied. An object with no DACL has no protection, and so access will be permitted. For example, a file on a FAT partition has no DACL and hence will not be protected by the NT security system.

Security Demonstration

We will illustrate user accounts and the NT security system with a simple example.

- User **amy** creates a file, **sensitive.txt**, in the root of an NTFS partition.
- She gives herself Read and Write access, gives Read access to **bob** and **carl**, and denies access to the group **Cowboys**.
- Log on on as **amy**, **bob**, and **carl** and observe the kind of access permitted.

Running the demo is a little tricky, because the default policy of Windows 2000 Server does not allow an ordinary user to log on to the domain controller, so with the default policy you cannot run the whole demo from the Server machine. Also, the default install of Windows 2000 Professional does not allow you to administer users from Professional. As a result, you cannot easily run the demo from either machine. The easiest solution, not requiring making any modifications to the configuration of either machine, is to do your ordinary user log ons on the Professional machine, and do all operations with user permissions on the Server machine.

1. Log on to Professional as **amy** and use Notepad to create a file, **sensitive.txt**, with a little sample text typed in. Save it on the root of an NTFS partition.
2. The next part should be done as **Administrator** on the Server machine. In Windows Explorer, right-click on **sensitive.txt** and choose Properties. Click on the Security tab. Notice that there are a number of permissions already for this file (which it has "inherited" from its parent directory). Select **Everyone** from the top list. Observe that **Everyone** has read and write access. See Figure 17–6.

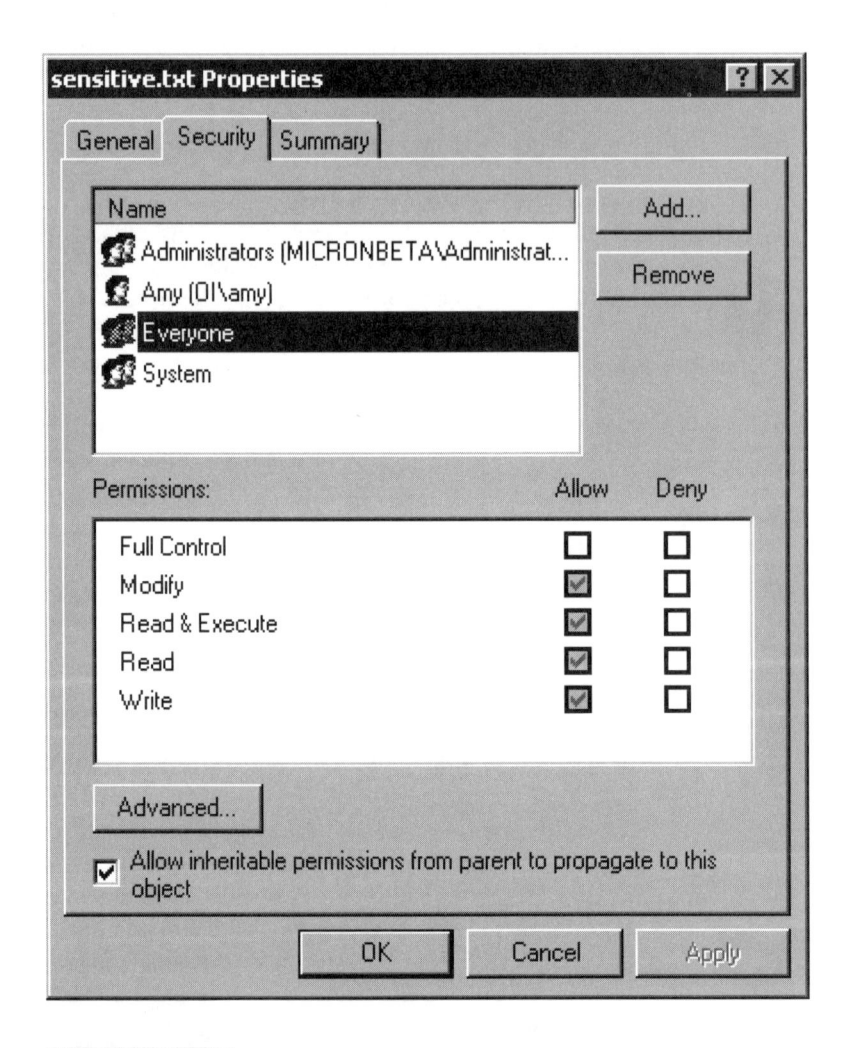

Figure 17–6 *By default Everyone has read and write access to a file*

NT Security

3. We are going to remove the permissions for **Everyone**. First clear the check box for "Allow inheritable permissions." Choose "Copy" from the message box that comes up. Now with **Everyone** selected, click "Remove."
4. Next, we grant permissions explicitly to **bob**, **carl**, and **Cowboys**. In the main Properties window for the file, click the "Add" button. In the "Select" dialog that comes up add **bob**, **carl**, and **Cowboys**. See Figure 17–7. Click OK.

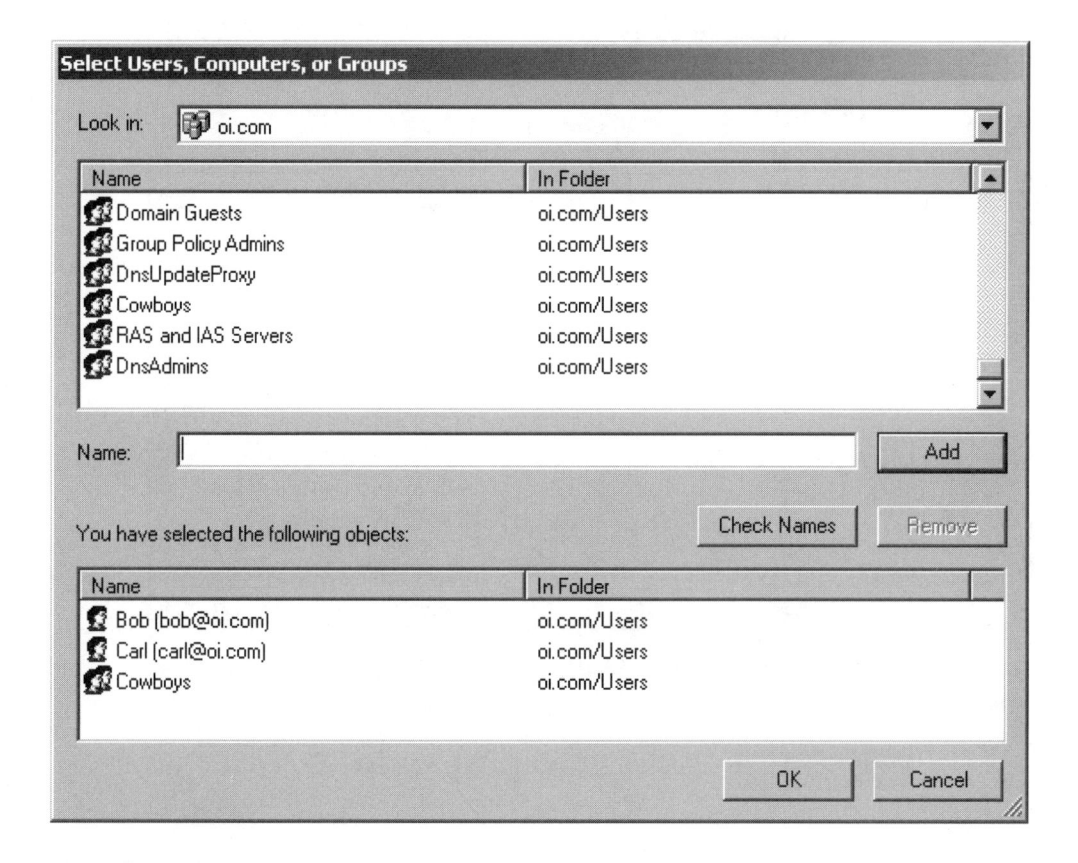

Figure 17–7 *We have added permissions for bob, carl, and Cowboys*

5. Back in the main Properties window you will see now that amy, bob, carl and Cowboys all have permission. Amy has all permissions (she created the file). Bob, carl and Cowboys have Read and Read & Execute permission. Select Cowboys and click the Deny box for Full Control. All the Deny boxes will now be checked, and all the Allow boxes have been cleared. See Figure 17–8.

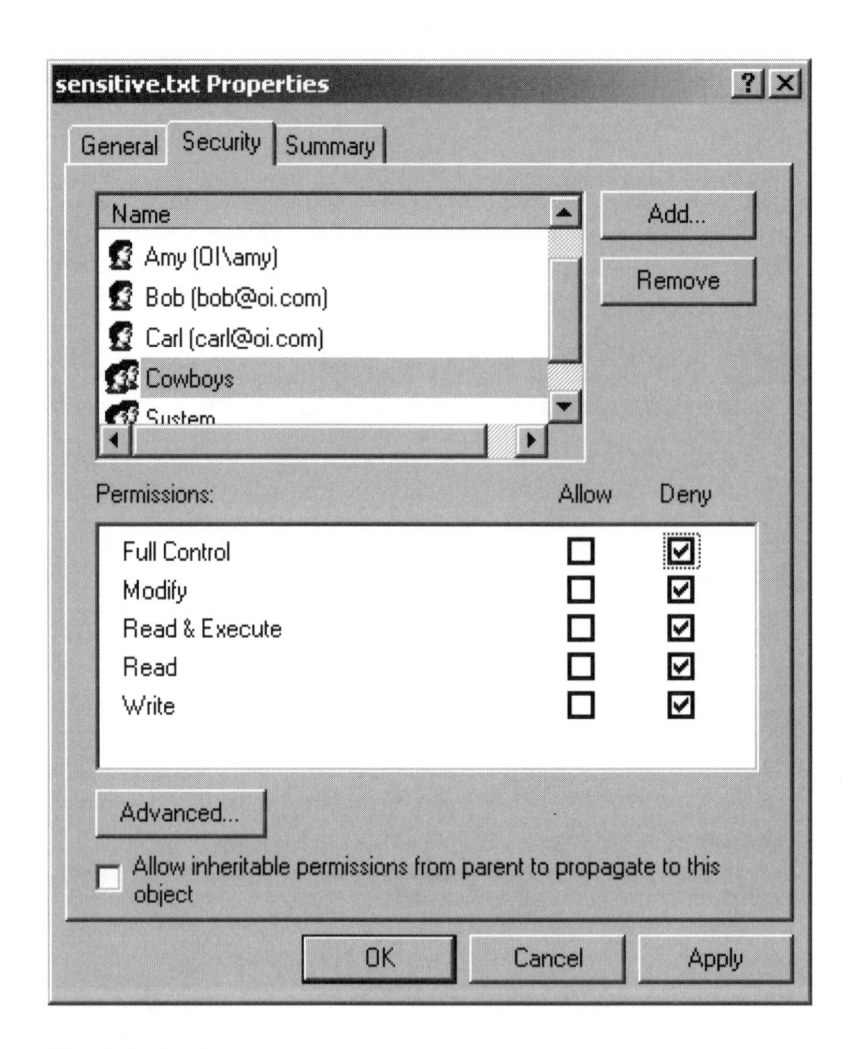

Figure 17-8 *We have denied all access for Cowboys*

6. Now go to the Professional machine and log on as **bob**. You will be able to read the file **sensitive.txt** but not write to it.

7. Now log on as **carl**. You won't be able to access the file at all. Even though **carl** has read permission, he is a member of **Cowboys**, a group that is denied all access. Deny takes precedence over Allow when walking a DACL.

COM Security

COM security is at a higher level of abstraction than NT security and is simpler than using NT security directly. Also, COM security addresses concerns of distributed security. COM security is implemented in two layers. The top layer is Authenticated RPC, which provides a secure communications layer. The bottom layer is implemented by a Security Support Provider (SSP), which implements a Security Support Provider Interface (SSPI), which is called by Authenticated RPC. Different underlying SSPs can be plugged in. Under NT 4.0 the NTLM (NT Lan Manager) SSP is used. Windows 2000 also provides the more powerful Kerberos SSP, which is the default. Figure 17–9 illustrates these layers,

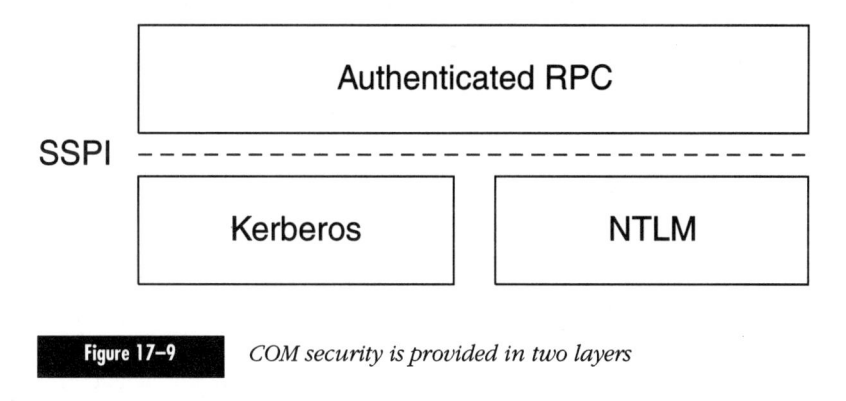

Figure 17–9 *COM security is provided in two layers*

Using these layers, COM handles security for you according to specifications you make in the Registry. You can conveniently adjust the Registry settings using the DCOMCNFG tool. COM handles the two basic security functions of authorization and authentication that we discussed at the beginning of the chapter. Also, COM has the issue of the identity under which the server component runs. We will see what this means and what the trade-offs are for making a choice. Finally, COM addresses the security issue of Impersonation, which is of interest in a multiple-tier architecture.

We will discuss all four issues. For the core topic of authorization, we will illustrate using the **Name** example from Chapters 9 and 10.

Authorization

As we have discussed, the basic problem of security is *authorizing* access to a resource. In the case of COM, the resource is a COM component. COM allows you to control both the launching of a component and also the access to the component once it has been launched. You can adjust Registry settings to specify launch and access permissions. We will go through the relevant settings using a specific example.

NAME EXAMPLE

Our example program is the **Name** EXE server we introduced in Chapter 9. There is a single interface **IMachine** with a single method **GetName**, which obtains the name of the machine the component is running on. You can find the server in **Chap17\Name** and the client test program in **Chap17\NameTest**. Build both programs.

Before exploring the security settings, let's run the example again as a straight illustration of DCOM. For your experiment to go smoothly, you should deploy the server on your Windows 2000 Server machine and the test program on your Windows 2000 Professional machine. Begin by unregistering the server on both machines, in case it was previously registered. Do that by running the two batch files **unreg_name.bat** and **unreg_nameps.bat**. Make sure that you are logged on as Administrator on both machines. Then do the following:

1. Register the server on your Server machine. Verify that the test program runs, and returns the name of your Server machine.
2. Register the server on your Professional machine. Verify that the test program runs, and returns the name of your Professional machine.
3. At this point, you could delete the EXE file **Name.exe** from your Professional machine, if you like. Go into DCOMCNFG on the Professional machine and change the Location to run the server on your Windows 2000 Server machine, as was explained in Chapter 10. If unsure of the details, refer back to that chapter. Now when you run the test program again, you should get back not the name of the local machine but the name of the remote machine.

If this demonstration does not work, there is probably some issue with your security settings, which you should be able to remedy after you have read the following discussion on security.

DEFAULT ACCESS AND LAUNCH PERMISSIONS

The starting point for looking at security settings is the Default Security tab of the main window of DCOMCNFG. Do this on your Windows 2000 Server machine. See Figure 17–10.

Under Default Access Permissions, click Edit Default. You will then see a list of users and groups who have permission to access a DCOM server that has not specified its own individual permissions. See Figure 17–11.

Note that for each user or group, you can specify Allow Access or Deny Access. Recall that in traversing a DACL, the Deny will take precedence over the Allow. There is a similar list of default launch permissions. Launch and access are different. A server may be already running, and then a client with access permission but not launch permission will succeed in talking to this server.

COM Security

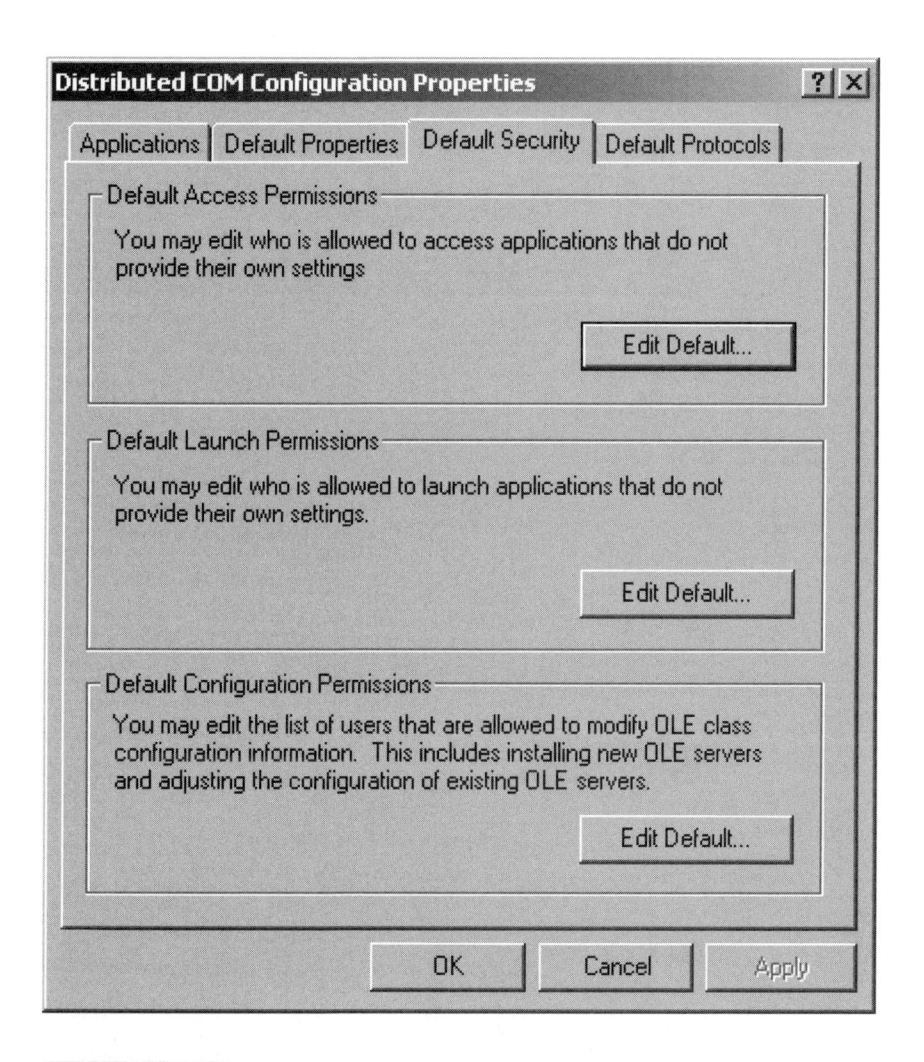

Figure 17-10 *You can set default access and launch permissions in DCOMCNFG*

We won't experiment with changing default permissions. This is normally not a good idea. You want to specify permissions appropriately for individual applications. One thing you may do with defaults is to make them more restrictive, decreasing the likelihood that an outside client can use an application on the server without being specifically enabled for a particular application.

We can verify the behavior of the defaults by trying to access the server from an ordinary user on the client (Professional) machine. Notice that **amy** does not have launch or access permission (we have just registered the server, so there is no chance of there being a special setting for the Name application).

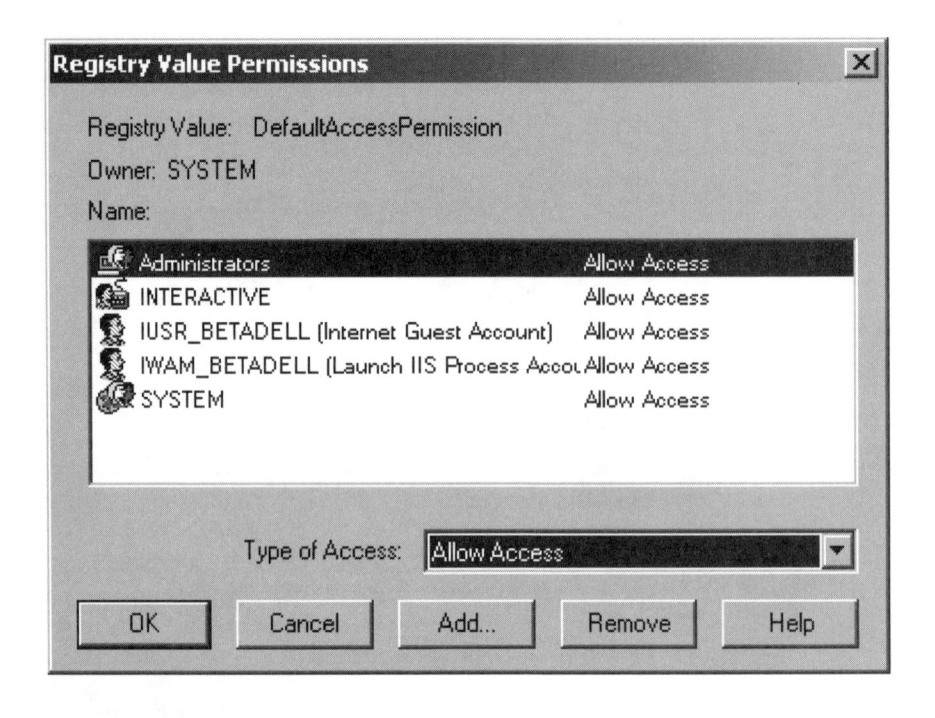

Figure 17–11 *Users and groups with default access permission*

Log on on as **amy** and try running the test program **NameTest.exe**. When you click "Get Name," you get an "access denied" error. See Figure 17–12.

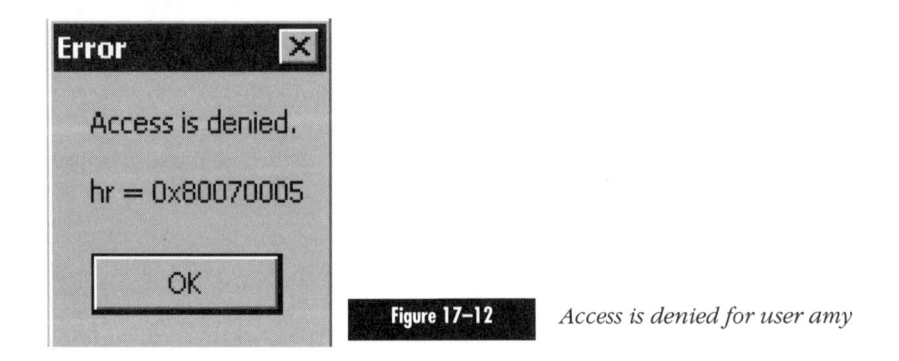

Figure 17–12 *Access is denied for user amy*

ACCESS AND LAUNCH PERMISSIONS FOR APPLICATIONS

You may modify access and launch permissions for individual applications. On your Windows 2000 Server machine, bring up DCOMCNFG and find the

"Name" application from the list. Choose "Properties." Select the Security tab, and click on the radio button for "Use custom access permissions." See Figure 17–13.

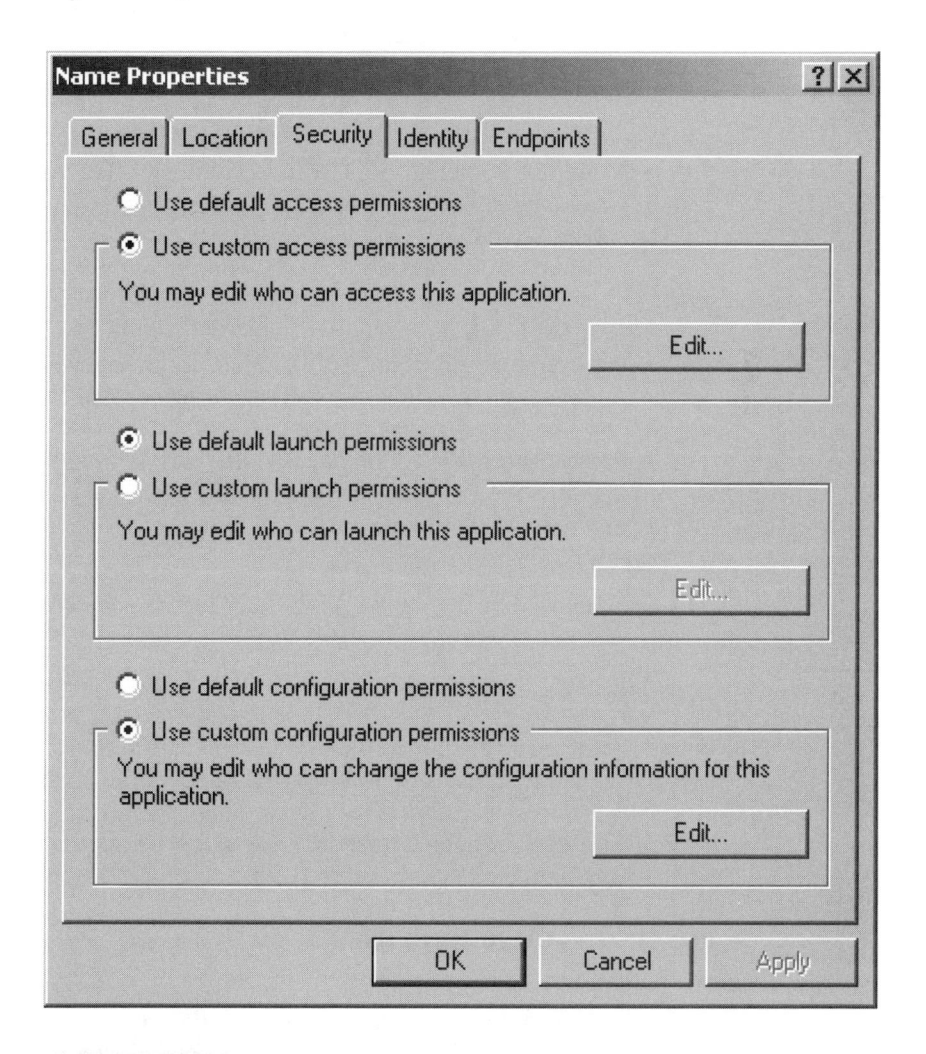

Figure 17–13 *You can specify custom access permissions for an application*

Click the "Edit" button. You can then proceed to add **bob** as a user who is Allowed permission to access the server. Also give **bob** permission to launch the application. Click OK out of DCOMCNFG, and then go to your Professional machine. Log **amy** off and log **bob** on. You should now be successful in running the client test program.

Authentication

Recall that authentication allows the client and server to check up on each other's identity. It is the foundation upon which authorization rests. A particular user may be authorized to use the server. But if an imposter succeeds in masquerading as this user, the authorization mechanism will be defeated. Hence, authentication is an essential part of the security infrastructure.

COM provides for six levels of authentication:

- **None**. No authentication. Without authentication you have no authorization either, and hence no security. This setting should never be used when you care about security.
- **Connect**. Authentication occurs when an connection is made to the server.
- **Call**. Authentication occurs when a RPC call is accepted by the server.
- **Packet**. Authentication that data has come from the identified client occurs with every packet (in a connectionless protocol such as UDP, Connect and Call are interpreted as Packet).
- **Packet Integrity**. Authentication that the data has come from the client and also that the data has not been modified.
- **Privacy**. All the checks of Packet Integrity, and the data in the packet is encrypted.

You can specify the authentication level using DCOMCNFG. Choose the Default Properties tab from the main window. See Figure 17–14.

Identity

When a remote server runs to handle method calls from a client, under what user ID does the server run? This user ID is needed to find out if the server process has access to various resources under the server machine's security system. You can change the user ID using the Identity tab in DCOMCNFG when examining the properties of a particular application. See Figure 17–15.

RUNNING AS LAUNCHING USER

The default setting is the "Launching User." For example, if **amy** logs on to a client machine and calls a remote server, the server process will handle method calls on behalf of **amy** using **amy**'s security credentials. This is intuitively reasonable behavior, but there are problems. The big problem is that the server will create a separate Windows station for each client, and Windows stations are very resource intensive (around 3 Mb of memory). A second problem is that the server only "impersonates" the launching user and has less capability. Also, running as the launching user means that the interactive desktop is not available to the server process. To understand the role of a Windows station and the interactive desktop, it will be useful to first understand what an NT service is.

COM Security **389**

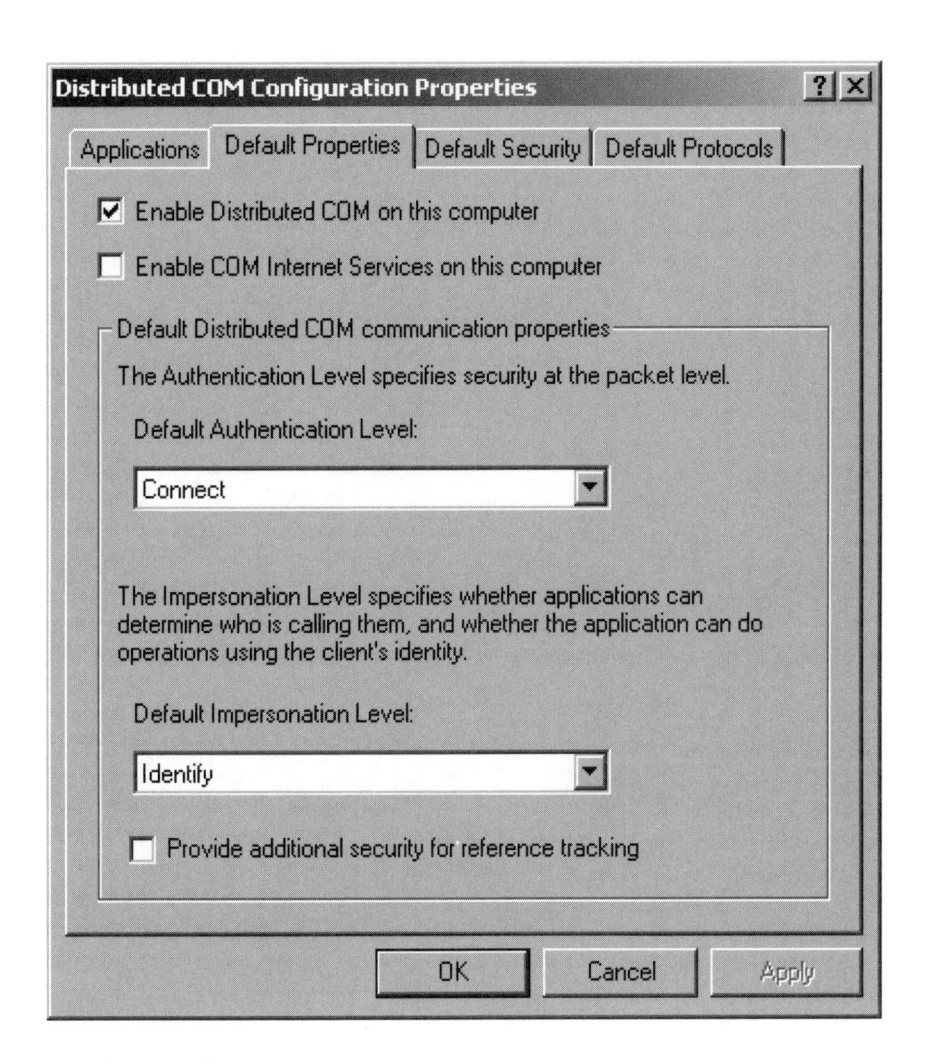

Figure 17-14 *You can specify authentication level in DCOMCNFG*

NT SERVICES

An *NT Service* is an application that runs in the background, independently of any particular logged on user. Services are started by the Service Control Manger (SCM). Services can be configured to run automatically at system startup, before any user has logged on. By default, services run under the built-in **System** account. Under Windows 2000, you administer services through the Computer Management snap-in. See Figure 17–16.

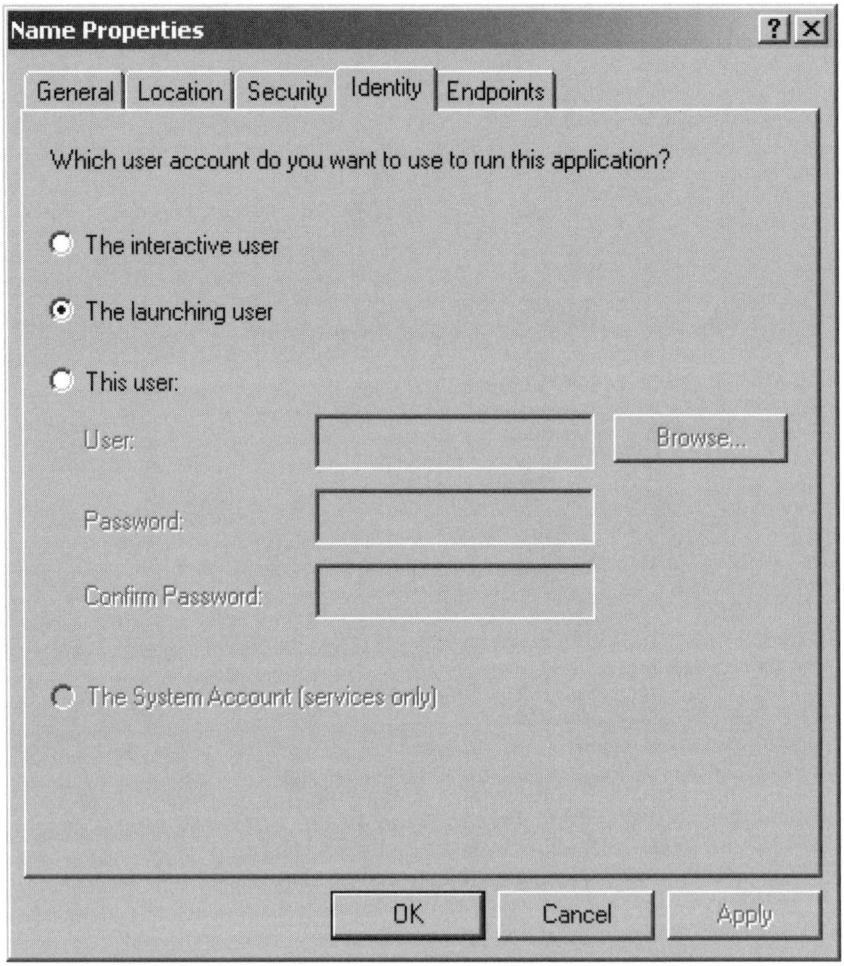

390 Chapter 17 • Windows 2000 and COM+ Security

Figure 17-15 *Setting the identity under which the server application runs*

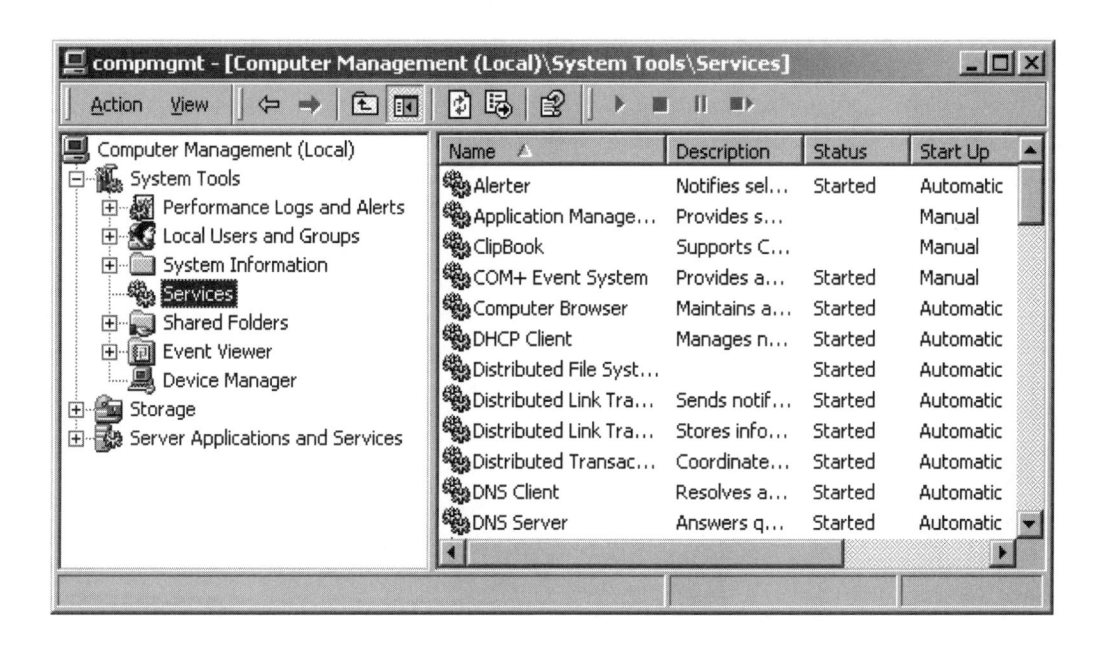

Figure 17-16 You can start and stop services and configure them to start automatically at system startup

WINDOW STATIONS AND DESKTOPS

When you log on as an interactive user you are given a desktop which presents a graphical user interface. GUI features such as windows are specific to this desktop. An NT service normally does not have a desktop. Message boxes put up by a service will not be displayed, so a service application can hang waiting for a message box (that is not shown) to be closed.

A *Windows station* is a Win32 entity that collects together the desktop, Clipboard, and some other resources. A Windows station is a large resource, around 3 Mb. Win32 functions are provided to create, open, and close Window stations; assign a Windows station to a particular process; etc.

RUNNING AS INTERACTIVE USER

In this case, the server runs under the access token of the interactive user currently logged on to the server machine. The desktop is available and windows can be displayed. There is no additional Windows station created for each client. There is no impersonation, and the server process can do everything that the interactive user can do. But there are problems here, too. The server cannot run at all if there is no logged-on user, and the server will terminate if it is running under one interactive user and that user logs off. Running as interactive user can be convenient during development. (But I would suggest you not put in message boxes, even temporarily. You can achieve the same results by logging to a file, as illustrated in Chapters 12 and 15. Then when the product ships you won't wind up with a message box you forgot to take out.)

RUNNING AS THIS USER

The third option is to run as a particular, designated user on the server machine. Only one additional Windows station is created that services all clients. There is no impersonation, and the server process can do everything the designated user can do. The server can run when there is no interactive user logged on. Generally, this is the preferred option.

Impersonation

We have seen that if the server runs under the identity of the launching user, the server "impersonates" this user, running under its security credentials. This impersonation feature can be useful in a multiple-tier application where the end component has its own security and does an access check against the identity of the client calling it. If the middle-tier component runs under a special account, this access check will fail. The solution is for the middle-tier process to impersonate the client process.

However, we do not want to incur the massive penalty of a separate Windows station for each logged-on user to achieve this impersonation. Such a solution is totally unacceptable if we wish to achieve scalability, and in fact under COM+ this option is not allowed.

Fortunately, COM allows a component do impersonate any user. You need to write a little code, which we will examine when we discuss COM+ security. An issue is the *level* of impersonation. What we would like is for the impersonation to be so perfect that the middle-tier process can do anything the end client does, including calling other tiers, which in turn can impersonate. This level is called *Delegation*, and was permitted for the first time under Windows 2000 with the Kerberos Security Support Provider.

Default impersonation levels can be set in Default Properties tab of DCOMCNFG:

- **Anonymous**, not currently supported in DCOM.
- **Identity**. The server can impersonate the client for the purpose of checking ACLs, but cannot access system level objects.
- **Impersonate**. The server can impersonate the client for ACL checking and can access system-level objects, but cannot impersonate the client for making calls to other (remote) servers.
- **Delegate**. The server can impersonate the client for ACL checking, can access system-level objects, and can impersonate the client for making calls to other servers (supported by Kerberos SSP in Windows 2000).

COM+ Security

COM+ provides a very capable security mechanism which is at the same time very flexible. You can administratively configure many security attributes which will enable security checking without any programming. If you need finer granularity of control, COM+ makes it easy to do programmatic security checking. In this section, we discuss the various ways security can be configured in COM+ and illustrate some simple programmatic security. Our program example will be a stub version of the Electronic Commerce Game™ case study.

Electronic Commerce Game Case Study

In our study so far we have worked with a number of quite simple programs. When working with some new programming technology it is usually a good idea to try something simple first, and indeed that has been the pattern for most of the examples in this book. However, in order to get a better understanding of how a number of concepts work in a more realistic setting, it will be helpful to have a somewhat larger example. In this book we provide a case study called "The Electronic Commerce Game." The basic concept is extremely simple—online buying and selling of products. It is structured as a game in which players take on the role of customer and compete to fulfill a shopping list by visiting various vendor sites and making purchases. There is also the possibility of a player temporarily assuming the role of a vendor and making purchases at wholesale to augment the inventory at a vendor site. Figure 17–17 illustrates one of the screens in the game, where a player is visiting "toyland.com."

The case study is described in detail in Appendix B. It is used extensively in Part 3 to illustrate concepts of COM+.

STUB VERSION OF ELECTRONIC COMMERCE GAME

The Electronic Commerce Game makes use of several databases. We begin our discussion of databases in the next chapter. For right now, we will use a stub version to illustrate concepts of security in COM+. There are two natural roles for players in the game, that of Customer and Vendor. The initial screen of the Electronic Commerce Game gives a player a choice of three sites to visit, **shopper.com**, **vendors.com**, and **wholesale.com**. The first site is for Customers and the third site is for Vendors. The second site is open to anyone and will simply provide a list of URLs of vendors, where customers can go to make purchases and vendors can go to adjust their inventory by buying at wholesale or returning products. The stub version of the game simply does a security check for access to the first and third sites. Message boxes in the client program show whether the player succeeded in getting to the site.

See **Chap17\EcStub\Server** for the server code and **Chap17\EcStub\Client** for the client code. Register the server and build the client.

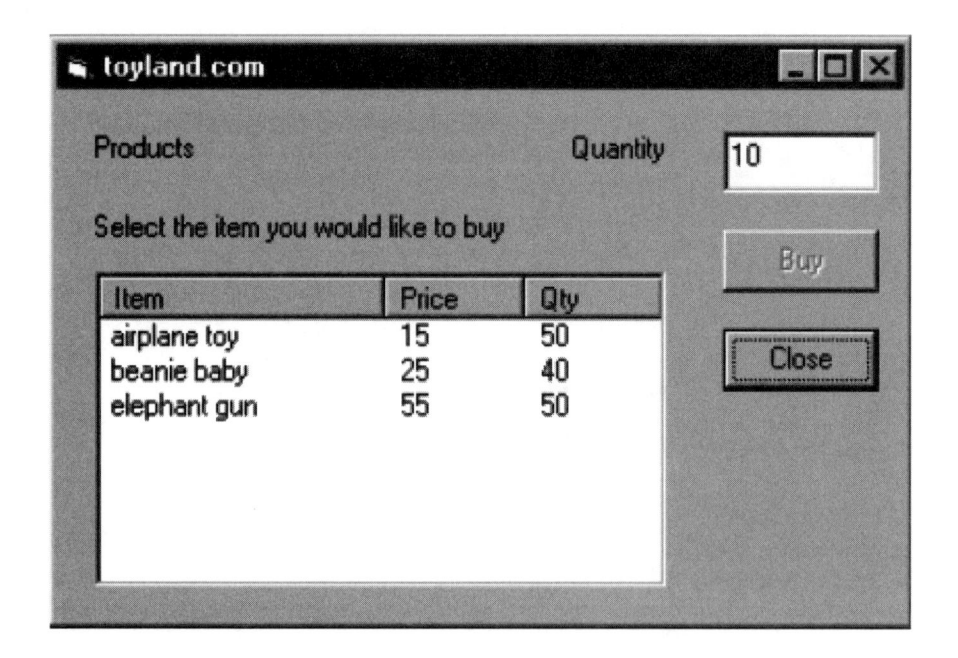

Figure 17-17 *Visiting a vendor site in the Electronic Commerce Game*

The Electronic Commerce Game is implemented in Visual Basic for the sake of simplicity. There is quite a bit of code in the final version of the game and we can illustrate concepts of COM+ most clearly by focusing on the use of COM+ and not on the coding details that would be required for a C++ implementation.

RUNNING THE STUB

Before starting to do any configuration or programming for security, it will be a good idea to run the stub program "as is," both locally on your Windows 2000 Server machine and also as a distributed application, with the server on your Server machine and the client on your Professional machine. We will go directly to running the program under COM+.

Create a new empty COM+ server application **EcStubApp** for the stub Electronic Commerce Game server. You should now understand the significance of the screen "Set Application Identity." For now, we continue to run as the interactive user. Then install the server by drag-and-drop. You should see two components in COM+ Explorer. See Figure 17–18.

Now you should be able to run the client program. First try visiting **shopper.com**. There are a few hardcoded players. "John Smith" is not one of them, but "amy" is a legal player (who has already played, and will be wel-

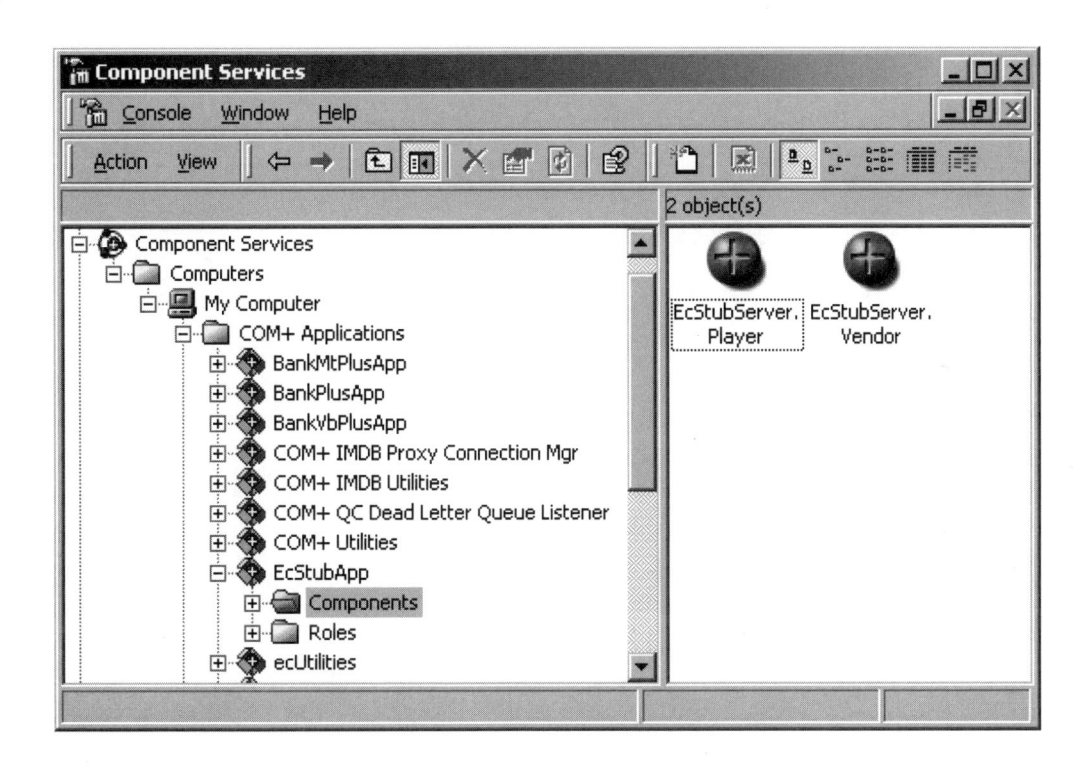

Figure 17–18 *The stub Electronic Commerce Game has two components*

comed back). Entering "amy" in the Player Login window will succeed. See Figure 17–19.

Also try visiting **wholesale.com**. That should succeed too. Note that for test purposes there is only one illegal ID in the log-on window, the number "0." You may wish to examine the source code to understand the logic of the stub programs, but don't worry about it. Our concern is not with the actual stub logic but with the security aspects of different logged-on users being able to access the components.

EXPORTING THE PROXY

As a final preliminary exercise we create a **.msi** file for exporting the proxy to another computer so that we can try running the program as a distributed application. In COM+ Explorer, right-click over **EcStubApp** and choose "Export" from the context menu. Browse to the **ComPlus\Deploy** directory and enter the name "EcStub" for the application file to be created. Choose "Application proxy." See Figure 17–20.

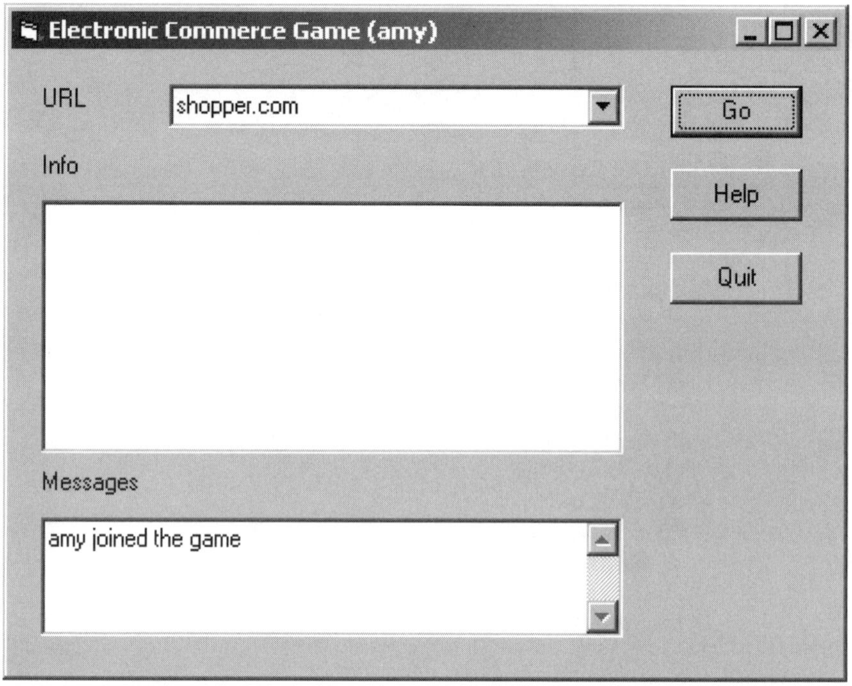

Chapter 17 • Windows 2000 and COM+ Security

Figure 17-19 *Logging in as amy at shopper.com succeeds*

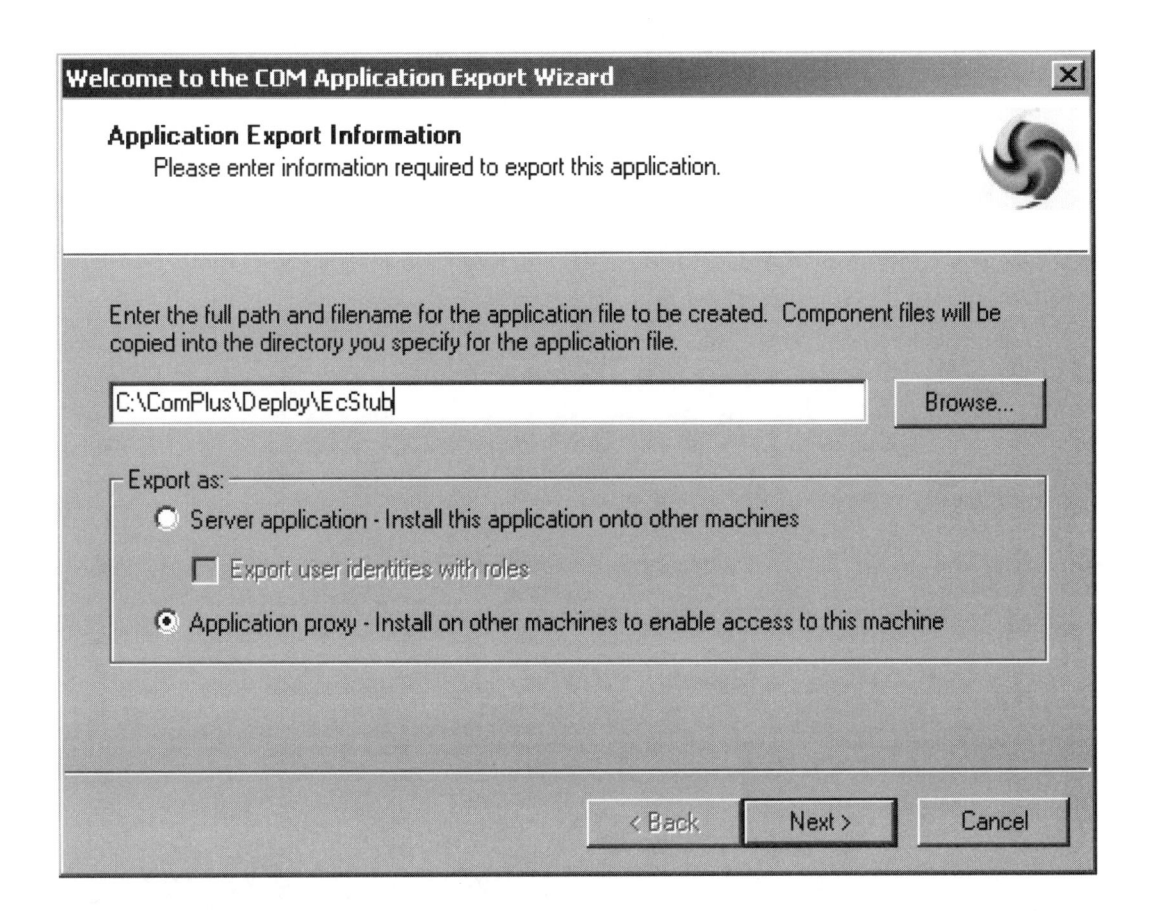

COM+ Security   **397**

Figure 17-20 *Creating application file for exporting the proxy*

Copy the files **EcStub.msi** and **EcStubClient.exe** to your remote client machine running Windows 2000 Professional. Install the proxy by double clicking on **EcStub.msi**. You should now be able to run the client program from the remote computer.

Configuring COM+ Security

We are now ready to begin our exploration of COM+ security. We begin by examining the various ways we can configure security in COM+. You will see a number of similarities to configuring security for straight COM in DCOM-CNFG, but the configuration options in COM+ are far more extensive. Authentication, Impersonation, and Identity are essentially the same. But there is much greater granularity in how you can configure access checking. In straight COM, you are limited to specifying security at the component level. In

COM+ you can specify security at the application, component, interface and method levels. You set configuration options at these different levels by bringing up the Properties window, as we discussed in Chapter 15.

Moreover, COM+ provides a whole new security abstraction, that of *roles*. We will discuss roles in a separate section.

APPLICATION-LEVEL SECURITY CONFIGURATION

At the application level, you can specify Authorization, Security Level, Authentication Level and Impersonation level. See Figure 17–21.

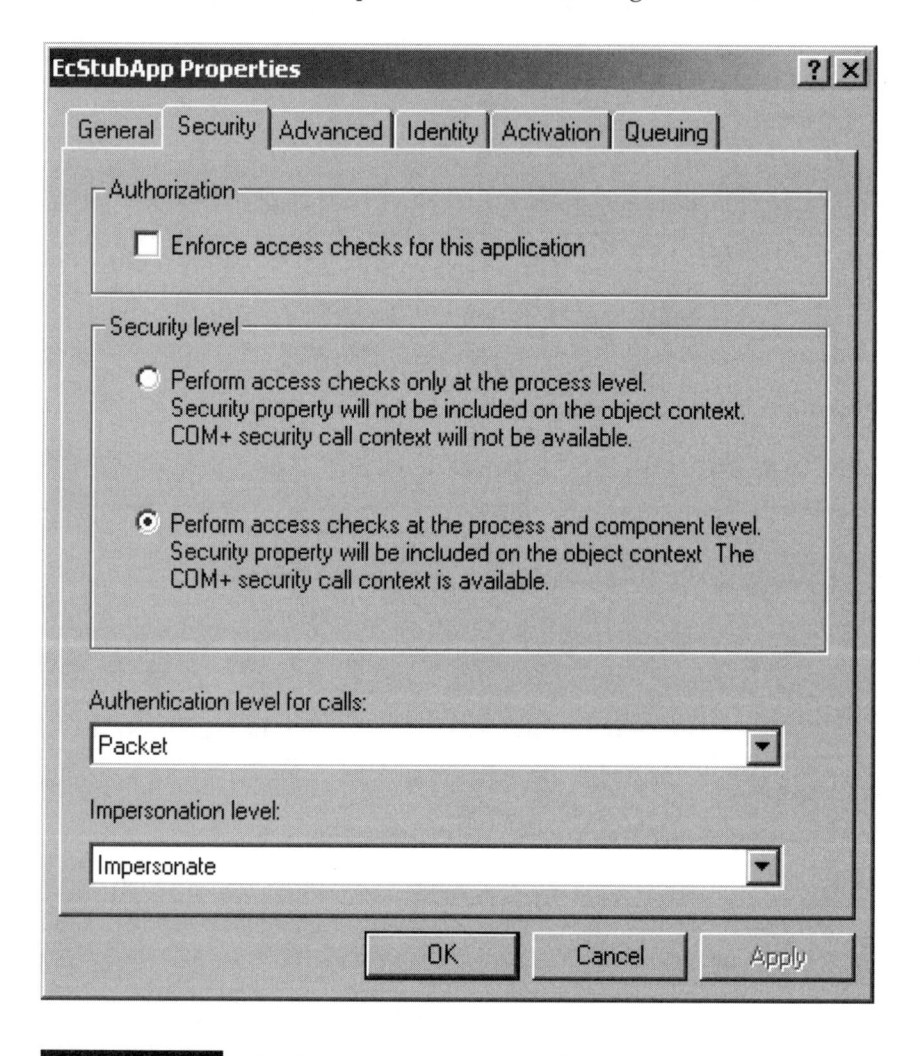

Figure 17-21 *Configuring security at the application level*

The Authorization check box is a master switch for access checking throughout the application. If this is unchecked (the default), no access checking whatever will be performed. You can verify this by logging in as an ordinary user (for instance, "amy") on your Professional machine. You should be able to do everything you were able to do as Administrator.

The Security Level option specifies whether security information will be included in the context object. The default is for such information to be included. We will examine how such context information is used when we investigate programmatic security.

The final two settings, Authentication level and Impersonation level, have the same significance as in straight COM. You set them here, not in DCOMCNFG. When your component(s) have been imported into COM+, you will specify all of your security settings using COM+ Explorer. You do not use DCOMCNFG at all.

Check the Authorization check box and click OK. You can now repeat your experiment of trying to run the application remotely logged on as an ordinary user. Now your client program may fail, with a "permission denied" error condition. See Figure 17–22.

Figure 17–22 *When access checking is enabled you may get "permission denied" failure*

In fact, if you now try to access the server from an Administrator account, access will again fail. COM+ is impartial. If access checking is enabled, *all* access is denied unless it is explicitly granted. In COM+, you grant access through *roles*, which is our next topic.

If you like, you could examine the Properties window at other levels (component, interface, and method), choosing the Security tab. You will see that at the component level there is a check box for specifying whether access checking is enabled at this level, and a box where you give role information. We have set up no roles yet, so this area is blank. The lower levels have spaces where you specify role information.

Role-Based Security

Role-based security was introduced with Microsoft Transaction Server and represents a substantial simplification in how you can configure and program security. A role is a logical group of users who are authorized to access a component, interface or method. A role can map into a natural business rule about who is allowed access to what. In short, roles are a good abstraction for specifying security *policy*. Now might be a good time to look back at Figure 17–1 for the big picture of security.

Roles are very intuitive, so without a lot of general discussion let's look at our example. We will define two roles, *Customer* and *Vendor*. A customer is allowed to play the game as a shopper. In our stub program, a customer can sign in at **shopper.com**. A vendor is allowed to log on to **wholesale.com**.

SETTING UP ROLES

You can set up roles using COM+ Explorer. As with all administrative procedures that you can perform with the tool, you could also automate the administration through scripts that use the COM+ Admin objects. You first create the roles, and then you populate them with users.

Open up "EcStubApp" and select "Roles." Right-click. From the context menu choose New | Role. For the first role, enter the name "Customer." Do this again, and for the second role enter "Vendor." Now in the tree view open up "Customer" and select "Users." Right-click and choose New | User. The "Select Users or Groups" dialog comes up. Add the following users: **amy**, **bob**, **carl**, and **Administrator**. See Figure 17–23.

In a similar way, populate the role of Vendor wth **vicky**, **wanda**, and **Administrator**.

CONFIGURING COMPONENT-LEVEL ACCESS

You can now configure component-level access. In COM+ Explorer select "EcStubServer.Player" under "Components" in the tree view. Right-click and choose Properties, and select the Security tab. Put a check next to the Customer role. See Figure 17–24.

Now COM+ will enforce a policy at run time which will allow users in the Customer role to access the Player component. No other users will be allowed access. You can now run the client program. Amy will now be allowed to log on to **shopper.com** but Vicky will not be allowed to. Nobody will be allowed to log on to **wholesale.com**, because we have not yet configured any roles for it.

We will now configure access to the other component, "EcStub-Server.Vendor." Put a check by both roles, Customer and Vendor. (We will later restrict access by some programmatic security checking.) If you are stilled logged on as Vicky on the client machine, you should now be able to

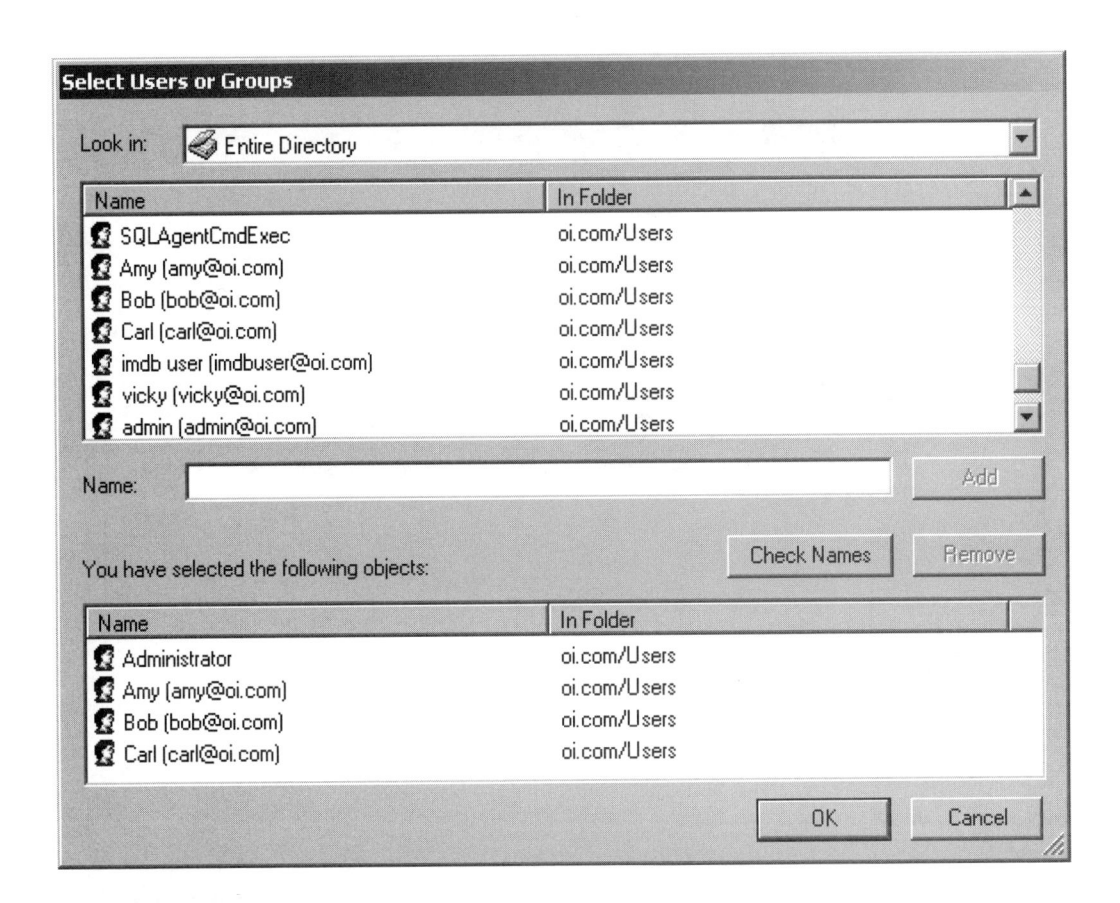

Figure 17-23 *Adding users to a role*

log on to **wholesale.com**. You would also be able to gain access as any of the other users, because right now we have access enabled for both roles.

Programmatic Security

COM+ makes it easy to do programmatic security checks. What makes this work is the fact that security information is part of the *context*. Just as you called methods like **SetComplete** and **SetAbort** on the context object, you may call a method **IsCallerInRole** to do a run time check on role membership.

The **IsCallerInRole** method is part of **IObjectContext**, the interface that was used in MTS. But in COM+, security has been refactored into its own interfaces, and it is preferable to use the interface **ISecurityCallContext**. In C++, you can obtain a pointer to this interface by calling **CoGetCallContext**. You may remember that when we were discussing context in COM+ we said that there are two kinds of context, object context and call context. The first is

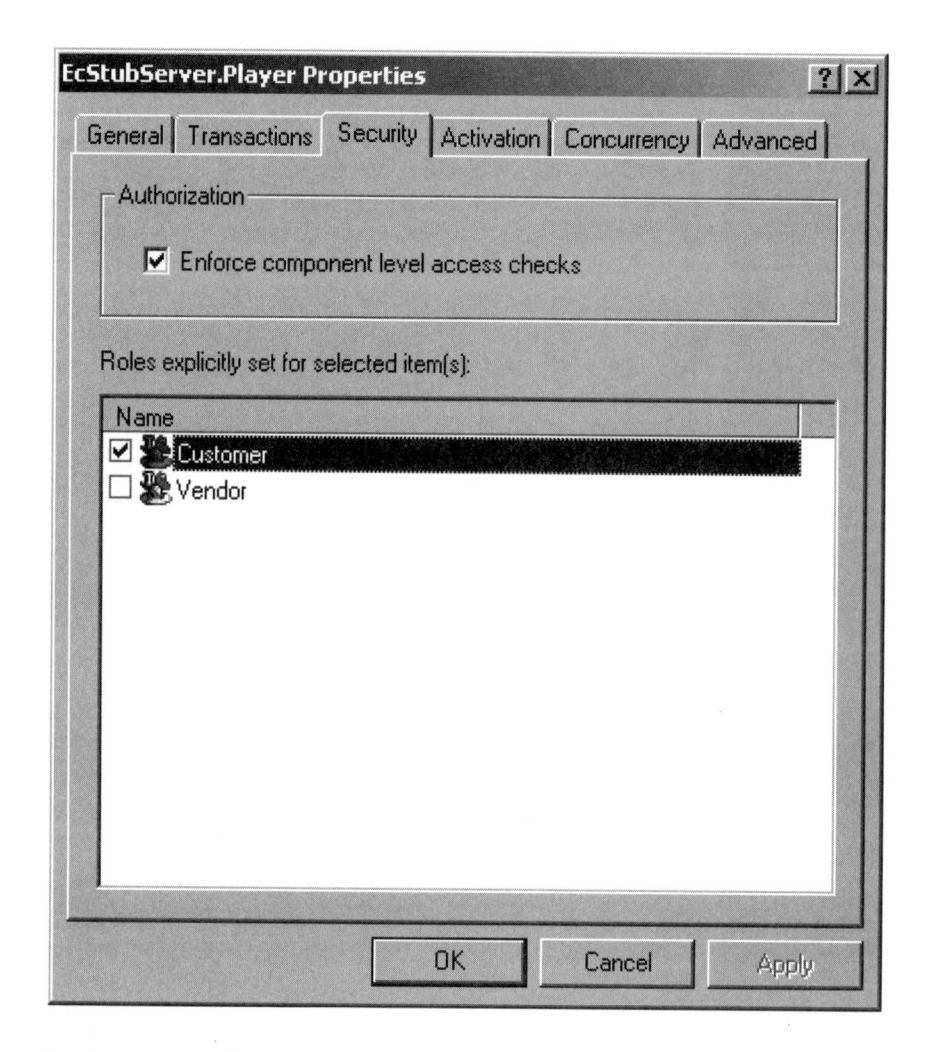

Figure 17-24 Granting Customers access to the Player component

valid while an object is active, and the second is valid during a particular call. Security makes use of the call context.

In Visual Basic, you call **GetSecurityContext** to obtain a reference to the call context object. The following code for the vendor class in **vendor.cls** in **Chap17\EcStub\Server** provides an example of using **IsCallerInRole** from Visual Basic. As you can see, the method takes as a parameter a single string, which you can use as the name of the role you are checking for. If there is a security violation, the function returns a special value of an enumerated type to pass error information to the client.

```
Public Enum LoginCodes
   ecOK = 0
   ecUrlNotFound = 1
   ecInvalidID = 2
   ecNew = 3
   ecOld = 4
   ecSecurityViolation = 5
End Enum

Public Function Login(ByVal url As String, _
         ByVal id As String) As LoginCodes
   'check for correct url and id (stub code)
   If url = "toyland.com" Then
      Login = ecOK
   ElseIf url = "petworld.com" Then
      Login = ecOK
   ElseIf url = "foodstore.com" Then
      Login = ecOK
   Else
      Login = ecUrlNotFound
   Exit Function
   End If

   'Do programmatic role check before checking ID
   If (GetSecurityCallContext.IsCallerInRole("Vendor")) Then
      If id <> "0" Then
         Login = ecOK
      Else
         Login = ecInvalidID
      End If
   Else
      Login = ecSecurityViolation
   End If
End Function
```

In this example, we check the URL against a few hardcoded values before doing the security check. This part of the code can be executed by any client in the allowed roles of Customer and Vendor. The rest of the code requires the caller to be in the role of Vendor.

The client code explicitly checks the return value for the type of error that was encountered. See the file **frmVendorLogin.frm** in **Chap17\ EcStubClient**.

```
...
Dim objVendor As New Vendor
Dim result As LoginCodes
result = objVendor.Login(txtURL, txtVendorID)
If result = ecUrlNotFound Then
   MsgBox txtURL & " not found, try again!", , "Login"
   txtVendorID.SetFocus
   SendKeys "{Home}+{End}"
```

```
      Exit Sub
    ElseIf result = ecSecurityViolation Then
      MsgBox "Security violation!", , "Login"
      txtVendorID.SetFocus
      SendKeys "{Home}+{End}"
      Exit Sub
    End If
    ...
```

Try running the client program from your Windows 2000 Professional machine. Try Amy and Vicky as two different users. Amy will not be able to succeed, but Vicky will, because Vicky is in the role of Vendor.

Identity in COM+

We have been running the client program under a variety of user accounts, but so far the server has always run as the Interactive User, which is the default. As was explained when we discussed COM security, the Interactive User is the user that is currently logged on to the server machine. There is a Windows station created for that user which provides a user interface, and message boxes will be displayed.

As a little experiment, add code to the vendor class to put up a message box when a vendor object is created. Now run the client remotely and visit **wholesale.com**. You should hear a beep coming from your server machine, and if you look on the task bar you should see a task for the message box, which you can now examine and close. When you close the message box on the server, you should see a message box on the client saying "Wholesale page goes here."

Continuing the experiment, log off from the server machine. Do not shut down. Now try running the client again to invoke one of the methods on the server. You will get an error message complaining about improper identity. The server needs to run under the identity of the Interactive User, but there is no Interactive User. See Figure 17–25.

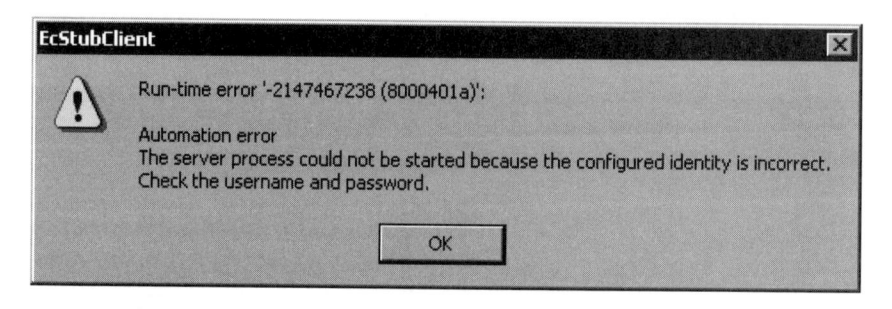

Figure 17–25   *Trying to use server when there is no logged-on user*

COM+ Security 405

Log back on to the server as Administrator. You will once again be able to access the server application. Now go into COM+ Explorer and bring up the Properties window for the **EcStubApp** application. Select the Identity tab. Change the account to one of the users you previously created, for instnce, **bob**. (Don't use the Administrator account for this demo.) See Figure 17–26. Click OK.

Now log off again and try running the client. This time the call to the client will succeed. Log back on as Administrator. Now try the client again. You can visit **shopper.com** just fine, but try to log on to **wholesale.com**. The client will hang. The server is putting up a message box, but it is *not* in the Win-

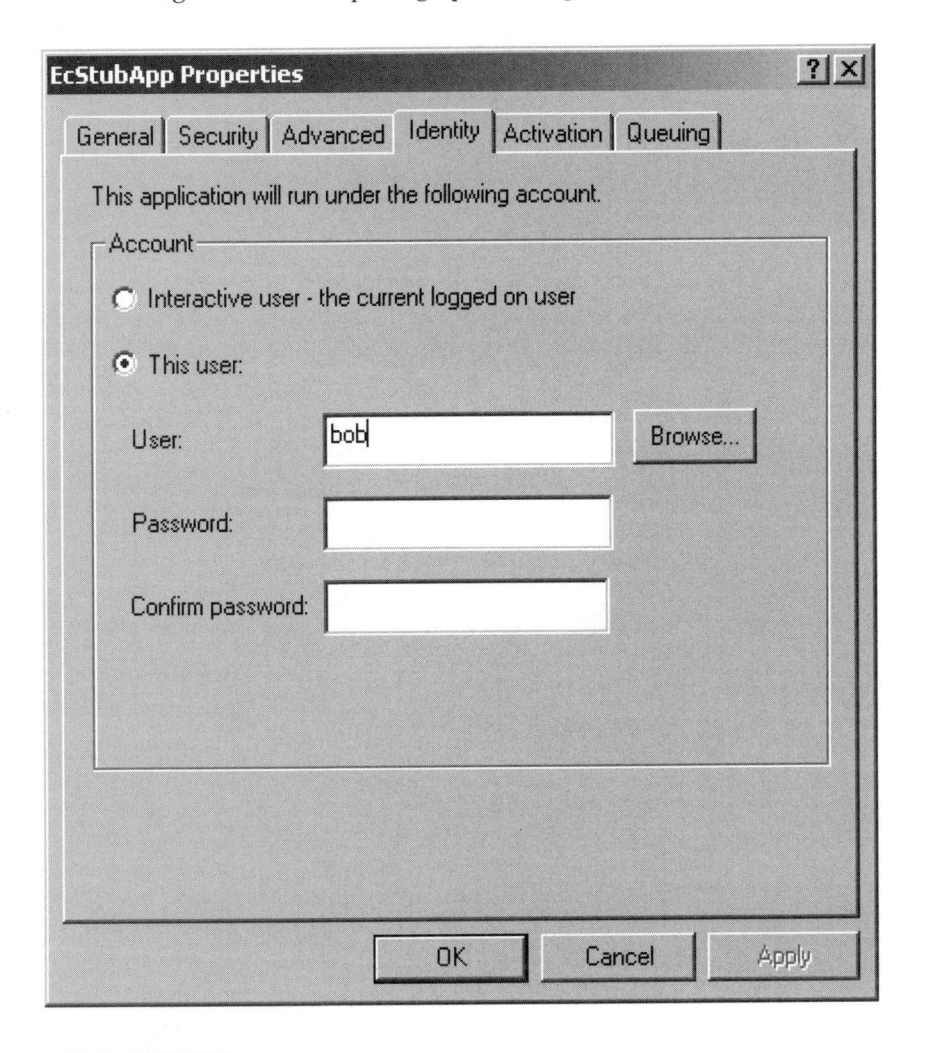

Figure 17–26 *Changing the identity under which the application will run*

dows station of the Interactive User. Hence, this message box is never displayed, and will never close. You can use the Task Manager to force your hung client to close.

Hopefully this little exercise will convince you *never* to use message boxes in server components. You could do so while debugging, but a better strategy is to write debug messages to a log file, as we explained in Chapter 12 and illustrated in Chapter 15.

If you look again at Figure 17–25, you will see that COM+ only gives you two options for the identity, not three as permitted under straight COM. The third choice, launching user, is a terrible one, because a separate Windows station is created for every client. Also, running the server under multiple identities defeats connection string pooling when talking to a database, which also works against scalability. This last point is also a drawback to using impersonation as part of your security strategy, the topic of the next section.

Impersonation

We already introduced the concept of impersonation while we were discussing COM security. Here we discuss when to use and not use impersonation, and also explain how to program for impersonation if you must use it.

To understand impersonation in more depth, consider the hypothetical four-tier application shown in Figure 17–27. Client C calls server S1, which calls server S2, which calls server S3. We designate the three successive calls ("hops") as X, Y and Z.

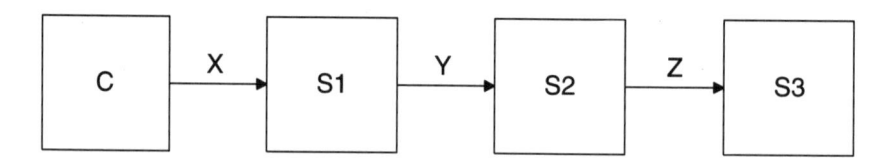

Figure 17–27 *A four-tier application that is a candidate for impersonation*

The question is, under whose security credentials is each of the calls made? For call X the answer is always the same—the credentials of the client C. Now if server S1 runs under its own account, it will have its own set of security credentials. If the impersonation level is "Impersonate" or "Delegate," S1 may "impersonate" C, and call Y will then also run under the security credentials of C. Now the difference between "Impersonate" and "Delegate" comes for the next call. If the level is "Impersonate," you are only allowed one remote "hop," and so call Z could *not* run under the security credentials of C. With the use of Kerberos as the Security Support Provider in Windows

2000, the "Delegate" impersonation level is enabled, and even in the case of remote calls you can continue to use the original client's security credentials.

Now why would you want to impersonate? The short answer is "only if you have to." Impersonation suffers several drawbacks. First, it is expensive from a performance standpoint, as you have to make multiple remote calls for security checking. Second, you don't find out until late that the access fails. The reason you may have to is if you are talking to a legacy server application whose whole security apparatus was geared on using the security credentials of the end client. As an example, suppose S3 is database code that relies on client identity for allowing connecting to the database and performing critical operations. Without rearchitecting the application, S2 will have to impersonate C. But now a third drawback surfaces. Every different client will involve server S2 using a different connection for talking to the database, defeating connection pooling. Indeed, one of the advantages of N-tier over client/server is the fact that the middle tier can pool resources., which you have now lost, limiting scalability.

OK, you probably don't want to use impersonation. But supposing you have to, how do you implement it? The answer is that it is quite easy, requiring just a little code on the client and on the server. We will not discuss the code in detail, just indicate the calls you have to make. You can check the documentation for details.

CLIENT SIDE OF IMPERSONATION

There are two considerations on the client side. The first is impersonation level. The client must indicate its willingness to have the server use its identity. The second is that the Active Directory supports a feature that can mark a user account as sensitive and cannot be delegated.

If the client does not indicate an impersonation level programmatically, a machinewide default is used. This default can be set in COM+ Explorer. Right-click over "My Computer" and choose Properties. In the "My Computer Properties" dialog, choose the "Default Properties" tab. Near the bottom you can specify default impersonation level. Notice that this window also provides the master switch by which you can enable or disable DCOM on the machine. See Figure 17–28.

The client can change the level of impersonation it will tolerate by calling the API function **CoSetProxyBlanket**, which can be called as often as desired. The impersonation level can also be specified by calling **CoInitializeSecurity**, which can be called only one time per process.

SERVER-SIDE IMPERSONATION

The server can start using the client's security credentials by calling **CoImpersonateClient**. When the server is done impersonating the client, it can start using its own security credentials again by calling **CoRevertToSelf**.

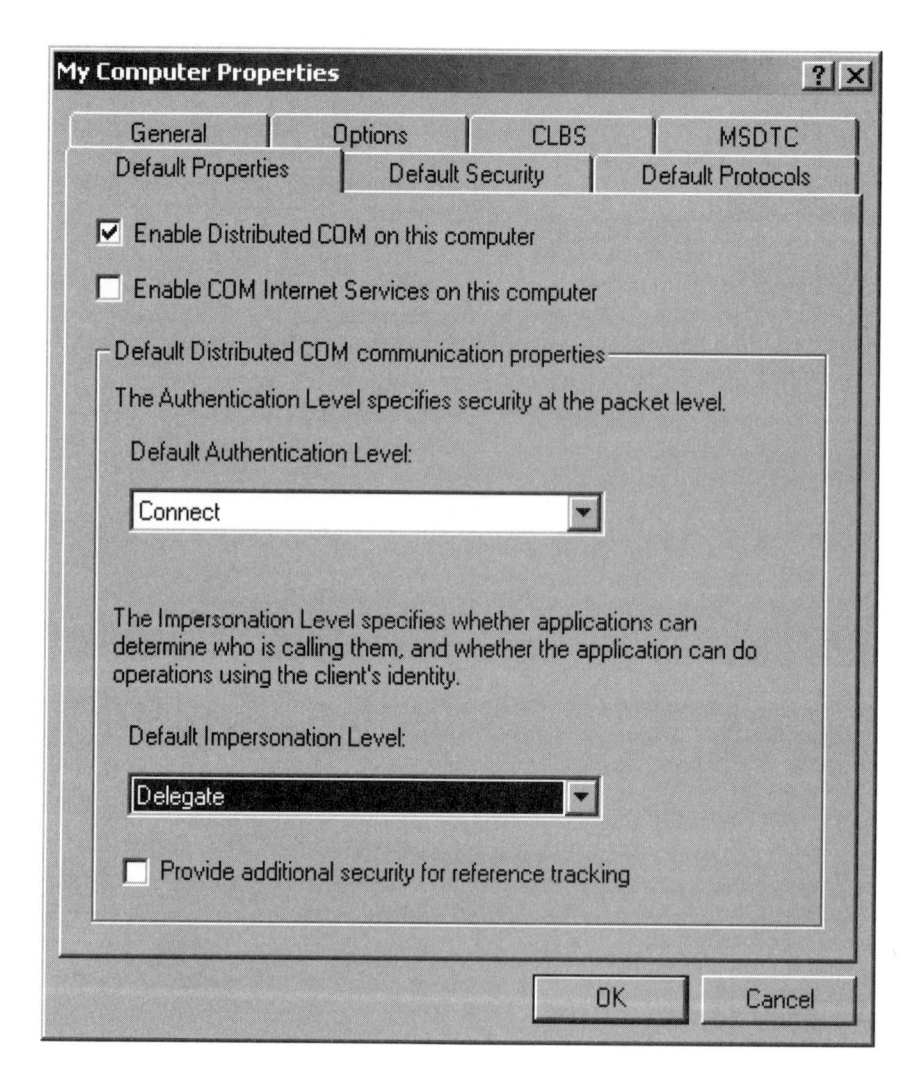

Figure 17-28   *Specifying machinewide default impersonation level*

Summary

This long chapter provided a fairly comprehensive overview of security in Windows 2000 and COM+. There are many details we have not covered, but you should have a good practical grasp of the fundamentals at this point. We first looked at the basic function of security as addressing the question "Who can do what to whom?" A Security Reference Monitor can apply a policy to validate requests for services. There are two aspects to security checking. The first is *authorizing* a request. Authorization depends on knowing who the parties are, which depends on *authentication*.

Security rests upon the operating system, so we looked at both how user accounts are administered and also at the underlying NT security model which Windows 2000 employs. We then examined COM security, which can specify permissions for launch and activation, an identity, an impersonation level, and an authentication level. These values are stored in the Registry and can be set using DCOMCNFG.

COM+ adds many more attributes, which can be set using COM+ Explorer or can be changed programmatically using the COM+ Admin objects. These attributes are much more flexible than provided by COM. Security can be configured at the application, component, interface, and method level.

COM+ provides a high-level abstraction called role-based security. Here policy can be specified by assigning users to roles, and the components can indicate which roles are permissible for doing operations. Roles can also be programmed using the call context.

We looked at the ramifications of the choice of identity under which a server application runs, and we concluded by looking in greater detail at the concept of impersonation, which allows a server to run under the security credentials of the client.

We used as our sample code a stub version of the Electronic Commerce Game. The "real" version of this game requires the use of databases, as does indeed the vast majority of commercial systems. In the next chapter we turn our attention to some database fundamentals in the Microsoft environment. We will then be in a position to pursue how COM+ facilitates a number of aspects of database programming.

EIGHTEEN

SQL Server and ADO Survival Guide

A very major part of much commercial programming involves databases. In this chapter we look at some essential parts of Microsoft's database technology that we need to understand in order to access databases using COM+. Of course COM+ architecture is independent of a particular database, and indeed one can work with Oracle databases, for example. But it will be very convenient for us to do all of our database examples using Microsoft technology, and it will also give us a more complete picture of Windows DNA.

We begin with an overview of SQL Server 7.0, which is an easy-to-use database management system. We show how to create a database, specify its schema, and perform queries. The rest of the chapter discusses database programming. We describe Microsoft's overall approach, called Uniform Data Access or UDA. We then look at ODBC, OLE DB, and ADO. We give a short tutorial on database programming using ADO, including an example of a three-tier application. This chapter provides the database fundamentals for implementing the Electronic Commerce Game™ case study, which will be used in the rest of this book. The chapter concludes with our first look at an implementation of this case study.

Getting Started with SQL Server 7.0

SQL Server is Microsoft's strategic database platform. It is derived from Sybase SQL Server. Microsoft and Sybase diverged several years ago, with Microsoft assuming full responsibility for moving forward its version of SQL Server on Microsoft operating systems. It is currently at revision 7.0, which is significantly easier to use than previous versions. It also now runs on Windows 95/98. It is the only DBMS we will work with in this book.

SQL Server 7.0 is easy to install. I suggest you install it on each of your test computers. That will give you convenience in being able to use the tools anywhere, and you will be able to test distributed transactions in the next chapter. The disk footprint is not too large, somewhat over 100 Mb for the desktop version, which is adequate for what we will be doing in this book. In any event, you will need it installed on at least one of your machines. You can accept all the suggested defaults when you install it.

After it is installed, the first thing to do is to start up the MSSQLServer service. You can do that from Start | Programs | Microsoft SQL Server 7.0 | Service Manager. This applet lets you start up the three services associated with SQL Server. (The other two are SQLServerAgent and MSDTC.) Start all three services. Since we are going to be working with databases for the next several chapters, it is convenient to configure them to auto start when the system boots. See Figure 18–1.

Figure 18–1 *Starting SQL Server services using the Service Manager*

Query Analyzer

The next tool to use, also in the Microsoft SQL Server 7.0 group, is Query Analyzer. This is an easy-to-use query tool, which will accept SQL statements in one pane and display results in another pane. You can also load SQL scripts from files and execute them.

Bring up Query Analyzer. A dialog box will come up for connecting to SQL Server. Right now use the (local) SQL Server. After you have registered other SQL Servers on your network, you can use Query Analyzer to connect to them and perform queries on them. We will register other SQL Servers in the next section. Accept the default of SQL Server authentication, using log-on name "sa" and blank password (the defaults). This will be easier for us in this chapter, when we are focusing on basic database functionality and not security. Click OK. See Figure 18–2.

Figure 18-2 *Connecting to SQL Server*

You now have a new query window open. You can type in a query and then execute it from the toolbar button with a green wedge-shaped arrow. You can also use the menu Query | Execute or the keyboard shortcut F5. Microsoft supplies a test database called "pubs," which you can use for testing before you have created any databases of your own. Choose this database

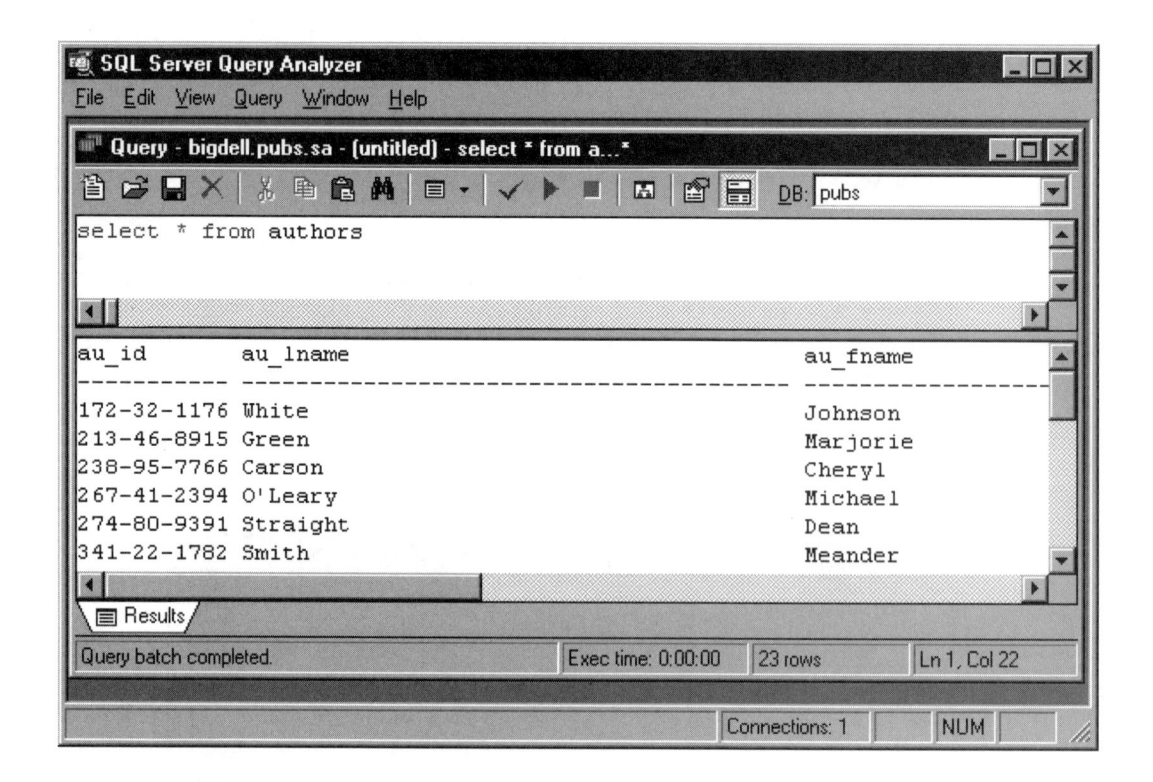

Figure 18-3 *Executing a simple query from Query Analyzer*

from the dropdown at the top right. Then enter a simple query **select * from authors** and execute it. A new pane will open up to show the results of the query. See Figure 18-3.

Enterprise Manager

The Enterprise Manager tool, as the name suggests, gives you the capability of managing from a single console all the SQL Servers that are installed in your enterprise. The Enterprise Manager is also in the Microsoft SQL Server 7.0 group that you get to from Start | Programs. It is another MMC snap-in. After you have installed SQL Server 7.0 on a new machine, it will be the only SQL Server you initially see from Enterprise Manager from that machine. See Figure 18-4.

You can add other SQL Servers by right-clicking over "Microsoft SQL Servers" and choosing "New SQL Server Registration" from the context menu. A wizard comes up which will enable you to add other servers. When you have SQL Server installed on other computers, you can mutually register

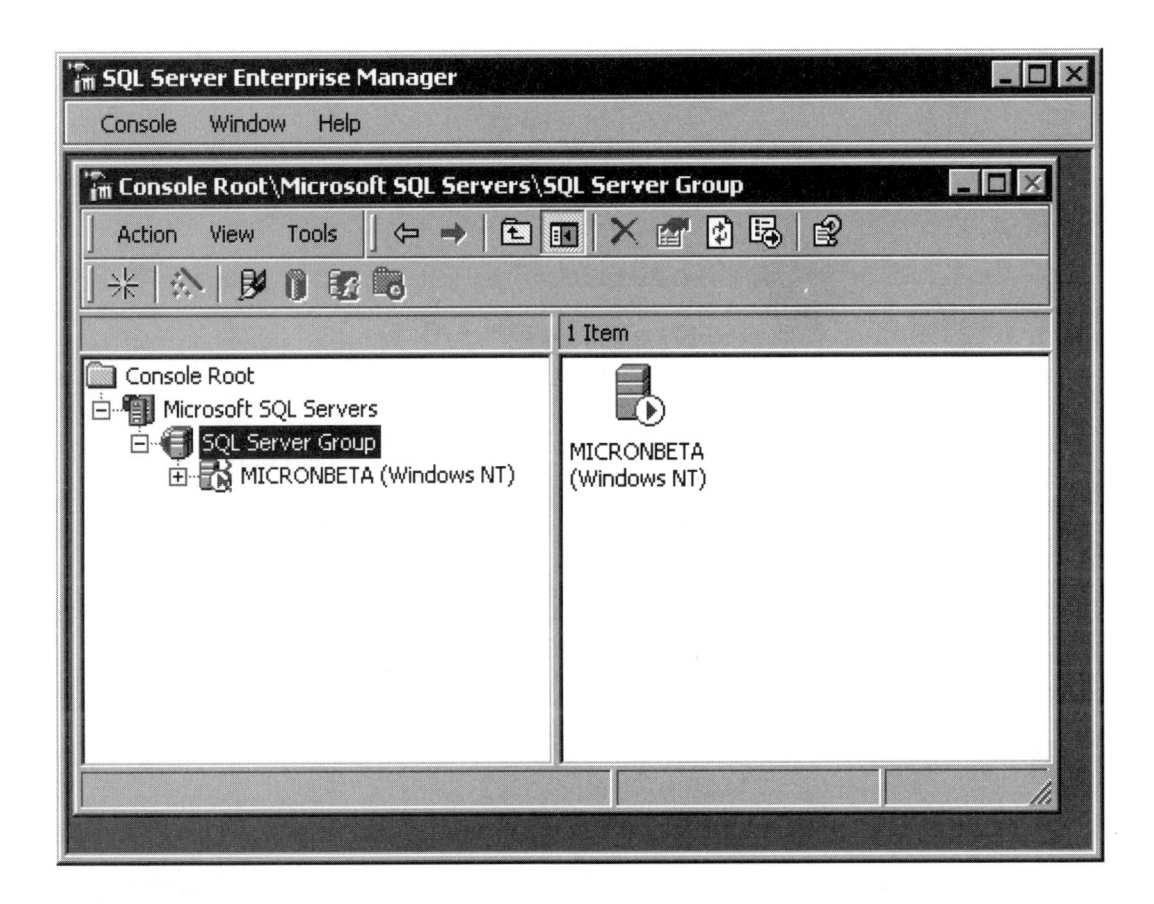

Figure 18-4 *Initially you see only one SQL Server in Enterprise Manager*

them. In the Authentication Mode window, you may wish to choose SQL Server Authentication for simplicity.

Once you have registered other SQL Servers, they now become available to you from Query Analyzer. You can now do queries against any SQL Server on your network.

Managing Databases Using SQL Server 7.0

Now that SQL Server 7.0 is up and running, you can start creating and managing your own databases. In this section, we will go through creating the databases that will be used for the Electronic Commerce Game case study. These databases will also be used for some smaller programming examples. We first outline the schema of these databases, and then we use Enterprise Manager and Query Analyzer to create the databases, add the tables, and populate the tables with some test data. Some of our work will involve using prepared scripts.

Databases for Case Study

There are three types of databases used in the Electronic Commerce Game case study and its associated programs. Please refer to Appendix B for more information about the Electronic Commerce Game. We give a brief description of each database in this section.

HISTORY

The History database is used to make a historical record of players who have played the game. It is not written to during the game itself, but by a special program that an administrator can run to move players from the active Game database to the History database. This program will be described in the next chapter. This database is very simple, and we will create its schema "by hand" using Enterprise Manager. There is one table, **Players**, with the columns **name**, **balance**, and **num_games**. The **name** column is used as a primary key.

GAME

The Game database stores information pertaining to players in the game and products they purchase. There is also a list of vendors. There are five tables:

1. **Players** is like the corresponding table in the History database, with the addition of an **active** field to indicate whether the player is currently playing the game or not.
2. **Shopping** provides an initial shopping list for each player.
3. **Products** provides a master list of all products and their wholesale prices.
4. **Items** keeps track of the purchases of each player.
5. **Vendors** provides a list of the vendors where players may go to buy products.

VENDOR DATABASES

There are three vendor databases, Toyland, Petworld, and Foodstore. These databases may be created on different machines. These databases share a common schema. There are two tables:

1. **Info** gives the URL and current balance of the vendor (one row).
2. **Inventory** maintains a list of items currently carried by the vendor, including the (retail) price and quantity on hand.

Creating a Database

It is extremely easy to create a database using SQL Server 7.0. You don't have to worry about a "database device," and you don't have to worry about initially allocating enough storage for the database, because SQL Server 7.0 can automatically "grow" databases as required. We will create five databases, History, Game, Toyland, Petworld, and Foodstore.

In Enterprise Manager, expand the tree view to show the databases on your machine. See Figure 18–5.

Right-click over "Databases." From the context menu that comes up, choose New Database. Enter "History" as the name of your new database. Accept all the defaults, and click OK. See Figure 18–6.

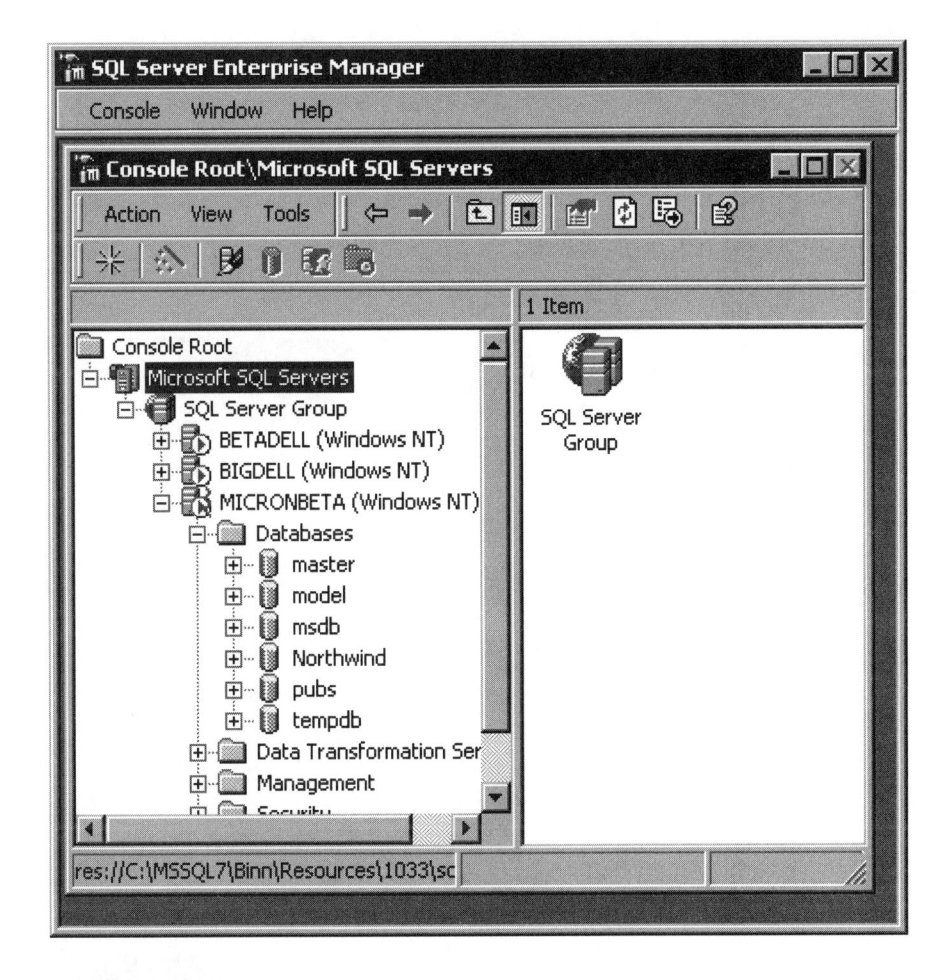

Figure 18–5 *Managing databases on your machine with Enterprise Manager*

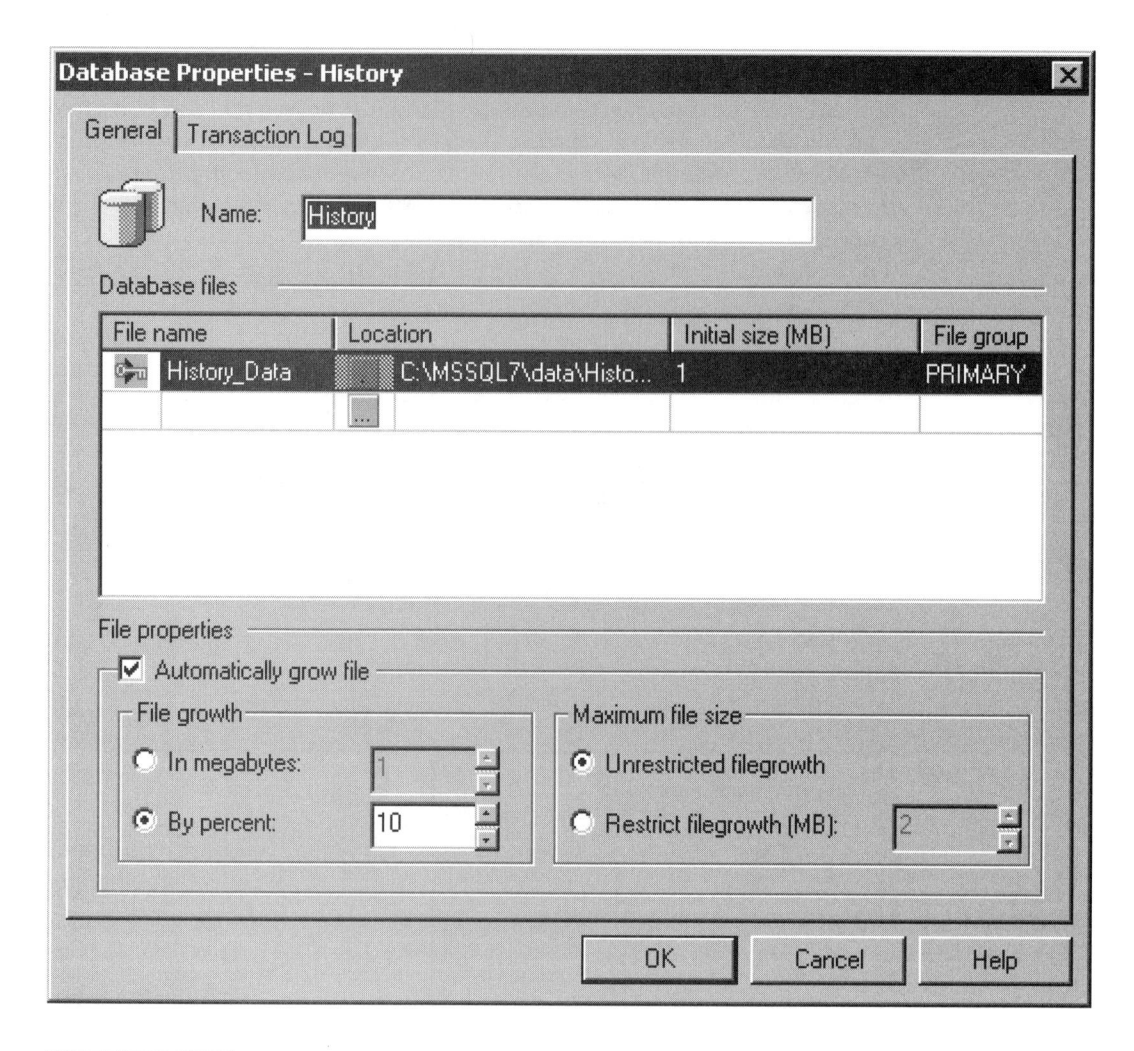

418 Chapter 18 • SQL Server and ADO Survival Guide

Figure 18-6 *Creating a new database using Enterprise Manager*

Creating a Table

You can also create tables using Enterprise Manager. Right-click over your new database "History." From the context menu choose New | Table. Enter the name "Players" for the new table. Enter the following information to define three columns:

```
Column Name   Data Type    Length

name          char         30
balance       money
num_games     int
```

Clear the check mark from the Allow Nulls. Right-click over the first column **name** and choose "Set Primary Key" from the context menu. The schema for your new table will now be as shown in Figure 18–7.

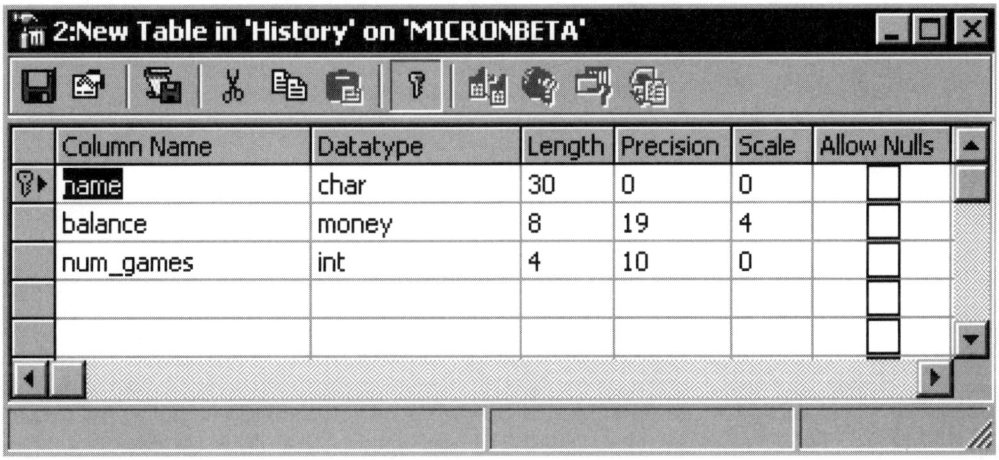

Figure 18–7   *Defining the schema for a table*

Close the window you were using to define the new table, and say "Yes" to saving the changes.

Inserting Data into a Table

You can insert data into your new table using either Enterprise Manager or Query Analyzer. We will do both, starting with Enterprise Manager. Select "Tables" in the left-hand pane. You will then see a list of tables in the right-hand pane. Select "Players" (there are a lot of system tables besides the one you defined yourself) and right-click. From the context menu, choose Open Table | Return all rows. In the window that comes up, you can type in data directly. Enter a couple of rows. See Figure 18–8.

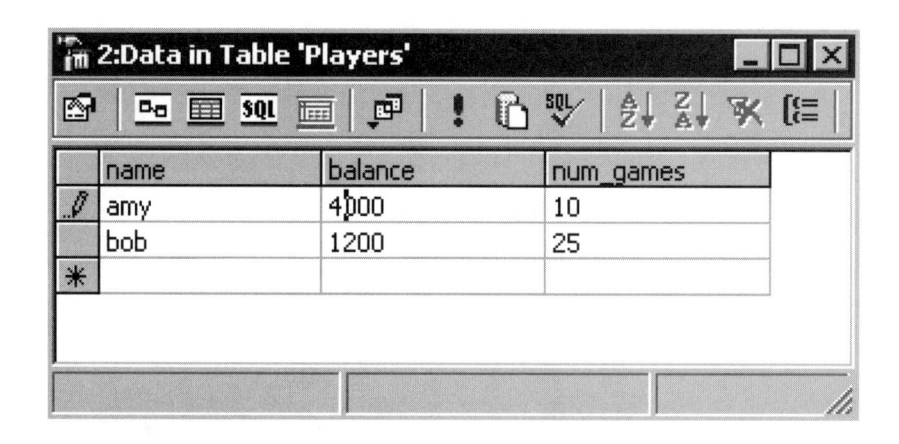

Figure 18-8 *Entering data into a table using Enterprise Manager*

You may also use Query Analyzer to insert data using an SQL INSERT statement. We already illustrated using Query Analyzer to run a SELECT statement against the Microsoft "pubs" database. Now bring up Query Analyzer again, and for the database choose "History." Type in the query:

```
insert into players values ('carl', 5000, 0)
```

You can execute this query. If you like, you can then perform a SELECT statement and verify that all of the data you provided is now in your table. Using the "Save" button from the toolbar (or command from the File menu), you can save your query. Save it under the file name **insert_history.sql** in the directory **Chap18\Demos**. A copy of all SQL Server scripts used in this chapter is provided in **CaseStudy\SqlScripts**.

Creating and Using SQL Scripts

We defined the schema for our History database manually. This would be tedious for a large database, especially one that will be set up on several machines. To automate the process, you can use SQL scripts. We just saw a simple example of a script created by saving a query that you entered through Query Analyzer. You may also have scripts created through Enterprise Manager. This is especially convenient for recreating a database schema.

Managing Databases Using SQL Server 7.0   **421**

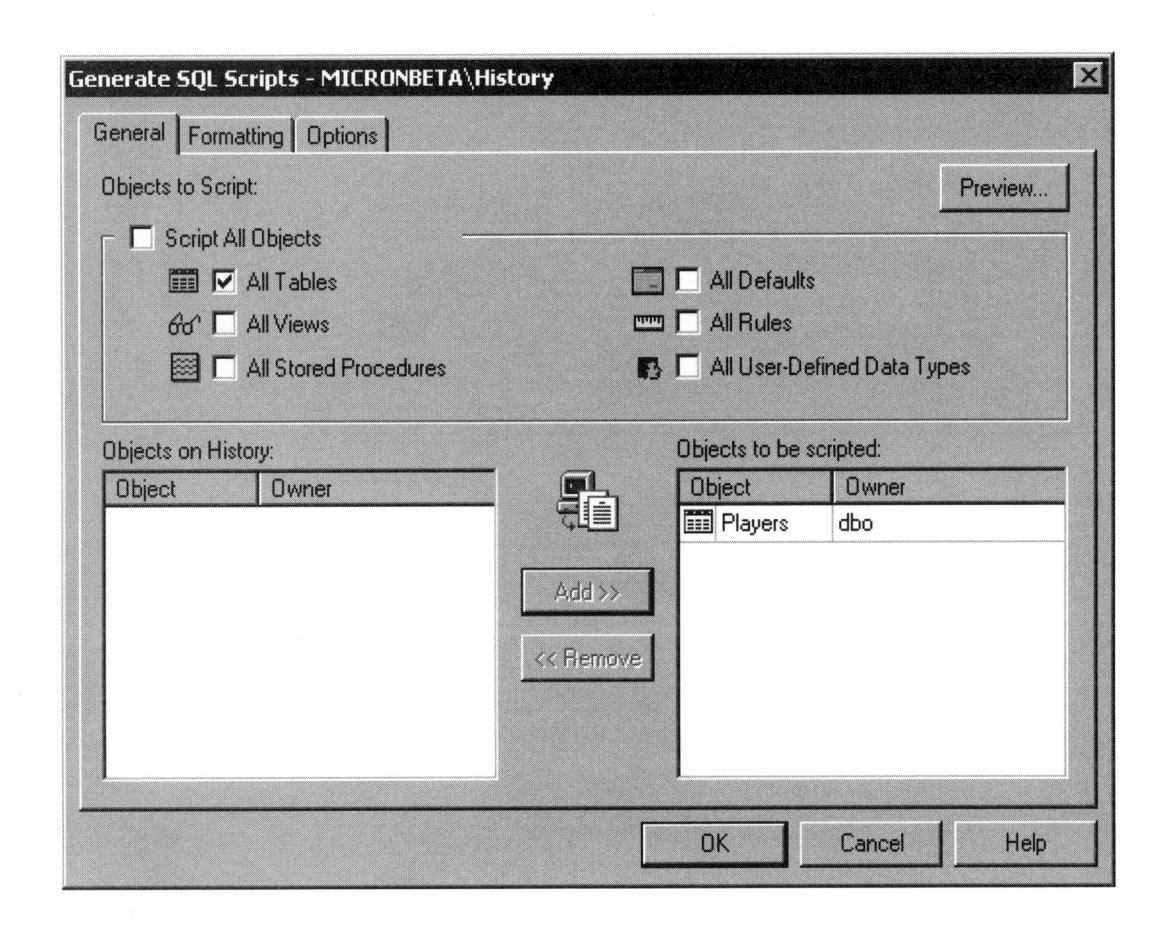

Figure 18–9   *Generating a script to create tables*

CREATING SCRIPTS

To illustrate, we will create a script for recreating the tables in the History database. Select "History" from the tree view and right-click. From the context menu, select All Tasks | Generate SQL Scripts. In the dialog that comes up, first use the "General" tab. Select what you want to script. In our case, it will be all the tables. See Figure 18–9. Then go, the "Options" tab and check "Script PRIMARY Key...." Click OK. In the "Save As" dialog, navigate to **Chap18\Demos** and save your script under the name **create_history _tables.sql**.

Here is the script that was produced.

```
if exists (select * from sysobjects where
  id = object_id(N'[dbo].[Players]') and
  OBJECTPROPERTY(id, N'IsUserTable') = 1)
drop table [dbo].[Players]
GO

CREATE TABLE [dbo].[Players] (
  [name] [char] (30) NOT NULL ,
  [balance] [money] NOT NULL ,
  [num_games] [int] NOT NULL
) ON [PRIMARY]
GO

ALTER TABLE [dbo].[Players] WITH NOCHECK ADD
  CONSTRAINT [PK_Players] PRIMARY KEY NONCLUSTERED
  (
    [name]
  ) ON [PRIMARY]
GO
```

When you compare your own script, please be sure that the ALTER TABLE portion was generated, so that the table has a primary key.

USING SCRIPTS

It is very easy to use a script. Just load the script in Query Analyzer and execute it. The only pitfall is that you must connect to the right server and must choose the right database (you don't want to create tables in the "master" database!).

As an exercise, you may want to go to another machine where you have SQL Server 7.0 installed, create a History database there, and run your scripts to create the tables and insert one row of data. In the next section, you will run some prepared scripts to set up the other databases needed for the Electronic Commerce Game case study.

Setting Up Databases for the Electronic Commerce Game

It will now be very easy for you to set up the databases required for the Electronic Commerce Game. In this section, you will create the databases, create the tables, and insert starting data. Before you begin, decide on what machine you want to do most of your database work from now on. Very likely it will be the machine running Windows 2000 Server. In this section you will just set the databases up. A little later, after we have discussed programming, you can run some programs against the databases, including the Electronic Commerce Game itself. Scripts needed can be found in **CaseStudy\SqlScripts**.

CREATING THE DATABASES

1. Use Enterprise Manager to create the database "Game" and the three vendor databases "Toyland," "Petworld," and "Foodstore."
2. Use Query Analyzer to run a number of scripts. First run **create_game_tables.sql** to create the tables for Games.
3. Run **insert_game_data.sql** to insert starting data into Games.
4. Run **create_vendor_tables.sql** to create the tables for Toyland, followed by **insert_toyland.sql**.
5. For the other two vendor databases, Petworld and Foodstore, run **create_vendor_tables.sql** followed by the corresponding script to insert data.

TESTING THE DATABASES

Right now we will just run some spot checks against the new databases by doing a couple of SELECT queries. Shortly you will have an opportunity to do some further checking by running some programs.

First run **select * from inventory** against Toyland. You should get the following results:

item	price	quantity
airplane toy	15.0000	50
beanie baby	25.0000	50
elephant gun	55.0000	50

(3 row(s) affected)

Next run **select* from products** against Game. You should get the following results:

item	price
airplane toy	10.0000
beanie baby	20.0000
cat carrier	30.0000
dog bone	5.0000
elephant gun	50.0000
fruit basket	10.0000

(6 row(s) affected)

Uniform Data Access

Now that we have some databases set up, we are in a position to do some database programming. But first let's look briefly at the big picture of Microsoft's data access architecture. Microsoft calls the overall architecture "Uniform Data Access." The goal is to provide a consistent set of programming interfaces that can be used by a wide variety of clients to talk to a wide variety of data sources, including both relational and nonrelational data.

ODBC

Microsoft's first initiative in this direction was ODBC, or Open Database Connectivity. ODBC provides a C interface to relational databases. Figure 18–10 illustrates the overall architecture of ODBC.

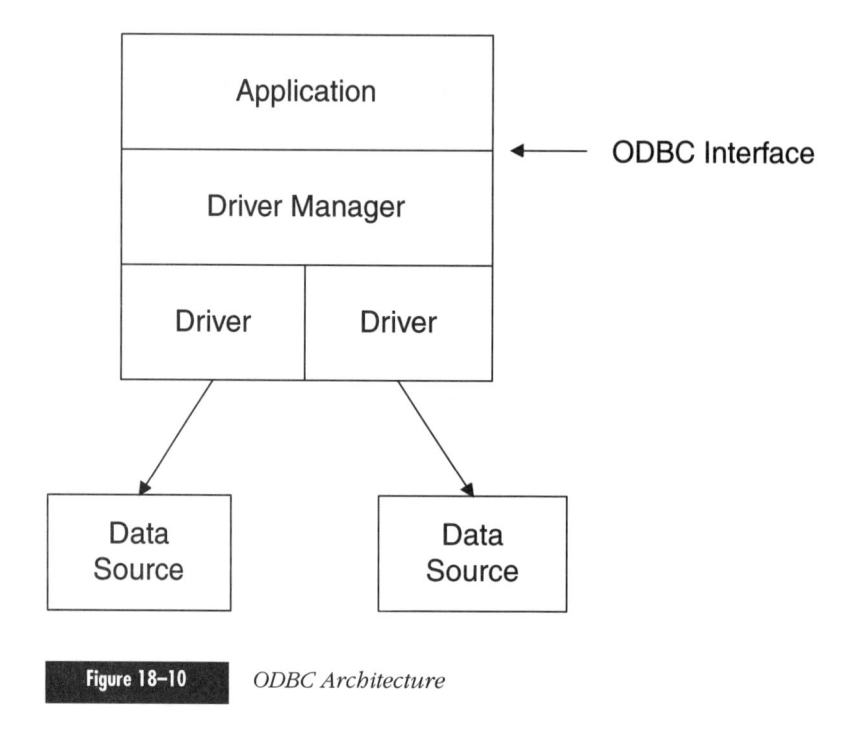

Figure 18-10 *ODBC Architecture*

Through this architecture, applications can talk to different relational databases using the same C interface. The ODBC standard has been widely adopted, and all major relational databases have provided ODBC drivers. In addition, some ODBC drivers have been written for nonrelational data sources, such as Excel spreadsheets.

Although successful, there are two main drawbacks to this approach. The first is the restriction to relational databases. As was pointed out, some ODBC drivers have been written to support ODBC talking to nonrelational data, but this approach puts a great burden on the driver to, in effect, emulate a relational database engine. And this code would have to be replicated in each such driver.

The second drawback is the C interface, which requires a programmer in any other language to first interface to C before being able to call ODBC.

OLE DB

Microsoft's improved strategy is based on COM. As we have seen, COM provides a language-independent interface, based on a binary standard. Thus any solution based on COM will improve the flexibility from the standpoint of the client program. Microsoft's set of COM database interfaces is referred to as "OLE DB," the original name when OLE was the all-embracing technology, and this name has stuck.

The other big feature is that OLE DB is not specific to relational databases. Any data source that wishes to expose itself to clients through OLE DB must implement an OLE DB *provider*. OLE DB itself provides much database functionality, including a cursor engine and a relational query engine. This code does not have to be replicated across many providers, unlike the case with ODBC drivers. Clients of OLE DB are referred to as *consumers*.

The first OLE DB provider was for ODBC. This at once gave OLE DB consumers access to all data sources supporting ODBC. The gain was a COM interface for clients. However, this solution imposed an additional layer between the client and the database.

Recently a number of *native* OLE DB providers have begun to appear, including one for SQL Server and Oracle. There is also a native provider for Microsoft's Jet database engine, which provides efficient access to desktop databases such as Access and dBase. Some object databases such as ObjectStore are also starting to furnish native OLE DB providers.

ActiveX Data Objects (ADO)

Although COM is based on a binary standard, all languages are not created equal with respect to COM. In its heart, COM "likes" C++. It is based on the C++ vtable interface mechanism, and C++ deals effortlessly with structures and pointers. Not so with many other languages, such as Visual Basic. If you provide a *dual* interface, which restricts itself to Automation-compatible data types, your components are much easier to access from Visual Basic.

OLE DB was architected for maximum efficiency for C++ programs. To provide an easy-to-use interface for Visual Basic, Microsoft created *ActiveX Data Objects* or ADO. The look and feel of ADO is somewhat similar to the popular Data Access Objects (DAO) that provides an easy-to-use object model for accessing Jet. The new ADO model has two advantages. One is that it is somewhat flattened and thus easier to use, without so much traversing down an object hierarchy. The great advantage of ADO is that it is based on OLE DB and thus will give programmers very broad reach in terms of data sources.

The end result of this technology is a very flexible range of interfaces available to the programmer. If you are accessing SQL Server, you have a choice of five main programming interfaces. One is embedded SQL, which is preprocessed from a C program. The other four interfaces are all run-time interfaces and are shown in Figure 18–11.

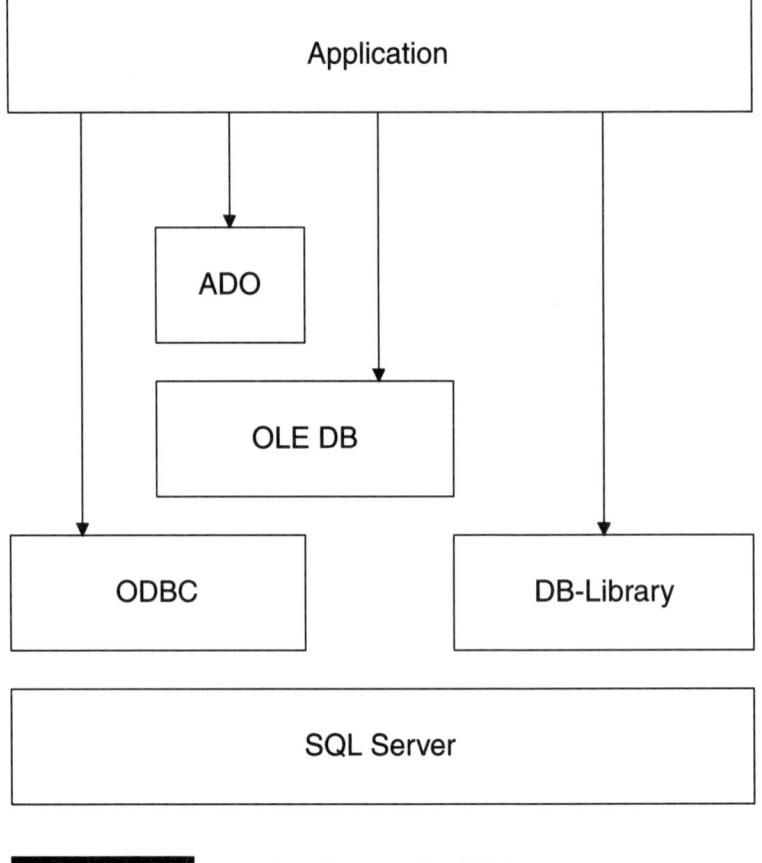

Figure 18-11 *Interfaces for accessing SQL Server*

DB-Library is the original run-time library for SQL Server. It is a layer on top of the SQL Server engine itself, which has a private interface not exposed to applications. An application can call DB-Library. This code is specific to SQL Server, and will not run on other databases, or on nonrelational data sources. It is a C interface. The second interface is ODBC. As we have seen, ODBC is also a C interface, but it will enable you to talk to many different relational databases.

If an application is written to OLE DB, it can access a wide variety of relational and nonrelational data sources. The range of data sources you can reach through OLE DB is a superset of ones that can be reached through ODBC, because there is an OLE DB provider for ODBC. SQL Server provides a native provider, so your application using OLE DB has a quite direct path to SQL Server. As was pointed out above, there are a number of native OLE DB providers to other databases, such as Oracle, and more are appearing all the time.

Finally, ADO is the highest level interface. It is very easy to use, and will be the one we use for illustrative purposes in this book. We will introduce programming in ADO later in this chapter.

A Tutorial in Database Programming

We can now dive in and do some database programming. We will write some code to access the History database. Our goal in this tutorial is to use the simplest techniques that will illustrate the basic concepts. We are not seeking to optimize performance. Thus we will use ADO as our programming interface, and our client program will be written in Visual Basic. We will go through ODBC, as it is easy to set up an ODBC data source, and an ODBC data source can be referenced through a simple connect string.

Creating an ODBC Data Source

First we will create an ODBC Data Source. Bring up the ODBC Data Source Administrator. On Windows 2000 Server, you can get to it from Start | Programs | Administrative Tools. On Windows 2000 Professional, you can also get it from the Administrative Tools group, but you get to the Administrative Tools group through Control Panel. (These directions reflect the Beta 3 release of Windows 2000. The final release may arrange things differently.) Select the "System DSN" tab. See Figure 18–12.

You need a DSN or "data source name" to connect to an ODBC data source. There are three kinds of DSNs: User, System, and File. The first two kinds are stored in an efficient binary manner by the operating system. A file DSN stores information in a text file. A file DSN is not as efficient, but is convenient for deploying across many computers. A user DSN is only valid under the account that created it, while a system DSN is valid for all accounts on the system. Our first example will be a system DSN. We will illustrate a file DSN later.

What we are going to do right now is add a new system DSN. Click the "Add" button. Select "SQL Server" from the "Create New Data Source" screen

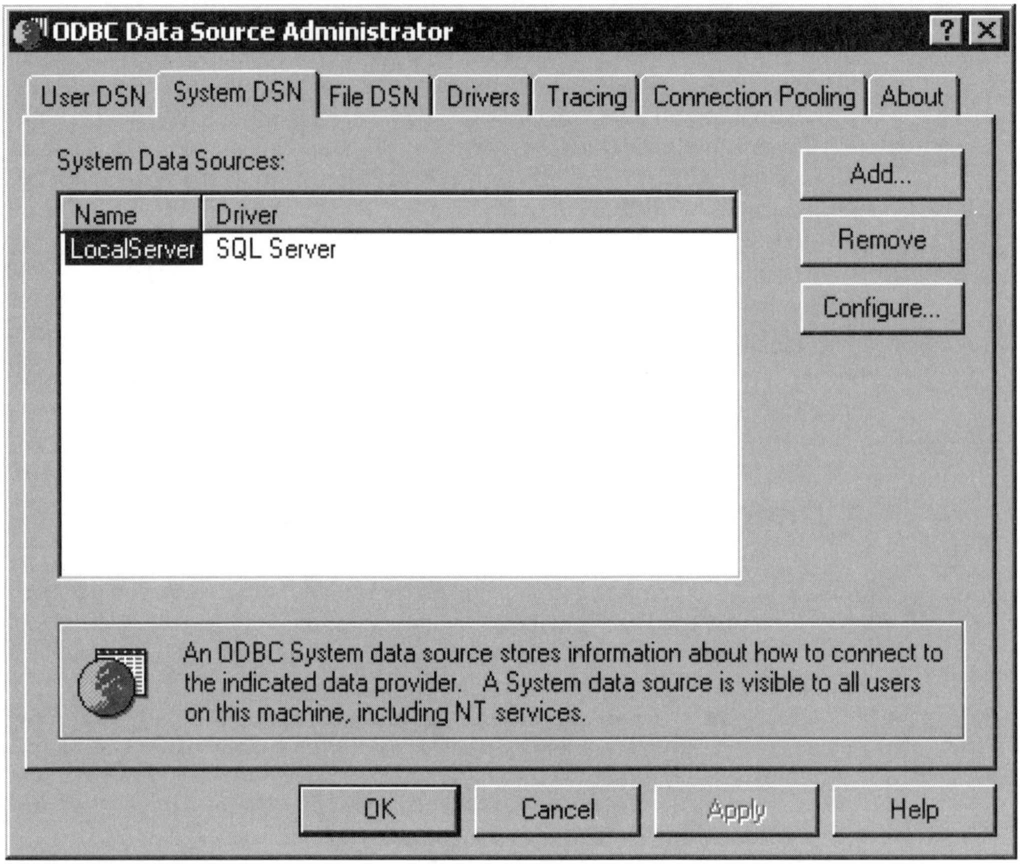

Figure 18-12 *The ODBC Data Source Administrator*

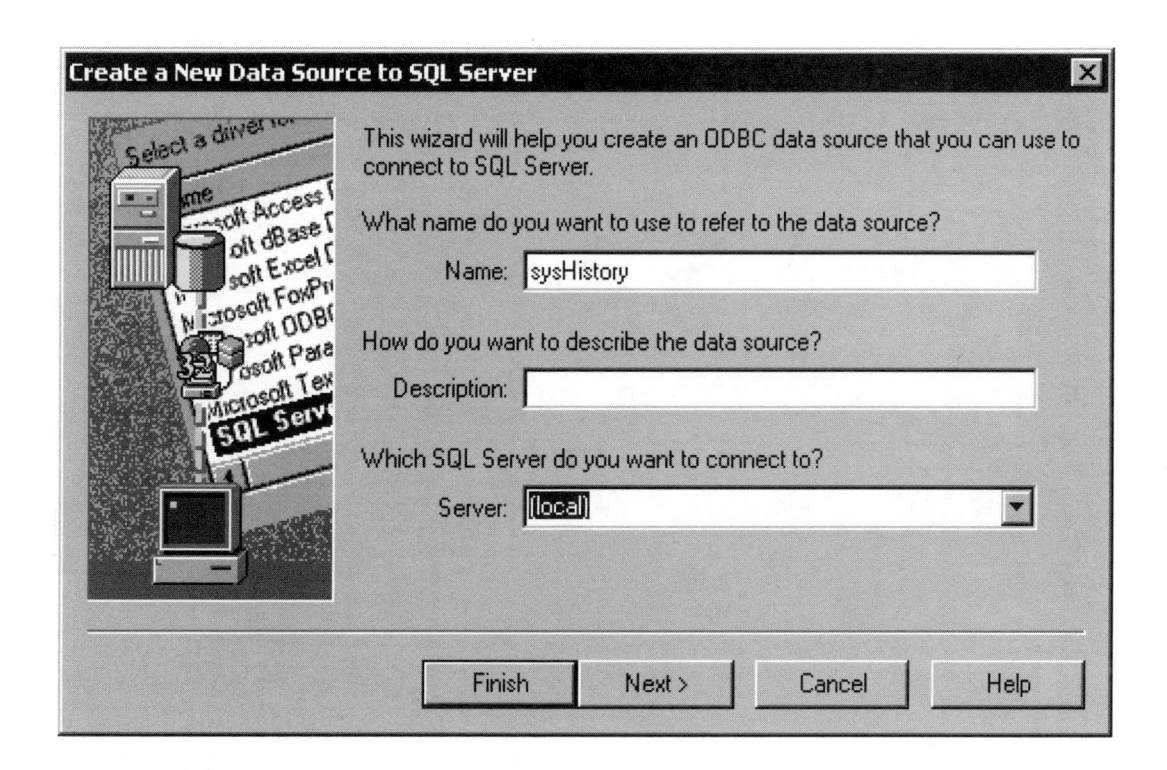

A Tutorial in Database Programming

Figure 18-13 *Creating a new DSN in SQL Server*

that comes up, and click "Finish." The next screen is "Create a New Data Source in SQL Server." See Figure 18–13.

Enter "sysHistory" as the name, and choose the local SQL Server. If you wanted to build a multiple-tier application with the data source on a different computer from the business logic, you could choose a remote computer here. Click Next. Choose SQL Server authentication, with log-on ID of "sa." See Figure 18–14.

Click Next. In the next screen that comes up, change the default database to History. Accept all the other choices on this screen. See Figure 18–15. Click Next and then Finish. On the final screen you can test your new data source. Click OK until you get out of the ODBC Data Source Administrator.

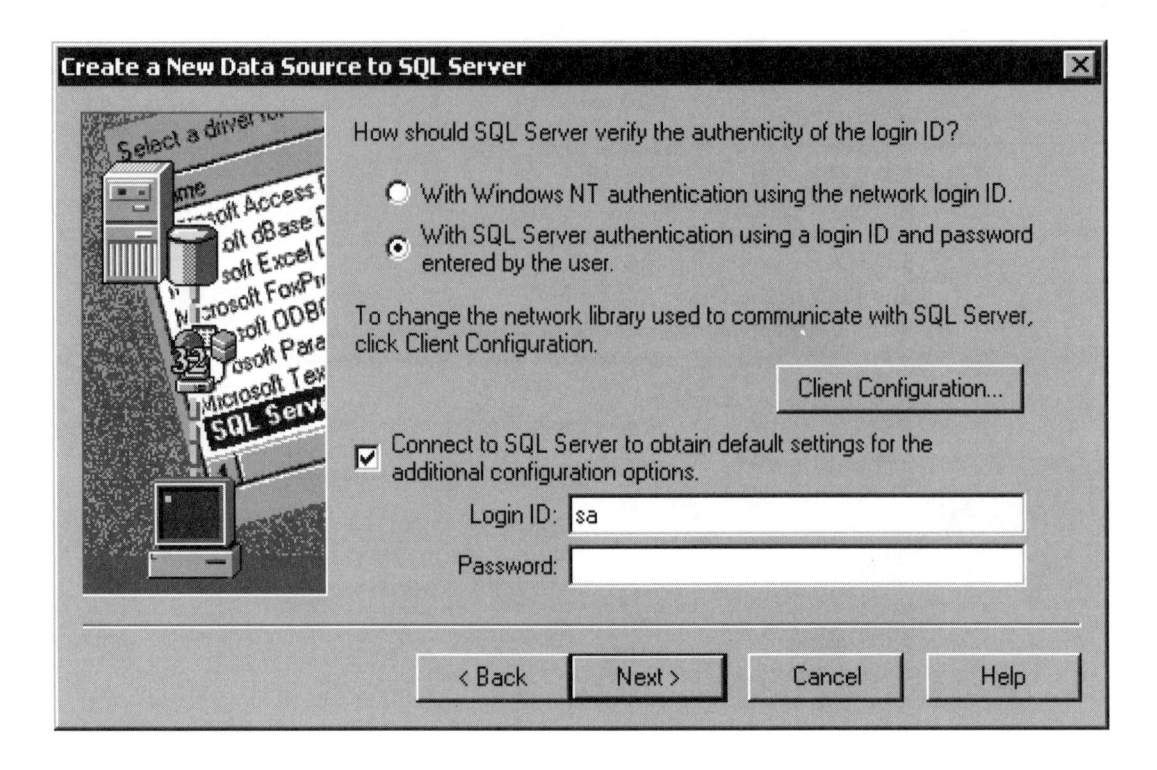

Figure 18-14 *We are using SQL Server authentication for simplicity*

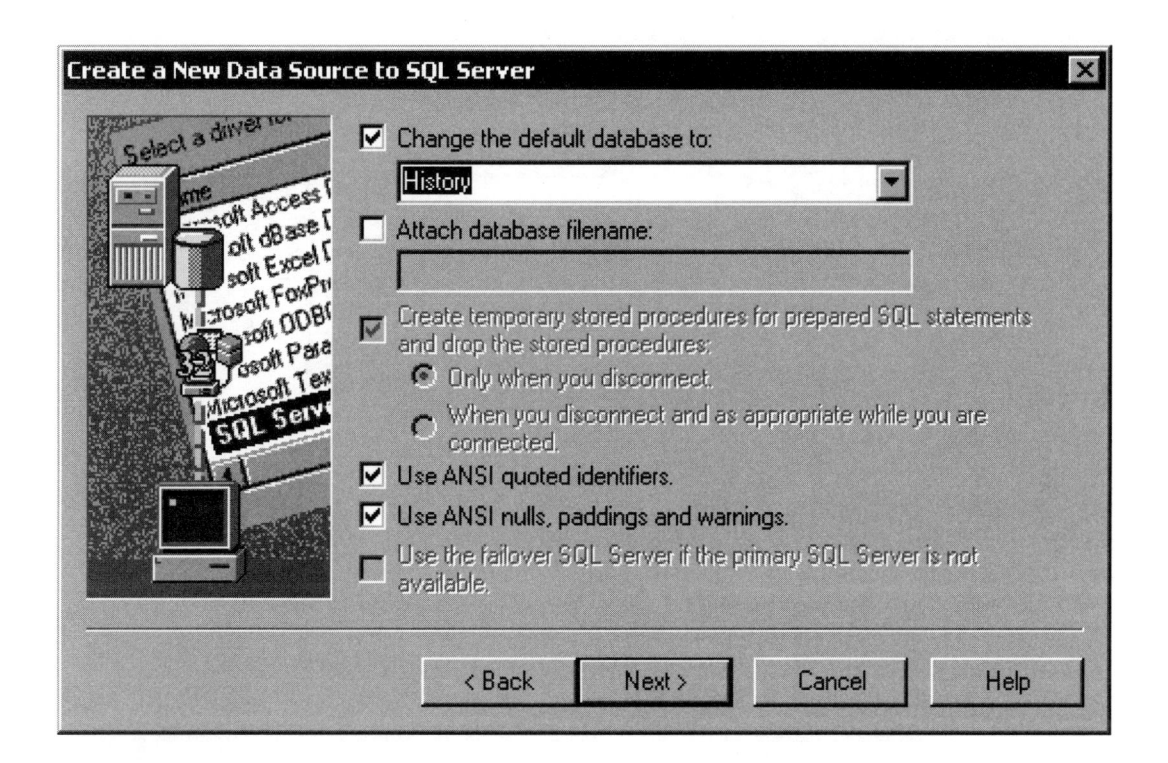

Figure 18–15 Choosing the History database for your new data source

An Administration Program for the History Database

Our example program is a simple GUI program to administer this small database. A user interface is provided that will allow you to find records, add or delete a record, update a record, and show all the records. The program is written in Visual Basic using ActiveX Data Objects. The program is located in **Chap18\HistoryAdminMonolithic**. This is a simple client/server program, the server being SQL Server. We will later restructure it to be a three-tier application.

Before examining the code and learning the rudiments of programming with ADO, it would be a good idea to run the program. This will also serve as a test that your database has been set up properly, and that you have a good DSN. Bring the program up in Visual Basic and run it. Assuming you previously inserted "carl" into the Players table, you should be able to find him now by clicking the "Find" button. See Figure 18–16.

You can now try out the various features of the program. Click the "Show Players" button to bring up a window showing the players in this his-

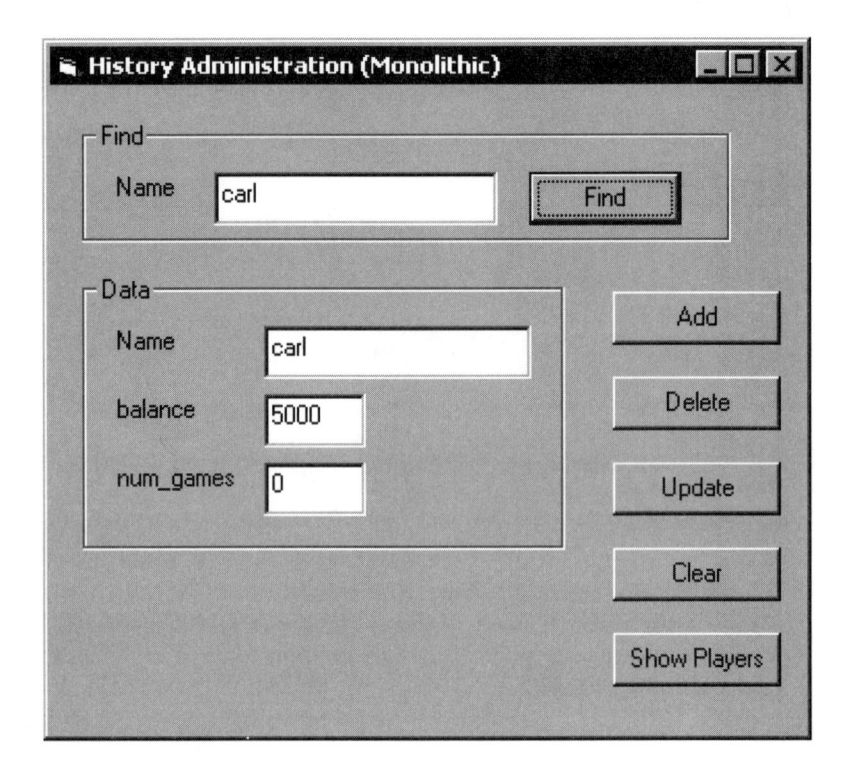

Figure 18-16 *Running administration program for History database*

tory file. Try adding a couple more players, deleting a player, updating information for a player. You can then show all the players again and verify that the operations have been performed correctly. Of course you can also examine the updated database using Query Analyzer.

Programming with ActiveX Data Objects

A popular high-level interface for database programming in current Microsoft technology is ActiveX Data Objects (ADO). It sits on top of OLE DB and thus connects to any database or other data source for which there is an OLE DB provider. ADO itself is an OLE DB consumer. In this section, we examine the ADO object model and then look at some programming examples which implement the History database administration program discussed in the previous section.

Our programming will be done in Visual Basic for simplicity. Be sure to add a reference to the Microsoft ActiveX Data Objects Library to your project. Choose the most recent version of the library. At the time of writing this book, the most recent version was 2.5.

ADO Object Model

ADO is structured as a family of COM classes ("objects") supporting dual interfaces. Thus ADO can be accessed through scripting languages as well as early-binding programming languages. This means that ADO can be used in Active Server Pages and hence works well in the middle tier of Web applications, providing the means of talking to the data tier, a topic we discuss in Chapter 20.

The classes in ADO are arranged in a hierarchy, as illustrated in Figure 18–17, which is somewhat simplified for clarity. Unlike previous hierarchies such as the one for DAO, this hierarchy is flatter, and also is not strict. Thus it is possible (and in fact quite common) in ADO to instantiate a lower-level object by itself, and the required higher-level object will be instantiated behind the scenes. The result is a programming model that is very easy to use.

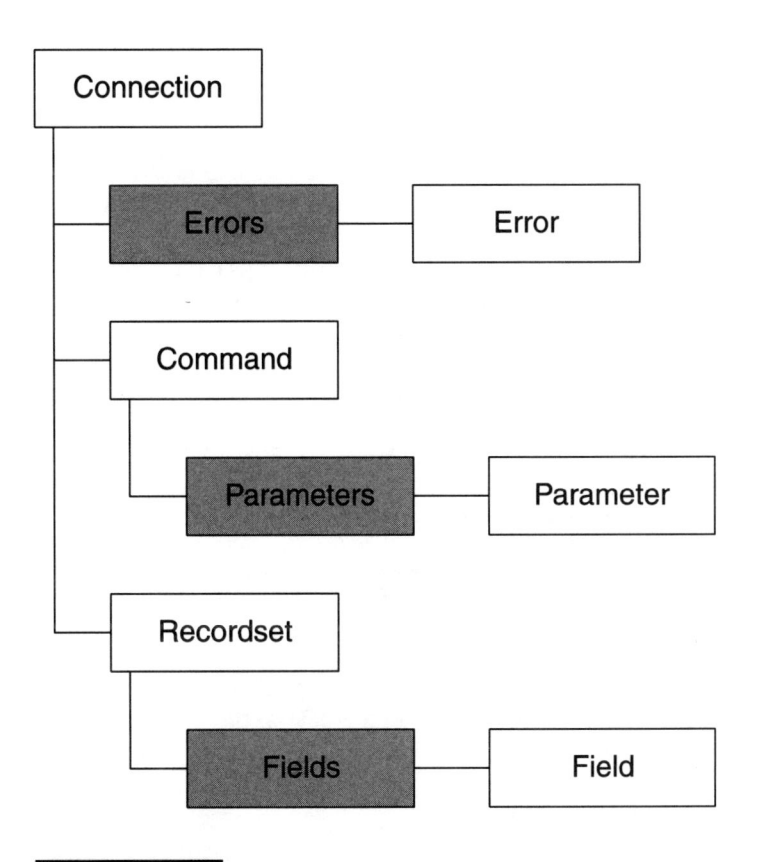

Figure 18-17 *Simplified ADO Object Model*

The object model contains both individual objects and collections of objects. In the diagram, collections are shown as shaded boxes.

Connection Object

In order to connect to a data source you need a connection object. Either you create one explicitly, or some other object will implicitly create one for your. The most important property of a connection object is **ConnectionString**, which is used by the underlying OLE DB provider to connect to the actual data source. One of the nice things about using ODBC is that there is a very simple connection string, such as "sysHistory" for our example. The connection string may be passed as the first parameter of the **Open** method.

ADO does connection pooling. This means that if you connect to a data source using a particular connection string, destroy the **Connection** object, and then later connect to the same data source using the exact same connection string, ADO may not have to reestablish an expensive database connection for you, but may be able to retrieve an already existing connection from a pool. This is one of the reasons we said in Chapter 17 that using impersonation is not a good security strategy when we want our application to scale. If multiple clients are each being impersonated by the server, each may connect to the database using a unique connection string which specifies a user id and password. Connection pooling is defeated. But if the middle-tier component runs under its own trusted account, all connections will have the same user id and password, and connection pooling can be used.

Once created, the **Connection** object may either be used directly by means of the **Execute** method or be passed to a **Recordset** object or a **Command** object.

The following code segment illustrates a simple use of the **Connection** object. It is used in the History Admin program to return information about all the Players in the game.

```
Public Function GetAll() As Recordset
  Dim conn As New Connection
  conn.Open "sysHistory"
  Set GetAll = conn.Execute("Players")
End Function
```

A connection object is created. The **Open** method is called, passing the connection string. Then the **Execute** method is called, passing the name of the table. This code will return all the data in the table, in the form of a recordset. The **Execute** method could also take a string representing any SQL statement.

Recordset Object

In ADO, as in other Microsoft database interfaces, a *recordset* is used for returning data from a database. A recordset may consist of multiple rows and multiple columns (fields). Thus a **Recordset** object contains a collection of **Field** objects. The collection is referred to as **Fields**. Sometimes you may want to refer to the **Fields** collection explicitly, such as interrogating a data source when you don't know the names of the fields. The **Fields** collection is also useful if you want to create your own recordset to store data, rather than populate a recordset with data from a database. But in many cases you don't need to explicitly work with the **Fields** collection. You can reference a particular field by using its name as a key. Thus if **rsHistory** is a recordset object, **rsHistory("balance")** can be used to refer to the "balance" field of the Players table.

A recordset may contain multiple rows, and you can navigate among these rows using methods like **MoveFirst** and **MoveNext**. When iterating through a recordset in this fashion, you are employing a database *cursor*, which is supplied by the underlying OLE DB provider.

As an example of iterating through a recordset and obtaining the data from individual fields, examine the following code which populates a list view with the data obtained from the Players table of the History database. Some of this code is concerned with using the list view control. The important database code is shown in bold.

```
Private Sub Form_Load()
   'Players table
   lvPlayer.ColumnHeaders.Add,,"Name", lvPlayer.Width * 0.4
   lvPlayer.ColumnHeaders.Add,,"Balance",lvPlayer.Width*0.3
   lvPlayer.ColumnHeaders.Add,,"Games", lvPlayer.Width* 0.3
   lvPlayer.View = lvwReport

   Dim objHistory As New dbHistory
   Dim rsHistory As New Recordset
   Set rsHistory = objHistory.GetAll
   Dim itmX As ListItem
   Do While Not rsHistory.EOF
      Set itmX = lvPlayer.ListItems.Add(, , _
           Trim(rsHistory("name")))
        itmX.SubItems(1) = CStr(rsHistory("balance"))
        itmX.SubItems(2) = CStr(rsHistory("num_games"))
      rsHistory.MoveNext
   Loop
   rsHistory.Close
End Sub
```

In this code example, the recordset was populated by the **GetAll** method of the **dbHistory** class, which we examined in the previous section. There, a recordset was populated by calling the **Execute** method of a **Connection** object.

SELECTING DATA FROM A TABLE

Another common way for a recordset to be populated is to explicitly instantiate a **Recordset** object and then call the **Open** method. The following code provides an illustration. Here, rather than obtaining all the data in the Players table, we are obtaining the players with a given name. (Since "name" is the primary key in the database, we will obtain either 0 or 1 row.)

```
Public Function GetByName(ByVal name As String, _
    ByRef balance As Currency, _
    ByRef num_games As Integer) As Boolean

  Dim strSQL As String
  Dim conn As New Connection
  Dim rsPlayers As New Recordset
  conn.Open "sysHistory"

  'Look for name in Players table
  strSQL = "SELECT * FROM Players WHERE name = " _
       & "'" & name & "'"
  rsPlayers.Open strSQL, conn, , adLockReadOnly, adCmdText

  'Check to see if name is found
  If rsPlayers.BOF Then
    GetByName = False
  Else
    balance = rsPlayers("balance")
    num_games = rsPlayers("num_games")
    GetByName = True
  End If
End Function
```

The last two examples illustrated use of the **BOF** and **EOF** properties. These **Boolean** values indicate whether the cursor for the recordset is just before the first or just after the last row. If you are iterating through a recordset and move beyond the last row, **EOF** becomes **True**. If a recordset is empty, both **BOF** and **EOF** are **True**.

UPDATING A RECORD

All the code examples presented so far illustrate only reading from the data source. There are some additional considerations when you are changing data in the data source. Our example code illustrates adding a record, deleting a record, and updating a record (changing one or more fields of an existing record).

Let's first look at updating a record. Our code example is very similar to the one we just looked at. We select the record with a particular name. But now in place of reading that record, we write to it. Here is the code. We show in bold the important parts that are different.

```
Public Function Update(ByVal name As String, _
    ByVal balance As Currency, _
    ByVal num_games As Integer) As Boolean

  Dim strSQL As String
  Dim conn As New Connection
  Dim rsPlayers As New Recordset
  conn.Open "sysHistory"

  'Look for name in Players table
  strSQL = "SELECT * FROM Players WHERE name = " _
      & "'" & name & "'"
  rsPlayers.Open strSQL,conn,, adLockOptimistic, adCmdText

  'Check to see if name is found
  If rsPlayers.BOF Then
    Update = False
  Else
    rsPlayers("balance") = balance
    rsPlayers("num_games") = num_games
    rsPlayers.Update
    Update = True
  End If
End Function
```

The first difference is in the way the recordset is opened. Before, the "locking" parameter was **adLockReadOnly**. We were only reading the data, and no lock was required. Now we are writing the data, and we must lock it to prevent inconsistencies. The two kinds of locks are "optimistic" and "pessimistic." The former keeps the lock open for the shortest period of time—only when you actually call the **Update** function to cause the change to be made in the database. "Pessimistic" locking sets the lock as soon as you start editing, and keeps the lock until you are done with **Update**. Normally you will get greater scalability with optimistic locking, but then for your code to be robust you must be prepared to deal with an error condition which ADO will raise if another client also modified the data.

The second difference is simply the direction of the assignment statements for individual fields. Here we are assigning data to the recordset.

The final difference is the call to the **Update** method. When you assign data to the recordset it is initially only stored in a buffer, not in the database itself. When you call **Update** you ask for the change to be made effective in the database itself.

An alternative to using a **Recordset** to update a record is to do the updating in straight SQL. Create a string for an SQL UPDATE statement, and pass that string to the **Execute** method of the **Connection** object. We illustrate this approach in the next chapter.

ADDING A RECORD

The **Recordset** class has an **AddNew** method, which you may use to add a new record to a recordset. Calling this method creates a buffer where the data for the new record is stored. The new record is added to the table in the database when you call **Update**. As with updating a record we need optimistic or pessimistic locking. The following code illustrates:

```
Public Sub Add(ByVal name As String, _
      ByVal balance As Currency, _
      ByVal num_games As Integer)

   Dim rsPlayers As New Recordset
     rsPlayers.Open "Players", "sysHistory", , _
       adLockOptimistic, adCmdTable
     rsPlayers.AddNew
     sPlayers("name") = name
     sPlayers("balance") = balance
     sPlayers("num_games") = num_games
     rsPlayers.Update
End Sub
```

As with updating a record, an alternative approach is to use straight SQL. Create a string with an SQL INSERT statement, and pass this string to the **Execute** method of the **Connection** object.

DELETING A RECORD

Finally, you can use a recordset to delete a record. Select the record you wish to delete and then call the **Delete** method. The delete takes effect in the database immediately—you do not need to subsequently call **Update**. The following code illustrates:

```
Public Function Delete(ByVal name As String) As Boolean
   Dim strSQL As String
   Dim conn As New Connection
   Dim rsPlayers As New Recordset
   conn.Open "sysHistory"

   'Look for name in Players table
   strSQL = "SELECT * FROM Players WHERE name = " _
         & "'" & name & "'"
   rsPlayers.Open strSQL, conn, , adLockOptimistic, _
         adCmdText

   'Check to see if name is found
   If rsPlayers.BOF Then
     Delete = False
```

```
    Else
        rsPlayers.Delete
        Delete = True
    End If
End Function
```

Once again an alternative approach is to use SQL directly via an SQL DELETE statement passed as a string to the **Connection** object's **Execute** method.

Errors Collection

Many kinds of errors can occur when working with ADO. Since ADO is layered on top of OLE DB, which in turn calls the database directly or goes through ODBC, errors can occur at many layers. In addition, if you are going across a network, you may get network errors. The standard COM HRESULT mechanism is totally inadequate to convey all the information you need. The extended error reporting interfaces provided by COM, which we discussed in Chapter 12, help but do not go far enough. You only get extended information about a single error.

In order to provide rich error information about multiple errors that can occur on a single call, ADO provides the **Errors** collection, which consists of **Error** objects, one object for each error. The collection has the **Count** property that provides a count of how many **Error** objects are in the collection. Then you can get detailed information from the individual **Error** objects through properties such as **Description**.

For an example, see the program **Chap18\Demos\PriceDemo** which illustrates doing a simple price lookup from the Products table of the Games database. This example uses the native OLE DB provider for SQL Server, which we discuss in the next section. It turns out that the connection string is very fussy, so it is hard to avoid getting an error the first time you try to create your own connection string. We have deliberately placed an error, and we have commented out a non-ADO error. An error-free version of the program can be found in **Chap18\PriceDemo**.

Before starting to iterate through the **Errors** collection, you should first check the **Count** property to make sure that the collection is not empty. You might have a non-ADO error. The sample code displays error(s) in a message box. If you are writing a middle-tier component you should of course not use message boxes but instead do some kind of error logging, as illustrated by our **Logger** component in Chapter 12, which we use in some of our examples in Part 3. Here is the code example.

Chapter 18 • SQL Server and ADO Survival Guide

```
Private Function FindPrice(ByVal server As String, _
    ByVal item As String) _
    As Currency

    On Error GoTo ErrorHandler
    Dim strSQL As String
    Dim rsProd As New Recordset
    Dim conn As New Connection
    strSQL = "SELECT * FROM Products WHERE item = " & "'" _
            & item & "'"
    'strSQL = 1 / 0
    conn.Provider = "SQLOLEDB"
    conn.ConnectionString = "Server=" & server & "; " _
            & "Database= Game;" _
            & "uid=sa;" _
            & "pwd=;"
    conn.Open
    rsProd.Open strSQL, conn, , adLockReadOnly, adCmdText

    'Check to see if item is found
    If rsProd.BOF Then
      FindPrice = -1
      Exit Function
    End If
    FindPrice = rsProd("price")
    Exit Function
ErrorHandler:
    Dim er As Error
    If conn.Errors.Count > 0 Then
      For Each er In conn.Errors
        MsgBox er.Description, , "ADO Error"
      Next er
    Else
      MsgBox Err.Description, , "Non-ADO error"
    End If
    FindPrice = -1
End Function
```

If you run the program as given in the **Chap18\Demos\PriceDemo** directory you will trip across an error in the connection string. Note the space between the = sign and "Game." This is an ADO error, and you should see the message box shown in Figure 18–18.

Figure 18-18 *An ADO error from the **Errors** collection*

Now uncomment the line

```
strSQL = 1/0
```

This will produce a non-ADO error. The error handler will be called, but the **Errors** collection will be empty. The result will be the message box shown in Figure 18–19.

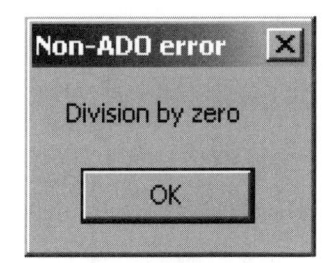

Figure 18-19 *The **Errors** collection is empty and you have a non-ADO error*

(If your message handler was not called when you ran the program from Visual Basic, check the "Error Trapping" option in Tools | Options, "General" tab. It should be either "Break in Class Module" or "Break on Unhandled Errors.")

Using Native SQL Server OLE DB Provider

Our last example illustrates using the native OLE DB provider of SQL Server. This is more efficient than using the ODBC provider. The **Connection** object has a property **Provider** which you use to specify the OLE DB Provider that ADO should use. The default is "MSDASQL," which is the ODBC provider. The native provider for SQL server is "SQLOLEDB." After you specify the **Provider** property, you should specify the **ConnectionString** property. You need to indicate four parts to the string, the **Server**, the **Database**, the **uid** (user ID) and **pwd** (password). A semicolon is used to terminate these parts, and there should be no embedded spaces. After the equal sign you should have the value given as a character string. If this value is blank, the semicolon should come immediately after the equal sign. As I said above, this syntax is fussy.

```
conn.Provider = "SQLOLEDB"
conn.ConnectionString = "Server=" & server & "; " _
                      & "Database=Game;" _
                      & "uid=sa;" _
                      & "pwd=;"
conn.Open
```

The string for "Server" can be left blank. Then it is assumed that the local server will be used. When you run the program you should be able to run the program using a blank for the server, using the name of your local server, or using the name of a remote server. See Figure 18–20 for an illustration of running the program, specifying a remote server. You should be able to look up the price of any item in the Products table of the Games database. You could practice changing data in the Products table of your remote database using Query Analyzer, and verify that you can lookup this new data.

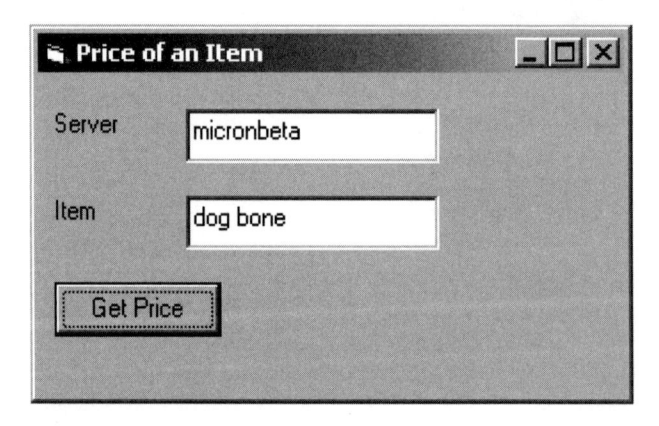

Figure 18–20 *Looking up a price on a remote server*

A Three-Tier COM+ Application

It is very easy to convert our "monolithic" application into a logical three-tier application. If you have three computers available, you can in fact deploy it on three separate computers. We will break apart our Visual Basic program

HistoryAdminMonolithic into a middle-tier server component **HistoryAdminServer** and a presentation-tier client program **HistoryAdminClient**. At this point, our application will be logically three tier, with the data tier being supplied by SQL Server.

We will then install the server into COM+ and create a client proxy. We can then run our program on two computers. The final step, if desired, is to reconfigure the ODBC data source to be a remote computer. Note that this last step is purely for didactic reasons. In practice, it is often desirable for the database to run on the same machine as the middle-tier server (to avoid another network hop).

Creating the Middle-Tier Server

The finished server code is in **Chap18\HistoryAdminServer**. If you wish to implement your own server as a demo, do your work in **Chap18\Demos\HistoryAdminServer**. All you have to do is create a new ActiveX DLL project, copy in the file **dbHistory.cls**, change its instancing property to "MultiUse," and add a reference to ActiveX Data Objects library. After you have built your DLL once, you will want to change the version compatibility to binary. That's it. This was easy, because we anticipated breaking up our monolithic applications and programmed our data access in a separate class module.

Creating the Presentation-Tier Client

The finished client code is in **Chap18\HistoryAdminClient**. If you wish to implement your own client as a demo, do your work in **Chap18\Demos\HistoryAdminClient**. All you have to do is create a new standard EXE file, copy in the files **Form1.frm** and **frmHistory.frm**, and add references to your own "HistoryAdminServer" and to Microsoft ActiveX Data Objects.

DISCONNECTED RECORDSETS

You may think that if you encapsulate your database access you should create your own collection to pass data to the client. This adds unnecessary processing to your program. The ADO **Recordset** class is designed so that it can operate in "disconnected" mode. Our example program illustrates this usage. The server's **GetAll** method returns a recordset. The recordset on the server side is created as a local variable. When the method returns, this recordset object will be closed and destroyed. A copy will be passed to the client. This new recordset is no longer connected to the database and cannot be used to update the database. But it is perfect for passing structured data to the client.

At this point, you should be able to run **HistoryAdminClient**. The behavior will be the same as your old monolithic program, but you now have three logical tiers.

Using COM+ to Create a Remote Proxy

You can import your component into COM+ and then export a remote proxy. You should know the drill now, so we will go over it very briefly. Use COM+ Explorer to create an empty application "HistoryAdminApp." Install your ActiveX DLL into this new application. You could try running the client, and it should work, and you may be able to see the ball spin. Next use the "Export" feature of COM+ to create a **.msi** file for an application proxy. Copy this **.msi** file to your remote Windows 2000 machine and double-click on it to install it. Then copy the client **.exe** file. You should now be able to run the remote client.

Running the Data Tier Remotely

Finally, it is easy to perform the data access from a third computer. On the machine where the middle tier is deployed you will just have to reconfigure your ODBC connection. Make sure that your have the History database set up on a remote machine running SQL Server. Now bring up the ODBC Administrator program. Choose the "System DSN" tab and select your DSN "sysHistory." Click the "Configure" button. On the first screen that comes up, select the remote server you want from the dropdown for "What SQL Server do you want to connect to?" See Figure 18–21.

The ODBC provider is very convenient for this administrative reconfiguration. If we had used the native OLE DB we would have had to do some more programming. To avoid hardcoding the name of the server we would need to provide some way at run time to get the name of the database server machine into the middle-tier server component. One approach in COM+ would be to create an object construction string. This could be initialized using COM+ Explorer. See Chapter 15 for a discussion and an example of using an object construction string.

Electronic Commerce Game Case Study

Now might be a good time for you to complete setting up the Electronic Commerce Game. We have mentioned the game several times, and will use it and related programs extensively in the remainder of this book. We used a stub version in Chapter 17 to illustrate security. We used the History database and the Products table from the Game database in this chapter. There is a complete, self-contained description of this case study in Appendix B, so we won't try to give any more general explanation here.

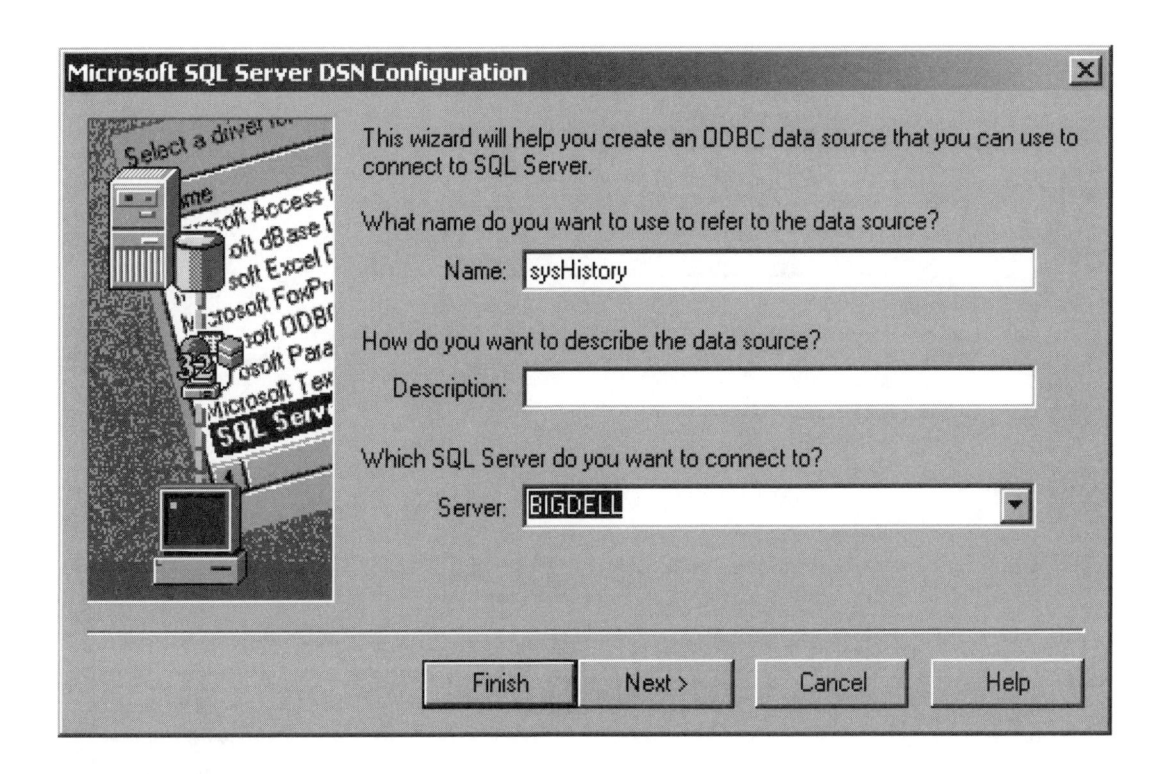

Figure 18-21 *Connecting to a remote server for data access*

What we will point out here is that you need to set up several more ODBC data sources in order to play the game. First we need data sources for the three vendor databases. Create system DSN's of "toyland.com," "petworld.com," and "foodstore.com" for the databases Toyland, Petworld, and Foodstore, respectively.

All the needed files for the case study are in the folder **CaseStudy**.

File DSN

The code that accesses the Game database illustrates a file DSN. A file DSN stores configuration information in a text file. The result is easier configuration at the expense of some run-time performance. We provide a file DSN **game.dsn** in **CaseStudy\SqlScripts.** Copy this file to the folder provided for ODBC data sources. On my machine, this folder was **Program Files\Common Files\ODBC\Data Sources** in the partition where Windows 2000 is installed. Now bring up the ODBC Data Source Administrator and choose the "File DSN" tab. You should see that there is now installed a DSN **game.dsn**. See Figure 18–22.

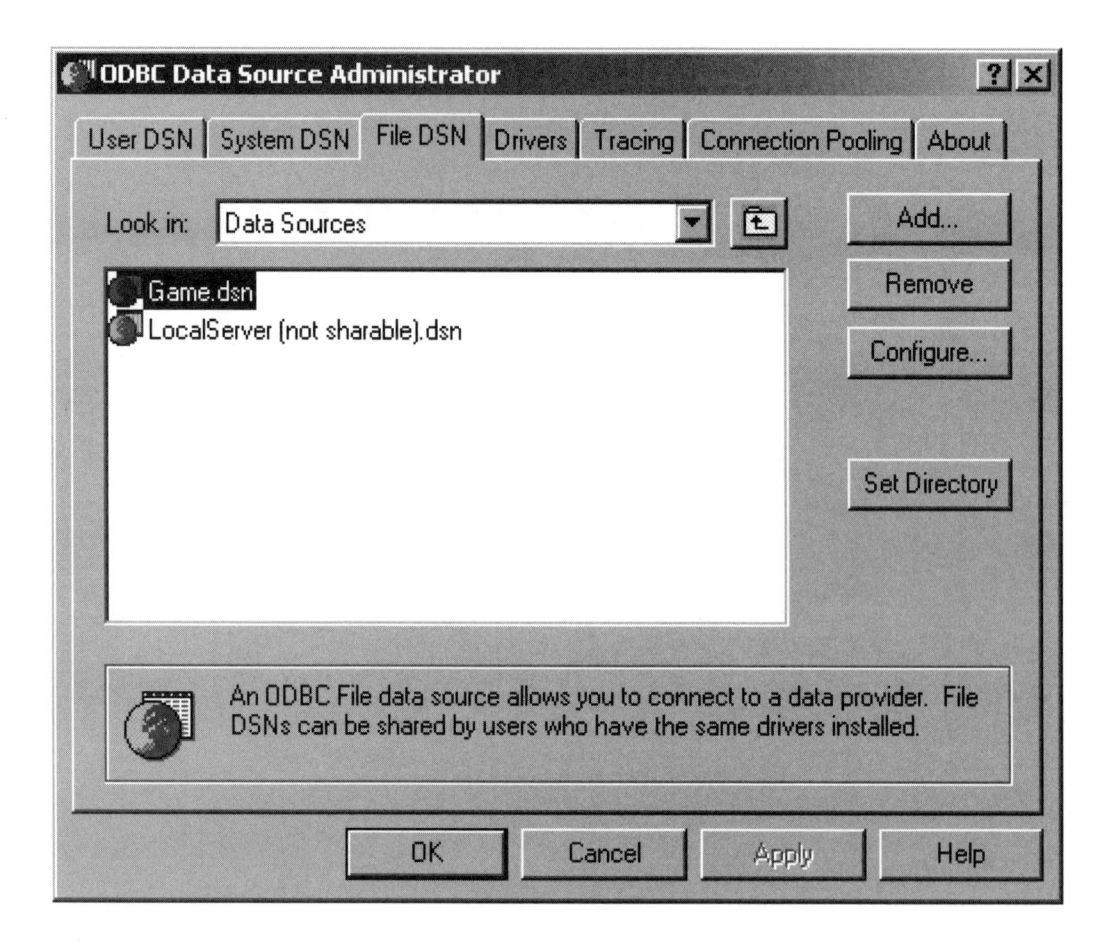

Figure 18-22 *The Game database is accessed through a file DSN*

To use a File DSN in your code you need to use a string like "FILEDSN=Game.DSN" for the connection string. The file **VendorList.cls** in **CaseStudy\Monolithic** illustrates.

```
Const fileDSN = "Game.DSN"

Public Function GetVendors() As Recordset
  Dim connGame As New Connection
  connGame.Open "FILEDSN=" & fileDSN
  Set GetVendors = connGame.Execute("Vendors")
End Function
```

Playing the Game

You can now verify that you have set up your databases and ODBC data sources correctly by playing the game. For now use the monolithic version of the game from the executable file **ClientBrowser.exe** in the folder **Case-Study\Monolithic**. If you have trouble running the EXE file, open up the project in Visual Basic, make sure the references resolve correctly on your system (for instance, proper version of ADO library, etc.).

Refer to Appendix B for a description of the game. Enjoy!

Summary

This chapter covered a lot of ground, because databases are very important. Even if you have not done any database programming before, you should find that the Microsoft tools make it fairly easy to get started. Naturally, depending on your experience, you may wish to do some more reading on SQL Server and on ADO. The purpose of this chapter was to get you up and running with the essentials you will need for using databases in the next two chapters.

We put so much stress on databases both because of their practical importance and because you need a database to illustrate transactions, one of the most important of all the COM+ services, which we will cover in the next chapter.

NINETEEN

Transactions in COM+

In this chapter, we cover the very important topic of transaction processing, and we see how COM+ greatly simplifies programming applications with transactional requirements. We begin with an overview of the principles of transaction processing, including the topic of distributed transactions. We then look at Microsoft's technology for implementing transactions, including OLE Transactions and Microsoft Distributed Transaction Coordinator (MS DTC). Then we describe how COM+ transparently uses OLE Transactions and MS DTC on behalf of an applications program. Transactions in COM+ provide an excellent illustration of how the concepts of context and interception are applied to solve a very important programming problem. The last section of the chapter presents a code example of transaction processing using COM+. We illustrate how to implement a distributed transaction that involves two SQL Server databases residing on different computers.

Principles of Transaction Processing

Transactions can be viewed as the key unifying principle in building robust distributed applications. They provide both a means of modularizing complex processing into simple logical units of work and a mechanism for ensuring correct operation of the overall system in the face of inevitable failures of individual components. Before delving into the details of Microsoft's technology for transaction processing, including especially COM+, it will help our overall understanding if we first look at the general principles. We describe the general characteristics of transactions, which can be applied to operations within a single database. Then we will examine distributed transaction processing.

Transactions

A transaction can be thought of as a unit of work. Transactions must satisfy four fundamental requirements, which have come to be known as the ACID properties.

- **Atomic**. A transaction is all or nothing. For example, a transfer transaction that combines a debit from one account and a credit to another account must not fail in the middle and leave the first account debited with no credit in the other account.

- **Consistent**. A transaction must not violate any integrity constraints of the state that is being managed. Databases are typically designed with various consistency requirements, and a transaction must respect them.

- **Isolated**. Concurrent transactions must not expose any of their internal state to each other. The system must operate as if first one transaction ran to completion before the other began. Thus transactions can be viewed as a high-level synchronization mechanism.

- **Durable**. Once a transaction has completed, any state modifications it made become permanent. If the system subsequently fails, upon recovery the state will reflect the results of the transaction.

In this chapter, we use a simple thematic example throughout, for which we provide code at the end. Our sample transaction is moving a database record from a table in an active database to a table in an archival "history" database. We definitely don't want only half of the operation to succeed, such as the record being deleted from one database without being added to the other. The operation must keep both databases consistent. For example, we would not want to allow deletion of a record that is referred to by another record, violating referential integrity. If there are concurrent move operations, we want them to be isolated from each other. And of course we require that the result of a move operation be permanent once it has been completed—both databases permanently go into a new state, one having one fewer record and the other one more.

Modern database systems normally provide a transaction mechanism within the database. You can group a series of operations together into a transaction. If all operations succeed, the transaction is *committed* and the changes become permanent. If any operation fails, the transaction is *aborted*, and the database reverts to its original state.

Principles of Transaction Processing 451

Distributed Transaction Processing

A more challenging problem in transaction processing is to deal with *distributed* transactions, in which operations within the transaction are applied to different data stores, which may be of different types and may reside on different computers. A complex operation might update two different databases on a LAN, send an e-mail message, and post a message to a queuing system for delivery to a remote application. One database might be SQL Server, another Oracle, the e-mail system might be Microsoft Exchange, and the queuing system MSMQ. Each of these data stores may individually be able to deal with transactions, but they have different APIs and protocols. How do we make them all cooperate and participate in a single distributed transaction?

The X/Open standards group introduced in 1991 the Distributed Transaction Processing (DTP) model and two standard interfaces. This model has been widely adopted, and the same conceptual model, although not the protocols, is used by Microsoft. So let us begin our study of distributed transaction processing by examining the DTP model

X/OPEN DTP MODEL

In the generic DTP model, applications talk to a *transaction manager* to coordinate transactions. Transactions are created by the transaction manager, and requests from the application to commit or abort the transaction are directed to the transaction manager. The data stores used by the application are each controlled by their own *resource manager*, which guarantees the ACID properties, commits changes to the data store, rolls back in case of failure, etc. The application communicates with the resource manager to request operations be done to the data store. The transaction manager talks to the resource manager to coordinate transactions affecting the data store managed by that resource manager. If there are multiple computers, each computer has its own transaction manager and one or more resource managers. The local transaction manager talks to the remote transaction managers to coordinate transactions affecting resources on the remote computers. The overall DTP architecture is illustrated in Figure 19–1, which has been simplified to show two resource managers on one computer.

X/Open defines two protocols as part of its DTP model. The first is **TX**, which provides a standard API for applications to use to talk to a transaction manager. The second is **XA**, which is a standard API for transaction managers to talk to resource managers. Every X/Open compliant transaction manager must support both TX and XA, and compliant resource managers must support XA.

To understand the operation of distributed transactions in this model, let's walk through the steps that occur when an application wishes to perform a transaction which involves an operation on each of the two resource managers:

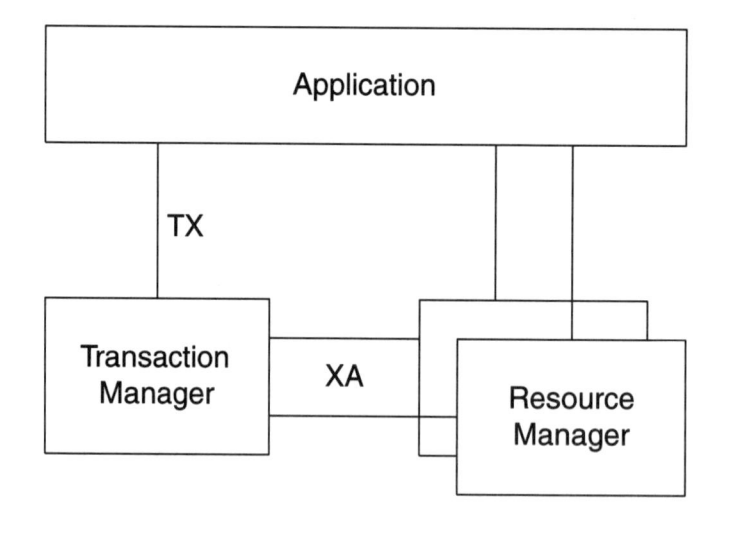

Figure 19-1 *X/Open model for Distributed Transaction Processing*

1. The application calls the transaction manager to create a transaction, getting back a reference to the new transaction.
2. The application calls each resource manager to do its piece of work. It passes the transaction reference.
3. Each resource manager calls the transaction manager to enlist in the transaction. The transaction manager now knows of all the resource managers with which it must coordinate when it comes time to commit the transaction.
4. Each resource manager does the work requested of it by the application and returns a success code back to the application. The resource manager may store the new state in a buffer, and will only update its data store if told to commit. As part of its operation, the resource manager will acquire locks to ensure isolation.
5. The application calls the transaction manager to commit or abort the transaction.

TWO-PHASE COMMIT

If the application calls for the transaction to be aborted, the transaction manager informs each resource manager that the transaction is to be aborted. The resource manager can discard any buffer of results not yet written to the data store and release any locks.

If the application calls for the transaction to be committed, the transaction manager initiates the two-phase commit, which brings about the following steps:

1. (Prepare phase) The transaction manager calls each resource manager that enlisted in the transaction and tells it to prepare to commit.
2. Each resource manager will vote yes or no. If it votes yes, it will write its result data to durable storage. This resource manager is now committed to carry out its part of the transaction, if requested, no matter what subsequent failures might occur. It has entered into a binding contract.
3. (Commit phase) If any resource manager voted no, the transaction is to be aborted, and the transaction manager will so notify the resource managers. They can then discard their changes and release their locks. If all the votes are yes, the transaction manager notifies the resource managers to commit the changes.
4. Each resource manager now writes its changes to the permanent data store. Its part of the transaction has now been carried out.

This protocol is robust with respect to failures of various kinds. Suppose, for example, that a resource manager goes down after voting to commit but before it receives the final commit order from the transaction manager. Since its results were written to durable storage, they will be there when the resource manager recovers. It then contacts the transaction manager for the results of the transaction and finishes up appropriately.

In the distributed case where there are multiple machines, each machine will have its own transaction manager. One transaction manager will be in charge of the overall transaction, and it will communicate with the resource managers on the remote machines through the other transaction managers, which act as intermediaries.

Microsoft Transactions Technology

Microsoft has supported transactions all along within its SQL Server database management system. With SQL Server 6.5, Microsoft introduced distributed transactions through a new NT service called Microsoft Distributed Transaction Coordinator (MS DTC), which plays the role of a transaction manager in the DTP model. Important data access products like SQL Server and MSMQ act as resource managers. Instead of implementing the TX and XA protocols, Microsoft introduced an object-oriented set of transaction interfaces called OLE Transactions, built upon COM. These interfaces fit much better into Microsoft's own system infrastructure based on COM. Interoperability with transaction processing systems adhering to the DTP standard is achieved through a mapping component.

The next step in the evolution of Microsoft's transaction processing technology was Microsoft Transaction Server (MTS), which extended COM to provide a very easy way for COM components to participate in transactions by simply "declaring" transactional requirements. MTS is now superseded by COM+. We will discuss in detail COM+ transaction processing in the following section. In this section we describe the underlying transaction services employed by COM+, namely OLE Transactions and MS DTC.

OLE Transactions

OLE Transactions are Microsoft's standard interfaces for communicating with transaction managers and resource managers. In the Microsoft transaction processing model, they fill the roles of the TX and XA interfaces in the DTP model. Microsoft chose to introduce its own interfaces for a number of reasons:

- Microsoft needed a COM-based standard in order to implement the higher-level, declarative-based transaction processing that was ultimately implemented in MTS and culminated in COM+.
- OLE Transactions are inherently more extensible than DTP, and in particular can be extended to a very wide variety of transaction-protected resources.
- OLE Transactions have some multithreading advantages over DTP.

Although OLE Transaction interfaces look like COM interfaces, they are somewhat different. Objects are created by special API functions or method calls and not by the standard **CoCreateInstanceEx** and related functions. OLE Transaction interfaces are designed to be always called within the same process, and there is no marshaling support. They are inherently free threaded, with no automatic apartment-based synchronization support. OLE Transactions are very much an underlying systems technology, and normally you will not need to work with them directly from your applications programs.

Microsoft Distributed Transaction Coordinator (MS DTC)

MS DTC provides the role of a transaction manager in Microsoft systems. From a high-level architecture perspective, Microsoft's distributed transaction processing model is identical to that of X/Open DTP. Thus, MS DTC is based upon a proven industry-standard model. To get a somewhat more concrete idea of how MS DTC works, let's look at a concrete example. Our application does a transaction that involves resources on two different computers. The resources are managed by resource managers RM1 and RM2 on these machines. Each machine has its own DTC, DTC1, and DTC2. Figure 19–2 illustrates.

This diagram is conceptually the same as Figure 19–1. Now we have a specific transaction manager, namely MS DTC. The resource managers reside on separate computers, and each resource manager communicates with its own local DTC. We will assume that DTC1 is the coordinating DTC. Let's walk through the steps of the application, invoking a transaction that updates resources controlled by the two resource managers on the two different machines. The general logic is the same as for the example we illustrated in the previous section for DTP, but now we will show a few more details for the specific case of using MS DTC and OLE Transactions.

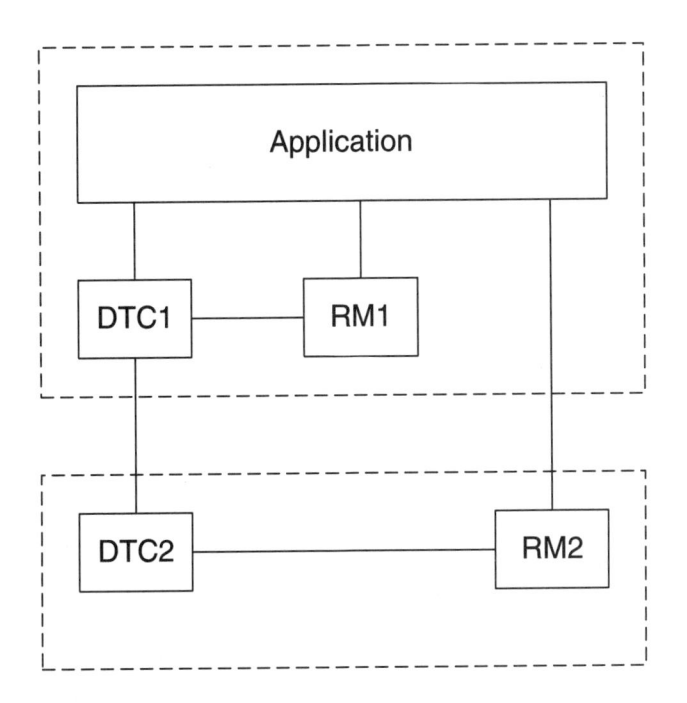

Microsoft Transactions Technology

Figure 19-2 *MS DTC coordinates a transaction across two computers*

1. The application connects to DTC1 by calling **DllGetTransactionManager**, getting back an interface pointer to **ITransactionDispenser**.
2. The application calls the **BeginTransaction** method through this interface, obtaining an **ITransaction** interface pointer.
3. The application connects to the resource managers, passing the **ITransaction** interface pointer.
4. The resource managers enlist in the transaction by calling the **Enlist** method of the **IResourceManager** interface, implemented by an object in the DTC.
5. The application calls the resource managers to do their work (for instance, issuing SQL statements to SQL Server, typically through ADO).
6. The resource managers do the work requested, storing the results in memory, and reporting success or failure back to the application.
7. The application calls DTC1 to commit or abort the application. It uses the **Commit** or **Abort** method of **ITransaction**.

Now DTC1 will initiate the two-phase commit protocol, using exactly the same logic as outlined in the previous section. DTC1 talks to RM1 directly, and it talks to RM2 through DTC2.

INTEROPERABILITY WITH XA

There are two ways in which MS DTC can work with resource managers to coordinate distributed transactions. It can use OLE Transactions for any resource manager that implements the OLE Transaction interfaces. It can also interoperate with resource managers that support the X/Open XA protocol through an XA Mapper component that translates between XA and OLE Transactions. Through this mapping, MS DTC can coordinate transactions that span both OLE Transactions and XA-compliant resource managers. Likewise, resource managers compliant with OLE Transactions, such as SQL Server can participate in transactions managed by a DTP-compliant transaction manager.

Automatic Transaction Processing Using COM+

COM+ effectively encapsulates this whole transaction processing model that we have been describing. The key to making it all work is using a three-tier architecture. The client application does not update resources directly but goes through a middle-tier component. This component can be configured through COM+ to have transactional attributes. Then at run time, through the standard COM+ interception model, COM+ can set up a distributed transaction on the component's behalf, a feature known as *automatic transactions*. In this section, we describe in detail how automatic transactions work, and in the following section present a programming example.

Transactional Components

A *transactional component* is one that has been imported into a COM+ application and been configured to support or require transactions through a transactional attribute. The transactional attribute can be used by COM+ in determining the context in which the component runs. As with COM+ components in general, a transactional component can share its caller's context, or it can be in a context of its own. One of the items stored in the context object is a *transaction identifier*, a GUID that uniquely identifies a transaction in which an object is participating.

If an object instance is participating in a transaction (or "running in a transaction"), resources touched by that object will be protected by the transaction. This means that changes made to the resource will not be made permanent until the transaction is committed, which may require the affirmative votes of multiple resource managers, as we have seen in the previous sections.

There are the following five choices for the transaction attribute:

- **Transactions disabled**. COM+ will ignore the transaction attribute in determining the context for a new object instance. This is the same behavior an unconfigured component would have.

- **Transactions not supported**. The component will never participate in a transaction. This is the default value of the transaction attribute.
- **Supports a transaction**. The component will run in its client's transaction. If the client is not running in a transaction, the component will not run in one either.
- **Requires a transaction**. The component will always run in a transaction. If the client is running in a transaction, the component will run in the same transaction. If the client is not running in a transaction, a new transaction will be created for the component.
- **Requires a new transaction**. The component will always run in a transaction of its own, especially created for it.

You can set the value of the transaction attribute from COM+ Explorer. See Figure 19–3.

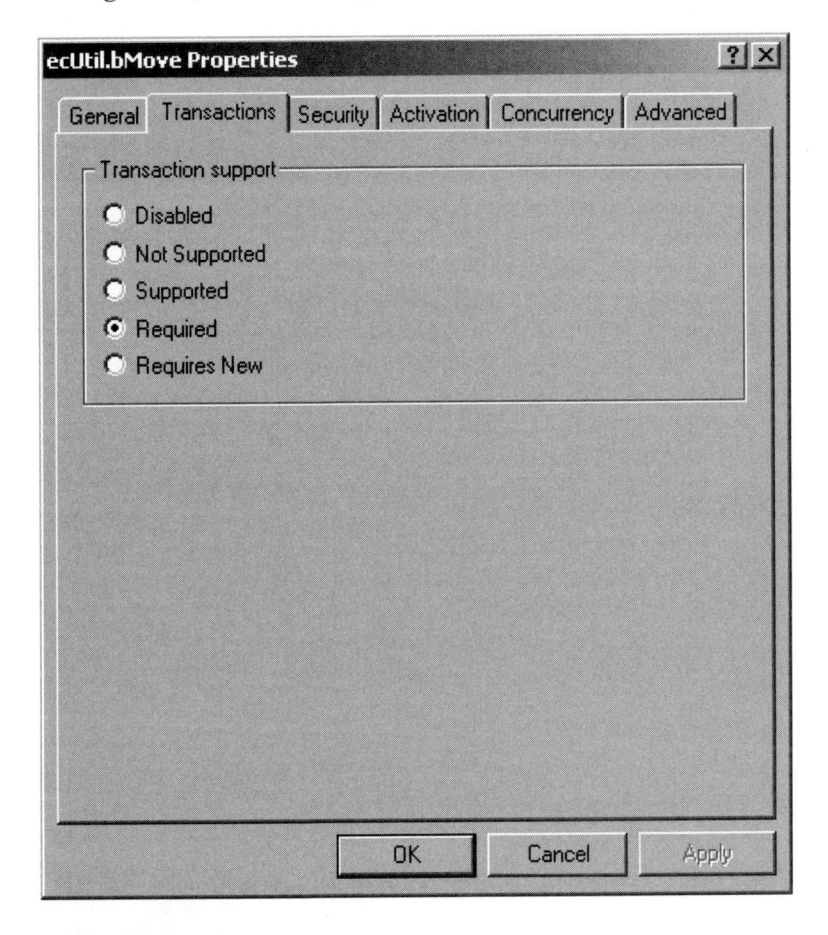

Figure 19-3 *Specifying the transaction attribute for a component*

DEPENDENT ATTRIBUTES

If you choose any of the last three values for the transaction attribute (specifying that a transaction may be used), some other attributes of the component are automatically selected. Just-in-time (JIT) activation is automatically enabled. This means that the object's lifetime will be governed by the "done" bit, and the object will be deactivated when **SetComplete** or **SetAbort** is called. This behavior goes along with ensuring the atomic behavior of a transaction. The Synchronization support attribute is set to "required," ensuring that COM+ will provide automatic serialization in accessing the object. This behavior goes along with the isolation requirement of a transaction. We discussed JIT in Chapter 14 and concurrency in Chapter 16. COM+ Explorer reflects the automatic setting of these dependent attributes by graying out the options to change them, as you can easily verify for yourself.

INTERIOR OBJECTS AND TRANSACTION BOUNDARIES

In COM+, you frequently decompose the overall processing required for a transaction that touches several resources into steps that are implemented by additional components, one for each resource. The top-level object, responsible for the transaction as a whole, is called the *root* object. Auxiliary objects created to carry out operations on individual resources are called *interior* objects. Figure 19-4 illustrates the run-time hierarchy of a root object "Move" that is responsible for the transaction of moving a record from the Players table of the Game database to the History database. It delegates its work to two interior objects "Delete Player" and "Add History." Informally, we might also say that Move is the "parent" of Delete Player and Add History.

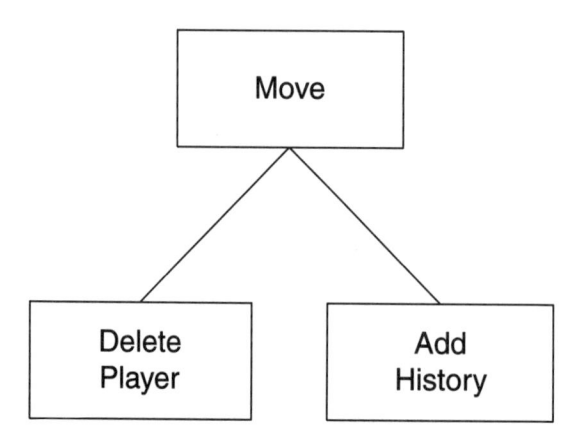

Figure 19-4 *Run-time hierarchy for "move" transaction*

The root object starts a new transaction and obtains a transaction identifier, which is stored in its context. This transaction identifier delineates the *transaction boundary*. The interior objects will have the same transaction identifier and are part of the same transaction.

CONSISTENCY AND DONE BITS

A transactional component has JIT enabled, and thus will pay attention to the done bit. When a method is called, the object is JIT activated. The done bit starts at false. When the method completes, it should set the done bit to true, which it can do by either calling **SetComplete** or **SetAbort**. The object will then be deactivated.

A transactional component will also pay attention to a consistency bit to determine how it will vote on committing a transaction. If the consistency bit is true, the vote will be to commit the transaction, and if it is false, the vote will be to abort the transaction.

The interface **IObjectContext** has the methods **SetComplete** and **SetAbort**, which affect both the done and consistency bits. Both methods set the done bit to true. **SetComplete** sets the consistency bit to true, and **SetAbort** sets it to false. The done and consistency bits can be set separately through the **IContextState** interface.

TRANSACTION FLAG ("DOOMED" BIT)

The transaction as a whole has a transaction flag, sometimes called the "doomed" bit. When the transaction is created, this flag is set to false, indicating that the transaction can potentially commit—it is not doomed. Whenever an object within the transaction boundary calls **SetAbort**, or in combination sets the done bit to true and the consistency bit to false, the doomed bit is set to true. This means that there is no way this transaction can ever commit. Hence when the root object is finished, COM+ will tell the DTC to abort the transaction.

Life Cycle of an Automatic Transaction

We have now described all the pieces of how COM+ deals with transactions, and we have a general understanding of how the underlying distributed transaction processing mechanism works. Let's try to tie these pieces together by tracing an example transaction.

The transaction is to move a record from the Players table of the Game database on one machine to the History database on another machine. Both databases are controlled by SQL Server as the resource manager, and MS DTC operates as the transaction manager. We will implement the transaction using COM+ components. The root component is "Move," which does its work by delegating to "Delete Player" and "Add History." We assume the delete operation fails and the add operation succeeds. If we were not operating under a transaction, we would get a record added to the History database without a corresponding deletion. Let's see how COM+ and the underlying mechanisms work together to bring about a correct result (which in this case is to abort the whole transaction). The transaction attributes are:

- "Move" requires a transaction.
- "Delete Player" supports transactions.
- "Add History" supports transactions.

Our example follows the same logic as is implemented in code in the next section, and is rather simplified. Only the root object in the example calls **SetComplete** or **SetAbort**. It should be a reasonable mental extension to visualize the interior objects doing voting on their own. The following steps are simplified, but should convey the essence of the processing that takes place.

1. The client calls "Move." This involves a cross-context call (because "Move" requires a transaction), so a COM+ interceptor is invoked.
2. The interceptor calls the DTC to obtain a new transaction. The transaction identifier is stored in the context of the root object "Move."
3. "Move" creates the interior objects "Delete Player" and "Add History." They run under the same transaction, and the transaction identifier is passed to their contexts.
4. Move calls the interior objects.
5. The interior objects call SQL Server through ADO.
6. Each SQL Server enlists in the transaction by calling the DTC on its machine.
7. "Delete Player" fails and there is no updating to its SQL Server.
8. "Add History" succeeds. Because there is a transaction, the result is not written to the database itself but only to a buffer, from where the change can be made permanent if the overall transaction is committed.
9. "Move" receives these notices of results and knows it has to abort the transaction. It calls **SetAbort**. The done bit is set to true and the consistency bit to false. Move now exits. The interior objects, which had been created as local variables, are now destroyed.
10. On the way back to the client, since it crosses a context boundary, control passes back to the interceptor.
11. The interceptor notices the consistency bit is false, and it calls the DTC to abort the transaction.
12. The DTC calls the local SQL Server to abort the transaction.
13. The DTC calls the remote DTC to notify its resource managers to abort the transaction.
14. The remote DTC calls its SQL Server to abort the transaction.
15. The interceptor returns to the client. No change has been made to either database.

Programming Transactions in COM+

We can now provide the code for the example we have just discussed and demonstrate how to set it up in the COM+ environment. After all our discussion, the code itself may seem anticlimactic. The implementation of mainstream transaction processing, even in the distributed case, is truly easy in COM+. That is the whole point. Our example also provides further examples of the type of database programming using ADO that we discussed in Chapter 18.

Player Administration Program

Our example program is a database administration program for the Players table of the Game database, which is part of our Electronic Commerce Game™ case study. The program allows you to find a player, add a player, delete a player, update information about a player, and to show the players. The program also allows you to add a player to the History database, and to show the players in the History database. Finally, you can move a player from the Game database to the History database. Figure 19–5 illustrates.

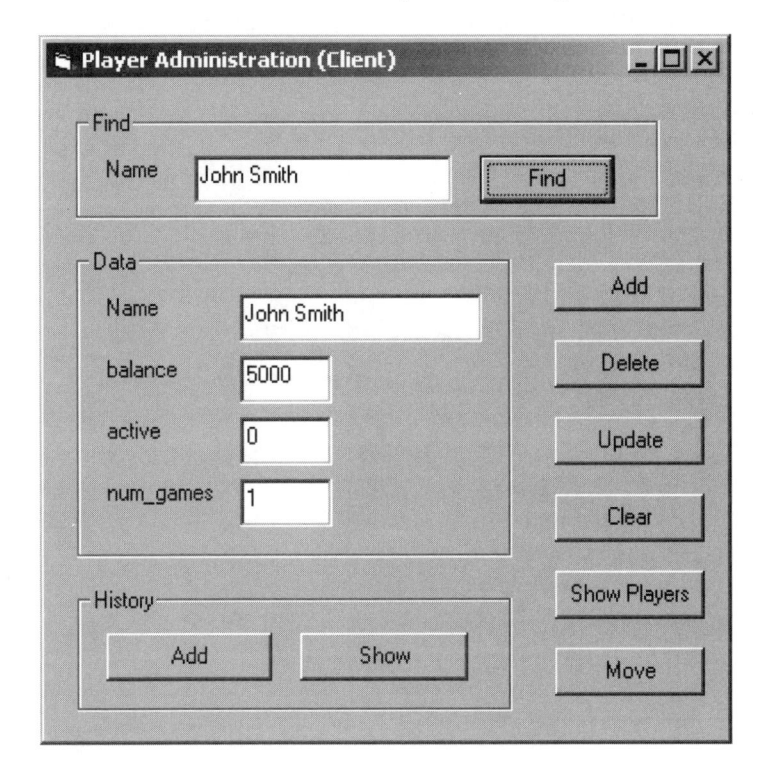

Figure 19–5 *Player administration program*

The "Move" command provides our transaction example. The way it works is to try to delete the record shown in the "Data" area from Game database and add it to the History database. Note that the record is identified by the "Name" field in the "Data" area, and so in fact there may not be any corresponding record in the Players field of the Game database—it may just be data that you typed in. In this case, "Delete Player" will fail. But if you have legal data in the fields, "Add History" will succeed. Thus we can easily simulate the scenario that we traced at the end of the preceding section.

If you would like to experiment with this program before building and installing the server in COM+, you can run a "monolithic" version of the program that is available in **Chap19\PlayerAdminMonolithic**. This version of the program is not transactional.

Middle-Tier Components

There are three components corresponding to the root object and the two interior objects. They are provided in the project in **Chap19\edUtil**—utilities for the Electronic Commerce Game. Create a new empty COM+ application called "ecUtilities" and then install the components implemented by **ecUtil.dll**. You should now see three components installed in the new application, as shown in Figure 19-6.

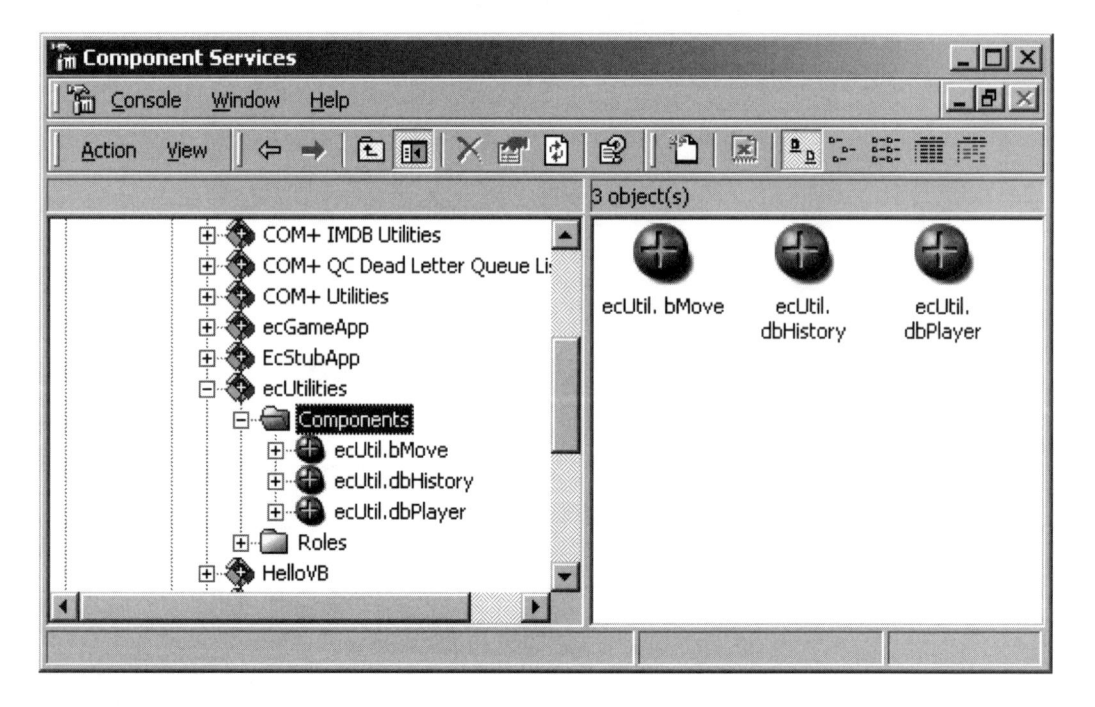

Figure 19-6 *Our example server has three components*

Next set the Transaction Support attribute of the three components as follows:

- **ecUtil.bMove** should be "Required."
- **ecUtil.dbPlayer** should be "Supported."
- **ecUtil.dbHistory** should be "Supported."

Now examine the code of the three components

ECUTIL.DBPLAYER

This component is a "database" component that encapsulates a variety of data access operations on the Players table of the Game database. You should recognize the ADO code as being very similar to programs we implemented in Chapter 18. The method which is required by our "move" transaction is **Delete**. This code (and the rest) is simplified. There is no error handling, for example.

```
Const fileDSN = "Game.DSN"

...

Public Function Delete(ByVal name As String)
    Dim strSQL As String
    Dim connGame As New Connection
    Dim objLog As New LogVb
    Dim ctx As ObjectContext
    Set ctx = GetObjectContext
    If ctx.IsInTransaction Then
       objLog.Writeln "In transaction (dbPlayer::Delete)"
    Else
       objLog.Writeln "Not in transaction (dbHistory::Delete)"
    End If

    connGame.Open "FILEDSN=" & fileDSN
    strSQL = "DELETE FROM Players WHERE name = " _
           & "'" & name & "'"
    Dim numrow As Long
    connGame.Execute strSQL, numrow
    If numrow = 0 Then
        Delete = False
        ctx.SetAbort
    Else
        Delete = True
        ctx.SetComplete
    End If
End Function
```

ECUTIL.DBHISTORY

This component in a similar way encapsulates data access to the History database. The method we are interested in for our transaction is **Add**.

```
Public Function Add(ByVal name As String, _
                    ByVal balance As Currency, _
                    ByVal num_games As Integer) As Boolean

    Dim connGame As New Connection
    Dim objLog As New LogVb
    Dim ctx As ObjectContext
    Set ctx = GetObjectContext
    If ctx.IsInTransaction Then
        objLog.Writeln "In transaction (dbHistory::Add)"
    Else
        objLog.Writeln "Not in transaction (dbHistory::Add)"
    End If
    On Error GoTo ErrorHandler
    connGame.Open "sysHistory"
    Dim strSQL As String
    strSQL = "INSERT INTO Players VALUES (" _
        & "'" & name & "'" & " , " _
        & balance & " , " _
        & num_games & ")"
    connGame.Execute strSQL
    ctx.SetComplete
    Add = True
    Exit Function
ErrorHandler:
    Dim er As Error
    If connGame.Errors.Count > 0 Then
      For Each er In connGame.Errors
         objLog.Writeln er.Description & " (ADO Error)"
      Next er
    Else
         objLog.Writeln Err.Description & " (Non-ADO error)"
    End If
    ctx.SetAbort
    Add = False
End Function
```

ECUTIL.BMOVE

This is our "business logic" which incorporates some functionality beyond interacting with a single data store. In our case this component implements the **Move** method, which tries to delete a record from the Players table of the Game database and add a record to the History database. It is here that we use the context object to call either **SetAbort** or **SetComplete**. The code is written so it could run either inside COM+ or outside. In the latter case there will be no context object, and so it would be illegal to call **SetAbort** or **Set-Complete**.

```
Public Function Move(ByVal name As String, _
                ByVal balance As Currency, _
                ByVal num_games As Integer) As Boolean
    'Add to History database and remove from
        Players table in Games database
    Dim objHistory As dbHistory
    Dim objPlayer As dbPlayer
    Dim ctx As ObjectContext
    Dim ok As Boolean
    Dim ok2 As Boolean
    Set ctx = GetObjectContext
    If ctx Is Nothing Then
        Set objHistory = New dbHistory
        Set objPlayer = New dbPlayer
        objHistory.Add name, balance, num_games
        ok = objPlayer.Delete(name)
        Move = ok
    Else
       'Set objHistory = ctx.CreateInstance("ecUtil.dbHistory")
       'Set objPlayer = ctx.CreateInstance("ecUtil.dbPlayer")
       Set objHistory = New dbHistory
       Set objPlayer = New dbPlayer
       ok = objHistory.Add(name, balance, num_games)
       ok2 = objPlayer.Delete(name)
       Move = ok And ok2
       If Move Then
           ctx.SetComplete
       Else
           ctx.SetAbort
       End If
    End If
End Function
```

The crucial code is shown in bold above. We instantiate the interior objects using the ordinary **New** operator. We call **Add** on **objHistory** and **Delete** on **objPlayer**. Either method may fail. Depending on the outcome, we call **SetAbort** or **SetComplete**.

Just before the code shown in bold are a few lines that have been commented out. This code is legal, but obsolete. With MTS you needed a special **CreateInstance** method on the context object in order to create an interior object. COM+ has done away with the requirement to create any objects in a special way. In COM+, the handling of context is uniformly a part of the standard COM infrastructure.

An ADO "Gotcha"?

A Workaround for Using Recordsets Inside COM+

I have run into a possible bug in ADO which appears to cause failures when you use recordsets inside COM+. The workaround is to avoid use of recordsets and to use SQL directly, passing a string containing an SQL statement to the **Execute** method of the **Connection** object. Two examples of this code are shown above. We performed the "add" operation by a SQL "INSERT" statement and the "delete" operation by a SQL "DELETE" statement. The alternative approach of using a recordset and calling the **AddNew/Update** or **Delete** methods worked just fine for me when the components were called outside of COM+ but failed when the components were imported into COM+.

Data Tier

The data tier is provided by SQL Server. Depending on your testbed, you may have the Game database and History database installed on the same machine or on two different machines. In the one-machine case, your configuration would be as illustrated in Figure 19–1 (except using OLE Transactions in place of the X/Open protocols). In the two-machine case, your configuration would be as illustrated in Figure 19–2.

To set up the History database to reside on a remote computer, you just need to create the database there, and to configure ODBC on the local computer to access the remote SQL Server, as illustrated in Figure 19–7.

Presentation Tier

A presentation tier client program puts up the user interface shown in Figure 19–5. This program is found in **Chap19\PlayerAdmin**. You should be able to run this program and observe the transactional behavior. All of the special COM+ coding and the handling of transactions is completely provided by the middle and data tiers. The client program is a plain vanilla COM client. Here is the easy code for the handler for the "Move" button, which will invoke our transaction:

```
Private Sub cmdMove_Click()
  Dim objMove As New bMove
  Dim ok As Boolean
  ok = objMove.Move(txtName, txtBalance, txtNumGames)
  If Not ok Then
    MsgBox "Could not move " & txtName
  End If
End Sub
```

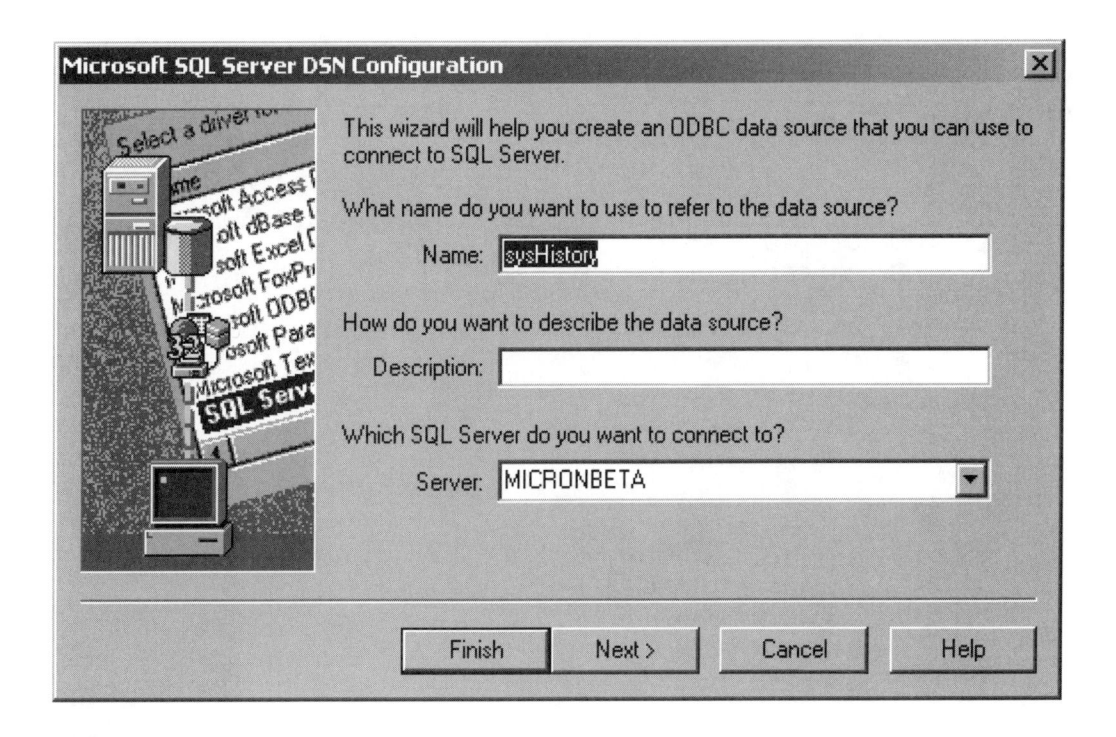

Figure 19-7 *Configuring ODBC data source for a remote SQL Server*

"Auto Done" Flag for a Method

We have seen that COM+ requires only a tiny amount of code in the middle tier to implement transactional behavior. It boils down to calling **SetComplete** or **SetAbort** appropriately. For mainstream transactional behavior, it is possible to shrink even this tiny amount of code by further configuration. In COM+ Explorer you can configure the **Move** method of the **_bMove** interface. Figure 19-8 illustrates opening up the component all the way to find this method.

To set the Auto Done flag you simply select the **Move** method and right-click. From the context menu, choose Properties. In the General tab, check "Automatically deactivate this method when the method returns." See Figure 19-9.

The name suggests that this flag sets the done bit to true when the method returns. This is true, but it also sets the consistency bit based on the HRESULT returned by the method. If the HRESULT indicates a success, the consistency bit is set to true, otherwise to false. In a C++ program, you return

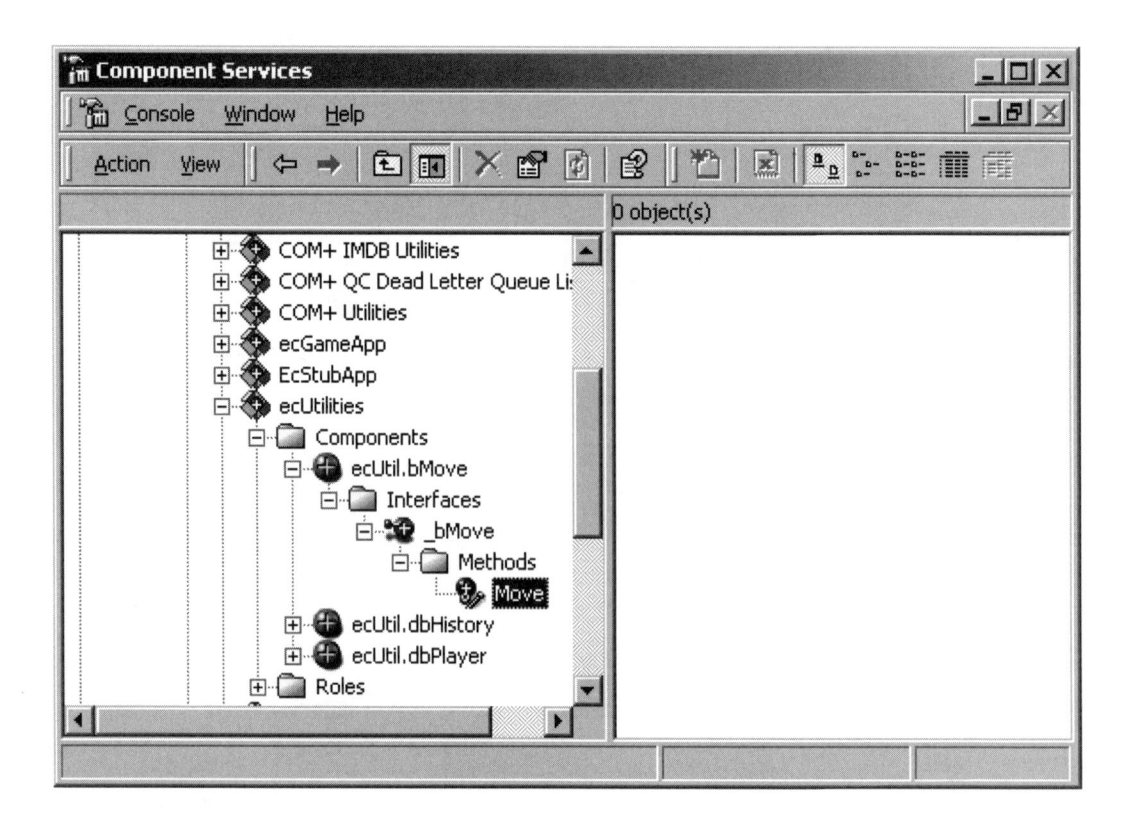

Figure 19-8 *Opening up an individual method inside COM+ Explorer*

an HRESULT explicitly. In a Visual Basic program, the HRESULT indicates a success unless an error is raised. So to obtain the desired behavior from a Visual Basic program, you should raise an error in the case that you are aborting. The example program does not do this, so you cannot demonstrate this feature by the example program.

Summary

Microsoft's transaction processing infrastructure is based on the X/Open DTP conceptual model that consists of transaction managers and resource managers. In place of the TX and XA protocols of X/Open, Microsoft uses its own COM-based OLE Transactions protocol. Through a mapping component, interoperability is achieved with XA-compliant resource managers, so you can program distributed transactions between SQL Server and Oracle, for example. The Microsoft Distributed Transaction Coordinator (MS DTC) plays the

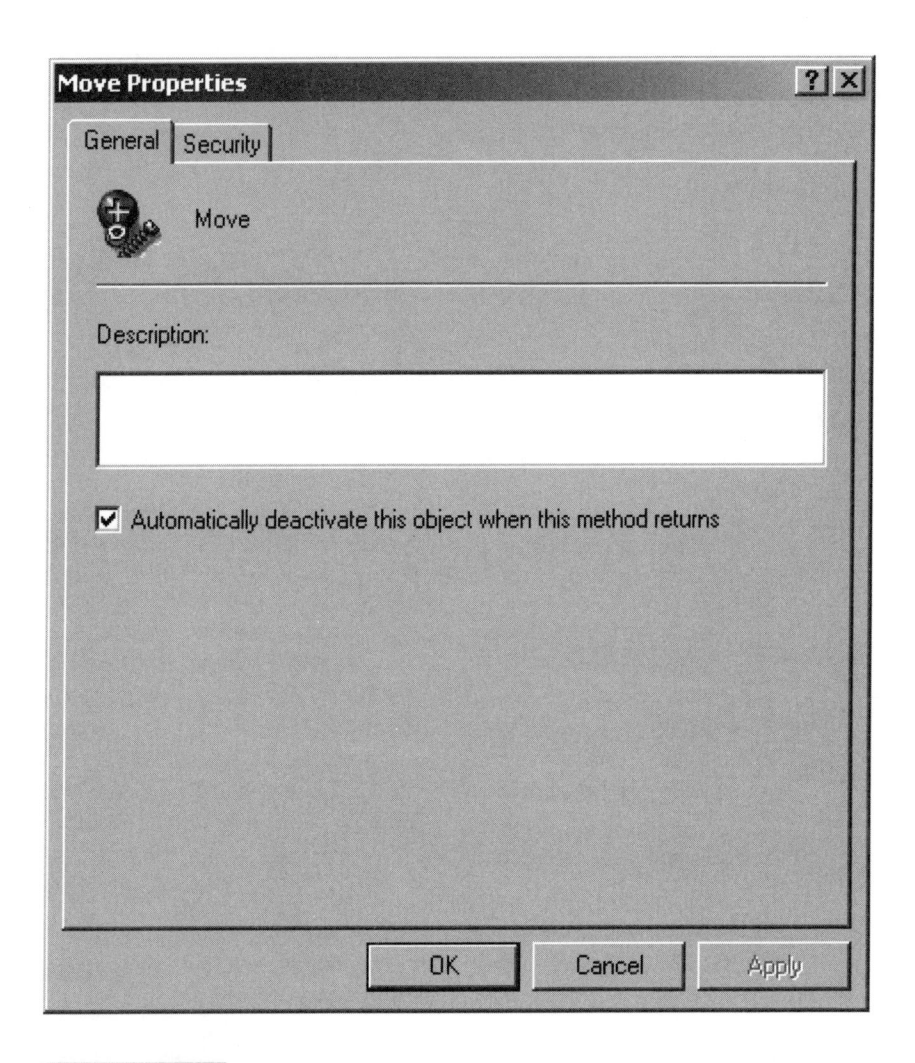

Figure 19-9 *Setting the Auto Done flag*

role of a transaction manager. COM+ provides the concept of automatic transactions, in which you achieve transactional behavior for your components by configuring them to support or require transactions. The standard COM+ interceptor mechanism provides the code required to interact with the DTC.

Continuing our work with databases, in the next chapter we look at how you can call a COM+ program that accesses a database from a thin client that is displayed inside a Web browser.

TWENTY

Web Applications Using COM+

*T*he Web is increasingly important as a means of deploying not only information content but also complete applications. The great advantage of the Web is ease of deployment. All that is needed on the client computer is a Web browser. There are no large client EXEs and DLLs that must be installed and maintained. Many companies are moving towards this style of application, and in the future doubtless many more will do so.

This chapter surveys the most important technologies for developing Web applications, culminating with the use of COM+ to develop three-tier distributed applications. The basic architecture is the same as we have already considered. The two main differences are that the presentation tier is a "thin" client hosted in a Web browser, and the communications protocol between the client and the middle tier is HTTP in place of DCOM.

In keeping with our endeavor to make this book as self-contained as possible, we do not assume a prior background in Web application development. We explain all the basic concepts. Naturally, in order to implement real applications you will need to dig deeper, but this chapter should be enough to get you started.

Classical Web Technology

The Internet originated in the early 1970s as an outgrowth of the ARPAnet, created for the U.S. Department of Defense and intended as a highly robust network connecting military research establishments. Through funding by the National Science Foundation, it was extended to academic institutions, and then commercial organizations became connected also.

The explosive growth of the Internet started in 1993 with the appearance of the first Web servers and the creation of the World Wide Web. The "Web" is a hypertext-based communications system allowing clients to access rich information (text, graphics, audio, etc.) from servers distributed across the Internet using multiple protocols. The Web was developed at CERN, the European Particle Physics Laboratory (www.cern.ch) as a new kind of information system enabling researchers to share information during a project. It was largely the work of one man, Tim Berners-Lee, who remains highly active. Hypertext technology was used to link together a Web of documents that could be traversed in any manner to find information. The Web was based on open specifications using Internet protocols with free sample implementations.

The role of *standards* in Web technology cannot be overemphasized. The Web provides the glue that connects diverse servers and clients all over the world. These servers and clients run on many different computer platforms. The only way they can be sure of being able to connect with each other is by adhering to agreed-upon standard protocols. There are three important standards in the classical Web:

- HTML or HyperText Markup Language for documents distributed over the Web.
- HTTP or HyperText Transfer Protocol as the communications protocol for Web clients to talk to Web servers.
- CGI or Common Gateway Interface as the protocol for Web servers to talk to application programs.

Hypertext and HTML

Hypertext is a nonlinear way of arranging information. Information resides on *pages*. A *link* leads directly to a different location on the same or on a different page, possibly on another Web site somewhere else in the world. The destination of a link is called an *anchor*. HyperText Markup Language (HTML) is a language for describing hypertext documents that can be accessed over the World Wide Web. HTML was invented by Tim Berners-Lee as part of his creation of the World Wide Web at CERN. HTML is an application of the Standard Generalized Markup Language (SGML).

HTML documents are plain (ASCII) text documents that can be created by any text editor. An *element* is a fundamental component of a document. Examples of elements are heads, paragraphs, and lists. *Tags* are used to denote the various elements in an HTML document. A tag consists of a left angle bracket (<), a tag name, and a right angle bracket (>). Tags are usually paired, with the end tag looking just like the beginning tag but with a slash (/).

```
<H1> Sample first level heading </H1>
```

Some elements may include *attributes* to include additional information within a start tag.

```
<P ALIGN=CENTER> A centered paragraph </P>
```

HTML is not case sensitive (except for some escape sequences).
    Here is the complete HTML for a hypothetical personal home page, based on an example Microsoft used to distribute with the Personal Web Server for Windows 95 (the file is **MyHomePage.htm** in the directory **Chap20\Html**, which contains several example HTML files).

```
<HTML>
<head>
<title>
   My Home Page
</title>
</head>
<body>

<h2 align=center>
   Bob's Home Page
</h2>
Welcome to my web server running on Windows 2000
<p>
<hr>

Here are some of my interests:

<ul>
<li> Movies
<li> Reading
<li> Computers

</ul>

<hr>
Here are some links to some other interesting Websites:
<p>
<a href="http://www.microsoft.com">www.microsoft.com</a>
<p>
<a href="http://
www.objectinnovations.com">www.objectinnovations.com</a>

</body>
</html>
```

UNIFORM RESOURCE LOCATORS

The World Wide Web uses Uniform Resource Locators (URLs) to specify the location of files (or other data) on servers throughout the Internet. The URL specifies the access method, the address of the server, and the address of the file (or other data).

```
scheme://host.domain [:port]/path/filename
```

Common schemes are

file	a file on your local system
ftp	a file on an FTP server
http	a file on a World Wide Web server

Port number can be usually omitted (HTTP servers normally use 80, the default).

WEB BROWSERS

A Web browser is a client program that can access and display content from the World Wide Web. It incorporates communications software to retrieve information using various protocols such as HyperText Transport Protocol (HTTP). It reads and displays HTML pages. If a browser does not know how to interpret a particular tag it, usually just ignores it.

The Web browser is what makes HTML "come alive." Instead of plain text, the tags make the page show many kinds of visual elements, and even nonvisual ones such as sound. Currently the most popular Web browsers are from Microsoft and Netscape. Figure 20–1 illustrates how the HTML page shown above will be displayed inside Microsoft's Internet Explorer. Note that Internet Explorer can display a local file on hard disk as well as one that has been fetched over the Internet.

HTML FORMS

The simplest kinds of HTML pages simply display information. This in itself is tremendously valuable, because of the ease with which a browser can enable you to "surf" the Web, retrieving information from all over the world. But you can do more. HTML provides a *forms* capability, allowing the user the ability to enter data, which will be sent to the Web server as part of the request. The Web server can then execute a program (by means we will discuss later), and send a customized response back to the user.

As an illustration, the following simple form has two text controls and one button. The user can enter the name of a server (where the price data is stored) and an item. Clicking the "Get Price" button will then send this infor-

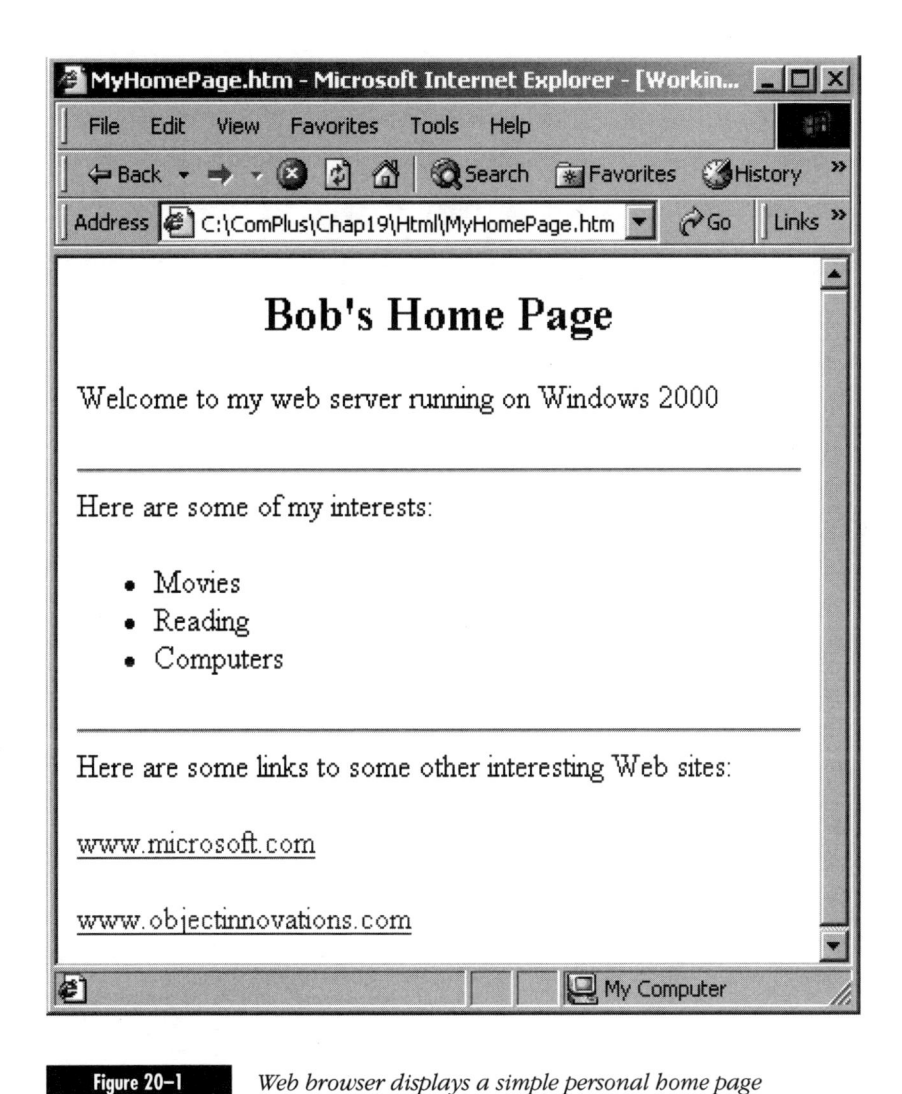

Figure 20-1 *Web browser displays a simple personal home page*

mation to the Web server, which will run a program to look up the price of the item and return a response back to the client. Figure 20-2 illustrates how this form will be shown in a browser. (You won't be able to "run" it until later, after we have set up the "PriceList.Price" COM component that is used in the background.)

476 Chapter 20 • Web Applications Using COM+

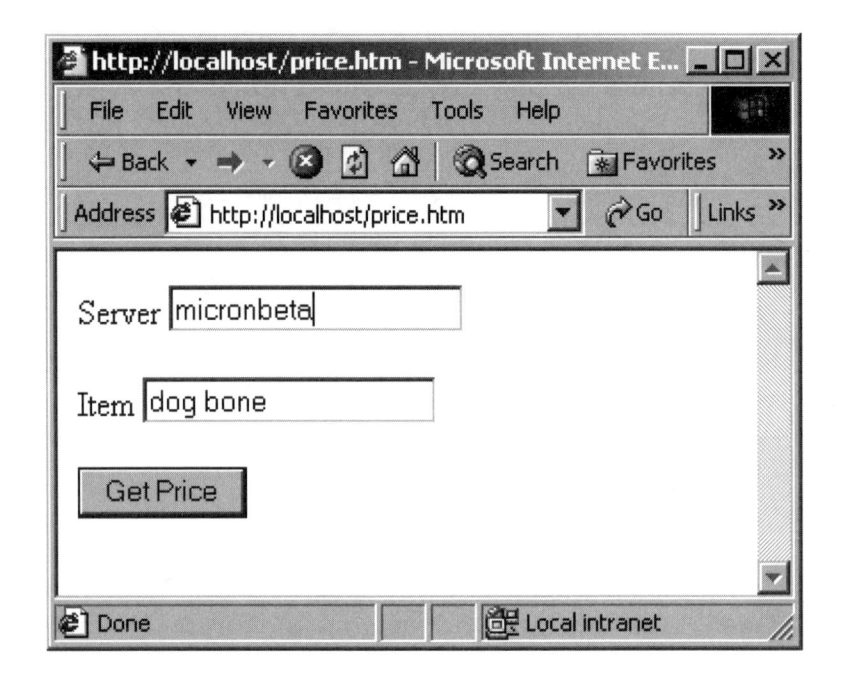

Figure 20-2 *An HTML form for looking up price information*

Here is the HTML code that will display this form:

```
<!-- price.htm -->
<HTML>
<HEAD>
<TITLE>Price of an Item</TITLE>
</HEAD>
<BODY>

<FORM METHOD="POST" ACTION="price.asp">
Server
<INPUT TYPE = "text" NAME="txtServer">
<P>
Item
<INPUT TYPE = "text" NAME="txtItem" VALUE = "dog bone">
<P>
<INPUT TYPE = "submit" NAME="btnGetPrice" VALUE = "Get Price">
</FORM>

</BODY>
</HTML>
```

The **METHOD = "POST"** portion of this HTML code is a directive to the HTTP that will be sent to the Web server.

Internet Servers

An *Internet server* provides the ability to publish information on the Internet or an intranet. A *Web server* publishes HTML pages for access over the World Wide Web using HyperText Transfer Protocol. Internet servers can also provide information using other protocols such as FTP and Gopher. While FTP is still very important as an efficient file transfer protocol, Gopher is fading in importance, and later versions of Microsoft Internet servers do not support it. An Internet server also provides for other services, such as security, logging and administration. Microsoft's latest product is called *Internet Information Services 5.0*, which comes bundled with Windows 2000. The acronym is IIS.

A Web server responds to requests from Web browsers by delivering an HTML document (or some other document type such as plain text). There are three kinds of HTML response pages:

- A static HTML page is prepared in advance of the request.
- A dynamic HTML page is created dynamically by the server in response to the request. The server may execute a CGI (Common Gateway Interface) script or an ISAPI (Internet Server API) DLL. Active Server Pages are an important Microsoft technology for generating dynamic HTML pages. We will discuss CGI, ISAPI and Active Server Pages later in this chapter.
- A directory listing. The server may be configured to support directory browsing, so that if there is no default "home page," it will send back a hypertext version of a directory listing.

HyperText Transfer Protocol (HTTP)

HyperText Transfer Protocol (HTTP) is used by Web clients to communicate with Web servers. A simple request will just ask for an HTML page (or other document type). A more complex request can submit form data gathered by an HTML form. HTTP uses plain text. HTTP by default uses port 80. HTTP is a stateless protocol. The connection between client and server is terminated after each response from the server. An HTTP session contains a header, a method, and request data.

The interaction of a Web browser and Web server is elegant in its simplicity. The client makes a request and gets a response. The interaction is over. The next request, perhaps initiated by a link in an HTML page, may be to another Web server. There is a request and a response; and so on. Figure 20–3 illustrates this simple architecture.

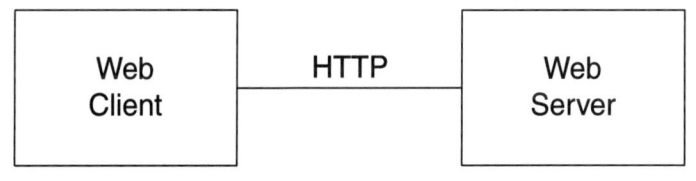

Figure 20-3 *Web client talks to Web server using HTTP*

HTTP HEADERS

A request header is sent by the client to the server and specifies the method used for the request and the capabilities of the client (for instance, the different kinds of file types that the client supports). A response header is sent by the server to the client and provides the status of the transaction (that is, success or failure) and the type of data that is being sent.

Here is an example of a request header where the client requests a static (preexisting) page from the server using the HTTP "GET" method.

```
GET /bylaws.htm HTTP/1.0
Accept: text/htm
Accept: text/plain
Accept: image/gif
...
User-Agent: Mozilla/2.0
From: bob@www.smallcompany.com
    --- blank line ---
```

Here is how this request is parsed:

- The client issues a GET request for **bylaws.htm**, via HTTP version 1.0.
- The client supplies a list of acceptable MIME (Multipurpose Internet Mail Extension) types.
- The user's browser is compatible with the HTTP "Mozilla/2.0" (this name was coined by Netscape as a combination of "Mosaic" and "Godzilla." They saw their browser as a "Mosaic killer." Microsoft emulated Netscape, so their requests would not be rejected by a Web server expecting to hear from a Netscape client).
- The user is identified in the "From" field.

WEB SERVER RESPONSE

Here is a typical response from a Web server:

```
HTTP/1.0 200 OK
Date: Tuesday, 07-Dec-99 20:55:00 EST
Server: IIS/5.0
MIME-version: 1.0
Last-modified: Monday, 02-Dec-99 7:15:00 EST
Content-type: text/plain
Content-length: 3500
    --- blank line ---
<data goes here>
```

And here is how this response is parsed:

- The server agrees to use HTTP 1.0 and sends success code 200.
- The date is sent, and the server is identified as IIS version 5.0.

- MIME version 1.0 is being used.
- The MIME type is specified in "Content-type." We are using plain text.
- A byte count of the data is given.
- The data itself follows after a blank line.

HTTP METHODS

The HTTP protocol has just four different methods that the client can choose. The most common are GET and POST.

GET   Get an HTML page and send any form results by concatenating onto the URL.

POST   Send form results separately as part of the data body rather than by concatenating onto the URL.

PUT   Replace contents of the specified URL by form data sent by client (overwrites existing information).

HEAD   Request transaction status and header information only (used typically for diagnostics).

Common Gateway Interface (CGI)

The Common Gateway Interface (CGI) is a standard for external gateway programs to interface to Web servers. Gateway programs are often called scripts and can be written in scripting languages such as Perl as well as in ordinary languages like C. A script is a stand-alone program and runs in a *separate process*. CGI specifies the mechanisms for scripts to receive and send data to the Web server. CGI uses environment variables, such as QUERY_STRING. The server can send data to the script through standard input. The script can send data to the server through standard output.

The fact that CGI programs run in a separate process makes them much less efficient than other mechanisms and raises a major impediment to scalability. We will examine other more efficient mechanisms later in this chapter. But CGI is a standard supported by all Web servers and is conceptually easy to understand, so we will study it briefly to gain a basic understanding of the principles of Web servers.

A DYNAMIC WEB PAGE

In place of requesting a preexisting Web page, a client may specify a *program* in a URL. The Web server recognizes from the URL that a program is to be called in place of delivering static data. It calls the program. The program and the Web server work cooperatively to create the Web page that is returned to the client via HTTP.

In our example, the client asks for the program **datetime.exe** to determine the date and time and return the values on a Web page. Here is a hypothetical request header:

```
GET /scripts/datetime.exe HTTP/1.0
Accept: text/htm
Accept: text/plain
Accept: image/gif
...
User-Agent: Mozilla/2.0
From: bob@www.smallcompany.com
     --- blank line ---
```

The Web server arranges for the following server side processing.

1. The Web server receives the HTTP request and calls the program **datetime.exe** indicated in the URL.
2. The **datetime.exe** program writes a header giving the content type it will return, a blank line, and then the data.

```
/* datetime.c */

#include <time.h>
#include <stdio.h>

void main()
{
  char dbuffer [9];
  char tbuffer [9];
    printf("content-type: text/plain\n");
    printf("\n");
  _strdate( dbuffer );
  printf( "The current date is %s \n", dbuffer );
  _strtime( tbuffer );
  printf( "The current time is %s \n", tbuffer );
}
```

3. The Web server creates the complete HTTP response.

```
HTTP/1.0 200 OK
...
Content-type: text/plain
...
     --- blank line ---
The current date is 12/04/99
The current time is 14:51:32
```

MORE ABOUT HTML FORMS

HTML provides a FORM tag that can be used to collect information from a client and specify an action to be performed by a server.

```
<FORM ACTION = "url"> ... </FORM>
```

The attributes are:
- ACTION gives the URL which can specify a script to be executed on the server.
- METHOD is the HTTP method, such as GET or POST.
- ENCTYPE specifies the encoding of the form contents, and is only used for POST. At present there is only one ENCTYPE defined:

```
application/x-www-form-urlencoded
```

Here is a sample HTML form (**Chap20\Club\getdate.htm**) which provides a button that can be used for invoking the **datetime.exe** program on the server.

```
<!-- getdate.htm -->
<HTML>
<HEAD>
<TITLE>Get Date</TITLE>
</HEAD>

<BODY>
<FORM ACTION="scripts\datetime.exe" METHOD="POST">
<P>
   <INPUT TYPE=SUBMIT VALUE="Get Date and Time">
</FORM>

</BODY>
</HTML>
```

An Internet Programming Testbed

At this point it would be a good idea to make sure that you have a good testbed for exercising Web applications. Later in this chapter, we show how to implement a three-tier distributed application that allows a client to talk to a SQL Server database through a COM+ component that is invoked through a Web server. There are a lot of pieces that have to be running for such an application to work. Rather than following a "big bang" approach and going for broke, I suggest you safeguard your bank account and exercise some simple Internet functionality first. These examples should also help solidify your understanding of the Internet fundamentals that we have been discussing.

Internet Explorer 5.0

Internet Explorer 5.0 comes bundled with all versions of Windows 2000 and is installed automatically when you install the operating system. It is integral to Windows, beginning with Window 98. It will start out as your default browser, and if you double-click on an **.htm** file on your local hard disk, you should find that Internet Explorer comes up and opens that file. Several example HTML files are in the folder **Chap20\Html**. As a tiny test, open the file **getdate.htm** that we discussed in the previous section. You will use this form to test a CGI script. (You will not be able to test the script until later, and you will need to access the HTML page using HTTP rather than as a local file.) Figure 20–4 illustrates what you should see. Figure 20–1 provides another example of an HTML page.

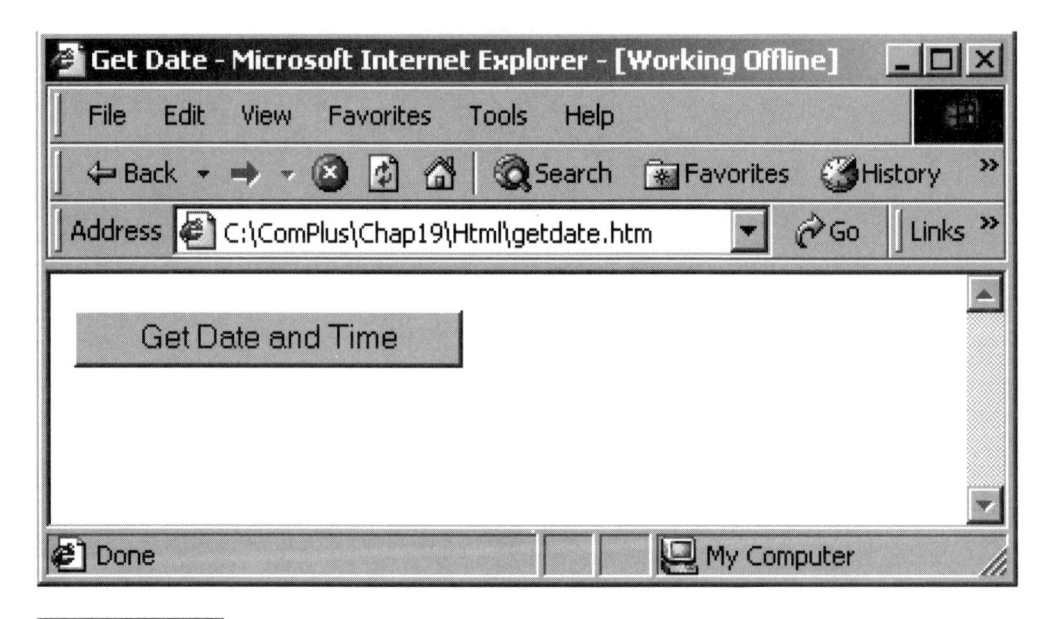

Figure 20–4 *An HTML form you will use to test a CGI script*

You will need to do some configuration of your browser to allow use of an "unsigned" ActiveX control. We will discuss that later.

Internet Information Services 5.0

Microsoft's Web server is provided by Internet Information Services 5.0. (The IIS acronym used to stand for Internet Information Server.) IIS is bundled with Windows 2000 (and later) Server and is installed by default. IIS is administered by (you guessed it) another MMC snap-in. Bring up this admin tool, from Start | Programs | Administrative Tools | Internet Services Manager. The first thing to check is that the Web service is running. In the admin tool, click on the name of your server under Internet Information Services. You should see a list of four services, all of which are running, including "Default Web Site," which has port 80, as you would expect. You can start, stop, and pause from toolbar buttons or by right-clicking over the service you are interested in. (You can also start and stop the services from the Computer Management snap-in. Click on Services under Tools.) Figure 20–5 illustrates the running services.

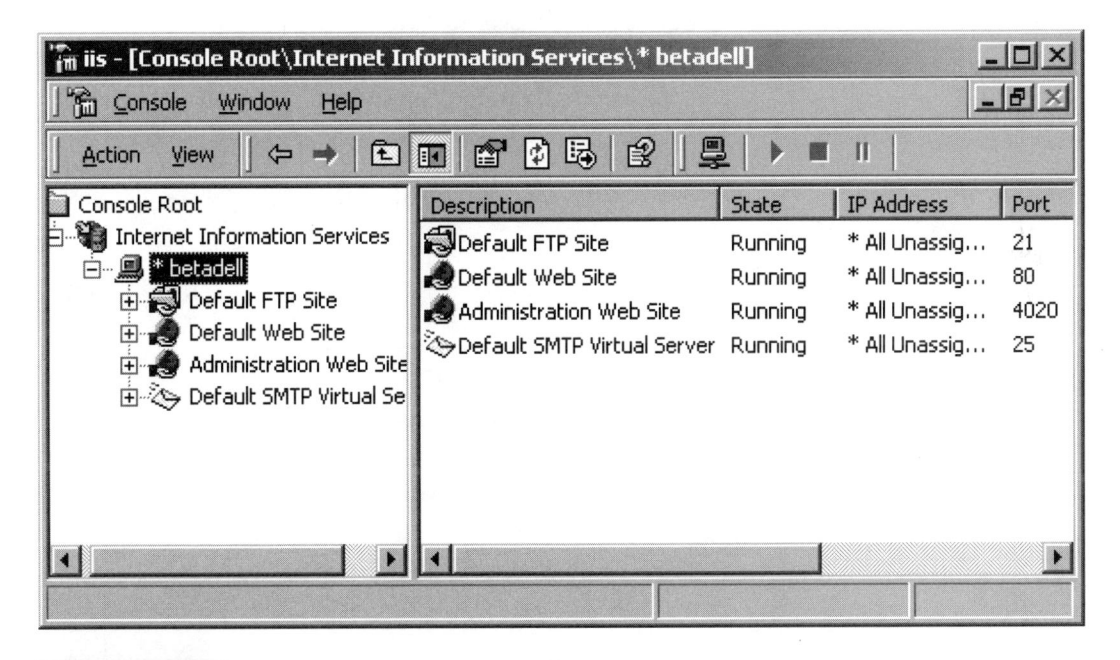

Figure 20–5 *You administer IIS from the Internet Services Manager snap-in*

PUBLISHING TO YOUR WEB SITE

You publish to your Web site by copying files to the folder **Inetpub\wwwroot**, which should be in the partition on which Windows 2000 is installed. By default, the Web server will look in the **wwwroot** directory for files to send back to the requesting browser. As a first example, copy **MyHomePage.htm** from **Chap20\Html** to **wwwroot**. You should now be able to access this file from anyplace on your LAN by using the URL:

```
http://yourservername/myhomepage.htm
```

where you put in the actual name of your server computer. If you are running Internet Explorer on the same machine as your server, you could use the following URL:

```
http://localhost/myhomepage.htm
```

where **localhost** is used as the name of the server.

Rather than risk disrupting any files in **wwwroot**, we will do all our work from now on in subfolders. Copy the folders **club** and **Html** from **Chap20** to **wwwroot**. From the browser you could give a complete path down to the particular file, for instance,

```
http://localhost/html/myhomepage.htm
```

But it is more convenient to change the home directory in the IIS admin program. To change the home directory to be **club**, right-click over "Default Web Site" and choose Properties from the context menu. Select the Home Directory tab. Specify **club** as a subdirectory in the local path. See Figure 20–6. Note the Directory Browsing check box. Don't check it now, but we will try that option shortly.

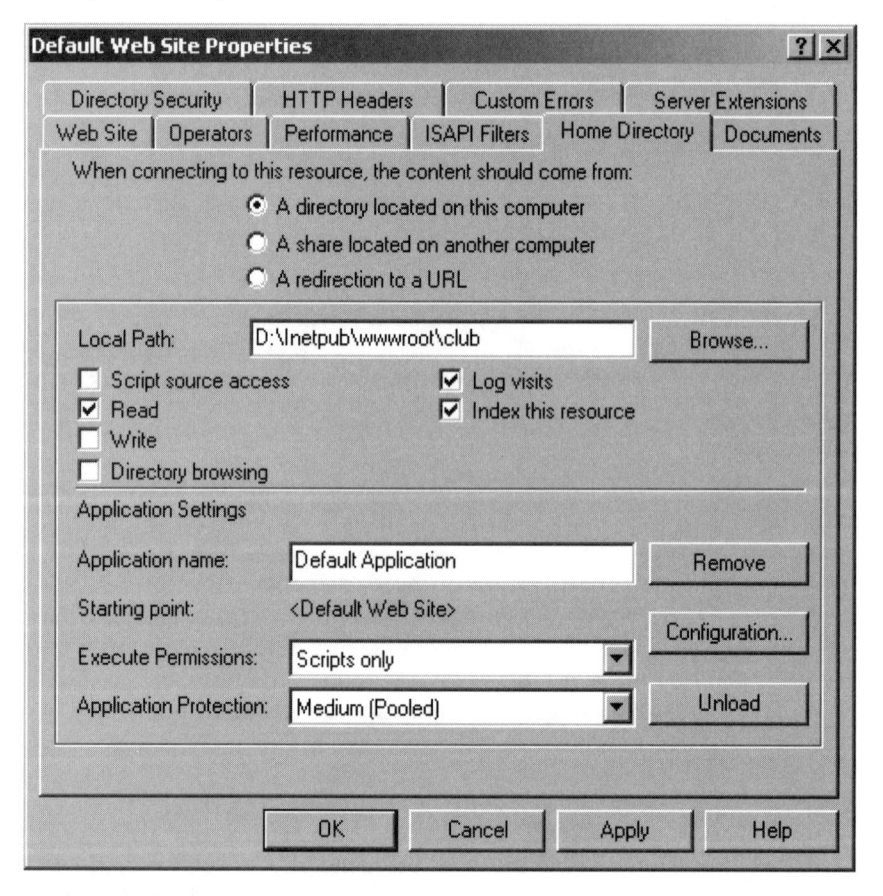

Figure 20–6 *Specifying a different home directory*

Now go back to your browser, and this time just type in the name of your computer, without any specific file:

```
http://localhost/
```

You are brought to the home page of the "Von Neumann Computer Club." See Figure 20–7.

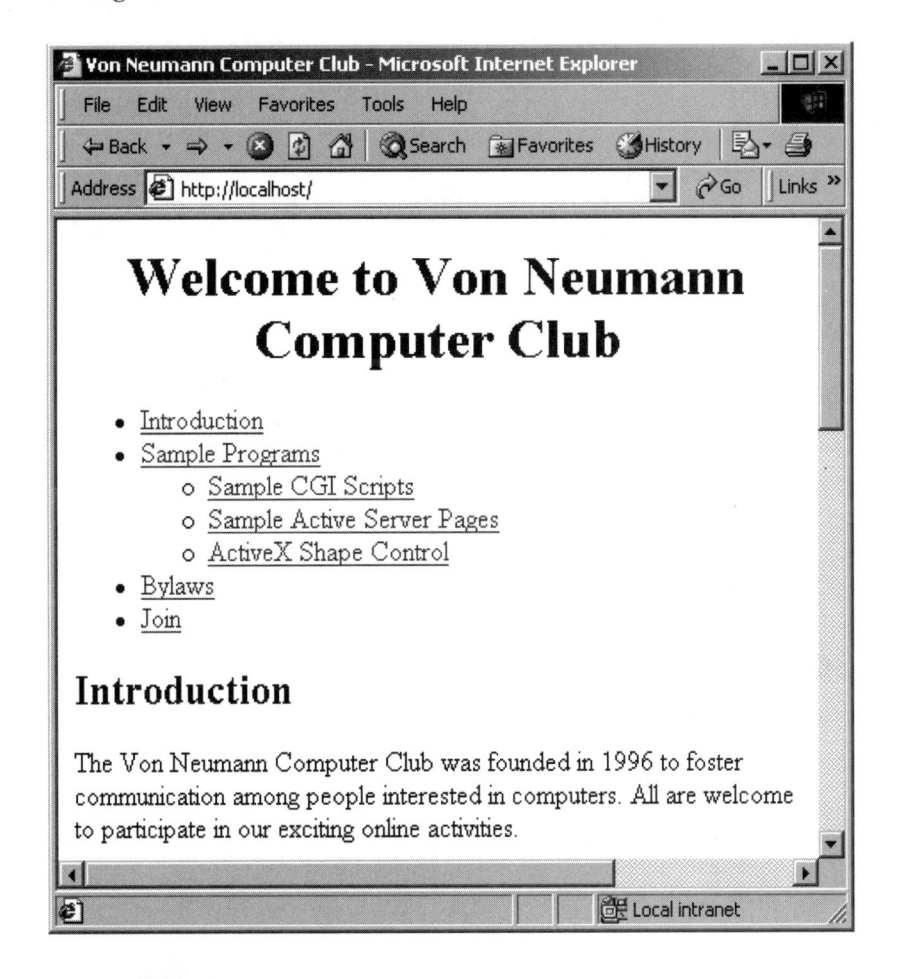

Figure 20–7 *Navigating to a default home page*

How did that happen? This happens all the time. You often just type in the name of a site, not a specific file (for instance, http://www.microsoft.com). All you need to do is name a page in the home directory **default.htm**. That is exactly what we did in the **club** directory, as you can easily verify.

DIRECTORY BROWSING

When we were talking about the responses a Web server can make to a request, we said there are three different types. The first is a static content page, typically in HTML. The second is a dynamic page generated by a program, for example, a CGI script. We will examine this case shortly. The third possibility is a directory listing. This can be enabled in the admin program, as was illustrated in Figure 20–6. Go back to the home directory properties, change the home directory to be the **html** subdirectory, and enable directory browsing. Now visit the following URL:

`http://localhost/`

There is no **default.htm** file, but directory browsing is enabled, so you get back a directory browsing with links to files (and subdirectories, if any). See Figure 20–8.

This option will be convenient for navigating among the various test pages—you can just click the link. Normally you would *not* want to enable directory browsing in a commercial site.

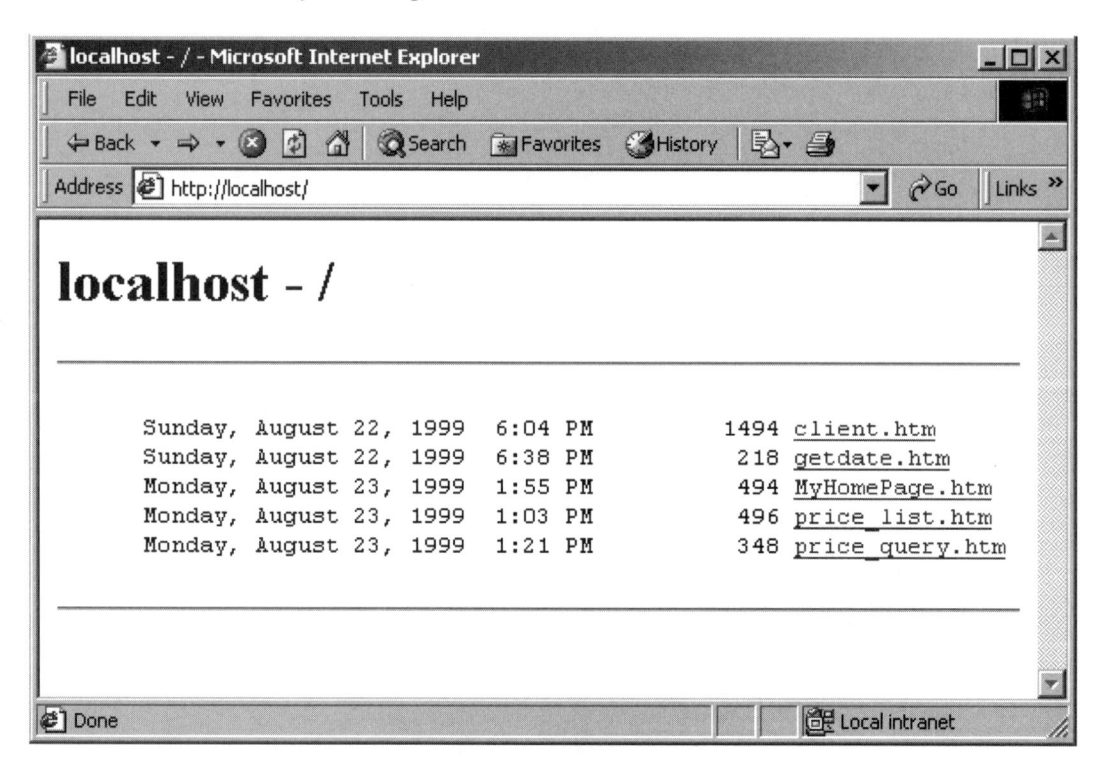

Figure 20–8 *Directory browsing has been enabled*

RUNNING CGI SCRIPTS

Now let's run some CGI scripts. Build the two programs in **Chap20\datetime** and **Chap20\homepage**. (Or you can use the prebuilt EXE files in **Chap20\Scripts**.) Copy the EXE files **datetime.exe** and **homepage.exe** to **Inetpubs\Scripts**.

First open **getdate.htm** in the browser and click the button. You should now have the **datetime.exe** script executed, and the result returned to your browser as shown in Figure 20–9.

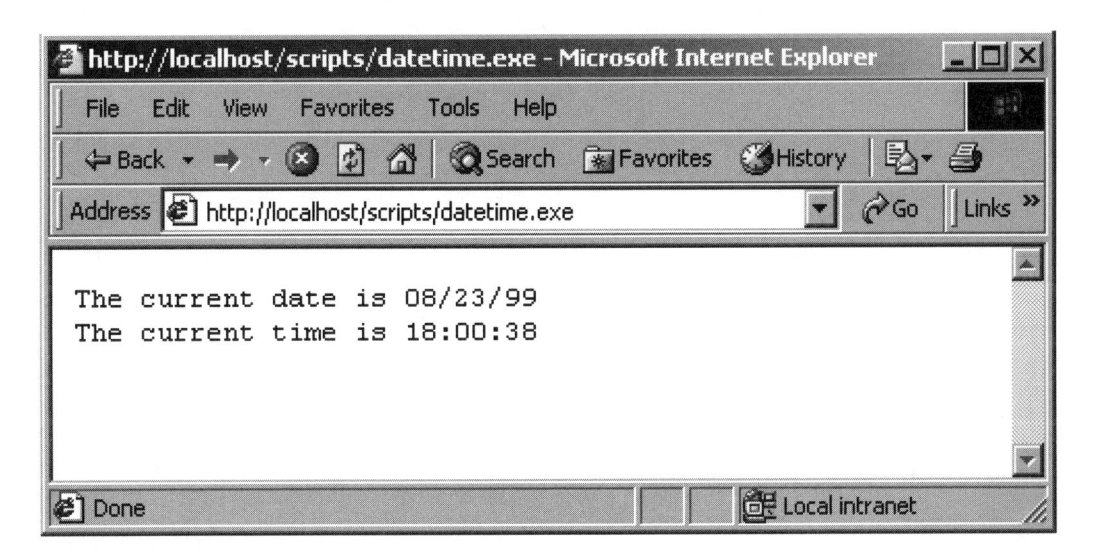

Figure 20–9 *Results from running a CGI script*

Note that you could get the same result by directly entering the URL:

```
http://localhost/scripts/datetime.exe
```

Next, we run the other script by opening the page **name.htm**. This example is a little more interesting. A simple form is displayed where you can enter a name. Try entering the name "John" and click the "Submit" button. You will now see a customized "home page" come up, with John's name in it. See Figure 20–10.

The CGI program wrote the HTML text to standard output, so that the Web server could compose a complete HTTP response header to send to the browser. You can inspect the example code in **Chap20\homepage\homepage.cpp**. The code is a little involved. It has to retrieve the information from the form sent by the browser. The CGI protocol calls for this information to

Chapter 20 • Web Applications Using COM+

Figure 20-10   *A customized home page created by a CGI script*

be passed via environment variables. We won't go through the details, because soon we will be using Active Server Pages, which is *much* easier.

Our purpose in presenting these examples is to show the basic mechanism of a Web server in its simplest guise (simple from the Web server perspective, not for the poor Web programmer). The architecture is illustrated in Figure 20–11. The Web client issues a request via HTTP to a Web server, possibly passing information from a form. The Web server passes this information on to a Web program, using the CGI protocol. The Web program creates part of the response, which it passes back to the Web server. The Web server completes the response header and sends the complete response to the client.

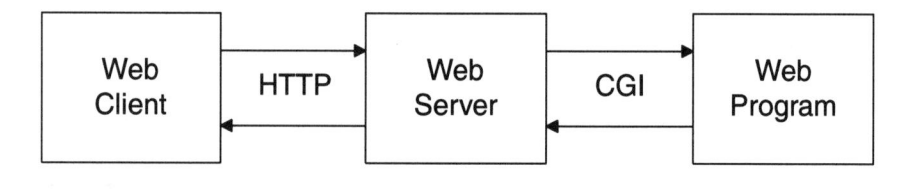

Figure 20-11   *Architecture of a dynamic page being created by a Web program*

If you try entering a complete name like "John Smith," you will see something funny displayed in the page that comes back: "John+Smith's home page." This is part of special encoding that HTTP does. If you are writing at the raw CGI level, you have to deal with it. Since we are not, we won't go into the details.

Another nuance is that the link to the Von Neumann computer club is currently not working. The page was set up with the assumption that **club** is the home directory. When we make **club** the home directory, this page works. We examine the complete "club" Web site after we look at the various Microsoft Internet technologies, many of which are illustrated in this site.

Microsoft Web Technologies

Microsoft emerged from nowhere on the Internet a few years ago to become one of the major players. The company really turned on a dime and embraced the new computing model (the technological part, not the "open" part). Microsoft introduced many new technologies of its own for developing Internet-based applications. If you plan to develop your own Internet applications using Microsoft tools, you need to be familiar with their core Internet technologies, which we survey in this section. There are many specialized products such as Site Server and Commerce Server which we do not cover. Our focus is on the fundamentals, laying the groundwork for a discussion of applying COM+ to Web application development.

Microsoft Client-Side Web Technologies

Microsoft's original focus was on the client, as was the initial focus of Java. In both cases, the objective was to enhance the client-side environment in various ways and to offload some processing from the server. Both initiatives have proved much more difficult to carry out in practice than was anticipated. The problem comes from the greatest strength of the Web—its universality. There are many different Web browsers, and an effective client-side technology should work in all of them, in order to attain universal reach. And that is impossible, because *some* users will use old browsers. The only common denominator is plain vanilla HTML.

An important distinction in the design of a Web-based application is whether it is to be deployed on the Internet or an intranet. The latter is a network within a company based on Internet protocols. But all the clients are within the company, so the company has control over both what is deployed on the server and what is deployed on the client. By contrast, on the Internet there are "outside" clients over which the company has no control. For example, a company's Web site is an Internet application. The company wants external users to be able to access its Web site and learn about its products and hopefully become customers. It would be self-defeating to employ some specialized client-side technology that only some clients would be able to use. On the other hand, an application to support its sales people in the field could rely on client-side technology, because all its sales people could be equipped with laptops having the proper software installed.

Although an application may be intended for an intranet, putting in dependencies on its always being an intranet application limits its flexibility. If the application is an Internet application from the start, new users can be easily accommodated. There is much more flexibility. We use the phrase "Web application" to be neutral, applying to both the Internet and to intranets.

Although the server side is emerging as more important, we begin with a discussion of client-side technologies. This order matches the historical development, and certain client technologies such as scripting apply also to the server.

We are starting to see renewed interest in client-side technologies such as DHTML (Dynamic HTML), because there are significant intrinsic benefits from doing some work on the client and presenting a richer user interface, and there will be pressure in the industry to converge on some universal standards.

SCRIPTING

In some cases, it is extremely useful to do some processing on the client—for example in validating input fields in an HTML form. How many times have you filled out a form on the Web and made a mistake that was not discovered until *after* the form was submitted to the server and then bounced back to you? Wouldn't it be better to do simple validation on the client *before* submitting it to the server? Client-side scripting is ideal for this kind of job.

The basic idea is very simple. Events like clicking a button invoke a handler function. An object model gives you access to data that is entered in the form. Your script code in the handler function can do necessary validation, and then, if valid, submit the request under program control. The file **valid.htm** in **Chap20\Html** provides an example. Access this file in Internet Explorer from the Web site on your local host, enter an invalid date, and click Submit. You should get an error message. See Figure 20–12.

If you go ahead and submit a valid date, your request should be submitted to the server. (The response is the current date and time—it has nothing to do with the date you entered—this program is only a demo.)

Here is the code. It should be largely self-explanatory. Note that the code is placed inside HTML comments, so that a browser that does not understand VBScript will simply ignore it, and not display something funny to the user.

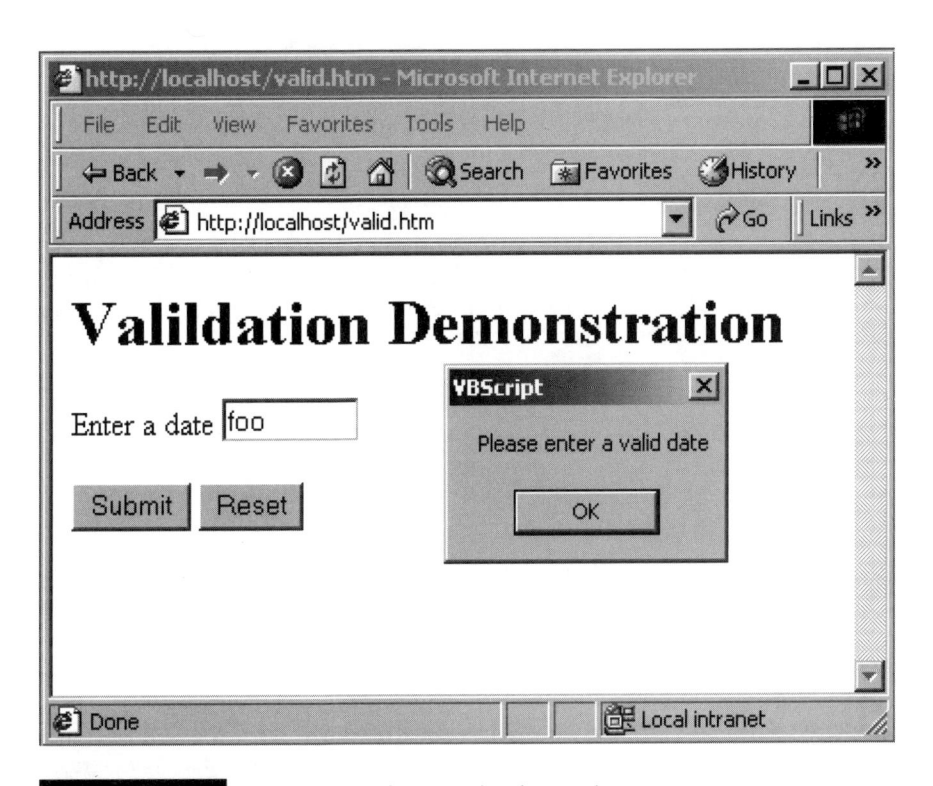

Microsoft Web Technologies

Figure 20-12 Validating a form on the client side

```
<!-- valid.htm -->
<HTML>
<HEAD>
<TITLE>Valiation Demonstration</TITLE>

<SCRIPT LANGUAGE="VBScript">
<!--
Sub btnSubmit_OnClick
  Dim form
  Set form = Document.Form1
  If IsDate(form.txtName.Value) Then
  MsgBox "Date is valid"
     form.Submit
  Else
    MsgBox "Please enter a valid date"
  End If
End Sub
-->
</SCRIPT>
</HEAD>
```

```
<BODY>
<H1>Validation Demonstration</H1>
<FORM NAME = "Form1" ACTION="scripts\datetime.exe"
METHOD="POST"
  ENCTYPE="application/x-www-form-urlencoded">
<P>
Enter a date <INPUT NAME="txtName" VALUE="" SIZE=8>
<P>
 <INPUT NAME="btnSubmit" TYPE=BUTTON VALUE="Submit">
 <INPUT TYPE=RESET VALUE="Reset">
</FORM>

</BODY>
</HTML>
```

VBSCRIPT AND JAVASCRIPT

All of our scripting examples are in VBScript. The reason is purely convenience. Since VBScript is a subset of Visual Basic, the syntax is widely known. We are using Visual Basic extensively in this book, so examples in VBScript should be readily understood.

In real life, you should seriously consider using JavaScript on the client, because it is more standardized. In particular, JavaScript will run in both Microsoft and Netscape Web browsers. You should stay away from advanced features, which are supported differently.

ACTIVEX CONTROLS

ActiveX controls are an especially rich kind of COM component. They plug into a client development environment. We saw in Chapter 1 how you could use the Web browser ActiveX control to very easily create a Web browser application using Visual Basic. It is almost as easy using Visual C++. Like all COM components, an ActiveX control is language neutral and can be used in many languages.

The great thing about ActiveX controls is that they plug right into your development environment and can be used by an applications programmer just like built-in controls. No knowledge of COM is required. Thousands of ActiveX controls are available from third-party vendors.

They way they play in Web applications is through a special OBJECT tag in HTML. Using this tag, an ActiveX control (indeed any COM object) can be placed in an HTML page. The CLSID is used to identify the control. You can call methods and set properties using scripting language. Here is a sample HTML page with a "Shape Preview" control inserted. See **client.htm** in **Chap20\club**.

```html
<!-- client.htm -->
<HTML>
<HEAD>
<TITLE>ActiveX Control Demo</TITLE>

</HEAD>
<BODY>
<H2>ActiveX Control Demo<BR>
</H2>
<script language = "vbscript">
<!--
sub NewShape
  if btnShape.Item(0).Checked then
    txtShape.Value = "Rectangle"
    Shape1.ShapeType = 0
  elseif btnShape.Item(1).Checked then
    txtShape.Value = "Ellipse"
    Shape1.ShapeType = 1
  else
    txtShape.Value = "No selection"
  end if
end sub

sub cmbColor_onChange
  if cmbColor.selectedIndex = 0 then
    txtColor.Value = "Red"
    Shape1.ForeColor = &H0000FF
  elseif cmbColor.selectedIndex = 1 then
    txtColor.Value = "Blue"
    Shape1.ForeColor = &HFF0000
  else
    txtColor.Value = "No selection"
  end if
end sub

-->
</script>
<P>
Select a shape and a color<BR>
<P>
Shape: <INPUT TYPE="RADIO" NAME="btnShape"
  VALUE="Rectangle" OnClick="NewShape">Rectangle
<INPUT TYPE="RADIO" NAME="btnShape"
  VALUE="Ellipse" OnClick="NewShape">Ellipse
<P>
Color: <SELECT NAME="cmbColor" >
<OPTION SELECTED VALUE="Red">Red
<OPTION VALUE="Blue">Blue</SELECT>  <BR>

<P>
```

```
Your selection is shown via text boxes<BR>
<P>
Shape: <INPUT NAME="txtShape" VALUE="" MAXLENGTH="25"
SIZE=25>
<P>
Color: <INPUT NAME="txtColor" VALUE="" MAXLENGTH="25"
SIZE=25>

<P>
Your selection is shown via an ActiveX Control<BR>
<P>

<object id ="Shape1" width=100 height=50
   classid="clsid:B1028D2C-35A7-11D1-A01B-00A024D06632"
   codebase="http://localhost/shape.dll"
>
</object>

</BODY>
</HTML>
```

To run this demo, first build the Shape Preview control in **Chap20\Shape**, which will register it. Then you can open up **client.htm** in Internet Explorer (either locally or through the Web site on your local host). Through radio buttons and a dropdown list box, you can set the shape and color of the control, which will be shown in both text boxes and "live" by the control itself.

"SAFETY" CONFIGURATION IN INTERNET EXPLORER

If you have the default settings in Internet Explorer, you will get an error message when you try to set any of the control properties (for example, click the "Rectangle" radio button). Figure 20–13 shows an error message announcing that your security settings prohibit running an "unsafe" ActiveX control.

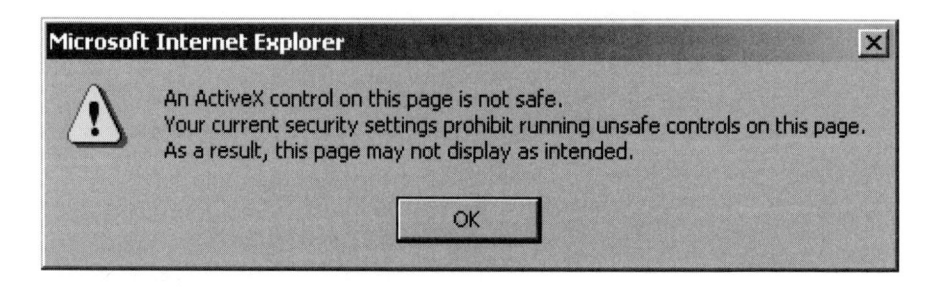

Figure 20–13 *Safety message from Internet Explorer*

To change the settings in Internet Explorer 5.0 so that you can run the control, go to the menu Tools | Internet Options. Select the Security tab. Click the "Custom Level" button, and in the dialog that comes up choose the "Prompt" radio button for the first three settings on ActiveX controls:

- Download signed ActiveX controls
- Download unsigned ActiveX controls
- Initialize and script ActiveX controls not marked as safe.

See Figure 20–14.

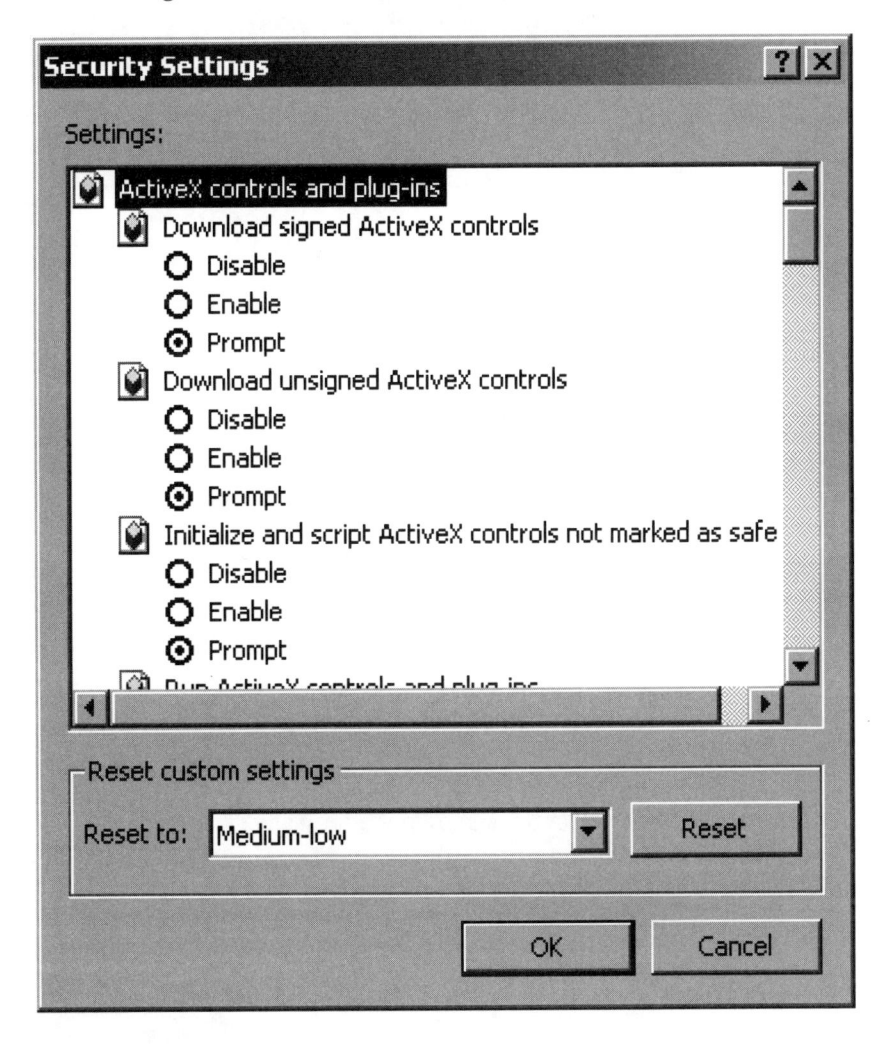

Figure 20–14 *Setting safety options in Internet Explorer 5.0*

Now go back to the demo. When you try to set one of the properties, you will receive a warning message box, not a fatal error. You can choose to let the scripts run. Do so. You should now be able to set the shape and color, and the shape and color will be reflected visually in the control, as illustrated in Figure 20–15.

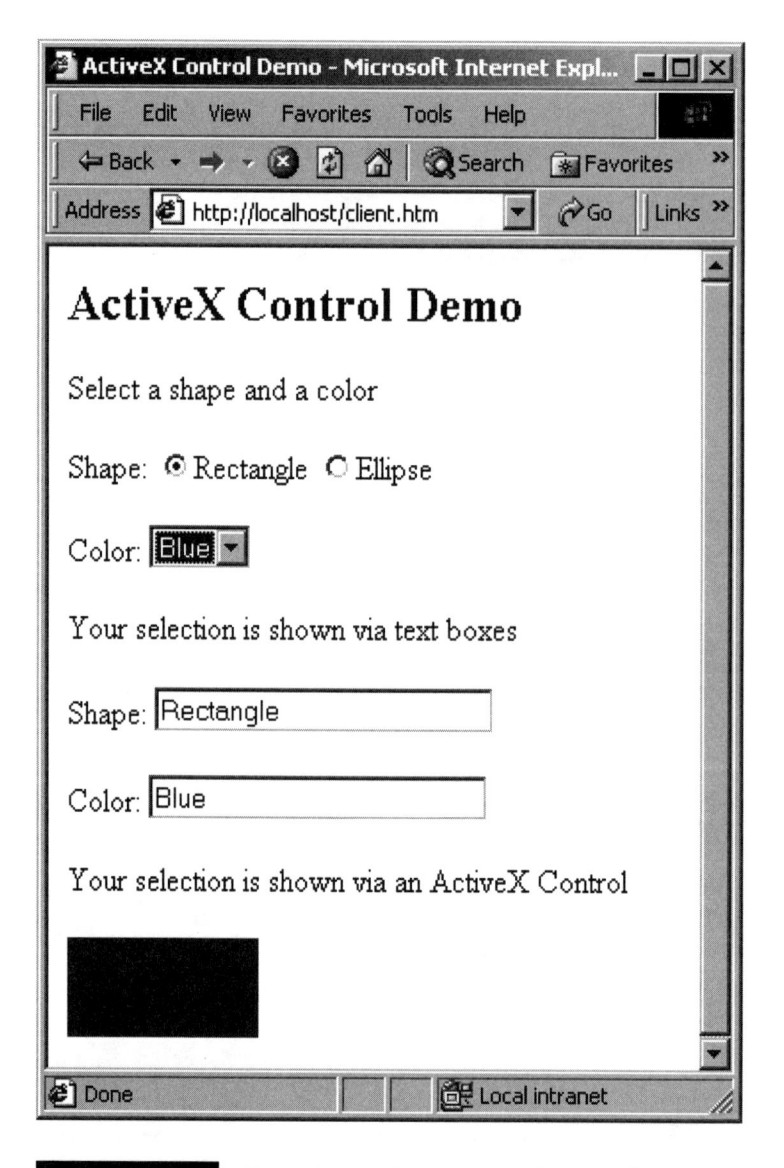

Figure 20–15 *Exercising an ActiveX control on a Web page*

The approach Microsoft took to safety with respect to ActiveX controls is different from Sun's original approach in Java. Sun originally prohibited Java applets from running outside a "sandbox," which prevented them from touching any system resources where they might do damage. Although this approach was safe, it also restricted the utility of Java applets. ActiveX controls have configurable security, as we have seen. "Marking" a control safe for scripting is something that the control developer does, placing a setting in the Registry that indicates the control is "safe." The developer should do extensive testing before so marking a control. But a user has no real way of knowing how safe a control really is just because it has been marked as safe.

The other safety settings concern "downloading" an ActiveX control, which we discuss next.

DOWNLOADING AN ACTIVEX CONTROL

Once we configured the safety setting for scripting, our control just ran, because it was already installed and registered on our system. But to require a user of an ActiveX control to separately obtain and install it defeats the idea of a "thin" client. The user is back in the business of having to install and maintain software on the client. What we want is the ability to download and automatically install an ActiveX control on demand. That capability is provided by the **codebase** attribute in the OBJECT tag. Look again at how the Shape Preview control was specified.

```
<object id ="Shape1" width=100 height=50
   classid="clsid:B1028D2C-35A7-11D1-A01B-00A024D06632"
   codebase="http://localhost/shape.dll"
>
</object>
```

The **codebase** specifies a URL where the control can be found and downloaded, if it is not currently installed on the local system. (This example is somewhat artificial. For convenience we specify "localhost" as the name of the server. We are going through the HTTP protocol, even though in this example we do not go to a remote machine.) To see how this works, unregister the control (you can run the **unreg_shape.bat** file in **Chap20\Shape**). Next copy **shape.dll** to the home directory on the Web server, which is currently **Inetpub\wwwroot\Html**. Now again visit **client.htm** using the URL **http://localhost/client.htm**. Refresh to make sure you are going to the Web server for the page. You should get a security warning. See Figure 20–16.

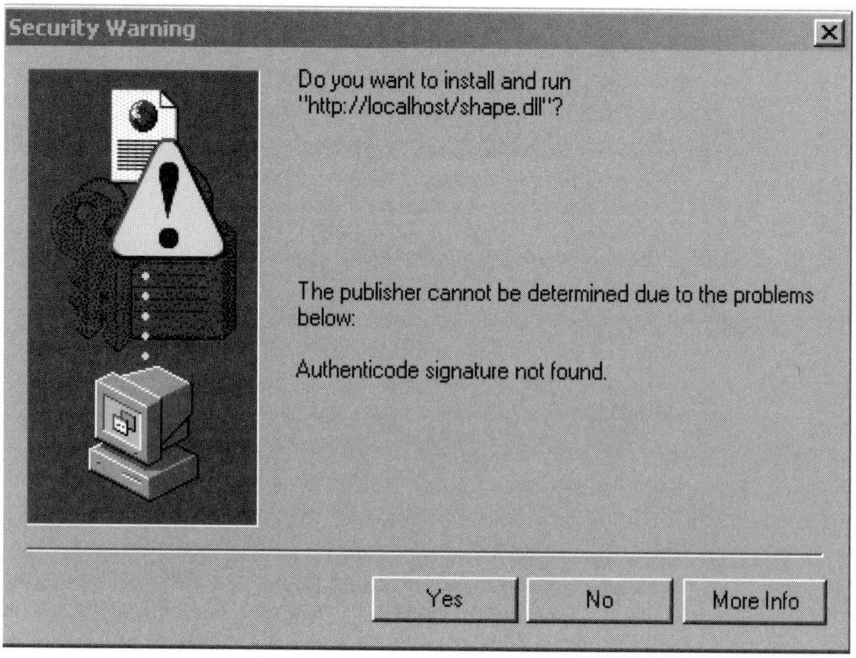

Figure 20-16 Security warning for an unsigned ActiveX control

Click "Yes." The control **shape.dll** will now be downloaded to your system and installed (registered). You should then be able to set the properties as before, and see the shape and color displayed by the control.

The Microsoft "Authenticode" technology uses a digital signature to sign controls. The digital signature is obtained from a signature authority, an independent company such as Verisign, which takes applications from individuals and companies for a digital signature. The digital signature can be used in various ways, such as providing robust identification of yourself in e-mail and electronic commerce. In the case of companies, the signature authority does some validation that the company is a legitimate business entity and then issues a certificate, which can be used for signing the ActiveX control. When the user brings up a Web page having a signed ActiveX control, the user will be shown the certificate, identifying the company. If the company is well known, the user may choose to go ahead and download the page. If the company is not known to the user, the user may choose not to download it for safety's sake. The choice is in the hands of the user.

Microsoft Server-Side Web Technologies

As we discussed in the introduction to the previous section, client-side technologies suffer the drawback that they are not universal. ActiveX controls, for example, require the user to be running Microsoft's Internet Explorer as the Web browser. The great advantage of server-side technology is that you can choose your own platform and tools for your servers, and if you stick to plain vanilla HTML (and possibly the core part of JavaScript), a very wide variety of clients will be able to run your applications.

INTERNET SERVER API (ISAPI)

The Common Gateway Interface (CGI) is standard and straightforward, but it suffers an enormous disadvantage. Every Web program that is launched by a Web server using CGI runs as a separate process. This both incurs significant overhead and severely limits scalability. Microsoft's solution is the *Internet Server API* or ISAPI, which defines an interface to server extensions which are implemented as DLLs. These DLLs run in the same address space as the Web server. Figure 20–17 shows the basic architecture.

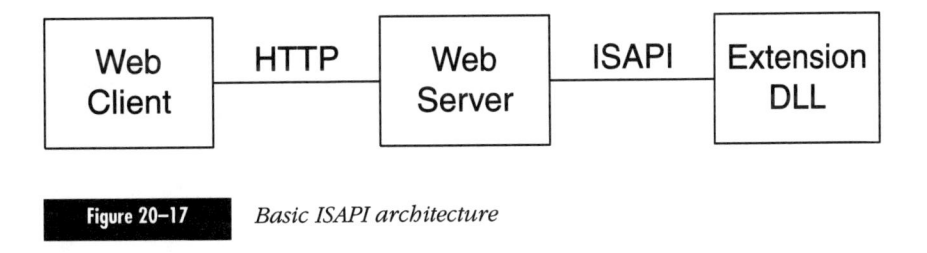

Figure 20-17   *Basic ISAPI architecture*

Conceptually, ISAPI works the same way as CGI. The Web server passes on a request from the Web client. In place of using environment variables the Web server communicates with the ISAPI DLL through an *Extension Control Block* or ECB. The Web server provides callback functions **ReadClient** and **WriteClient** to read and write data from the Web server (which is done through **stdin** and **stdout** with CGI). The extension DLL parses the data received from the server and composes its response, which it passes back to the server. The server then adds the header information and sends a complete response back to the Web client.

Visual C++ makes it easy to create ISAPI extension DLLs through an ISAPI Extension Wizard. Several MFC classes are provided to wrap the ISAPI server functionality. You might enjoy doing a small demo. Create a new Visual C++ project called "Hello" in the **ComPlus\Chap20\Demos** directory. A completed version of the program is in the **ComPlus\Chap20\Hello** directory. The project type should be "ISAPI Extension Wizard." See Figure 20–18.

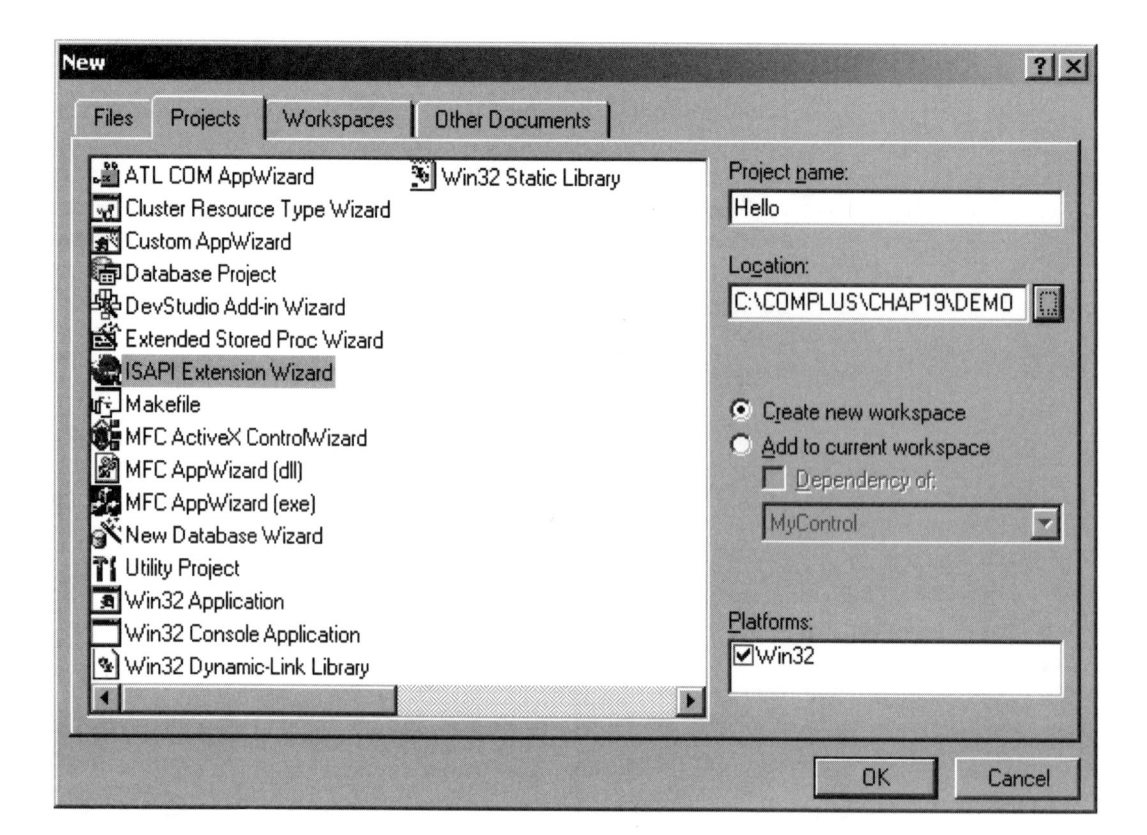

Figure 20-18 *Creating a new ISAPI extension project using Visual C++*

In the next screen, accept the default to generate a Server Extension object. Click Finish. In the generated project, edit the **Default** method of the **CHelloExtension** class to simply return the message "Hello from ISAPI."

```
void CHelloExtension::Default(CHttpServerContext* pCtxt)
{
  StartContent(pCtxt);
  WriteTitle(pCtxt);

  *pCtxt << _T("Hello from ISAPI\r\n");

  EndContent(pCtxt);
}
```

Build the DLL. Copy **hello.dll** to the **Inetpub\Scipts** directory. You can then invoke your extension DLL through the URL

```
http://localhost/scripts/hello.dll
```

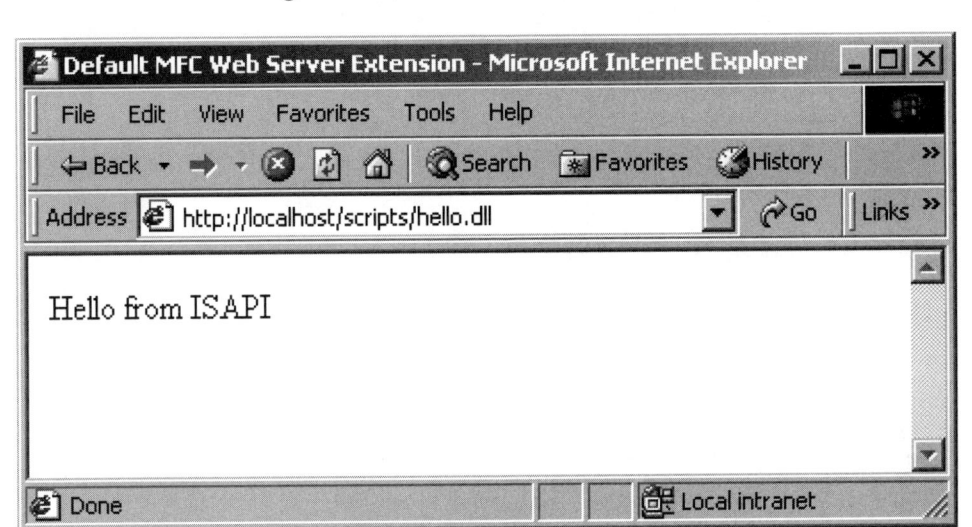

Figure 20-19 shows the result.

Figure 20-19 *Invoking an ISAPI extension DLL through Internet Explorer*

A slightly more interesting example is provided by **join.htm** in the Von Neumann Computer Club Web site. To get ready for this example, first build the ISAPI project in the directory **Chap20\clubisap** and copy **clubisap.dll** to **Inetpub\Scripts**. (A prebuilt copy of the DLL can be found in **Chap20\Scripts**.)

Next go back to Internet Services Manager and change the home directory to be **wwwroot\club**. Also turn off directory browsing. See Figure 20–6. Since there is a **default.htm** file in the **club** directory, you can now bring up the club's home page from the URL **http://localhost/**. Click the "Join" link. You will then be brought to a simple form where you can enter your name. See Figure 20–20.

Type in your name and click "Join now." You will see a debugging message referring to a file opening succeeding and adding a string to the file. The **clubisap.dll** extension DLL writes data to a flat file. The file is created the first time the server writes to it. You may try adding some more members to the club, and then click "List Members." You should get back a list of the members in the club, as recorded in the flat file.

Naturally in real life you would probably use a database rather than a flat file. We will in fact call database code from the Web server when we make use of COM+ applications on the Web server.

ISAPI is the technology of choice when you are looking for absolutely the best performance in a Web application. Programming with ISAPI is somewhat low level, and for everyday use Microsoft has provided a higher level technology called Active Server Pages, the subject of the next section.

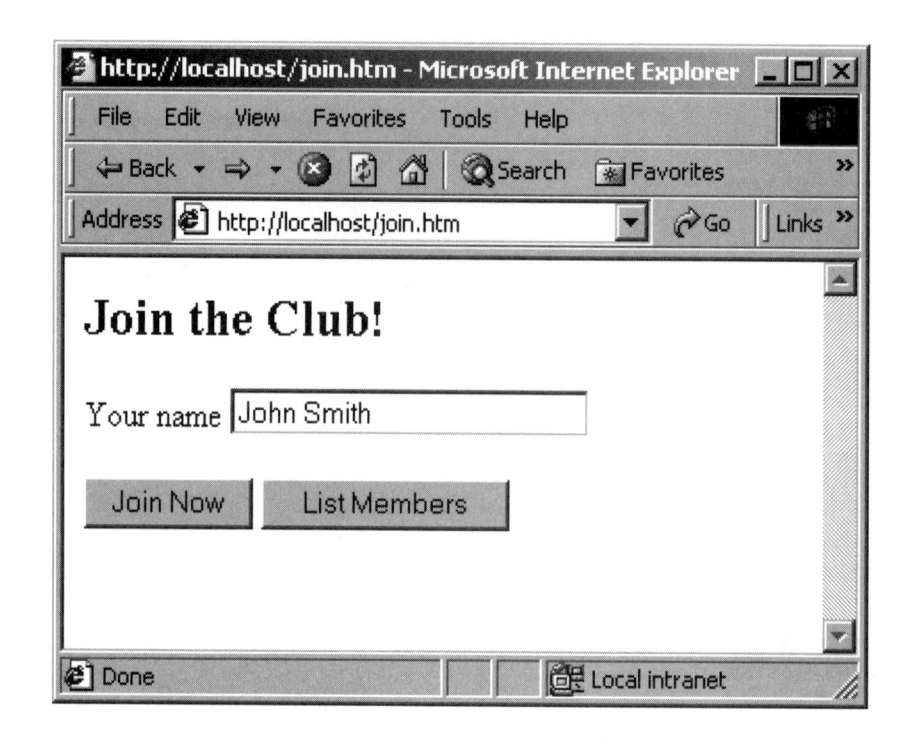

Figure 20–20 *A form for joining the club*

ACTIVE SERVER PAGES (ASP)

Active Server Pages (ASP) have become the most popular Microsoft technology for implementing Web applications. They run on the server, thus avoiding the various problems we have discussed concerning client-side technology. They are efficient, and they are easy to program.

ASP differs from CGI and ISAPI in the way it gets invoked. An Active Server Page is actually an extended HTML file with additional script content. It is not a separate file that gets executed by the server. Thus a browser may point directly to an ASP file. In fact, any HTML file can be made into an ASP file simply by renaming its extension. This makes it possible to easily migrate static HTML files to dynamic ASP files.

To get started, let's look at an example. Our ASP examples are in the folder **Chap20\ASP**. Copy the folder **ASP** to **Inetpub\wwwroot**. Bring up the Internet Services Manager to make **ASP** your home directory. While you are there, check to make sure that the Execute Permissions include Scripts. Also, you may wish to enable Directory Browsing for your convenience. Figure 20–21 illustrates the proper settings.

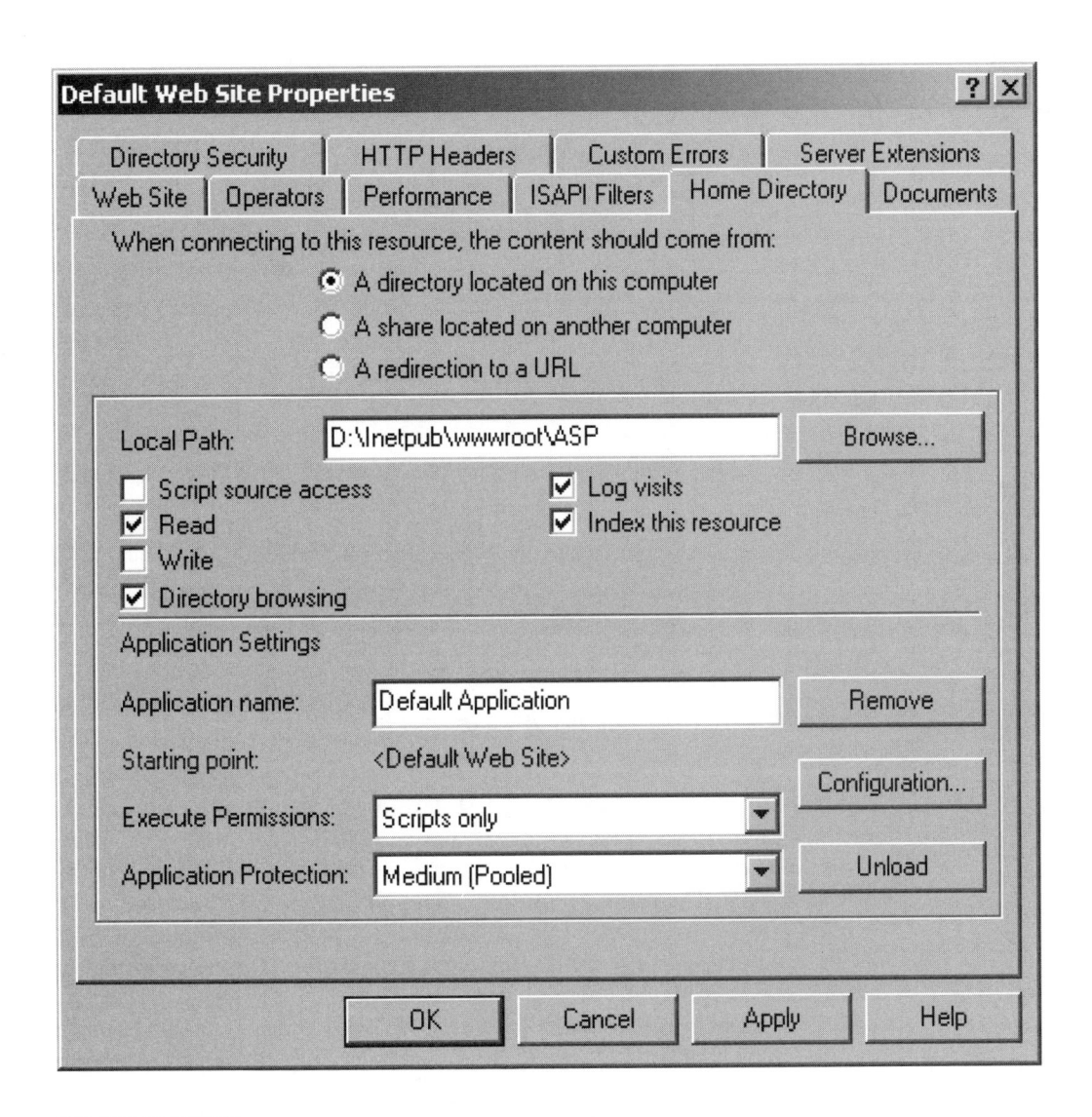

Figure 20-21   *The directory where your ASP files reside must grant execute permission to scripts*

Now view the file **datetime.asp**. Be sure to go through HTTP to the Web server, using the URL **http://localhost/datetime.asp**. You should see the date and time displayed. They are in a slightly different format, because the script code ran VBScript functions rather than C library functions, as was the case with our previous CGI example. Figure 20–22 illustrates what the browser will display for this page.

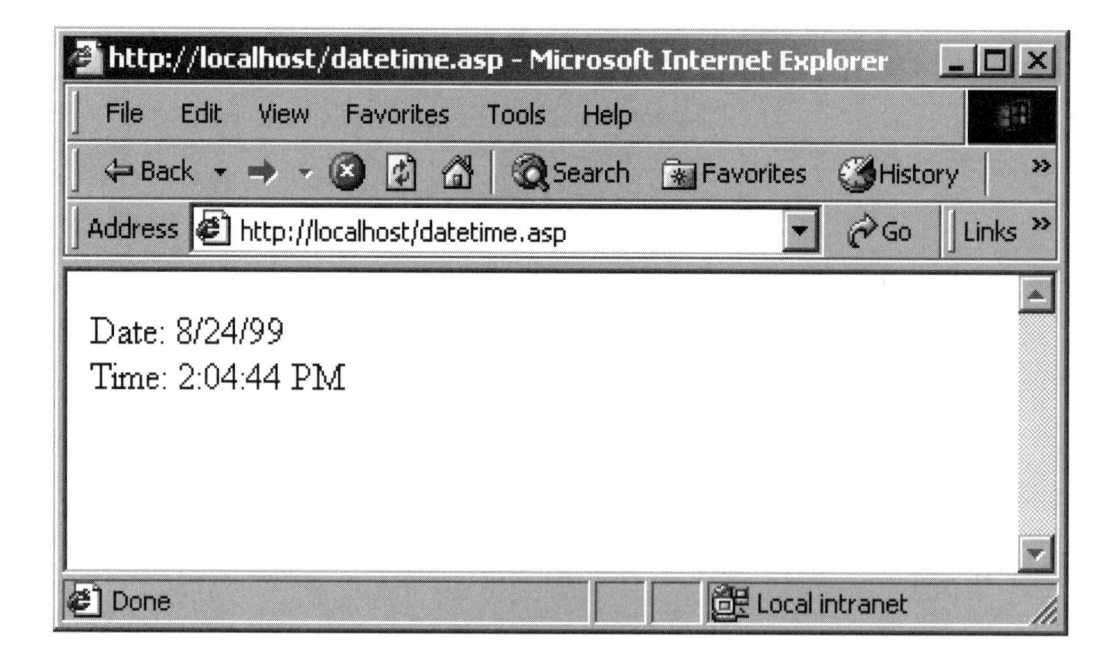

Figure 20-22 *Displaying an ASP page where script called built-in functions*

The big difference between the ASP and CGI examples is in how the functions got invoked. With CGI, there was an HTML page which contained a button the user pressed. An HTTP request went to the server, which called a script using CGI. The script, running in a separate process, wrote data that the Web server used to create the HTTP response that went to the client. With ASP, the script code is directly on the initial page requested by the client. Recognizing the **.asp** extension, the Web server calls an ISAPI extension DLL **asp.dll** which runs in the same process as the Web server. This DLL executes the script, which calls the date and time functions. The Web server builds the HTTP response and sends it to the client. Here is the Active Server Pages file. Notice it is just like HTML, with the addition of the script.

```
<!-- datetime.asp -->
<html>
<head>
<title> Date and Time Using ASP </title>
</head>
<body BGCOLOR=WHITE>
Date: <% = Date %> <br>
Time: <% = Time %> <br>
</body>
</html>
```

The script code is bracketed inside the <% ... %> delimiters. This script gets executed on the server, not on the client. You can have both client- and server-side scripts on the same page. Client-side scripts use different delimiters—the SCRIPT tag, as we have already seen.

Active Server Pages and COM+

The real power of Active Server Pages comes from its coupling with COM/COM+. We have seen that Active Server Pages get invoked through an ISAPI DLL and run in-process with the Web server. Thus they are efficient. But once the scripting code starts executing, the efficiency goes out the window. The script code is interpreted and thus runs much more slowly than compiled code.

Scripts are great when they are short and do their processing within compiled functions that they call. The example we looked at above fits this case exactly. Each line of script code is only one line long, and all the script does is call a built-in function. There are only a limited number of built-in functions. What will make the whole model extensible is to provide a way for scripts to invoke any compiled code that you write. This capability is exactly what COM provides. And COM is object oriented, to boot.

Besides providing the ability to call COM components, Active Server Pages themselves are implemented using COM. There is an object model for Active Server Pages. Thus programming with Active Server Pages is quite seamlessly object-oriented. You invoke the various built-in objects provided by ASP, and you can also invoke your own custom COM objects, sometimes called "Active Server Components" when used in this context.

ADO is an example of an Active Server Component. You can call ADO directly from an ASP script to do database programming. Even better, however, is to encapsulate your database program into your own COM components, which are the ones that call ADO (or OLE DB directly). These COM components can be imported into COM+ and then enjoy all the power of COM+ applications, such as automatic transactions.

Active Server Pages Object Model

There are five built-in objects provided by Active Server Pages.

- The **Server** object provides general purpose utility functions and through the **CreateObject** method the ability to instantiate COM components that are not built-in.
- The **Application** object can be used to share information among all users of an application.
- The **Session** object can be used to store information for a particular user of an application.

- The **Request** object provides all the information associated with a user's request and contains several collection objects, including the **Forms** collection.
- The **Response** object can be used to send information to the user and contains the **Cookies** collection.

The workhorse objects are the **Request** and **Response** objects. From the **Request** object you can read information that was submitted by the user by filling in an HTML form. The **Response** object is used for writing information that is to be sent to the client. The **Request** object contains five collections:

- The **ClientCertificate** collection retrieves certificate information sent via "secure HTTP" (URL begins with **https**).
- With the **Cookies** collection, you can retrieve the value of "cookies" sent in an HTTP request.
- The **Form** collection contains values from HTML form elements.
- With the **QueryString** collection, you can retrieve values from the HTTP query string.
- With the **ServerVariables** collection, you can retrieve the values of server environment variables (the ones used in CGI programming).

Request and Response Using Active Server Pages

We will illustrate use of the **Request** and **Response** objects with a minimal example which echos back a name submitted by the client. Open up **echo.htm** in the browser, and enter a name. See Figure 20–23.

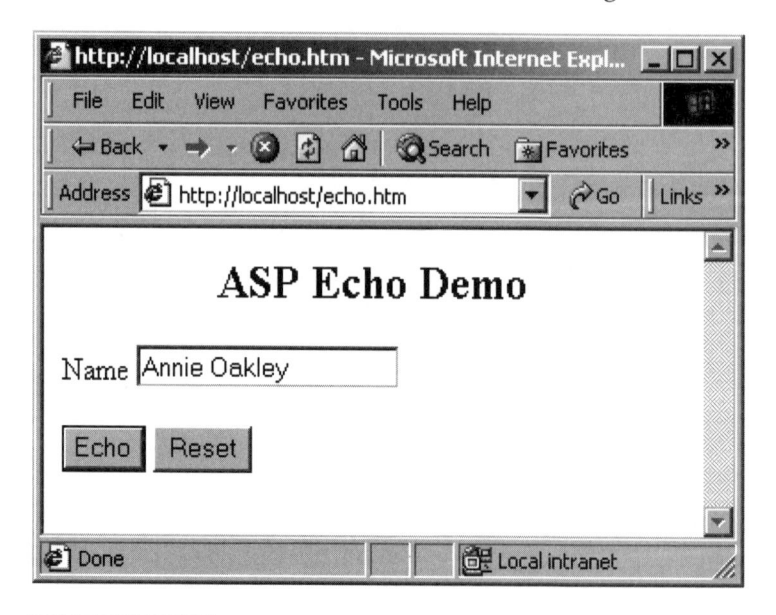

Figure 20–23 *A form for entering a name which will be echoed back*

Click the "Echo" button, and you should see the name echoed back. Here is the HTML code:

```
!-- echo.htm --><HTML>
<HEAD>
<TITLE>Name Input</TITLE>
</HEAD>

<BODY>
<FORM ACTION="echoback.asp" METHOD="POST">
<P>
Name <INPUT NAME="txtName" VALUE="" MAXLENGTH="25" SIZE=25>
<P>
   <INPUT TYPE=SUBMIT VALUE="Submit">
   <INPUT TYPE=RESET VALUE="Reset">
</FORM>

</BODY>
</HTML>
```

The form's ACTION parameter simply specifies an ASP file. That file uses the **Request** object to obtain the name that was submitted. The **Form** collection is used, keying off **txtName**, which was NAME attribute of the INPUT box. A greeting message is then sent back to the client, incorporating the name that was entered.

```
<!-- echoback.asp -->
<%@ LANGUAGE = VBScript %>
<HTML>
<HEAD>
<TITLE>Echo Back</TITLE>
</HEAD>
<BODY>
<%
name = Request.Form("txtName")
Response.Write("Hello, " & name)
%>
</BODY>
</HTML>
```

A Three-Tier Web Application Using COM+

All the pieces are now in place for understanding the principles of a three-tier Web application that employs COM+ on the middle tier. Conceptually it is the same as a three-tier DCOM application, but there are several twists due to the presence of Web components. Figure 20–24 outlines the overall architecture. The dotted line going directly from the client to the business logic shows the DCOM alternative.

Figure 20-24 *Three-tier Web application architecture*

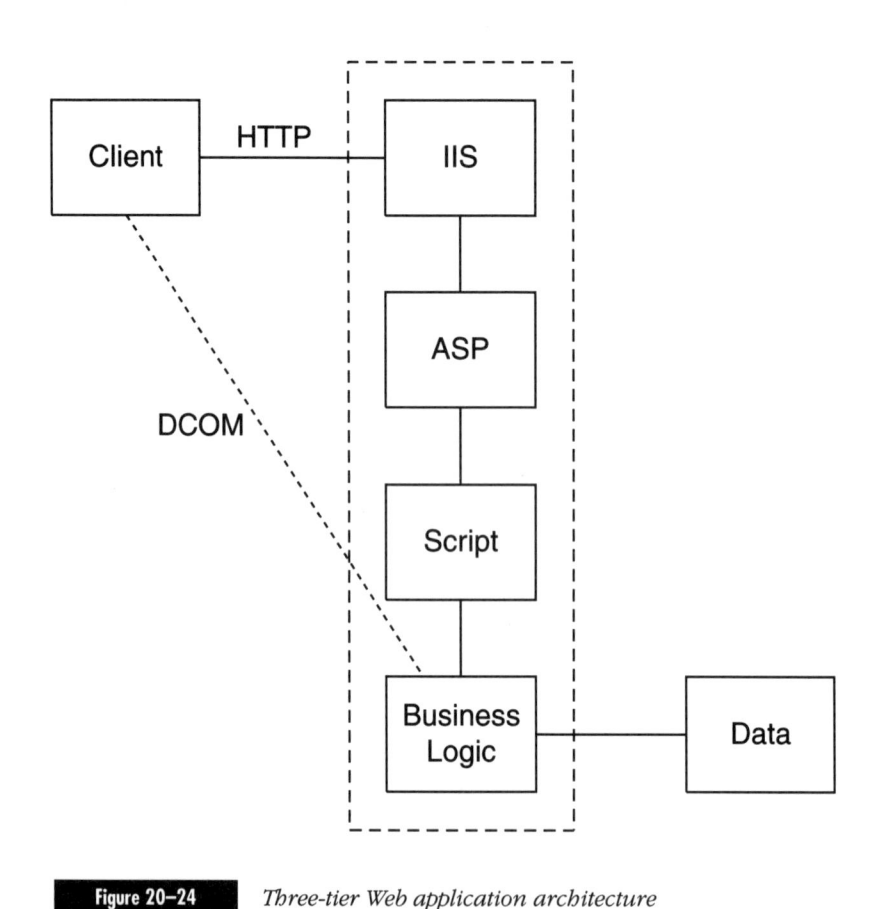

Looking at the diagram, you might be thinking that DCOM would generally be the preferred alternative. With HTTP there are all those layers. But consider first that ASP runs in-process with IIS and runs the scripting engine in-process. Interpreting the script does slow things down, but a properly designed script will not be long, and will call out to a COM component (the business logic) for the bulk of the processing.

The great advantage of the HTTP client is ease of deployment. The client can run anywhere in the world, using the Internet to connect to the Web server (IIS). DCOM might be excellent with an intranet deployed on a LAN. But if you try to run DCOM over the Internet you will run into problems. You may face firewall problems in connecting to your server. If you get through the firewall, you have to worry about keeping your connection over a wide area network.

Both DCOM and HTTP have their place. HTTP is more flexible, and we will probably see more deployments of Web-based applications, which is why this chapter is important. Chapter 21 shows a third alternative, using MSMQ, which can be attractive over a wide area network.

PRICE LIST EXAMPLE COM+ APPLICATION

Our example program is a simple price lookup. The client can either look up the price of a single item or can ask for a list of all items and their prices. The information is stored in the **Products** table of the SQL Server **Game** database that we set up in Chapter 18. We use the native SQL Server OLE DB provider, so you don't have to worry about having an ODBC data source set up. It would be a good idea to verify that you have the Game database on your computer, and go back to Chapter 18 if you do not. Bring up SQL Server Enterprise Manager and open up the Products table of the Game database. See Figure 20–25. Note that, for illustrative purposes, we have changed the price of a dog bone from 5 to 500 on one of our servers (we left it alone on the other server). You can change data using Enterprise Manager simply by typing in new data after you have opened up a table.

Now build the server program in **Chap20\PriceList**. Create an empty COM+ application **PriceApp** and install the DLL **PriceList.dll**. There will now be one component "PriceList.Price." There is the interface **_Price** having methods **FindPrice** and **ListPrices**. See Figure 20–26.

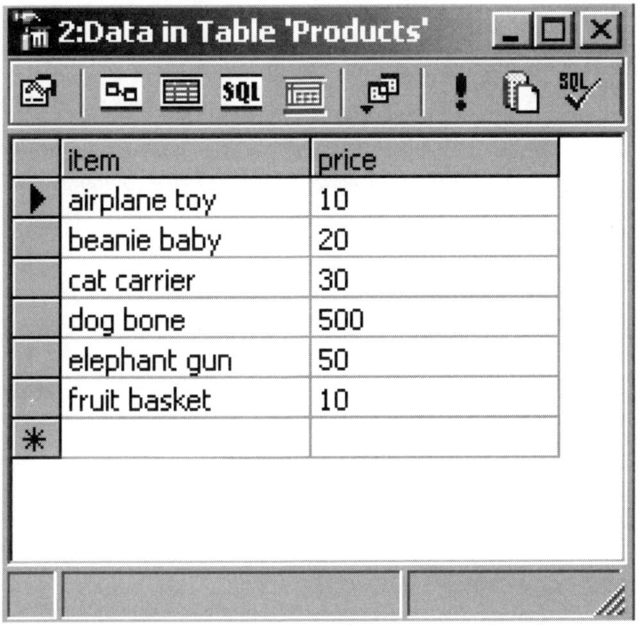

item	price
airplane toy	10
beanie baby	20
cat carrier	30
dog bone	500
elephant gun	50
fruit basket	10

Figure 20–25 *Examining the Products table in the Game database*

Chapter 20 • Web Applications Using COM+

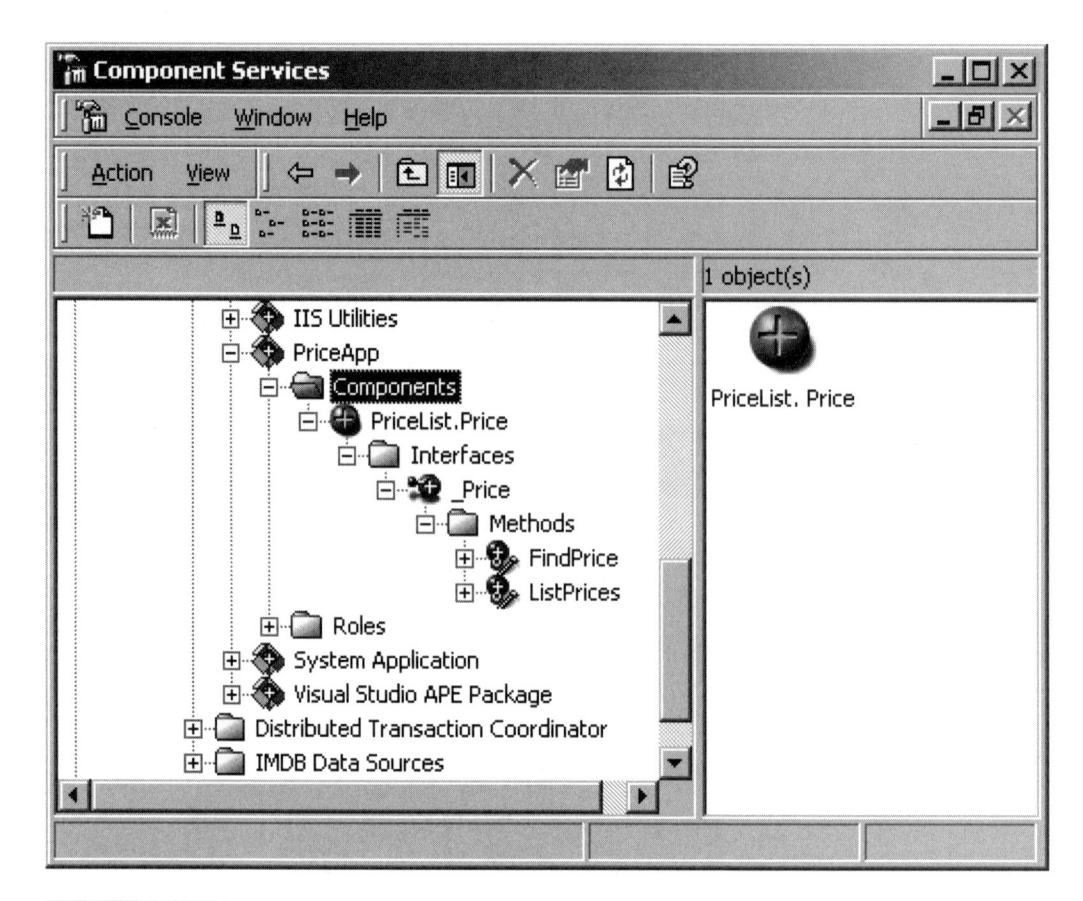

Figure 20-26 *A COM+ application containing the PriceList.Price component*

Here is the Visual Basic source code:

```
Public Function FindPrice(ByVal server As String, _
                          ByVal item As String) _
                          As Currency

    Dim strSQL As String
    Dim rsProd As New Recordset
    Dim conn As New Connection
    strSQL = "SELECT * FROM Products WHERE _
        item = " & "'" & item & "'"
    conn.Provider = "SQLOLEDB"
    conn.ConnectionString = "Server=" & server & "; " _
                          & "Database=Game;" _
                          & "uid=sa;" _
                          & "pwd=;"
```

```
    conn.Open
    rsProd.Open strSQL, conn, , adLockReadOnly, adCmdText

    'Check to see if item is found
    If rsProd.BOF Then
      FindPrice = -1
      Exit Function
    End If
    FindPrice = rsProd("price")
End Function

Public Function ListPrices(ByVal server As String) _
                    As Recordset
    Dim strSQL As String
    Dim rsProd As New Recordset
    Dim conn As New Connection
    strSQL = "SELECT * FROM Products "
    conn.Provider = "SQLOLEDB"
    conn.ConnectionString = "Server=" & server & "; " _
                        & "Database=Game;" _
                        & "uid=sa;" _
                        & "pwd=;"
    conn.Open
    rsProd.Open strSQL, conn, , adLockReadOnly, adCmdText

    Set ListPrices = rsProd

End Function
```

You can test out this COM+ application by using the client program in the folder **Chap20\PriceClient**. When you run the program, you can leave the server field blank, in which case you will be looking for data from a SQL Server running on your local machine. Or you may put in the name of a remote server, as illustrated in Figure 20–27.

USING COM/COM+ OBJECTS FROM ACTIVE SERVER PAGES

The key to building a sophisticated Web application is the ability to use COM/COM+ objects in Active Server Pages. We saw in Chapter 11 how Automation enables COM objects to be used from scripting languages. An Active Server Page is controlled by scripting, so it can create and use COM objects. If the COM component is a configured component, we have the full power of COM+ at our disposal.

Since a script language such as VBScript uses late binding, we will use **CreateObject** to instantiate our object. We must pass it the program ID. Then we can invoke methods and properties as usual.

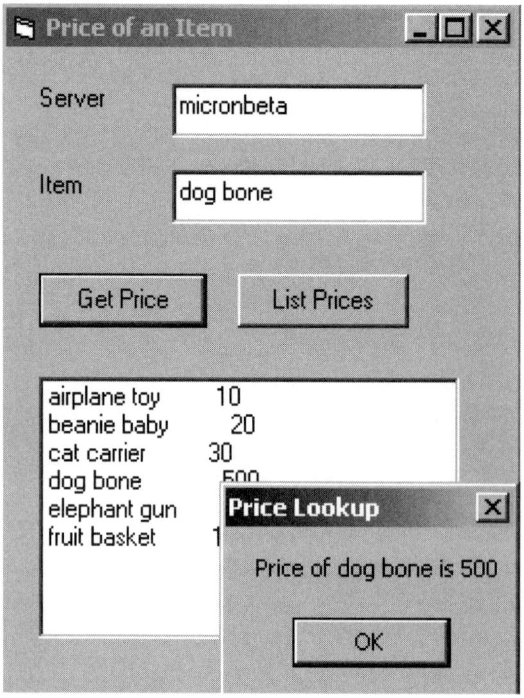

512 Chapter 20 • Web Applications Using COM+

Figure 20-27 *A standard rich client exercises the PriceList server*

As an illustration, here is the ASP page that will do a price lookup, calling the **FindPrice** method of our "PriceList.Price" component. See **Chap20\ASP\price.asp**.

```
<!-- price.asp -->
<%@ LANGUAGE = VBScript %>
<HTML>
<HEAD>
<TITLE>Price of an Item</TITLE>
</HEAD>
<BODY>
<%
set objPrice = server.CreateObject("PriceList.Price")
serverName = Request.Form("txtServer")
item = Request.Form("txtItem")
price = objPrice.FindPrice(serverName, item)
If price >= 0 Then
  str = "Price of " & item & " is " & CStr(price)
Else
  str = txtItem & " was not found"
```

```
End If
Response.Write(str)
%>
</BODY>
</HTML>
```

WEB VERSION OF PRICE LIST APPLICATION

We can now look at the Web version of our Price List application. It consists of the following parts:

- The COM component "PriceList.Price" that we installed in the COM+ application "PriceApp."
- One HTML page, **price_query.htm**.
- Two Active Server Pages, **price.asp** and **pricelist.asp**.

We have already built and installed the COM component, and we examined the code at the start of this section. There is nothing to build for the HTML and ASP pages. If you have already copied the **ASP** folder from **Chap20** to **Inetpub\wwwroot** and made **wwwroot\ASP** your home directory, you are all set to run the Web application. Use Internet Explorer to open up **price_query.htm** using the URL

```
http://localhost/price_query.htm
```

You will now see a simple HTML form where you can specify an Item (with starting value of "dog bone"). There are buttons for "Get Price" and "List Prices." If you leave the Server field blank, the program will use the SQL Server on the machine where the Web server is running. Figure 20–28 shows this form.

Here is the HTML source. Note that we have two forms. The ACTION attributes in the different forms specify different Active Server Pages, allowing us to load a different Active Server Page for each button. (This solution is not entirely correct. It is presented first for the sake of simplicity. See the final subsection for a note on a fully correct solution.)

```
<!-- price_query.htm -->
<HTML>
<HEAD>
<TITLE>Price of an Item</TITLE>
</HEAD>
<BODY>

<FORM METHOD="POST" ACTION="price.asp">
Server
<INPUT TYPE = "text" NAME="txtServer">
<P>
Item
<INPUT TYPE = "text" NAME="txtItem" VALUE = "dog bone">
```

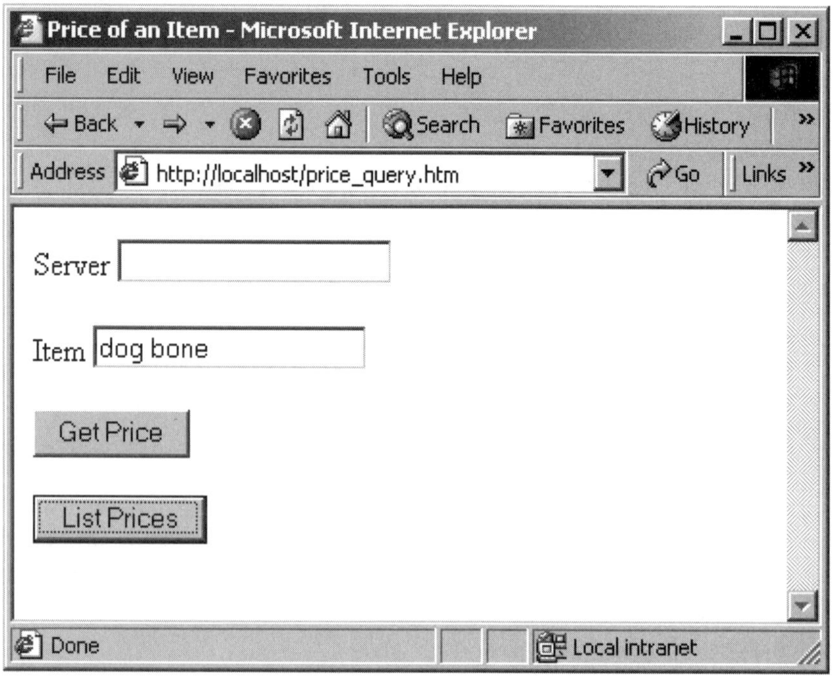

514   Chapter 20 •   Web Applications Using COM+

[Browser screenshot: Price of an Item - Microsoft Internet Explorer, address http://localhost/price_query.htm, with fields Server (empty), Item "dog bone", and buttons "Get Price" and "List Prices"]

Figure 20-28   *HTML form for price list application*

```
<P>
<INPUT TYPE = "submit" NAME="btnGetPrice" VALUE = "Get Price">
</FORM>
```

`<FORM METHOD="POST" ACTION="pricelist.asp" id=form1`
```
name=form1>
<INPUT TYPE = "submit" NAME="btnListPrices" VALUE = "List
Prices">
</FORM>

</BODY>
</HTML>
```

Try first clicking the "Get Price" button. The **price.asp** Active Server Page will be loaded, which will look up the price of the specified item and write a line of plain text, which will be sent back to the browser. Figure 20-29 shows the response that will be displayed by the browser. The ASP source code was shown in the previous subsection.

Finally try clicking the "List Prices" button. The **pricelist.asp** Active Server Page will be loaded, which will create an HTML table displaying the complete price list, as shown in Figure 20-30.

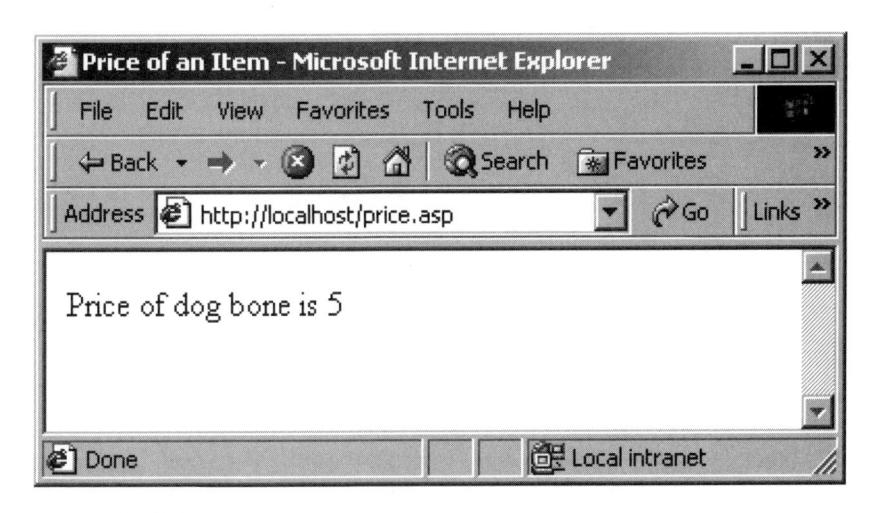

Figure 20–29   *Response for price lookup of a single item*

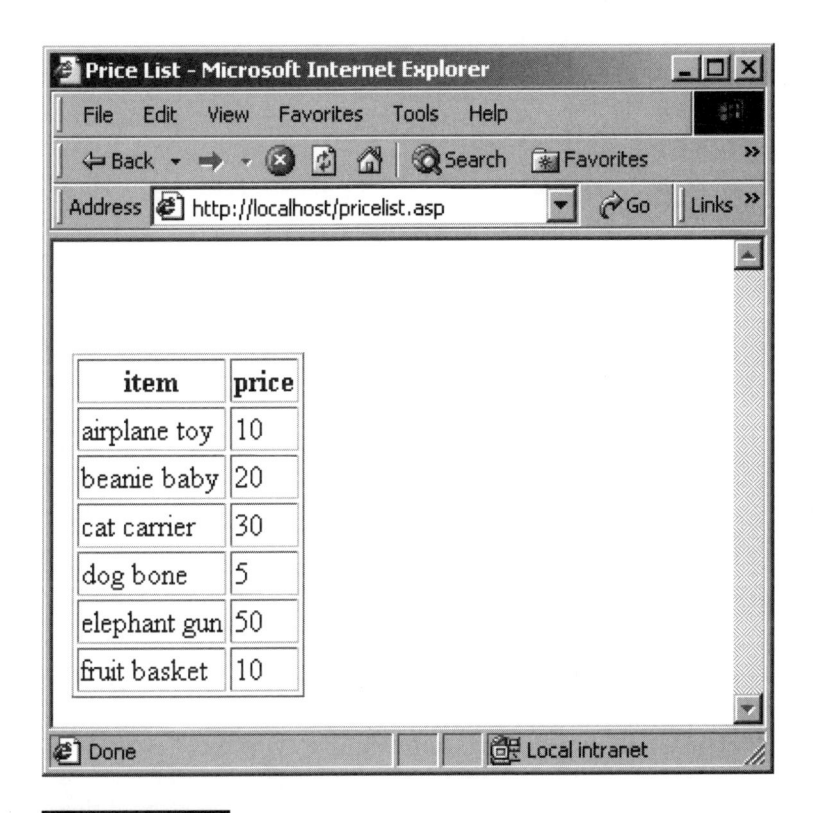

Figure 20–30   *Response which displays a table showing the complete price list*

The Active Server Page code again calls **CreateObject** and this time calls the **ListPrices** method, which returns a recordset. The script code loops through this recordset and builds an HTML table. Here is the **pricelist.asp** source.

```
<!-- pricelist.asp -->
<%@ LANGUAGE = VBScript %>
<HTML>
<HEAD>
<TITLE>Price List</TITLE>
</HEAD>
<BODY>

<%
  set objPrice = createobject("PriceList.Price")
  serverName = Request.Form("txtServer")
  set rs = objPrice.ListPrices(serverName)
%>

<TABLE BORDER>
<CAPTION ALIGN=TOP>
<b><FONT size = 6>
<BR>
</b></FONT>
</CAPTION>

<TH> item </TH>
<TH> price </TH>

<% do until rs.eof %>
<TR>
  <% for i = 0 to rs.fields.count - 1 %>
    <TD> <%= rs.fields(i).value %> </TD>
  <% next %>
  </TR>
  <% rs.movenext %>
<% loop %>

</TABLE>
</BODY>
</HTML>
```

A WEB PROGRAMMING ADDENDUM

I said that the HTML page **price_query.htm** was not completely correct. The problem comes when you try using another server. The first button "Find Price" will use the server you specify, but the second button will still use the default, local server.

The problem comes from the fact that the INPUT controls are in the first form and not the second. Hence the **Form** collection in **pricelist.asp** is not populated with the input data. The line of code

```
serverName = Request.Form("txtServer")
```

then returns an empty string, which corresponds to the case of no server specified, and the local server is used.

One solution is to use the HTTP GET method for passing "query string" information to the Web server as part of the URL. To see what information to pass, you can put a duplicate of the server INPUT box in the second form and manually fill in the name of the server you want to use. See **price_query2.htm**. If you look at this page in the browser and click the "List Prices" button, you will see a long URL in the "address" window of the browser:

```
http://localhost/
pricelist2.asp?txtServer=micronbeta&btnListPrices=List+Prices
```

After the name of the Active Server Page **pricelist2.asp** comes a question mark, followed by a list of parameters separated by ampersands. Spaces are replaced by plus signs.

All you care about is **tstServer**. Also, the first part, **http://localhost/**, will be prefixed automatically. So a sufficient URL to employ will be

```
pricelist2.asp?txtServer=micronbeta
```

where the proper name of the server is used. Now you can create the "real" HTML page, which has only one form with only one INPUT box for the server. A little bit of VBScript code is provided for handling the event of clicking the "List Prices" button. This code will use the **Navigate** method of the built-in **Window** object to send the request to the server with the specified URL. The complete code is provided in **price_query_get.htm**.

The final piece of code is a revised Active Server Page **pricelist2.asp**, which uses the **QueryString** collection of the **Request** object in place of the **Form** collection in order to extract the value from the **txtServer** INPUT box.

You can try this solution by opening **price_query_get.htm** in Internet Explorer and trying both buttons with both local and remote data servers.

Summary

This has been a long chapter, the longest in the book. The subject is a large one because there is a great deal of Web technology that is employed in building and running a Web application. We began with an overview of the classic Web, which consisted of HTML pages displayed in a Web browser, the HTTP communications protocol, and Web servers which can service requests received from Web clients and send responses back, typically HTML pages. These HTML pages can either be static or else created dynamically. Dynamic Web pages are created on the fly by a Web program. The classic interface to Web programs is the Common Gateway Interface (CGI), which spawns a separate process for each request.

We then examined Microsoft Web technology. Microsoft's initial emphasis was on the client. VBScript provided a scripting language for HTML pages, and ActiveX controls could provide the addition of rich user interface components. Microsoft uses a configurable security system, including the "signing" of ActiveX controls, in contrast to the Java sandbox.

More important are the server technologies, because they are more widely applicable, not depending on the client platform. While intranet applications can make assumptions about the client, an Internet application should run on as wide a range of browsers as possible. Microsoft's base server technology is ISAPI, which provides an efficient DLL mechanism for running Web programs in-process.

We concluded with an introduction to Active Server Pages, which are easy to create and can be scripted using VBScript or JavaScript (like the client). COM/COM+ components can be instantiated using the **CreateObject** function, and the full power of COM and COM+ can be brought to bear. We provided an illustration of a three-tier Web application that performed a price lookup from a table in a SQL Server database.

If you have not done Web programming before, you have another learning curve in store, but it is a very worthwhile one. Web applications have the tremendous advantage of ease of deployment. All that is needed on the part of a client is a Web browser, and clients can reach the application from anywhere in the world. The server capability can be arbitrarily powerful, using the full capabilities of COM+.

In the next chapter, we examine the third protocol, MSMQ, which is an alternative to DCOM and HTTP. We will look at Queued Components, which are based on MSMQ.

TWENTY ONE

MSMQ and Queued Components

*M*icrosoft Message Queue (MSMQ) *is the third of the major protocols used in building distributed applications on Microsoft platforms. The first two protocols, DCOM and HTTP, although quite different in architecture and usage, share one fundamental attribute—they are* synchronous. *When a client calls a method, the call does not return until after the message has been processed. In the case of DCOM, the server does required processing and then returns, and in the case of HTTP the Web server sends back a response in the form of an HTML page or other content. MSMQ, on the other hand, is* asynchronous. *A client makes a request by sending a message. MSMQ places the message on a queue and then immediately returns. The client is not tied up waiting for a response. The server reads messages from the queue and, if a response is wanted by the client, sends a message.*

Message queuing can improve the responsiveness of clients in a distributed application, because they do not have to wait for a network hop plus processing. In fact, message queuing can enable a client to make requests while not even connected to the server. Requests are placed in a queue on the client. When the client is later connected, the queuing system will send the message from the client queue to a server queue, from which the server can process the request.

COM+ makes it easier for applications to use MSMQ by providing a service called "Queued Components." By configuring a component as "queued" you can enable COM+ to utilize MSMQ on your behalf. The client instantiates the object using a special "queue" moniker and then makes an ordinary method call, and COM+ will marshal the parameters into an MSMQ message structure and send this message to a queue. Thus the programmer does not have to learn the MSMQ API but can rely on COM+ using MSMQ under the hood.

This chapter begins with an introduction to message queuing and to MSMQ itself, including presenting some programming examples. Although Queued Components are useful, they cannot do everything that can be done by using MSMQ directly. Also, it is a good idea to gain a basic conceptual understanding of how MSMQ works, and a knowledge of basic administration and configuration procedures. We then discuss Queued Components.

Message Queuing and MSMQ

This section discusses message queuing in general and then describes Microsoft's implementation, called Microsoft Message Queue or MSMQ.

Message Queuing

Message queuing is a conceptually simple model for building distributed systems. An application creates a message and sends it to a queue. Another application can read the message from the queue. The receiving application can then send another message to another queue. This other queue may be read by the original sender or by yet another application. Message queuing is asynchronous. As soon as the message has been posted in the queue, the sending application can go on to other work, without waiting for the message to be read. Message queuing permits offline work—a message can be queued while the application is not connected to the network, and then routed to its queue once a network connection is reestablished. Message queuing can be very robust. The queue can be saved on persistent storage, and queue operation can be retried when the system is back after a failure. Figure 21–1 illustrates this basic message queuing structure.

Message queuing and remote procedure call (RPC) are both valid high-level models for communication among applications, and each has its uses. DCOM is an object-oriented communication model built on RPC. For synchro-

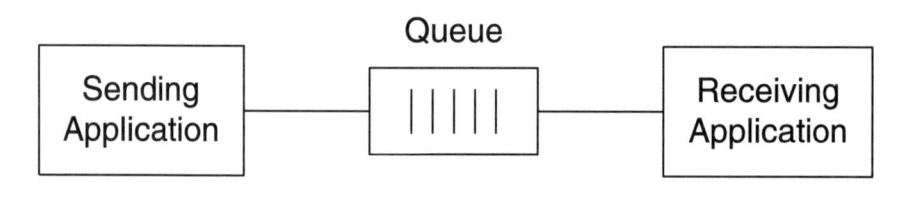

Figure 21-1 *Basic message queuing structure*

nous operations where the caller depends on results from the server before proceeding, you typically should use RPC. If the sending and the receiving application may run at different times, use message queuing. If the sender does not care which receiver processes a message, use message queuing. In message queuing, the sender posts a message to a queue, which may be read by many different servers. With RPC, the client typically talks to a specific server.

A major issue in many distributed systems is interoperability. *Data* can be accessed from multiple systems using a standard data access technique such as ODBC. But what if the *business rules* are running on a "foreign" system? Message queuing provides a simple model that is implemented on many systems. There is a whole category of "middleware" products called "message-oriented middleware," or MOM, designed for interoperability across diverse systems.

Microsoft Message Queue

Microsoft Message Queue (MSMQ) is Microsoft's implementation of message queuing on Windows platforms. There are three major components to MSMQ:

- An API for applications to send and receive messages.
- *Messages* that get created by an application and are then sent to other applications.
- *Queues* to which messages are sent and from which they are retrieved.

Queues are managed by a *queue manager*.

MSMQ APPLICATIONS

There are three main kinds of MSMQ applications. The most complete is an *MSMQ server*, which contains queues and a queue manager, support for the API, routing software, and more. An MSMQ server runs only on Windows 2000 (or NT) Server or higher. There must be at least one MSMQ server in any MSMQ system.

An MSMQ *independent client* contains support for queues and the API. Messages can be queued while the client is not connected to the network. Messages will be sent on to the server when the client reconnects.

An MSMQ *dependent client* contains only support for the API. The client must be connected at all times to the network to perform any queuing operation.

MSMQ ARCHITECTURE

The whole MSMQ network is called the *enterprise*. An enterprise is divided into *connected networks*, within which the same protocol is used (for instance, TCP/IP). A connected network may be wide area (WAN). A *site* consists of computers that are physically close—on a LAN.

One server is the *Primary Enterprise Controller* (PEC) and contains the configuration information for the entire enterprise. A server in a site is the *Primary Site Controller* (PSC) and maintains a local copy of the configuration. There may be one or more *Backup Site Controllers* (BSC). Some server machines may be *Routing Servers*.

Connector Servers provide connections to non-Window systems. Level8's FalconMQ provides connections to a number of non-Windows message queuing systems, including IBM's MQ Series.

MESSAGE QUEUE STORAGE

A message queue holds messages that are in transit. A *recoverable* queue is disk-based and will be used in robust systems. An *express* queue is RAM-based and can provide high performance. Messages are stored in native format for the system they are on.

A data store is needed for location information. In NT 4.0, SQL Server is used for location information, and thus is required for MSMQ. In Windows 2000, Active Directory Services is used, and SQL Server becomes unnecessary.

PUBLIC AND PRIVATE QUEUES

Queues in MSMQ may be either *public* or *private*. Public queues are registered with Active Directory and so can be located throughout the enterprise by MSMQ applications. Public queues are persistent, and their registration information can be backed up. Private queues are registered on the local computer. Normally, private queues are not seen by other applications, but they can be exposed by passing the other application the "format name" of the queue. Private queues are not registered with Active Directory, and so operating on them is faster.

REFERENCING QUEUES

Queues can be referenced in three different ways. Queues are created by specifying a *pathname*. A pathname has one of the following forms:

- MachineName\QueueName
- MachineName\PRIVATE\QueueName
- .\QueueName, where the dot is used to refer to the local machine.

A *queue handle* is returned to an application when it opens a queue. It is used as a parameter when an application calls other API functions. The queue handle is used directly by a programmer using the C API, and it is encapsulated by the COM object model.

The *format name* of a queue is a unique name generated by MSMQ when the queue is created. It contains a queue GUID, guaranteeing uniqueness. The format name can be retrieved by various API functions and used in others.

MSMQ API

There are two forms of the API for MSMQ. The first is a standard C language API. You must populate various structures and you pass these structures as parameters to the function calls. The second is a set of COM objects. You can use these COM objects from any language supporting COM, including Visual C++ and Visual Basic. We will focus on the COM objects API in this chapter.

MSMQ OBJECT MODEL

MSMQ has an object model similar to other object models in COM, with a root object and various other objects you create off the root. One twist is a "list" of objects which is not a COM collection.

- **MSMQQuery** is the top-level object of MSMQ. You use it to query the enterprise to obtain queues.
- **MSMQQueueInfos** is a "list" (not a VB-style collection) of queues.
- **MSMQQueueInfo** represents a single queue object. You work with a queue's properties and methods from this object.
- **MSMQQueue** represents an *open instance* of a queue. (A queue can be opened by more than one application at a time.)
- **MSMQMessage** is used for messages. You use it to create and send messages and also to refer to messages that have been received.

There are a number of other objects, including **MSMQApplication, MSMQEvent, MSMQTransaction,** etc.

MSMQ AND TRANSACTIONS

A very important feature of MSMQ is that it is a resource manager and hence can participate in distributed transactions. Figure 21–2 illustrates an application performing a transaction that involves both updating a SQL Server database and sending a message to a queue using MSMQ.

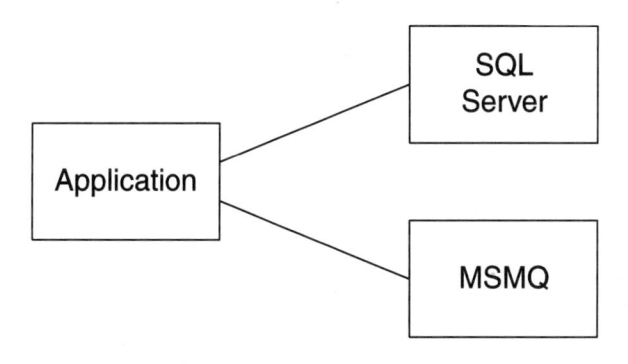

Figure 21-2   *A transaction involving SQL Server and MSMQ*

Using and Programming MSMQ

This section discusses installing and testing MSMQ, performing administration, and doing some simple programming. In order to use Queued Components you must install MSMQ—it is not installed as a default with Windows 2000.

Installing and Testing MSMQ

On your primary computer you should have Active Directory installed, and it should have been promoted to a domain controller. You can now proceed to install Microsoft Message Queue. You should install MSMQ as a server on your primary machine. On your second Windows 2000 machine, you could install MSMQ as an "independent client." This means that it will be possible to post messages to a queue on the client while the server is offline. Then when the server comes up, it can service messages in the queue. In this chapter, however, we will confine our hands-on work to using MSMQ on a single machine. After MSMQ has been installed, you can do a little testing with an API test program that has been provided with the Platform SDK.

INSTALLING MSMQ

You will do the installation on your primary machine running Windows 2000 Server. Bring up "Configure Your Server" (from Start | Programs | Administrative Tools). Click on "Advanced." From the dropdown, click on "Message Queuing." Click on "Learn More" and read the documentation provided. In particular, you will want to refer to the checklists. Separate checklists are provided for installing Message Queue servers and clients. You will install a server on your domain controller. Optionally, you could install a client on your machine running Windows 2000 Professional.

MSMQ API TEST PROGRAM

The Platform SDK supplies a useful test program for the MSMQ API. You can find this program in directory **Samples\COM\MessageQueuing\MqApiTst** in the directory where the SDK is installed (normally **Program Files\Platform SKD**). Build this program using Visual C++ and run **MqApiTst.exe**. You can now exercise the Create, Open and Send API functions to create a queue called **queue1**, open it in Send mode, and then send some messages to it. Figure 21–3 shows the feedback we get from the API test program. Notice the format name that is displayed for the public queue that is created.

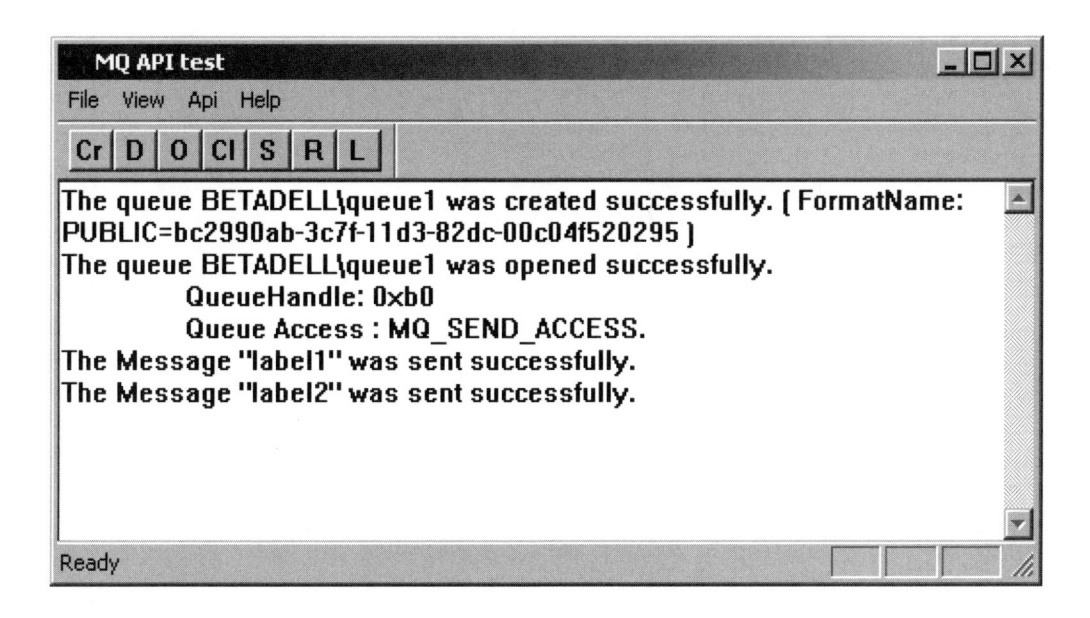

```
      MQ API test                                    _ □ ×
    File  View  Api  Help
     Cr  D  O  Cl  S  R  L
    The queue BETADELL\queue1 was created successfully. ( FormatName:
    PUBLIC=bc2990ab-3c7f-11d3-82dc-00c04f520295 )
    The queue BETADELL\queue1 was opened successfully.
            QueueHandle: 0xb0
            Queue Access : MQ_SEND_ACCESS.
    The Message "label1" was sent successfully.
    The Message "label2" was sent successfully.



    Ready
```

Figure 21-3 *Invoking MSMQ API functions*

Administering MSMQ

We can administer queues using a tool sometimes called the "MSMQ Explorer." Like so many administrative tools in Windows 2000, it is a Microsoft Management Console (MMC) snap-in. You can bring this tool up from Start | Programs | Administrative Tools | Computer Management. Open up the node "Server Applications and Services" and you will find a node for "Message Queuing," where you can view all the queues. See Figure 21-4.

You can open up the public queues and find the queue **queue1** we created using the API test program, and you can find the messages in this queue. You could now use the API test program to receive messages from the queue, and then observe that the messages have been drained from the queue. You may have to Refresh.

Example Programs

To illustrate programming with MSMQ, we provide a suite of four programs:
- **QueueCreate** creates a queue.
- **QSendObj** is a component which will send a message to a queue.
- **QueueSend** provides a user interface allowing a user to specify a queue and send a message to it, using the **QSendObj** component.

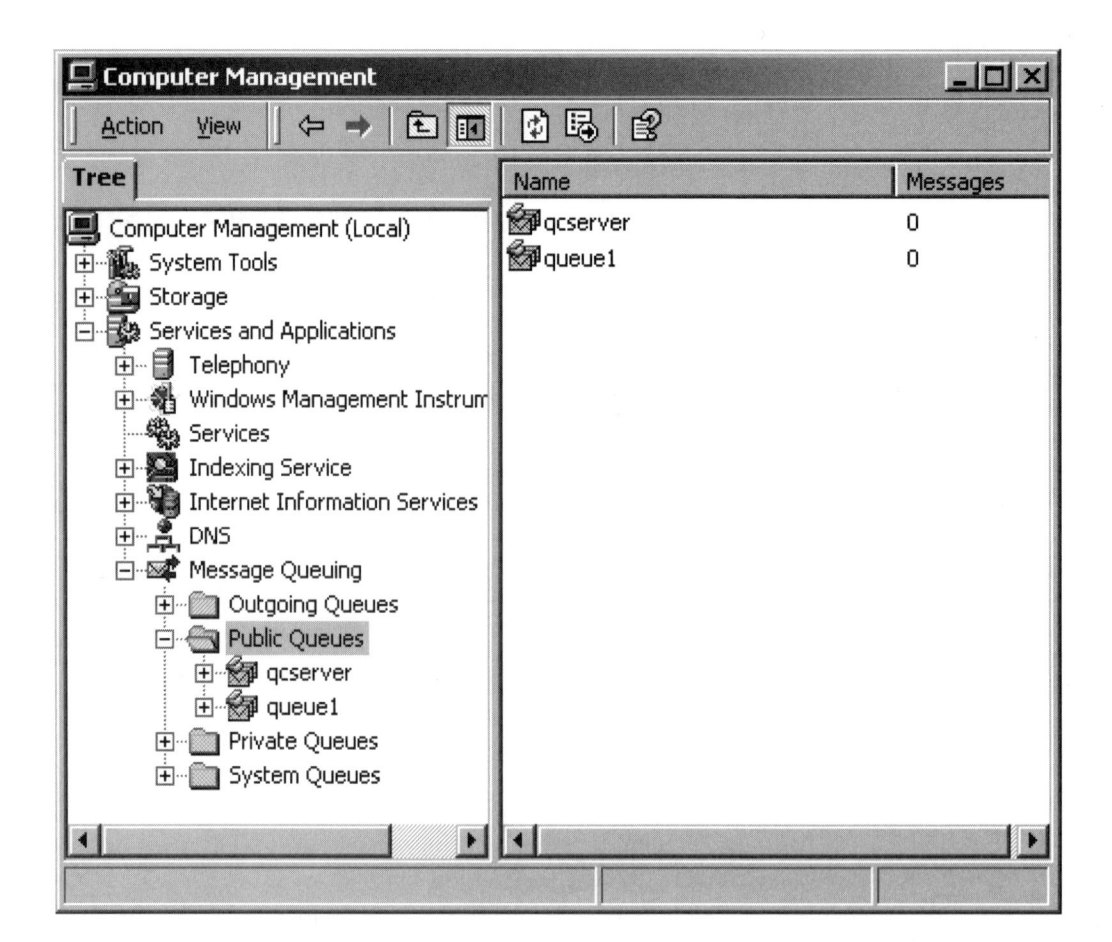

526 Chapter 21 • MSMQ and Queued Components

Figure 21-4 *The MSMQ snap-in is available from the Computer Management tool*

- **QueueReceive** provides a user interface allowing a user to receive messages from the queue.

Figure 21-5 illustrates the relationship of these programs and the queue.

The programs are in Visual Basic and make use of the COM object model for MSMQ that was outlined in the previous section.

QUEUECREATE

The **QueueCreate** program (**Chap21\QueueCreate**) is used to create a queue. A pathname derived from the name of the local machine, is suggested for the queue with "queue2" suggested as the name of the queue. A label name of "queue2" is also suggested. The user may change these names. See Figure 21-6.

Using and Programming MSMQ **527**

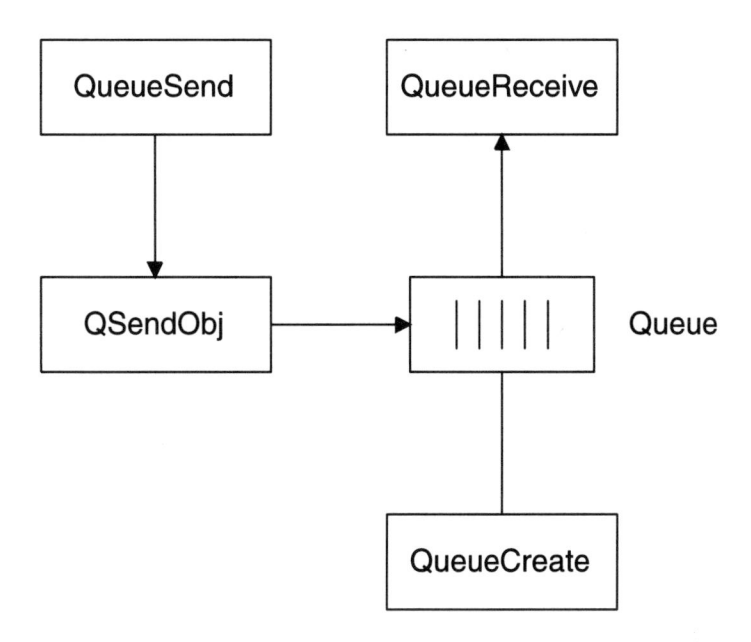

Figure 21-5 *Relationship of example queuing programs and the queue*

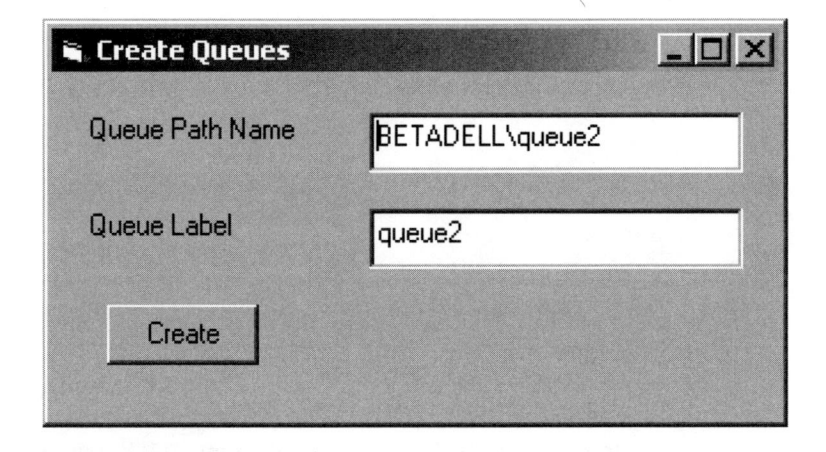

Figure 21-6 *User interface for creating a queue*

Here is the Visual Basic source code.

```
Private Declare Function GetComputerNameAPI Lib "kernel32"
_ Alias "GetComputerNameA" _(ByVal lpBuffer As String,
nSize As Long) As Long

Function GetComputerName() As String
    ' Set or retrieve the name of the computer.
    Dim strBuffer As String
    Dim lngLen As Long

    strBuffer = Space(255 + 1)
    lngLen = Len(strBuffer)
    If CBool(GetComputerNameAPI(strBuffer, lngLen)) Then
        GetComputerName = Left$(strBuffer, lngLen)
    Else
        GetComputerName = ""
    End If
End Function

Private Sub cmdCreate_Click()
    If txtLabel = "" Then
        Dim pos As Integer
        pos = InStr(1, txtPathName, "\") + 1
        txtLabel = Mid(txtPathName, pos)
    End If
    Dim objQueueInfo As New MSMQQueueInfo
    objQueueInfo.PathName = txtPathName
    objQueueInfo.Label = txtLabel
    On Error GoTo ErrorHandler
    objQueueInfo.Create
    Exit Sub
ErrorHandler:
    MsgBox Err.Description
End Sub

Private Sub Form_Load()
    txtPathName = GetComputerName & "\" & "queue2"
End Sub
```

To create a queue programmatically, you need first to create a **MSMQ-QueueInfo** object. You must assign the **PathName** property. You can optionally assign other properties. In our program, we assigned the **Label** property. Then you call the **Create** method. An optional **Boolean** parameter in the **Create** method can be used to specify that the new queue will be transactional. A transactional queue will participate in a DTC transaction.

The program makes use of the "Microsoft Message Queue 2.0 Object Library." Figure 21–7 shows the references in the Visual Basic program.

Using and Programming MSMQ

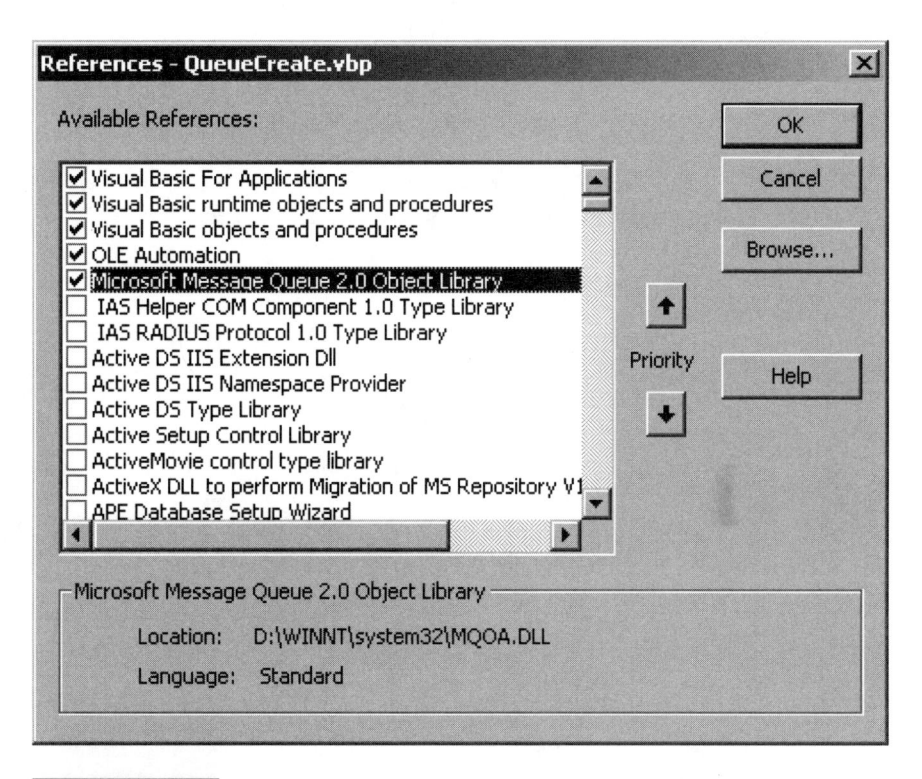

Figure 21–7 *You need a reference to the MSMQ object library*

Run the program to create the queue "queue2." You can then use MSMQ Explorer to verify that the queue has been created. Refresh if you have to.

QSENDOBJ

The **QSendObj** COM component (**Chap21\QSendObj**) has a single method **Send** that is used for sending a message to a queue. Parameters are a **MSMQ-Queue** object specifying the queue, and strings for the message label and message body. A message is created by instantiating an **MSMQMessage** object and filling in the **label** and **body** properties. The sending is done using the **Send** method of the **MSMQMessage** object., passing the queue as a parameter. Here is the code:

```
Public Sub Send(ByVal queue As MSMQQueue, _
                ByVal label As String, _
                ByVal body As String)
    Dim message As New MSMQMessage
    On Error GoTo ErrorHandler
    message.label = label
    message.body = body
    message.Send queue
```

```
    Exit Sub
ErrorHandler:
    MsgBox Err.Description
End Sub
```

Register this component, either by running the batch file **reg_QSendObj.bat** or by building the project.

QUEUESEND

The **QueueSend** program (**Chap21\QueueSend**) is used to send messages. A queue will be found from its label, and you can enter strings for the message label and message. You first try to open the queue with the specified label. If successful, you can then send a message. You can send many messages by entering new information and clicking "Send" again. See Figure 21–8.

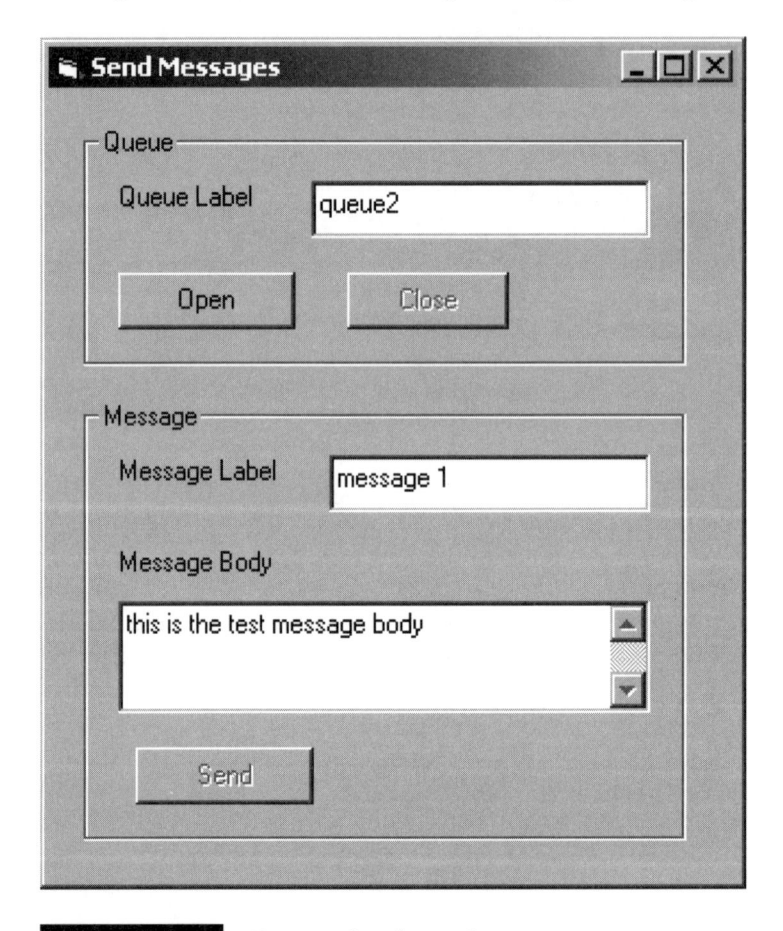

Figure 21–8   *User interface for sending a message*

Using and Programming MSMQ 531

Here is the Visual Basic source code.

```
Dim queue As MSMQQueue

Private Sub cmdClose_Click()
    queue.Close
    cmdOpen.Enabled = True
    cmdClose.Enabled = False
    cmdSend.Enabled = False
End Sub

Private Sub cmdOpen_Click()
    Dim query As New MSMQQuery
    Dim qinfos As MSMQQueueInfos
    Dim qinfo As MSMQQueueInfo
    On Error GoTo ErrorHandler

    'Locate queue with given label
    Set qinfos = query.LookupQueue(Label:=txtQueueLabel)
    Set qinfo = qinfos.Next
    If qinfo Is Nothing Then
        MsgBox "Queue not found"
        Exit Sub
    End If
    Set queue = qinfo.Open(MQ_SEND_ACCESS, MQ_DENY_NONE)
    cmdOpen.Enabled = False
    cmdClose.Enabled = True
    cmdSend.Enabled = True
    Exit Sub
ErrorHandler:
    MsgBox Err.Description
End Sub

Private Sub cmdSend_Click()
    Dim objSend As New Sender
    objSend.Send queue, txtMsgLabel, txtMsgBody
    On Error GoTo ErrorHandler
    Exit Sub
ErrorHandler:
    MsgBox Err.Description
End Sub
```

The heart of the code is the handler for the "Open" button and illustrates working with the MSMQ object model. You first create a **MSMQQuery** object, which is at the root of the object hierarchy. Use this object to create a **MSMQQueueInfos** object, which contains a list of queues. Search this list to find the specific one we want, in this case one matching our label. Assign the queue that is found to a **MSMQQueueInfo** object, which can then be used for opening the queue, getting back a **MSMQQueue** object. We actually send the message by calling our **QSendObj** component.

Use this program to send a couple of messages to the queue that you created using the **QueueCreate** program. You can then look for the messages using MSMQ Explorer. As usual, you may have to Refresh.

QUEUERECEIVE

The **QueueReceive** program (**Chap21\QueueReceive**) is used to receive messages. A queue will again be found from its label. You first try to open the queue with the specified label. If successful, you can then receive messages. Figure 21–9 illustrates the first message received from the queue.

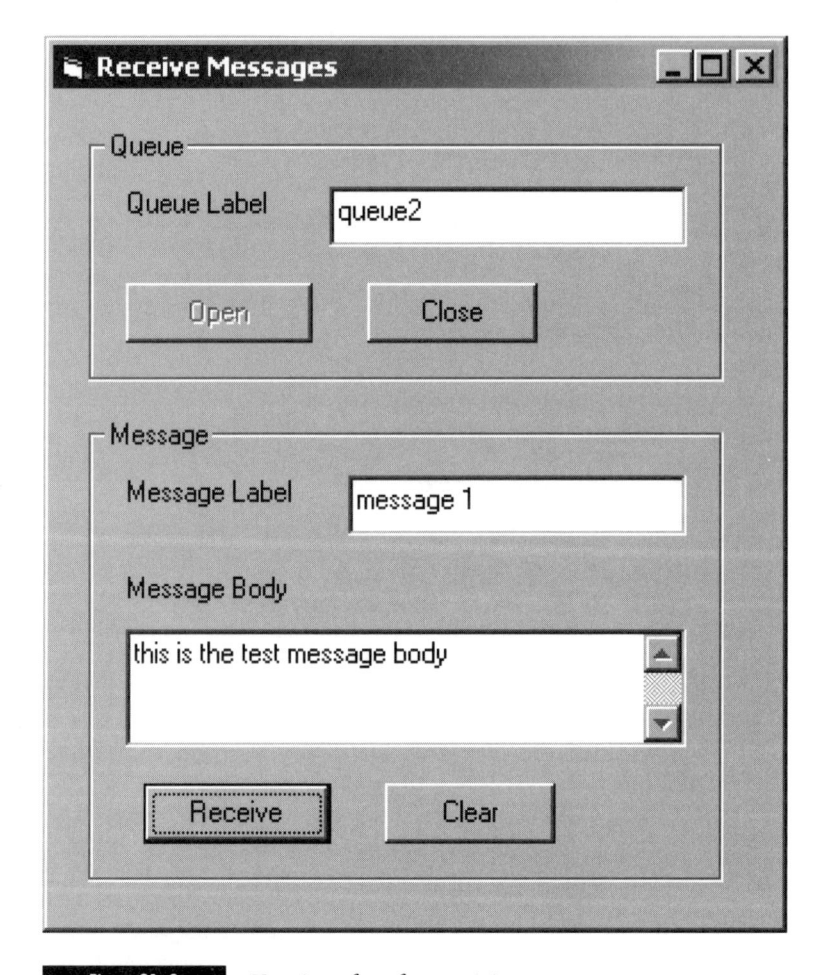

Figure 21-9   *User interface for receiving a message*

Here is the Visual Basic source code:

```vb
Dim queue As MSMQQueue

Private Sub cmdClear_Click()
    txtMsgLabel = ""
    txtMsgBody = ""
End Sub

Private Sub cmdClose_Click()
    queue.Close
    cmdOpen.Enabled = True
    cmdClose.Enabled = False
    cmdReceive.Enabled = False
End Sub

Private Sub cmdOpen_Click()
    Dim query As New MSMQQuery
    Dim qinfos As MSMQQueueInfos
    Dim qinfo As MSMQQueueInfo
    On Error GoTo ErrorHandler

    'Locate queue with given label
    Set qinfos = query.LookupQueue(Label:=txtQueueLabel)
    Set qinfo = qinfos.Next
    If qinfo Is Nothing Then
        MsgBox "Queue not found"
        Exit Sub
    End If
    Set queue = qinfo.Open(MQ_RECEIVE_ACCESS, MQ_DENY_NONE)
    cmdOpen.Enabled = False
    cmdClose.Enabled = True
    cmdReceive.Enabled = True
    Exit Sub
ErrorHandler:
    MsgBox Err.Description
End Sub

Private Sub cmdReceive_Click()
    Dim message As MSMQMessage
    On Error GoTo ErrorHandler
    Set message = queue.Receive(ReceiveTimeout:=1000)
    If Not message Is Nothing Then
        txtMsgLabel = message.Label
        txtMsgBody = message.Body
    Else
        txtMsgLabel = "*** TIMEOUT ***"
        txtMsgBody = ""
    End If
    Exit Sub
ErrorHandler:
    MsgBox Err.Description
End Sub
```

The code for opening the queue is similar to that for the send program, the main part being locating a queue from its label. When you open the queue this time, you specify receive access. To receive a message, you create an **MSMQMessage** object and call the **Receive** method, specifying a destination queue. This method call times out if no message is received within the time-out period. When you have received the message, you can then read its properties.

You can use this program to receive the messages that you sent using the **QueueSend** program.

Queued Components

MSMQ provides very useful functionality, enabling asynchronous communication between client and server. The programming model is reasonably straightforward, but even in simple cases you have to write a fair amount of code. In keeping with the overall COM+ objective of simplifying the development of distributed applications, COM+ provides a service called *Queued Components* that automates much of the work in using MSMQ. Using Queued Components, you can call a component using exactly the same method calls and have the delivery be done by MSMQ in place of RPC.

In this section, we look first at the overall architecture of Queued Components and then at the details of configuring and programming with Queued Components.

Queued Components Architecture

COM+ processes method calls to a queued component using a special kind of proxy called the *Recorder*. The Recorder exports the same interfaces as the target component. But, unlike an RPC proxy, the Recorder uses MSMQ as the transport mechanism. The Recorder receives the method call, marshals the parameters into an MSMQ message, and then sends this message to a queue that is associated with the component. On the receiving side, the *Listener* takes messages off the queue and passes them on the *Player*. The Player unmarhsals the parameters from the message and calls the target component. Figure 21–10 illustrates this architecture.

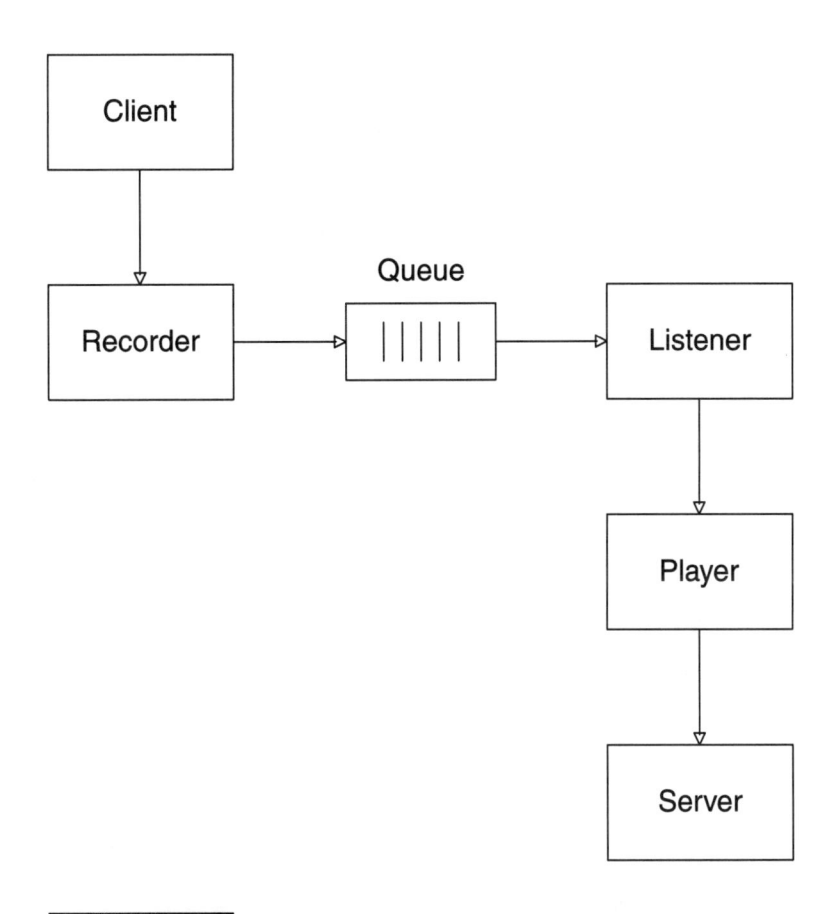

Figure 21-10 *Queued components architecture*

Using Queued Components

It is quite easy to use Queued Components. The same COM component, provided it satisfies certain requirements, can be accessed either by queuing or via straight DCOM. The component is unaware of how it is being accessed on any given method call. The component must be installed in a COM+ application and configured for queuing in the Catalog. Security must be configured properly. The client uses a special mechanism of a "queue moniker" to obtain the initial interface pointer. Finally, the server is activated somewhat differently from straight COM/DCOM. In this section, we go through these various considerations, leaving the configuration details to a separate section.

REQUIREMENTS FOR A QUEUED COMPONENT

A Queued Component must satisfy the normal requirements for a COM+ component, such as being self-registering and having a type library. In addition, a Queued Component must have only **in** parameters in all of its methods and must not return a result value. This restriction is required by the asynchronous nature of invoking methods on a Queued Component. The method call results in a message being placed on a queue, not in actually calling the server. All method calls are one-way. In order to get a response back, the server must itself make a one-way method call back to the client.

CONFIGURATION OF A QUEUED COMPONENT

The COM+ application containing a Queued Component must be configured as Queued. This does not mean that every method call is going to come in through MSMQ, but that queuing is supported so that COM+ will be able to create the Player, etc. In addition, each interface that will support queued invocation must be marked as Queued. This configuration can be performed using the Component Services snap-in or via the admin API. An interface can be marked as QUEUEABLE using IDL.

```
[
    odl,
    uuid(650D1702-3550-11D3-82D3-00C04F520295),
    version(1.0),
    hidden,
    dual,
    nonextensible,
    oleautomation,
    QUEUEABLE
]
interface _Name : IDispatch {
    [id(0x60030000)]
    HRESULT Add([in] BSTR str);
};
```

SECURITY CONSIDERATIONS

You need to have an internal MSMQ security certificate for each user. This is a digital signature that MSMQ employs to authenticate users. You can obtain an internal MSMQ certificate using the MSMQ Control Panel applet. Select the Security tab and click "Renew Internal Certificate." We will illustrate this when we go through the configuration of our sample application.

QUEUE MONIKER

A client program does not use the normal **CoCreateInstanceEx** mechanism for obtaining an interface pointer for a Queued Component. Instead it calls

CoGetObject and passes a "queue moniker." A Visual Basic program does not use **New** but calls **GetObject**.

A *moniker* is a special kind of COM object whose whole purpose in life is to obtain an interface pointer to another COM object. Monikers were invented to support links in OLE. A link is really a name for an object. OLE 1.0 did not have the notion of a moniker but instead used pathnames to identify linked objects. OLE 2.0 introduced monikers, which are much more flexible. A linked object can now be a great many things, not just a file which had a name in the file system. For example, you can link to a range of cells in a spreadsheet via a moniker. The moniker is an "intelligent name" that knows how to find the object that it refers to. When you "bind" a moniker to its object, you get back an interface pointer to the object that the moniker names. The moniker then drops out of the picture, and after that you are talking directly to the object (possibly through a proxy).

After the original use of monikers in OLE, it has turned out that there are many different kinds of monikers that have proved useful in COM. For example, a URL moniker can be used to reference an object on the Internet, using its Uniform Resource Locator as its name. You rarely, if ever, will have occasion to implement a moniker yourself, but you may frequently find yourself employing a system-supplied moniker.

Queued Components introduced two new kinds of monikers. The first is called a **new** moniker, and it can be used to obtain an interface pointer giving a class ID or a program ID. Here is some Visual Basic code that obtains an object reference using **GetObject** and the **new** moniker:

```
Dim objName As Name
Set objName = GetObject("new:qcServer.Name")
```

Monikers can be composed. You obtain an interface pointer for a Queued Component by composing the **queue** moniker with the **new** moniker. Here is some Visual Basic code that obtains an object reference for a Queued Component:

```
Dim objName As Name
Set objName = GetObject("queue:/new:qcServer.Name")
```

The object reference you obtain turns out to refer to the COM+ Recorder rather than to the target object itself. The Recorder will receive the method call and place a corresponding message in the queue that is associated with the component.

Notice that COM+ handles Queued Components somewhat differently from using the normal interceptor mechanism based on contexts. We still have declarative attributes (in this case, Queued). But rather than always going through an interceptor, the client has a choice of making an ordinary synchronous RPC call to the component or making an asynchronous call using MSMQ. In the latter case, the client uses the queue moniker to obtain the interface pointer. Once the interface pointer is obtained, subsequent calls to methods of the component are identical to what they would be in the ordinary synchronous case.

STARTING A QUEUED APPLICATION

Queued Components also differ from standard components in how they are started. With COM and DCOM, the Service Control Manager starts ("launches") a component as necessary to satisfy a method call. This happens synchronously with the call. In the case of Queued Components, the server does not have to be launched synchronously. In fact, in the disconnected case, the server may not actually be launched until sometime after the client has placed the request in the queue. So it is not the method call itself that triggers the activation of the server.

What needs to happen is for the Listener to be started. For this to happen, the Listener must first of all be configured as enabled in the Catalog. Second, the application must be started, which can be done either through the Component Services snap-in or by using the admin API. As an alternative, the component can be started by making a nonqueued method call (even the same method call that will later be called through queuing). Once the component is started and the Listener is running, messages that arrive at the queue will be taken off the queue as they arrive and be packaged up as calls to the server.

Programming Example

We provide a simple illustration of Queued Components. The server is **qcServer** (in the folder **Chap21\qcServer**), and the client is **qcClient** (in **Chap21\qcClient**). The program simply adds a name to a list of names. Rather than using a database, the server writes the name passed to it by writing to a log file, using the **Logger** component we introduced in Chapter 12. Here is the complete Visual Basic source code for the server:

```
Public Sub Add(ByVal str As String)
    Dim objLog As New Log
    objLog.Write str
End Sub
```

The program ID of this server is "qcServer.Name."

The client program provides a user interface for entering a name and three buttons. The "Add" button does an ordinary instantiation of an object and makes a synchronous method call. The "Add via New" button gets the object reference via **GetObject** and the new moniker. The method call is synchronous in this case also. The "Add via Server Queue" button gets the object reference via **GetObject** and the queue moniker. In this case, the call goes through MSMQ, and messages will pile up on the queue until the server is activated. When the server is active, it will drain messages from the queue as they arrive. Figure 21–11 shows the user interface of the client program.

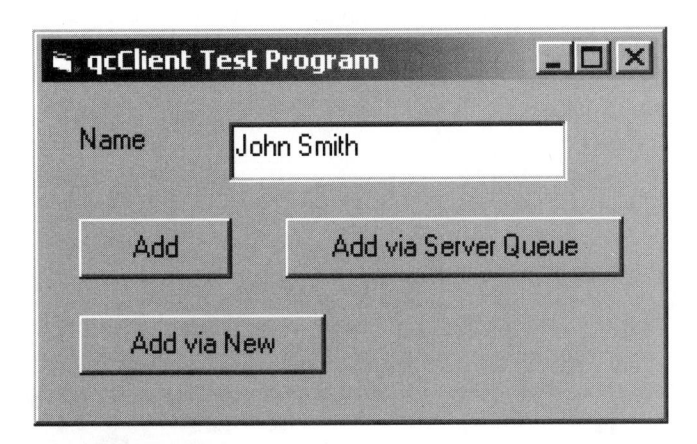

Figure 21-11 *User interface for program illustrating synchronous and asynchronous calls*

Here is the Visual Basic source code:

```
Private Sub cmdAdd_Click()
    Dim objName As New Name
    objName.Add txtName
End Sub

Private Sub cmdAddNew_Click()
    Dim objName As Name
    Set objName = GetObject("new:qcServer.Name")
    objName.Add txtName
End Sub

Private Sub cmdAddQueue_Click()
    Dim objName As Name
    Set objName = GetObject("queue:/new:qcServer.Name")
    objName.Add txtName
End Sub
```

Configuring a Queued Component

Before doing anything else, make sure the Logger component from Chjapter 12 is registered by running the batch file **reg_logger.bat** (or by making the **logger.dll**). To run this example as a Queued Component, you must first create an empty COM+ application, "qcServer." Install **qcServer.dll** into your new application. Now you should be able to run the client program to add some names via the "Add" and "Add via New" buttons. Check by looking at the log file that is created, **c:\logfile.txt**.

After we are done we want to make sure the server is not running. To that end, bring up the Task Manager and kill all the **dllhost.exe** processes that you can. You can easily find the **dllhost.exe** project by clicking twice on the "Image Name" header of the list view control showing the processes. See Figure 21–12.

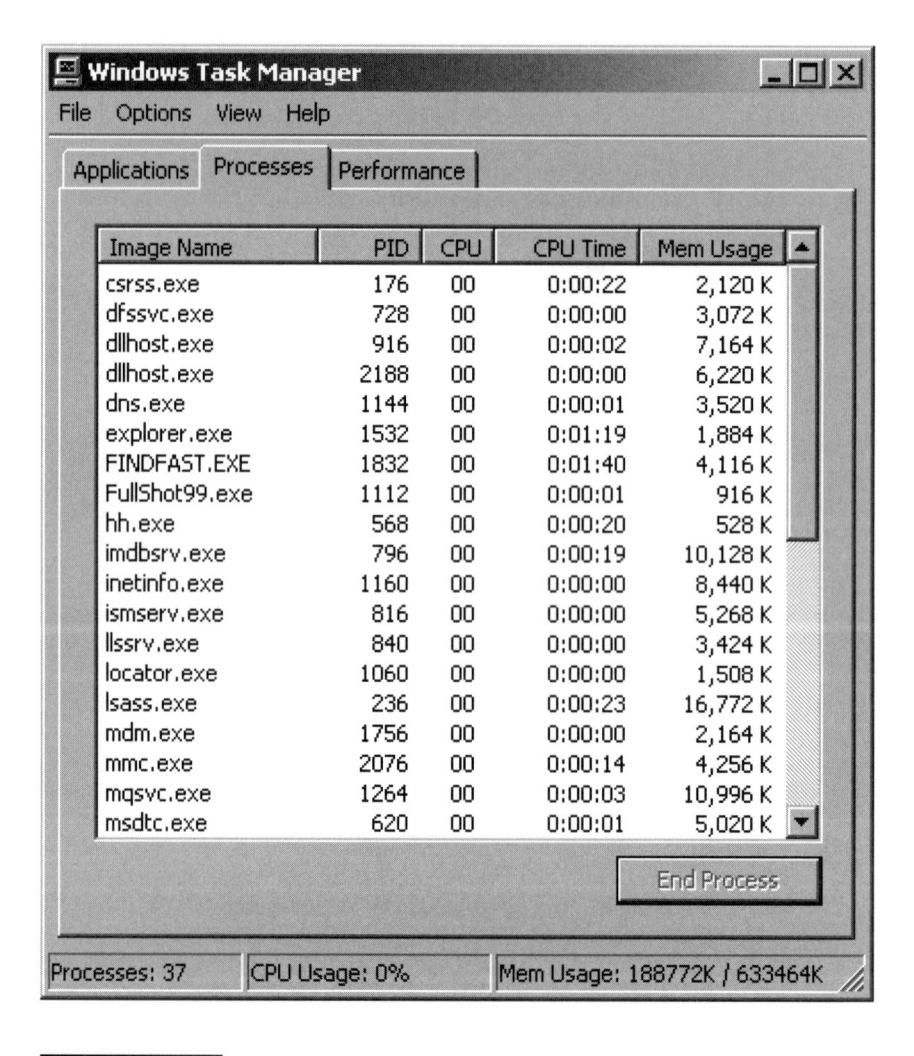

Image Name	PID	CPU	CPU Time	Mem Usage
csrss.exe	176	00	0:00:22	2,120 K
dfssvc.exe	728	00	0:00:00	3,072 K
dllhost.exe	916	00	0:00:02	7,164 K
dllhost.exe	2188	00	0:00:00	6,220 K
dns.exe	1144	00	0:00:01	3,520 K
explorer.exe	1532	00	0:01:19	1,884 K
FINDFAST.EXE	1832	00	0:01:40	4,116 K
FullShot99.exe	1112	00	0:00:01	916 K
hh.exe	568	00	0:00:20	528 K
imdbsrv.exe	796	00	0:00:19	10,128 K
inetinfo.exe	1160	00	0:00:00	8,440 K
ismserv.exe	816	00	0:00:00	5,268 K
llssrv.exe	840	00	0:00:00	3,424 K
locator.exe	1060	00	0:00:00	1,508 K
lsass.exe	236	00	0:00:23	16,772 K
mdm.exe	1756	00	0:00:00	2,164 K
mmc.exe	2076	00	0:00:14	4,256 K
mqsvc.exe	1264	00	0:00:03	10,996 K
msdtc.exe	620	00	0:00:01	5,020 K

Processes: 37   CPU Usage: 0%   Mem Usage: 188772K / 633464K

Figure 21–12   *You can use Task Manager to kill **dllhost.exe** processes*

CONFIGURING APPLICATION AS QUEUED

The first unique step for configuring a Queued Component is to mark the application as Queued. In the Component Services snap-in, right-click on "qcServer" and select Properties from the context menu. Select the "Queuing" tab. Check both the "Queued" and "Listen" check boxes. See Figure 21–13.

As soon as you have performed this step, COM+ will create a public queue called "qcserver," as you can verify using the MSMQ snap-in. There will also be a number of private queues created.

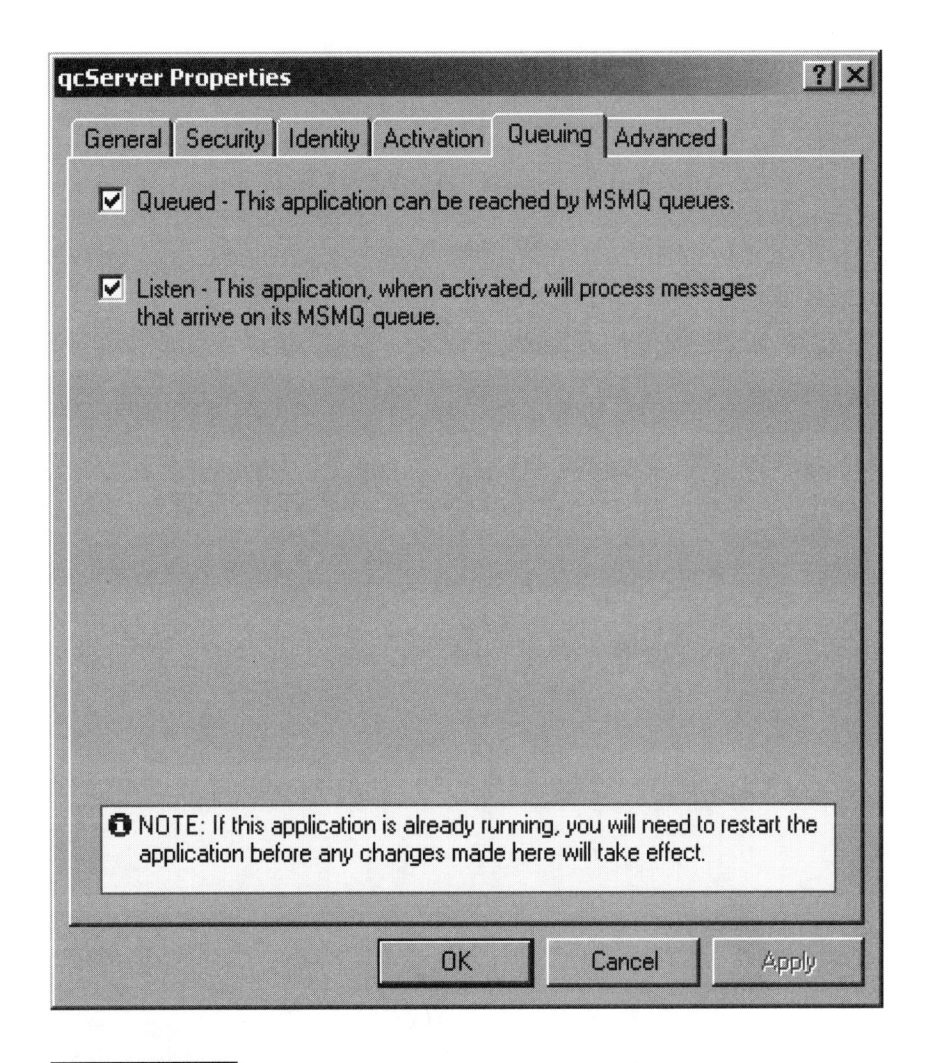

Figure 21-13 *Configuring a COM+ application as Queued*

CONFIGURING INTERFACE AS QUEUED

Next you have to configure the interface as queued. (The server was written in Visual Basic, so you do not have access to the IDL. If you wrote the server in Visual C++, you could add a "queueable" attribute to the IDL to automate this step.) In the Component Services snap-in, open up the "qcServer.Name" component to show the interfaces, and right-click on "_Name." From the context menu choose "Properties." Select the "Queuing" tab and check "Queued." See Figure 21–14.

If you run your client program at this point and try the "Add via Server Queue" button, you will find no error messages, but no messages get added to the "qcserver" queue.

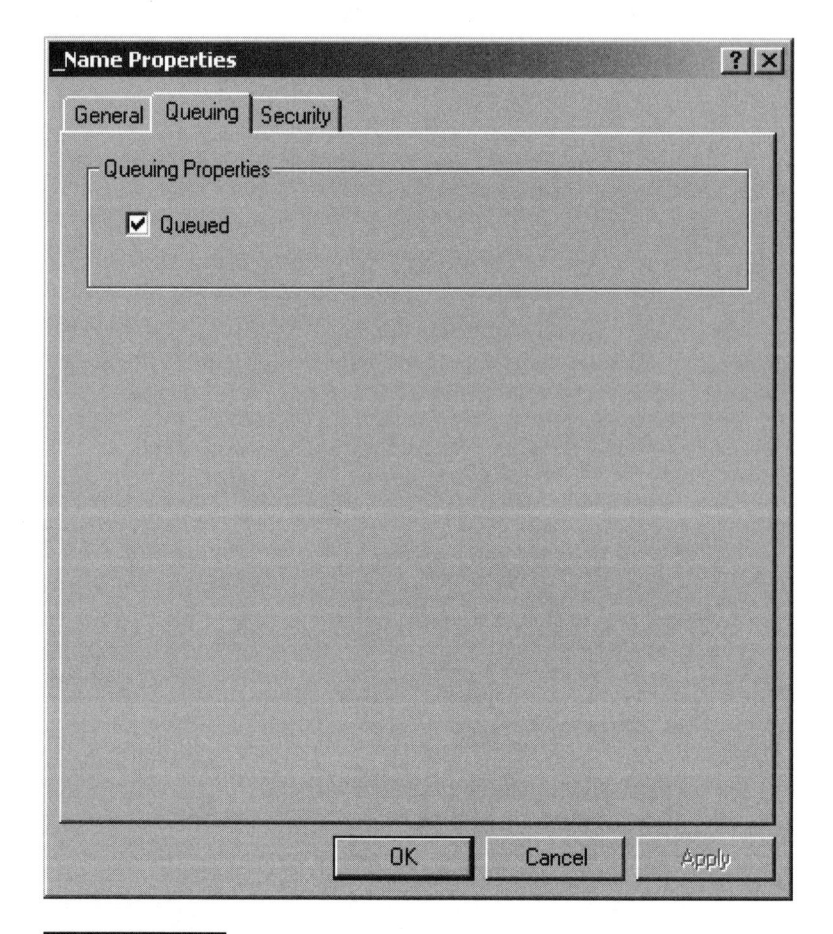

Figure 21-14 *Marking an interface as Queued*

OBTAINING AN MSMQ SECURITY CERTIFICATE

The next step is to obtain an MSMQ internal security certificate for each user account that you want to be able to use Queued Components. If you are doing all your work under Administrator, you just need to do this once. The easiest way to obtain this certificate is to bring up the Message Queuing applet from the Control Panel. Select the Security tab and click "Renew Internal Security Certificate." See Figure 21–15.

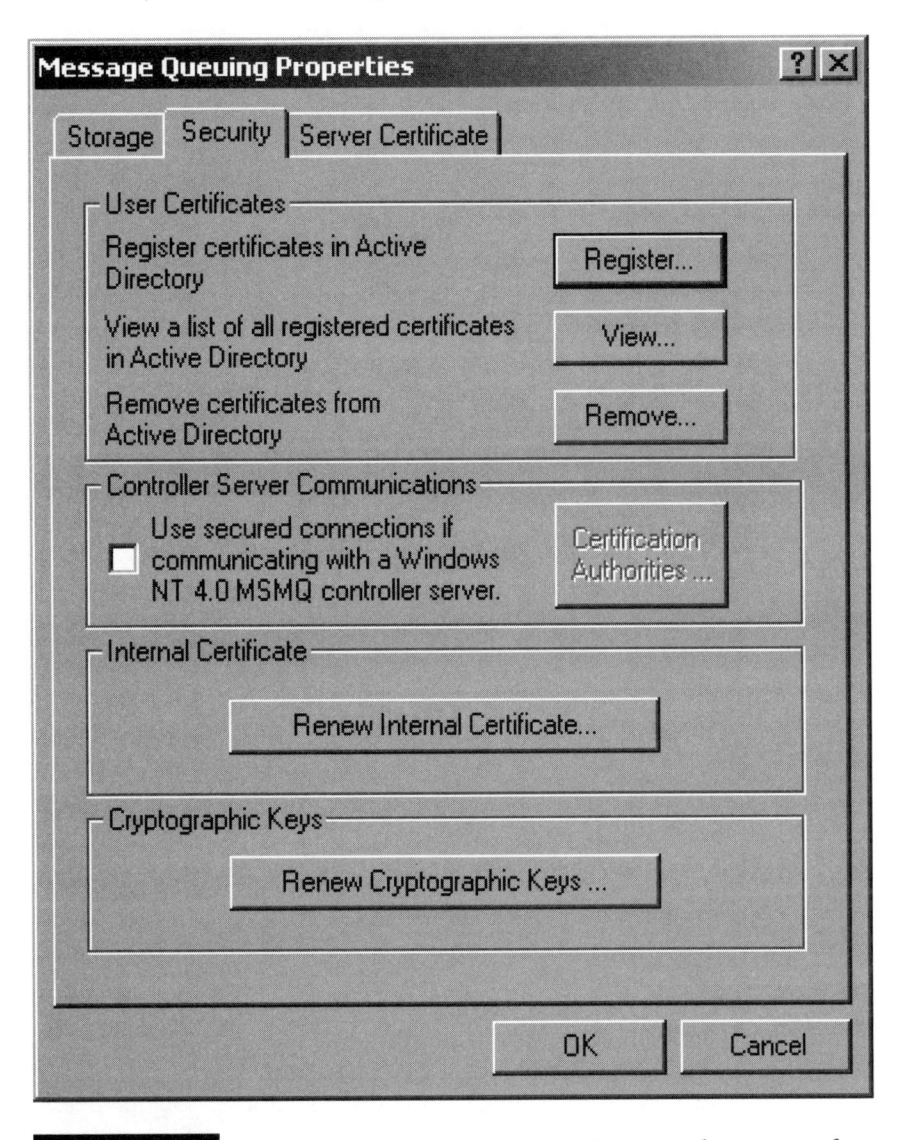

Figure 21–15 *Using the Control Panel to renew MSMQ internal security certificate*

ADDING REQUESTS TO THE QUEUE

Now you can run your client program and you should at this point be able to see requests get added to the "qcserver" queue. Add three names using the "Add via Server Queue" button. DO NOT use either of the other two buttons at this point. Check out the queue using the MSMQ snap-in. You should see three messages (don't forget to Refresh). See Figure 21–16.

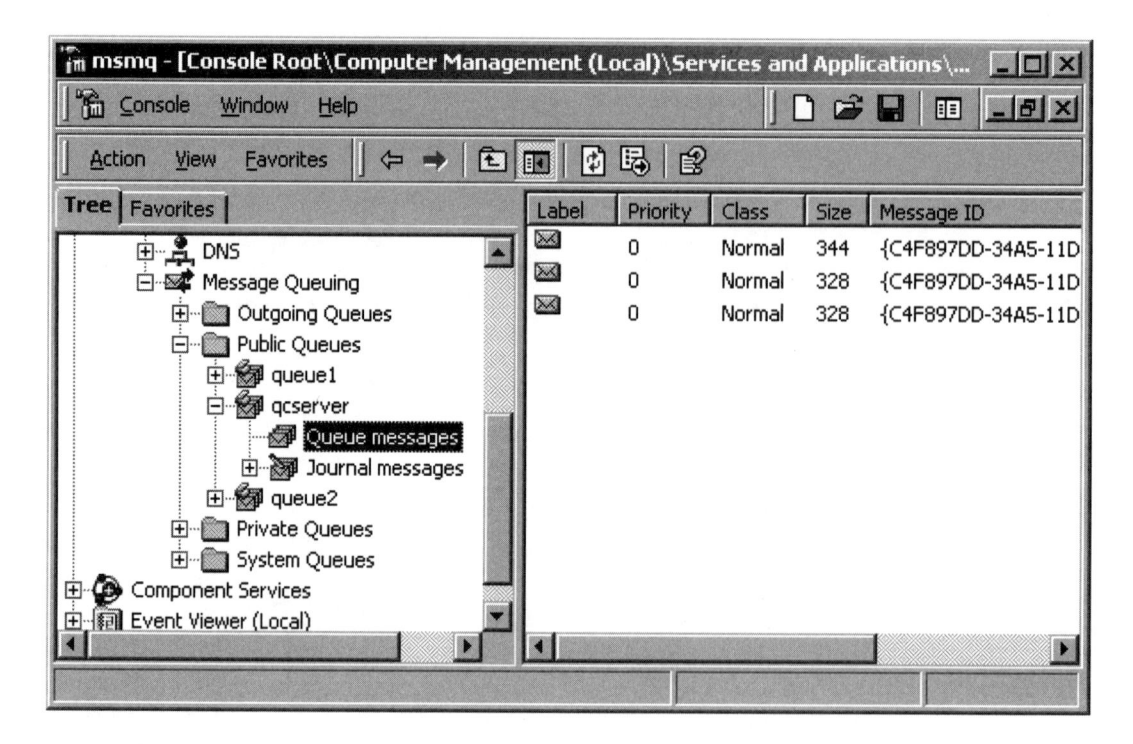

Figure 21–16 *Method calls for a Queued Component get placed in a queue*

STARTING A QUEUED APPLICATION

Finally, we have to start the server. We can do that from the Component Services snap-in by right-clicking over the application and choosing "Start" from the context menu. You can initiate shutdown of the application from the "Shut Down" command of the same menu. "Start" should happen immediately, but you may find that the shutdown may take a while. You can use Task Manager to observe start and shutdown via noticing **dllhost.exe** in the list of processes.

Queued Components 545

Once the application starts, the queue should immediately drain, and you should see names reflected in the log file **c:\logfile.txt**.

You may notice some boundary effects when the application first starts, such as not all the names written out to the log file immediately or in the order you expect. But once the application is running, you should see all names processed.

USING ADMIN OBJECTS

You can control application start and shutdown with just a little admin code. All you need is the one object **COMAdminCatalog** and a single method call. The program **appStarter** in the folder **Chap21\appStarter** illustrates. See Figure 21-17.

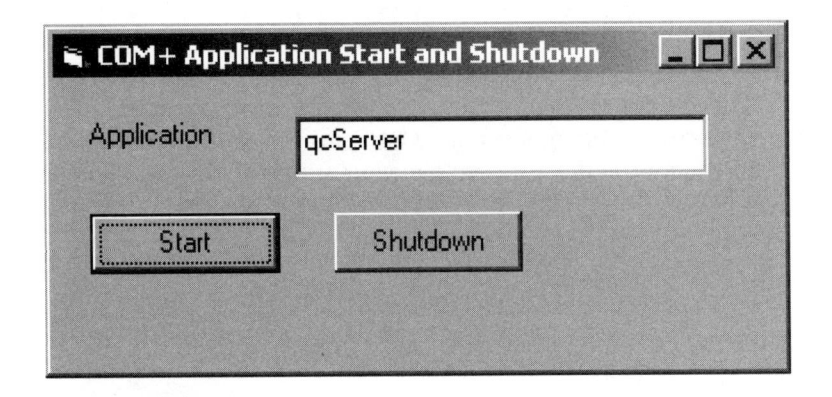

Figure 21-17 *User interface for admin program to start and shut down COM+ applications*

Here is the Visual Basic source code for this program:

```
Private Sub txtShutdown_Click()
    Dim cat
    Set cat = CreateObject("COMAdmin.COMAdminCatalog")
    cat.ShutdownApplication txtApp
End Sub

Private Sub txtStart_Click()
    Dim cat
    Set cat = CreateObject("COMAdmin.COMAdminCatalog")
    cat.StartApplication txtApp
End Sub
```

Summary

Message queuing provides an alternative to RPC for invoking services from a server. While RPC is synchronous, message queuing is asynchronous. In a distributed environment, message queuing offers various advantages, including greater robustness. You cannot expect 100 percent reliability of any network, especially a wide area one. Message queuing can store messages in persistent, recoverable queues, providing a guaranteed delivery. Microsoft's implementation of message queuing is called Microsoft Message Queue or MSMQ. It can be programmed using a COM object model.

Queued Components is a COM+ service that can automate the use of MSMQ. If your component permits, by having only **in** parameters in method calls, you can mark it as "Queued." Then COM+ can do the work for you of packaging up your method calls and using MSMQ as a transport mechanism.

We have been extending the reach of COM in various ways, going beyond the straight COM/DCOM protocol of a client making a synchronous call of a server using RPC. The first alternative we looked at was HTTP. We have just examined using MSMQ as a transport. In the next chapter, we discuss an event model that COM+ provides which facilitates sending event notifications in the opposite direction, from the server to the client.

TWENTY TWO

COM+ Events

*E*vents have long been a part of standard COM, and indeed a core concept in the Windows programming model. Through "events," a program can receive notifications of occurrences outside the program. Graphical user interfaces need to deal with many different events associated with user interaction with the computer, such as clicking the mouse, choosing a menu item, selecting an item from a listbox, etc. With an "event" abstraction, the program implements event handlers to respond to these external events. In Chapter 11 we saw how to work with events in Visual Basic, which are built on a COM technology known as "connection points."

The same concept of events arises in distributed applications. Whether in process control, factory automation, patient monitoring, or many other kinds of applications, there is frequently a need for a program to receive notifications of outside occurrences. COM connection points can be used for implementing events in the distributed case, but they are not an ideal solution because they set up a "tight" coupling between the sender and receiver of the event notifications. COM+ provides a *loosely coupled* event system based on the notions of *publishers* and *subscribers*.

In this chapter, we first examine the classical COM event system based on connection points, and we then describe the COM+ loosely coupled event model of publishers and subscribers. We will provide a programming example of loosely coupled events.

Events and Connection Points in COM

In this section, we look at standard tightly coupled events in COM, which provides a background for our subsequent discussion of the loosely coupled event model of COM+. To help make things concrete, we will work with a common programming example to illustrate both technologies. Our example is illustrated in Visual Basic, but we will also look at the underlying COM connection point mechanism.

Event Example

Our example is a prototype of an event structure for the Electronic Commerce Game™. We want to provide the capability for players of the game to receive notifications when a new player joins the game and when a player quits the game. It is like an online chat room, where you receive a notification of a new person joining the chat or leaving the chat.

To run the demo, register the server component in **Chap22\VbEvent** by making the DLL or by running the registration batch file **reg_VbEvent.bat**. Then you can run the client program in **Chap22\VbEventClient**. Figure 22–1 illustrates the user interface of the client.

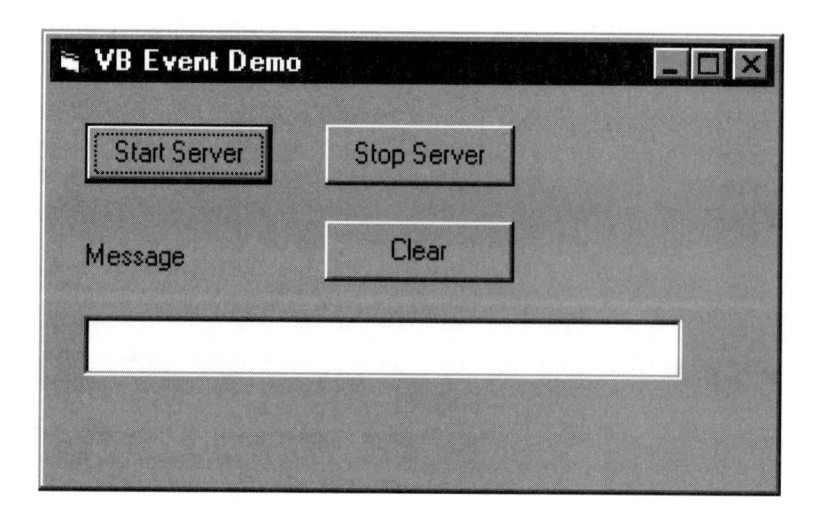

Figure 22-1 *User interface of client program for event demonstration*

When you click "Start Server," the server component **Player** is instantiated. It puts up a user interface, which will enable you to "fire" events back to the client. Figure 22–2 illustrates the user interface of the server component. You can then enter a name for a player and click either "Join" or "Quit." You should see in the client window a message displayed saying that a certain player either joined or quit the game. When you are done in the client program, click the "Stop Server" button and the server object will be destroyed.

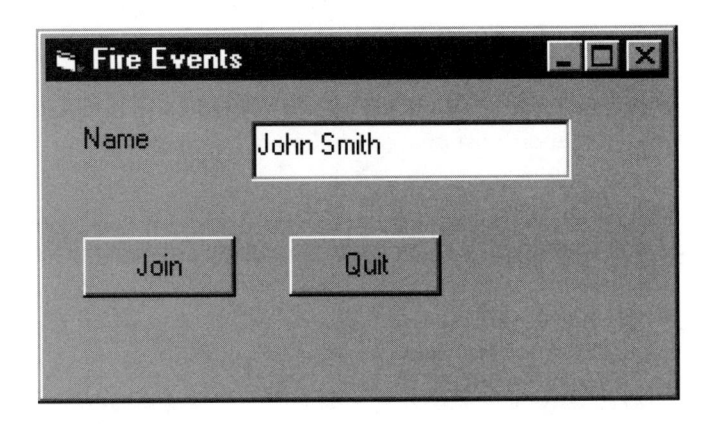

Figure 22-2 *User interface of server component for event demonstration*

SERVER

The server component is **VbEvent**. It provides a class **Player** that implements the events **Join** and **Quit**. When the class is initialized (object instance created), a form is loaded. This form provides the user interface for "firing" the events. In Visual Basic, you fire events through the **RaiseEvent** statement, which must be called from the class. To enable the events to be fired from the form, the class provides two helper functions, **FireJoin** and **FireQuit**. Here is the Visual Basic source code for the class **Player**.

```
Public Event Join(ByVal name As String)
Public Event Quit(ByVal name As String)

Private Sub Class_Initialize()
    Load Form1
    Set Form1.objEvent = Me
    Form1.Visible = True
End Sub

Public Sub FireJoin(ByVal name As String)
    RaiseEvent Join(name)
End Sub

Public Sub FireQuit(ByVal name As String)
    RaiseEvent Quit(name)
```

```
End Sub

Public Sub StopServer()
    Set Form1.objEvent = Nothing
    Unload Form1
End Sub
```

And here is the simple code of the form, which handles the buttons by calling the helper functions to fire the corresponding event.

```
Public objEvent As Player

Private Sub cmdJoin_Click()
    objEvent.FireJoin txtName
End Sub

Private Sub cmdQuit_Click()
    objEvent.FireQuit txtName
End Sub
```

CLIENT

The client program does a **Dim WithEvents** of a **Player** object. In response to "Start Server," a **Player** object is instantiated. Event handlers are provided for the **Join** and **Play** events. These handlers simply display a suitable message in the textbox. Here is the Visual Basic source code:

```
Dim WithEvents objPlayer As Player

Private Sub cmdClear_Click()
    txtMessage = ""
End Sub

Private Sub cmdStartServer_Click()
    Set objPlayer = New Player
End Sub

Private Sub cmdStopServer_Click()
    objPlayer.StopServer
    Set objPlayer = Nothing
End Sub

Private Sub objPlayer_Join(ByVal name As String)
    txtMessage = name & " has joined the game"
End Sub

Private Sub objPlayer_Quit(ByVal name As String)
    txtMessage = name & " has quit the game"
End Sub
```

Connection Point Architecture

Under the hood, Visual Basic employs *connection points* to implement events. Connection points are a generic COM mechanism used by *connectable* objects to notify their client when an event has occurred. To send such notifications (or "fire events"), the object defines "outgoing" interfaces (specified in the type library). Although the server *defines* the interface, the client *implements* the interface. The object that sends the notification is called the *source*, and the object receiving the notification is called the *sink*. Figure 22–3 illustrates a connectable object with one ordinary ("incoming") interface and one outgoing interface, along with the client and its sink.

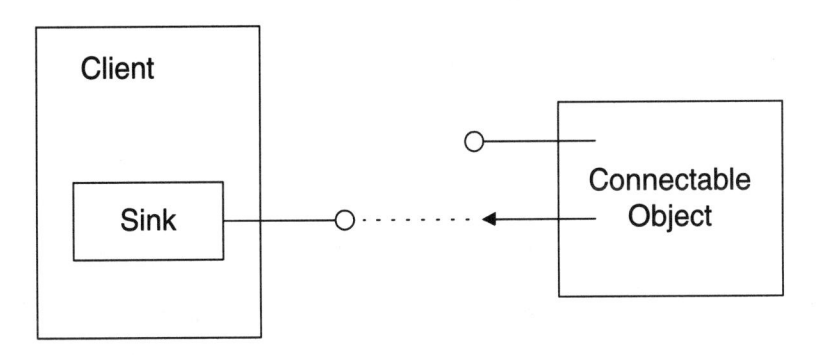

Figure 22–3 *A connectable object specifies an outgoing interface, which is implemented by a sink object in the client*

INCOMING AND OUTGOING INTERFACES

An ordinary COM object supports *incoming* interfaces. A client calls into the object. A *connectable* object also supports one or more *outgoing* interfaces. The object defines the interface and the client implements the interface. The object calls the client through the outgoing interface. An outgoing interface is sometimes called a "source" interface, because the object itself is the source of method calls that go through the interface—that is, the object makes the method calls. Outgoing interfaces are designated by the attribute **source** in IDL. Here is the relevant part of the IDL of the **VbEvent.Player** class. A source interface is always a dispatch interface.

```
coclass Player {
    [default] interface _Player;
    [default, source] dispinterface __Player;
};

[
```

```
        uuid(5298DD8B-5FAD-11D3-9060-00105AA45BDC),
        version(1.0),
        hidden,
        nonextensible
    ]
dispinterface __Player {
  properties:
  methods:
    [id(0x00000001)]
    void Join([in] BSTR name);
    [id(0x00000002)]
    void Quit([in] BSTR name);
};
```

CLIENT-OBJECT-SINK

There are three components in the interaction supported by connectable objects:

• The **Object** is a COM object that supports one or more ordinary incoming interfaces.

• The **Client** makes calls into the incoming interfaces supported by the Object.

• The **Sink** is an object associated with the Client which implements the interfaces the Object calls.

The Client is responsible for "connecting" the Sink to the Object. The Client instantiates a Sink object, obtaining an interface pointer. The Client passes this interface pointer to the Object by calling a method of one of the Object's incoming interfaces. The Object then uses this Sink interface pointer to make calls into the Sink.

ICONNECTIONPOINT

The connectable object has a *connection point* object for each of its outgoing interfaces. The connection point supports the **IConnectionPoint** interface. **IConnectionPoint** is the interface by which the client can pass its sink interface pointer to the connectable object. Note that it is the connection point and not the connectable object that supports the **IConnectionPoint** interface (see Figure 22-4, which we will discuss a little later). Important methods provided by **IConnectionPoint** include:

• **Advise** is used to establish a connection. The input parameter is the sink interface pointer and the output parameter is a "cookie" that can be saved by the client and used later when breaking the connection.

• **Unadvise** is used to terminate the connection described by the cookie returned from calling **Advise**.

• **EnumConnections** returns an enumerator that can be used for enumerating all the open connections set up via **Advise**.

ICONNECTIONPOINTCONTAINER

Through the **IConnectionPointContainer** interface, the client can find out about the connectable object's outgoing interfaces. **IConnectionPointContainer** is provided by the connectable object itself. **IConnectionPointContainer** has two methods:

- **FindConnectionPoint** is used to obtain an **IConnectionPoint** interface pointer given an IID.
- **EnumConnectionPoints** returns an interface pointer to an enumerator, which can be used to enumerate all the connection points supported by the object.

CONNECTION POINT ARCHITECTURE

We can now examine the overall connection point architecture. The Client reads the type library of the Object, making note of the outgoing interfaces specified there. It can then create any needed Sink objects to receive method calls when the Object "fires" events. The Object supports the **IConnectionPointContainer** interface and contains one or more connection points, each of which supports the **IConnectionPoint** interface. The Client uses the **IConnectionPointContainer** interface to obtain the **IConnectionPoint** interface pointers for the connection points. The Client can then call the **Advise** method of a connection point to pass the interface pointer of its Sink object. The connection point can then fire events by making methods calls on the Sink interface. Figure 22–4 illustrates this architecture.

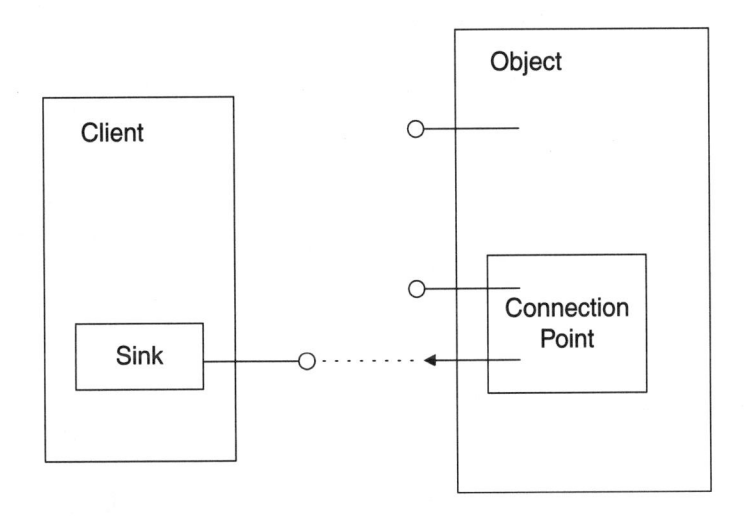

Figure 22–4 *The Object supports **IConnectionPointContainer** interface and the connection points support **IConnectionPoint**. The connection points call the Sink.*

TIGHTLY COUPLED EVENTS

A precursor of this event architecture was developed for OLE 1.0, which provided a sink in an OLE compound document container that could receive change notifications from an embedded object. The connection point architecture was developed as a more generic mechanism, which was applied to OLE Controls (now ActiveX controls). The kind of event model used in both cases is sometimes referred to as "tightly coupled events," or TCE. The Client expecting the notifications knows ahead of time which specific Object is going to provide them, and the two parties have to agree on specific interfaces ahead of time. Their lifetimes must overlap. Both Client and Object have to be running when the Client calls the **Advise** method to inform the Object of the Sink interface pointer. And both Client and Object have to be running when the Object fires events to the Sink.

This kind of event model is appropriate both for compound documents and ActiveX controls when indeed there is a natural close coupling between a container and an embedded object or control. But it is not so appropriate for the case of enterprise applications, where a loosely coupled mechanism offers far more flexibility.

Loosely Coupled Events and the Publisher/Subscriber Model in COM+

COM+ provides a new, general event system called "loosely coupled events," or LCE, designed to meet the needs of distributed computing. The general problem to be solved is delivering timely information to interested parties without necessarily knowing ahead of time who they are, and certainly without having to implement closely coupled programming interfaces between them.

A new terminology has been developed in the industry to describe a suitable programming model for such systems. "Clients" and "servers" does not convey who is passing information to whom. Clients call servers but with events, the servers call the clients. The alternative terminology is "publishers" and "subscribers." The publisher provides information, and the subscriber consumes it. As soon as new information becomes available from the publisher, we would like for the subscribers to be able to receive it, without a need to continually poll the publisher. The publisher notifies the subscriber through events.

In COM+, publishers and subscribers are loosely coupled. Event information from different publishers is stored in the COM+ catalog, and subscribers specify what information they wish to receive by registering for it. In addition, they can filter what information they receive, so that they receive event notifications selectively based on criteria they specify. This event registration information is known as a "subscription" and exists independently of the publisher or subscriber. Figure 22–5 illustrates the COM+ publisher/subscriber model, with the COM+ event system mediating between the publishers and subscribers.

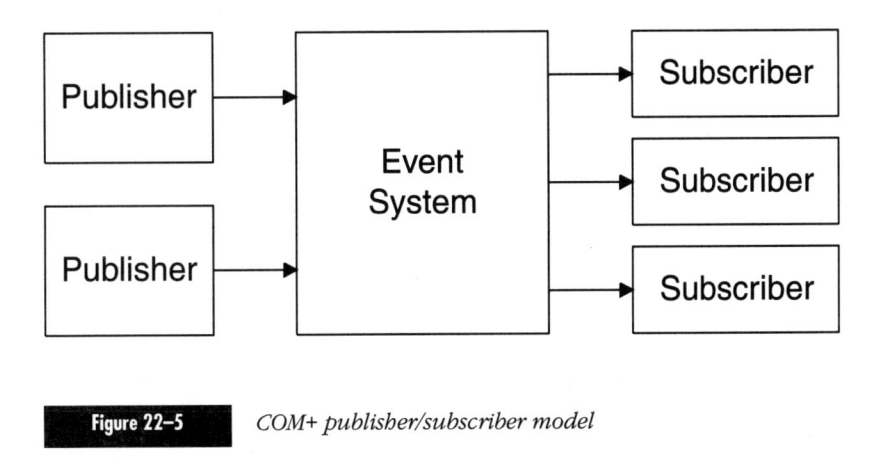

Figure 22–5 *COM+ publisher/subscriber model*

This section describes the overall COM+ event system architecture, and the following section will present a programming example and illustrate the use of the Component Services snap-in to install subscription information in the COM+ catalog.

COM+ Event System Architecture

As with the rest of COM+, the event system is constructed in such a way that much of the infrastructure is provided automatically by COM+ with minimal work required by the programmer, and much functionality declared administratively. You must implement an *EventClass* component and specify *Subscriptions*. The EventClass contains interfaces whose methods are called by the publisher to fire events. The COM+ run time synthesizes an event object that implements the interfaces of the EventClass. Subscribers must implement the interfaces of the EventClass. The subscribers get called by the event object. Subscriptions are used to specify which subscribers get called. Both the EventClass and the subscriptions are set up administratively, either by using the Component Services snap-in or by calling the Admin API. Figure 22–6 illustrates this architecture.

Figure 22-6 COM+ event system architecture

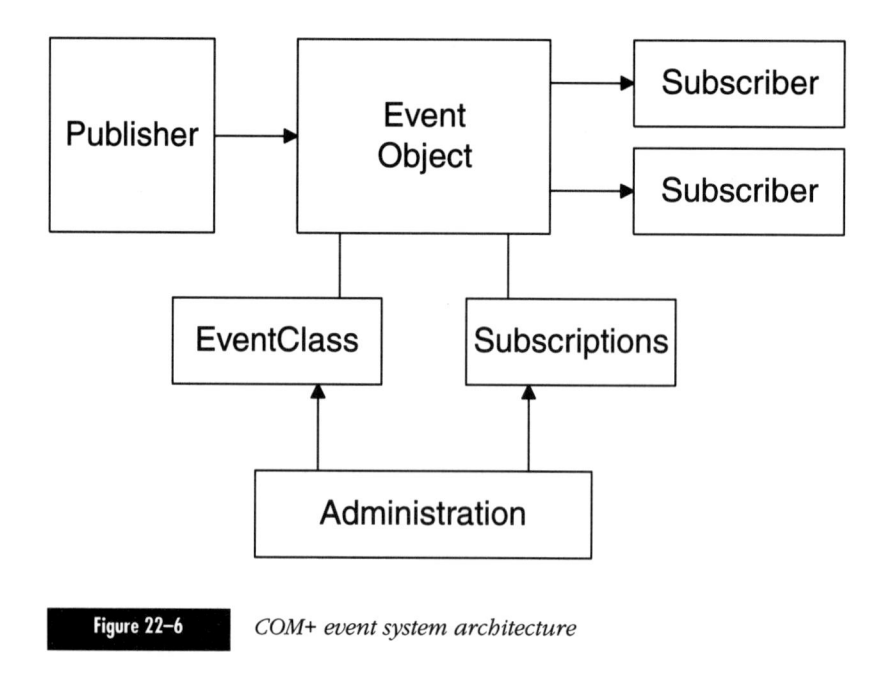

EventClass

The EventClass is a COM+ component that establishes the connection between the publisher and the subscribers. Each of its interfaces are called *event interfaces*, and the methods are called *event methods* or just *events*. Event methods, like the methods of queued components, can contain only input parameters and must return an HRESULT. (You cannot get a result back from an event method because the call can go to multiple subscribers, and it is possible that different subscribers would return different values.)

The EventClass component itself provides only dummy implementations of the event methods, which never get called. Instead, the event system will synthesize its own implementation of the methods, which will call the appropriate subscribers. The EventClass must provide a type library and be self-registering. The EventClass has a CLSID, and it must also provide a ProgID.

You must register the EventClass so that subscribers can find it and subscribe to it. This registration can be done by the Component Services snap-in by using the "Install New Event Classes" button when creating a new COM+ application. It can also be done by calling **ICOMAdminCatalog::InstallEventClass** from the Admin API.

Subscriptions

Subscriptions are what enable the loose-coupling between publishers and subscribers, making a connection between them. A subscription includes the following information:

- Identification of the publisher
- Identification of the EventClass
- Event interface
- Event method
- Identification of the subscriber (may be a CLSID, queue moniker, or an interface pointer)
- Filtering information.

Subscriptions are stored in the COM+ Catalog. Subscribers may set up their own subscriptions through the Admin API. Subscriptions can also be set up using the Component Services snap-in.

PERSISTENT SUBSCRIPTIONS

A *persistent* subscription is stored persistently in the COM+ Catalog and will survive a system restart. A persistent subscription is independent of the subscriber's lifetime. A persistent subscription will create a new subscriber from the CLSID (or from a queue moniker if the subscriber is a queued component). The subscriber object is released after the event method completes. Persistent subscriptions may be created using the Component Services snap-in.

TRANSIENT SUBSCRIPTIONS

A *transient* subscription is tied to a particular subscriber, which must already exist prior to creating the subscription. The subscription is created through the Admin API. The subscriber is specified by passing an interface pointer to a subscriber object. You must manage the lifetime of a transient subscription yourself, and you cannot use the Component Services snap-in to create a transient subscription.

Subscribers

In COM+, a subscriber is simply an ordinary configured COM component. You do not have to implement any special interfaces. You do have to manage setting up subscriptions in some way. In the case of transient subscriptions, you will call the Admin API. For persistent subscriptions, you can use the Component Services snap-in, which we will explain in the next section. Under the interfaces section for the component there is a Subscriptions section, as illustrated by Figure 22–9 in the next section.

Publishers

Likewise in COM+, there are no special interfaces that the publisher has to implement (such as **IConnectionPointContainer** or **IConnectionPoint** that had to be implemented by a connectable object). Subscribers find publishers through subscriptions and the COM+ event system, not through special interfaces implemented by the publisher. In order to fire events, the publisher simply instantiates an object of the EventClass and calls methods on its interfaces. The COM+ event system takes care of propagating the events to the appropriate subscribers.

Filtering

A useful feature of the COM+ event system is filtering capability, which does not exist at all in the tightly coupled connection point architecture. There are two techniques for filtering: publisher filtering and parameter filtering, and the two can be used together.

PUBLISHER FILTERING

Publisher filtering provides complete programmatic control of event firing. You can control which subscribers will receive an event and the order in which they are fired. You need to implement a publisher filter class. This class gets hooked into the event system either through setting the **MultiPublisherFilterCLSID** property of the EventClass (using the Admin API) or by calling **IEventControl::SetPublisherFilter**. The former method is preferred because it allows your events to work with queued components.

The publisher filter class must support one of the interfaces **IPublisherFilter** or **IMultiPublisherFilter**. The latter supports multiple event interfaces in the EventClass. The **Initialize** method is called once by the event system, which passes an **IEventSystem** interface pointer, which can be used to obtain an enumerator for a list of subscriptions. When the publisher fires an event, the event system calls the **PrepareToFire** method of the filter class, passing in the name of the method to be fired and an **IFiringControl** interface pointer. You may then call **IFiringControl::FireSubscription** to fire the event to the subscribers you wish and in the order you wish. For finer granularity of control, you can implement the event interfaces themselves in the publisher filter, and then you can make use of parameters in event method invocations to use in your logic to determine firings.

PARAMETER FILTERING

A much simpler filtering mechanism uses a filter criteria string that is a property of the subscription. This filtering is done on a per-method, per-subscription basis. You can specify this string using parameter names from the type library. Standard relational operators, nested parentheses and the keywords

AND, OR and NOT are recognized. The string can be specified through the Component Services snap-in or by using the Admin API.

Parameter filtering composes with publisher filtering and occurs after publisher filtering, when **IFiringControl::FireSubscription** is called.

COM+ Event Example

In this section we provide a complete programming example to illustrate the COM+ event system. We use the same example used earlier for demonstrating the older event technology based on connection points. We again use Visual Basic for the sake of simplicity, to focus on the concepts and not on coding details.

Our example is a prototype of an event structure for the Electronic Commerce Game. We want to provide the capability for players of the game to receive notifications when a new player joins the game and when a player quits the game. The structure of our example is more straightforward than with the connection point illustration, where we were constrained by the tight coupling. We need to provide three components:

- An EventClass specifying an event interface with event methods **Join** and **Quit**. Only dummy implementations are provided of the methods. An ActiveX DLL is created and installed in a COM+ application as an EventClass.

- A Subscriber, which provides real implementations of the event methods. It is installed in a COM+ application, and the Component Services snap-in is used to create several persistent subscriptions.

- A Publisher, which provides a user interface for firing the events. It merely has to instantiate an EventClass object and call the event methods.

EventClass

The EventClass is specified through the ActiveX DLL in **Chap22\ecEventVb**. The code simply provides dummy implementations of the methods **Join** and **Quit** of the class **Player**.

```
Public Sub Join(ByVal name As String)
   'empty
End Sub

Public Sub Quit(ByVal name As String)
   'empty
End Sub
```

Perform the following steps to register this component as an EventClass in the COM+ catalog. You will be using the Component Services snap-in.

1. Create an empty COM+ application called **ecEventApp**.
2. Select Components for your new application and right-click. From the context menu, choose New | Component. In the COM Component Install Wizard, choose "Install new event class(es). See Figure 22–7.

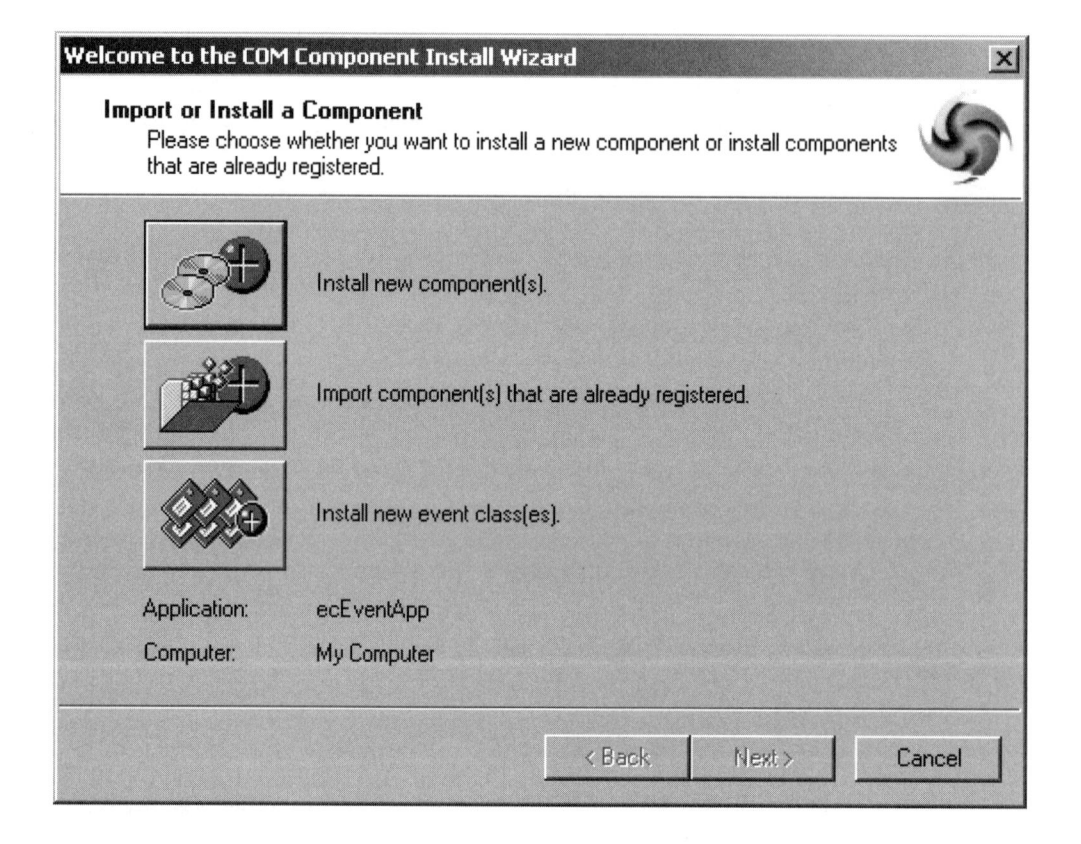

Figure 22–7 *Using Component Services snap-in to install an event class*

3. In the "Select files to install" dialog navigate to **Chap22\ecEventVb\ecEventVb.dll** and click "Open."
4. You will be shown your file **ecEventVb.dll** and the event class **Player** that was found. See Figure 22–8. Click Next and then Finish.

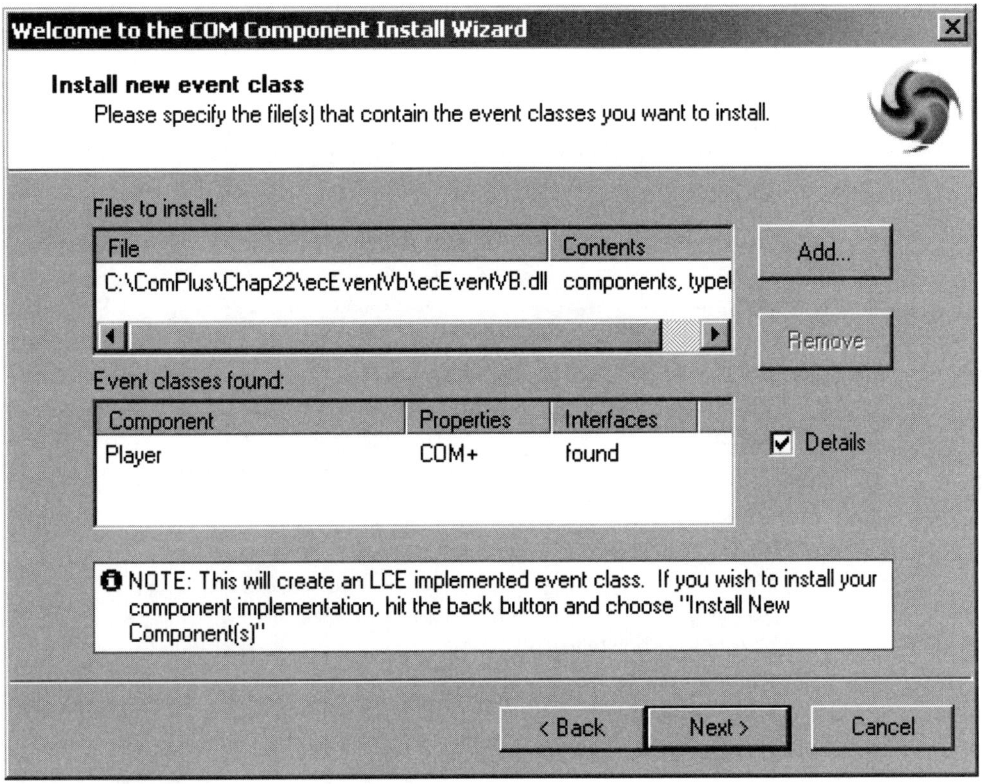
Welcome to the COM Component Install Wizard
Install new event class
Please specify the file(s) that contain the event classes you want to install.
Files to install:
File
Contents
C:\ComPlus\Chap22\ecEventVb\ecEventVB.dll
components, typel
Add...
Remove
Event classes found:
Component
Properties
Interfaces
Player
COM+
found
Details
NOTE: This will create an LCE implemented event class. If you wish to install your component implementation, hit the back button and choose "Install New Component(s)"
< Back
Next >
Cancel

Figure 22–8 *Specifying files and event classes*

Subscriber

The Subscriber is specified through the ActiveX DLL in **Chap22\SubDemoVb**. This project contains a reference to **ecEventVB**. It provides "real" implementations of the methods of the event interface. For our demo program we merely display message boxes.

```
Implements Player

Private Sub Player_Join(ByVal name As String)
  MsgBox name & " has joined the game"
End Sub

Private Sub Player_Quit(ByVal name As String)
  MsgBox name & " has quit the game"
End Sub
```

Chapter 22 • COM+ Events

Perform the following steps to install the Subscriber as a COM+ component and create some subscriptions. You will again be using the Component Services snap-in.

1. Create an empty COM+ application called **ecSubApp**.
2. Install **SubDemoVb.dll** as an ordinary component (not an event class).
3. In the tree view, open up the new component **SubDemoVb.SubEventVb**. You will see folders for both Interfaces and Subscriptions. See Figure 22–9.

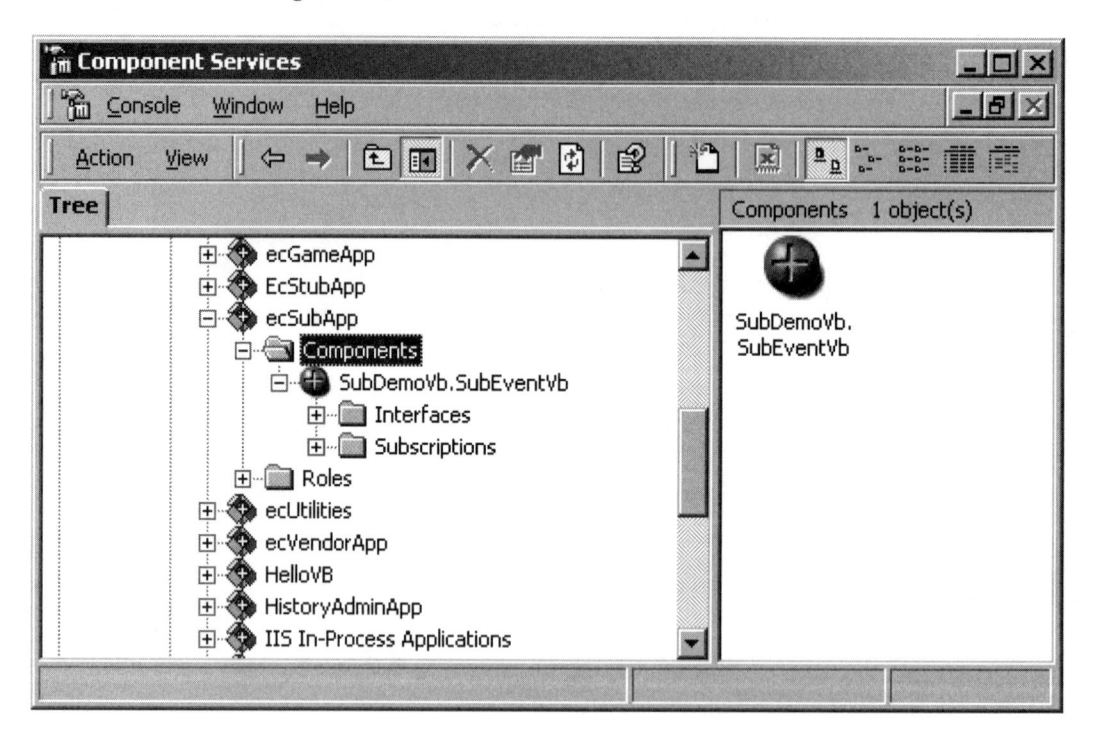

Figure 22–9   *You can manage subscriptions using Component Services snap-in*

4. Select Subscriptions and right-click. From the context menu choose New | Subscriptions. The COM New Subscription Wizard will come up. For the first subscription, select the **_Player** interface. This will subscribe to all event methods of the interface. See Figure 22–10. Click Next.

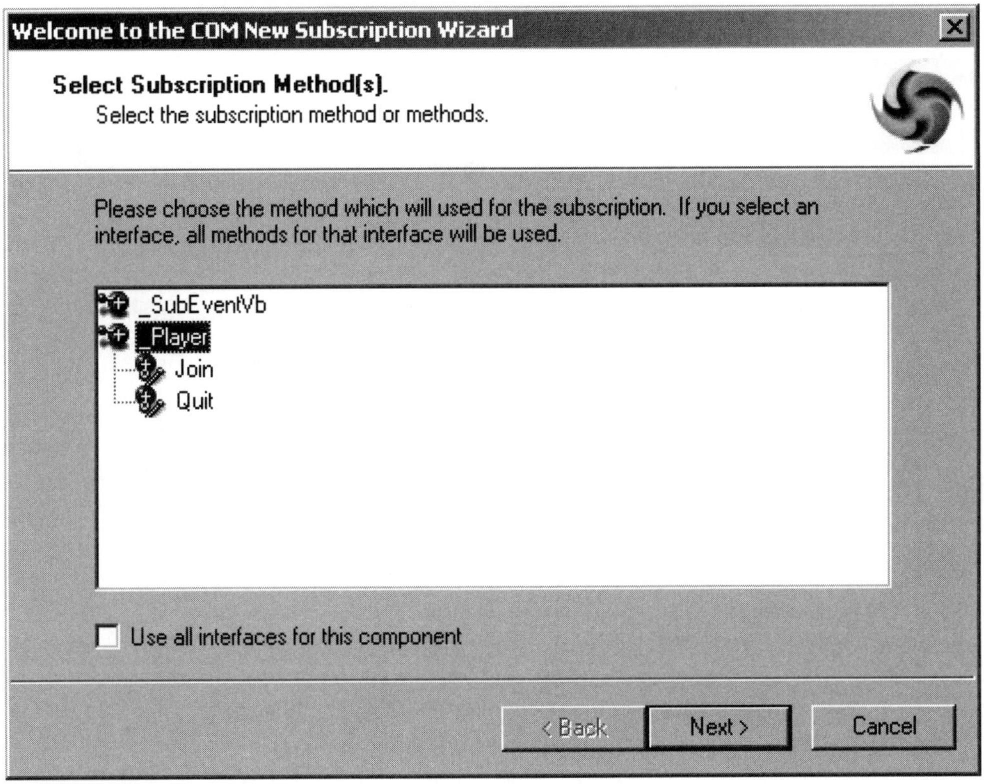

Figure 22–10 *Subscribing to an interface, which will include all the methods*

5. In the following step you choose the event class for the interface you selected. We have only one, with ProgID "ecEventVB.Player." Select that and click Next.
6. Specify a name "All Events" for this subscription, and check the box "Enable this subscription immediately." Click Next and Finish.
7. Now repeat the above steps to create a second subscription. For this one, we subscribe only to the **Join** method. See Figure 22–11. For the name of this subscription specify "Only Join."

Chapter 22 • COM+ Events

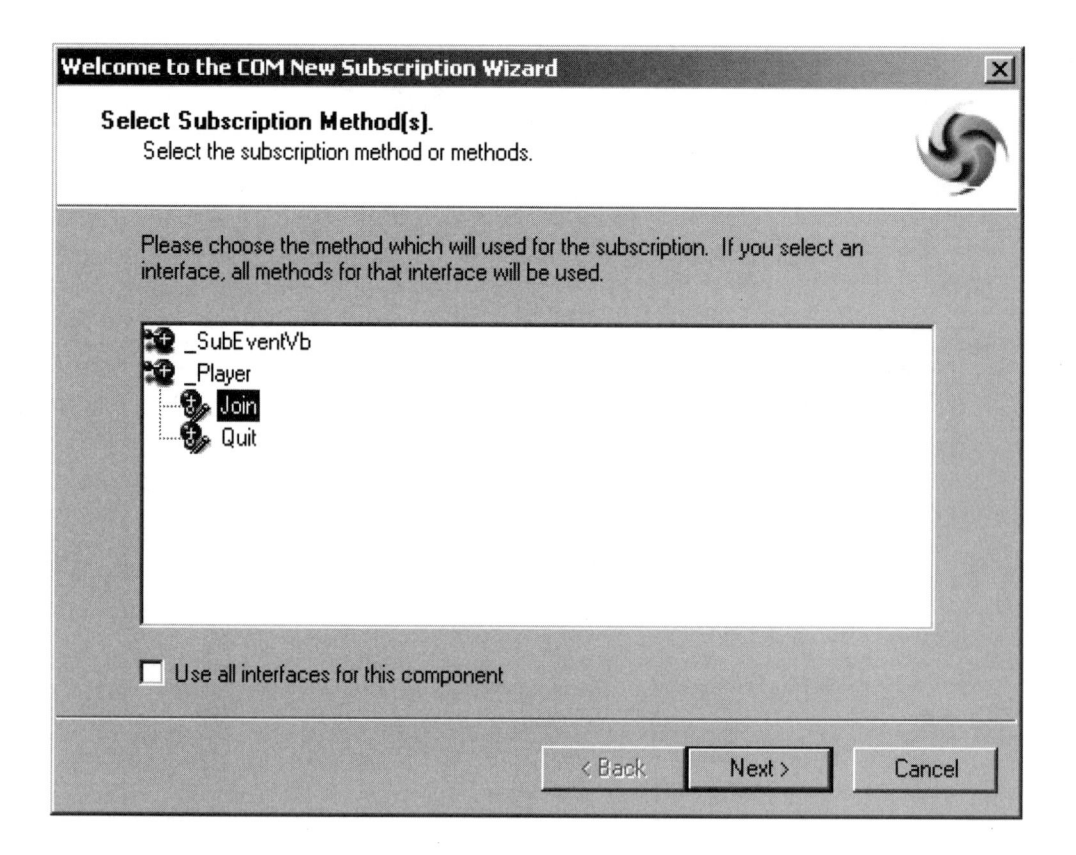

Figure 22-11 *Subscribing to only the Join method*

ADDING A FILTER

Here we add a filter to the "All Events" subscription. Thinking about the Electronic Commerce Game application that we are prototyping, when a new player joins the game we want to send an event notification to all the other players, but it would be redundant to send this notification to the player who has just joined. We illustrate a suitable filter with a filter criteria which specifies that the Name be different from one we specify (hardcoded in our prototype).

In the tree view, open up the "Subscriptions" folder and select "All Events." Right-click and, from the context menu, choose Properties. Choose the Options tab. For the Filter criteria give the string

```
name != "Bob"
```

See Figure 22–12. Click OK.

COM+ Event Example **565**

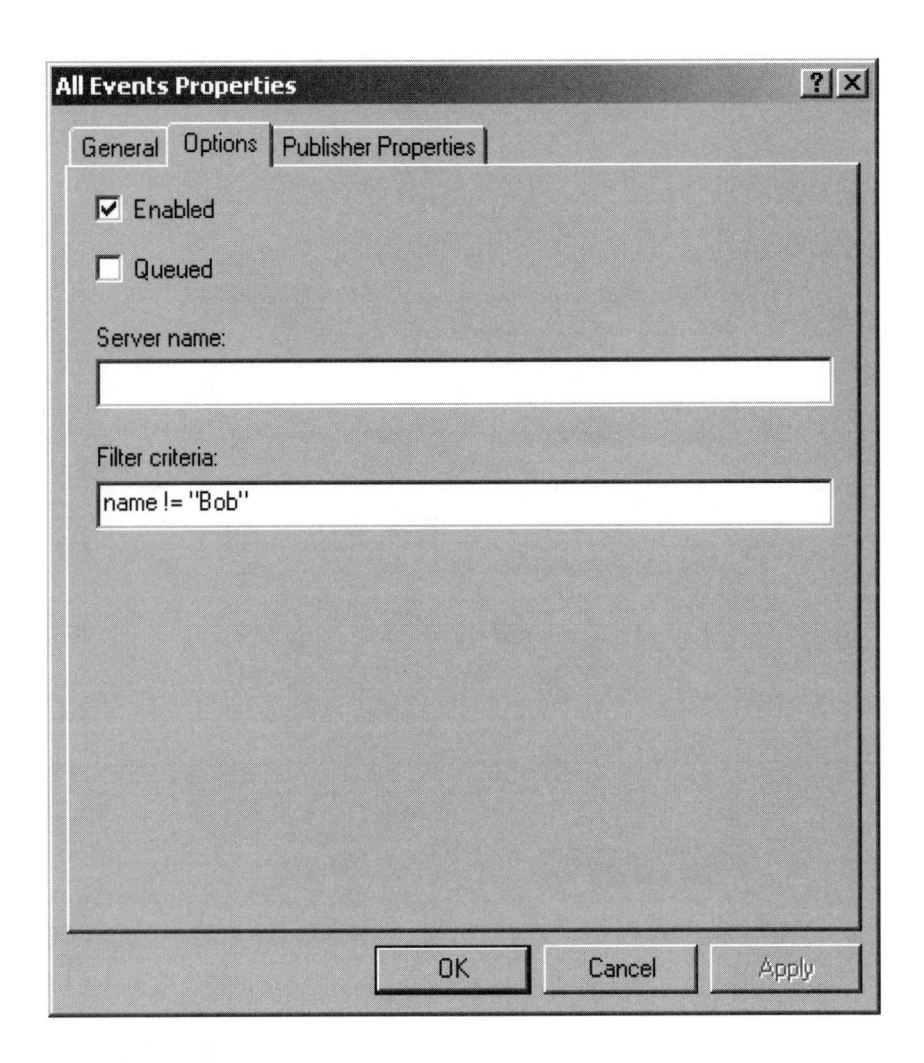

Figure 22-12 *Specifying a parametric filter*

Publisher

Finally, we examine the code for the Publisher. It is very simple, just a Visual Basic application, in the folder **Chap22\PubDemo**. It contains a reference to **ecEventVB**. It provides a user interface for firing the **Join** and **Quit** event methods, passing the name entered in the text box. This publisher merely instantiates an event object and calls the methods. Here is the code:

```
Dim objEventVb As New ecEventVB.Player

Private Sub cmdJoin_Click()
  objEventVb.Join txtName
End Sub

Private Sub cmdQuit_Click()
  objEventVb.Quit txtName
End Sub
```

Try running the program. You will see the user interface shown in Figure 22–13.

Figure 22-13 *User interface for publisher program*

Try clicking the Join button for the suggested name of "John Smith." You should see two message boxes, one for each of the subscriptions. Now try clicking the Quit button. This time you should see only one message box, because the second subscription was for only the **Join** method. As a final experiment, try "Bob" as the name. Now if you click the Join button you should see only a single message box. The "All Events" subscription has a filter that filters out method calls with the name "Bob." If you click Quit, you should now see no message box at all.

Summary

A common requirement in distributed systems is to provide appropriate notifications to interested parties of events that occur in the system. COM has long provided a "tightly coupled" event system using connection points for events. Visual Basic events make use of this architecture. These tightly coupled events suffer from a number of limitations, including the requirement that both parties adhere to specific interfaces such as **IConnectionPoint** and the requirement that the lifetimes of both components must overlap.

COM+ provides a "loosely coupled" event system that is both easier to program and more flexible. You must supply an "EventClass" that is simply an ActiveX DLL with dummy implementations of event methods. This class must be registered in the COM+ Catalog, which can be done using the Admin API or by using the Component Services snap-in. The subscriber provides real implementations of these event methods and gets called by the COM+ event system according to subscriptions. Subscriptions can be specified using the Admin API or by the Component Services snap-in. The publisher fires events merely by instantiating an EventClass object and calling its methods. Events can be filtered both programmatically and by specifying a simple filter criteria string.

We have not discussed the distributed aspects of events in this chapter. The fact is that version 1.0 of COM+ events does not provide a distributed event store. It would not be difficult for you to have all events routed to a single computer, which will fire them to the appropriate subscribers on various machines. Such an architecture would put this central computer in the role of a single point of failure, and also limit scalability.

In the final chapter, we survey some of the additional features of COM+ that can enhance scalability, including important clustering technology. Through a cluster of computers you can eliminate a single point of failure, and you can achieve enhanced scalability.

TWENTY THREE

COM+ and Scalability

The raison d'être of COM+ is to facilitate the development of distributed enterprise applications. COM+ provides many useful services, which we have been examining throughout this book. One of the important themes is scalability. *We have already discussed some of the features of COM+ that enhance scalability, such as just-in-time activation. We also mentioned object pooling. In this final chapter, we take a closer look at object pooling and we also discuss* clustering, *which can increase scalability by adding additional processing nodes. Microsoft provides several different clustering technologies, which we will examine briefly to provide a basic orientation. We will look in more detail at the ability of COM+ to distribute a component workload among multiple nodes. COM+ provides a* load balancing ser*vice to optimize the assignment of component work to nodes.*

In the final section I will share with you some thoughts about the overall significance of COM+. What does it all mean now? What are the implications for your own development work?

Microsoft Clustering Technologies

A natural approach to handling an increased workload is to add hardware. You can buy a bigger system to replace the current one, but that is disruptive and expensive. It also tops out at the size of the largest single system, which is limited in the PC arena on which Microsoft concentrates. A more incremental approach is to employ multiple processors. You can add more processors as the workload requires. There are two basic kinds of multiprocessor systems, tightly coupled and loosely coupled. The most common type of tightly-coupled multiprocessor is a symmetric, Shared-memory MultiProcessor (SMP). Such a system runs a single copy of the operating system, and transparently schedules threads among the processors. Such a system is largely transparent to applications. An SMP is limited in scalability due to bus contention for accessing the shared memory. Also SMP does not provide any fault tolerance.

Loosely coupled multiprocessors or *clusters* offer a more scalable solution and can also provide for fault tolerance. A cluster consists of independent nodes, each with its own CPU and memory and running its own copy of the operating system. Since nodes in a cluster do not share memory, they are more highly scalable than SMP. And since each node runs its own copy of the operating system, one node can crash without bringing down the whole system.

In this section, we examine three different clustering technologies offered by Microsoft. Each has its own area of applicability, and they can be employed together to create very scalable and robust Web-based applications.

Microsoft Cluster Server (MSCS or "Wolfpack")

Microsoft's first clustering product is Microsoft Cluster Server, still sometimes referred to by its code name of "Wolfpack." This product leverages industry-proven technologies which Microsoft licensed from Digital and Tandem. It shipped with NT Server 4.0 Enterprise Edition. The initial product supports a two-node cluster with "failover" to provide a high degree of availability. Later releases are planned to scale up to multiple nodes. The basic architecture is shown in Figure 23–1.

Clients connect to the servers over a LAN. The servers have a high-speed interconnect which maintains a "heartbeat." The servers run independently, but through the heartbeat know if the other server is running properly. Each server has its own disk or disk array. Each disk is connected to both servers through SCSI, but at any one time is only serving one server. Note that the server machines may be SMP multiprocessors.

There are two software models for sharing resources in a cluster. In the "shared disk" model, software running on any server can access any disk. Thus data can be shared across the servers, and so access to the shared data must be serialized, via a Distributed Lock Manager (DLM). This synchronization provided by the DLM causes overhead, which reduces scalability. MSCS employs a "shared nothing" model. Each server in the cluster owns a subset of the resources, and only one server can access a particular resource at any given time. On a server failure the system can be dynamically reconfigured so that the other server now controls the resource.

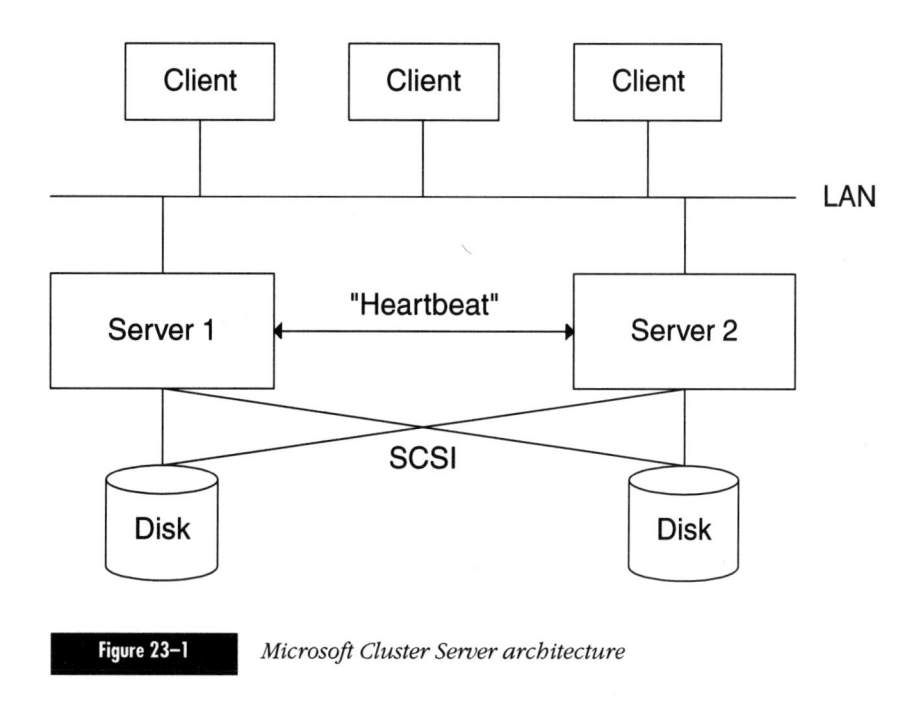

Microsoft Clustering Technologies

[Figure 23-1: Microsoft Cluster Server architecture — diagram showing three Clients connected via LAN to Server 1 and Server 2, which are connected by a "Heartbeat" link and share two Disks via SCSI.]

Figure 23-1 *Microsoft Cluster Server architecture*

The "heartbeat" between the servers is used to detect a failed application or a failed server. If an application fails, MSCS can try to restart the application on the same server. If that fails, it will move the application's resources to the other server and restart from there. If an entire server goes down, all applications can be moved to the surviving server. There will be a brief downtime during this "failover" operation, typically less than a minute. MSCS can be configured to provide automatic "failback" to restore applications to the failed server when it comes back online.

Application or server failure is not transparent to client applications. For example, a remote procedure call may fail. The client application may then retry the operation during a time interval, and finally fail after a specified timeout period. If the application has been restarted on another server within the timeout period, the retry will succeed. By configuring the timeout period on the client to be long enough for typical server recovery, the client application can be kept going under most failures. This approach, of course, requires appropriate coding of the client application. In some cases the end user may be presented with an "Abort, Retry or Cancel" dialog box. By retrying, the user may succeed in continuing her work on the other server, without being aware that a different server is now being used.

SQL Server 7.0 has been designed to work with MSCS, so the two working together can provide a high availability solution for the data tier of a three-tier application.

Windows Load Balancing Service (WLBS or "Convoy")

Microsoft Windows NT Load Balancing Service (WLBS) provides a clustering solution for load balancing IP traffic. Its typical application is to scale Web servers by distributing incoming IP traffic among multiple nodes in the cluster. Higher workloads can be supported by adding more nodes. Up to 32 nodes can be supported. WLBS also supports failover capability, so if one node fails, its workload can be transferred to another node. WLBS is based on Convoy Cluster Software, which was developed by Valence Research Inc., recently acquired by Microsoft. It ships with Windows NT Server 4.0 Enterprise Edition. Figure 23–2 illustrates its architecture.

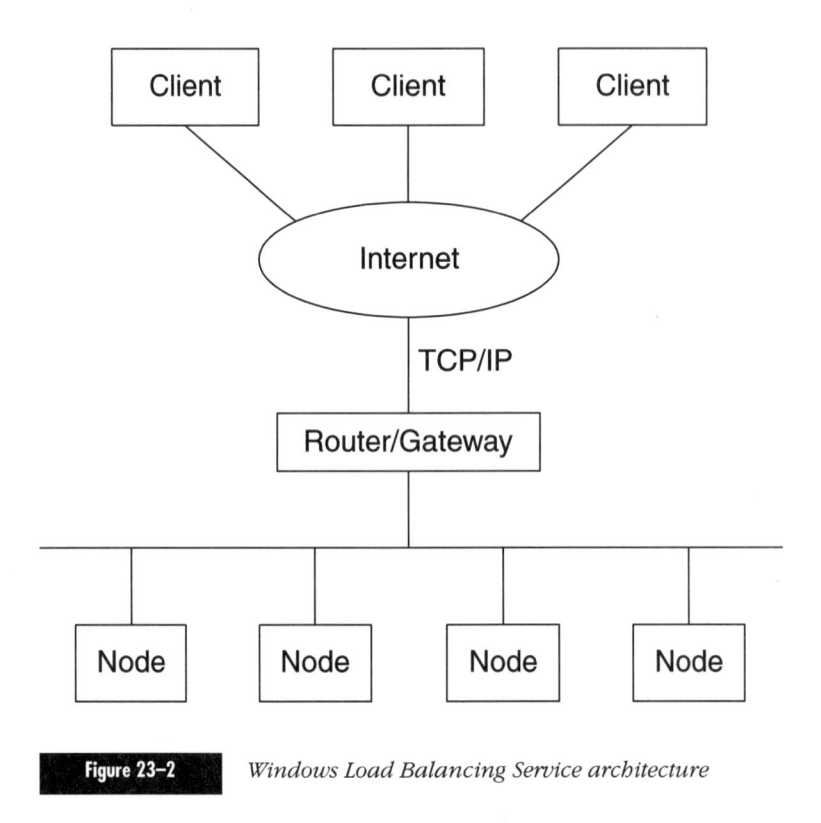

Figure 23-2   *Windows Load Balancing Service architecture*

WLBS is a standard NT networking driver that is installed on each server (or "node") of the cluster. These servers are placed on the same subnet. WLBS is transparent to both server applications and TCP/IP clients. The clients can access the cluster using a single IP address, and incoming requests will be routed to one of the nodes. If one node fails, WLBS redirects network traffic to the other nodes.

WLBS can load balance "stateless" services, such as Web servers accessing static Web pages, because these servers can independently handle a portion of the workload. WLBS cannot directly load balance "stateful" services, such as ones updating a shared database, due to coordination requirements in the access to the shared data. WLBS works well in a multiple-tier architecture, providing a front end for requests to update data, which can be handled by another tier.

Component Load Balancing (CLB)

Microsoft's third cluster solution is Component Load Balancing (CLB), one of the services provided by COM+. Originally part of Windows 2000, CLB is now part of an add-on product, called AppCenter Server. Through CLB you can configure Windows 2000 servers on an ordinary LAN to participate as members of an "application cluster." You install a COM+ application on multiple nodes, and then incoming requests to create an object can be load balanced among these nodes. The incoming client requests are handled by a "CLB server," which acts in a routing capacity to direct an object creation request to one of the application servers in the cluster. Figure 23–3 illustrates the architecture, which we will discuss in detail in the next section.

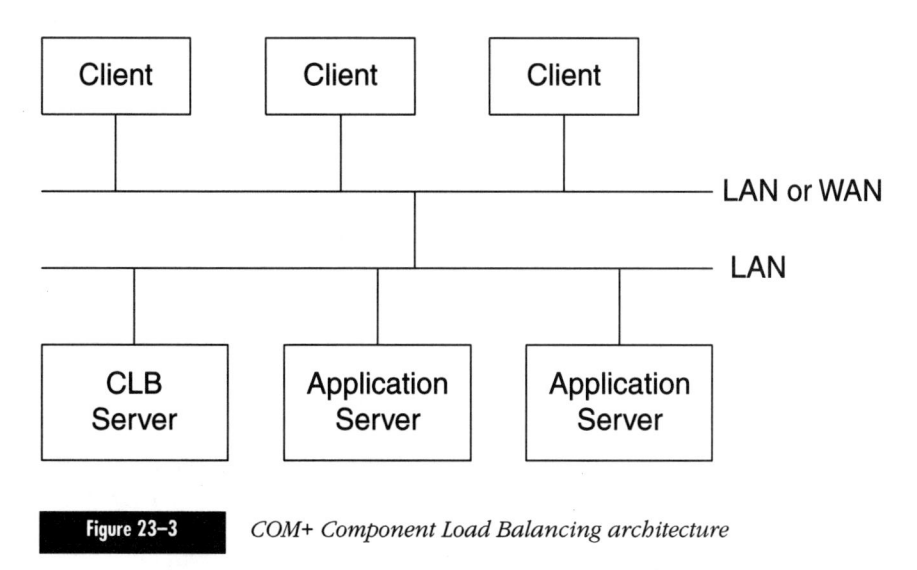

Figure 23-3 *COM+ Component Load Balancing architecture*

Note that the CLB server is a peer of the application servers, and in fact can be an application server itself. The servers can run both load-balanced applications and applications that are not load balanced. Requests for the load-balanced applications go through the CLB Server, and requests for applications that are not load balanced go directly to the appropriate server.

COM+ Component Load Balancing

You should now have some perspective on the clustering solutions available from Microsoft. You can use MSCS to create a highly available data tier and in other places where high availability is important. You can use WLBS to scale incoming IP requests for a Web application. For the middle tier application layer, if you have implemented it as COM+ components, you can use Component Load Balancing to achieve greater scalability.

In this section we discuss Component Load Balancing in some detail.

Load Balancing

The basic idea of a cluster is that work can be distributed among the nodes, increasing the total amount of work that can get done. There is also enhanced flexibility, since you can add or remove nodes as conditions warrant. But to achieve good results, we need to ensure that there is some kind of balance among the nodes. If one of the nodes is doing all the work and the other nodes are idle, we have gained nothing.

Load balancing could be left to the clients. In fact, straight DCOM could distribute a workload among multiple servers without any special software merely by having the clients designate different servers. Such an approach would be cumbersome to administer. A much better approach is to have the servers balance the load transparently to the client. The basic way that works in COM+ is for client requests to go through a routing server (the CLB Server), as shown in Figure 23–3. The CLB Server will use some algorithm (to be discussed later) to determine which application server has the lightest load and would be best equipped to handle the request.

When we are balancing a workload, the granularity of the work units becomes significant. If we have very large work units, it becomes difficult to achieve an even distribution. With small units of work, we can achieve good balance, but the overhead is higher, as we must go through the routing for all these small pieces of work.

The unit of work for COM+ load balancing is component activation. An incoming **CoCreateInstance(Ex)** or **CoGetObject** call is handled by the CLB server. It determines the target machine in the cluster with the lightest load and directs the request to the target machine. An interface pointer is returned back to the client. After that, the client is talking to the component on the machine where the object was instantiated, without any indirection through the CLB server. Once the object has been activated, it is bound to the server it was created on for its lifetime.

Note that the presence of load balancing does not change the programming model for the client. The client may still obtain an object reference and hold on to it for a long time. If just-in-time activation is enabled, the object will be deactivated on the completion of a method call. Then a new method call will cause the component to be activated again, and load balancing will occur. This time the object may be instantiated on a different server. The client's object reference is to a proxy, and so the "real" object may at different times reside on different machines, without the client being aware of it.

Load Balancing Algorithm

Two approaches to selecting a server for an incoming request are *round-robin* and *response time*. With round-robin, the routing server simply maintains a list of application servers, and directs each request to the next server on the list. When the end of the list is reached, the router starts again at the beginning of the list. With response time, the router gathers statistics about the response time of the different application servers and directs a request to the server currently offering the best response time.

COM+ currently employs a hybrid algorithm. The CLB server periodically polls the application servers for response time data and constructs a list of application servers, ordered by response time. Then until the next polling interval requests are serviced round-robin from this list. If the polling interval is long, this algorithm is mainly round-robin. If the polling interval is short, the algorithm is mainly response time.

Composing Clustering Technologies

A nice thing about Microsoft's clustering technologies is that they are not an either-or proposition, but can be used together to advantage. In COM+ Component Load Balancing, the CLB server is a single point of failure. If it goes down, none of the application servers can do any work for load-balanced applications. (They can continue to service applications that are not load-balanced.) Because of its critical role, the CLB server is a good candidate for MSCS, which will offer a high degree of availability for the component routing service.

MSCS is also a good candidate for the backend data tier, offering high availability for data access. If the DBMS is cluster aware, as is SQL Server 7.0, you can also get enhanced scalability by using MSCS on the data tier.

If the distributed application is Web-based, you can get additional scalability by using WLBS to route incoming IP traffic.

Finally, the individual nodes of the machines in the clusters can be high-end SMP multiprocessors. When SMP multiprocessors appear using the 64-bit Merced chip, we should see some very highly scalable systems appear in the Microsoft space.

Configuring Component Load Balancing

It is quite easy to configure Component Load Balancing on a Windows 2000 network. First of all, you need to run Windows 2000 Advanced Server or Windows 2000 Datacenter Server on the machine that will be your CLB server. (As noted above, you also need the add-on product, AppCenter Server.) Then you can configure that machine as your CLB server through the Component Services snap-in. Right-click on "My Computer," and from the context menu choose Properties. Select the "CLBS" tab. Check "Use this computer as the load balancing server." Click the Add button to add application servers. Figure 23–4 illustrates a CLB server that is being configured for two application servers.

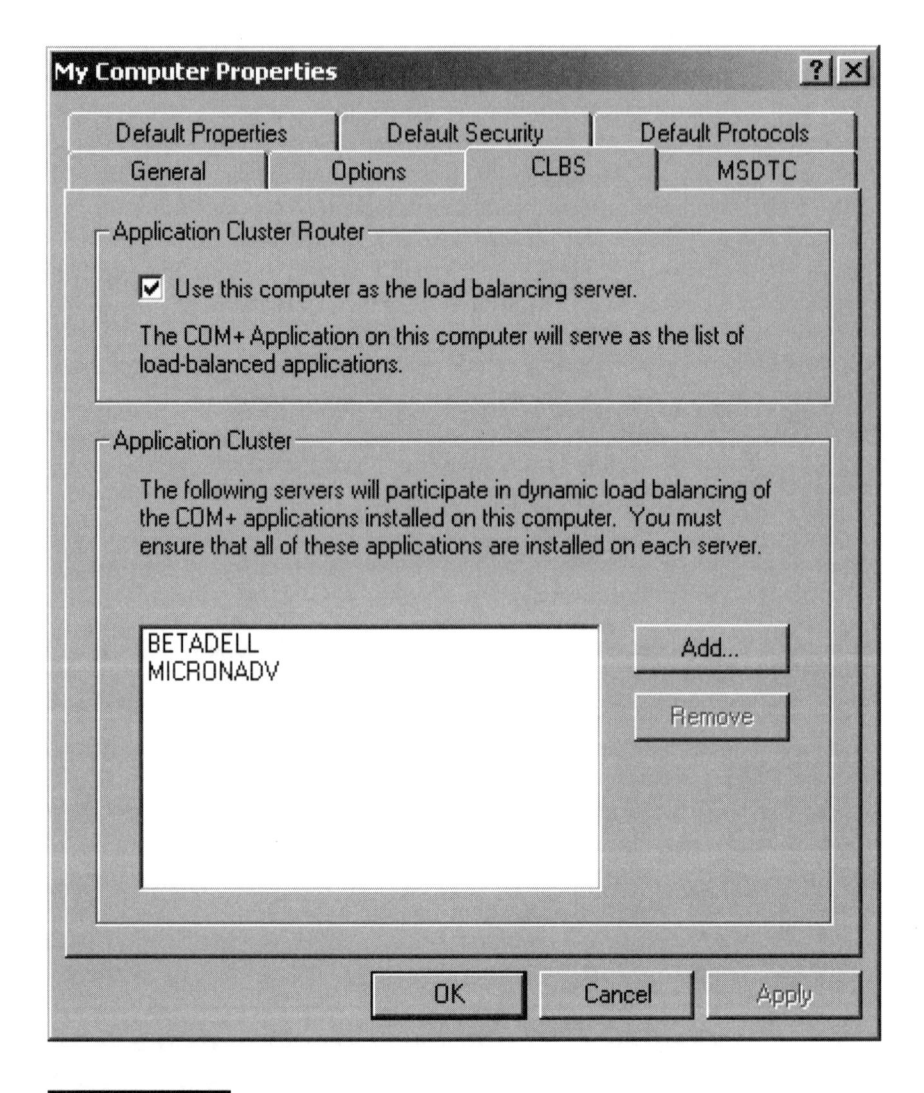

Figure 23–4 *Configuring a server to be the CLB server*

You also have to configure all the components you wish to be load balanced. In Component Services snap-in, bring up the properties for the component you want to configure. Select the "Activation" tab. Check "Component supports dynamic load balancing." See Figure 23–5.

You need to install the configured applications with load-balanced components on each application server. Then when you make a **CoCreateInstanceEx** call from a client using DCOM, you specify the CLB server as the server name (either using the Registry or through the COSERVERINFO structure).

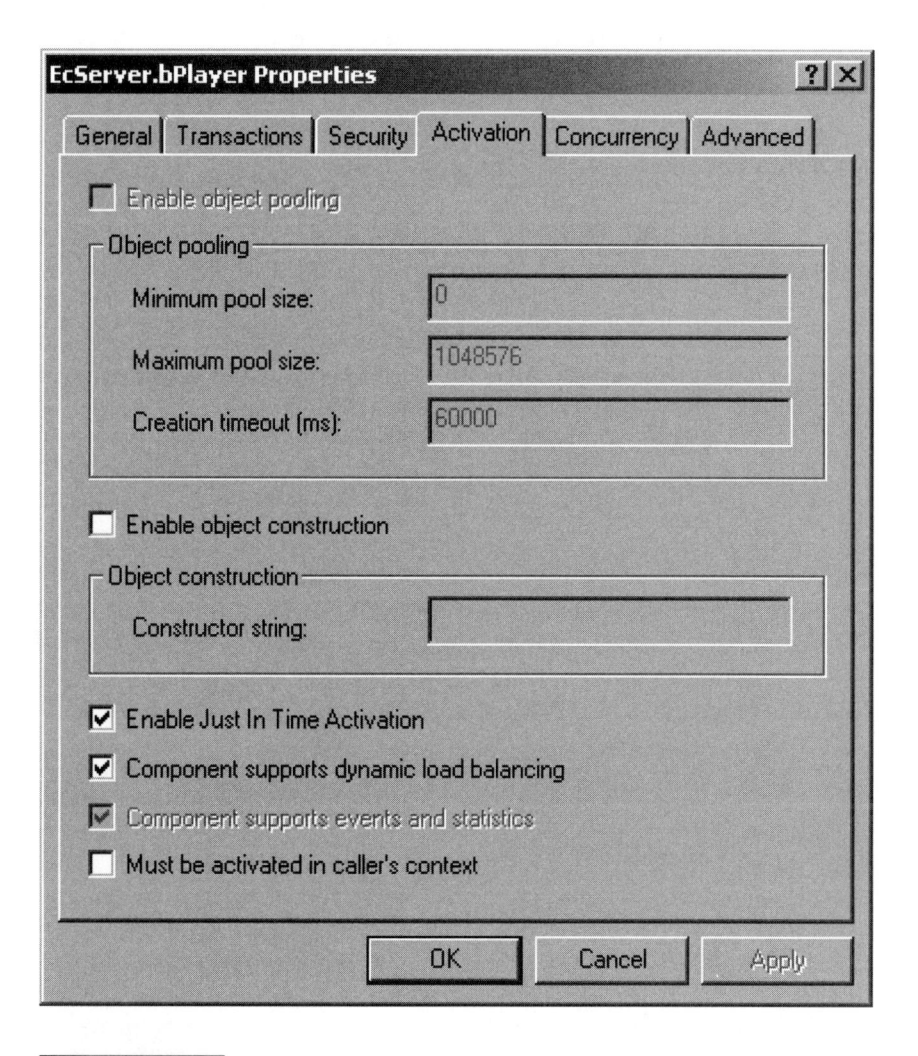

Figure 23–5 *Configuring a component to be load balanced*

Fault Tolerance with Component Load Balancing

Component load balancing permits implementing some degree of fault tolerance in a distributed application. Consider what happens when an application server fails between method calls. If the component has enabled just-in-time activation, the next method call will bring about activation. The CLB server will determine an application server on which to activate the component. The failed server is not available, but if another server is available in the cluster, the activation request can be routed there, and the client call succeeds, without the client being the wiser about the server failure.

If JIT is not enabled, the second method call in the same scenario will time out. The client could then release the object reference and try to create a new object instance. We will then be back to the situation where the CLB determines an application server for the newly activated object instance. If an application server is available in the cluster, the call will succeed. The error has been recovered, and the client application can continue running.

Design Issues for Load-Balanced Components

There are some design issues for load-balanced components. Your component cannot have any affinity for a particular machine. An object instance might hop around from machine to machine, and your program logic must be able to handle this movement of the object instance. You should not store object state in shared memory, because that is local to a particular machine. You should also not store state in a temporary file that resides on the machine where the object is running. A load-balanced component also cannot make use of object pooling, as we discuss in the following section.

Performance

Performance is a critical issue in enterprise applications. When you are trying to achieve scalability in your application, you need to ensure that you will provide adequate performance for your clients. This may be hard to benchmark, because your development lab will typically have far fewer machines than will be used in deployment. Microsoft has developed a Windows DNA Performance kit that contains tools and documentation to help you make performance measurements on distributed applications. It contains a driver that can simulate multiple clients, including make provision for "think time." There are also included summaries of a number of interesting Microsoft performance studies. For example, they found that, using load balancing, they could get roughly linear performance improvement as they added application servers. This was a good result, because they tested under the worst-case scenario of just-in-time activation, with an object created and routed to the appropriate server on every method call.

You can download the performance kit from the following Web address:

www.microsoft.com/com/resources/WinDNAPerf.asp

Object Pooling

There are a number of issues in achieving highly scalable applications. The basic obstacle is limitation of resources of one kind or another. You may be limited by processor power, and a way to overcome this limitation is through adding more processors, such as through clustering. Other kinds of limits include memory and database connections. The activation model of COM+, which was derived from Microsoft Transaction Server, addresses this issue through just-in-time activation. Objects which use a lot of resources can be deactivated and the resources released when the object is not in use. There may be a great many clients holding object references, but resources are in use only when they are actually needed. (But recall, as we pointed out in Chapter 14, that the resource usage of an inactive component does not drop to zero. There may be several hundred bytes of memory required to keep the stub alive.)

A possible problem with JIT is that object creation and initialization may be expensive. A possible solution is to create a *pool* of object instances. Then a newly activated object can obtain its instance from the pool rather than creating it from scratch. Upon deactivation, the object instance can be returned to the pool.

Using Object Pooling

Assuming that your component(s) have been implemented in a manner which supports object pooling, using object pooling is quite easy. Pooling is done on a per-component basis. You configure each component you wish to pool using the Component Services snap-in. Open up the Properties for the component and select the Activation tab. Check the box for "Enable object pooling" (this box will be grayed out if the component cannot be pooled). Then specify the minimum pool size, the maximum pool size, and the timeout value. See Figure 23–6.

When the application starts up, the object pools will be populated by creating the number of objects specified by the minimum pool size. Each pooled component will have its own pool of homogeneous objects, all having the same CLSID. As objects get activated, they will come from the pool as long as there are objects available in the pool. If no object is available in the pool, but the maximum pool size has not been reached, a new object will be created. When an object is deactivated it will be returned to the pool. If a request comes in for an object and there is no object in the pool and the maximum pool size has been reached, the request will wait for the specified timeout period. If no object has been returned to the pool during this interval, the client will receive a timeout error return code.

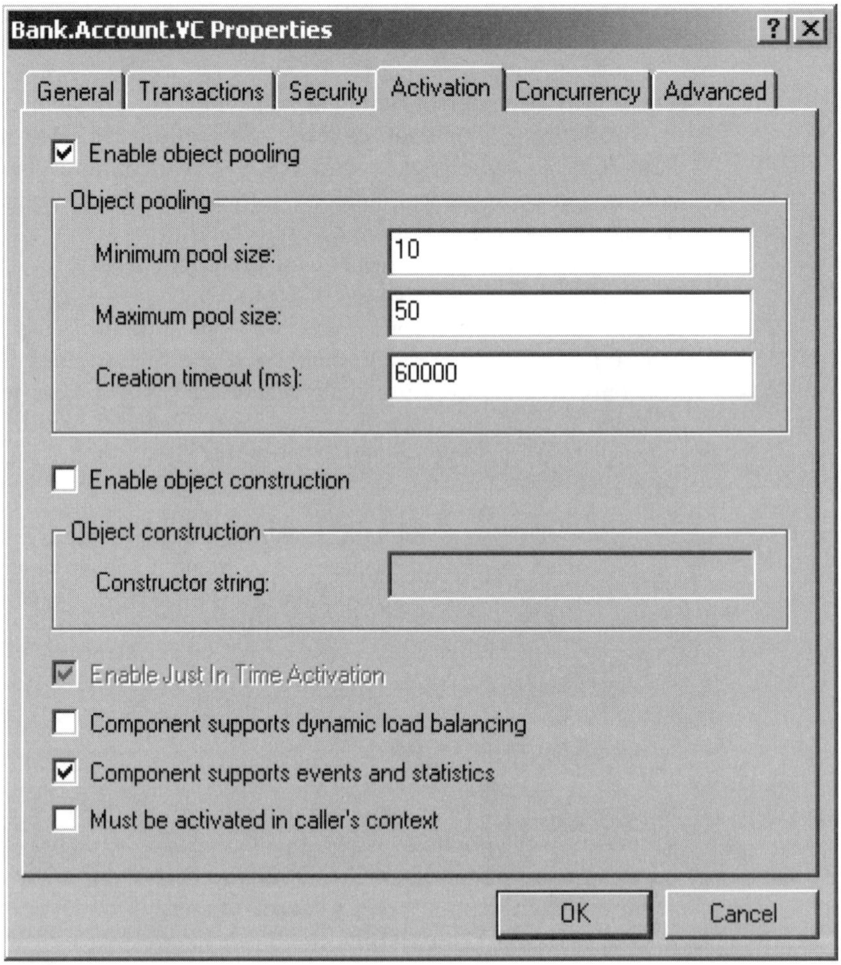

Figure 23-6 *Configuring a component for object pooling*

IObjectControl

Objects in a poolable component are responsible for monitoring their state and determining whether it will be all right to be returned to the pool when deactivated. The component should implement the **IObjectControl** interface. The object must return an appropriate value when **IObjectControl::CanBePooled** is called. A pooled object when created is aggregated inside an outer object that manages the object's lifetime. This outer object calls the methods of **IObjectControl**.

- **Activate** is called once each time the object is activated, before any other methods on the component are called.

- **Deactivate** is called when the object is deactivated, such as when **SetComplete** or **SetAbort** are called.

- **CanBePooled** is called when an object is about to be returned to the pool. If the object is in a bad state and should not be reused, it should return FALSE, and the object will be released. Otherwise the object should return TRUE, and it will go back into the pool.

A legacy nontransactional component that meets the requirements for a poolable component listed below does not need to implement **IObjectControl**. Such an object will not participate in managing its lifetime. COM+ will assume that it can always be pooled and hence will always be reused until the pool reaches its maximum size.

Requirements for an Object That Is Pooled

There are a number of requirements on an object to enable it to be pooled. There are two basic constraints that drive the requirements. The first is that a pooled object needs to be able to service different clients during its lifetime. The second is that the pooled object has to be able to work with the COM+ run-time system, which in particular will need to aggregate the object. The requirements include the following:

- **Stateless.** Since a pooled object may be used by multiple clients, it should not maintain any client state. Such state that is correct for one client is probably incorrect for another client.

- **No Thread Affinity.** A poolable object must not be bound to a particular thread. Otherwise there could be excessive thread-switching overhead when it is run by different clients. Hence the component must be marked for the Multiple Thread Apartment or the Neutral Apartment. This requirement precludes Visual Basic as a development language for a poolable component, because Visual Basic components are always apartment threaded. Also, the component should not use any thread local storage.

- **Aggregatable.** At run time, COM+ controls the lifetime of a poolable object by aggregating it into a larger object, which calls the methods of **IObjectControl**. This requirement precludes the use of Visual J++ for a poolable component because Visual J++ does not support creating a component that can be aggregated.

- **Manually Enlist in Transactions.** The most difficult aspect of implementing a poolable component arises for a transactional component. You cannot rely on COM+ to automatically enlist in a transaction but must do this coding yourself.

Pooling and Load Balancing

A pooled component cannot be load balanced. A pool of objects resides in memory on a particular machine. Hence the object cannot run on different machines in a cluster. A "shared" pool that crosses machines would not make sense, because the overhead involved in crossing the network would be excessive.

The Significance of COM+

We have come on a long journey together. Was it worth the trip? What is the value of the things we have studied? In this final section I'd like to offer my own perspective.

The Effectiveness of COM

COM+ is built on the Component Object Model or COM. This foundation has proved to be very durable and effective. Its original role was as the foundation of OLE. While OLE itself now occupies rather a niche as a particular technology for integrating desktop applications that manage documents, COM has emerged as the ubiquitous infrastructure throughout Microsoft's entire system architecture. Almost all of the new APIs that Microsoft brings out are based on COM.

COM is effective because it meets its original design objective of providing a binary standard for objects to interoperate. A C style interface is OK for C/C++ programs, but becomes difficult for other languages. Even C++ programs like to provide object-oriented wrappers around C style interfaces to simplify the programming model. Class libraries such as Microsoft Foundation Classes (MFC) became important for C++ programmers. But C++ class libraries only work for C++ programs, offering no benefit for other languages, and they make for another layer in the software architecture. A library based on COM is usable by all languages which support COM. In the Microsoft world, this is extremely important because of the widespread use of the various versions of Visual Basic. You can easily call COM components from C++, Visual Basic, and Visual J++, as well as from many third-party development languages and tools.

COM components can be very full blown. ActiveX controls can implement a great deal of functionality, and at the same time be very easy to use, plugging into a development environment to function just like built-in controls.

COM is effective because it is efficient, dispatching method calls by a single indirection through a table of function pointers. COM is not "middleware." It mediates the connection between an object and its client, but once the connection is set up, COM gets out of the way and the client talks directly to the object.

COM is effective because it is inherently distributed. No extra bells and whistles had to be grafted onto COM in order to enable clients to talk to remote COM objects. COM's basic architecture provides for location transparency. A client talks to an object in the same way, whether the object is in-process, in an EXE on the same machine, or resides on another machine.

And COM turns out to be effective for a number of other reasons. Through its interface negotiation mechanism COM effectively handles versioning issues, allowing clients and servers to independently upgrade to new versions and continue to interoperate. The COM apartment abstraction facilitates the use of COM components in multithreaded applications, relieving the component writer and application programmer from having to explicitly deal with threading issues, unless needed for maximum performance. (But, as we saw in Chapter 16, the COM+ synchronization attribute-based mechanism largely supercedes the use of apartments.)

The Power of COM+

COM+ builds on the robust foundation of COM to provide many effective services for the development of distributed enterprise applications. To provide these services, COM+ needs to offer a middleware layer, which COM itself does not. The mechanism that COM+ uses for invoking the middleware is very skillful, not compromising the basic efficiency of COM. Contexts provide the needed abstraction. A method call within a context is handled by straight COM, without any added overhead. But when a method calls crosses a context boundary, COM+ invokes an interceptor as a middleware layer to do the work required to harmonize the differences in context.

COM+ provides a declarative model for specifying contexts. Thus if a component requires that its work be protected by a transaction, this requirement can simply be declared as an attribute of the component, stored in the COM+ Catalog. Then when a method call is made the interceptor that gets invoked will call the required code to enlist in a distributed transaction. There is a great deal of sophisticated processing that is done by COM+ on your behalf, greatly simplifying your job as an application programmer.

In this book we surveyed many of the COM+ services, and I will not try to summarize them here. You should have a reasonable feel for the extent of the services that COM+ provides.

Comparing Architectures

I am much less enamored than I once was of finding and evangelizing for the "best" architecture. At one time in my career, I worked as a software engineer in a hardware CPU group. I became very interested in CPU architecture and had many interesting discussions with hardware engineers about the merits of RISC versus CISC. I was very taken by the articles I was reading at the time about RISC ("reduced instruction set computer") and believed we could design a faster CPU if we adopted a RISC design. I even won a lunch bet with the director of our group over this issue, when he became convinced of the merits of RISC.

Around this time our company got a new Vice President of R&D. He shared his experience with seeing CPU designs evolve. He observed that over time different architectures would tend to converge in bottom-line performance. Each has different trade-offs but can be optimized when worked at hard enough. As a practical matter, reasonable architectures are equivalent. I tend now to think he was basically right.

For a time RISC processors did have a performance advantage, because they made more effective use of scare real estate on chips. And we saw the emergence in the marketplace of a number of RISC processors such as SPARC, MIPS, the RS6000, and Alpha. But as circuit density continued to increase, CISC ("complex instruction set architecture") designs could be adequately implemented on-chip and still leave room for large caches, and we have tended to see a convergence in performance. The Intel family of CISC processors appears to be quite competitive.

While writing this book, I read about Compaq dropping their support of the Alpha chip for NT, and Microsoft followed suit. For a while NT ran on Alpha, MIPS, the PowerPC (based on RS6000) as well as Intel. Now Intel is the only platform left.

Many factors determine the success of a computer product, and architecture is only one consideration. You need a reasonable architecture, or the product will be fundamentally flawed and will not prove effective. But once an architecture is "good enough," other factors take precedence.

Today there are software religious wars over COM, CORBA, Java, etc. I do not believe that spinning one's wheels over which is the "best" is productive. All of these software architectures can produce effective results. You should examine the requirements of your system and look at practical issues like tools and training, and then make a pragmatic choice of what you think will work best for you.

Raising the Level of Abstraction

Apart from any particular merit of COM/COM+ as a software architecture, there is an extremely important development consideration that COM+ exemplifies. The level of abstraction in software development is getting higher and higher. Your own program relies on many layers of software that you do not write yourself, and you rely on many tools. While this relieves you of much code that you do not have to write, you are now also increasingly dependent on these "black boxes." You have to learn how these black boxes behave, and they work not according to natural laws but reflect the fact that they are artifacts.

Configuration issues are becoming increasingly important in software development, and COM+ carries the amount of configuration you need to be concerned about to a much higher level. You may sometimes find you need some "magic switch" set correctly in order for your application to work. As an example, while writing this book I had difficulty getting my queued components example to work. It turned out that there was nothing wrong with my program logic or with my understanding of how queued components work. I had neglected to go to the Message Queuing applet in the Control Panel and click "Renew Internal Security Certificate." There are inevitably many such configuration gotchas in a highly configurable system, and this is an area where it is difficult to acquire an adequate conceptual model.

The Importance of Quality

Quality has always been important for software, but today it is more vital than ever. Software systems affect more people in more ways than ever before. Software systems are more complex, so it becomes harder to achieve quality. It may also be more difficult for you as an individual programmer to ship a relatively bug-free product, because your software relies so much on other layers, and so the overall product quality relies not only on the quality of the software that you wrote but also on the quality of the layers on which you rely.

Distributed systems raise many more challenges in creating high quality applications because correct behavior is not merely dependent on the logical functioning of your program but also upon the behavior of a complex networked system. You need to think about error processing and recovery throughout your application.

A system based on components raises its own issues for quality. On the one hand, using components can be a great boost for quality, because the system is more modular. Although it is easier to design and debug a component than a complete system, testing a component has different requirements than testing a system. While a QA engineer who is not a programmer can test an end-user system, you need to test a component by writing programs. And a reusable component should behave properly under *all* uses, not just those of a particular system.

Quality means more than the absence of bugs. You should design your components and systems so that the user (a programmer in case of a component and an end user in the case of a system) can form an adequate conceptual model. Without this mental model the system becomes an amalgam of features, which becomes difficult to understand and use, even if every feature functions "properly."

Summary

In this final chapter, we looked at the fundamental problem of scalability for COM+ applications, which is one of the main driving issues of COM+. We looked at two ways of achieving scalability: clustering and object pooling. The most important of these technologies is clustering. COM+ provides the capability to automatically load balance components across a cluster of application servers. This Component Load Balancing service provided by COM+ can work in conjunction with Microsoft's other clustering products. Windows Load Balancing Service can enable you to route incoming IP traffic to up to 32 servers, providing a high degree of scalability for Web-based applications. Microsoft Cluster Server offers a high-availability solution based on two servers with failover capability.

Object pooling is more of a niche capability that can be implemented using COM+. Object pooling works in conjunction with just-in-time activation to save on the overhead of creating objects from scratch every time they need to be activated. It is only suitable when the initial creation/initialization overhead is large and reinitialization overhead is small. There are a number of requirements on a component for it to be poolable. These requirements at present preclude both Visual Basic and Visual J++ as development languages for a component that is to be pooled. More significantly, pooling an object creates an affinity for the machine the object was created on, and hence a pooled component cannot be load balanced across a cluster.

I concluded the chapter with some observations about the significance of COM+. I hope you have enjoyed this book, and would like to wish you the very best of success in applying COM+ to your development work.

APPENDIX A

Learning Resources

*T*he subject matter covered by this book is vast. I have tried to make this book itself as self-contained as possible, so that there are no requirements on other learning resources, other than the software and its documentation. Thus I included substantial introductions to Windows 2000 security, SQL Server and database programming, and Web programming. And Part 2 of this book contained a complete treatment of the fundamentals of COM required for understanding COM+ and for implementing COM+ applications. But there is much more to learn than can be covered by any one book. This appendix contains a list of resources that I believe you will find helpful.

The single most important resource is the Microsoft Software Developers Network (MSDN). The quarterly library is now distributed on CD-ROM and DVD. It is quite extensive, currently requiring 3 CDs, containing much more information than you would like to download from the Web.

Next comes the Web. Here are three Web sites, which, besides providing information themselves, can point you to other useful sites:

- **http://msdn.microsoft.com** is the online site for MSDN.
- **http://www.microsoft.com/com** is Microsoft's COM site.
- **http://www.ObjectInnovations.com** is the site for Object Innovations, which maintains up-to-date information about COM+, including updates for the CD-ROM that comes with this book. There is also information about training courses developed by Object Innovations.

Next come periodicals. Currently the two most useful periodicals in this field are the ones published by Microsoft, *Microsoft Systems Journal* and *Microsoft Internet Developer*.

Finally, there are many books in the field. COM+ itself is very new, but there are many useful books on the underlying COM and related technologies. Here are some suggestions:

Abernathy, Randy, *COM/DCOM Unleashed*, Sams Publishing, 1999.

Bernstein, Philip A. and Newcomer, Eric, *Principles of Transaction Processing*, Morgan Kaufmann, 1997.

Box, Don, *Essential COM*, Addison-Wesley, 1998.

Box et al., *Effective COM*, Addison-Wesley, 1999.

Dickman, Alan, *Designing Applications with MSMQ*, Addison-Wesley, 1998.

Gray, Jim and Reuter, Andreas, *Transaction Processing: Concepts and Techniques*, Morgan Kaufmann, 1993.

Grimes, Richard, *Professional ATL COM Programming*, Wrox, 1998.

Grimes, Richard, *Professional DCOM Programming*, Wrox, 1997.

Homer, Alex and Sussman, David, *Professional MTS and MSMQ with VB and ASP*, Wrox Press, 1998.

Kirtland, Mary, *Designing Component-Based Applications*, Microsoft Press, 1999.

Li, Sing and Economopoulos, Panos, *Professional COM Applications with ATL*, Wrox, 1998.

Maloney, Jim, *Distributed COM Application Development Using Visual Basic 6.0*, Prentice Hall, 1999.

Pinnock, Jonathan, *Professional DCOM Application Development*, Wrox, 1998.

Platt, David, *Understanding COM+*, Microsoft Press, 1999.

Rector, Brent and Sells, Chris, *ATL Internals*, Addison-Wesley, 1999.

Soukup, Ron and Kelaney, Karen, *Inside Microsoft SQL Server 7.0*, Microsoft Press, 1999.

Thui, Thuan L., *Learning DCOM*, O'Reilly, 1999.

APPENDIX B

Electronic Commerce Game Case Study

The Electronic Commerce Game™ is designed as an entertaining introduction to distributed objects. It can be implemented in several different technologies, among them COM+, CORBA, and Java. The case study can be used as both a learning tool and as a research vehicle for comparing implementation techniques for distributed systems. It has been used in this book for illustrating COM+ programming techniques. This appendix provides complete, self-contained documentation for setting up and playing the game. It is assumed that you are familiar with SQL Server 7.0. Please refer to the SQL Server Survival Guide in Chapter 18 if you need help with SQL Server 7.0.

The first section of this appendix gives a concise summary of the steps needed to set up the databases and ODBC data sources. The second section gives a player's guide to the game, using a "monolithic" version of the game that runs on one computer. The final section describes how to set up the distributed version of the game.

Setup

This section gives a concise summary of the steps needed to set up the databases. Chapter 18 presented this information along with tutorial information about using SQL Server 7.0. Once you are familiar with SQL Server 7.0 and

ODBC, you should find it easy to set the game up on a fresh computer using the instructions given here.

Databases

1. Use SQL Server Enterprise manager to create new databases having the names **Game**, **Foodstore**, **Petworld** and **Toyland**.
2. Use SQL Server Query Analyzer to run the script **create_game_tables.sql** to create the tables for the **Game** database. All the scripts you need are in **CaseStudy\SqlScripts**.
3. Use Query Analyzer to run the script **create_vendor_tables.sql** to create the tables for the **Foodstore**, **Petworld**, and **Toyland** databases.
4. Run the script **Insert_game_data.SQL** to insert initial data into the **Game** database. As a spot check, run the query **select * from products**. You should get the following data:

```
item                      price
-------------------       --------------------
airplane toy              10.0000
beanie baby               20.0000
cat carrier               30.0000
dog bone                   5.0000
elephant gun              50.0000
fruit basket              10.0000
```

5. Run the script **create_vendor_tables.sql** to create the tables for each of the databases **Foodstore**, **Petworld**, and **Toyland**.
6. Run the three scripts **Insert_foodstore.SQL**, **Insert_petworld.SQL**, and **Insert_toyland.SQL** to insert data into the three vendor databases. As a spot check, run the query **select * from inventory** on the **Toyland** database. You should get the following data:

```
item              price       quantity
---------------   ---------   ----------
airplane toy      15.0000     50
beanie baby       25.0000     50
elephant gun      55.0000     50
```

ODBC Data Sources

1. Use the ODBC Data Source Administrator to create system DSNs of "foodstore.com," "petworld.com," and "toyland.com" for the corresponding vendor databases **Foodstore**, **Petworld**, and **Toyland**.
2. Copy the file **Game.dsn** from the folder **CaseStudy\SqlScripts** to the folder provided for ODBC data sources. On my machine, this folder is

Program Files\Common Files\ODBC\Data Sources on the partition where Windows 2000 is installed. You could verify that a corresponding file DSN is now installed by bringing up the ODBC Data Source Administrator and choosing the File DSN tab.

Player's Guide

The basic concept of the game is extremely simple—online buying and selling of products. It is structured as a game in which players compete to fulfill a shopping list by visiting various vendor sites and making purchases.

Introduction

Players take on the role of Customer (and may temporarily assume the role of a Vendor if they can discover a Vendor ID). Vendors carry different products, which they buy at wholesale and sell at retail. Vendors decide what products to stock, what inventory level to maintain, and what retail prices to charge for their products. They may adjust their product list, prices, and inventory during the game. All Vendors are given the same starting capital, and they earn more money by selling products to Customers. Their balance declines when they buy products at wholesale for their inventory. The winning Vendor is the one with the most money when the game is over. A Vendor whose balance drops below zero is disqualified.

At the beginning of a game, all Customers are supplied with an identical starting balance and an identical shopping list, specifying items to be purchased from Vendors. Customers pay for their purchases out of their balance. The winning Customer is the one who has purchased all the items on the shopping list and has the largest balance. A Customer whose balance drops below zero is disqualified.

There are multiple Customers, and there are preassigned Vendors with various starting inventories. The game is won by buying all the items on the shopping list without the balance dropping below zero. The ending balance gives the score for the game. The Customer may temporarily assume the role of a Vendor by visiting the **wholesale.com** Web page.

All transactions are carried out through a simulated Web. Players run a browser program, and they navigate by entering Web addresses to bring up Web pages. A Web page either displays information or runs a program. The following standard pages are available:

vendors.com	Displays Web addresses of all Vendors.
shopper.com	Displays a personalized shopping page, which shows customer name, current balance and shopping list.

wholesale.com Runs a program that enables Vendors to buy products at wholesale, return products, and change the retail price charged for a product.

In addition, each Vendor has a home page (listed at **vendors.com**) that runs a program enabling Customers to buy the products that the Vendor carries. The following vendor pages are provided in the standard setup:

- **toyland.com**
- **petworld.com**
- **foodstore.com**

Playing the Game

You can now run the single machine version of the "monolithic" application without further setup. Just open and run **ClientBrowser.vbp** in directory **CaseStudy\Monolithic**.

MAIN WINDOW

The main window has a dropdown combobox for entering the URL of the "Web" page you wish to visit. See Figure B–1.

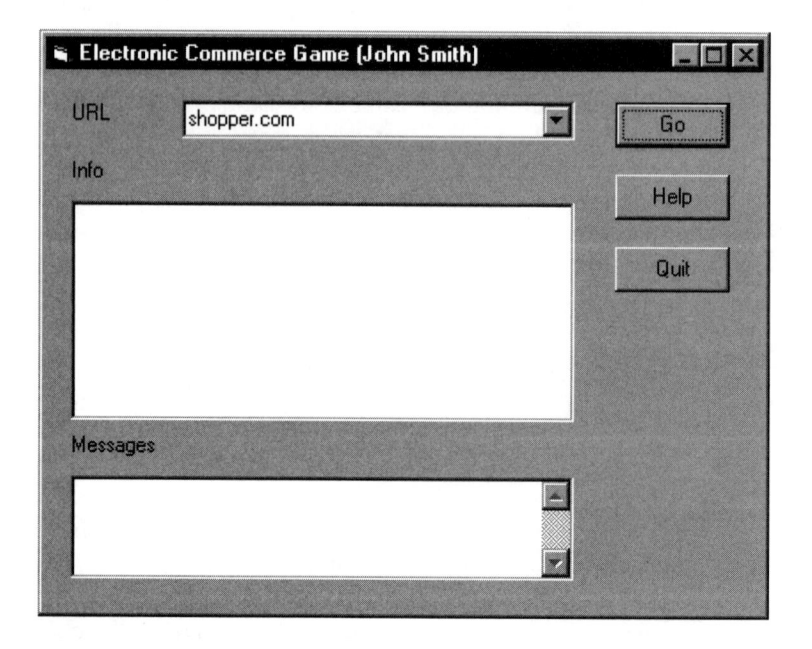

Figure B–1 *Main window of Electronic Commerce Game*

Three pages are hardwired into the program:

shopper.com   Visit to get your shopping list.
vendors.com   Displays Web addresses of all Vendors in Info box.
wholesale.com Runs a program that enables Vendors to buy products at wholesale, return products, and change the retail price charged for a product (requires a valid Vendor logon).

You may also type in any other Web address. In this game, the only other valid addresses are those of vendors, which are stored in the **Vendors** table of the **Game** database. You obtain a list of vendors by visiting **vendors.com**. You can then copy and paste a vendor address into the URL text box. Once you have visited a particular vendor, the vendor's address is added to the dropdown list, making it easy to visit a second time. Once you have chosen a URL, you simply click the "Go" button.

Unlike "real" browsers, our simulated browser will generally open up a new window to show the page you are visiting. The one exception is **vendors.com**, where the list of available vendors is shown in the Info box.

The Messages box can show various messages. At the current level of the game there are no messages. In more advanced levels, messages can be displayed, such as announcing a new player entering the game or a player leaving the game.

The name of the player is shown in the title of the main window (after a player has logged on).

PLAYER LOGON

At this point you should enter **shopper.com** in order to obtain your initial shopping list. You will then be presented with a logon screen (with default player "John Smith"). See Figure B–2.

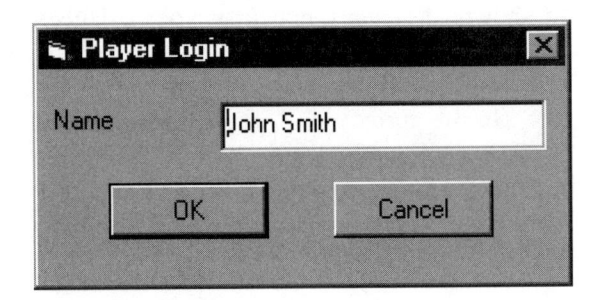

Figure B–2   *Player logon window*

Click OK and you will either be welcomed as a new player or welcomed back.

SHOPPING PAGE

After you have logged on, you will be shown a shopping page. Figure B–3 shows the initial shopping page for John Smith.

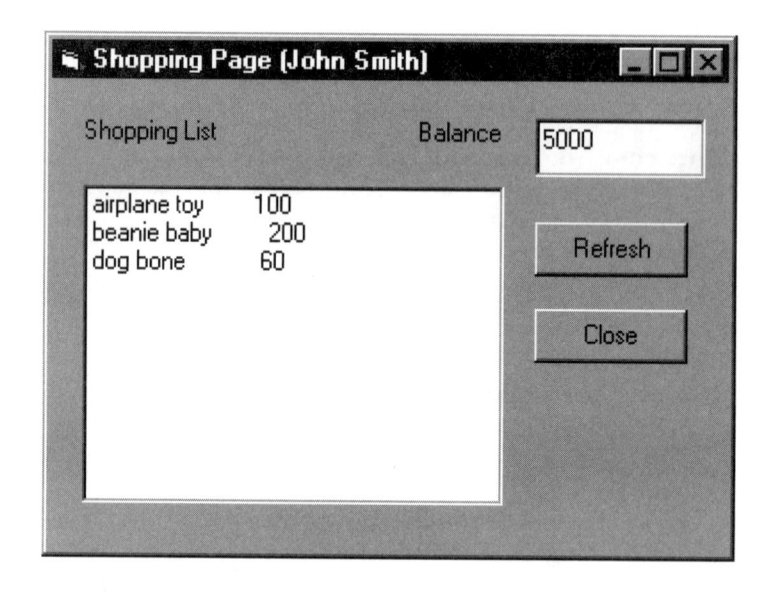

```
Shopping Page (John Smith)

Shopping List              Balance    5000

airplane toy      100
beanie baby       200                 Refresh
dog bone           60
                                       Close
```

Figure B–3   *An initial shopping page*

As you buy items, the quantity remaining to buy will decrease. You can always get an up-to-date shopping list by visiting **shopper.com**. Your current balance is also shown. Be careful not to let your balance drop below zero! This form is modeless, so you may leave it up throughout the game, if you wish. To obtain and show the latest data from the database, click the "Refresh" button. (In the current level, if you close the shopping page, you will be logged off. You can easily log back on—it will just mean that you are playing another game, picking up from where you left off.)

LIST OF VENDORS

You should next visit **vendors.com** to obtain a list of Vendors, where you can buy the items on your shopping list. See Figure B–4.

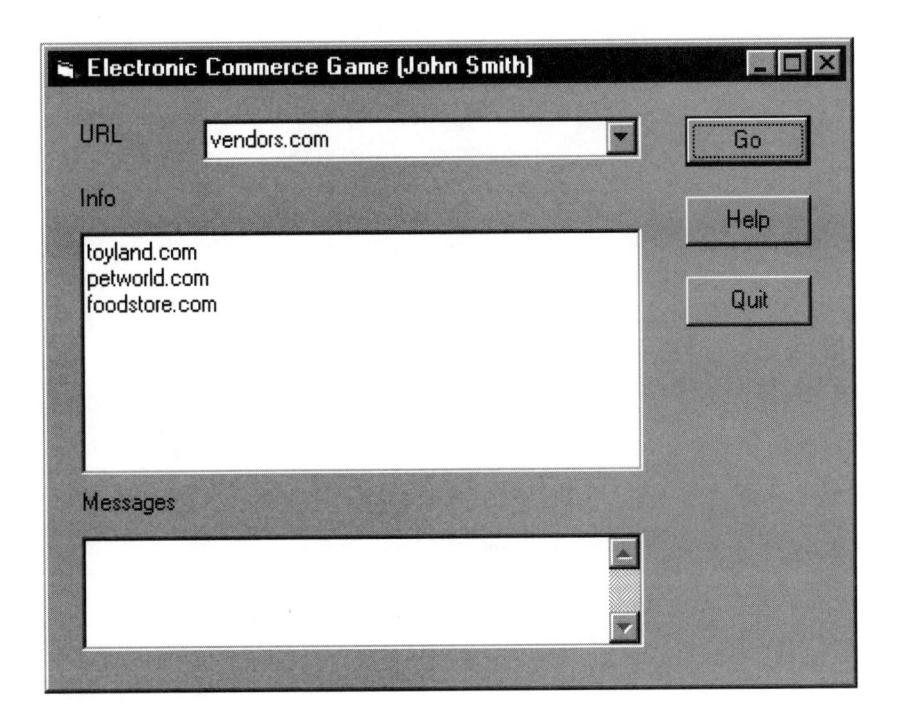

Figure B–4 Visit **vendors.com** to obtain a list of vendors

A PARTICULAR VENDOR'S PAGE

At this point, you can start visiting Vendors and buying products. For example, if you enter **toyland.com** for the address, you will see the window shown in Figure B–5.

The vendor's inventory is shown—all items that are carried, the retail price, and the quantity that the vendor currently has on hand. To buy an item, select it from the list box. The "Buy" button is enabled. Enter the quantity you want and click Buy. You may buy other products. The form is modal, so you will have to close it to move on.

As an example, buy 10 beanie babies. That will cost you $250. The vendor's stock of this item has been reduced. See Figure B–6.

Close **toyland.com** and go back to **shopper.com** (if you left it open, click Refresh). Your balance has been reduced by $250 to $4750, and the required number of beanie babies you have to buy is now only 190. See Figure B–7.

Figure B–5 *Vendor page for **toyland.com***

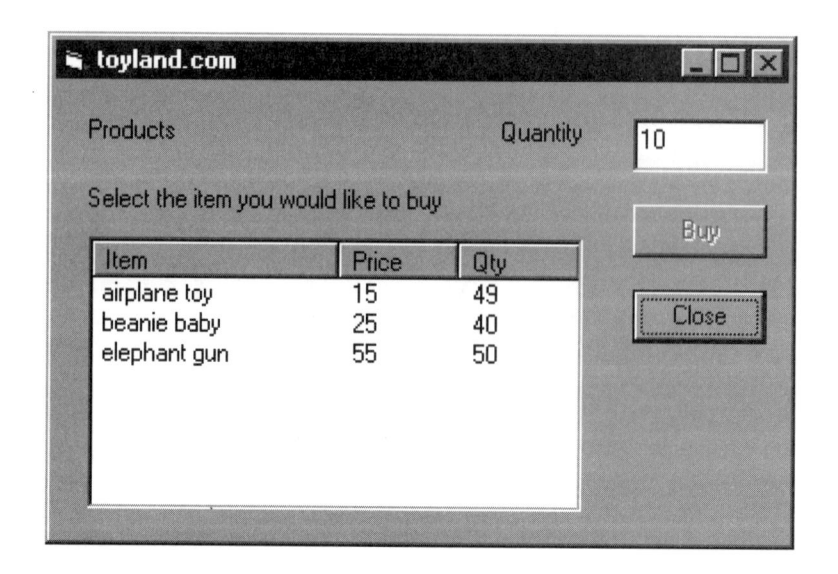

Figure B–6 *Customer has purchased 10 beanie babies*

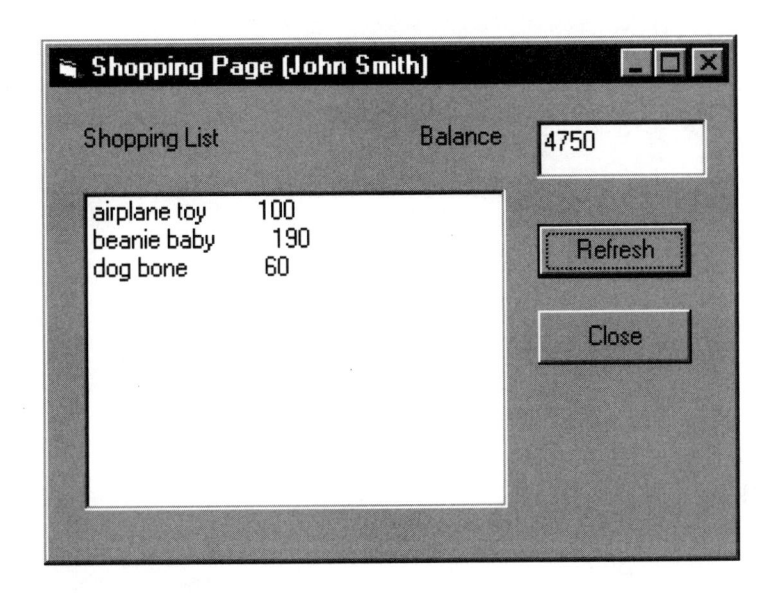

Figure B–7 Shopping page reflects the purchase of 10 beanie babies

Now try to finish the game on your own. Visit other vendors, and try to buy all the items on the list, without going bankrupt! Good luck!

Distributed Version of Game

You can set up a distributed version of the game using the server project in the folder **CaseStudy\EcServer** and the client project in **CaseStudy\Client-Browser**. Create an empty COM+ application, for example, **EcGameApp**. Install your ActiveX DLL **EcServer.dll** into this new application. This will bring 8 components into the application. See Figure B–8. You can try running the client, and it should work.

Next use the "Export" feature of COM+ to create a **.msi** file for an application proxy. Copy this **.msi** file to your remote Windows 2000 machine and double-click on it to install it. Then copy the client **.exe** file. You should now be able to run the remote client.

Running the Data Tier Remotely

Finally, it is easy to perform the data access from another computer. On the machine where the middle tier is deployed you will just have to reconfigure your ODBC data sources. Make sure that your have the databases set up on a

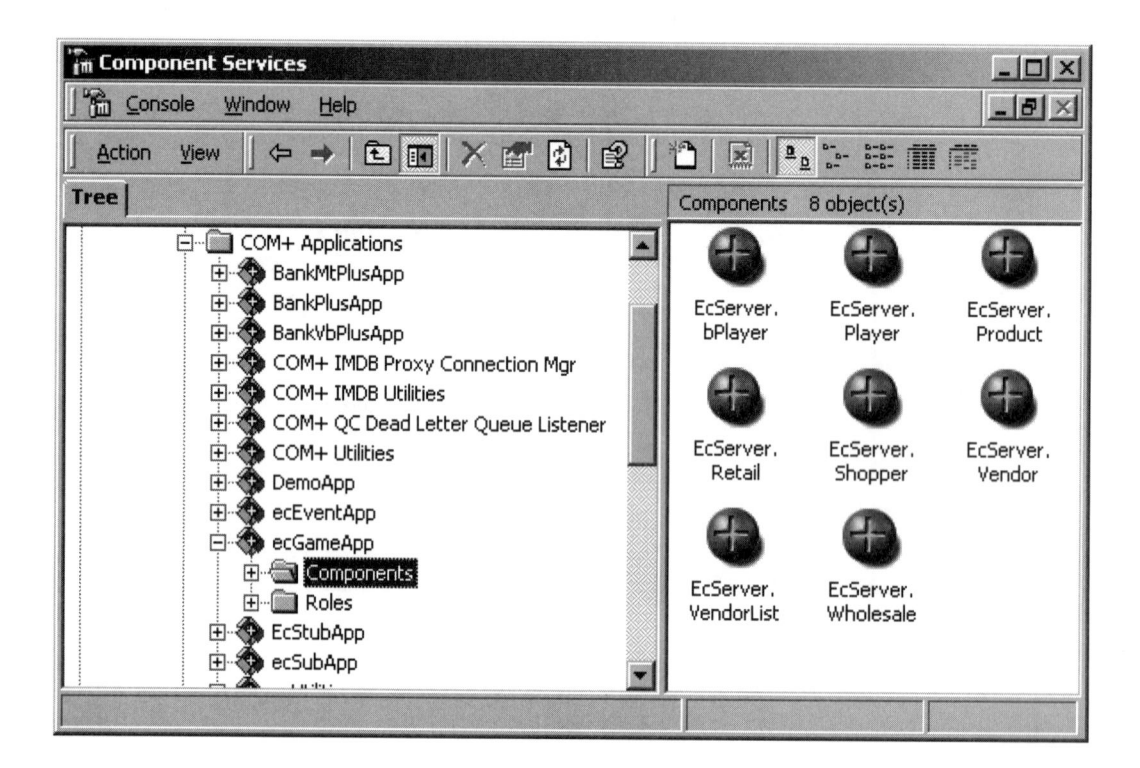

598 Appendix B • Electronic Commerce Game Case Study

Figure B-8 *Server for Electronic Commerce Game has been installed in COM+ application*

remote machine running SQL Server. Now bring up the ODBC Administrator program. Select a DSN. Click the "Configure" button. On the first screen that comes up, select the remote server you want from the dropdown for "What SQL Server do you want to connect to?"

A simulation of an Internet version of the game would be to have the **Game** database installed on the same machine as the COM+ application, and to have the various vendor databases deployed on remote machines.

INDEX

A

Aborted transactions, 450
Abstraction, 5-6
   level of, 584-85
Abstraction hierarchy, 5
Access control entry (ACE), 377, 379
Access control list (ACL), 379
Access tokens, 377, 378
ACID properties, transactions, 308, 325, 450
Activate method, **IObjectControl** interface, 345, 581
Activation, 306, 317, 319-21
   bank account example, 320-21
   flowing context properties, 319-20
   forcing in caller's context, 321
   See also Just-in-time (JIT) activation
Active Directory, 36, 58-61, 376-77
   installing, 59
   joining a domain, 59-60
   managing users, 60-61
Active Server Pages (ASP), 42, 477, 502-5
   and COM+, 505-17
   object model, 505-6
   price list example COM+ application, 509-11
      Web version, 513-16
   Request and **Response** objects, 506-7
   three-tier Web application using COM+, 507-17
   using COM/COM+ objects from, 511-13
   Web programming addendum, 516-17
Active Template Library (ATL), 23, 111, 149-73
   AppWizard, 125, 156-57, 197
   ATL COM server demo, 155-63
      ATL COM AppWizard, 156-57, 197
      attributes, 158-59
      building the server, 160
      class names, 158
      client test program, 163
      defining the implementation class, 162-63
      defining the methods, 160
      IDL file, 162
      implementing the methods, 163
      Object Wizard, 158
   boilerplate COM code, 150
   CComObject, 153
   class declaration, 151-52
   class implementation, 152
   coclass, 169-70
   code walkthrough, 164-67
      CComModule, 164, 167
      DllCanUnloadNow, 165
      DllGetClassObject, 165
      DllMain, 165
      implementing **IClassFactory**, 167
      MIDL generated code, 164
      REGSVR32.exe, 167
      self-registration, 166-67
   enumerator classes, 247
   example program, 153-54
   EXE servers using, 196-201
      demo, 197-98
      EXE server files, 201
      proxies/stubs, 199-201
      self-registration for EXE servers, 198-99
   IDL file, 162, 168-71
   implementation of **IUnknown**, 151
   instantiating an ATL-based COM object, 152-53
   and Microsoft Foundation Class (MFC) Library, 150
   multiple interfaces, 168-71
   multithreading support, 291-92
   Object Wizard, 158, 257-58
   second interface:
      adding in IDL, 168-70
      C++ code for, 170-71
   tracing support, 272-73
      QueryInterface calls, 272
      tracing output, 272-73
   type library, 169
   and Visual C++, 154-67
      ATL code walkthrough, 164-67
      ATL COM server demo, 155-63
      COM support, 155
   wrapper classes, 171-73
      CComBSTR, 172
      smart pointers, 172-73
ActiveX, 13
   controls, 22-23, 38, 107, 492-94
   downloading, 497-98
ActiveX Data Objects (ADO), 46, 425-27, 505
   ADO object model, 433-34
   advantage of, 426
   Application object, 505
   classes in, 433
   Connection object, 434
   Errors collection, 439-41
   programming with, 432-42
   recordset, defined, 434-35
   Recordset object, 434-39
      adding a record, 438
      deleting a record, 438-39
      selecting data from a table, 436
      updating a record, 436-37
   Request object, 506
   Server object, 505
   Session object, 505
Ada, 23
AddRef, 86, 118, 121-22, 123, 153, 172, 176
Administration objects, COM+, 354-56
ADO, *See* ActiveX Data Objects (ADO)
ADO object model, 433-34

599

600 Index

Advise method, **IConnectionPoint**, 552
afxdisp.h, 141
Algol, 6
Anchor, 472
Anonymous impersonation level, 392
Apartment architecture, 309-10, 313
Apartments, 284-90
    apartment threading model, 287-88
    defined, 284-85
    multithreaded, 285-86
    single-threaded, 285, 309-10
    and synchronization, 359-61
    multithreaded bank account example, 360
    neutral apartments, 361
    synchronization through apartments, 360-61
AppCenter Server, 573, 576
AppID Registry entries:
    for DCOM, 212
    for a local EXE server, 210-12
Application attributes, 337-39
Application ID (AppID), 210-12
Application proxy, COM+, 316
Applications:
    COM+, 305-6, 315
        deploying remotely, 356-57
        preinstalled, 316
        types of, 316
Application servers:
    three-tier systems, 34
    two-tier systems, 32-33
appStarter program, 545
AppWizard, 125, 156-57, 197
APSE (Ada Programming and Support Environment), 23
Architecture:
    COM+, 317-26
        activation, 319-21
        context, 16, 305-6
        fundamentals of, 305-27
        interception, 16, 317, 321-23
        just-in-time (JIT) activation, 323-25
        object construction, 325-26
        object pooling, 325
ASP, *See* Active Server Pages (ASP)
ATL, *See* Active Template Library (ATL)
atlbase.h, 171
Attributes:
    COM+, 305, 309-10, 337-41
        application attributes, 337-39
        component attributes, 339-40
        interface attributes, 340
        method attributes, 340-41
Authentication, 371
Authorization, 371
Automatic transactions, 308, 456-60
    consistency/done bits, 459
    dependent attributes, 458
    interior objects/transaction boundaries, 458-59
    life cycle, 459-60
    transactional components, 456-59
    transaction flag ("doomed" bit), 459
Automation, 229-50
    with Active Template Library (ATL), 233-37
    collections, 246-49
        enumerators, 247
        example, 248-49
        implementing, 248-49
    and object models, 246-47
    controller, 230
    dual interfaces, 231
    IDispatch interface, 231, 237
    late binding, 230
    methods, 230
    properties, 230
    tagVARIANT structure, 232-33
    type information, 231
    VARIANTS, 232-33
    with VBScript, 233, 234-35
        VBScript Automation processing, 237
    and Visual Basic, 240-46
        client program that handles events, 244-45
        default properties, 241
        events, 242-46
        events in COM servers, 243
        IDL for an event interface, 245-46
        IDL for a dispatch interface, 241-42
        properties, 240-42
        read-only/write-only properties, 241
    Visual C++ Automation controllers, 237-40
        calling **IDispatch** directly, 238-39
        using **CComDispatchDriver**, 239-40

B

Backup domain controller (BDC), 376
Backup Site Controllers (BSC), 522
Bank Account Server example program, 72-73
BeginTransaction method, 455
Behavior, class, 4
_bMove interface, **move** method, 467
Boilerplate COM code, 150
Brockschmidt, Kraig, 15
BSTR, 97
bstr, 97
_bstr_t, 180
Business layer, three-tier systems, 33-34
Business logic layer, 40-45
    Internet Information Server, 40-42
    Microsoft Message Queue (MSMQ), 44-45
    Microsoft Transaction Server and COM+, 42-44
ByRef, 74
Bytecode, 7
ByVal, 74

C

C, 5-6, 12
C++, 6, 12, 105-28
    classes, 108-9
    class identification, 108
    constructors, 109
    distributed objects, 111
    encapsulation, 108
    implementing a COM class using, 111-27
        bank account object example, 112
        binary representation of interfaces, 112-13
        C++ representation of interfaces, 113-14
        class factories, 118
        COM status and error reporting, 124-25
        globally unique identifiers (GUID), 116-17
        IAccount interface, 127
        IDisplay interface, 126-27
        implementing a COM object, 118-19
        interface implementation, 120-23

Index 601

interface specification, 119-20
IUnknown interface, 117-18
  object creation function, 123-24
  QueryInterface, 117-18
  reference counting, 118
  using a COM object, 125-26
interfaces, 108-9
object creation, 109
object lifetime, 110
primary goal of, 108
reuse, 111
static data members, 109-10
versioning/interface negotiation, 110-11
virtual functions, 114-16
CanBePooled method, **IObject Control** interface, 324, 345, 581
CaseStudy subdirectory, 19
Catalog, 306, 310-12
  and Microsoft Management Console snap-in, 311
Catalog Manager, 310
CComBSTR, 172
CComCoClass, 167
  Error method, 258, 261
CComDispatchDriver, 230, 239-40
CComIEnum, 247
CComIEnumImpl, 247
CComModule, 166-68
CComObject, 153
CComObjectRootEx, 151, 153
CComQIPtr, 172
CD-ROM, installing, 19
CException, 267
Classes, 4-5, 73, 81, 108-9
  in ADO, 433
  behavior, 4
  data, 4
  methods, 4-5
Class factory, 118, 130-31
  registering, 192-93
  revoking, 193
Class ID (CLSID), 78, 85, 118, 131, 579
  and the system registry, 131
Class identification, 108
Class libraries, 23
Class name, 85
Class object, 109, 130
ClassWizard, 125
CLB, *See* Component Load Balancing (CLB)
Client, 28, 31
  COM, 71-104
  COM client programming, 90-95
  connectable objects, 552
  Electronic Commerce Game, 550-51
  fat/rich, 25, 38-39
  thin, 25, 38-39
Client/server systems, 28-33
CLogging, 276
Clustering, 36-37
  Microsoft clustering technologies, 569-73
    Component Load Balancing (CLB), 573, 574-78
    Microsoft Cluster Server (MSCS/Wolfpack), 570-71
    Windows Load Balancing Service (WLBS/Convoy), 572-73
Clusters, 570

Coclass (COM class), identifying, 78-79
CoCreateInstance, 83, 101, 104, 123, 125, 140-41, 163, 216, 237
CoCreateInstanceEx, 82, 104, 214, 216, 217, 220, 222, 454, 536, 574, 577
codebase attribute, OBJECT tag, 497
CoFreeUnusedLibraries, 141
CoGetCallContext, 318, 401
CoGetClassObject, 140, 141, 192, 216, 220
CoGetInterfaceAndReleaseStream, 295
CoGetObject, 537, 574
CoGetObjectContext, 318
COIeDispatchException, 267-68
CoImpersonateClient, 407
CoInitialize, 192
CoInitializeEx, 361
CoInitializeSecurity, 407
Collections, 246-49
  enumerators, 247
  example, 248-49
  implementing, 248-49
  and object models, 246-47
COM+:
  and Active Server Pages (ASP), 505-17
  administration objects, 354-56
  application proxy, 316
  applications, 305-6, 315
    deploying remotely, 356-57
    preinstalled, 316
    types of, 316
  architecture, 317-26
  activation, 319-21
    context, 16, 305-6
    fundamentals of, 305-27
    interception, 16, 317, 321-23
    just-in-time (JIT) activation, 323-25
    object construction, 325-26
    object pooling, 325
  attributes, 305, 309-10, 337-41
    application attributes, 337-39
    component attributes, 339-40
    interface attributes, 340
    method attributes, 340-41
  automatic transactions, 308
  basics of, 3-24
  Catalog, 310-12
  complexity, 308
  component model, 16
  components, 7-8, 315-16
    configured/unconfigured, 316
  concurrency in, 359-67
  declarative programming, 309-10
  deploying on a remote computer, 66-67
  events, 547-68
  event system architecture, 555-56
  Explorer, 311-12
  library application, 316
  Microsoft's road to, 8-15
    Component Object Model (COM), 11-13
    dynamic link libraries (DLLs), 8-9
    Microsoft Message Queue (MSMQ), 14-15
    Microsoft Transaction Server (MTS), 13-14
    object linking and embedding (OLE), 9-11
    Windows Open System Architecture (WOSA), 9
  object-oriented languages, 5-7

objects, 4-5
  life cycle of, 319
  power of, 583
  preview of, 64-68
  reliability of, 307
  scalability of, 306-7, 569-86
  security, 369-409
  services, 16-18
    concurrency, 17
    load-balancing service, 18
    message queuing, 17-18
    publish and subscribe event service, 18
    security, 17
    transactions, 17
  significance of, 582-85
  terminology, 314-16
  transactions, 308-9, 449-70
    declaring requirements, 310
  tutorial, 329-58
    Visual Basic COM+ component, 330-48
    Visual C++ COM+ component, 348-54
  Web applications using, 471-518
  See also COM+ security; Events; Security
COM+ Explorer, 311-12
COM+ security, 369-409
  configuring, 397-99
    application-level security configuration, 398-99
  electronic commerce game case study, 393-97
    exporting the proxy, 395-97
    running the stub, 394-95
    stub version of game, 393-94
  identity, 404-6
  impersonation, 406-8
    client-side, 407
    server-side, 407-8
  programmatic security, 401-4
  role-based security, 400-401
    configuring component-level access, 400-401
    setting up roles, 400
COM, 3, 11-13
  ActiveX, 13
  apartment architecture, 309-10, 313
  as binary standard, 12
  and C++, 6, 12, 105-28
  classes, 81, 108-9, 313
  class identification, 108
  class object, 109
  client programming model, 90
  clients, 71-104
    programming, 90-95
  components, structure of, 131-32
  concepts, 79-89
  defined, 107-8
  distributed objects, 111
  effectiveness of, 582-83
  encapsulation, 108
  identifiers, 84-86
    class name, 85
    globally unique identifier (GUID), 84-85
    program ID (ProgID), 85
    "user" names, 85-86
  interface negotiation, 87-89, 110-11
    QueryInterface using Visual Basic, 88
    QueryInterface using Visual C++, 87-88
  interfaces, 80-81, 108-9, 112, 313

IUnknown interface, 80-81, 86, 89, 106, 111, 112, 117-20, 135-36, 223, 315
  methods, 313
  multithreading in, 279-301
  object creation, 109
  object instantiation, 82-84
    CoCreateInstance (C++), 83, 101, 104, 123, 125, 140-41, 163, 216
    CreateObject (Visual Basic), 84
    New operator (Visual Basic), 83-84
  object lifetime, 86-87, 110
    in Visual Basic, 87
  objects, 81-82, 313
  power of, 18-24
  reuse, 111
  security, 383-92
  server, 89, 313-14
  status and error reporting mechanism, 124-25
  terminology, 79-89, 313-14
  type library, 89
  and Windows Registry, 98-104
  See also COM++; COM classes; COM clients; COM security
CoMarshalInterThreadInterfaceInStream, 295
COM classes:
  implementing in a DLL, 129-48
  implementing using C++, 111-27
COM client programming, 90-95
  BSTR, 97
  COM library, 97-98
  Unicode, 95-97
    converting using macros, 96
    converting using Win32, 96
  Visual Basic COM client program, 90-92
  Visual C++ COM client program:
    console, 92-94
    using MFC, 94-95
COM clients, 71-104
_com_error, 180-81, 262-63, 278
COM error interfaces, 256-64
  IErrorInfo, 256
  ISupportErrorInfo, 256
  returning error information, 256
COM interfaces, 80-81, 108-9, 112
COM library programming, 97-98
Committed transactions, 450
Common Gateway Interface (CGI), 40, 479-81, 487-89
  dynamic Web page, 479-80
  HTML forms, 481
COM objects:
  test programs for, 125-26
    COM account object example program, 126
  using, 125-26
Complexity, COM+, 308
ComPlus directory, 19
Component attributes, 339-40
Component Load Balancing (CLB), 573, 574-78
  composing clustering technologies, 575
  configuring, 575-77
  design issues, 578
  fault tolerance with, 578
  load balancing, 574-75
  load balancing algorithm, 575
  performance, 578
Component Object Model, *See* COM

Component Object Model (COM), 11-13
Component objects, 106
Components:
    COM+, 7-8, 315-16
        configured/unconfigured, 316
    Components dialog, 22-23
    Component Services, 15
    Component software, 106-7
COM security, 383-92
    authentication, 388
    authorization, 383-88
        access and launch permissions for applications, 386-87
        default access/launch permissions, 384-86
        name example, 384
    identity, 388-92
        NT services, 389
        running as interactive user, 391-92
        running as launching user, 388
        running as this user, 392
        Window stations/desktops, 391
    impersonation, 392
COM servers, 129-48
    bootstrapping an object, 130
    class factories, 130-31
    class IDs and the system registry, 131
    class object, 109, 130
    concepts, 129-35
    Interface Definition Language (IDL), 75-79
        identifying the coclass (COM class), 78-79
        identifying the type library, 77-78
        interfaces, 79
        methods, 79
        properties, 79
    local/remote transparency, 130
    OLE/COM Object Viewer (OLE View), 74-75
    structure of a component, 131-32
    structure of, 73-79
    Visual Basic Object Browser, 20-21, 73-74
    Windows Registry, 132
        Registry Editor (REGEDIT), 132
        registry entry files, 132-33
        registry information, 133-35
    working with DLLs, 141-42
    See also In-process COM server
Concrete class, 121
Concurrency, 279, 359-67
    programming example, 364-66
    synchronization and activities, 361-64
        activities defined, 361-62
        relationship with other attributes, 364
        "rental" threading model, 364
        synchronization attribute, 362-64
    synchronization and apartments, 359-61
        multithreaded bank account example, 360
        neutral apartments, 361
        synchronization through apartments, 360-61
Concurrent programming, 280-84
    automatically serializing data access, 281
    race condition example, 280
    serializing access to shared data, 280-81
    Windows message queue demo, 281-84
        DelayDeposit method, 282
        exercising the test program, 282
        hidden window, 283
        trying for a race condition, 282-83

Configuration, 50-53
    roadmap, 51
    timeline, 52-53
Configured components, COM+, 316
Connectable objects, 551
Connection point architecture, 551-54
    Client-Object-Sink, 552
    IConnectionPoint, 552
    IConnectionPointAdvise method, 553
    incoming/outgoing interfaces, 551-52
Connection points, 551
Connector Servers, 522
Consistency/done bits, 459
Construct method, **IObjectConstruct** interface, 326, 352-53
Constructors, 109
Consumers, 425
Context, 16, 305-6, 317-18
    call context, 318
    context object, 318
    default, 317
Contract, 5
Convoy Cluster Software, 572
CORBA (Common Object Request Broker Architecture), 12, 24, 32, 107, 111
Core elements, NT security model, 377-79
CoRegisterClassObject, 193, 216, 225, 275
CoRevertToSelf, 407
CoServerInfo, 217
CoSetProxyBlanket, 407
CreateInstance method, **IClassFactory**, 130, 137, 140
CreateObject function, 82, 84, 236
CWinApp, 164

D

Data, 4-5
Data access layer, 45-46
Database programming tutorial, 427-32
    administration program for History database, 431-32
    ODBC Data Source, creating, 427-31
Database servers, 28-31
Data hiding, 5-6
DB-Library, 426-27
DbMon utility, 273-74
DCOM, 12, 14, 32, 111, 203-28
    architecture, 224-27
    implementation, 216-20
        client code example, 218-19
        CoCreateInstanceEx, 217
        CoServerInfo, 217
        execution context, 216
        _MULTI_QI, 218
    launching a server over the network, 224-25
    moving data between machines, 225
    multithreading issues, 226-27
    network architecture, 225-26
    network traffic:
        IMultiQI interface, 222-23
        optimizations by the DCOM infrastructure, 223-24
        optimizing, 220-24
    programming for, 212-24
        client specifies the server, 213-16
        remoting an existing COM object, 204-12

Index **603**

604 Index

COM server, 204
DCOM demo, 204-6
Registry entries, 209-12
security issue, 207-8
security, 224
server operation over the network, 225-26
and the Windows Registry, 220
dcomconfg.exe, 204, 207
Deactivate method, **IObjectControl** interface, 345, 581
DebugBreak function, 275
Declarative programming, 309-10
Default context, 317
Default impersonation levels, 392
Default method, **CHelloExtension** class, 500
Delegate impersonation level, 392
Delete method, **CException**, 267
demosdk.reg, 191, 194
Development tools, 61-64
Platform SDK, 64, 273
Visual Basic, 7, 12, 18-19, 31, 61, 62, 71, 230
Visual C++, 61, 62-63, 71
Visual InterDev, 63
Discretionary access control list (DACL), 377-79
Distributed COM, *See* DCOM
Distributed Computing Environment (DCE), 84
Distributed interNet Applications (DNA) architecture, 34
Distributed Lock Manager (DLM), 570
Distributed objects, 111
Distributed systems:
evolution of, 26-34
one-tier systems, 26-27
PC LANs, 27-28
three-tier systems, 33-34
two-tier systems, 28-33
Distributed transactions, 42-44
processing, 451-53
two-phase commit, 452-53
X/Open DTP model, 451-52
DllCanUnloadNow, 138, 139-40, 141, 164, 165, 315
DllGetClassObject, 138-39, 165, 315
DllGetObject, 164
DllGetTransactionManager, 455
dllhost.exe, 224-25, 314, 323, 325, 338, 540, 544
DllRegisterServer, 103, 166-67, 315
DLLs, 8-9
exported functions, 138
module definition file, 138
working with, 141-42
DllUnregisterServer, 103, 166-67, 315
Domain Admins group, 373-74
Domain controllers, 58, 377
Domain Name System (DNS), 57-58
Domains, 36, 376-77
joining, 59-60
Domain Users group, 373-74
Dual interfaces, 231
Dynamic Data Exchange (DDE), 10-11, 188
Dynamic HTML, 39
Dynamic HTML page, 477
Dynamic link libraries (DLLs), 8-9, 89

E

Early binding, 230, 231
ecEventVb.dll, 560-61, 565

EcStubApp, 394-95
EcStubClient.exe, 397
EcStub.msi, 397
ecSubApp, 562
ecUtil.bMove, 463, 464-65
ecUtil.dbHistory, 463, 464
ecUtil.dbPlayer, 463
ecUtil.dll, 462-63
Eiffel, 6
Electronic Commerce Game, 411, 548-50
case study, 393-97, 444-47, 589-98
client, 550-51
databases, 416, 590
Game database, 416, 461-62
History database, 416, 461-62
vendor databases, 416
distributed version of, 597-98
exporting the proxy, 395-97
File DSN, 445-46
game description, 591-92
main window, 592-93
ODBC data sources, 590-91
player logon, 593-94
player's guide, 591-97
playing, 447, 592-97
running data tier remotely, 597-98
running the stub, 394-95
server, 549-50
setting up databases for, 422-23
database creation, 423
database testing, 423
setup, 589-91
shopping page, 594
stub version of game, 393-94
vendor list, 594-95
vendor pages, 595-97
Elements, HTML documents, 472
Encapsulation, 5, 108
Enterprise Manager, SQL Server 7.0, 414-15
EnumConnections method:
IConnectionPoint, 552
IConnectionPointContainer, 553
Enumerators, 247
Error codes:
looking up, 253-54
and naming conventions, 253
ErrorMessage function, 177
Error method, **CComCoClass**, 258, 261
Error processing/debugging, 251-78
Automation exceptions, 264-68
COIeDispatchException, 267-68
EXCEPINFO, 264-65
MFC support for, 265-68
COM error interfaces, 256-64
client code and error information, 261-62
example, 258-60
GetErrorInfo, 256
ICreateErrorInfo, 256
IErrorInfo, 256
ISupportErrorInfo, 256-57
returning error information, 256
returning error information using ATL, 257-58
server code and error information, 260-61
SetErrorInfo, 256
Visual C++ compiler smart pointer error support, 262-64

Index 605

error handling in Visual Basic, 268-71
    default error handling, 268-69
    On Error statement, 269-71
  HRESULT, 252-55
    displaying error descriptions, 254-55
    error codes and naming conventions, 253
    facility codes, 252
    looking up error codes, 253-54
  tracing/debugging, 272-78
    ATL tracing support, 272-73
    breaking into program execution, 273-76
    tracing in SDK, 273
Event interfaces, 556
Event methods, 556
Events, 547-69
  COM+ event example, 559-66
    EventClass, 559-60
    filtering, 564-65
    Publisher, 565-66
    Subscriber, 561-65
  connection point architecture, 551-54
    Client-Object-Sink, 552
    IConnectionPoint, 552
    IConnectionPointAdvise method, 553
    IConnectionPointContainer, 553
    incoming/outgoing interfaces, 551-52
  and connection points in COM, 548-50
  example, 548-50
    client, 550-51
    server, 549-50
  loosely coupled events, 554-59
    COM+ event system architecture, 555-56
    EventClass component, 556
    filtering, 558-59
    publishers, 558
    subscribers, 557
    subscriptions, 557
  tightly coupled events, 554
EXCEPINFO, 264-65
Execution context, 130, 141, 216
EXE servers, 183-202
  application integration, 187-88
    and OLE, 183-84
  main window, hiding, 194-95
  OLE 1.0, 185
  OLE demonstration, 186-87
  OLE server, interfaces for, 188-89
  structure of, 189-96
    "demo" object as a local server, 191
    marshaling, 189-90
    proxy, 191-92
    REGCLS enumeration, 193
    registering a class factory, 192-93
    revoking class factory, 193
  and surrogates, 188
  unloading the application, 195-96
  using ATL, 196-201
    EXE server demo, 197-98
    EXE server files, 201
    proxies/stubs, 199-201
    self-registration, 198-99
  window messages and DDE, 184-85
Express queue, 522

F

Facility codes, 252

Fat clients, 25, 31, 38-39
Fault tolerance, with Component Load Balancing (CLB), 578
Filtering, 558-59
  parameter, 558-59
  publisher, 558
FormatMessage, 254
Format name, queues, 522
Forms, HTML, 474-76, 481
free threading model, 288

G

GetBalance method, 240, 354
GetClassID method, **IPersist** interface, 197, 198
GetComputerName, 199
get_ConstructString, 326
GetErrorInfo, 256, 261
GetIDsOfNames, 231, 237
GetName method, **IMachine** interface, 199, 384
GetObject, 537-38
GetObjectContext, 318, 342
GetSecurityContext, 402
GetTypeInfo, 231
GetTypeInfoCount, 231
Globally unique identifier (GUID), 77, 84-85, 89, 111, 116-17
  GUIDGEN, 116-17
Graphical User Interface (GUI), 7, 27
GUIDGEN, 116-17

H

Hello.dll, 65
hello.exe, 195
HelloVBClient.exe, 65, 67
HelloVB.dll, 64-65
HelloVB.msi, 67
Hives, 132
Host name, 57
HRESULT, 80, 252-55, 556
  displaying error descriptions, 254-55
  error codes and naming conventions, 253
  facility codes, 252
  looking up error codes, 253-54
HTTP, *See* HyperText Transfer Protocol (HTTP)
Hypertext, 472
HyperText Markup Language (HTML), 13, 472-76
  elements, 472
  forms, 474-76, 481
  tags, 472-73
  Uniform Resource Locators (URLs), 474
  Web browsers, 474
HyperText Transfer Protocol (HTTP), 25, 35-36, 44, 474, 477-79
  headers, 478
  methods, 479
  Web server response, 478-79

I

IAccount interface, 79, 81, 83-84, 88, 92, 112, 124, 127, 156, 158, 160-61, 168, 220, 258
_IAccount interface, 340
IAccount interface:
  implementation of methods, 123
  interface specification of, 119
IAccountPtr, 177
IBank interface, 365

IClassFactory interface, 118, 120, 129, 130, 136
    methods, 130
        CreateInstance method, 130, 137, 140
        LockServer method, 130, 137-38
IClientSecurity interface, 192
IConnectionPointContainer interface, 553, 558
    IConnectionPointAdvise method, 553
IConnectionPoint interface, 552, 567
IContextState, 318, 324
ICreateErrorInfo, 256
ICreateTypeInfo, 231
ICreateTypeLib, 231
IDE (integrated development environment), 23
Identifiers, 84-86
    class name, 85
    globally unique identifier (GUID), 77, 84-85, 89, 111, 116-17
    program ID (ProgID), 85
    "user" names, 85-86
Identity impersonation level, 392
IDispatch interface, 231, 237-39
    calling directly, 238-39
    CComDispatchDriver, 230, 239-40
IDisplay interface, 79, 81, 88, 92, 112, 126-27, 156, 168, 170, 220, 231, 233, 333, 336
_IDisplay interface, 340
IDL, *See* Interface Definition Language (IDL)
IDL file, 162, 168-71
IEnumVARIANT, 246-47, 248
IEnumXXX, 247, 248
IErrorInfo, 256, 261, 264, 267
IGreet interface, 79, 92, 171
IMachine interface, 199, 204, 384
IMalloc, 95
IMarshal interface, 192, 225
Impersonate impersonation level, 392
Impersonation:
    COM+ security, 406-8
        client-side, 407
        server-side, 407-8
    COM security, 392
IMultiPublisherFilter interface, 558
IMultiQI interface, 192, 222-23, 225
    QueryMultipleInterfaces method, 222
Incoming interfaces, 551-52
Independent Software Vendors (ISVs), 8
In-process COM servers, 130
    implementing using C++, 135-41
        class factory definition, 136
        class factory implementation, 136-38
        client access to the class factory, 140
        CoCreateInstance, 140
        CoFreeUnusedLibraries, 141
        execution context, 141
        exported functions of the DLL, 138
        exposing the class factory to COM, 139
        linking to COM libraries, 141
        unloading mechanism, 139-40
    implementing using Visual Basic, 142-47
        building the DLL, 145
        class module for **IDisplay** interface, 144
        client test program, 146-47
        creating a new ActiveX DLL project, 143
        creating the server, 143-46
        implementing **IDisplay** in **Account** class, 145
        providing code for **Account.cls** class module, 144
        setting binary version compatibility, 145-46
Install.exe, 19
Interception, 16, 306, 317, 321-23
    interceptors, 17, 321, 322
    interface pointer marshaling, 322-23
Interface attributes, 340
Interface Definition Language (IDL), 75-79, 80, 119, 242
    for an event interface, 245-46
    coclass (COM class), identifying, 78-79
    for a dispatch interface, 241-42
    interfaces, 79
    methods, 79
    properties, 79
    type library, identifying, 77-78
Interface ID, 209
Interface negotiation, 87-89
    QueryInterface:
        using Visual Basic, 88
        using Visual C++, 87-88
Interface pointer, marshaling, 290, 322-23
Interfaces, 79, 80-81
    binary representation of, 112-13
    C++, 108-9, 113-14
    implementing, 120-23
        concrete class, 121
        IAccount methods, 123
        reference counting, 122-23
    IUnknown, 80-81, 86-87, 89, 106, 111, 112, 117-20, 135-36, 223, 315
    naming conventions, 120
    QueryInterface, 12, 87-88, 90, 107, 117-18, 121-22, 125, 151, 172, 222
InterfaceSupportsErrorInfo method, 257, 260, 261
InterlockedDecrement, 227
InterlockedIncrement, 227
Internet Explorer 5.0, 482
Internet Information Server, 40-42
Internet Information Services 5.0, 477, 482-89
Internet programming testbed, 481-89
    Internet Explorer 5.0, 482
    Internet Information Services 5.0, 482-89
        directory browsing, 486
        publishing to your Web site, 483-85
        running CGI scripts, 487-89
Internet server API (ISAPI), 41, 499-502
Internet servers, 477
IObjectConstruct interface, 326, 350-52
    Construct method, 326, 352-53
IObjectConstructString, 326
IObjectContextActivity, 318
IObjectContextInfo, 318
IObjectContext interface, 318, 324, 351-52
    IsCallerInRole method, 401, 402
IObjectControl interface, 324, 330, 350-52, 580-81
    Activate method, 345, 581
    CanBePooled method, 324, 345, 581
    Deactivate method, 345, 581
IPersistFile, 197
IPersist interface, 191, 195-97
IPersistStorage, 197
IPersistStream, 197
IProxyManager interface, 192

Index

IPublisherFilter interface, 558
IResourceManager interface, 455
ISAPI (Internet Services Application Programming Interface), 41, 499-502
IsCallerInRole method, **IObjectContext** interface, 401, 402
ISecurityCallContext interface, 318, 401
ISupportErrorInfo interface, 256-57, 258, 261
ITransactionDispenser, 455
ITransaction interface pointer, 455
ITypeInfo, 231
IUnknown interface, 80-81, 86-87, 89, 106, 111, 112, 117-20, 135-36, 192, 223, 315

J

Java, 7, 12, 32, 107
　Remote Method Invocation (RMI) in, 32
Java Beans, 107
JavaScript, 40, 42, 492
Java Virtual Machine (JVM), 7
Just-in-time (JIT) activation, 323-25
　disabling, 344-45
　"done" bit, 324
　hooking object activation/deactivation, 324
　limits to scalability, 323-24
　state in COM+ components, 325

L

Late binding, 230, 231
Learning resources, 587-88
Library application, COM+, 316
library statement, 169
Lightweight Directory Access Protocol (LDAP), 58
Lightweight remote procedure call (LRPC) protocol, 11
Links, 10-11
Load balancing, and object pooling, 582
Local/remote transparency, 130
Local server, 130
Location transparency, 12, 50
LockServer method, **IClassFactory**, 130, 137-38
Logger component, 276-78
loosely coupled events, 554-59
　COM+ event system architecture, 555-56
　EventClass component, 556
　filtering, 558-59
　publishers, 558
　subscribers, 557
　subscriptions, 557

M

Marshaling, 189-90
　interface pointer, 290, 322-23
Message-oriented middleware (MOM), 14, 32, 45, 521
Message queuing, 17-18, 519, 520-21
　basic structure, 520
　defined, 520
　message-oriented middleware (MOM), 521
　and remote procedure call (RPC), 520-21
Methods, 4-5, 73-74, 79, 80, 230
　attributes, 340-41
　signature of, 73-74
Microsoft "Authenticode" technology, 498
Microsoft client-side web technologies, 489-98
　ActiveX controls, 492-94

JavaScript, 492
　"safety" configuration in Internet Explorer, 494-97
　scripting, 490-92
　VBScript, 492
Microsoft clustering technologies, 569-73
　Component Load Balancing (CLB), 573, 574-78
　　composing clustering technologies, 575
　　configuring, 575-77
　　design issues, 578
　　fault tolerance with, 578
　　load balancing, 574-75
　　load balancing algorithm, 575
　　performance, 578
　Microsoft Cluster Server (MSCS/Wolfpack), 570-71
　Windows Load Balancing Service (WLBS/Convoy), 572-73
Microsoft Cluster Server (MSCS/Wolfpack), 570-71
Microsoft Distributed Transaction Coordinator (MSDTC), 43, 412, 454-56
Microsoft Foundation Class (MFC) Library, 150
Microsoft Management Console (MMC), 54
　snap-in, and Catalog, 311
Microsoft Message Queue (MSMQ), 14-15, 24, 32, 36, 40, 44-45, 64, 519-46
　administering, 525
　API, 14-15, 523
　API test program, 524-25
　applications, 521
　architecture, 521-22
　BackupSite Controllers (BSC), 522
　components, 14
　Connector Servers, 522
　dependent clients, 521
　enterprise, 521
　example programs, 525-34
　　QSendObj COM component, 529-30
　　QueueCreate program, 526-29
　　QueueReceive program, 532-34
　　QueueSend program, 530-32
　express queue, 522
　format name, 522
　independent clients, 521
　installing, 524
　message queue storage, 5232
　message queuing, 17-18, 520-21
　MSMQMessage, 523
　MSMQQuery, 523
　MSMQQueue, 523
　MSMQQueueInfo, 523
　MSMQQueueInfos, 523
　MSMQ security certificate, obtaining, 543
　object model, 523
　pathnames, 522
　Primary Enterprise Controller (PEC), 522
　public and private queues, 522
　Queued Components, 45, 534-45
　　adding requests to the queue, 544
　　architecture, 534-35
　　configuration of, 536, 539-45
　　configuring application as queued, 541
　　configuring interface as queued, 542
　　Listener, 534
　　Player, 534
　　programming example, 538-39

Index

queue moniker, 536-38
Recorder, 534
requirements for, 536
security, 536
starting a queued application, 538, 544-45
using, 535-38
using **admin** objects, 545
queue handle, 522
recoverable queue, 522
referencing queues, 522
and RPC, 14
and transactions, 523
Microsoft server-side web technologies, 499-505
Active Server Pages (ASPs), 502-5
Internet server API (ISAPI), 499-502
Microsoft Transaction Server (MTS), 13-14, 17, 33-34, 42-44, 453-56
Microsoft transactions technology, 453-56
Microsoft Distributed Transaction Coordinator (MS DTC), 454-56
OLE Transactions, 454
Microsoft Visual Studio, 61, 116-17, 125
Microsoft Web technologies, 489-505
Microsoft client-side web technologies, 489-98
ActiveX controls, 492-94
downloading an ActiveX control, 497-98
JavaScript, 492
"safety" configuration in Internet Explorer, 494-97
scripting, 490-92
VBScript, 492
Microsoft server-side web technologies, 499-505
Active Server Pages (ASP), 502-5
Internet server (ISAPI), 499-502
Microsoft Windows 2000 Beta Training Kit, 55-56
Middleware, 12, 14
MIDL.EXE, 119
Module definition file, 138
Move method, **_bMove** interface, 467
MQSeries (IBM), 32
MSDN Library, 61
MSDTC, *See* Microsoft Distributed Transaction Coordinator (MSDTC)
MSMQ, *See* Microsoft Message Queue (MSMQ)
MSMQMessage object, 534
MSMQQuery object, 531-32
MSMQQueueInfo object, 531-32
MSMQQueueInfos object, 531
MTS Explorer, 13-14
_MULTI_QI, 218
Multithreading, 279-301
apartments, 284-90
crossing apartment boundaries, 289-90
EXE and DLL servers, 286
multithreaded apartments, 285-86
threading models, 286-89
ATL support for, 291-92
concurrent programming, 280-84
automatically serializing data access, 281
race condition example, 280
serializing access to shared data, 280-81
Windows message queue demo, 281-84
implementing in COM, 290-300
DLL server example, 292-300
interface pointer, marshaling, 290, 322-23
threading models, 286-89

apartment threading model, 287-88
"both" threading model, 289
free threading model, 288
neutral threading model, 289
single threading model, 286-87

N

Name.exe, 207, 212, 384
nameps.dll, 209
Nametest.exe, 204-5
NetBios/NetBEUI (LAN Manager), 27, 32
NetWare, 27, 32
Network DDE, 188
Network Directory Service (NDS), 58
Networking, 35-36, 56-57
Neutral apartments, 361
neutral threading model, 289
New operator (Visual Basic), 83-84
NT objects, 377, 378
NT security model, 377-79
access control entry (ACE), 377, 379
access tokens, 377, 378
core elements, 377-79
discretionary access control list (DACL), 377, 379
NT objects, 377, 378
security descriptors, 377, 378
security IDs (SIDs), 377, 378

O

Object, connectable objects, 552
Object Browser, 20-21, 73-74
Object construction, 325-26, 352-54
configuring the constructor string, 353
running the program, 354
Object creation, C++, 109
Object instantiation, 82-84
CoCreateInstance (C++), 83, 101, 104, 123, 125, 140-41, 163, 216
New operator (Visual Basic), 83-84
Objective C, 6
Object lifetime, 86-87
in Visual Basic, 87
Object linking and embedding (OLE), 9-11
demonstration, 186-87
OLE 1.0, 10-11, 185
OLE 2.0, 11, 186
Object model, 246-47
Active Server Pages (ASP), 505-6
ADO object model, 433-34
Component Object Model (COM), 11-13
Microsoft Message Queue (MSMQ), 523
Object-oriented languages, 5-7
Object pooling, 306, 319, 325, 579-82
configuring a component for, 580
IObject Control, 580-81
and load balancing, 582
requirements for, 581
using, 579
Objects, 4-5, 58, 81-82, 376
bootstrapping, 130
class object, 109, 130
interfaces, 12
Object Wizard, 158, 257-58
OCX (OLE Custom Control), 13
ODBC, 5, 6, 9, 11, 12, 31, 45-46, 424-25
architecture, 10

Data Source, creating, 427-31
Data Source Administrator, 428
OLE 1.0, 10-11, 185
OLE 2.0, 11, 186
ole32.dll, 190
ole32.lib, 141
OLE, *See* Object linking and embedding (OLE)
OLE/COM Object Viewer, 74-75, 99-101
    Bank.Account.1, 101
    CLSID, 101
    instantiating an object, 101
    TYPELIB, 101
OLE controls (OCXs), 188
OLE DB, 425
OLE DB providers, 425
OLE server, interfaces for, 188-89
OLE Transactions, 454
On Error statement, 268-71, 278
One-tier systems, 26-27
Open Database Connectivity, *See* ODBC
Oracle, 9, 31
ORB (Object Request Broker), 12
Outgoing interfaces, 551-52
OutputDebugString function, 273
Owner SID, 378

P

Parameter filtering, 558-59
Pathnames, queues, 522
PC LANs, 27-28
Peer-to-peer, defined, 376
Persistent subscriptions, 557
"Pinging" computers on a network, 57
Platform SDK, 64
    tracing in, 273
Pooling, *See* Object pooling
PowerBuilder, 31
ppv, 139
Preinstalled applications, COM+, 316
Presentation layer, 38-40
    rich clients, 25, 38-39
    scripting/components, 40
    thin clients, 38-39
Primary domain controller (PDC), 376
Primary Enterprise Controller (PEC), 522
Private data, 5-6
Private queues, 522
Program ID (ProgID), 85
Programmable component, 230
Properties, 73-74, 79, 230
Public data, 5
Public queues, 522
Publisher, 547, 558, 565-66
Publisher filtering, 558
PutBalance method, 240-41
pwszName field, 217

Q

qcServer.dll, 539-40
QSendObj COM component, 525, 529-30
Quality, level of, 585
Query Analyzer, SQL Server 7.0, 29, 413-14
QueryInterface, 12, 87-88, 90, 107, 117-18, 123-24, 125, 127, 151, 172, 175, 222, 272
    implementing, 121-22
    using Visual Basic, 88

using Visual C++, 87-88
QueryMultipleInterfaces method, **IMultiQI** interface, 222
QueueCreate program, 525, 526-29, 532
Queue handle, 522
QueueReceive program, 526, 532-34
QueueSend program, 525, 530-32

R

rclsid, 139
Recoverable queue, 522
Reference counting, 110, 118
    implementation of, 122-23
Referencing queues, 522
Regdb, 310
REGEDIT (Registry Editor), 98, 101-2, 131-32
.reg files, 19
regsvr32.exe, 103
Release method, 86, 118, 122, 125, 163, 172, 175, 176, 223-24
Reliability, COM+, 307
Remote Method Invocation (RMI), Java, 32
Remote procedure call (RPC), 12, 14, 32, 111
    and message queuing, 520-21
Remoting an existing COM object, 204-12
    COM server, 204
    DCOM demo, 204-6
    Registry entries, 209-12
        AppID, 210-12
        proxy/stub, 209-10
        security issue, 207-8
Resource manager, 451
Response time approach, to selecting a server for an incoming request, 575
Reuse, C++, 111
Rich clients, 25, 31, 38-39
riid, 139
Role-based security, 400-401
    configuring component-level access, 400-401
    setting up roles, 400
Root domain, 57
Round robin approach, to selecting a server for an incoming request, 575
RPC, *See* Remote procedure call (RPC)
rpcss.exe, 225

S

Scalability, 306-7, 569-86
    Component Load Balancing (CLB), 573, 574-78
    Microsoft clustering technologies, 569-73
        Component Load Balancing (CLB), 573, 574-78
        Microsoft Cluster Server (MSCS/Wolfpack), 570-71
        Windows Load Balancing Service (WLBS/Convoy), 572-73
    object pooling, 306, 319, 325, 579-82
        configuring a component for, 580
        IObject Control interface, 580-81
        and load balancing, 582
        requirements for, 581
        using, 579
Scripting, 490-92
SDK, tracing in, 273
Second-level domains, 57
Security, 36, 369-409

610 Index

authentication, 371
authorization, 371
COM+, 393-408
COM, 383-92
demonstration, 379-82
fundamental problem of, 370-71
Microsoft Message Queue (MSMQ), 536
NT security model, 377-79
    access control entry (ACE), 377, 379
    access tokens, 377, 378
    core elements, 377-79
    discretionary access control list (DACL), 377, 379
    NT objects, 377, 378
    security descriptors, 377, 378
    security IDs (SIDs), 377, 378
policy, 370
Security Reference Monitor, 370
Windows 2000 system administration tutorial, 371-75
Security descriptors, 377, 378
Security IDs (SIDs), 377, 378
Security Reference Monitor, 370
Servers, 130
Server self-registration, 103
Service Control Manager (SCM), 131
SetAbort, 44, 324, 325, 346-47, 401, 459-60, 464-65, 467
SetComplete, 44, 324, 325, 341, 342-44, 346-47, 354, 401, 459-60, 464-65, 467
SetDeactivateOnReturn, 324
SetErrorInfo, 256
shape.dll, 498
ShowError, 254-55, 259
Show method, **IDisplay** interface, 220
ShowWindow, 194
Shrink-wrapped applications, 9
Simula, 6
Single-threaded apartment (STA), 285, 309-10
Sink, 551, 552
Sites, 377, 521
Smalltalk, 6-7
Smart pointers, 172-73
Software components, 22-24
SPX/IPX, 32
SQL: Access group (SAG) SQL CAE specification, 9
SQL Server 7.0, 412-23, 571
    databases:
        for case study, 416-17
        creating, 417
        setting up for Electronic Commerce Game, 422-23
    Enterprise Manager, 414-15
    installation of, 412
    managing databases using, 415-23
    Query Analyzer, 413-14
    SQL scripts, creating/using, 420-22
    table:
        creating, 418-19
        inserting data into, 419-20
SQL Server, 31
    native OLE DB provider of, 441-42
SQLServerAgent, 412
STA, *See* Single-threaded apartment (STA)
Standard C Library, 8
Standard Generalized Markup Language (SGML), 472

Static data members, 109-10
Static HTML page, 477
Static libraries, 8
Status and error reporting mechanism, 124-25
stdafx.h, 141
str.exe, 190
Stroustrup, Bjarne, 6
Subscriber, 547, 557, 561-65
Subscriptions, 557
Surrogate, 188
Synchronization:
    and activities, 361-64
        activities defined, 361-62
        relationship with other attributes, 364
        "rental" threading model, 364
        synchronization attribute, 362-64
    and apartments, 359-61
        multithreaded bank account example, 360
        neutral apartments, 361
    through apartments, 360
Synchronization attribute, 360
SysAllocString, 97
SysFreeString, 97
System Access Control List (SACL), 378
System account, 373, 389
System registry, 131
    and class ID (CLSID), 131

T

Tags, HTML, 472-73
tagVARIANT structure, 232-33
TCP/IP, 32
Template library, 23
Thin clients, 25, 38-39
Threading models, 286-89
    apartment threading model, 287-88
    "both" threading model, 289
    free threading model, 288
    neutral threading model, 289
    single threading model, 286-87
Three-tier COM+ application, 442-44
    data tier, running remotely, 444
    middle-tier server, creating, 443
    presentation-tier client, creating, 443-44
    using COM+ to create a remote proxy, 444
Three-tier systems, 33-34
    architecture, 34
Tightly coupled events, 554
Top-level domains, 57
Transaction identifier, 456
Transaction manager, 451
Transactions, 308-9, 449-70
    aborted, 450
    ACID properties, 308, 325, 450
    automatic transactions in COM+, 456-60
        consistency/done bits, 459
        dependent attributes, 458
        interior objects/transaction boundaries, 458-59
        life cycle, 459-60
        transactional components, 456-59
        transaction flag ("doomed" bit), 459
    committed, 450
    declaring requirements, 310
    distributed transaction processing, 451-53
        two-phase commit, 452-53

Index

X/Open DTP model, 451-52
and Microsoft Message Queue (MSMQ), 523
Microsoft transactions technology, 453-56
    Microsoft Distributed Transaction Coordinator (MS DTC), 454-56
    OLE Transactions, 454
principles of transaction processing, 449-50
programming in COM+, 461-68
    "Auto Done" flag for a method, 467-68
    data tier, 466
    ecUtil.bMove, 463, 464-65
    ecUtil.dbHistory, 463, 464
    ecUtil.dbPlayer, 463
    middle-tier components, 462-66
    player administration program, 461-62
    presentation tier, 466
Transient subscriptions, 557
Tutorial:
    COM+, 329-58
    database programming, 427-32
    Windows 2000 system administration, 371-75
Two-tier systems, 28-33
    application servers, 32-33
    database servers, 28-31
Type information, 89, 231
Type library, 73, 77-78, 89, 169

U

UDA, *See* Uniform Data Access (UDA)
Unadvise method, **IConnectionPoint**, 552
Unconfigured components, COM+, 316
Unicode, 95-96
    converting using macros, 96
    converting using Win32, 96
Uniform Data Access (UDA), 46, 424-27
    ActiveX Data Objects (ADO), 425-27
    ODBC, 424-25
    OLE DB, 425
Uniform Resource Locators (URLs), 474
Universally unique identifier (UUID), 77, 84, 116
"User" names of classes, 85-86

V

VARIANTS, 232-33
VBScript, 40, 42, 230, 492
    Automation with, 233, 234-35
    VBScript Automation processing, 237
VBX, 7-8, 13
Virtual functions, C++, 114-16
Visual Basic, 7, 12, 18-19, 31, 61, 62, 71, 230
    and Automation, 240-46
        client program that handles events, 244-45
        default properties, 241
        events, 242-46
        events in COM servers, 243
        IDL for an event interface, 245-46
        IDL for a dispatch interface, 241-42
        properties, 240-42
        read-only/write-only properties, 241
    and coclass, 169-70
    COM client program, 90-92
    event abstraction, 243
    logging from, 278
    object lifetime in, 87
    version 6.0, 18-19
Visual Basic COM+ component, 330-48

activation and state, 341-48
    activation/deactivation at runtime, 343-44
    automatic deactivation, 346-48
    disabling just-in-time activation, 344-45
    hooking into activation/deactivation in Visual Basic, 345-46
    programming with context in Visual Basic, 342-43
attributes, 337-41
    application attributes, 337-39
    component attributes, 339-40
    interface attributes, 340
    method attributes, 340-41
configured component, 332-37
    creating in empty COM + application, 332
    installation/registration, 334-35
    installing a new component, 332-33
    running the COM+ application, 336-37
    using drag-and-drop, 333-34
    viewing the component(s) in COM+ Explorer, 335-36
roadmap, 330
unconfigured component, 331-32
    testing the bank account component, 331-32
    using the **Logger** component, 331
Visual Basic Extension, *See* VBX
Visual Basic Object Browser, 20-21, 73-74
Visual C++, 61, 62-63, 71
    and Active Template Library (ATL), 154-67
    Automation controllers, 237-40
        calling **IDispatch** directly, 238-39
    COM client demo, 176-78
        namespaces, 179-80
        starter project, 176
        testing/error handling, 177-78
        using the smart pointer, 176-77
        using the type library, 176
    COM client program:
        console, 92-94
        using MFC, 94-95
    and COM clients, 175-76
    COM support, 175-82
    COM support classes, 180-81
        _bsatr_t, 180
        _com_error, 180-81
    disambiguating in, 179-80
    logging from, 276-77
Visual C++ Automation controllers, 237-40
    calling **IDispatch** directly, 238-39
    using **CComDispatchDriver**, 239-40
Visual C++ COM+ component, 348-54
    example program:
        creating, 348-49
        installing/running, 349-50
    IObjectControl and **IObjectConstruct** interfaces, 350-52
        accessing the object context, 351-52
    object construction, 352-54
Visual InterDev, 63
Visual J++, 12
Visual Studio, 61, 116-17, 125

W

Web browsers, 474
    building, 18-22
    demonstration, 19-22

Web server, 477
Web technology, 472-81
    Common Gateway Interface (CGI), 40, 479-81, 487-89
    HTML, 472-76
    hypertext, 472
    HyperText Transfer Protocol (HTTP), 477-79
    Internet servers, 477
Windows 2000, 36, 50, 53-55
    Component Services, 15
    hardware requirements, 53
    Professional version, 53-55
        finding your way around, 54
Windows 2000 Server, 55-61
    Active Directory, 58-61
        installing, 59
        joining a domain, 59-60
        managing users, 60-61
    Domain Name System (DNS), 57-58
    networking, 56-57
    opening screen, 55
    using, 55-56
Windows 2000 system administration tutorial, 371-75
    Active Directory, 376-77
    domains in NT 4.0, 376
    user accounts, 371-75
        adding users, 372
        built-in accounts, 372-73
        groups, 373-75
    workgroups, 376
Windows DNA:
    business logic layer, 40-45
        Internet Information Server, 40-42
        Microsoft Message Queue (MSMQ), 44-45
        Microsoft Transaction Server and COM+, 42-44
    data access layer, 45-46
    development tools, 61-64
        Platform SDK, 64
        Visual Basic, 62
        Visual C++, 62-63
        Visual InterDev, 63
    general services, 35-37
        Active Directory, 36
        clustering, 36-37
        networking, 35-36
        security, 36
    "glue" technology, 37-38
        COM, 37
        COM+, 37-38
    layers, 38-46
    overall structure of, 35-38
    presentation layer, 38-40
        rich clients, 25, 38-39
        scripting/components, 40
        thin clients, 38-39
    testbed for, 49-68
Windows Load Balancing Service (WLBS/Convoy), 572-73
    defined, 572
Windows Open System Architecture (WOSA), 9, 31
Windows Registry, 132
    and COM, 98-104
    and DCOM, 220
    interfaces in, 134-35
    OLE/COM Object Viewer, 99-101
        Bank.Account.1, 101
        CLSID, 101
        instantiating an object, 101
        TYPELIB, 101
    REGEDIT (Registry Editor), 98, 101-2
    Registry Editor (REGEDIT), 132
    registry entry files, 132-33
    registry information, 133-35
    server self-registration, 103
Windows station, 391
WLBS, *See* Windows Load Balancing Service (WLBS/Convoy)
Wolfpack, *See* Microsoft Cluster Server (MSCS/Wolfpack)
Workgroups, 36, 376
WOSA, 9, 31
Wrapper classes, 171-73
    CComBSTR, 172
    smart pointers, 172-73

X

X/Open DTP model, 451-52, 454

Z

ZooColl, 247-48

LICENSE AGREEMENT AND LIMITED WARRANTY

READ THE FOLLOWING TERMS AND CONDITIONS CAREFULLY BEFORE OPENING THIS CD PACKAGE, Understanding and ProgrammingCOM+: A Practical Guide to Windows 2000 DNA. THIS LEGAL DOCUMENT IS AN AGREEMENT BETWEEN YOU AND PRENTICE-HALL, INC. (THE "COMPANY"). BY OPENING THIS SEALED CD PACKAGE, YOU ARE AGREEING TO BE BOUND BY THESE TERMS AND CONDITIONS. IF YOU DO NOT AGREE WITH THESE TERMS AND CONDITIONS, DO NOT OPEN THE CD PACKAGE. PROMPTLY RETURN THE UNOPENED CD PACKAGE AND ALL ACCOMPANYING ITEMS TO THE PLACE YOU OBTAINED THEM FOR A FULL REFUND OF ANY SUMS YOU HAVE PAID.

1. **GRANT OF LICENSE:** In consideration of your purchase of this book, and your agreement to abide by the terms and conditions of this Agreement, the Company grants to you a nonexclusive right to use and display the copy of the enclosed software program (hereinafter the "SOFTWARE") on a single computer (i.e., with a single CPU) at a single location so long as you comply with the terms of this Agreement. The Company reserves all rights not expressly granted to you under this Agreement.

2. **OWNERSHIP OF SOFTWARE:** You own only the magnetic or physical media (the enclosed CD) on which the SOFTWARE is recorded or fixed, but the Company and the software developers retain all the rights, title, and ownership to the SOFTWARE recorded on the original CD copy(ies) and all subsequent copies of the SOFTWARE, regardless of the form or media on which the original or other copies may exist. This license is not a sale of the original SOFTWARE or any copy to you.

3. **COPY RESTRICTIONS:** This SOFTWARE and the accompanying printed materials and user manual (the "Documentation") are the subject of copyright. The individual programs on the CD are copyrighted by the authors of each program. Some of the programs on the CD include separate licensing agreements. If you intend to use one of these programs, you must read and follow its accompanying license agreement. You may not copy the Documentation or the SOFTWARE, except that you may make a single copy of the SOFTWARE for backup or archival purposes only. You may be held legally responsible for any copying or copyright infringement which is caused or encouraged by your failure to abide by the terms of this restriction.

4. **USE RESTRICTIONS:** You may not network the SOFTWARE or otherwise use it on more than one computer or computer terminal at the same time. You may physically transfer the SOFTWARE from one computer to another provided that the SOFTWARE is used on only one computer at a time. You may not distribute copies of the SOFTWARE or Documentation to others. You may not reverse engineer, disassemble, decompile, modify, adapt, translate, or create derivative works based on the SOFTWARE or the Documentation without the prior written consent of the Company.

5. **TRANSFER RESTRICTIONS:** The enclosed SOFTWARE is licensed only to you and may not be transferred to any one else without the prior written consent of the Company. Any unauthorized transfer of the SOFTWARE shall result in the immediate termination of this Agreement.

6. **TERMINATION:** This license is effective until terminated. This license will terminate automatically without notice from the Company and become null and void if you fail to comply with any provisions or limitations of this license. Upon termination, you shall destroy the Documentation and all copies of the SOFTWARE. All provisions of this Agreement as to warranties, limitation of liability, remedies or damages, and our ownership rights shall survive termination.

7. **MISCELLANEOUS:** This Agreement shall be construed in accordance with the laws of the United States of America and the State of New York and shall benefit the Company, its affiliates, and assignees.

8. **LIMITED WARRANTY AND DISCLAIMER OF WARRANTY:** The Company warrants that the SOFTWARE, when properly used in accordance with the Documentation, will operate in substantial conformity with the description of the SOFTWARE set forth in the Documentation. The

Company does not warrant that the SOFTWARE will meet your requirements or that the operation of the SOFTWARE will be uninterrupted or error-free. The Company warrants that the media on which the SOFTWARE is delivered shall be free from defects in materials and workmanship under normal use for a period of thirty (30) days from the date of your purchase. Your only remedy and the Company's only obligation under these limited warranties is, at the Company's option, return of the warranted item for a refund of any amounts paid by you or replacement of the item. Any replacement of SOFTWARE or media under the warranties shall not extend the original warranty period. The limited warranty set forth above shall not apply to any SOFTWARE which the Company determines in good faith has been subject to misuse, neglect, improper installation, repair, alteration, or damage by you. EXCEPT FOR THE EXPRESSED WARRANTIES SET FORTH ABOVE, THE COMPANY DISCLAIMS ALL WARRANTIES, EXPRESS OR IMPLIED, INCLUDING WITHOUT LIMITATION, THE IMPLIED WARRANTIES OF MERCHANTABILITY AND FITNESS FOR A PARTICULAR PURPOSE. EXCEPT FOR THE EXPRESS WARRANTY SET FORTH ABOVE, THE COMPANY DOES NOT WARRANT, GUARANTEE, OR MAKE ANY REPRESENTATION REGARDING THE USE OR THE RESULTS OF THE USE OF THE SOFTWARE IN TERMS OF ITS CORRECTNESS, ACCURACY, RELIABILITY, CURRENTNESS, OR OTHERWISE.

IN NO EVENT, SHALL THE COMPANY OR ITS EMPLOYEES, AGENTS, SUPPLIERS, OR CONTRACTORS BE LIABLE FOR ANY INCIDENTAL, INDIRECT, SPECIAL, OR CONSEQUENTIAL DAMAGES ARISING OUT OF OR IN CONNECTION WITH THE LICENSE GRANTED UNDER THIS AGREEMENT, OR FOR LOSS OF USE, LOSS OF DATA, LOSS OF INCOME OR PROFIT, OR OTHER LOSSES, SUSTAINED AS A RESULT OF INJURY TO ANY PERSON, OR LOSS OF OR DAMAGE TO PROPERTY, OR CLAIMS OF THIRD PARTIES, EVEN IF THE COMPANY OR AN AUTHORIZED REPRESENTATIVE OF THE COMPANY HAS BEEN ADVISED OF THE POSSIBILITY OF SUCH DAMAGES. IN NO EVENT SHALL LIABILITY OF THE COMPANY FOR DAMAGES WITH RESPECT TO THE SOFTWARE EXCEED THE AMOUNTS ACTUALLY PAID BY YOU, IF ANY, FOR THE SOFTWARE.

SOME JURISDICTIONS DO NOT ALLOW THE LIMITATION OF IMPLIED WARRANTIES OR LIABILITY FOR INCIDENTAL, INDIRECT, SPECIAL, OR CONSEQUENTIAL DAMAGES, SO THE ABOVE LIMITATIONS MAY NOT ALWAYS APPLY. THE WARRANTIES IN THIS AGREEMENT GIVE YOU SPECIFIC LEGAL RIGHTS AND YOU MAY ALSO HAVE OTHER RIGHTS WHICH VARY IN ACCORDANCE WITH LOCAL LAW.

ACKNOWLEDGMENT

YOU ACKNOWLEDGE THAT YOU HAVE READ THIS AGREEMENT, UNDERSTAND IT, AND AGREE TO BE BOUND BY ITS TERMS AND CONDITIONS. YOU ALSO AGREE THAT THIS AGREEMENT IS THE COMPLETE AND EXCLUSIVE STATEMENT OF THE AGREEMENT BETWEEN YOU AND THE COMPANY AND SUPERSEDES ALL PROPOSALS OR PRIOR AGREEMENTS, ORAL, OR WRITTEN, AND ANY OTHER COMMUNICATIONS BETWEEN YOU AND THE COMPANY OR ANY REPRESENTATIVE OF THE COMPANY RELATING TO THE SUBJECT MATTER OF THIS AGREEMENT.

Should you have any questions concerning this Agreement or if you wish to contact the Company for any reason, please contact in writing at the address below.

>Robin Short

>Prentice Hall PTR

>One Lake Street

>Upper Saddle River, New Jersey 07458

ABOUT UCI CORPORATION

*T*he evolution of UCI Corporation mirrors the rapid rate of change in the software industry.

In 1984 UCI Corporation began providing consulting and training services to professional programmers and systems engineers on Digital Equipment Corporation's VMS operating system.

UCI business grew to include training in the UNIX environment with training for Programmers and Systems engineers in the late eighties.

With the emergence of Microsoft as an industry leader, UCI became one of the first Certified Microsoft Training organizations in the world in 1992.

With this background UCI instructors possess a clear understanding of the issues faced by IT organizations in an industry where the only constant is change.

The founder of UCI, Andrew Scoppa, is a nationally recognized leader in software training.

This book is one of the UCI Series on Microsoft technology published by Prentice Hall PTR. The series topics include Distributed COM application development, E-commerce, Windows NT Cluster, Device Driver Development, and SQL Server Optimization and Tuning. These books are written by UCI instructors and provide valuable technical information for programmers and systems engineers. We are very interested in your comments on our series of books. Please send email to UCI at info@ucicorp.com.

UCI Corporation headquarters are in Massachusetts. To reach UCI call 800-884-1772, or email info@ucicorp.com. For more information on currently available courses and project driven curriculum visit the UCI web site at http://www.ucicorp.com.

PRENTICE HALL
Professional Technical Reference
Tomorrow's Solutions for Today's Professionals.

Keep Up-to-Date with
PH PTR Online!

We strive to stay on the cutting-edge of what's happening in professional computer science and engineering. Here's a bit of what you'll find when you stop by **www.phptr.com**:

Special interest areas offering our latest books, book series, software, features of the month, related links and other useful information to help you get the job done.

Deals, deals, deals! Come to our promotions section for the latest bargains offered to you exclusively from our retailers.

Need to find a bookstore? Chances are, there's a bookseller near you that carries a broad selection of PTR titles. Locate a Magnet bookstore near you at www.phptr.com.

What's New at PH PTR? We don't just publish books for the professional community, we're a part of it. Check out our convention schedule, join an author chat, get the latest reviews and press releases on topics of interest to you.

Subscribe Today! **Join PH PTR's monthly email newsletter!**

Want to be kept up-to-date on your area of interest? Choose a targeted category on our website, and we'll keep you informed of the latest PH PTR products, author events, reviews and conferences in your interest area.

Visit our mailroom to subscribe today! **http://www.phptr.com/mail_lists**